TCP/IP Network
Administration

THIRD EDITION

TCP/IP Network Administration

Craig Hunt

O'REILLY®

Beijing · Cambridge · Farnham · Köln · Paris · Sebastopol · Taipei · Tokyo

TCP/IP Network Administration, Third Edition

by Craig Hunt

Published by O'Reilly & Associates, Inc., 1005 Gravenstein Highway North, Sebastopol, CA 95472.

O'Reilly & Associates books may be purchased for educational, business, or sales promotional use. Online editions are also available for most titles (*safari.oreilly.com*). For more information contact our corporate/institutional sales department: (800) 998-9938 or *corporate@oreilly.com*.

Editors:	Mike Loukides and Debra Cameron
Production Editor:	Emily Quill
Cover Designer:	Edie Freedman
Interior Designer:	Melanie Wang

Printing History:

August 1992:	First Edition.
January 1998:	Second Edition.
April 2002:	Third Edition.

ISBN: 0-596-00297-1

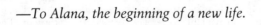

—To Alana, the beginning of a new life.

Table of Contents

Preface . . . . **xi**

1. Overview of TCP/IP **1**
TCP/IP and the Internet   2
A Data Communications Model   6
TCP/IP Protocol Architecture   9
Network Access Layer   11
Internet Layer   12
Transport Layer   18
Application Layer   22
Summary   23

2. Delivering the Data **24**
Addressing, Routing, and Multiplexing   24
The IP Address   25
Internet Routing Architecture   35
The Routing Table   37
Address Resolution   43
Protocols, Ports, and Sockets   44
Summary   50

3. Network Services **51**
Names and Addresses   51
The Host Table   52
DNS   54
Mail Services   62
File and Print Servers   75
Configuration Servers   76
Summary   82

4. Getting Started **84**
Connected and Non-Connected Networks 85
Basic Information 86
Planning Routing 97
Planning Naming Service 101
Other Services 104
Informing the Users 106
Summary 107

5. Basic Configuration **108**
Kernel Configuration 108
Startup Files 124
The Internet Daemon 129
The Extended Internet Daemon 132
Summary 133

6. Configuring the Interface **134**
The ifconfig Command 134
TCP/IP Over a Serial Line 150
Installing PPP 153
Summary 169

7. Configuring Routing **170**
Common Routing Configurations 170
The Minimal Routing Table 171
Building a Static Routing Table 173
Interior Routing Protocols 178
Exterior Routing Protocols 188
Gateway Routing Daemon 191
Configuring gated 193
Summary 204

8. Configuring DNS **205**
BIND: Unix Name Service 205
Configuring the Resolver 207
Configuring named 211
Using nslookup 228
Summary 232

9. Local Network Services **233**

The Network File System 233

Sharing Unix Printers 252

Using Samba to Share Resources with Windows 259

Network Information Service 268

DHCP 272

Managing Distributed Servers 277

Post Office Servers 280

Summary 283

10. sendmail **285**

sendmail's Function 285

Running sendmail as a Daemon 286

sendmail Aliases 288

The sendmail.cf File 290

sendmail.cf Configuration Language 297

Rewriting the Mail Address 309

Modifying a sendmail.cf File 319

Testing sendmail.cf 323

Summary 332

11. Configuring Apache **333**

Installing Apache Software 334

Configuring the Apache Server 338

Understanding an httpd.conf File 341

Web Server Security 361

Managing Your Web Server 378

Summary 380

12. Network Security **381**

Security Planning 382

User Authentication 387

Application Security 402

Security Monitoring 404

Access Control 409

Encryption 418

Firewalls 425

Words to the Wise 433

Summary 434

13. **Troubleshooting TCP/IP** **435**
   Approaching a Problem   435
   Diagnostic Tools   438
   Testing Basic Connectivity   440
   Troubleshooting Network Access   443
   Checking Routing   450
   Checking Name Service   456
   Analyzing Protocol Problems   471
   Protocol Case Study   474
   Summary   478

A. **PPP Tools** **479**

B. **A gated Reference** **503**

C. **A named Reference** **548**

D. **A dhcpd Reference** **586**

E. **A sendmail Reference** **599**

F. **Solaris httpd.conf File** **661**

G. **RFC Excerpts** **679**

Index **687**

Preface

The first edition of *TCP/IP Network Administration* was written in 1992. In the decade since, many things have changed, yet some things remain the same. TCP/IP is still the preeminent communications protocol for linking together diverse computer systems. It remains the basis of interoperable data communications and global computer networking. The underlying Internet Protocol (IP), Transmission Control Protocol, and User Datagram Protocol (UDP) are remarkably unchanged. But change has come in the way TCP/IP is used and how it is managed.

A clear symbol of this change is the fact that my mother-in-law has a TCP/IP network connection in her home that she uses to exchange electronic mail, compressed graphics, and hypertext documents with other senior citizens. She thinks of this as "just being on the Internet," but the truth is that her small system contains a functioning TCP/IP protocol stack, manages a dynamically assigned IP address, and handles data types that did not even exist a decade ago.

In 1991, TCP/IP was a tool of sophisticated users. Network administrators managed a limited number of systems and could count on the users for a certain level of technical knowledge. No more. In 2002, the need for highly trained network administrators is greater than ever because the user base is larger, more diverse, and less capable of handling technical problems on its own. This book provides the information needed to become an effective TCP/IP network administrator.

TCP/IP Network Administration was the first book of practical information for the professional TCP/IP network administrator, and it is still the best. Since the first edition was published there has been an explosion of books about TCP/IP and the Internet. Still, too few books concentrate on what a system administrator really needs to know about TCP/IP administration. Most books are either scholarly texts written from the point of view of the protocol designer, or instructions on how to use TCP/IP applications. All of those books lack the practical, detailed network information needed by the Unix system administrator. This book strives to focus on TCP/IP and Unix and to find the right balance of theory and practice.

I am proud of the earlier editions of *TCP/IP Network Administration*. In this edition, I have done everything I can to maintain the essential character of the book while making it better. Dynamic address assignment based on Dynamic Host Configuration Protocol (DHCP) is covered. The Domain Name System material has been updated to cover BIND 8 and, to a lesser extent, BIND 9. The email configuration is based on current version of sendmail 8, and the operating system examples are from the current versions of Solaris and Linux. The routing protocol coverage includes Routing Information Protocol version 2 (RIPv2), Open Shortest Path First (OSPF), and Border Gateway Protocol (BGP). I have also added a chapter on Apache web server configuration, new material on xinetd, and information about building a firewall with iptables. Despite the additional topics, the book has been kept to a reasonable length.

TCP/IP is a set of communications protocols that define how different types of computers talk to each other. *TCP/IP Network Administration* is a book about building your own network based on TCP/IP. It is both a tutorial covering the "why" and "how" of TCP/IP networking, and a reference manual for the details about specific network programs.

Audience

This book is intended for everyone who has a Unix computer connected to a TCP/IP network.* This obviously includes the network managers and the system administrators who are responsible for setting up and running computers and networks, but it also includes any user who wants to understand how his or her computer communicates with other systems. The distinction between a "system administrator" and an "end user" is a fuzzy one. You may think of yourself as an end user, but if you have a Unix workstation on your desk, you're probably also involved in system administration tasks.

Over the last several years there has been a rash of books for "dummies" and "idiots." If you really think of yourself as an "idiot" when it comes to Unix, this book is not for you. Likewise, if you are a network administration "genius," this book is probably not suitable either. If you fall anywhere between these two extremes, however, you'll find this book has a lot to offer.

This book assumes that you have a good understanding of computers and their operation and that you're generally familiar with Unix system administration. If you're not, the Nutshell Handbook *Essential System Administration* by Æleen Frisch (published by O'Reilly & Associates) will fill you in on the basics.

---

* Much of this text also applies to non-Unix systems. Many of the file formats and commands and all of the protocol descriptions apply equally well to Windows 9x, Windows NT/2000, and other operating systems. If you're an NT administrator, you should read *Windows NT TCP/IP Network Administration* (O'Reilly).

Organization

Conceptually, this book is divided into three parts: fundamental concepts, tutorial, and reference. The first three chapters are a basic discussion of the TCP/IP protocols and services. This discussion provides the fundamental concepts necessary to understand the rest of the book. The remaining chapters provide a "how-to" tutorial. Chapters 4–7 discuss how to plan a network installation and configure the basic software necessary to get a network running. Chapters 8–11 discuss how to set up various important network services. Chapters 12 and 13 cover how to perform the ongoing tasks that are essential for a reliable network: security and troubleshooting. The book concludes with a series of appendixes that are technical references for important commands and programs.

This book contains the following chapters:

Chapter 1, *Overview of TCP/IP*, gives the history of TCP/IP, a description of the protocol architecture, and a basic explanation of how the protocols function.

Chapter 2, *Delivering the Data*, describes addressing and how data passes through a network to reach the proper destination.

Chapter 3, *Network Services*, discusses the relationship between clients and server systems and the various services that are central to the function of a modern internet.

Chapter 4, *Getting Started*, begins the discussion of network setup and configuration. This chapter discusses the preliminary configuration planning needed before you configure the systems on your network.

Chapter 5, *Basic Configuration*, describes how to configure TCP/IP in the Unix kernel, and how to configure the system to start the network services.

Chapter 6, *Configuring the Interface*, tells you how to identify a network interface to the network software. This chapter provides examples of Ethernet and PPP interface configurations.

Chapter 7, *Configuring Routing*, describes how to set up routing so that systems on your network can communicate properly with other networks. It covers the static routing table, commonly used routing protocols, and gated, a package that provides the latest implementations of several routing protocols.

Chapter 8, *Configuring DNS*, describes how to administer the name server program that converts system names to Internet addresses.

Chapter 9, *Local Network Services*, describes how to configure many common network servers. The chapter discusses the DHCP configuration server, the LPD print server, the POP and IMAP mail servers, the Network File System (NFS), the Samba file and print server, and the Network Information System (NIS).

Chapter 10, *sendmail*, discusses how to configure sendmail, which is the daemon responsible for delivering electronic mail.

Chapter 11, *Configuring Apache*, describes how the Apache web server software is configured.

Chapter 12, *Network Security*, discusses how to live on the Internet without excessive risk. This chapter covers the security threats introduced by the network, and describes the plans and preparations you can make to meet those threats.

Chapter 13, *Troubleshooting TCP/IP*, tells you what to do when something goes wrong. It describes the techniques and tools used to troubleshoot TCP/IP problems and gives examples of actual problems and their solutions.

Appendix A, *PPP Tools*, is a reference guide to the various programs used to configure a serial port for TCP/IP. The reference covers dip, pppd, and chat.

Appendix B, *A gated Reference*, is a reference guide to the configuration language of the gated routing package.

Appendix C, *A named Reference*, is a reference guide to the Berkeley Internet Name Domain (BIND) name server software.

Appendix D, *A dhcpd Reference*, is a reference guide to the Dynamic Host Configuration Protocol Daemon (dhcpd).

Appendix E, *A sendmail Reference*, is a reference guide to sendmail syntax, options, and flags.

Appendix F, *Solaris httpd.conf File*, lists the contents of the Apache configuration file discussed in Chapter 11.

Appendix G, *RFC Excerpts*, contains detailed protocol references taken directly from the RFCs that support the protocol troubleshooting examples in Chapter 13. This appendix explains how to obtain your own copies of the RFCs.

Unix Versions

Most of the examples in this book are taken from Red Hat Linux, currently the most popular Linux distribution, and from Solaris 8, the Sun operating system based on System V Unix. Fortunately, TCP/IP software is remarkably standard from system to system, and because of this uniformity, the examples should be applicable to any Linux, System V, or BSD-based Unix system. There are small variations in command output or command-line options, but these should not present a problem.

Some of the ancillary networking software is identified separately from the Unix operating system by its own release number. Many such packages are discussed, and when appropriate are identified by their release numbers. The most important of these packages are:

BIND

Our discussion of the BIND software is based on version 8 running on a Solaris 8 system. BIND 8 is the version of the BIND software delivered with Solaris, and supports all of the standard resource records. There are relatively few administrative differences between BIND 8 and the newer BIND 9 release for basic configurations.

sendmail

Our discussion of sendmail is based on release 8.11.3. This version should be compatible with other releases of sendmail v8.

Conventions

This book uses the following typographical conventions:

Italic

is used for the names of files, directories, hostnames, domain names, and to emphasize new terms when they are introduced.

`Constant width`

is used to show the contents of files or the output from commands. It is also used to represent commands, options, and keywords in text.

`Constant width bold`

is used in examples to show commands typed on the command line.

`Constant width italic`

is used in examples and text to show variables for which a context-specific substitution should be made. (The variable `filename`, for example, would be replaced by some actual filename.)

%, #

Commands that you would give interactively are shown using the default C shell prompt (%). If the command must be executed as root, it is shown using the default superuser prompt (#). Because the examples may include multiple systems on a network, the prompt may be preceded by the name of the system on which the command was given.

[option]

When showing command syntax, optional parts of the command are placed within brackets. For example, ls [-l] means that the -l option is not required.

We'd Like to Hear from You

We have tested and verified all of the information in this book to the best of our ability, but you may find that features have changed (or even that we have made mistakes!). Please let us know about any errors you find, as well as your suggestions for future editions, by writing:

O'Reilly & Associates, Inc.
1005 Gravenstein Highway North
Sebastopol, CA 95472
(800) 998-9938 (in the United States or Canada)
(707) 829-0515 (international or local)
(707) 829-0104 (fax)

There is a web page for this book, where we list errata, examples, or any additional information. You can access this page at:

http://www.oreilly.com/catalog/tcp3

To comment or ask technical questions about this book, send email to:

bookquestions@oreilly.com

For more information about books, conferences, Resource Centers, and the O'Reilly Network, see our web site at:

http://www.oreilly.com

To find out what else Craig is doing, visit his web site, *http://www.wrotethebook.com*.

Acknowledgments

I would like to thank the many people who helped in the preparation of this book. All of the people who contributed to the first and second editions deserve thanks because so much of their input lives on in this edition. For the first edition that's John Wack, Matt Bishop, Wietse Venema, Eric Allman, Jeff Honig, Scott Brim, and John Dorgan. For the second edition that's Eric Allman again, Bryan Costales, Cricket Liu, Paul Albitz, Ted Lemon, Elizabeth Zwicky, Brent Chapman, Simson Garfinkel, Jeff Sedayao, and Æleen Frisch.

The third edition has also benefited from many contributors—a surprising number of whom are authors in their own right. They set me straight about the technical details and improved my prose. Three authors are due special thanks. Cricket Liu, one of the authors of the best book ever written about DNS, provided many comments that improved the sections on Domain Name System. David Collier-Brown, one of the authors of *Using Samba*, did a complete technical review of the Samba material. Charles Aulds, author of a best-selling book on Apache administration, provided insights into Apache configuration. All of these people helped me make this book better than earlier editions. Thanks!

All the people at O'Reilly & Associates have been very helpful. Deb Cameron, my editor, deserves a special thanks. Deb kept everything moving forward while balancing the demands of a beautiful newborn daughter, Bethany Rose. Emily Quill was the production editor and project manager. Jeff Holcomb and Jane Ellin performed quality control checks. Leanne Soylemez provided production assistance. Tom Dinse wrote the index. Edie Freedman designed the cover, and Melanie Wang designed the interior format of the book. Neil Walls converted the book from Microsoft Word to Framemaker. Chris Reilley and Robert Romano's illustrations from the earlier editions have been updated by Robert Romano and Jessamyn Read.

Finally, I want to thank my family—Kathy, Sara, David, and Rebecca. They keep my feet on the ground when the pressure to meet deadlines is driving me into orbit. They are the best.

## CHAPTER 1

In this chapter:
- TCP/IP and the Internet
- A Data Communications Model
- TCP/IP Protocol Architecture
- Network Access Layer
- Internet Layer
- Transport Layer
- Application Layer

Overview of TCP/IP

All of us who use a Unix desktop system—engineers, educators, scientists, and business people—have second careers as Unix system administrators. Networking these computers gives us new tasks as network administrators.

Network administration and system administration are two different jobs. System administration tasks such as adding users and doing backups are isolated to one independent computer system. Not so with network administration. Once you place your computer on a network, it interacts with many other systems. The way you do network administration tasks has effects, good and bad, not only on your system but on other systems on the network. A sound understanding of basic network administration benefits everyone.

Networking your computers dramatically enhances their ability to communicate—and most computers are used more for communication than computation. Many mainframes and supercomputers are busy crunching the numbers for business and science, but the number of these systems in use pales in comparison to the millions of systems busy moving mail to a remote colleague or retrieving information from a remote repository. Further, when you think of the hundreds of millions of desktop systems that are used primarily for preparing documents to communicate ideas from one person to another, it is easy to see why most computers can be viewed as communications devices.

The positive impact of computer communications increases with the number and type of computers that participate in the network. One of the great benefits of TCP/IP is that it provides interoperable communications between all types of hardware and all kinds of operating systems.

The name "TCP/IP" refers to an entire suite of data communications protocols. The suite gets its name from two of the protocols that belong to it: the Transmission Control Protocol (TCP) and the Internet Protocol (IP). TCP/IP is the traditional name for this protocol suite and it is the name used in this book. The TCP/IP protocol suite is also called the Internet Protocol Suite (IPS). Both names are acceptable.

This book is a practical, step-by-step guide to configuring and managing TCP/IP networking software on Unix computer systems. TCP/IP is the leading communications software for local area networks and enterprise intranets, and it is the foundation of the worldwide Internet. TCP/IP is the most important networking software available to a Unix network administrator.

The first part of this book discusses the basics of TCP/IP and how it moves data across a network. The second part explains how to configure and run TCP/IP on a Unix system. Let's start with a little history.

TCP/IP and the Internet

In 1969 the Advanced Research Projects Agency (ARPA) funded a research and development project to create an experimental packet-switching network. This network, called the *ARPAnet*, was built to study techniques for providing robust, reliable, vendor-independent data communications. Many techniques of modern data communications were developed in the ARPAnet.

The experimental network was so successful that many of the organizations attached to it began to use it for daily data communications. In 1975 the ARPAnet was converted from an experimental network to an operational network, and the responsibility for administering the network was given to the Defense Communications Agency (DCA).* However, development of the ARPAnet did not stop just because it was being used as an operational network; the basic TCP/IP protocols were developed after the network was operational.

The TCP/IP protocols were adopted as Military Standards (MIL STD) in 1983, and all hosts connected to the network were required to convert to the new protocols. To ease this conversion, DARPA† funded Bolt, Beranek, and Newman (BBN) to implement TCP/IP in Berkeley (BSD) Unix. Thus began the marriage of Unix and TCP/IP.

About the time that TCP/IP was adopted as a standard, the term *Internet* came into common usage. In 1983 the old ARPAnet was divided into MILNET, the unclassified part of the Defense Data Network (DDN), and a new, smaller ARPAnet. "Internet" was used to refer to the entire network: MILNET plus ARPAnet.

In 1985 the National Science Foundation (NSF) created NSFNet and connected it to the then-existing Internet. The original NSFNet linked together the five NSF supercomputer centers. It was smaller than the ARPAnet and no faster: 56Kbps. Still, the

---

* DCA has since changed its name to Defense Information Systems Agency (DISA).

† During the 1980s, ARPA, which is part of the U.S. Department of Defense, became Defense Advanced Research Projects Agency (DARPA). Whether it is known as ARPA or DARPA, the agency and its mission of funding advanced research have remained the same.

creation of the NSFNet was a significant event in the history of the Internet because NSF brought with it a new vision of the use of the Internet. NSF wanted to extend the network to every scientist and engineer in the United States. To accomplish this, in 1987 NSF created a new, faster backbone and a three-tiered network topology that included the backbone, regional networks, and local networks. In 1990 the ARPA-net formally passed out of existence, and in 1995 the NSFNet ceased its role as a primary Internet backbone network.

Today the Internet is larger than ever and encompasses hundreds of thousands of networks worldwide. It is no longer dependent on a core (or backbone) network or on governmental support. Today's Internet is built by commercial providers. National network providers, called tier-one providers, and regional network providers create the infrastructure. Internet Service Providers (ISPs) provide local access and user services. This network of networks is linked together in the United States at several major interconnection points called Network Access Points (NAPs).

The Internet has grown far beyond its original scope. The original networks and agencies that built the Internet no longer play an essential role for the current network. The Internet has evolved from a simple backbone network, through a three-tiered hierarchical structure, to a huge network of interconnected, distributed network hubs. It has grown exponentially since 1983—doubling in size every year. Through all of this incredible change one thing has remained constant: the Internet is built on the TCP/IP protocol suite.

A sign of the network's success is the confusion that surrounds the term *internet*. Originally it was used only as the name of the network built upon IP. Now *internet* is a generic term used to refer to an entire class of networks. An internet (lowercase "i") is any collection of separate physical networks, interconnected by a common protocol, to form a single logical network. The Internet (uppercase "I") is the worldwide collection of interconnected networks, which grew out of the original ARPAnet, that uses IP to link the various physical networks into a single logical network. In this book, both "internet" and "Internet" refer to networks that are interconnected by TCP/IP.

Because TCP/IP is required for Internet connection, the growth of the Internet spurred interest in TCP/IP. As more organizations became familiar with TCP/IP, they saw that its power can be applied in other network applications as well. The Internet protocols are often used for local area networking even when the local network is not connected to the Internet. TCP/IP is also widely used to build enterprise networks. TCP/IP-based enterprise networks that use Internet techniques and web tools to disseminate internal corporate information are called *intranets*. TCP/IP is the foundation of all of these varied networks.

TCP/IP Features

The popularity of the TCP/IP protocols did not grow rapidly just because the protocols were there, or because connecting to the Internet mandated their use. They met an important need (worldwide data communication) at the right time, and they had several important features that allowed them to meet this need. These features are:

- Open protocol standards, freely available and developed independently from any specific computer hardware or operating system. Because it is so widely supported, TCP/IP is ideal for uniting different hardware and software components, even if you don't communicate over the Internet.

- Independence from specific physical network hardware. This allows TCP/IP to integrate many different kinds of networks. TCP/IP can be run over an Ethernet, a DSL connection, a dial-up line, an optical network, and virtually any other kind of physical transmission medium.

- A common addressing scheme that allows any TCP/IP device to uniquely address any other device in the entire network, even if the network is as large as the worldwide Internet.

- Standardized high-level protocols for consistent, widely available user services.

Protocol Standards

Protocols are formal rules of behavior. In international relations, protocols minimize the problems caused by cultural differences when various nations work together. By agreeing to a common set of rules that are widely known and independent of any nation's customs, diplomatic protocols minimize misunderstandings; everyone knows how to act and how to interpret the actions of others. Similarly, when computers communicate, it is necessary to define a set of rules to govern their communications.

In data communications, these sets of rules are also called *protocols*. In homogeneous networks, a single computer vendor specifies a set of communications rules designed to use the strengths of the vendor's operating system and hardware architecture. But homogeneous networks are like the culture of a single country—only the natives are truly at home in it. TCP/IP creates a heterogeneous network with open protocols that are independent of operating system and architectural differences. TCP/IP protocols are available to everyone and are developed and changed by consensus, not by the fiat of one manufacturer. Everyone is free to develop products to meet these open protocol specifications.

The open nature of TCP/IP protocols requires an open standards development process and publicly available standards documents. Internet standards are developed by the Internet Engineering Task Force (IETF) in open, public meetings. The protocols developed in this process are published as *Requests for Comments* (RFCs).* As the title "Request for Comments" implies, the style and content of these documents are much less rigid than in most standards documents. RFCs contain a wide range of interesting and useful information, and are not limited to the formal specification of data communications protocols. There are three basic types of RFCs: standards (STD), best current practices (BCP), and informational (FYI).

RFCs that define official protocol standards are STDs and are given an STD number in addition to an RFC number. Creating an official Internet standard is a rigorous process. *Standards track* RFCs pass through three *maturity levels* before becoming standards:

Proposed Standard
> This is a protocol specification that is important enough and has received enough Internet community support to be considered for a standard. The specification is stable and well understood, but it is not yet a standard and may be withdrawn from consideration to be a standard.

Draft Standard
> This is a protocol specification for which at least two independent, interoperable implementations exist. A draft standard is a final specification undergoing widespread testing. It will change only if the testing forces a change.

Internet Standard
> A specification is declared a standard only after extensive testing and only if the protocol defined in the specification is considered to be of significant benefit to the Internet community.

There are two categories of standards. A *Technical Specification* (TS) defines a protocol. An *Applicability Statement* (AS) defines when the protocol is to be used. There are three *requirement levels* that define the applicability of a standard:

Required
> This standard protocol is a required part of every TCP/IP implementation. It must be included for the TCP/IP stack to be compliant.

Recommended
> This standard protocol should be included in every TCP/IP implementation, although it is not required for minimal compliance.

Elective
> This standard is optional. It is up to the software vendor to implement it or not.

Two other requirements levels (*limited use* and *not recommended*) apply to RFCs that are not part of the standards track. A "limited use" protocol is used only in special

---

* Interested in finding out how Internet standards are created? Read RFC 2026, *The Internet Standards Process*.

circumstances, such as during an experiment. A protocol is "not recommended" when it has limited functionality or is outdated. There are three types of *non-standards track* RFCs:

Experimental
> An experimental RFC is limited to use in research and development.

Historic
> A historic RFC is outdated and no longer recommended for use.

Informational
> An informational RFC provides information of general interest to the Internet community; it does not define an Internet standard protocol.

A subset of the informational RFCs is called the FYI (For Your Information) notes. An FYI document is given an FYI number in addition to an RFC number. FYI documents provide introductory and background material about the Internet and TCP/IP networks. FYI documents are not mentioned in RFC 2026 and are not included in the Internet standards process. But there are several interesting FYI documents available.*

Another group of RFCs that go beyond documenting protocols are the Best Current Practices (BCP) RFCs. BCPs formally document techniques and procedures. Some of these document the way that the IETF conducts itself; RFC 2026 is an example of this type of BCP. Others provide guidelines for the operation of a network or service; RFC 1918, *Address Allocation for Private Internets*, is an example of this type of BCP. BCPs that provide operational guidelines are often of great interest to network administrators.

There are now more than 3,000 RFCs. As a network system administrator, you will no doubt read several. It is as important to know which ones to read as it is to understand them when you do read them. Use the RFC categories and the requirements levels to help you determine which RFCs are applicable to your situation. (A good starting point is to focus on those RFCs that also have an STD number.) To understand what you read, you need to understand the language of data communications. RFCs contain protocol implementation specifications defined in terminology that is unique to data communications.

A Data Communications Model

To discuss computer networking, it is necessary to use terms that have special meaning. Even other computer professionals may not be familiar with all the terms in the networking alphabet soup. As is always the case, English and computer-speak are

---

* To find out more about FYI documents, read RFC 1150, *FYI on FYI: An Introduction to the FYI Notes*.

not equivalent (or even necessarily compatible) languages. Although descriptions and examples should make the meaning of the networking jargon more apparent, sometimes terms are ambiguous. A common frame of reference is necessary for understanding data communications terminology.

An architectural model developed by the International Standards Organization (ISO) is frequently used to describe the structure and function of data communications protocols. This architectural model, which is called the *Open Systems Interconnect (OSI) Reference Model*, provides a common reference for discussing communications. The terms defined by this model are well understood and widely used in the data communications community—so widely used, in fact, that it is difficult to discuss data communications without using OSI's terminology.

The OSI Reference Model contains seven *layers* that define the functions of data communications protocols. Each layer of the OSI model represents a function performed when data is transferred between cooperating applications across an intervening network. Figure 1-1 identifies each layer by name and provides a short functional description for it. Looking at this figure, the protocols are like a pile of building blocks stacked one upon another. Because of this appearance, the structure is often called a *stack* or *protocol stack*.

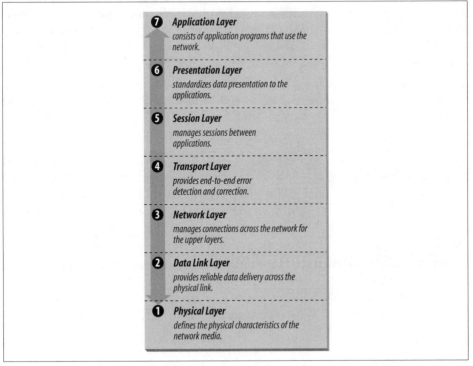

Figure 1-1. The OSI Reference Model

A layer does not define a single protocol—it defines a data communications function that may be performed by any number of protocols. Therefore, each layer may contain multiple protocols, each providing a service suitable to the function of that layer. For example, a file transfer protocol and an electronic mail protocol both provide user services, and both are part of the Application Layer.

Every protocol communicates with its peers. A *peer* is an implementation of the same protocol in the equivalent layer on a remote system; i.e., the local file transfer protocol is the peer of a remote file transfer protocol. Peer-level communications must be standardized for successful communications to take place. In the abstract, each protocol is concerned only with communicating to its peers; it does not care about the layers above or below it.

However, there must also be agreement on how to pass data between the layers on a single computer, because every layer is involved in sending data from a local application to an equivalent remote application. The upper layers rely on the lower layers to transfer the data over the underlying network. Data is passed down the stack from one layer to the next until it is transmitted over the network by the Physical Layer protocols. At the remote end, the data is passed up the stack to the receiving application. The individual layers do not need to know how the layers above and below them function; they need to know only how to pass data to them. Isolating network communications functions in different layers minimizes the impact of technological change on the entire protocol suite. New applications can be added without changing the physical network, and new network hardware can be installed without rewriting the application software.

Although the OSI model is useful, the TCP/IP protocols don't match its structure exactly. Therefore, in our discussions of TCP/IP, we use the layers of the OSI model in the following way:

Application Layer
> The Application Layer is the level of the protocol hierarchy where user-accessed network processes reside. In this text, a TCP/IP application is any network process that occurs above the Transport Layer. This includes all of the processes that users directly interact with as well as other processes at this level that users are not necessarily aware of.

Presentation Layer
> For cooperating applications to exchange data, they must agree about how data is represented. In OSI, the Presentation Layer provides standard data presentation routines. This function is frequently handled within the applications in TCP/IP, though TCP/IP protocols such as XDR and MIME also perform this function.

Session Layer
> As with the Presentation Layer, the Session Layer is not identifiable as a separate layer in the TCP/IP protocol hierarchy. The OSI Session Layer manages the

sessions (connections) between cooperating applications. In TCP/IP, this function largely occurs in the Transport Layer, and the term "session" is not used; instead, the terms "socket" and "port" are used to describe the path over which cooperating applications communicate.

Transport Layer

Much of our discussion of TCP/IP is directed to the protocols that occur in the Transport Layer. The Transport Layer in the OSI reference model guarantees that the receiver gets the data exactly as it was sent. In TCP/IP, this function is performed by the *Transmission Control Protocol* (TCP). However, TCP/IP offers a second Transport Layer service, *User Datagram Protocol* (UDP), that does not perform the end-to-end reliability checks.

Network Layer

The Network Layer manages connections across the network and isolates the upper layer protocols from the details of the underlying network. The Internet Protocol (IP), which isolates the upper layers from the underlying network and handles the addressing and delivery of data, is usually described as TCP/IP's Network Layer.

Data Link Layer

The reliable delivery of data across the underlying physical network is handled by the Data Link Layer. TCP/IP rarely creates protocols in the Data Link Layer. Most RFCs that relate to the Data Link Layer discuss how IP can make use of existing data link protocols.

Physical Layer

The Physical Layer defines the characteristics of the hardware needed to carry the data transmission signal. Features such as voltage levels and the number and location of interface pins are defined in this layer. Examples of standards at the Physical Layer are interface connectors such as RS232C and V.35, and standards for local area network wiring such as IEEE 802.3. TCP/IP does not define physical standards—it makes use of existing standards.

The terminology of the OSI reference model helps us describe TCP/IP, but to fully understand it, we must use an architectural model that more closely matches the structure of TCP/IP. The next section introduces the protocol model we'll use to describe TCP/IP.

TCP/IP Protocol Architecture

While there is no universal agreement about how to describe TCP/IP with a layered model, TCP/IP is generally viewed as being composed of fewer layers than the seven used in the OSI model. Most descriptions of TCP/IP define three to five functional levels in the protocol architecture. The four-level model illustrated in Figure 1-2 is based on the three layers (Application, Host-to-Host, and Network Access) shown in the DOD Protocol Model in the *DDN Protocol Handbook Volume 1*, with the addition of a separate Internet layer. This model provides a reasonable pictorial representation of the layers in the TCP/IP protocol hierarchy.

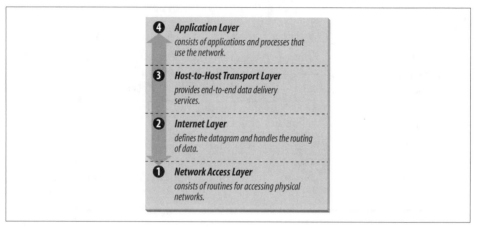

Figure 1-2. The TCP/IP architecture

As in the OSI model, data is passed down the stack when it is being sent to the network, and up the stack when it is being received from the network. The four-layered structure of TCP/IP is seen in the way data is handled as it passes down the protocol stack from the Application Layer to the underlying physical network. Each layer in the stack adds control information to ensure proper delivery. This control information is called a *header* because it is placed in front of the data to be transmitted. Each layer treats all the information it receives from the layer above as data, and places its own header in front of that information. The addition of delivery information at every layer is called *encapsulation*. (See Figure 1-3 for an illustration of this.) When data is received, the opposite happens. Each layer strips off its header before passing the data on to the layer above. As information flows back up the stack, information received from a lower layer is interpreted as both a header and data.

Each layer has its own independent data structures. Conceptually, a layer is unaware of the data structures used by the layers above and below it. In reality, the data structures of a layer are designed to be compatible with the structures used by the surrounding layers for the sake of more efficient data transmission. Still, each layer has its own data structure and its own terminology to describe that structure.

Figure 1-4 shows the terms used by different layers of TCP/IP to refer to the data being transmitted. Applications using TCP refer to data as a *stream*, while applications using UDP refer to data as a *message*. TCP calls data a *segment*, and UDP calls its data a *packet*. The Internet layer views all data as blocks called *datagrams*. TCP/IP uses many different types of underlying networks, each of which may have a different terminology for the data it transmits. Most networks refer to transmitted data as *packets* or *frames*. Figure 1-4 shows a network that transmits pieces of data it calls *frames*.

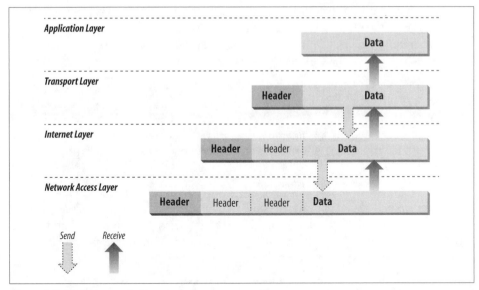

Figure 1-3. Data encapsulation

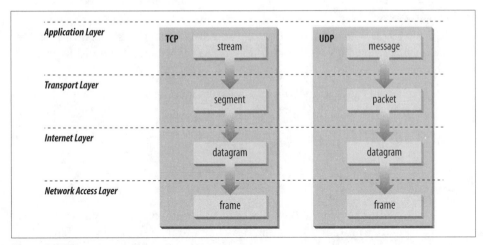

Figure 1-4. Data structures

Let's look more closely at the function of each layer, working our way up from the Network Access Layer to the Application Layer.

Network Access Layer

The *Network Access Layer* is the lowest layer of the TCP/IP protocol hierarchy. The protocols in this layer provide the means for the system to deliver data to the other devices on a directly attached network. This layer defines how to use the network to transmit an IP datagram. Unlike higher-level protocols, Network Access Layer protocols must know the details of the underlying network (its packet structure, addressing, etc.) to correctly format the data being transmitted to comply with the network constraints. The TCP/IP Network Access Layer can encompass the functions of all three lower layers of the OSI Reference Model (Network, Data Link, and Physical).

The Network Access Layer is often ignored by users. The design of TCP/IP hides the function of the lower layers, and the better-known protocols (IP, TCP, UDP, etc.) are all higher-level protocols. As new hardware technologies appear, new Network Access protocols must be developed so that TCP/IP networks can use the new hardware. Consequently, there are many access protocols—one for each physical network standard.

Functions performed at this level include encapsulation of IP datagrams into the frames transmitted by the network, and mapping of IP addresses to the physical addresses used by the network. One of TCP/IP's strengths is its universal addressing scheme. The IP address must be converted into an address that is appropriate for the physical network over which the datagram is transmitted.

Two RFCs that define Network Access Layer protocols are:

- RFC 826, *Address Resolution Protocol (ARP)*, which maps IP addresses to Ethernet addresses
- RFC 894, *A Standard for the Transmission of IP Datagrams over Ethernet Networks*, which specifies how IP datagrams are encapsulated for transmission over Ethernet networks

As implemented in Unix, protocols in this layer often appear as a combination of device drivers and related programs. The modules that are identified with network device names usually encapsulate and deliver the data to the network, while separate programs perform related functions such as address mapping.

Internet Layer

The layer above the Network Access Layer in the protocol hierarchy is the *Internet Layer*. The Internet Protocol (IP) is the most important protocol in this layer. The release of IP used in the current Internet is IP version 4 (IPv4), which is defined in RFC 791. There are more recent versions of IP. IP version 5 is an experimental Stream Transport (ST) protocol used for real-time data delivery. IPv5 never came into operational use. IPv6 is an IP standard that provides greatly expanded addressing capacity. Because IPv6 uses a completely different address structure, it is not interoperable with IPv4. While IPv6 is a standard version of IP, it is not yet widely used in operational, commercial networks. Since our focus is on practical, operational networks, we do not cover IPv6 in detail. In this chapter and throughout the main body of the text, "IP" refers to IPv4. IPv4 is the protocol you will configure on your system when you want to exchange data with remote systems, and it is the focus of this text.

The Internet Protocol is the heart of TCP/IP. IP provides the basic packet delivery service on which TCP/IP networks are built. All protocols, in the layers above and below IP, use the Internet Protocol to deliver data. All incoming and outgoing TCP/IP data flows through IP, regardless of its final destination.

Internet Protocol

The Internet Protocol is the building block of the Internet. Its functions include:

- Defining the datagram, which is the basic unit of transmission in the Internet
- Defining the Internet addressing scheme
- Moving data between the Network Access Layer and the Transport Layer
- Routing datagrams to remote hosts
- Performing fragmentation and re-assembly of datagrams

Before describing these functions in more detail, let's look at some of IP's characteristics. First, IP is a *connectionless protocol*. This means that it does not exchange control information (called a "handshake") to establish an end-to-end connection before transmitting data. In contrast, a *connection-oriented protocol* exchanges control information with the remote system to verify that it is ready to receive data before any data is sent. When the handshaking is successful, the systems are said to have established a *connection*. The Internet Protocol relies on protocols in other layers to establish the connection if they require connection-oriented service.

IP also relies on protocols in the other layers to provide error detection and error recovery. The Internet Protocol is sometimes called an *unreliable protocol* because it contains no error detection and recovery code. This is not to say that the protocol cannot be relied on—quite the contrary. IP can be relied upon to accurately deliver your data to the connected network, but it doesn't check whether that data was correctly received. Protocols in other layers of the TCP/IP architecture provide this checking when it is required.

The datagram

The TCP/IP protocols were built to transmit data over the ARPAnet, which was a *packet-switching network*. A *packet* is a block of data that carries with it the information necessary to deliver it, similar to a postal letter, which has an address written on its envelope. A packet-switching network uses the addressing information in the packets to switch packets from one physical network to another, moving them toward their final destination. Each packet travels the network independently of any other packet.

The *datagram* is the packet format defined by the Internet Protocol. Figure 1-5 is a pictorial representation of an IP datagram. The first five or six 32-bit words of the datagram are control information called the *header*. By default, the header is five words long; the sixth word is optional. Because the header's length is variable, it includes a field called *Internet Header Length* (IHL) that indicates the header's length in words. The header contains all the information necessary to deliver the packet.

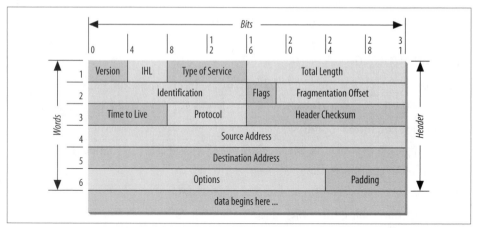

Figure 1-5. IP datagram format

The Internet Protocol delivers the datagram by checking the *Destination Address* in word 5 of the header. The Destination Address is a standard 32-bit IP address that identifies the destination network and the specific host on that network. (The format of IP addresses is explained in Chapter 2.) If the Destination Address is the address of a host on the local network, the packet is delivered directly to the destination. If the Destination Address is not on the local network, the packet is passed to a gateway for delivery. *Gateways* are devices that switch packets between the different physical networks. Deciding which gateway to use is called *routing*. IP makes the routing decision for each individual packet.

Routing datagrams

Internet gateways are commonly (and perhaps more accurately) referred to as *IP routers* because they use Internet Protocol to route packets between networks. In traditional TCP/IP jargon, there are only two types of network devices—*gateways* and *hosts*. Gateways forward packets between networks, and hosts don't. However, if a host is connected to more than one network (called a *multi-homed host*), it can forward packets between the networks. When a multi-homed host forwards packets, it acts just like any other gateway and is in fact considered to be a gateway. Current data communications terminology makes a distinction between gateways and routers,[*] but we'll use the terms *gateway* and *IP router* interchangeably.

---

[*] In current terminology, a gateway moves data between different protocols, and a router moves data between different networks. So a system that moves mail between TCP/IP and X.400 is a gateway, but a traditional IP gateway is a router.

Figure 1-6 shows the use of gateways to forward packets. The hosts (or *end systems*) process packets through all four protocol layers, while the gateways (or *intermediate systems*) process the packets only up to the Internet Layer where the routing decisions are made.

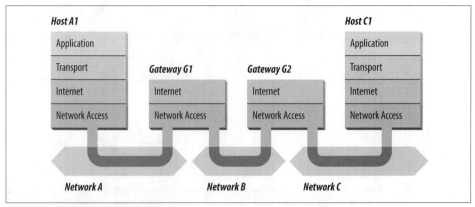

Figure 1-6. Routing through gateways

Systems can deliver packets only to other devices attached to the same physical network. Packets from *A1* destined for host *C1* are forwarded through gateways *G1* and *G2*. Host *A1* first delivers the packet to gateway *G1*, with which it shares network *A*. Gateway *G1* delivers the packet to *G2* over network *B*. Gateway *G2* then delivers the packet directly to host *C1* because they are both attached to network *C*. Host *A1* has no knowledge of any gateways beyond gateway *G1*. It sends packets destined for both networks *C* and *B* to that local gateway and then relies on that gateway to properly forward the packets along the path to their destinations. Likewise, host *C1* sends its packets to *G2* to reach a host on network *A*, as well as any host on network *B*.

Figure 1-7 shows another view of routing. This figure emphasizes that the underlying physical networks a datagram travels through may be different and even incompatible. Host *A1* on the token ring network routes the datagram through gateway *G1* to reach host *C1* on the Ethernet. Gateway *G1* forwards the data through the X.25 network to gateway *G2* for delivery to *C1*. The datagram traverses three physically different networks, but eventually arrives intact at *C1*.

Fragmenting datagrams

As a datagram is routed through different networks, it may be necessary for the IP module in a gateway to divide the datagram into smaller pieces. A datagram received from one network may be too large to be transmitted in a single packet on a different network. This condition occurs only when a gateway interconnects dissimilar physical networks.

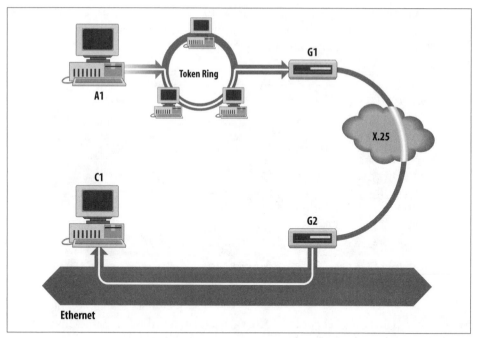

Figure 1-7. Networks, gateways, and hosts

Each type of network has a *maximum transmission unit* (MTU), which is the largest packet that it can transfer. If the datagram received from one network is longer than the other network's MTU, the datagram must be divided into smaller *fragments* for transmission. This process is called *fragmentation*. Think of a train delivering a load of steel. Each railway car can carry more steel than the trucks that will take it along the highway, so each railway car's load is unloaded onto many different trucks. In the same way that a railroad is physically different from a highway, an Ethernet is physically different from an X.25 network; IP must break an Ethernet's relatively large packets into smaller packets before it can transmit them over an X.25 network.

The format of each fragment is the same as the format of any normal datagram. Header word 2 contains information that identifies each datagram fragment and provides information about how to re-assemble the fragments back into the original datagram. The Identification field identifies what datagram the fragment belongs to, and the Fragmentation Offset field tells what piece of the datagram this fragment is. The Flags field has a "More Fragments" bit that tells IP if it has assembled all of the datagram fragments.

Passing datagrams to the transport layer

When IP receives a datagram that is addressed to the local host, it must pass the data portion of the datagram to the correct Transport Layer protocol. This is done by using the *protocol number* from word 3 of the datagram header. Each Transport Layer protocol has a unique protocol number that identifies it to IP. Protocol numbers are discussed in Chapter 2.

You can see from this short overview that IP performs many important functions. Don't expect to fully understand datagrams, gateways, routing, IP addresses, and all the other things that IP does from this short description; each chapter will add more details about these topics. So let's continue on with the other protocol in the TCP/IP Internet Layer.

Internet Control Message Protocol

An integral part of IP is the *Internet Control Message Protocol* (ICMP) defined in RFC 792. This protocol is part of the Internet Layer and uses the IP datagram delivery facility to send its messages. ICMP sends messages that perform the following control, error reporting, and informational functions for TCP/IP:

Flow control
> When datagrams arrive too fast for processing, the destination host or an intermediate gateway sends an ICMP Source Quench Message back to the sender. This tells the source to stop sending datagrams temporarily.

Detecting unreachable destinations
> When a destination is unreachable, the system detecting the problem sends a Destination Unreachable Message to the datagram's source. If the unreachable destination is a network or host, the message is sent by an intermediate gateway. But if the destination is an unreachable port, the destination host sends the message. (We discuss ports in Chapter 2.)

Redirecting routes
> A gateway sends the ICMP Redirect Message to tell a host to use another gateway, presumably because the other gateway is a better choice. This message can be used only when the source host is on the same network as both gateways. To better understand this, refer to Figure 1-7. If a host on the X.25 network sent a datagram to *G1*, it would be possible for *G1* to redirect that host to *G2* because the host, *G1*, and *G2* are all attached to the same network. On the other hand, if a host on the token ring network sent a datagram to *G1*, the host could not be redirected to use *G2*. This is because *G2* is not attached to the token ring.

Checking remote hosts
> A host can send the ICMP Echo Message to see if a remote system's Internet Protocol is up and operational. When a system receives an echo message, it replies and sends the data from the packet back to the source host. The ping command uses this message.

Transport Layer

The protocol layer just above the Internet Layer is the *Host-to-Host Transport Layer*, usually shortened to *Transport Layer*. The two most important protocols in the Transport Layer are *Transmission Control Protocol* (TCP) and *User Datagram Protocol* (UDP). TCP provides reliable data delivery service with end-to-end error detection and correction. UDP provides low-overhead, connectionless datagram delivery service. Both protocols deliver data between the Application Layer and the Internet Layer. Applications programmers can choose whichever service is more appropriate for their specific applications.

User Datagram Protocol

The User Datagram Protocol gives application programs direct access to a datagram delivery service, like the delivery service that IP provides. This allows applications to exchange messages over the network with a minimum of protocol overhead.

UDP is an unreliable, connectionless datagram protocol. As noted, "unreliable" merely means that there are no techniques in the protocol for verifying that the data reached the other end of the network correctly. Within your computer, UDP will deliver data correctly. UDP uses 16-bit *Source Port* and *Destination Port* numbers in word 1 of the message header to deliver data to the correct applications process. Figure 1-8 shows the UDP message format.

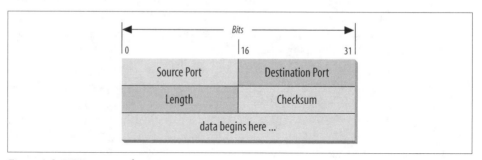

Figure 1-8. UDP message format

Why do applications programmers choose UDP as a data transport service? There are a number of good reasons. If the amount of data being transmitted is small, the overhead of creating connections and ensuring reliable delivery may be greater than the work of re-transmitting the entire data set. In this case, UDP is the most efficient choice for a Transport Layer protocol. Applications that fit a *query-response* model are also excellent candidates for using UDP. The response can be used as a positive acknowledgment to the query. If a response isn't received within a certain time period, the application just sends another query. Still other applications provide their own techniques for reliable data delivery and don't require that service from the

Transport Layer protocol. Imposing another layer of acknowledgment on any of these types of applications is inefficient.

Transmission Control Protocol

Applications that require the transport protocol to provide reliable data delivery use TCP because it verifies that data is delivered across the network accurately and in the proper sequence. TCP is a *reliable, connection-oriented, byte-stream* protocol. Let's look at each of these characteristics in more detail.

TCP provides reliability with a mechanism called *Positive Acknowledgment with Retransmission* (PAR). Simply stated, a system using PAR sends the data again *unless* it hears from the remote system that the data arrived OK. The unit of data exchanged between cooperating TCP modules is called a *segment* (see Figure 1-9). Each segment contains a checksum that the recipient uses to verify that the data is undamaged. If the data segment is received undamaged, the receiver sends a *positive acknowledgment* back to the sender. If the data segment is damaged, the receiver discards it. After an appropriate timeout period, the sending TCP module re-transmits any segment for which no positive acknowledgment has been received.

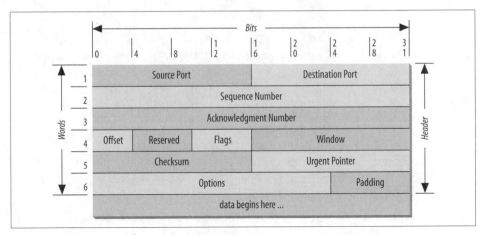

Figure 1-9. TCP segment format

TCP is connection-oriented. It establishes a logical end-to-end connection between the two communicating hosts. Control information, called a *handshake*, is exchanged between the two endpoints to establish a dialogue before data is transmitted. TCP indicates the control function of a segment by setting the appropriate bit in the Flags field in word 4 of the segment header.

The type of handshake used by TCP is called a *three-way handshake* because three segments are exchanged. Figure 1-10 shows the simplest form of the three-way handshake. Host *A* begins the connection by sending host *B* a segment with the "Synchronize sequence numbers" (SYN) bit set. This segment tells host *B* that *A* wishes to set up a connection, and it tells *B* what sequence number host *A* will use as a starting number for its segments. (Sequence numbers are used to keep data in the proper order.) Host *B* responds to *A* with a segment that has the "Acknowledgment" (ACK) and SYN bits set. *B*'s segment acknowledges the receipt of *A*'s segment, and informs *A* which sequence number host *B* will start with. Finally, host *A* sends a segment that acknowledges receipt of *B*'s segment, and transfers the first actual data.

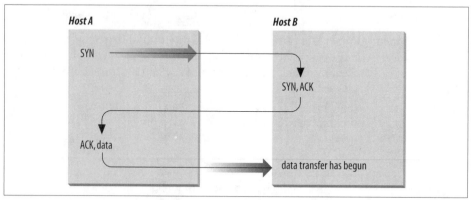

Figure 1-10. Three-way handshake

After this exchange, host *A*'s TCP has positive evidence that the remote TCP is alive and ready to receive data. As soon as the connection is established, data can be transferred. When the cooperating modules have concluded the data transfers, they will exchange a three-way handshake with segments containing the "No more data from sender" bit (called the FIN bit) to close the connection. It is the end-to-end exchange of data that provides the logical connection between the two systems.

TCP views the data it sends as a continuous stream of bytes, not as independent packets. Therefore, TCP takes care to maintain the sequence in which bytes are sent and received. The Sequence Number and Acknowledgment Number fields in the TCP segment header keep track of the bytes.

The TCP standard does not require that each system start numbering bytes with any specific number; each system chooses the number it will use as a starting point. To keep track of the data stream correctly, each end of the connection must know the other end's initial number. The two ends of the connection synchronize byte-numbering systems by exchanging SYN segments during the handshake. The Sequence Number field in the SYN segment contains the *Initial Sequence Number* (ISN), which is the starting point for the *byte-numbering system*. For security reasons the ISN should be a random number.

Each byte of data is numbered sequentially from the ISN, so the first real byte of data sent has a Sequence Number of ISN+1. The Sequence Number in the header of a data segment identifies the sequential position in the data stream of the first data byte in the segment. For example, if the first byte in the data stream was sequence number 1 (ISN=0) and 4000 bytes of data have already been transferred, then the first byte of data in the current segment is byte 4001, and the Sequence Number would be 4001.

The Acknowledgment Segment (ACK) performs two functions: *positive acknowledgment* and *flow control*. The acknowledgment tells the sender how much data has been received and how much more the receiver can accept. The Acknowledgment Number is the sequence number of the next byte the receiver expects to receive. The standard does not require an individual acknowledgment for every packet. The acknowledgment number is a positive acknowledgment of all bytes up to that number. For example, if the first byte sent was numbered 1 and 2000 bytes have been successfully received, the Acknowledgment Number would be 2001.

The Window field contains the *window*, or the number of bytes the remote end is able to accept. If the receiver is capable of accepting 6000 more bytes, the window would be 6000. The window indicates to the sender that it can continue sending segments as long as the total number of bytes that it sends is smaller than the window of bytes that the receiver can accept. The receiver controls the flow of bytes from the sender by changing the size of the window. A zero window tells the sender to cease transmission until it receives a non-zero window value.

Figure 1-11 shows a TCP data stream that starts with an Initial Sequence Number of 0. The receiving system has received and acknowledged 2000 bytes, so the current Acknowledgment Number is 2001. The receiver also has enough buffer space for another 6000 bytes, so it has advertised a window of 6000. The sender is currently sending a segment of 1000 bytes starting with Sequence Number 4001. The sender has received no acknowledgment for the bytes from 2001 on, but continues sending data as long as it is within the window. If the sender fills the window and receives no acknowledgment of the data previously sent, it will, after an appropriate timeout, send the data again starting from the first unacknowledged byte.

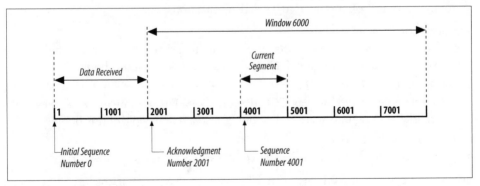

Figure 1-11. TCP data stream

In Figure 1-11 re-transmission would start from byte 2001 if no further acknowledgments are received. This procedure ensures that data is reliably received at the far end of the network.

TCP is also responsible for delivering data received from IP to the correct application. The application that the data is bound for is identified by a 16-bit number called the *port number*. The *Source Port* and *Destination Port* are contained in the first word of the segment header. Correctly passing data to and from the Application Layer is an important part of what the Transport Layer services do.

Application Layer

At the top of the TCP/IP protocol architecture is the *Application Layer*. This layer includes all processes that use the Transport Layer protocols to deliver data. There are many applications protocols. Most provide user services, and new services are always being added to this layer.

The most widely known and implemented applications protocols are:

Telnet
> The Network Terminal Protocol, which provides remote login over the network.

FTP
> The File Transfer Protocol, which is used for interactive file transfer.

SMTP
> The Simple Mail Transfer Protocol, which delivers electronic mail.

HTTP
> The Hypertext Transfer Protocol, which delivers web pages over the network.

While HTTP, FTP, SMTP, and Telnet are the most widely implemented TCP/IP applications, you will work with many others as both a user and a system administrator. Some other commonly used TCP/IP applications are:

Domain Name System (DNS)
> Also called *name service*, this application maps IP addresses to the names assigned to network devices. DNS is discussed in detail in this book.

Open Shortest Path First (OSPF)
> Routing is central to the way TCP/IP works. OSPF is used by network devices to exchange routing information. Routing is also a major topic of this book.

Network File System (NFS)
> This protocol allows files to be shared by various hosts on the network.

Some protocols, such as Telnet and FTP, can be used only if the user has some knowledge of the network. Other protocols, like OSPF, run without the user even knowing that they exist. As the system administrator, you are aware of all these applications and all the protocols in the other TCP/IP layers. And you're responsible for configuring them!

Summary

In this chapter we discussed the structure of TCP/IP, the protocol suite upon which the Internet is built. We have seen that TCP/IP is a hierarchy of four layers: Applications, Transport, Internet, and Network Access. We have examined the function of each of these layers. In the next chapter we look at how the IP datagram moves through a network when data is delivered between hosts.

CHAPTER 2
Delivering the Data

In this chapter:
- Addressing, Routing, and Multiplexing
- The IP Address
- Internet Routing Architecture
- The Routing Table
- Address Resolution
- Protocols, Ports, and Sockets

In Chapter 1, we touched on the basic architecture and design of the TCP/IP protocols. From that discussion, we know that TCP/IP is a hierarchy of four layers. In this chapter, we explore in finer detail how data moves between the protocol layers and the systems on the network. We examine the structure of Internet addresses, including how addresses route data to its final destination and how address structure is locally redefined to create subnets. We also look at the protocol and port numbers used to deliver data to the correct applications. These additional details move us from an overview of TCP/IP to the specific implementation issues that affect your system's configuration.

Addressing, Routing, and Multiplexing

To deliver data between two Internet hosts, it is necessary to move the data across the network to the correct host, and within that host to the correct user or process. TCP/IP uses three schemes to accomplish these tasks:

Addressing
> IP addresses, which uniquely identify every host on the network, deliver data to the correct host.

Routing
> Gateways deliver data to the correct network.

Multiplexing
> Protocol and port numbers deliver data to the correct software module within the host.

Each of these functions—addressing between hosts, routing between networks, and multiplexing between layers—is necessary to send data between two cooperating applications across the Internet. Let's examine each of these functions in detail.

To illustrate these concepts and provide consistent examples, we'll use an imaginary corporate network. Our imaginary company brings together authors to write computer books and conduct training. Our company network is made up of several networks at our training facilities and publishing office, as well as a connection to the Internet. We are responsible for managing the Ethernet in the computing center. This network's structure, or *topology*, is shown in Figure 2-1.

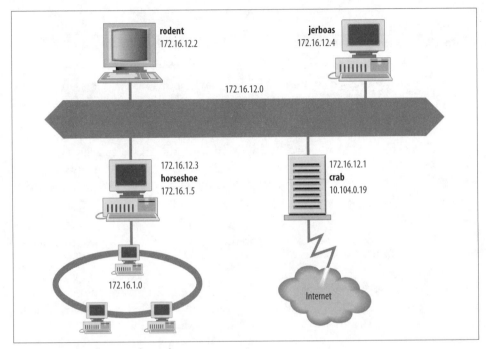

Figure 2-1. Sample network topology

The icons in the figure represent computer systems. There are, of course, several other imaginary systems on our imaginary network, but we'll use the hosts *rodent* (a workstation) and *crab* (a system that serves as a gateway) for most of our examples. The thick line is our computer center Ethernet, and the oval is the local network that connects our various corporate networks. The cloud is the Internet, and the numbers are IP addresses.

The IP Address

An IP address is a 32-bit value that uniquely identifies every device attached to a TCP/IP network. IP addresses are usually written as four decimal numbers separated by dots (periods) in a format called *dotted decimal notation.*[*] Each decimal number

---

[*] Addresses are occasionally written in other formats, e.g., as hexadecimal numbers. Whatever the notation, the structure and meaning of the address are the same.

represents an 8-bit byte of the 32-bit address, and each of the four numbers is in the range 0–255 (the decimal values possible in a single byte).

IP addresses are often called host addresses. While this is common usage, it is slightly misleading. IP addresses are assigned to network interfaces, not to computer systems. A gateway, such as *crab* (see Figure 2-1), has a different address for each network to which it is connected. The gateway is known to other devices by the address associated with the network that it shares with those devices. For example, *rodent* addresses *crab* as 172.16.12.1 while external hosts address it as 10.104.0.19.

Systems can be addressed in three different ways. Individual systems are directly addressed by a host address, which is called a *unicast address*. A unicast packet is addressed to one individual host. Groups of systems can be addressed using a *multicast address*, e.g., 224.0.0.9. Routers along the path from the source to the destination recognize the special address and route copies of the packet to each member of the multicast group.* All systems on a network are addressed using the broadcast address, e.g., 172.16.255.255. The broadcast address depends on the broadcast capabilities of the underlying physical network.

The broadcast address is a good example of the fact that not all network addresses or host addresses can be assigned to a network device. Some host addresses are reserved for special uses. On all networks, host numbers 0 and 255 are reserved. An IP address with all host bits set to 1 is a *broadcast address*.† The broadcast address for network 172.16 is 172.16.255.255. A datagram sent to this address is delivered to every individual host on network 172.16. An IP address with all host bits set to 0 identifies the network itself. For example, 10.0.0.0 refers to network 10, and 172.16.0.0 refers to network 172.16. Addresses in this form are used in routing tables to refer to entire networks.

Network addresses with a first byte value greater than 223 cannot be assigned to a physical network, because those addresses are reserved for special use. There are two other network addresses that are used only for special purposes: network 0.0.0.0 designates the *default route* and network 127.0.0.0 is the *loopback address*. The default route is used to simplify the routing information that IP must handle. The loopback address simplifies network applications by allowing the local host to be addressed in the same manner as a remote host. These special network addresses play an important part when configuring a host, but these addresses are not assigned to devices on real networks. Despite these few exceptions, most addresses are assigned to physical devices and are used by IP to deliver data to those devices.

---

* This is only partially true. Multicasting is not supported by every router. Sometimes it is necessary to tunnel through routers and networks by encapsulating the multicast packet inside a unicast packet.

† There are configuration options that affect the default broadcast address. Chapter 5 discusses these options.

The Internet Protocol moves data between hosts in the form of datagrams. Each datagram is delivered to the address contained in the Destination Address (word 5) of the datagram's header. The Destination Address is a standard 32-bit IP address, which contains sufficient information to uniquely identify a network and a specific host on that network.

Address Structure

An IP address contains a *network part* and a *host part*, but the format of these parts is not the same in every IP address. The number of address bits used to identify the network and the number used to identify the host vary according to the prefix length of the address. The prefix length is determined by the address bit mask.

An address bit mask works like this: if a bit is on in the mask, that equivalent bit in the address is interpreted as a network bit; if a bit in the mask is off, the bit belongs to the host part of the address. For example, if address 172.22.12.4 is given the network mask 255.255.255.0, which has 24 bits on and 8 bits off, the first 24 bits are the network number and the last 8 bits are the host address. Combining the address and the mask tells us that this is the address of host 4 on network 172.22.12.

Specifying both the address and the mask in dotted decimal notation is cumbersome when writing out addresses. A shorthand notation is available for writing an address with its associated address mask. Instead of writing network 172.31.26.32 with a mask of 255.255.255.224, we can write 172.31.26.32/27. The format of this notation is *address/prefix-length*, where *prefix-length* is the number of bits in the network portion of the address. Without this notation, the address 172.31.26.32 could easily be misinterpreted.

Organizations usually obtain official IP addresses by purchasing a block of addresses from their Internet service provider. The ISP normally assigns a single organization a continuous block of addresses that is appropriate for the needs of the organization. For example, a moderately large business might purchase 192.168.16.0/20 while a small business might buy 192.168.32.0/24. Because the prefix shows the length of the network portion of the address, the number of host addresses that are available to an organization (the host portion of the address) is determined by subtracting the prefix from the total number of bits in an address, which is 32. Thus a prefix of 20 leaves 12 bits that are available to be locally assigned. This is called a "12-bit block" of addresses. A prefix of 24 creates an "8-bit block." Of the two sample address blocks, the first is a 12-bit block that encompasses 4,096 addresses from 192.168.16.0 to 192.168.31.255, and the second is an 8-bit block that includes the 256 addresses from 192.168.32.0 to 192.168.32.255.

Each of these address blocks appears to the outside world to be a single "network" address. Thus external routers have one route to the block 192.168.16.0/20 and one route to the block 192.168.32.0/24, regardless of the size of the address block.

Internally, however, the organization may have several separate physical networks within the address block. The flexibility of address masks means that service providers can assign arbitrary length blocks of addresses to their customers, and the customers can subdivide those address blocks using different length masks.

Subnets

The structure of an IP address can be locally modified by using host address bits as additional network address bits. Essentially, the "dividing line" between network address bits and host address bits is moved, creating additional networks but reducing the maximum number of hosts that can belong to each network. These newly designated network bits define an address block within the larger address block, which is called a *subnet*.

Organizations usually decide to subnet in order to overcome topological or organizational problems. Subnetting allows decentralized management of host addressing. With the standard addressing scheme, a central administrator is responsible for managing host addresses for the entire network. By subnetting, the administrator can delegate address assignment to smaller organizations within the overall organization—which may be a political expedient, if not a technical requirement. If you don't want to deal with the data processing department, for example, assign them their own subnet and let them manage it themselves.

Subnetting can also be used to overcome hardware differences and distance limitations. IP routers can link dissimilar physical networks together, but only if each physical network has its own unique network address. Subnetting divides a single address block into many unique subnet addresses, so that each physical network can have its own unique address.

A subnet is defined by changing the bit mask of the IP address. A *subnet mask* functions in the same way as a normal address mask: an "on" bit is interpreted as a network bit; an "off" bit belongs to the host part of the address. The difference is that a subnet mask is only used locally. On the outside, the address is still interpreted using the address mask known to the outside world.

Assume you have a small real estate business that has been assigned the address block 192.168.32.0/24. The bit mask associated with that address block is 255.255.255.0, and the block contains 256 addresses. Further, assume that your business has 10 offices, each with a half-dozen computers, and that you want to allocate some addresses to each office and keep some for future expansion. You can subdivide the 256 address block with a subnet mask that extends the network portion of the address by a few additional bits.

To subdivide 192.168.32.0/24 into 16 subnets, use the mask 255.255.255.240, i.e., 192.168.32.0/28. The first three bytes contain the original network address block; the fourth byte is divided between the subnet address and the address of the host on that subnet. Applying this mask defines the four high-order bits of the fourth byte as the subnet part of the address, and the remaining four bits—the last four bits of the fourth byte—as the host portion of the address. This creates 16 subnets that each contain 14 host addresses, which is better suited to the network topology of your small real estate business. Table 2-1 shows the subnets and host addresses produced by applying this subnet mask to network address 192.168.32.0/24.

Table 2-1. Effects of a subnet mask

Network number	Host address range	Broadcast address
192.168.32.0	192.168.32.1 – 192.168.32.14	192.168.32.15
192.168.32.16	192.168.32.17 – 192.168.32.30	192.168.32.31
192.168.32.32	192.168.32.33 – 192.168.32.46	192.168.32.47
192.168.32.48	192.168.32.49 – 192.168.32.62	192.168.32.63
192.168.32.64	192.168.32.65 – 192.168.32.78	192.168.32.79
192.168.32.80	192.168.32.81 – 192.168.32.94	192.168.32.95
192.168.32.96	192.168.32.97 – 192.168.32.110	192.168.32.111
192.168.32.112	192.168.32.113 – 192.168.32.126	192.168.32.127
192.168.32.128	192.168.32.129 – 192.168.32.142	192.168.32.143
192.168.32.144	192.168.32.145 – 192.168.32.158	192.168.32.159
192.168.32.160	192.168.32.161 – 192.168.32.174	192.168.32.175
192.168.32.176	192.168.32.177 – 192.168.32.190	192.168.32.191
192.168.32.192	192.168.32.193 – 192.168.32.206	192.168.32.207
192.168.32.208	192.168.32.209 – 192.168.32.222	192.168.32.223
192.168.32.224	192.168.32.225 – 192.168.32.238	192.168.32.239
192.168.32.240	192.168.32.241 – 192.168.32.254	192.168.32.255

In Table 2-1, the first row describes a subnet with a subnet number that is all 0s (the first four bits of the fourth byte are all set to 0). The last row in the table describes a subnet with a subnet number that is all 1s (the first four bits of the fourth byte are all set to 1). Originally, the RFCs implied that you should not use subnet numbers of all 0s or all 1s. However, RFC 1812, *Requirements for IP Version 4 Routers*, makes it clear that subnets of all 0s and all 1s are legal and should be supported by all routers. Some older routers did not allow the use of these addresses despite the newer RFCs. Today's router software and hardware should make it possible for you to reliably use all subnet addresses.

You don't have to manually calculate a table like this to know what subnets and host addresses are produced by a subnet mask. The calculations have already been done for you. RFC 1878, *Variable Length Subnet Table For IPv4*, lists all possible subnet masks and the valid addresses they produce.

RFC 1878 describes all 32 prefix values. But little documentation is needed because the prefix is easy to understand and remember. Writing 10.104.0.19 as 10.104.0.19/8 shows that this address has 8 bits for the network number and therefore 24 bits for the host number. Unfortunately, things are not always this neat. Sometimes the address is not given an explicit address mask, and you need to know how to determine the natural mask that an address will be assigned by default.

The Natural Mask

Originally, the IP address space was divided into a few fixed-length structures called *address classes*. The three main address classes were *class A*, *class B*, and *class C*. IP software determined the class, and therefore the structure, of an address by examining its first few bits. Address classes are no longer used, but the same rules that were used to determine the address class are now used to create the default address mask, which is called the *natural mask*. These rules are as follows:

- If the first bit of an IP address is 0, the default mask is 8 bits long (prefix 8). This is the same as the old class A network address format. The first 8 bits identify the network, and the last 24 bits identify the host.

- If the first 2 bits of the address are 1 0, the default mask is 16 bits long (prefix 16), which is the same as the old class B network address format. The first 16 bits identify the network, and the last 16 bits identify the host.

- If the first 3 bits of the address are 1 1 0, the default mask is 24 bits long (prefix 24). This mask is the same as the old class C network address format. The first 24 bits are the network address, and the last 8 bits identify the host.

- If the first 4 bits of the address are 1 1 1 0, it is a multicast address. These addresses were sometimes called *class D* addresses, but they don't really refer to specific networks. Multicast addresses are used to address groups of computers all at one time. They identify a group of computers that share a common application, such as a videoconference, as opposed to a group of computers that share a common network. All bits in a multicast address are significant for routing, so the default mask is 32 bits long (prefix 32).

When an IP address is written in dotted decimal format, it is sometimes easier to think of the address as four 8-bit bytes instead of as a 32-bit value. We can look at the address as composed of full bytes of network address and full bytes of host address when using the natural mask, because the three default masks all create prefix lengths that are multiples of 8. A simple way to determine the default mask is to look at the first byte of the address. If the value of the first byte is:

- Less than 128, the default address mask is 8 bits long; the first byte is the network number, and the next three bytes are the host address.

- From 128 to 191, the default address mask is 16 bits long; the first two bytes identify the network, and the last two bytes identify the host.

- From 192 to 223, the default address mask is 24 bits long; the first three bytes are the network address, and the last byte is the host number.
- From 224 to 239, the address is multicast. The entire address identifies a specific multicast group; therefore the default mask is 32 bits.
- Greater than 239, the address is reserved. We can ignore reserved addresses.

Figure 2-2 illustrates the two techniques for determining the default address structure. The first address is 10.104.0.19. The first bit of this address is 0; therefore, the first 8 bits define the network and the last 24 bits define the host. Explained in a byte-oriented manner, the first byte is less than 128, so the address is interpreted as host 104. 0.19 on network 10. One byte specifies the network and three bytes specify the host.

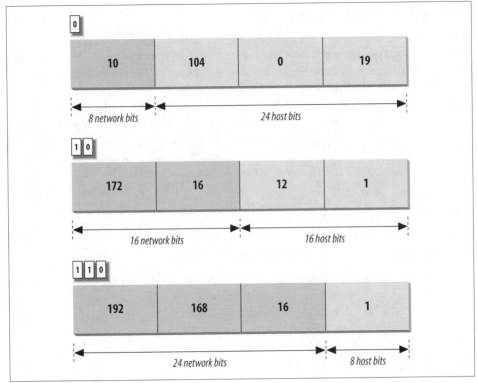

Figure 2-2. Default IP address formats

The second address is 172.16.12.1. The two high-order bits are 1 0, meaning that 16 bits define the network and 16 bits define the host. Viewed in a byte-oriented way, the first byte falls between 128 and 191, so the address refers to host 12.1 on network 172.16. Two bytes identify the network and two identify the host.

Finally, in the address 192.168.16.1, the three high-order bits are 1 1 0, indicating that 24 bits represent the network and 8 bits represent the host. The first byte of this address is in the range from 192 to 223, so this is the address of host 1 on network 192.168.16—three network bytes and one host byte.

Evaluating addresses according to the class rules discussed above limits the length of network numbers to 8, 16, or 24 bits—1, 2, or 3 bytes. The IP address, however, is not really byte-oriented. It is 32 contiguous bits. The address *bit mask* provides a flexible way to define the network and host portions of an address. IP uses the network portion of the address to route the datagram between networks. The full address, including the host information, is used to identify an individual host. Because of the dual role of IP addresses, the flexibility of address masks not only makes more addresses available for use, but also has a positive impact on routing.

CIDR Blocks and Route Aggregation

The IP address, which provides universal addressing across all of the networks of the Internet, is one of the great strengths of the TCP/IP protocol suite. However, the original class structure of the IP address had weaknesses. The TCP/IP designers did not envision the enormous scale of today's network. When TCP/IP was being designed, networking was limited to large organizations that could afford substantial computer systems. The idea of a powerful Unix system on every desktop did not exist. At that time, a 32-bit address seemed so large that it was divided into classes to reduce the processing load on routers, even though dividing the address into classes sharply reduced the number of host addresses actually available for use. For example, assigning a large network a single class B address instead of six class C addresses reduced the load on the router because the router needed to keep only one route for that entire organization. However, an organization that was assigned the class B address probably did not have 64,000 computers, so most of the host addresses available to the organization were never used.

The class-structured address design was critically strained by the rapid growth of the Internet. At one point it appeared that all class B addresses might be rapidly exhausted. The rapid depletion of the class B addresses showed that three primary address classes were not enough: class A was much too large and class C was much too small. Even a class B address was too large for many networks, but was used because it was better than the alternatives.

The obvious solution to the class B address crisis was to force organizations to use multiple class C addresses. There were millions of these addresses available and they were in no immediate danger of depletion. As is often the case, the obvious solution was not as simple as it seemed. Each class C address requires its own entry within the routing table. Assigning thousands or millions of class C addresses would cause the routing table to grow so rapidly that the routers would soon be overwhelmed. The solution required the new way of looking at addresses that address masks provide; it also required a new way of assigning addresses.

Originally network addresses were assigned in more or less sequential order as they were requested. This worked fine when the network was small and centralized. However, it did not take network topology into account. Thus, only random chance determined if the same intermediate routers would be used to reach network 195.4.12.0 and network 195.4.13.0, which makes it difficult to reduce the size of the routing table. Addresses can be aggregated only if they are contiguous numbers and are reachable through the same route. For example, if addresses are contiguous for one service provider, a single route can be created for that aggregation because that service provider will have a limited number of connections to the Internet. But if one network address is in France and the next contiguous address is in Australia, creating a consolidated route for these addresses is not possible.

Today, large, contiguous blocks of addresses are assigned to large network service providers in a manner that better reflects the topology of the network. The service providers then allocate chunks of these address blocks to the organizations to which they provide network services. Because the assignment of addresses reflects the topology of the network, it permits route aggregation. Under this scheme, we know that network 195.4.12.0 and network 195.4.13.0 are reachable through the same intermediate routers. In fact, both of these addresses are in the range of the addresses assigned to Europe, 194.0.0.0 to 195.255.255.255.

Assigning addresses that reflect the topology of the network enables route aggregation but does not implement it. As long as network 195.4.12.0 and network 195.4.13.0 were interpreted as separate class C addresses, they still required separate entries in the routing table. The development of address masks not only increased the usable address space, but it improved routing.

The use of an address mask instead of the old address classes to determine the destination network is called *Classless Inter-Domain Routing* (CIDR).[*] CIDR requires modifications to the routers and routing protocols. The protocols need to distribute, along with the destination addresses, address masks that define how the addresses are interpreted. The routers and hosts need to know how to interpret these addresses as "classless" addresses and how to apply the bit mask that accompanies the address. All new operating systems and routing protocols support address masks.

CIDR was intended as an interim solution, but it has proved much more durable than its designers imagined. CIDR has provided address and routing relief for many years and is capable of providing it for many more years to come. The long-term solution for address depletion is to replace the current addressing scheme with a new one. In the TCP/IP protocol suite, addressing is defined by the IP protocol. Therefore, to define a new address structure, the Internet Engineering Task Force (IETF) created a new version of IP called IPv6.

---

[*] CIDR is pronounced "cider."

IPv6

IPv6 is an improvement on the IP protocol based on 20 years of operational experience. The original motivation for the new protocol was the threat of address depletion. IPv6 has a very large 128-bit address, so address depletion is not an issue. The large address also makes it possible to use a hierarchical address structure to reduce the burden on routers while still maintaining more than enough addresses for future network growth. But large addresses are only one of the benefits of the new protocol. Other benefits of IPv6 are:

- Improved security built into the protocol
- Simplified, fixed-length, word-aligned headers to speed header processing and reduce overhead
- Improved techniques for handling header options

IPv6 has several good features, but it is still not widely used. This is partly because enhancements to IPv4, improvements in hardware performance, and changes in the way that networks are configured have reduced the demand for the new features of IPv6.

A critical shortage of addresses did not materialize for three reasons:

- CIDR makes the assignment of addresses more flexible, which in turn makes more addresses available and permits aggregation to reduce the burden on routers.
- Private addresses and NAT have greatly reduced the demand for official addresses. Many organizations prefer to use private addresses for all systems on their internal networks because private addresses reduce the administrative burden and improve security.
- Permanent, fixed address assignment is less common than dynamic address assignment. The majority of systems use dynamic addresses temporarily assigned by the configuration protocol DHCP.

The creation of the IPsec standards for IPv4 lessened the need for the security enhancements of IPv6. In fact, many of the security tools and features available for IPv4 systems are not being fully utilized, indicating that the demand for tools that secure the link may have been overestimated.

IPv6 eliminates hop-by-hop segmentation, has a more efficient header design, and features enhanced option processing. These things make it more efficient to process IPv6 packets than to handle IPv4 packets. However, for the vast majority of systems, this increased efficiency is not needed because processing IP datagrams is a very minor task. Most systems are at the edge of the network and handle relatively few communications packets. Processor speed and memory have increased enormously while hardware prices have fallen. Most managers would rather buy more hardware using the proven IPv4 protocol than risk implementing the new IPv6 protocol just to save a few machine cycles. Only those systems located near the core of the network would truly benefit from this efficiency, and although important, those systems are relatively few in number.

All of these things have worked together to lessen the demand for IPv6. This lack of demand has limited the number of organizations that have adopted IPv6 as their primary communications protocol, and a large user community is the one thing that a protocol needs to be truly successful. We use communications protocols to communicate with other people. If there are not enough people using the protocol, we don't feel the need to use it. IPv6 is still in the early-adopter phase. Most organizations do not use IPv6 at all, and many that do use it only for experimental purposes.* Between organizations, most IPv6 communications are encapsulated inside IPv4 datagrams and sent over the Internet inside IPv4 tunnels. It will be some time before it is the primary protocol of operational networks.

If you run an operational network, you should not be overly concerned with IPv6. The current generation of TCP/IP (IPv4), with the enhancements that CIDR and other extensions provide, should be more than adequate for your current network needs. On your network and the Internet, you will use IPv4 and 32-bit IP addresses.

Internet Routing Architecture

Chapter 1 described the evolution of the Internet architecture over the years. Along with these architectural changes have come changes in the way that routing information is disseminated within the network.

In the original Internet structure, there was a hierarchy of gateways. This hierarchy reflected the fact that the Internet was built upon the existing ARPAnet. When the Internet was created, the ARPAnet was the backbone of the network: a central delivery medium to carry long-distance traffic. This central system was called the *core*, and the centrally managed gateways that interconnected it were called the *core gateways*.

In that hierarchical structure, routing information about all of the networks on the Internet was passed into the core gateways. The core gateways processed the information and then exchanged it among themselves using the *Gateway to Gateway Protocol* (GGP). The processed routing information was then passed back out to the external gateways. The core gateways maintained accurate routing information for the entire Internet.

Using the hierarchical core router model to distribute routing information has a major weakness: every route must be processed by the core. This places a tremendous processing burden on the core, and as the Internet grew larger the burden

---

* Both Solaris and Linux include support for IPv6 if you wish to experiment with it.

increased. In network-speak, we say that this routing model does not "scale well." For this reason, a new model emerged.

Even in the days of a single Internet core, groups of independent networks called autonomous systems existed outside of the core. The term *autonomous system* (AS) has a formal meaning in TCP/IP routing. An autonomous system is not merely an independent network. It is a collection of networks and gateways with its own internal mechanism for collecting routing information and passing it to other independent network systems. The routing information passed to the other network systems is called *reachability information*. Reachability information simply says which networks can be reached through that autonomous system. In the days of a single Internet core, autonomous systems passed reachability information into the core for processing. The *Exterior Gateway Protocol* (EGP) was the protocol used to pass reachability information between autonomous systems and into the core.

The new routing model is based on co-equal collections of autonomous systems called *routing domains*. Routing domains exchange routing information with other domains using *Border Gateway Protocol* (BGP). Each routing domain processes the information it receives from other domains. Unlike the hierarchical model, this model does not depend on a single core system to choose the "best" routes. Each routing domain does this processing for itself; therefore, this model is more expandable. Figure 2-3 represents this model with three intersecting circles. Each circle is a routing domain. The overlapping areas are border areas, where routing information is shared. The domains share information but do not rely on any one system to provide all routing information.

The problem with this model is: how are "best" routes determined in a global network if there is no central routing authority, like the core, that is trusted to determine the "best" routes? In the days of the NSFNET, the *policy routing database* (PRDB) was used to determine whether the reachability information advertised by an autonomous system was valid. But now, even the NSFNET does not play a central role.

To fill this void, NSF created the *Routing Arbiter* (RA) servers when it created the *Network Access Points* (NAPs) that provide interconnection points for the various service provider networks. A route arbiter is located at each NAP. The server provides access to the *Routing Arbiter Database* (RADB), which replaced the PRDB. ISPs can query servers to validate the reachability information advertised by an autonomous system.

The RADB is only part of the *Internet Routing Registry* (IRR). As befits a distributed routing architecture, there are multiple organizations that validate and register routing information. Europeans were the pioneers in this. The Reseaux IP Europeens (RIPE) Network Control Center (NCC) provides the routing registry for European IP networks. Big network carriers provide registries for their customers. All of the registries share a common format based on the RIPE-181 standard.

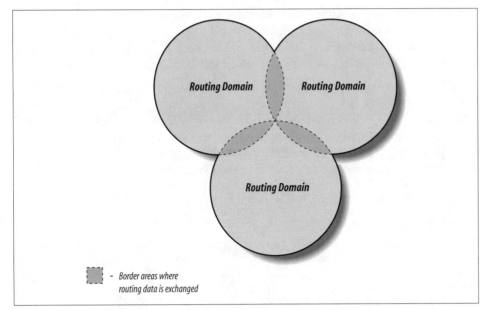

Figure 2-3. *Routing domains*

Many ISPs do not use the route servers. Instead they depend on formal and informal bilateral agreements, where two ISPs get together and decide what reachability information each will accept from the other. They create, in effect, private routing policies. Small ISPs have criticized the routing policies of the tier-one providers, claiming that they limit competition. In response, most tier-one providers have promised to make the policies public, which should clarify the basis for the current architecture and may even spark more changes.

Creating an effective routing architecture continues to be a major challenge for the Internet, and the routing architecture will certainly evolve over time. No matter how it is derived, the routing information eventually winds up in your local gateway, where it is used by IP to make routing decisions.

The Routing Table

Gateways route data between networks, but all network devices, hosts as well as gateways, must make routing decisions. For most hosts, the routing decisions are simple:

- If the destination host is on the local network, the data is delivered to the destination host.
- If the destination host is on a remote network, the data is forwarded to a local gateway.

IP routing decisions are simply table lookups. Packets are routed toward their destinations as directed by the *routing table* (also called the *forwarding table*). The routing table maps destinations to the router and network interface that IP must use to reach that destination. Examining the routing table on a Linux system shows this.

On a Linux system, use the route command with the -n option to display the routing table.* The -n option prevents route from converting IP addresses to hostnames, which gives a clearer display. Here is a routing table from a sample Red Hat system:

```
# route -n
Kernel IP routing table
Destination    Gateway       Genmask          Flags Metric Ref    Use Iface
172.16.55.0    0.0.0.0       255.255.255.0    U     0      0        0 eth0
172.16.50.0    172.16.55.36  255.255.255.0    UG    0      0        0 eth0
127.0.0.0      0.0.0.0       255.0.0.0        U     0      0        0 lo
0.0.0.0        172.16.55.1   0.0.0.0          UG    0      0        0 eth0
```

On a Linux system, the route -n command displays the routing table with the following fields:

Destination

> The value against which the destination IP address is matched.

Gateway

> The router to use to reach the specified destination.

Genmask

> The address mask used to match an IP address to the value shown in the Destination field.

Flags

> Certain characteristics of this route. The possible Linux flag values are:†

> U   Indicates that the route is up and operational.

> H   Indicates that this is a route to a specific host (most routes are to networks).

> G   Indicates that the route uses an external gateway. The system's network interfaces provide routes to directly connected networks. All other routes use external gateways. Directly connected networks do not have the G flag set; all other routes do.

> R   Indicates a route that was installed, probably by a dynamic routing protocol running on this system, using the reinstate option.

> D   Indicates that this route was added because of an ICMP Redirect Message. When a system learns of a route via an ICMP Redirect, it adds the route to

---

* The netstat command is used to examine the routing table on Solaris 8 systems. A Solaris example is covered later in this chapter.

† The flags R, M, C, I, and ! are specific to Linux. The other flags are used on most Unix systems.

its routing table so that additional packets bound for that destination will not need to be redirected. The system uses the D flag to mark these routes.

M   Indicates a route that was modified, probably by a dynamic routing protocol running on this system, using the mod option.

A   Indicates a cached route that has an associated entry in the ARP table.

C   Indicates that this route came from the kernel routing cache. Most systems use two routing tables: the Forwarding Information Base (FIB), which is the table we are interested in because it is used for the routing decision, and the kernel routing cache, which lists the source and destination of recently used routes. This flag is documented, but I have never seen the C flag in a routing table listing, even when listing the routing cache.

L   Indicates that the destination of this route is one of the addresses of this computer. These "local routes" are found only in the routing cache.

B   Indicates a route whose destination is a broadcast address. These "broadcast routes" are found only in the routing cache. Solaris assigns the flag to both broadcast addresses and network addresses; i.e., both 172.16.255.255 and 172.16.0.0 are given the B flag by Solaris systems that live on network 172.16.0.0/16.

I   Indicates a route that uses the loopback interface for some purpose other than addressing the loopback network. These "internal routes" are found only in the routing cache.

!   Indicates that datagrams bound for this destination will be rejected. Linux permits you to manually install "negative" routes. These are routes that explicitly block data bound for a specific destination. This is Linux-specific and rarely used, but it is a possible flag setting.

Metric
The "cost" of the route. The metric is used to sort duplicate routes if any appear in the table. Beyond this, a dynamic routing protocol is required to make use of the metric.

Ref
The number of times the route has been referenced to establish a connection. This value is not used by Linux systems.

Use
The number of times this route was looked up by IP.

Iface
The name of the network interface* used by this route.

---

* The *network interface* is the network access hardware and software that IP uses to communicate with the physical network. See Chapter 6 for details.

Each entry in the routing table starts with a *destination value*. The destination value is the key against which the IP address is matched to determine if this is the correct route to use to reach the IP address. The destination value is usually called the "destination network," although it does not need to be a network address. The destination value can be a host address, a multicast address, an address block that covers an aggregation of many networks, or a special value for the default route or loopback address. In all cases, however, the Destination field contains the value against which the destination address from the IP packet is matched to determine if IP should deliver the datagram using this route.

The Genmask field is the bit mask that IP applies to the destination address from the packet to see if the address matches the destination value in the table. If a bit is on in the bit mask, the corresponding bit in the destination address is significant for matching the address. Thus, the address 172.16.50.183 would match the second entry in the sample table because ANDing the address with 255.55.255.0 yields 172.16.50.0.

When an address matches an entry in the table, the Gateway field tells IP how to reach the specified destination. If the Gateway field contains the IP address of a router, the router is used. If the Gateway field contains all 0s (0.0.0.0 when route is run with -n) or an asterisk (* when route is run without -n), the destination network is a directly connected network and the "gateway" is the computer's network interface. The last field displayed for each table entry is the network interface used for the route. In the example, it is either the first Ethernet interface (*eth0*) or the loopback interface (*lo*). The destination, gateway, mask, and interface define the route.

The remaining four fields (Ref, Use, Flags, and Metric) display supporting information about the route. These informational fields are of only marginal value. Some systems keep an accurate count in the Ref field; others, such as Linux, don't really use it. Linux uses the Use field to count the number of times a route needed to be looked up because it was not in the routing cache when IP needed it. Some other systems show the number of packets transmitted via the route in the Use field. The Flags field displays information that is often obvious even without the flags: every route has the U flag set because every route in the routing table is up by definition, and looking at the Gateway field tells you whether or not an external gateway is used without looking for the G flag. The Metric value is used only if you run some version of the Routing Information Protocol (RIP) on your system. Don't be distracted by this information. The heart of the routing table is the route, which is composed of the destination, the mask, the gateway, and the interface.

IP uses the information from the routing table (the forwarding table) to construct the routes used for active connections. The routes associated with active connections are stored in the routing cache. On Linux systems, the routing cache can be examined by adding the -C argument to the route command line:

```
$ route -Cn
Kernel IP routing cache
```

Source	Destination	Gateway	Flags	Metric	Ref	Use	Iface
127.0.0.1	127.0.0.1	127.0.0.1	l	0	0	0	lo
192.203.230.10	172.16.55.3	172.16.55.3	l	0	0	0	lo
172.16.55.1	172.16.55.255	172.16.55.255	ibl	0	0	243	lo
172.16.55.2	172.16.55.255	172.16.55.255	ibl	0	0	15	lo
172.16.55.3	192.203.230.10	172.16.55.1		0	0	0	eth0
127.0.0.1	127.0.0.1	127.0.0.1	l	0	0	0	lo
172.16.55.3	132.163.4.9	172.16.55.1		0	0	0	eth0
172.16.55.2	172.16.55.3	172.16.55.3	il	0	0	149	lo
172.16.55.3	172.16.55.2	172.16.55.2		0	1	0	eth0
132.163.4.9	172.16.55.3	172.16.55.3	l	0	0	0	lo

The routing cache is different from the routing table because the cache shows established routes. The routing table is used to make routing decisions; the routing cache is used *after* the decision is made. The routing cache shows the source and destination of a network connection and the gateway and interface used to make that connection.

Linux provides a good example for showing the contents of the routing table because the Linux route command displays the table so clearly. On Solaris systems, the route command has a very different syntax. When running Solaris, display the routing table's contents with the netstat -nr command. The -r option tells netstat to display the routing table, and the -n option tells netstat to display the table in numeric form.[*]

```
% netstat -nr
Routing Table: IPv4
```

Destination	Gateway	Flags	Ref	Use	Interface
127.0.0.1	127.0.0.1	UH	1	298	loo
default	172.16.12.1	UG	2	50360	
172.16.12.0	172.16.12.2	U	40	111379	dnet0
172.16.2.0	172.16.12.3	UG	4	1179	
172.16.1.0	172.16.12.3	UG	10	1113	
172.16.3.0	172.16.12.3	UG	2	1379	
172.16.4.0	172.16.12.3	UG	4	1119	

The first table entry is the *loopback route* for the local host. This is the loopback address mentioned earlier as a reserved network number. Because every system uses the loopback route to send datagrams to itself, an entry for the loopback interface is in every host's routing table. The H flag is set because Solaris creates a route to a specific host (127.0.0.1), not a route to an entire network (127.0.0.0). We'll see the loopback facility again when we discuss kernel configuration and the ifconfig command. For now, however, our real interest is in external routes.

Another unique entry in this routing table is the one with the word "default" in the destination field. This entry is for the *default route*, and the gateway specified in this

---

[*] Linux incorporates the address mask information in the routing table display. Solaris 8 supports address masks; it just doesn't show them when displaying the routing table.

entry is the *default gateway*. The default route is the other reserved network number mentioned earlier: 0.0.0.0. The default gateway is used whenever there is no specific route in the table for a destination network address. For example, this routing table has no entry for network 192.168.16.0. If IP receives any datagrams addressed to this network, it will send them via the default gateway 172.16.12.1.

All of the gateways that appear in the routing table are on networks directly connected to the local system. In the sample shown above, this means that the gateway addresses all begin with 172.16.12 regardless of the destination address. This is the only network to which this sample host is directly attached, and therefore it is the only network to which it can directly deliver data. The gateways that a host uses to reach the rest of the Internet must be on its subnet.

In Figure 2-4, the IP layer of two hosts and a gateway on our imaginary network is replaced by a small piece of a routing table, showing destination networks and the gateways used to reach those destinations. Assume that the address mask used for network 172.16.0.0 is 255.255.255.0. When the source host (172.16.12.2) sends data to the destination host (172.16.1.2), it applies the address mask to determine that it should look for the destination network address 172.16.1.0 in the routing table. The routing table in the source host shows that data bound for 172.16.1.0 is sent to gateway 172.16.12.3. The source host forwards the packet to the gateway. The gateway does the same steps and looks up the destination address in its routing table. Gateway 172.16.12.3 then makes direct delivery through its 172.16.1.5 interface. Examining the routing tables in Figure 2-4 shows that all systems list only gateways on networks to which they are directly connected. This is illustrated by the fact that 172.16.12.1 is the default gateway for both 172.16.12.2 and 172.16.12.3, but because 172.16.1.2 cannot reach network 172.16.12.0 directly, it has a different default route.

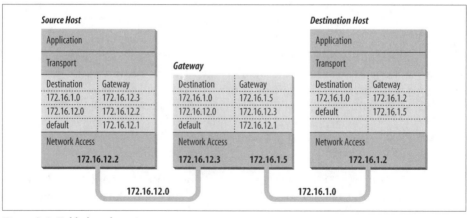

Figure 2-4. Table-based routing

A routing table does not contain end-to-end routes. A route points only to the next gateway, called the *next hop*, along the path to the destination network.* The host relies on the local gateway to deliver the data, and the gateway relies on other gateways. As a datagram moves from one gateway to another, it should eventually reach one that is directly connected to its destination network. It is this last gateway that finally delivers the data to the destination host.

IP uses the network portion of the address to route the datagram between networks. The full address, including the host information, is used to make final delivery when the datagram reaches the destination network.

Address Resolution

The IP address and the routing table direct a datagram to a specific physical network, but when data travels across a network, it must obey the physical layer protocols used by that network. The physical networks underlying the TCP/IP network do not understand IP addressing. Physical networks have their own addressing schemes, and there are as many different addressing schemes as there are different types of physical networks. One task of the network access protocols is to map IP addresses to physical network addresses.

The most common example of this Network Access Layer function is the translation of IP addresses to Ethernet addresses. The protocol that performs this function is *Address Resolution Protocol* (ARP), which is defined in RFC 826.

The ARP software maintains a table of translations between IP addresses and Ethernet addresses. This table is built dynamically. When ARP receives a request to translate an IP address, it checks for the address in its table. If the address is found, it returns the Ethernet address to the requesting software. If the address is not found, ARP broadcasts a packet to every host on the Ethernet. The packet contains the IP address for which an Ethernet address is sought. If a receiving host identifies the IP address as its own, it responds by sending its Ethernet address back to the requesting host. The response is then cached in the ARP table.

The arp command displays the contents of the ARP table. To display the entire ARP table, use the arp -a command. Individual entries can be displayed by specifying a hostname on the arp command line. For example, to check the entry for *rodent* in the ARP table on *crab*, enter:

```
% arp rodent
rodent (172.16.12.2) at 0:50:ba:3f:c2:5e
```

---

* As we'll see in Chapter 7, some routing protocols, such as OSPF and BGP, obtain end-to-end routing information. Nevertheless, the packet is still passed to the next-hop router.

Checking all entries in the table with the -a option produces the following output:

```
% arp -a

Net to Media Table: IPv4
Device   IP Address             Mask       Flags   Phys Addr
------   -------------------    ---------------    -----   ----------------
dnet0    rodent                 255.255.255.255            00:50:ba:3f:c2:5e
dnet0    crab                   255.255.255.255 SP         00:00:c0:dd:d4:da
dnet0    224.0.0.0              240.0.0.0       SM         01:00:5e:00:00:00
```

This table tells you that when *crab* forwards datagrams addressed to *rodent*, it puts those datagrams into Ethernet frames and sends them to Ethernet address 00:50:ba:3f:c2:5e.

One of the entries in the sample table (*rodent*) was added dynamically as a result of queries by *crab*. Two of the entries (*crab* and *224.0.0.0*) are static entries added as a result of the configuration of *crab*. We know this because both these entries have an S, for "static," in the Flags field. The special *224.0.0.0* entry is for all multicast addresses. The M flag means "mapping" and is used only for the multicast entry. On a broadcast medium like Ethernet, the Ethernet broadcast address is used to make final delivery to a multicast group.

The P flag on the *crab* entry means that this entry will be "published." The "publish" flag indicates that when an ARP query is received for the IP address of *crab*, this system answers it with the Ethernet address 00:00:c0:dd:d4:da. This is logical because this is the ARP table on *crab*. However, it is also possible to publish Ethernet addresses for other hosts, not just for the local host. Answering ARP queries for other computers is called *proxy ARP*.

For example, assume that *24seven* is the server for a remote system named *clock* connected via a dial-up telephone line. Instead of setting up routing to the remote system, the administrator of *24seven* could place a static, published entry in the ARP table with the IP address of *clock* and the Ethernet address of *24seven*. Now when *24seven* hears an ARP query for the IP address of *clock*, it answers with its own Ethernet address. The other systems on the network therefore send packets destined for *clock* to *24seven*. *24seven* then forwards the packets on to *clock* over the telephone line. Proxy ARP is used to answer queries for systems that can't answer for themselves.

ARP tables normally don't require any attention because they are built automatically by the ARP protocol, which is very stable. However, if things go wrong, the ARP table can be manually adjusted. See "Troubleshooting with the arp Command" in Chapter 13.

Protocols, Ports, and Sockets

Once data is routed through the network and delivered to a specific host, it must be delivered to the correct user or process. As the data moves up or down the TCP/IP layers, a mechanism is needed to deliver it to the correct protocols in each layer. The system must be able to combine data from many applications into a few transport protocols, and from the transport protocols into the Internet Protocol. Combining many sources of data into a single data stream is called *multiplexing*.

Data arriving from the network must be *demultiplexed*: divided for delivery to multiple processes. To accomplish this task, IP uses *protocol numbers* to identify transport protocols, and the transport protocols use *port numbers* to identify applications.

Some protocol and port numbers are reserved to identify *well-known services*. Well-known services are standard network protocols, such as FTP and Telnet, that are commonly used throughout the network. The protocol numbers and port numbers are assigned to well-known services by the Internet Assigned Numbers Authority (IANA). Officially *assigned numbers* are documented at *http://www.iana.org*. Unix systems define protocol and port numbers in two simple text files.

Protocol Numbers

The protocol number is a single byte in the third word of the datagram header. The value identifies the protocol in the layer above IP to which the data should be passed.

On a Unix system, the protocol numbers are defined in */etc/protocols*. This file is a simple table containing the protocol name and the protocol number associated with that name. The format of the table is a single entry per line, consisting of the official protocol name, separated by whitespace from the protocol number. The protocol number is separated by whitespace from the "alias" for the protocol name. Comments in the table begin with #. An */etc/protocols* file is shown below:

```
% cat /etc/protocols
#ident  "@(#)protocols  1.5     99/03/21 SMI"   /* SVr4.0 1.1   */

#
# Internet (IP) protocols
#
ip          0    IP           # pseudo internet protocol number
icmp        1    ICMP         # internet control message protocol
ggp         3    GGP          # gateway-gateway protocol
tcp         6    TCP          # transmission control protocol
egp         8    EGP          # exterior gateway protocol
pup         12   PUP          # PARC universal packet protocol
udp         17   UDP          # user datagram protocol
hmp         20   HMP          # host monitoring protocol
xns-idp     22   XNS-IDP      # Xerox NS IDP
rdp         27   RDP          # "reliable datagram" protocol

#
# Internet (IPv6) extension headers
#
hopopt      0    HOPOPT       # Hop-by-hop options for IPv6
ipv6        41   IPv6         # IPv6 in IP encapsulation
```

```
ipv6-route    43    IPv6-Route    # Routing header for IPv6
ipv6-frag     44    IPv6-Frag     # Fragment header for IPv6
esp           50    ESP           # Encap Security Payload for IPv6
ah            51    AH            # Authentication Header for IPv6
ipv6-icmp     58    IPv6-ICMP     # IPv6 internet control message protocol
ipv6-nonxt    59    IPv6-NoNxt    # IPv6No next header extension header
ipv6-opts     60    IPv6-Opts     # Destination Options for IPv6
```

The listing above is the contents of the */etc/protocols* file from a Solaris 8 workstation. This list of numbers is by no means complete. If you refer to the Protocol Numbers section of the IANA web site, you'll see many more protocol numbers. However, a system needs to include only the numbers of the protocols that it actually uses. Even the list shown above is more than this specific workstation needed; for example, the second half of this table is used only on systems that run IPv6. Don't worry if your system doesn't use IPv6 or many of these other protocols. The additional entries do no harm.

What exactly does this table mean? When a datagram arrives and its destination address matches the local IP address, the IP layer knows that the datagram has to be delivered to one of the transport protocols above it. To decide which protocol should receive the datagram, IP looks at the datagram's protocol number. Using this table, you can see that if the datagram's protocol number is 6, IP delivers the datagram to TCP; if the protocol number is 17, IP delivers the datagram to UDP. TCP and UDP are the two transport layer services we are concerned with, but all of the protocols listed in the first half of the table use IP datagram delivery service directly. Some, such as ICMP, EGP, and GGP, have already been mentioned. Others haven't, but you don't need to be concerned with the minor protocols in order to configure and manage a TCP/IP network.

Port Numbers

After IP passes incoming data to the transport protocol, the transport protocol passes the data to the correct application process. Application processes (also called *network services*) are identified by port numbers, which are 16-bit values. The source port number, which identifies the process that sent the data, and the destination port number, which identifies the process that will receive the data, are contained in the first header word of each TCP segment and UDP packet.

Port numbers below 1024 are reserved for well-known services (like FTP and Telnet) and are assigned by the IANA. Well-known port numbers are considered "privileged ports" that should not be bound to a user process. Ports numbered from 1024 to 49151 are "registered ports." IANA tries to maintain a registry of services that use these ports, but it does not officially assign port numbers in this range. The port numbers from 49152 to 65535 are the "private ports." Private port numbers are available for any use.

Port numbers are not unique between transport layer protocols; the numbers are unique only within a specific transport protocol. In other words, TCP and UDP can and do assign the same port numbers. It is the combination of protocol and port numbers that uniquely identifies the specific process to which the data should be delivered.

On Unix systems, port numbers are defined in the */etc/services* file. There are many more network applications than there are transport layer protocols, as the size of the */etc/services* table shows. A partial */etc/services* file from a Solaris 8 workstation is shown here:

```
rodent% head -22 /etc/services
#ident  "@(#)services   1.25    99/11/06 SMI"   /* SVr4.0 1.8   */
#
#
# Copyright (c) 1999 by Sun Microsystems, Inc.
# All rights reserved.
#
# Network services, Internet style
#
tcpmux          1/tcp
echo            7/tcp
echo            7/udp
discard         9/tcp           sink null
discard         9/udp           sink null
systat          11/tcp          users
daytime         13/tcp
daytime         13/udp
netstat         15/tcp
chargen         19/tcp          ttytst source
chargen         19/udp          ttytst source
ftp-data        20/tcp
ftp             21/tcp
telnet          23/tcp
```

The format of this file is very similar to the */etc/protocols* file. Each single-line entry starts with the official name of the service separated by whitespace from the port number/protocol pairing associated with that service. The port numbers are paired with transport protocol names because different transport protocols may use the same port number. An optional list of aliases for the official service name may be provided after the port number/protocol pair.

The */etc/services* file, combined with the */etc/protocols* file, provides all of the information necessary to deliver data to the correct application. A datagram arrives at its destination based on the destination address in the fifth word of the datagram header. Using the protocol number in the third word of the datagram header, IP delivers the data from the datagram to the proper transport layer protocol. The first word of the data delivered to the transport protocol contains the destination port number that tells the transport protocol to pass the data up to a specific application. Figure 2-5 shows this delivery process.

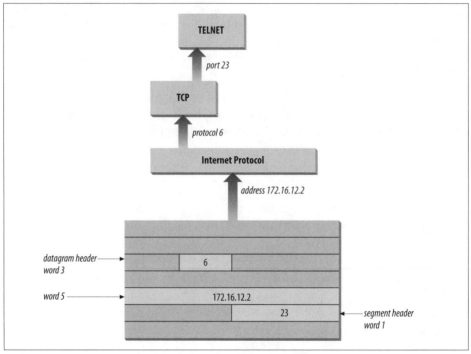

Figure 2-5. Protocol and port numbers

Despite its size, the */etc/services* file does not contain the port number of every important network service. You won't find the port number of every *Remote Procedure Call* (RPC) service in the *services* file. Sun developed a different technique for reserving ports for RPC services that doesn't involve getting a well-known port number assignment from IANA. RPC services generally use registered port numbers, which do not need to be officially assigned. When an RPC service starts, it registers its port number with the portmapper. The portmapper is a program that keeps track of the port numbers being used by RPC services. When a client wants to use an RPC service, it queries the portmapper running on the server to discover the port assigned to the service. The client can find portmapper because it is assigned well-known port 111. portmapper makes it possible to install widely used services without formally obtaining a well-known port.

Sockets

Well-known ports are standardized port numbers that enable remote computers to know which port to connect to for a particular network service. This simplifies the connection process because both the sender and receiver know in advance that data bound for a specific process will use a specific port. For example, all systems that offer Telnet do so on port 23.

Equally important is a second type of port number called a *dynamically allocated port*. As the name implies, dynamically allocated ports are not pre-assigned; they are assigned to processes when needed. The system ensures that it does not assign the same port number to two processes, and that the numbers assigned are above the range of well-known port numbers, i.e., above 1024.

Dynamically allocated ports provide the flexibility needed to support multiple users. If a telnet user is assigned port number 23 for both the source and destination ports, what port numbers are assigned to the second concurrent telnet user? To uniquely identify every connection, the source port is assigned a dynamically allocated port number, and the well-known port number is used for the destination port.

In the telnet example, the first user is given a random source port number and a destination port number of 23 (telnet). The second user is given a different random source port number and the same destination port. It is the *pair* of port numbers, source and destination, that uniquely identifies each network connection. The destination host knows the source port because it is provided in both the TCP segment header and the UDP packet header. Both hosts know the destination port because it is a well-known port.

Figure 2-6 shows the exchange of port numbers during the TCP handshake. The source host randomly generates a source port, in this example 3044. It sends out a segment with a source port of 3044 and a destination port of 23. The destination host receives the segment and responds back using 23 as its source port and 3044 as its destination port.

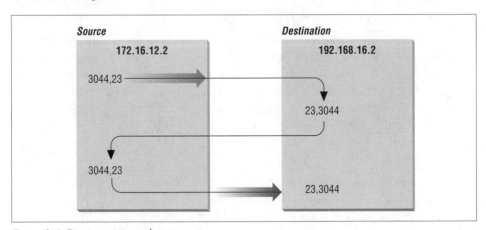

Figure 2-6. Passing port numbers

The combination of an IP address and a port number is called a *socket*. A socket uniquely identifies a single network process within the entire Internet. Sometimes the terms "socket" and "port number" are used interchangeably. In fact, well-known services are frequently referred to as "well-known sockets." In the context of this discussion, a "socket" is the combination of an IP address and a port number. A pair of sockets, one socket for the receiving host and one for the sending host, define the connection for connection-oriented protocols such as TCP.

Let's build on the example of dynamically assigned ports and well-known ports. Assume a user on host 172.16.12.2 uses Telnet to connect to host 192.168.16.2. Host 172.16.12.2 is the source host. The user is dynamically assigned a unique port number, 3382. The connection is made to the telnet service on the remote host, which is, according to the standard, assigned well-known port 23. The socket for the source side of the connection is 172.16.12.2.3382 (IP address 172.16.12.2 plus port number 3382). For the destination side of the connection, the socket is 192.168.16.2.23 (address 192.168.16.2 plus port 23). The port of the destination socket is known by both systems because it is a well-known port. The port of the source socket is known by both systems because the source host informed the destination host of the source socket when the connection request was made. The socket pair is therefore known by both the source and destination computers. The combination of the two sockets uniquely identifies this connection; no other connection in the Internet has this socket pair.

Summary

This chapter has shown how data moves through the global Internet from one specific process on the source computer to a single cooperating process on the other side of the world. TCP/IP uses globally unique addresses to identify any computer on the Internet. It uses protocol numbers and port numbers to uniquely identify a single process running on that computer.

Routing directs the datagrams destined for a remote process through the maze of the global network. Routing uses part of the IP address to identify the destination network. Every system maintains a routing table that describes how to reach remote networks. The routing table usually contains a default route that is used if the table does not contain a specific route to the remote network. A route only identifies the next computer along the path to the destination. TCP/IP uses hop-by-hop routing to move datagrams one step closer to the destination until the datagram finally reaches the destination network.

At the destination network, final delivery is made by using the full IP address (including the host part) and converting that address to a physical layer address. Address Resolution Protocol (ARP) is an example of the type of protocol used to convert IP addresses to physical layer addresses. It converts IP addresses to Ethernet addresses for final delivery.

These first two chapters described the structure of the TCP/IP protocol stack and the way in which it moves data across a network. In the next chapter, we move up the protocol stack to look at the type of services the network provides to simplify configuration and use.

In this chapter:
- Names and Addresses
- The Host Table
- DNS
- Mail Services
- File and Print Servers
- Configuration Servers

Network Services

Some network servers provide essential computer-to-computer services. These differ from application services in that they are not directly accessed by end users. Instead, these services are used by networked computers to simplify the installation, configuration, and operation of the network.

The functions performed by the servers covered in this chapter are varied:

- Name service for converting IP addresses to hostnames
- Configuration servers that simplify the installation of networked hosts by handling part or all of the TCP/IP configuration
- Electronic mail services for moving mail through the network from the sender to the recipient
- File servers that allow client computers to transparently share files
- Print servers that allow printers to be centrally maintained and shared by all users

Servers on a TCP/IP network should not be confused with traditional PC LAN servers. Every Unix host on your network can be both a server and a client. The hosts on a TCP/IP network are "peers." All systems are equal, and the network is not dependent on any one server. All of the services discussed in this chapter can be installed on one or several systems on your network.

We begin with a discussion of name service. It is an essential service that you will certainly use on your network.

Names and Addresses

The Internet Protocol document[*] defines names, addresses, and routes as follows:

> A name indicates what we seek. An address indicates where it is. A route indicates how to get there.

---

[*] RFC 791, *Internet Protocol*, Jon Postel, ISI, 1981, page 7.

Names, addresses, and routes all require the network administrator's attention. Routes and addresses were covered in the previous chapter. This section discusses names and how they are disseminated throughout the network. Every network interface attached to a TCP/IP network is identified by a unique 32-bit IP address. A name (called a *hostname*) can be assigned to any device that has an IP address. Names are assigned to devices because, compared to numeric Internet addresses, names are easier to remember and type correctly. Names aren't required by the network software, but they do make it easier for humans to use the network.

In most cases, hostnames and numeric addresses can be used interchangeably. A user wishing to telnet to the workstation at IP address 172.16.12.2 can enter:

```
% telnet 172.16.12.2
```

or use the hostname associated with that address and enter the equivalent command:

```
% telnet rodent.wrotethebook.com
```

Whether a command is entered with an address or a hostname, the network connection always takes place based on the IP address. The system converts the hostname to an address before the network connection is made. The network administrator is responsible for assigning names and addresses and storing them in the database used for the conversion.

Translating names into addresses isn't simply a "local" issue. The command telnet rodent.wrotethebook.com is expected to work correctly on every host that's connected to the network. If *rodent.wrotethebook.com* is connected to the Internet, hosts all over the world should be able to translate the name *rodent.wrotethebook.com* into the proper address. Therefore, some facility must exist for disseminating the hostname information to all hosts on the network.

There are two common methods for translating names into addresses. The older method simply looks up the hostname in a table called the *host table*.[*] The newer technique uses a distributed database system called the *Domain Name System* (DNS) to translate names to addresses. We'll examine the host table first.

The Host Table

The *host table* is a simple text file that associates IP addresses with hostnames. On most Unix systems, the table is in the file */etc/hosts*. Each table entry in */etc/hosts* contains an IP address separated by whitespace from a list of hostnames associated with that address. Comments begin with #.

---

[*] Sun's Network Information Service (NIS) is an improved technique for accessing the host table. NIS is discussed later in this chapter.

The host table on *rodent* might contain the following entries:

```
#
# Table of IP addresses and hostnames
#
172.16.12.2      rodent.wrotethebook.com rodent
127.0.0.1        localhost
172.16.12.1      crab.wrotethebook.com crab loghost
172.16.12.4      jerboas.wrotethebook.com jerboas
172.16.12.3      horseshoe.wrotethebook.com horseshoe
172.16.1.2       ora.wrotethebook.com ora
172.16.6.4       linuxuser.articles.wrotethebook.com linuxuser
```

The first entry in the sample table is for *rodent* itself. The IP address 172.16.12.2 is associated with the hostname *rodent.wrotethebook.com* and the alternate hostname (or alias) *rodent*. The hostname and all of its aliases resolve to the same IP address, in this case 172.16.12.2.

Aliases provide for name changes, alternate spellings, and shorter hostnames. They also allow for "generic hostnames." Look at the entry for 172.16.12.1. One of the aliases associated with that address is *loghost*. *loghost* is a special hostname used by Solaris in the *syslog.conf* configuration file. Some systems preconfigure programs like syslogd to direct their output to the host that has a certain generic name. You can direct the output to any host you choose by assigning it the appropriate generic name as an alias. Other commonly used generic hostnames are *lprhost*, *mailhost*, and *dumphost*.

The second entry in the sample file assigns the address 127.0.0.1 to the hostname *localhost*. As we have discussed, the network address 127.0.0.0/8 is reserved for the loopback network. The host address 127.0.0.1 is a special address used to designate the loopback address of the local host—hence the hostname *localhost*. This special addressing convention allows the host to address itself the same way it addresses a remote host. The loopback address simplifies software by allowing common code to be used for communicating with local or remote processes. This addressing convention also reduces network traffic because the *localhost* address is associated with a loopback device that loops data back to the host before it is written out to the network.

Although the host table system has been superseded by DNS, it is still widely used for the following reasons:

- Most systems have a small host table containing name and address information about the important hosts on the local network. This small table is used when DNS is not running, such as during the initial system startup. Even if you use DNS, you should create a small */etc/hosts* file containing entries for your host, for *localhost*, and for the gateways and servers on your local net.

- Sites that use NIS use the host table as input to the NIS host database. You can use NIS in conjunction with DNS, but even when they are used together, most NIS sites create host tables that have an entry for every host on the local network. Chapter 9 explains how to use NIS with DNS.

- Very small sites that are not connected to the Internet sometimes use the host table. If there are few local hosts and the information about those hosts rarely changes, and there is also no need to communicate via TCP/IP with remote sites, then there is little advantage to using DNS.

The old host table system is inadequate for the global Internet for two reasons: inability to scale and lack of an automated update process. Prior to the development of DNS, an organization called the Network Information Center (NIC) maintained a large table of Internet hosts called the *NIC host table*. Hosts included in the table were called *registered hosts*, and the NIC placed hostnames and addresses into this file for all sites on the Internet.

Even when the host table was the primary means of translating hostnames to IP addresses, most sites registered only a limited number of key systems. But even with limited registration, the table grew so large that it became an inefficient way to convert hostnames to IP addresses. There is no way that a simple table could provide adequate service for the enormous number of hosts on today's Internet.

Another problem with the host table system is that it lacks a technique for automatically distributing information about newly registered hosts. Newly registered hosts can be referenced by name as soon as a site receives the new version of the host table. However, there is no way to guarantee that the host table is distributed to a site, and no way to know who had a current version of the table and who did not. This lack of guaranteed uniform distribution is a major weakness of the host table system.

DNS

DNS overcomes both major weaknesses of the host table:

- DNS scales well. It doesn't rely on a single large table; it is a distributed database system that doesn't bog down as the database grows. DNS currently provides information on approximately 100,000,000 hosts, while fewer than 10,000 were listed in the host table.

- DNS guarantees that new host information will be disseminated to the rest of the network as it is needed.

Information is automatically disseminated, and only to those who are interested. Here's how it works. If a DNS server receives a request for information about a host for which it has no information, it passes on the request to an *authoritative server*. An authoritative server is any server responsible for maintaining accurate information about the domain being queried. When the authoritative server answers, the local server saves, or *caches*, the answer for future use. The next time the local server receives a request for this information, it answers the request itself. The ability to control host information from an authoritative source and to automatically disseminate accurate information makes DNS superior to the host table, even for networks not connected to the Internet.

In addition to superseding the host table, DNS also replaces an earlier form of name service. Unfortunately, both the old and new services were called *name service*. Both are listed in the */etc/services* file. In that file, the old software is assigned UDP port 42 and is called *nameserver* or *name*; DNS name service is assigned port 53 and is called *domain*. Naturally, there is some confusion between the two name servers. There shouldn't be—the old name service is outdated. This text discusses DNS only; when we refer to "name service," we always mean DNS.

The Domain Hierarchy

DNS is a distributed hierarchical system for resolving hostnames into IP addresses. Under DNS, there is no central database with all of the Internet host information. The information is distributed among thousands of name servers organized into a hierarchy similar to the hierarchy of the Unix filesystem. DNS has a *root domain* at the top of the domain hierarchy that is served by a group of name servers called the *root servers*.

Just as directories in the Unix filesystem are found by following a path from the root directory through subordinate directories to the target directory, information about a domain is found by tracing pointers from the root domain through subordinate domains to the target domain.

Directly under the root domain are the *top-level domains*. There are two basic types of top-level domains—geographic and organizational. Geographic domains have been set aside for each country in the world and are identified by a two-letter country code. Thus, this type of domain is called a *country code top-level domain* (ccTLD). For example, the ccTLD for the United Kingdom is *.uk*, for Japan it is *.jp*, and for the United States it is *.us*. When *.us* is used as the top-level domain, the second-level domain is usually a state's two-letter postal abbreviation (e.g., *.wy.us* for Wyoming). U.S. geographic domains are usually used by state governments and K-12 schools but are not widely used for other hosts.

Within the United States, the most popular top-level domains are organizational— that is, membership in a domain is based on the type of organization (commercial, military, etc.) to which the system belongs.[*] These domains are called *generic top-level domains* or *general-purpose top-level domains* (gTLDs).

---

[*] There is no relationship between the organizational and geographic domains in the U.S. Each system belongs to either an organizational domain *or* a geographic domain, not both.

The official generic top-level domains are:

com
> Commercial organizations

edu
> Educational institutions

gov
> Government agencies

mil
> Military organizations

net
> Network support organizations, such as network operation centers

int
> International governmental or quasi-governmental organizations

org
> Organizations that don't fit into any of the above, such as nonprofit organizations

aero
> Organizations involved in the air-transport industry

biz
> Businesses

coop
> Cooperatives

museum
> Museums

pro
> Professionals, such as doctors and lawyers

info
> Sites providing information

name
> Individuals

These are the fourteen current gTLDs. The first seven domains in the list (*com*, *edu*, *gov*, *mil*, *net*, *int*, and *org*) have been part of the domain system since the beginning. The last seven domains in the list (*aero*, *biz*, *coop*, *museum*, *pro*, *info*, and *name*) were added in 2000 to increase the number of top-level domains. One motivation for creating the new gTLDs is the huge size of the *.com* domain. It is so large that it is difficult to maintain an efficient *.com* database. Whether or not these new gTLDs will be effective in drawing registrations away from the *.com* domain remains to be seen.

Figure 3-1 illustrates the domain hierarchy using six of the original organizational top-level domains. At the top is the root. Directly below the root domain are the top-level domains. The root servers have complete information only about the top-level domains. No servers, not even the root servers, have complete information about all domains, but the root servers have pointers to the servers for the second-level domains.[*] So while the root servers may not know the answer to a query, they know who to ask.

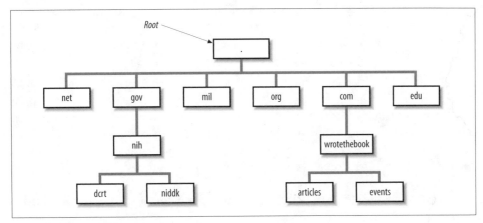

Figure 3-1. Domain hierarchy

Creating Domains and Subdomains

Several domain name registrars have been authorized by the Internet Corporation for Assigned Names and Numbers (ICANN), a nonprofit organization that was formed to take over the responsibility for allocating domain names and IP addresses. (Previously, the U.S. government oversaw this process.) ICANN has authorized these registrars to allocate domains. To obtain a domain, you apply to a registrar for authority to create a domain under one of the top-level domains. (The details of applying for a domain name are covered in Chapter 4.) Once the authority to create a domain is granted, you can create additional domains, called *subdomains*, under your domain. Let's look at how this works at our imaginary company.

Our company is a commercial, profit-making (we hope) enterprise. It clearly falls into the *com* domain. We apply for authority to create a domain named *wrotethebook* within the *com* domain. The request for the new domain contains the hostnames and addresses of the servers that will provide name service for the new domain. When the registrar approves the request, it adds pointers in the *com* domain to the new

---

[*] Figure 3-1 shows two second-level domains: *nih* under *gov* and *wrotethebook* under *com*.

domain's name servers. Now when queries are received by the root servers for the *wrotethebook.com* domain, the queries are referred to the new name servers.

The registrar's approval grants us complete authority over our new domain. Any registered domain has authority to divide its domain into subdomains. Our imaginary company can create separate domains for the division that handles special events (*events.wrotethebook.com*) and for the division that coordinates the preparation of magazine articles (*articles.wrotethebook.com*) without consulting the registrar or any other "higher authority." The decision to add subdomains is completely up to the local domain administrator. The registrars delegate authority and distribute control over names to individual organizations. Once that authority has been delegated, the individual organization is responsible for managing the names it has been assigned.

A new subdomain becomes accessible when pointers to the servers for the new domain are placed in the domain above it (see Figure 3-1). Remote servers cannot locate the *wrotethebook.com* domain until a pointer to its server is placed in the *com* domain. Likewise, the subdomains *events* and *articles* cannot be accessed until pointers to them are placed in *wrotethebook.com*. The DNS database record that points to the name servers for a domain is the NS (*name server*) record. This record contains the name of the domain and the name of the host that is a server for that domain. Chapter 8 discusses the actual DNS database. For now, let's just think of these records as pointers.

Figure 3-2 illustrates how the NS records are used as pointers. A local server has a request to resolve *linuxuser.articles.wrotethebook.com* into an IP address. The server has no information on *wrotethebook.com* in its cache, so it queries a root server (*a. root-servers.net* in our example) for the address. The root server replies with an NS record that points to *crab.wrotethebook.com* as the source of information on *wrotethebook.com*. The local server queries *crab*, which points it to *linuxmag.articles. wrotethebook.com* as the server for *articles.wrotethebook.com*. The local server then queries *linuxmag.articles.wrotethebook.com* and finally receives the desired IP address. The local server caches the A (address) record and each of the NS records. The next time it has a query for *linuxuser.articles.wrotethebook.com*, it will answer the query itself. And the next time the server has a query for other information in the *wrotethebook.com* domain, it will go directly to *crab* without involving a root server.

Figure 3-2 provides examples of both recursive and nonrecursive searches. The remote servers are examples of *nonrecursive* servers. The remote servers tell the local server who to ask next. The local server must follow the pointers itself. The local server is an example of a *recursive* server. In a *recursive* search, the server follows the pointers and returns the final answer for the query. The root servers generally perform only *nonrecursive* searches. Most other servers perform recursive searches.

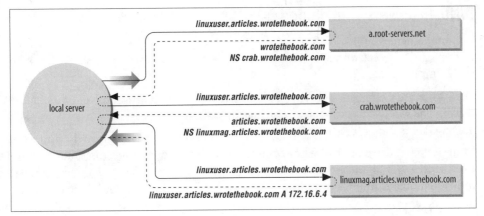

Figure 3-2. A DNS query

Domain Names

Domain names reflect the domain hierarchy. They are written from most specific (a hostname) to least specific (a top-level domain), with each part of the domain name separated by a dot.* A *fully qualified domain name* (FQDN) starts with a specific host and ends with a top-level domain. *rodent.wrotethebook.com* is the FQDN of workstation *rodent*, in the *wrotethebook* domain, of the *com* domain.

Domain names are not always written as fully qualified domain names. They can be written relative to a *default domain* in the same way that Unix pathnames are written relative to the current (default) working directory. DNS adds the default domain to the user input when constructing the query for the name server. For example, if the default domain is *wrotethebook.com*, a user can omit the *wrotethebook.com* extension for any hostnames in that domain. *crab.wrotethebook.com* could be addressed simply as *crab*; DNS adds the default domain *wrotethebook.com*.

On most systems, the default domain name is added only if there is no dot in the requested hostname. For example, *linuxuser.articles* would not be extended and would therefore not be resolved by the name server because *articles* is not a valid top-level domain. But the hostname *crab*, which contains no dot, would be extended with *wrotethebook.com*, giving the valid domain name *crab.wrotethebook.com*. Like almost everything on a Unix system, this behavior is configurable, as you'll see in Chapter 8.

How the default domain is used and how queries are constructed vary depending on the software configuration. For this reason, you should exercise caution when embedding a hostname in a program. Only a fully qualified domain name or an IP address is immune from changes in the name server software.

---

* The root domain is identified by a single dot; i.e., the root name is a null name written simply as ".".

BIND, Resolvers, and named

The implementation of DNS used on Unix systems is the *Berkeley Internet Name Domain* (BIND) software. Descriptions in this text are based on the BIND name server implementation.

DNS software is conceptually divided into two components—a resolver and a name server. The *resolver* is the software that forms the query; it asks the questions. The *name server* is the process that responds to the query; it answers the questions.

The resolver does not exist as a distinct process running on the computer. Rather, the resolver is a library of software routines (called the *resolver code*) that is linked into any program that needs to look up addresses. This library knows how to ask the name server for host information.

Under BIND, all computers use resolver code, but not all computers run the name server process. A computer that does not run a local name server process and relies on other systems for all name service answers is called a *resolver-only* system. Resolver-only configurations are common on single-user systems. Larger Unix systems usually run a local name server process.

The BIND name server runs as a distinct process called *named* (pronounced "name" "d"). Name servers are classified differently depending on how they are configured. The three main categories of name servers are:

Master
> The *master server* (also called the *primary server*) is the server from which all data about a domain is derived. The master server loads the domain's information directly from a disk file created by the domain administrator. Master servers are *authoritative*, meaning they have complete information about their domain and their responses are always accurate. There should be only one master server for a domain.

Slave
> *Slave servers* (also known as *secondary servers*) transfer the entire domain database from the master server. A particular domain's database file is called a *zone file*; copying this file to a slave server is called a *zone file transfer*. A slave server assures that it has current information about a domain by periodically transferring the domain's zone file. Slave servers are also authoritative for their domain.

Caching-only
> *Caching-only servers* get the answers to all name service queries from other name servers. Once a caching server has received an answer to a query, it caches the information and will use it in the future to answer queries itself. Most name servers cache answers and use them in this way. What makes the caching-only server unique is that this is the only technique it uses to build its domain database. Caching servers are *non-authoritative*, meaning that their information is second-hand and incomplete, though usually accurate.

The relationship between the different types of servers is an advantage that DNS has over the host table for most networks, even very small networks. Under DNS, there should be only one primary name server for each domain. DNS data is entered into the primary server's database by the domain administrator. Therefore, the administrator has central control of the hostname information. An automatically distributed, centrally controlled database is an advantage for a network of any size. When you add a new system to the network, you don't need to modify the /etc/hosts files on every node in the network; you modify only the DNS database on the primary server. The information is automatically disseminated to the other servers by full zone transfers or by caching single answers.

Network Information Service

The Network Information Service (NIS)* is an administrative database system developed by Sun Microsystems. It provides central control and automatic dissemination of important administrative files. NIS can be used in conjunction with DNS or as an alternative to it.

NIS and DNS have similarities and differences. Like DNS, the Network Information Service overcomes the problem of accurately distributing the host table, but unlike DNS, it provides service only for local area networks. NIS is not intended as a service for the Internet as a whole. Another difference is that NIS provides access to a wider range of information than DNS—much more than name-to-address conversions. It converts several standard Unix files into databases that can be queried over the network. These databases are called *NIS maps*.

NIS converts files such as /etc/hosts and /etc/networks into maps. The maps can be stored on a central server where they can be centrally maintained while still being fully accessible to the NIS clients. Because the maps can be both centrally maintained and automatically disseminated to users, NIS overcomes a major weakness of the host table. But NIS is not an alternative to DNS for Internet hosts because the host table, and therefore NIS, contains only a fraction of the information available to DNS. For this reason DNS and NIS are usually used together.

This chapter has introduced the concept of hostnames and provided an overview of the various techniques used to translate hostnames into IP addresses. This is by no means the complete story. Assigning hostnames and managing name service are important tasks for the network administrator. These topics are revisited several times in this book and discussed in extensive detail in Chapter 8.

Name service is not the only service that you will install on your network. Another service that you are sure to use is electronic mail.

---

* NIS was formerly called the "Yellow Pages," or *yp*. Although the name has changed, the abbreviation *yp* is still used.

Mail Services

Users consider electronic mail the most important network service because they use it for interpersonal communications. Some applications are newer and fancier; others consume more network bandwidth; and others are more important for the continued operation of the network. But email is the application people use to communicate with each other. It isn't very fancy, but it is vital.

TCP/IP provides a reliable, flexible email system built on a few basic protocols. These protocols are *Simple Mail Transfer Protocol* (SMTP), *Post Office Protocol* (POP), *Internet Message Access Protocol* (IMAP), and *Multipurpose Internet Mail Extensions* (MIME). There are other TCP/IP mail protocols that have some interesting features, but they are not yet widely implemented.

Our coverage concentrates on the four protocols you are most likely to use building your network: SMTP, POP, IMAP, and MIME. We start with SMTP, the foundation of all TCP/IP email systems.

Simple Mail Transfer Protocol

SMTP is the TCP/IP mail delivery protocol. It moves mail across the Internet and across your local network. SMTP is defined in RFC 821, *A Simple Mail Transfer Protocol*. It runs over the reliable, connection-oriented service provided by *Transmission Control Protocol* (TCP), and it uses well-known port number 25.* Table 3-1 lists some of the simple, human-readable commands used by SMTP.

Table 3-1. SMTP commands

Command	Syntax	Function
Hello	HELO *<sending-host>*	Identify sending SMTP
	EHLO *<sending-host>*	
From	MAIL FROM:*<from-address>*	Sender address
Recipient	RCPT TO:*<to-address>*	Recipient address
Data	DATA	Begin a message
Reset	RSET	Abort a message
Verify	VRFY *<string>*	Verify a username
Expand	EXPN *<string>*	Expand a mailing list
Help	HELP *[string]*	Request online help
Quit	QUIT	End the SMTP session

---

* Most standard TCP/IP applications are assigned a well-known port so that remote systems know how to connect the service.

SMTP is such a simple protocol you can literally do it yourself. telnet to port 25 on a remote host and type mail in from the command line using the SMTP commands. This technique is sometimes used to test a remote system's SMTP server, but we use it here to illustrate how mail is delivered between systems. The example below shows mail that Daniel on *rodent.wrotethebook.com* manually input and sent to Tyler on *crab.wrotethebook.com*.

```
$ telnet crab 25
Trying 172.16.12.1...
Connected to crab.wrotethebook.com.
Escape character is '^]'.
220 crab.wrotethebook.com ESMTP Sendmail 8.9.3+Sun/8.9.3; Thu, 19 Apr 2001 16:28:01-
0400 (EDT)
HELO rodent.wrotethebook.com
250 crab.wrotethebook.com Hello rodent [172.16.12.2], pleased to meet you
MAIL FROM:<daniel@rodent.wrotethebook.com>
250 <daniel@rodent.wrotethebook.com>... Sender ok
RCPT TO:<tyler@crab.wrotethebook.com>
250 <tyler@crab.wrotethebook.com>... Recipient ok
DATA
354 Enter mail, end with "." on a line by itself
Hi Tyler!
.
250 QAA00316 Message accepted for delivery
QUIT
221 crab.wrotethebook.com closing connection
Connection closed by foreign host.
```

The user input is shown in bold type. All of the other lines are output from the system. This example shows how simple it is. A TCP connection is opened. The sending system identifies itself. The *From* address and the *To* address are provided. The message transmission begins with the DATA command and ends with a line that contains only a period (.). The session terminates with a QUIT command. Very simple, and very few commands are used.

There are other commands (SEND, SOML, SAML, and TURN) defined in RFC 821 that are optional and not widely implemented. Even some of the commands that are implemented are not commonly used. The commands HELP, VRFY, and EXPN are designed more for interactive use than for the normal machine-to-machine interaction used by SMTP. The following excerpt from a SMTP session shows how these odd commands work.

```
HELP
214-This is Sendmail version 8.9.3+Sun
214-Topics:
214-    HELO    EHLO    MAIL    RCPT    DATA
214-    RSET    NOOP    QUIT    HELP    VRFY
214-    EXPN    VERB    ETRN    DSN
214-For more info use "HELP <topic>".
214-For local information contact postmaster at this site.
214 End of HELP info
```

```
HELP RSET
214-RSET
214-    Resets the system.
214 End of HELP info
VRFY <jane>
250 <jane@brazil.wrotethebook.com>
VRFY <mac>
250 Kathy McCafferty <<mac>>
EXPN <admin>
250-<sara@horseshoe.wrotethebook.com>
250 David Craig <<david>>
250-<tyler@wrotethebook.com>
```

The HELP command prints out a summary of the commands implemented on the system. The HELP RSET command specifically requests information about the RSET command. Frankly, this help system isn't very helpful!

The VRFY and EXPN commands are more useful but are often disabled for security reasons because they provide user account information that might be exploited by network intruders. The EXPN <admin> command asks for a listing of the email addresses in the mailing list *admin*, and that is what the system provides. The VRFY command asks for information about an individual instead of a mailing list. In the case of the VRFY <mac> command, *mac* is a local user account, and the user's account information is returned. In the case of VRFY <jane>, *jane* is an alias in the */etc/aliases* file. The value returned is the email address for *jane* found in that file. The three commands in this example are interesting but rarely used. SMTP depends on the other commands to get the real work done.

SMTP provides direct end-to-end mail delivery. Other mail systems, like UUCP and X.400, use *store and forward* protocols that move mail toward its destination one hop at a time, storing the complete message at each hop and then forwarding it on to the next system. The message proceeds in this manner until final delivery is made. Figure 3-3 illustrates both store-and-forward and direct-delivery mail systems. The UUCP address clearly shows the path that the mail takes to its destination, while the SMTP mail address implies direct delivery.*

Direct delivery allows SMTP to deliver mail without relying on intermediate hosts. If the delivery fails, the local system knows it right away. It can inform the user that sent the mail or queue the mail for later delivery without reliance on remote systems. The disadvantage of direct delivery is that it requires both systems to be fully capable of handling mail. Some systems cannot handle mail, particularly small systems such as PCs or mobile systems such as laptops. These systems are usually shut down at the end of the day and are frequently offline. Mail directed from a remote host fails with a "cannot connect" error when the local system is turned off or is offline. To handle these cases, features in the DNS system are used to route the message to a

---

* The address doesn't have anything to do with whether a system is store and forward or direct delivery. It just happens that UUCP provides an address that helps to illustrate this point.

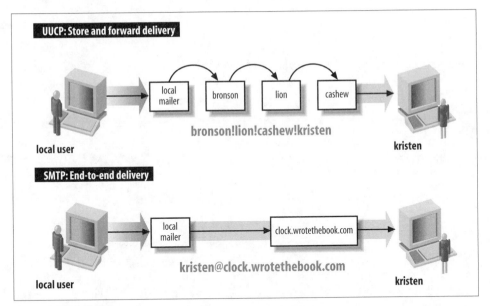

UUCP: Store and forward delivery

bronson!lion!cashew!kristen

local user

kristen

SMTP: End-to-end delivery

kristen@clock.wrotethebook.com

local user

kristen

Figure 3-3. Mail delivery systems

mail server in lieu of direct delivery. The mail is then moved from the server to the client system when the client is back online. One of the protocols TCP/IP networks use for this task is POP.

Post Office Protocol

There are two versions of Post Office Protocol: POP2 and POP3. POP2, defined in RFC 937, uses port 109, and POP3, defined in RFC 1725, uses port 110. These are incompatible protocols that use different commands, although they perform the same basic functions. The POP protocols verify the user's login name and password and move the user's mail from the server to the user's local mail reader. POP2 is rarely used anymore, so this section focuses on POP3.

A sample POP3 session clearly illustrates how a POP protocol works. POP3 is a simple request/response protocol, and just as with SMTP, you can type POP3 commands directly into its well-known port (110) and observe their effect. Here's an example with the user input shown in bold type:

```
% telnet crab 110
Trying 172.16.12.1 ...
Connected to crab.wrotethebook.com.
Escape character is '^]'.
+OK crab POP3 Server Process 3.3(1) at Mon 16-Apr-2001 4:48PM-EDT
USER hunt
+OK User name (hunt) ok. Password, please.
PASS Watts?Watt?
+OK 3 messages in folder NEWMAIL (V3.3 Rev B04)
STAT
```

```
+OK 3 459
RETR 1
+OK 146 octets
...The full text of message 1...
DELE 1
+OK message # 1 deleted
RETR 2
+OK 155 octets
...The full text of message 2...
DELE 2
+OK message # 2 deleted
RETR 3
+OK 158 octets
...The full text of message 3...
DELE 3
+OK message # 3 deleted
QUIT
+OK POP3 crab Server exiting (0 NEWMAIL messages left) Connection closed by foreign
host.
```

The USER command provides the username, and the PASS command provides the password for the account of the mailbox that is being retrieved. (This is the same username and password the user would use to log into the mail server.) In response to the STAT command, the server sends a count of the number of messages in the mailbox and the total number of bytes contained in those messages. In the example, there are three messages that contain a total of 459 bytes. RETR 1 retrieves the full text of the first message. DELE 1 deletes that message from the server. Each message is retrieved and deleted in turn. The client ends the session with the QUIT command. Simple! Table 3-2 lists the full set of POP3 commands.

Table 3-2. POP3 commands

Command	Function
USER *username*	The user's account name
PASS *password*	The user's password
STAT	Display the number of unread messages/bytes
RETR *n*	Retrieve message number *n*
DELE *n*	Delete message number *n*
LAST	Display the number of the last message accessed
LIST [*n*]	Display the size of message *n* or of all messages
RSET	Undelete all messages; reset message number to 1
TOP *n l*	Print the headers and *l* lines of message *n*
NOOP	Do nothing
QUIT	End the POP3 session

The retrieve (RETR) and delete (DELE) commands use message numbers that allow messages to be processed in any order. Additionally, there is no direct link between retrieving a message and deleting it. It is possible to delete a message that has never been read or to retain a message even after it has been read. However, POP clients do not normally take advantage of these possibilities. On an average POP server, the entire contents of the mailbox are moved to the client and either deleted from the server or retained as if never read. Deletion of individual messages on the client is not reflected on the server because all of the messages are treated as a single unit that is either deleted or retained after the initial transfer of data to the client. Email clients that want to remotely maintain a mailbox on the server are more likely to use IMAP.

Internet Message Access Protocol

Internet Message Access Protocol (IMAP) is an alternative to POP. It provides the same basic service as POP and adds features to support mailbox synchronization, which is the ability to read individual mail messages on a client or directly on the server while keeping the mailboxes on both systems completely up to date. IMAP provides the ability to manipulate individual messages on the client or the server and to have those changes reflected in the mailboxes of both systems.

IMAP uses TCP for reliable, sequenced data delivery. The IMAP port is TCP port 143.[*] Like the POP protocol, IMAP is also a request/response protocol with a small set of commands. The IMAP command set is somewhat more complex than the one used by POP because IMAP does more, yet there are still fewer than 25 IMAP commands. Table 3-3 lists the basic set of IMAP commands as defined in RFC 2060, *Internet Message Access Protocol - Version 4rev1*.

Table 3-3. IMAP4 commands

Command	Function
CAPABILITY	List the features supported by the server
NOOP	Literally "No Operation"
LOGOUT	Close the connection
AUTHENTICATE	Request an alternate authentication method
LOGIN	Provide the username and password for plain-text authentication
SELECT	Open a mailbox
EXAMINE	Open a mailbox as read-only
CREATE	Create a new mailbox
DELETE	Remove a mailbox
RENAME	Change the name of a mailbox
SUBSCRIBE	Add a mailbox to the list of active mailboxes

[*] The */etc/services* file lists two different ports for IMAP: 143 and 220. Port 220 is used by IMAP 3. IMAP 4 uses port number 143, which is the same port used by IMAP 2

Table 3-3. IMAP4 commands (continued)

Command	Function
UNSUBSCRIBE	Delete a mailbox name from the list of active mailboxes
LIST	Display the requested mailbox names from the set of all mailbox names
LSUB	Display the requested mailbox names from the set of active mailboxes
STATUS	Request the status of a mailbox
APPEND	Add a message to the end of the specified mailbox
CHECK	Force a checkpoint of the current mailbox
CLOSE	Close the mailbox and remove all messages marked for deletion
EXPUNGE	Remove from the current mailbox all messages marked for deletion
SEARCH	Display all messages in the mailbox that match the specified search criterion
FETCH	Retrieve a message from the mailbox
STORE	Modify a message in the mailbox
COPY	Copy the specified messages to the end of the specified mailbox
UID	Locate a message based on the message's unique identifier

This command set clearly illustrates the "mailbox" orientation of IMAP. The protocol is designed to remotely maintain mailboxes that are stored on the server. The protocol commands show that. Despite the increased complexity of the protocol, it is still possible to run a simple test of your IMAP server using telnet and a small number of the IMAP commands.

```
$ telnet localhost 143
Trying 127.0.0.1...
Connected to rodent.wrotethebook.com.
Escape character is '^]'.
* OK rodent.wrotethebook.com IMAP4rev1 v12.252 server ready
a0001 LOGIN craig Wats?Watt?
a0001 OK LOGIN completed
a0002 SELECT inbox
* 3 EXISTS
* 0 RECENT
* OK [UIDVALIDITY 965125671] UID validity status
* OK [UIDNEXT 5] Predicted next UID
* FLAGS (\Answered \Flagged \Deleted \Draft \Seen)
* OK [PERMANENTFLAGS (\* \Answered \Flagged \Deleted \Draft \Seen)] Permanent flags
* OK [UNSEEN 1] first unseen message in /var/spool/mail/craig
a0002 OK [READ-WRITE] SELECT completed
a0003 FETCH 1 BODY[TEXT]
* 1 FETCH (BODY[TEXT] {1440}
... an e-mail message that is 1440 bytes long ...
* 1 FETCH (FLAGS (\Seen))
a0003 OK FETCH completed
a0004 STORE 1 +FLAGS \DELETED
* 1 FETCH (FLAGS (\Seen \Deleted))
a0004 OK STORE completed
a0005 CLOSE
```

```
a0005 OK CLOSE completed
a0006 LOGOUT
* BYE rodent.wrotethebook.com IMAP4rev1 server terminating connection
a0006 OK LOGOUT completed
Connection closed by foreign host.
```

The first three lines and the last line come from telnet; all other messages come from IMAP. The first IMAP command entered by the user is LOGIN, which provides the username and password from */etc/passwd* used to authenticate this user. Notice that the command is preceded by the string A0001. This is a *tag*, which is a unique identifier generated by the client for each command. Every command must start with a tag. When you manually type in commands for a test, you are the source of the tags.

IMAP is a mailbox-oriented protocol. The SELECT command selects the mailbox that will be used. In the example, the user selects a mailbox named "inbox". The IMAP server displays the status of the mailbox, which contains three messages. Associated with each message are a number of flags. The flags are used to manage the messages in the mailbox by marking them as Seen, Unseen, Deleted, and so on.

The FETCH command downloads a message from the mailbox. In the example, the user downloads the text of the message, which is what you normally see when reading a message. It is possible, however, to download only the headers or flags.

After the message is downloaded, the user deletes it. This is done by writing the Deleted flag with the STORE command. The DELETE command is not used to delete messages; it deletes entire mailboxes. Individual messages are marked for deletion by setting the Delete flag. Messages with the Delete flag set are not deleted until either the EXPUNGE command is issued or the mailbox is explicitly closed with the CLOSE command, as is done in the example. The session is then terminated with the LOGOUT command.

Clearly, the IMAP protocol is more complex than POP; it is just about at the limits of what can reasonably be typed in manually. Of course, you don't really enter these commands manually. The desktop system and the server exchange them automatically. They are shown here only to give you a sense of the IMAP protocol. About the only IMAP test you would ever do manually is to test if imapd is up and running. To do that, you don't even need to log in; if the server answers the telnet, you know it is up and running. All you then need to do is send the LOGOUT command to gracefully close the connection.

Multipurpose Internet Mail Extensions

The last email protocol on our quick tour is *Multipurpose Internet Mail Extensions* (MIME).* As its name implies, MIME is an extension of the existing TCP/IP mail

---

* MIME is also an integral part of the Web and HTTP.

system, not a replacement for it. MIME is more concerned with what the mail system delivers than with the mechanics of delivery. It doesn't attempt to replace SMTP or TCP; it extends the definition of what constitutes "mail."

The structure of the mail message carried by SMTP is defined in RFC 822, *Standard for the Format of ARPA Internet Text Messages*. RFC 822 defines a set of mail headers that are so widely accepted they are used by many mail systems that do not use SMTP. This is a great benefit to email because it provides a common ground for mail translation and delivery through gateways to different mail networks. MIME extends RFC 822 into two areas not covered by the original RFC:

- Support for various data types. The mail system defined by RFC 821 and RFC 822 transfers only 7-bit ASCII data. This is suitable for carrying text data composed of U.S. ASCII characters, but it does not support several languages that have richer character sets, nor does it support binary data transfer.

- Support for complex message bodies. RFC 822 doesn't provide a detailed description of the body of an electronic message. It concentrates on the mail headers.

MIME addresses these two weaknesses by defining encoding techniques for carrying various forms of data and by defining a structure for the message body that allows multiple objects to be carried in a single message. RFC 1521, *Multipurpose Internet Mail Extensions Part One: Format of Internet Message Bodies*, defines two headers that give structure to the mail message body and allow it to carry various forms of data. These are the *Content-Type* header and the *Content-Transfer-Encoding* header.

As the name implies, the *Content-Type* header defines the type of data being carried in the message. The header has a Subtype field that refines the definition. Many subtypes have been defined since the original RFC was released. A current list of MIME types can be obtained from the Internet.[*] The original RFC defines seven initial content types and a few subtypes:

text
    Text data. RFC 1521 defines text subtypes *plain* and *richtext*. More than 30 subtypes have since been added, including *enriched*, *xml* and *html*.

application
    Binary data. The primary subtype defined in RFC 1521 is *octet-stream*, which indicates the data is a stream of 8-bit binary bytes. One other subtype, *Post-Script*, is defined in the standard. Since then more than 200 subtypes have been defined. They specify binary data formatted for a particular application. For example, *msword* is an application subtype.

image
    Still graphic images. Two subtypes are defined in RFC 1521: *jpeg* and *gif*. More than 20 additional subtypes have since been added, including widely used image data standards such as *tiff*, *cgm*, and *g3fax*.

---

[*] Go to *ftp://ftp.isi.edu/in-notes/iana/assignments/media-types* to retrieve the file *media-types*.

video

Moving graphic images. The initially defined subtype was *mpeg*, which is a widely used standard for computer video data. A few others have since been added, including *quicktime*.

audio

Audio data. The only subtype initially defined for audio was *basic*, which means the sounds are encoded using pulse code modulation (PCM). About 20 additional audio types, such as *MP4A-LATM*, have since been added.

multipart

Data composed of multiple independent sections. A multipart message body is made up of several independent parts. RFC 1521 defines four subtypes. The primary subtype is *mixed*, which means that each part of the message can be data of any content type. Other subtypes are *alternative*, meaning that the same data is repeated in each section in different formats; *parallel*, meaning that the data in the various parts is to be viewed simultaneously; and *digest*, meaning that each section is data of the type *message*. Several subtypes have since been added, including support for voice messages (*voice-message*) and *encrypted* messages.

message

Data that is an encapsulated mail message. RFC 1521 defines three subtypes. The primary subtype, *rfc822*, indicates that the data is a complete RFC 822 mail message. The other subtypes, *partial* and *External-body*, are both designed to handle large messages. *partial* allows large encapsulated messages to be split among multiple MIME messages. *External-body* points to an external source for the contents of a large message body so that only the pointer, not the message itself, is contained in the MIME message. Two additional subtypes that have been defined are *news* for carrying network news and *http* for HTTP traffic formatted to comply with MIME content typing.

The *Content-Transfer-Encoding* header identifies the type of encoding used on the data. Traditional SMTP systems forward only 7-bit ASCII data with a line length of less than 1000 bytes. Since the data from a MIME system may be forwarded through gateways that support only 7-bit ASCII, the data can be encoded. RFC 1521 defines six types of encoding. Some types are used to identify the encoding inherent in the data. Only two types are actual encoding techniques defined in the RFC. The six encoding types are:

7bit

U.S. ASCII data. No encoding is performed on 7-bit ASCII data.

8bit

Octet data. No encoding is performed. The data is binary, but the lines of data are short enough for SMTP transport; i.e., the lines are less than 1000 bytes long.

binary

Binary data. No encoding is performed. The data is binary and the lines may be longer than 1000 bytes. There is no difference between *binary* and *8bit* data except the line length restriction; both types of data are unencoded byte (octet) streams. MIME does not modify unencoded bitstream data.

quoted-printable

Encoded text data. This encoding technique handles data that is largely composed of printable ASCII text. The ASCII text is sent unencoded, while bytes with a value greater than 127 or less than 33 are sent encoded as strings made up of the equals sign followed by the hexadecimal value of the byte. For example, the ASCII form feed character, which has the hexadecimal value of 0C, is sent as =0C. Naturally, there's more to it than this—for example, the literal equals sign has to be sent as =3D, and the newline at the end of each line is not encoded. But this is the general idea of how *quoted-printable* data is sent.

base64

Encoded binary data. This encoding technique can be used on any byte-stream data. Three octets of data are encoded as four 6-bit characters, which increases the size of the file by one-third. The 6-bit characters are a subset of U.S. ASCII, chosen because they can be handled by any type of mail system. The maximum line length for *base64* data is 76 characters. Figure 3-4 illustrates this 3-to-4 encoding technique.

x-token

Specially encoded data. It is possible for software developers to define their own private encoding techniques. If they do so, the name of the encoding technique must begin with *X-*. Doing this is strongly discouraged because it limits interoperability between mail systems.

The number of supported data types and encoding techniques grows as new data formats appear and are used in message transmissions. New RFCs constantly define new data types and encoding. Read the latest RFCs to keep up with MIME developments.

MIME defines data types that SMTP was not designed to carry. To handle these and other future requirements, RFC 1869, *SMTP Service Extensions*, defines a technique for making SMTP *extensible*. The RFC does not define new services for SMTP; in fact, the only service extensions mentioned in the RFC are defined in other RFCs. What this RFC does define is a simple mechanism for systems to negotiate which SMTP extensions are supported. The RFC defines a new *hello* command (EHLO) and the legal responses to that command. One response is for the receiving system to return a list of the SMTP extensions it supports. This response allows the sending system to know what extended services can be used, and to avoid those that are not implemented on the remote system. SMTP implementations that support the EHLO command are called Extended SMTP (ESMTP).

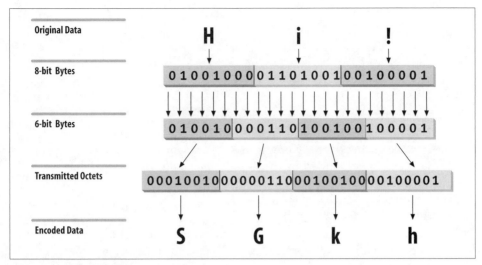

Figure 3-4. base64 encoding

Several ESMTP service extensions have been defined for MIME mailers. Table 3-4 lists some of these. The table lists the EHLO keyword associated with each extension, the number of the RFC that defines it, and its purpose. These service extensions are just an example. Other have been defined to support SMTP enhancements.

Table 3-4. SMTP service extensions

Keyword	RFC	Function
8BITMIME	1652	Accept 8bit binary data
CHUNKING	1830	Accept messages cut into chunks
CHECKPOINT	1845	Checkpoint/restart mail transactions
PIPELINING	1854	Accept multiple commands in a single send
SIZE	1870	Display maximum acceptable message size
DSN	1891	Provide delivery status notifications
ETRN	1985	Accept remote queue processing requests
ENHANCEDSTATUSCODES	2034	Provide enhanced error codes
STARTTLS	2487	Use Transport Layer Security to encrypt the email exchange
AUTH	2554	Use strong authentication to identify the email source

It is easy to check which extensions are supported by your server by using the EHLO command. The following example is from a generic Solaris 8 system, which comes with sendmail 8.9.3:

```
> telnet localhost 25
Trying 127.0.0.1...
Connected to localhost.
Escape character is '^]'.
```

```
220 crab.wrotethebook.com ESMTP Sendmail 8.9.3+Sun/8.9.3; Mon, 23 Apr 2001 11:00:35-
0400 (EDT)
EHLO crab
250-crab.wrotethebook.com Hello localhost [127.0.0.1], pleased to meet you
250-EXPN
250 HELP
250-8BITMIME
250-SIZE
250-DSN
250-ETRN
250-VERB
250-ONEX
250-XUSR
QUIT
221 crab.foobirds.org closing connection
Connection closed by foreign host.
```

The sample system lists nine commands in response to the EHLO greeting. Two of these, EXPN and HELP, are standard SMTP commands that aren't implemented on all systems (the standard commands are listed in Table 3-1). 8BITMIME, SIZE, DSN, and ETRN are ESMTP extensions, all of which are described in Table 3-4. The last three keywords in the response are VERB, ONEX, and XUSR. All of these are specific to sendmail version 8. None is defined in an RFC. VERB simply places the sendmail server in verbose mode. ONEX limits the session to a single message transaction. XUSR is equivalent to the -U sendmail command-line argument.* As the last three keywords indicate, the RFCs allow for private ESMTP extensions.

The specific extensions implemented on each system are different. For example, on a generic Solaris 2.5.1 system, only three keywords (EXPN, SIZE, and HELP) are displayed in response to EHLO. The extensions available depend on the version of sendmail that is running and on how sendmail is configured.† The purpose of EHLO is to identify these differences at the beginning of the SMTP mail exchange.

ESMTP and MIME are important because they provide a standard way to transfer non-ASCII data through email. Users share lots of application-specific data that is not 7-bit ASCII. Many users depend on email as a file transfer mechanism.

SMTP, POP, IMAP, and MIME are essential parts of the mail system, but other email protocols may also be essential in the future. The one certainty is that the network will continue to change. You need to track current developments and include helpful technologies in your planning. Two technologies that users find helpful are file sharing and printer sharing. In the next section we look at file and print servers.

---

* See Appendix E for a list of the sendmail command-line arguments.

† See Chapter 10 for the details of sendmail configuration.

File and Print Servers

File and print services make the network more convenient for users. Not long ago, disk drives and high-quality printers were relatively expensive, and diskless workstations were common. Today, every system has a large hard drive and many have their own high-quality laser printers, but the demand for resource-sharing services is higher than ever.

File Sharing

File sharing is not the same as file transfer; it is not simply the ability to move a file from one system to another. A true file-sharing system does not require you to move files across the network. It allows files to be accessed at the record level so that it is possible for a client to read a record from a file located on a remote server, update that record, and write it back to the server—without moving the entire file from the server to the client.

File sharing is transparent to the user and to the application software running on the user's system. Through file sharing, users and programs access files located on remote systems as if they were local files. In a perfect file-sharing environment, the user neither knows nor cares where files are actually stored.

File sharing didn't exist in the original TCP/IP protocol suite. It was added to support diskless workstations. Several TCP/IP protocols for file sharing have been defined, but two hold the lion's share of the file sharing market:

NetBIOS/Server Message Block
NetBIOS was originally defined by IBM. It is the basic networking used on Microsoft Windows systems. Unix systems can act as file and print servers for Windows clients by running the Samba software package that implements NetBIOS and Server Message Block (SMB) protocols.

Network File System
NFS was defined by Sun Microsystems to support their diskless workstations. NFS is designed primarily for LAN applications and is implemented for all Unix systems and many other operating systems.

For file sharing between Unix systems, you will probably use NFS, as it is the most widely used Unix file-sharing protocol. If you need to support Windows clients using Unix servers, you will probably use Samba. For a detailed discussion of both of these tools, see Chapter 9.

Print Services

A print server allows printers to be shared by everyone on the network. Printer sharing is not as important as file sharing, but it is a useful network service. The advantages of printer sharing are:

- Fewer printers are needed, and less money is spent on printers and supplies.
- Reduced maintenance. There are fewer machines to maintain, and fewer people spending time fiddling with printers.
- Access to special printers. Very high-quality color printers and very high-speed printers are expensive and needed only occasionally. Sharing these printers makes the best use of expensive resources.

There are two techniques commonly used for sharing printers on a corporate network. One technique is to use the sharing services provided by Samba. This is the technique preferred by Windows clients. The other approach is to use the traditional Unix lpr command and an lpd server. Print server configuration is also covered in Chapter 9.

This chapter concludes with a discussion of the various types of TCP/IP configuration servers. Unlike email, file sharing, and print servers, configuration servers are not used on every network. However, the demand for easier installation and improved mobility makes configuration servers an important part of many networks.

Configuration Servers

The powerful features that add to the utility and flexibility of TCP/IP also add to its complexity. TCP/IP is not as easy to configure as some other networking systems. TCP/IP requires that the configuration provide hardware, addressing, and routing information. It is designed to be independent of any specific underlying network hardware, so configuration information that can be built into the hardware in some network systems cannot be built in for TCP/IP. The information must be provided by the person responsible for the configuration. This assumes that every system is run by people who are knowledgeable enough to provide the proper information to configure the system. Unfortunately, this assumption does not always prove correct.

Configuration servers make it possible for the network administrator to control TCP/IP configuration from a central point. This relieves the end user of some of the burden of configuration and improves the quality of the information used to configure systems.

TCP/IP has used three protocols to simplify the task of configuration: RARP, BOOTP, and DHCP. We begin with RARP, the oldest and most basic of these configuration tools.

Reverse Address Resolution Protocol

RARP, defined in RFC 903, is a protocol that converts a physical network address into an IP address, which is the reverse of what Address Resolution Protocol (ARP) does. A Reverse Address Resolution Protocol server maps a physical address to an IP address for a client that doesn't know its own IP address. The client sends out a broadcast using the broadcast services of the physical network.* The broadcast packet contains the client's physical network address and asks if any system on the network knows what IP address is associated with the address. The RARP server responds with a packet that contains the client's IP address.

The client knows its physical network address because it is encoded in the Ethernet interface hardware. On most systems, you can easily check the value with a command. For example, on a Solaris 8 system, the superuser can type:

```
# ifconfig dnet0
dnet0: flags=1000843<UP,BROADCAST,RUNNING,MULTICAST,IPv4> mtu 1500 index 2
        inet 172.16.12.1 netmask ffffff00 broadcast 172.16.12.255
        ether 0:0:c0:dd:d4:da
```

The ifconfig command can set or display the configuration values for a network interface.† *dnet0* is the device name of the Ethernet interface. The Ethernet address is displayed after the *ether* label. In the example, the address is 0:0:c0:dd:d4:da.

The RARP server looks up the IP address that it uses in its response to the client in the */etc/ethers* file. The */etc/ethers* file contains the client's Ethernet address followed by the client's hostname. For example:

```
2:60:8c:48:84:49        clock
0:0:c0:a1:5e:10         ring
0:80:c7:aa:a8:04        24seven
8:0:5a:1d:c0:7e         limulus
8:0:69:4:6:31           arthropod
```

To respond to a RARP request, the server must also resolve the hostname found in the */etc/ethers* file into an IP address. DNS or the *hosts* file is used for this task. The following *hosts* file entries could be used with the *ethers* file shown above:

```
clock           172.16.3.10
ring            172.16.3.16
24seven         172.16.3.4
limulus         172.16.3.7
arthropod       172.16.3.21
```

---

* Like ARP, RARP is a Network Access Layer protocol that uses physical network services residing below the Internet Layer. See the discussion of TCP/IP protocol layers in Chapter 1.

† See Chapter 6 for information about the ifconfig command.

Given these sample files, if the server receives a RARP request that contains the Ethernet address 0:80:c7:aa:a8:04, it matches it to *24seven* in the */etc/ethers* file. The server uses the name *24seven* to look up the IP address. It then sends the IP address 172.16.3.4 out as its ARP response.

RARP is a useful tool, but it provides only the IP address. There are still several other values that need to be manually configured. Bootstrap Protocol (BOOTP) is a more flexible configuration tool that provides more values than just the IP address and can deliver those values via the network.

BOOTP is defined in RFCs 951 and 1532. The RFCs describe BOOTP as an alternative to RARP; when BOOTP is used, RARP is not needed. BOOTP, however, is a more comprehensive configuration protocol than RARP. It provides much more configuration information and has the potential to offer still more. The original specification allowed vendor extensions as a vehicle for the protocol's evolution. RFC 1048 first formalized the definition of these extensions, which have been updated over time and are currently defined in RFC 2132. BOOTP and its extensions became the basis for the Dynamic Host Configuration Protocol (DHCP). DHCP has superseded BOOTP, so DHCP is the configuration protocol that you will use on your network.

Dynamic Host Configuration Protocol

Dynamic Host Configuration Protocol (DHCP) is defined in RFCs 2131 and 2132. It's designed to be compatible with BOOTP. RFC 1534 outlines interactions between BOOTP clients and DHCP servers and between DHCP clients and BOOTP servers. DHCP is the correct configuration protocol for your network because DHCP exceeds the capabilities of BOOTP while maintaining support for existing BOOTP clients.

DHCP uses the same UDP ports as BOOTP (67 and 68) and the same *basic* packet format. But DHCP is more than just an update of BOOTP. The new protocol expands the function of BOOTP in two areas:

- The configuration parameters provided by a DHCP server include everything defined in the *Requirements for Internet Hosts* RFC. DHCP provides a client with a complete set of TCP/IP configuration values.
- DHCP permits automated allocation of IP addresses.

DHCP expands the original BOOTP packet in order to indicate the DHCP packet type and to carry a complete set of configuration information. DHCP calls the values in this part of the packet *options*. To handle the full set of configuration values from the *Requirements for Internet Hosts* RFC, the Options field is large and has a variable format.

You don't usually need to use the full set of configuration values. Don't get me wrong; it's not that the values are unnecessary—all the parameters are needed for a complete TCP/IP configuration. It's just that you don't need to *define* values for them. Default values are provided in most TCP/IP implementations, and the defaults need to be changed only in special circumstances. The expanded configuration parameters of DHCP make it a more complete protocol than BOOTP, but they are not the most useful features of DHCP.

For most network administrators, automatic allocation of IP addresses is a more interesting feature. DHCP allows addresses to be assigned in four ways:

Permanent fixed addresses
> As always, the administrator can continue to assign addresses without using the DHCP system. While this happens completely outside of DHCP, DHCP makes allowances for it by permitting addresses to be excluded from the range of addresses under the control of the DHCP server. Most networks have some permanently assigned addresses.

Manual allocation
> The network administrator keeps complete control over addresses by specifically assigning them to clients in the DHCP configuration. This is exactly the same way that addresses are handled under BOOTP. Manual allocation fails to take full advantage of the power of DHCP but might be needed if you have BOOTP clients.

Automatic allocation
> The DHCP server permanently assigns an address from a pool of addresses. The administrator is not involved in the details of assigning a client an address. This technique fails to take advantage of the DHCP server's ability to collect and reuse addresses.

Dynamic allocation
> The server assigns an address to a DHCP client for a limited period of time. The limited life of the address is called a *lease*. The client can return the address to the server at any time but must request an extension from the server to retain the address longer than the time permitted. The server automatically reclaims the address after the lease expires if the client has not requested an extension. Dynamic allocation uses the full power of DHCP.

Dynamic allocation is useful in any network, particularly a large distributed network where many systems are being added and deleted. Unused addresses are returned to the pool of addresses without relying on users or system administrators to deliberately return them. Addresses are used only when and where they're needed. Dynamic allocation allows a network to make the maximum use of a limited set of addresses. It is particularly well suited to mobile systems that move from subnet to subnet and therefore must be constantly reassigned addresses appropriate for their current network location. Even in the smallest network, dynamic allocation simplifies the network administrator's job.

Dynamic address allocation does not work for every system. Name servers, email servers, login hosts, and other shared systems are always online, and they are not mobile. These systems are accessed by name, so a shared system's domain name must resolve to the correct address. Shared systems are manually allocated permanent, fixed addresses.

Dynamic address assignment has major repercussions for DNS. DNS is required to map hostnames to IP addresses. It cannot perform this job if IP addresses are constantly changing and DNS is not informed of the changes. To make dynamic address assignment work for all types of systems, we need a DNS that can be dynamically updated by the DHCP server. *Dynamic DNS* (DDNS) is available, but it is not yet widely used.* When fully deployed, it will help make dynamic addresses available to systems that provide services and to those that use them.

Given the nature of dynamic addressing, most sites assign permanent fixed addresses to shared servers. This happens through traditional system administration and is not handled by DHCP. In effect, the administrator of the shared server is given an address and puts that address in the shared server's configuration. Using DHCP for some systems doesn't mean it must be used for all systems.

DHCP servers can support BOOTP clients. However, a DHCP client is needed to take full advantage of the services offered by DHCP. BOOTP clients do not understand dynamic address leases. They do not know that an address can time out and that it must be renewed. BOOTP clients must be manually or automatically assigned permanent addresses. True dynamic address assignment is limited to DHCP clients.

Therefore, most sites that use DHCP have a mixture of:

- Permanent addresses assigned to systems that can't use DHCP
- Manual addresses assigned to BOOTP clients
- Dynamic addresses assigned to all DHCP clients

All of this begs the question of how a client that doesn't know its own address can communicate with a server. DHCP defines a simple packet exchange that allows the client to find a server and obtain a configuration.

How DHCP works

The DHCP client broadcasts a packet called a *DHCPDISCOVER* message that contains, at a minimum, a transaction identifier and the client's DHCP identifier, which is normally the client's physical network address. The client sends the broadcast using the address 255.255.255.255, which is a special address called the *limited broadcast address*.† The client waits for a response from the server. If a response is

---

* See Chapter 8 for more information about DDNS.

† This address is useful because, unlike the normal broadcast address, it doesn't require the system to know the address of the network it is on.

not received within a specified time interval, the client retransmits the request. DHCP uses UDP as a transport protocol and, unlike RARP, does not require any special Network Access Layer protocols.

The server responds to the client's message with a *DHCPOFFER* packet. DHCP uses two different well-known port numbers. UDP port number 67 is used for the server, and UDP port number 68 is used for the client. This is very unusual. Most software uses a well-known port on the server side and a randomly generated port on the client side. (How and why random source port numbers are used is described in Chapter 1.) The random port number ensures that each pair of source/destination ports identifies a unique path for exchanging information. A DHCP client, however, is still in the process of booting. It probably does not know its IP address. Even if the client generates a source port for the *DHCPDISCOVER* packet, a server response that is addressed to that port and the client's IP address won't be read by a client that doesn't recognize the address. Therefore, DHCP sends the response to a specific port on all hosts. A broadcast sent to UDP port 68 is read by all hosts, even by a system that doesn't know its specific address. The system then determines if it is the intended recipient by checking the transaction identifier and the physical network address embedded in the response.

The server fills in the *DHCPOFFER* packet with the configuration data it has for the client. A DHCP server can provide every TCP/IP configuration value a client needs, provided the server is properly configured. Chapter 9 is a tutorial on setting up a DHCP server, and Appendix D is a complete list of all of the DHCP configuration parameters.

As the name implies, the *DHCPOFFER* packet is an *offer* of configuration data. That offer has a limited lifetime—typically 120 seconds. The client must respond to the offer before the lifetime expires. This is done because more than one server may hear the *DHCPDISCOVER* packet from the client and respond with a *DHCPOFFER*. If the servers did not require a response from the client, multiple servers might commit resources to a single client, thus wasting resources that could be used by other clients. If a client receives multiple *DHCPOFFER* packets, it responds to only one and ignores the others.

The client responds to the *DHCPOFFER* with a *DHCPREQUEST* message. The *DHCPREQUEST* message asks the server to assign the client the configuration information that was offered. The server checks the information in the *DHCPREQUEST* to make sure that the client got everything right and that all of the offered data is still available. If everything is correct, the server sends the client a *DHCPACK* message letting the client know that it is now configured to use all of the information from the original *DHCPOFFER* packet. Figure 3-5 shows the normal packet flow when DHCP is used to configure a client.

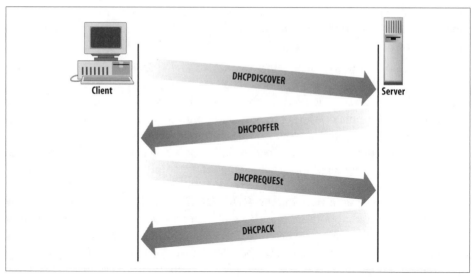

Figure 3-5. DHCP client/server protocol

Summary

TCP/IP provides some network services that simplify network installation, configuration, and use. Name service is one such service and it is used on every TCP/IP network.

Name service can be provided by the host table, Domain Name System (DNS), and Network Information Service (NIS). The host table is a simple text file stored in */etc/hosts*. Most systems have a small host table, but it cannot be used for all applications because it is not scalable and does not have a standard method for automatic distribution. NIS, the Sun "yellow pages" server, solves the problem of automatic distribution for the host table but does not solve the problem of scaling. DNS, which superseded the host table as a TCP/IP standard, does scale. DNS is a hierarchical, distributed database system that provides hostname and address information for all of the systems in the Internet.

Simple Mail Transfer Protocol (SMTP), Post Office Protocol (POP), Internet Message Access Protocol (IMAP), and Multipurpose Internet Mail Extensions (MIME) are the building blocks of a TCP/IP email network. SMTP is a simple request/response protocol that provides end-to-end mail delivery. Sometimes end-to-end mail delivery is not suitable, and the mail must be routed to a mail server. TCP/IP mail servers can use POP or IMAP to move the mail from the server to the end system, where it is read by the user. SMTP can deliver only 7-bit ASCII data. MIME extends the TCP/IP mail system so that it can carry a wide variety of data.

Network File System (NFS) is the leading Unix file-sharing protocol. It allows server systems to export directories that are then mounted by clients and used as if they were local disk drives. The Unix LPD/LPR protocol can be used for printer sharing on a TCP/IP network. Samba provides similar file and print sharing services for Windows clients.

Many configuration values are needed to install TCP/IP. These values can be provided by a configuration server. Three protocols have been used by TCP/IP for distributing configuration information:

RARP

> *Reverse Address Resolution Protocol* tells a client its IP address. The RARP server does this by mapping the client's Ethernet address to its IP address. The Ethernet to IP address mappings are stored on the server in the */etc/ethers* file.

BOOTP

> *Bootstrap Protocol* provides a wide range of configuration values.

DHCP

> *Dynamic Host Configuration Protocol* replaced BOOTP with a service that provides the full set of configuration parameters defined in the *Requirements for Internet Hosts* RFC. It also provides for dynamic address allocation, which allows a network to make maximum use of a limited set of addresses.

This chapter concludes our introduction to the architecture, protocols, and services of a TCP/IP network. In the next chapter, we begin to look at how to install a TCP/IP network by examining the process of planning an installation.

CHAPTER 4
Getting Started

In this chapter:
- Connected and Non-Connected Networks
- Basic Information
- Planning Routing
- Planning Naming Service
- Other Services
- Informing the Users

In this chapter, our emphasis shifts from how TCP/IP functions to how it is configured. While Chapters 1 through 3 described the TCP/IP protocols and how they work, now we begin to explore the network configuration process. The first step in this process is planning. Before configuring a host to run TCP/IP, you must have certain information. At the very least, every host must have a unique IP address and hostname. You should also resolve the following issues before configuring a system:

Default gateway address

If the system communicates with TCP/IP hosts that are not on its local network, a default gateway address may be needed. Alternatively, if a routing protocol is used on the network, each device needs to know that protocol.

Name server addresses

To resolve hostnames into IP addresses, each host needs to know the addresses of the domain name servers.

Domain name

Hosts using the domain name system must know their correct domain name.

Subnet mask

To communicate properly, each system on a network must use the same subnet mask.

If you're adding a system to an existing network, make sure you find out the answers from your network administrator before putting the system online. The network administrator is responsible for making and communicating decisions about overall network configuration. If you have an established TCP/IP network, you can skip several sections in this chapter, but you may still want to read about selecting hostnames, planning mail systems, and other topics that affect mature networks as much as they do new networks.

If you are creating a new TCP/IP network, you will have to make some basic decisions. Will the new network connect to the Internet? If so, how will the connection be made? How should the network number be chosen? How do I register a domain name? How do I choose hostnames? In the following sections, we cover the information you need to make these decisions.

Connected and Non-Connected Networks

First, you must decide whether your new network will be fully connected to the Internet. A *connected network* is directly attached to the Internet and is fully accessible to other networks on the Internet. A *non-connected network* is not directly attached to the Internet, and its access to Internet networks is limited. An example of a non-connected network is a TCP/IP network that attaches to the outside world via a network address translation (NAT) box or a proxy server. Users on the non-connected network can access remote Internet hosts, but remote users cannot directly access hosts on the non-connected network. Because non-connected networks do not provide services to the outside world, they are also known as *private networks*.

Private networks that interconnect the various parts of an organization are often called *enterprise networks*. When those private networks use the information services applications that are built on top of TCP/IP, particularly web servers and browsers, to distribute internal information, those networks are called *intranets*.

There are a few basic reasons why many sites do not fully connect to the Internet. One reason is security. Connecting to any network gives more people access to your system. Connecting to a global network with millions of users is enough to scare any security expert. There is no doubt about it: connecting to the Internet increases the security risks for your network. Chapter 12 covers some techniques for reducing this risk.

Cost is another consideration. Many organizations do not see sufficient value in a full Internet connection for every desktop. For some organizations, low use or limited requirements, such as needing only email access, make the cost of connecting the entire network to the Internet exceed the benefit. For others, the primary reason for an Internet connection is to provide information about their products. It is not necessary to connect the entire enterprise network to the Internet to do this. It is often sufficient to connect a single web server to the local Internet Service Provider (ISP) or to work with a web hosting company to provide information to your customers.

Other organizations consider an Internet connection an essential requirement. Educational and research institutions depend on the Internet as a source of information, and many companies use it as a means of delivering service and support to their customers.

You may have both types of networks: a non-connected enterprise network sitting behind a security firewall, and a small connected network that provides services to your external customers and proxy service for your internal users.

Unless you have carefully determined what your needs are and what an Internet connection will cost, you cannot know whether connecting your entire network to the Internet is right for your organization. Your local ISPs can give you the various cost and performance alternatives. Ask them about services as well as prices. Some ISPs specialize in providing low-cost service to home users. They emphasize price. However, if you are connecting a full network to the Internet, you may want an ISP that can provide network addresses, name service, web hosting, and other features that your network might need.

Basic Information

Regardless of whether you decide to connect your network to the Internet, one thing is certain: you will build your enterprise network using the TCP/IP protocols. All TCP/IP networks, whether or not they connect to the Internet, require the same basic information to configure the physical network interface. As we will see in Chapter 6, the network interface needs an IP address and may also need a subnet mask and broadcast address. The decision of whether to connect to the Internet affects how you obtain the values needed to configure the interface. In this section, we look at how the network administrator arrives at each of the required values.

Obtaining an IP Address

Every interface on a TCP/IP network must have a unique IP address. If a host is part of the Internet, its IP address must be unique within the entire Internet. If a host's TCP/IP communications are limited to a local network, its IP address only needs to be unique locally. Administrators whose networks will not be connected to the Internet can select an address from RFC 1918, *Address Allocation for Private Intranets*, which lists network numbers that are reserved for private use.* The private network numbers are:

- Network 10.0.0.0 (10/8 prefix) is a 24-bit block of addresses.
- Networks 172.16.0.0 to 172.31.0.0 (172.16/12 prefix) is a 20-bit block of addresses.
- Networks 192.168.0.0 to 192.168.255.0 (192.168/16 prefix) is a 16-bit block of addresses.

The disadvantage of using a network address from RFC 1918 is that you may have to change your address in the future if you connect your full network to the Internet. The advantages to choosing a private network address are:

---

* The address used in this book (172.16.0.0) is treated as an official address, but it is a private network number set aside for use by non-connected enterprise networks. Feel free to use this address on your network if it will not be connected to the Internet.

- It's easy. You do not have to apply for an official address or get anyone's approval.
- It's friendly. You save address space for those who need to connect to the Internet.
- It's free. RFC 1918 addresses cost nothing—official addresses cost money.

If you do choose an address from RFC 1918, the hosts on your network can still have access to systems on the Internet. But it will take some effort. You'll need a *network address translation* (NAT) box or a proxy server. NAT is available as a separate piece of hardware or as an optional piece of software in some routers and firewalls. It works by converting the source address of datagrams leaving your network from your private address to your official address. Address translation has several advantages:

- It conserves IP addresses. Most network connections are between systems on the same enterprise network. Only a small percentage of systems need to connect to the Internet at any one time. Therefore, far fewer official IP addresses are needed than the total number of systems on an enterprise network. NAT makes it possible for you to use a large address space from RFC 1918 for configuring your enterprise network while using only a small official address space for Internet connections.
- It reduces address spoofing, a security attack in which a remote system pretends to be a local system. The addresses in RFC 1918 cannot be routed over the Internet. Therefore, even if a datagram is routed off your network toward the remote system, the fact that the datagram contains an RFC 1918 destination address means that the routers in the Internet will discard the datagram as a *martian.*
- It eliminates the need to renumber your hosts when you connect to the Internet.

Network address translation also has disadvantages:

Cost
: NAT may add cost for new hardware or optional software. However, these costs tend to be very low.

Performance
: Address translation adds overhead to the processing of every datagram. When the address is changed, the checksum must be recalculated. Furthermore, some upper-layer protocols carry a copy of the IP address that also must be converted.

Reliability
: Routers never modify the addresses in a datagram header, but NAT does. This might introduce some instability. Additionally, protocols and applications that embed addresses in their data may not function correctly with NAT.

---

* A martian is a datagram with an address that is known to be invalid.

Security

> NAT limits the use of end-to-end encryption and authentication. Authentication schemes that include the header within the calculation do not work because the router changes the addresses in the header. Encryption does not work if the encrypted data includes the source address.

Proxy servers provide many of the same advantages as NAT boxes. In fact, these terms are often used interchangeably. But there are differences. Proxy servers are application gateways originally created as part of firewall systems to improve security. Internal systems connect to the outside world through the proxy server, and external systems respond to the proxy server. Proxy servers are application-specific. A network might have one proxy web server and another proxy FTP server—each server dedicated to serving connections for one type of application. Therefore, the difference between NAT boxes and proxy servers is that NAT maps IP addresses regardless of the application; the true proxy server focuses on one application.

Proxy servers often have added security features. Address translation can be done at the IP layer. Proxy services require the server to handle data up to the application layer. Security filters can be put in proxy servers that filter data at all layers of the protocol stack.

Given the differences discussed here, network address translation servers should scale better than proxy servers, and proxy servers should provide better security. However, over time these technologies have merged and are now largely indistinguishable. Before you decide to use either NAT or proxy services, make sure they are suitable for your network needs.

Combining NAT with a private network address gives every host on your network access to the outside world, but it does not allow outside users access into your network. For that, you need to obtain an official IP address.

Obtaining an official network address

Networks that are fully connected to the Internet must obtain official network addresses. An official address is needed for every system on your network that is *directly* accessible to remote Internet hosts. Every network that communicates with the Internet, even those that use NAT, have at least one official address, although that address may not be permanently assigned. The first step toward obtaining a block of addresses is to determine how many addresses you need.

Determining your "organizational type" helps you assess your address needs and how you should satisfy those needs. RFC 2901, *Administrative Internet Infrastructure Guide*, describes four different organizational types:

Internet end user

> A small- to medium-sized organization focused on connecting itself to the Internet. This could be as small as a single user connecting to the Internet with a

dynamic address assigned by the ISP's DHCP server, or as large as a network of thousands of hosts using NAT on the enterprise network and official addresses on a limited number of publicly accessible systems. What categorizes this organizational type is that it wants to use the Internet while limiting the number of systems it makes available to remote users. "Internet end user" organizations obtain official addresses from their ISP. From the point of view of the Internet, all Internet end user organizations appear small because they use only a limited number of official addresses.

High-volume end user

A medium-sized to large organization that distributes official addresses to systems throughout its network. This type of organization tends to have a distributed management under which divisions within the overall organization are allowed to make systems remotely accessible. "High-volume end user" organizations usually satisfy their address requirements through their ISP or a Local Internet Registry. If the organization needs more than 8,000 addresses, it may go directly to a Regional Internet Registry. While in reality a high-volume end user organization may not be any larger than an Internet end user organization, it appears to be larger from the point of view of the Internet because it exposes more systems to the Internet.

Internet Service Provider

An organization that provides Internet connection services to other organizations and provides those organizations with official addresses. Even an ISP connects to the Internet in some way. If it connects through another ISP, that ISP is its *upstream provider*. The upstream provider assigns addresses to the ISP. If it connects directly to a network access point (NAP), as described in Chapter 2, the ISP requests addresses from the Local Internet Registry or the Regional Internet Registry.

Local Internet Registry

An organization that provides addresses to ISPs. In effect, a Local Internet Registry is an organization that provides addresses to other organizations that provide addresses. A Local Internet Registry must obtain its addresses from a Regional Internet Registry.

RFC 2901 lists four organizational types in order to be thorough, but most organizations are either Internet end users or high-volume end users. In all likelihood, your organization is one of these, and you will obtain all of your addresses from your ISP.

Your ISP has been delegated authority over a group of network addresses and should be able to assign you a network number. If your local ISP cannot meet your needs, perhaps the ISP's upstream provider can. Ask your local ISP who it receives service from and ask that organization for an address. If all else fails, you may be forced to go directly to an Internet registry. If you are forced to take your request to a registry, you will need to take certain steps before you make the application.

You need to prepare a detailed network topology. The topology must include a diagram that shows the physical layout of your network and highlights its connections to the Internet. You should include network engineering plans that, in addition to diagramming the topology, describe:

- Your routing plans, including the protocols you will use and any constraints that forced your routing decisions.

- Your subnetting plans, including the mask you will use and the number of networks and hosts you will have connected during the next year. RFC 2050, *Internet Registry IP Allocation Guidelines*, suggests the following details in your subnet plan:

  — A table listing all subnets.

  — The mask for each subnet. The use of variable-length subnet masks (VLSMs) is strongly encouraged. VLSMs are described later in this chapter under "Defining a Subnet Mask."

  — The estimated number of hosts.

  — A descriptive remark explaining the purpose of each subnet.

The biggest challenge is accurately predicting your future requirements for addresses. If you have previously been assigned an address block, you may be required to provide a history of how that address block was used. Even if it is not requested by the Internet registry, a history can be a helpful tool for your own planning. Additionally, you will be asked to prepare a network deployment plan. This plan typically shows the number of hosts you currently have that need official addresses and the number you expect to have in six months, one year, and two years.

One factor used to determine how much address space is needed is the *expected utilization rate*. The expected utilization rate is the number of hosts assigned official addresses divided by the total number of hosts possible for the network. The deployment plans must show the number of hosts that will be assigned addresses over a two-year period. The total number of possible hosts can be estimated from the total number of employees in your organization and the number of systems that have been traditionally deployed per employee. Clearly you need to have a global knowledge of your organization and its needs before applying for an official address assignment.

In addition to providing documentation that justifies the address request, obtaining an official address requires a formal commitment of resources. Most address applications require at least two contacts: an administrative contact and a technical contact. The administrative contact should have the authority to deal with administrative issues ranging from policy violations to billing disputes. The technical contact must be a skilled technical person who can deal with technical problems and answer technical questions. The registries require that these contacts live in the same country as the organization that they represent. You must provide the names, addresses, telephone numbers, and email addresses of these people. Don't kid yourself—these are not honorary positions. These people have targets on their backs when things go wrong.

The registry includes this contact information in the whois database, which provides publicly available contact information about the people responsible for networks. Once your name is in the whois database, you're given a NIC handle, which is a unique identifier linked to your whois database record. For example, my NIC handle is cwh3. Many official applications request your NIC handle.

In addition to human resources, you need to commit computer resources. You should have systems set up, running, and ready to accept the new addresses before you apply for official addresses.

When all of the background work is done, you're ready to present your case to an Internet registry. A three-level bureaucracy controls the allocation of IP addresses:

IANA
> The Internet Assigned Numbers Authority allocates large blocks of addresses to regional Internet registries.

Regional Internet Registry
> Regional Internet Registries (IRs) have been given authority by the IANA to allocate addresses within a large region of the world. There are three IRs:

> *APNIC*
>> The Asian Pacific Network Information Center has address allocation authority for Asia and the Pacific region.

> *ARIN*
>> The American Registry for Internet Numbers has address allocation authority for the Americas.

> *RIPE*
>> Reseaux IP Europeens has address allocation authority for Europe.

Local Internet Registry
> Local IRs are given authority, either by IANA or by a regional IR, to allocate addresses within a specific area. An example might be a national registry or a registry created by a consortium of ISPs.

Regardless of how much address space you need, you should start at the bottom of the hierarchy and work your way up. Always start with your local ISP. If they cannot handle your needs, ask them if there is a local IR that can help you. As a last resort, take your request to the regional IR that serves your part of the world.

If you're in the APNIC region, first fill out the membership application. The APNIC membership application is available at *http://www.apnic.net/member/application. html*. Once you become a member of APNIC, you can request an address.

ARIN does not require that you become a member before applying for an address. If you're a high-volume end user, use the application form at *http://www.arin.net/ templates/networktemplate.txt* to apply for an address. If you're an ISP, use *http:// www.arin.net/templates/isptemplate.txt*. In either case, send the completed application to *hostmaster@arin.net*.

End user organization in the RIPE region must use a local IR. RIPE only allocates addresses to local IRs that are members of RIPE. End user organizations cannot apply to RIPE for address allocations. See the document *ftp://ftp.ripe.net/ripe/docs/ ripe-159.txt* for more information.

Regardless of where your network is located, the most important thing to remember is that most organizations never have to go through this process because they do not want to expose the bulk of their computers to the Internet. For security reasons, they use private address numbers for most systems and have only a limited number of official IP addresses. That limited number of addresses can usually be provided by a local ISP.

Obtaining an IN-ADDR.ARPA domain

When you obtain an official IP address, you should also apply for an *in-addr.arpa* domain. This special domain is sometimes called a *reverse domain*. Chapter 8 contains more information about how the *in-addr.arpa* domain is set up and used, but basically the reverse domain maps numeric IP addresses into domain names. This is the reverse of the normal domain name lookup process, which converts domain names to addresses. If your ISP provides your name service or assigned you an address from a block of its own addresses, you may not need to apply for an *in-addr.arpa* domain on your own. Check with your ISP *before* applying. If, however, you obtain a block of addresses from a Regional Internet Registry, you probably need to get your own *in-addr.arpa* domain. If you do need to get a reverse domain, you will register it with the same organization from which you obtained your address assignment.

- For address blocks obtained from APNIC, use the form *ftp://ftp.apnic.net/apnic/ docs/in-addr-request* and mail the completed form to *domreg@rs.apnic.net*.
- For address blocks obtained from ARIN, use the form *http://www.arin.net/templates/modifytemplate.txt* and mail the completed form to *hostmaster@arin.net*.
- For address blocks obtained from RIPE, a domain object needs to be entered into the RIPE database. Mail the completed object to *auto-inaddr@ripe.net*.

As an example, assume that your network is located in the RIPE region. You would need to provide the information needed to create a RIPE domain object for your network. The domain object for the RIPE database illustrates the type of information that is required to register a reverse domain. The RIPE database object has ten fields:

domain:

This is the domain name. How reverse domain names are derived is described in detail in Chapter 8, but the name is essentially the address reversed with *in-addr. arpa* added to the end. For our 172.16/16 address allocation, the reverse domain name is *16.172.in-addr.arpa*.

descr:

A text description of the domain. For example, "The address allocation for wrotethebook.com."

admin-c:

The NIC handle of the administrative contact.

tech-c:

The NIC handle of the technical contact.

zone-c:

The NIC handle of the domain administrator, also called the zone contact.

nserver:

The name or address of the master server for this domain.

nserver:

The name or address of a slave server for this domain.

nserver:

For RIPE, this third server is always *ns.ripe.net*.

changed:

The email address of the maintainer who submitted this database object and the date it was submitted.

source:

For addresses allocated by RIPE, the value of this field is always *RIPE*.

Again, the most important thing to note about reverse address registration is that most organizations don't have to do this. If you obtain your address from your ISP, you probably do not have to take care of this paperwork yourself. These services are one of the reasons you pay your ISP.

Assigning Host Addresses

So far we have been discussing *network numbers*. Our imaginary company's network was assigned network number 172.16.0.0/16. The network administrator assigns individual host addresses within the range of IP addresses available to the network address; i.e., our administrator assigns the last two bytes of the four-byte address.[*] The portion of the address assigned by the administrator cannot have all bits 0 or all

---

[*] The range of addresses is called the *address space*.

bits 1; i.e., 172.16.0.0 and 172.16.255.255 are not valid host addresses. Beyond these two restrictions, you're free to assign host addresses in any way that seems reasonable to you.

Network administrators usually assign host addresses in one of two ways:

One address at a time
> Each individual host is assigned an address, perhaps in sequential order, through the address range.

Groups of addresses
> Blocks of addresses are delegated to departments within the organization, which then assign the individual host addresses.

The assignment of groups of addresses is most common when the network is subnetted and the address groups are divided along subnet boundaries. But assigning blocks of addresses does not require subnetting. It can be just an organizational device for delegating authority. Delegating authority for groups of addresses is often very convenient for large networks, while small networks tend to assign host addresses one at a time. No matter how addresses are assigned, someone must retain sufficient central control to prevent duplication and to ensure that the addresses are recorded correctly on the domain name servers.

Addresses can be assigned statically or dynamically. Static assignment is handled through manually configuring the boot file on the host computer. Dynamic address assignment is always handled by a server, such as a DHCP server. One advantage of dynamic address assignment is that the server will not accidentally assign duplicate addresses. Thus, dynamic address assignment is desirable not only because it reduces the administrator's workload but also because it reduces errors.

Before installing a server for dynamic addressing, make sure it is useful for your purposes. Dynamic PPP addressing is useful for servers that handle many remote dial-in clients that connect for a short duration. If the PPP server is used to connect various parts of the enterprise network and has long-lived connections, dynamic addressing is probably unnecessary. Likewise, the dynamic address assignment features of DHCP are of most use if you have mobile systems in your network that move between subnets and therefore need to change addresses frequently. See Chapter 6 for information on PPP, and Chapters 3 and 9 for details about DHCP.

Clearly, you must make several decisions about obtaining and assigning addresses. You also need to decide what bit mask will be used with the address. In the next section we look at the subnet mask, which changes how the address is interpreted.

Defining the Subnet Mask

As the prefix number indicates, a network address is assigned with a specific address mask. For example, the prefix of 16 in the network address 172.16.0.0/16 means that

ARIN assigned our imaginary network the block of addresses defined by the address 172.16.0.0 and the 16-bit mask 255.255.0.0.* Unless you have a reason to change the interpretation of your assigned network number, you do not have to define a subnet mask. Chapter 2 described the structure of IP addresses and touched upon the reasons for subnetting. The decision to subnet is commonly driven by topological or organizational considerations.

The topological reasons for subnetting include:

Overcoming distance limitations
> Some network hardware has very strict distance limitations. The original 10 Mbps Ethernet is the most common example. The maximum length of a "thick" Ethernet cable is 500 meters; the maximum length of a "thin" cable is 300 meters; the total length of a 10 Mbps Ethernet, called the maximum diameter, is 2500 meters.† If you need to cover a greater distance, you can use IP routers to link a series of Ethernet cables. Individual cable still must not exceed the maximum allowable length, but using this approach, every cable is a separate Ethernet. Therefore the total length of the IP network can exceed the maximum length of an Ethernet.

Interconnecting dissimilar physical networks
> IP routers can be used to link networks that have different and incompatible underlying network technologies. Figure 4-1 later in this chapter shows a central token ring subnet, 172.16.1.0, connecting two Ethernet subnets, 172.16.6.0 and 172.16.12.0.

Filtering traffic between networks
> Local traffic stays on the local subnet. Only traffic intended for other networks is forwarded through the gateway.

Subnetting is not the only way to solve topology problems. Networks are implemented in hardware and can be altered by changing or adding hardware, but subnetting is an effective way to overcome these problems at the TCP/IP level.

Of course, there are non-technical reasons for creating subnets. Subnets often serve organizational purposes such as:

Simplifying network administration
> Subnets can be used to delegate address management, troubleshooting, and other network administration responsibilities to smaller groups within the overall organization. This is an effective tool for managing a large network with a

---

* Even though 172.16.0.0 is an RFC 1918 private network number, this text treats 172.16.0.0 as if it were an officially assigned network number, for the sake of example.

† The faster the Ethernet, the smaller its network diameter. For this reason, high-speed Ethernet technologies use switches instead of a daisy chain cable to connect nodes.

limited staff. It places the responsibility for managing the subnet on the people who benefit from its use.

Recognizing organizational structure

The structure of an organization (or simply office politics) may require independent network management for some divisions. Creating independently managed subnets for these divisions is preferable to having them go directly to an ISP to get their own independent network numbers.

Isolating traffic by organization

Certain organizations may prefer to have their local traffic isolated to a network that is primarily accessible only to members of that organization. This is particularly appropriate when security is involved. For example, the payroll department might not want its network packets on the engineering network where some clever person could figure out how to intercept them.

Isolating potential problems

If a certain segment is less reliable than the remainder of the net, you may want to make that segment a subnet. For example, if the research group puts experimental systems on the network from time to time or experiments with the network itself, this part of the network will be unstable. You would make it a subnet to prevent experimental hardware or software from interfering with the rest of the network.

The network administrator decides if subnetting is required and defines the subnet mask for the network. The subnet mask has the same form as an IP address mask. As described in Chapter 2, it defines which bits form the "network part" of the address and which bits form the "host part." Bits in the "network part" are turned on (i.e., 1) while bits in the "host part" are turned off (i.e., 0).

The subnet mask used on our imaginary network is 255.255.255.0. This mask sets aside 8 bits to identify subnets, which creates 256 subnets. The *network* administrator has decided that this mask provides enough subnets and that the individual subnets have enough hosts to effectively use the address space of 254 hosts per subnet. The upcoming Figure 4-1 shows an example of this type of subnetting. Applying this subnet mask to the addresses 172.16.1.0 and 172.16.12.0 causes them to be interpreted as the addresses of two different networks, not as two different hosts on the same network.

Once a mask is defined, it must be disseminated to all hosts on the network. There are two ways this is done: manually, through the configuration of network interfaces, and automatically, through configuration protocols like DHCP. Routing protocols can distribute subnet masks, but in most environments host systems do not run routing protocols. In this case, every device on the network must use the same subnet mask because every computer believes that the entire network is subnetted in exactly the same way as its local subnet.

Because routing protocols distribute address masks for each destination, it is possible to use variable-length subnet masks (VLSMs). Using variable-length subnet masks increases the flexibility and power of subnetting. Assume you wanted to divide 192.168.5.0/24 into three networks: one network of 110 hosts, one network of 50 hosts, and one network of 60 hosts. Using traditional subnet masks, a single subnet mask would have to be chosen and applied to the entire address space. At best, this would be a compromise. With variable-length subnet masks you could use a mask of 255.255.255.128 to create subnets of 126 hosts for the large subnet, and a mask of 255.255.255.192 to create subnets of 62 hosts for the smaller subnets. VLSMs, however, require that every router on the network knows how to store and use the masks and runs routing protocols that can transmit them. (See Chapter 7 for more information on routing.) Routing is an essential part of a TCP/IP network. Like other key components of your network, routing should be planned before you start configuration.

Planning Routing

In Chapter 2, we learned that hosts communicate directly only with other computers connected to the same network. Gateways are needed to communicate with systems on other networks. If the hosts on your network need to communicate with computers on other networks, a route through a gateway must be defined. There are two ways to do this:

- Routing can be handled by a *static routing table* built by the system administrator. Static routing tables are most useful when the number of gateways is limited. Static tables do not dynamically adjust to changing network conditions, so each change in the table is made manually by the network administrator. Complex environments require a more flexible approach to routing than a static routing table provides.

- Routing can be handled by a *dynamic routing table* that responds to changing network conditions. Dynamic routing tables are built by routing protocols. Routing protocols exchange routing information that is used to update the routing table. Dynamic routing is used when there are multiple gateways on a network; it's essential when more than one gateway can reach the same destination.

Many networks use a combination of both static and dynamic routing. Some systems on the network use static routing tables while others run routing protocols and have dynamic tables. While it is often appropriate for hosts to use static routing tables, gateways usually run routing protocols.

The network administrator is responsible for deciding what type of routing to use and for choosing the default gateway for each host. Make these decisions before you start to configure your system.

Here are a few guidelines to help you plan routing. If you have:

A network with no gateways to other TCP/IP networks
> No special routing configuration is required in this case. The gateways referred to in this discussion are IP routers that interconnect TCP/IP networks. If you are not interconnecting TCP/IP networks, you do not need an IP router. Neither a default gateway nor a routing protocol needs to be specified.

A network with a single gateway
> If you have only one gateway, don't run any routing protocols. Specify the single gateway as the default gateway in a static routing table.

A network with internal gateways to other subnets and a single gateway to the world
> Here, there is a real choice. You can statically specify each subnet route and make the gateway to the world your default route, or you can run a routing protocol. Decide which you want to do based on the effort involved in maintaining a static table versus the slight overhead of running a routing protocol on your hosts and networks. If you have more than a few hosts, running a routing protocol is probably easiest.

A network with multiple gateways to the world
> If you have multiple gateways that can reach the same destination, use a routing protocol. This allows the gateways to adapt to network changes, giving you redundant access to the remote networks.

Figure 4-1 shows a subnetted network with five gateways identified as *A* through *E*. A central subnet (172.16.1.0) interconnects five other subnets. One of the subnets has a gateway to an external network. The network administrator would probably choose to run a routing protocol on the central subnet (172.16.1.0) and perhaps on subnet 172.16.12.0, which is attached to an external network. Dynamic routing is appropriate on these subnets because they have multiple gateways. Without dynamic routing, the administrator would need to update every one of these gateways manually whenever any change occurred in the network—for example, whenever a new subnet was added. A mistake during the manual update could disrupt network service. Running a routing protocol on these two subnets is simpler and more reliable.

On the other hand, the administrator would probably choose static routing for the other subnets (172.16.3.0, 172.16.6.0, and 172.16.9.0). These subnets each use only one gateway to reach all destinations. Changes external to the subnets, such as the addition of a new subnet, do not change the fact that these three subnets still have only one routing choice. Newly added networks are still reached through the same gateway. The hosts on these subnets specify the subnet's gateway as their default route. In other words, the hosts on subnet 172.16.3.0 specify *B* as the default gateway, while the hosts on subnet 172.16.9.0 specify *D* as the default, no matter what happens on the external networks.

Some routing decisions are thrust upon you by the external networks to which you connect. In Figure 4-1, the local network connects to an external network that

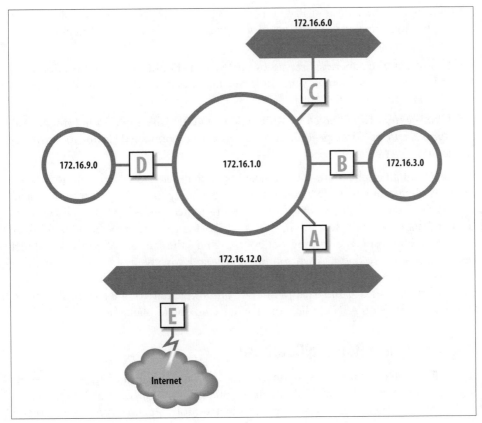

Figure 4-1. Routing and subnets

requires that Border Gateway Protocol (BGP) be used for routing. Therefore, gateway E has to run BGP to exchange routes with the external network.

Obtaining an autonomous system number

The Border Gateway Protocol (BGP) requires that gateways have a special identifier called an *autonomous system number* (ASN).[*] Most sites do not need to run BGP. Even when a site does run BGP, it usually runs it using the ASN of its ISP or one of the ASNs that have been set aside for private use, which are the numbers from 64512 to 65535. Coordinate your ASN selection with your border gateway peers to avoid any possible conflicts. If you connect to the Internet through a single ISP, you almost certainly do not need an official ASN. If after discussions with your service provider you find that you *must* obtain an official ASN, obtain the application from the Regional Internet Registry that services your country.

---

[*] Refer to the section "Internet Routing Architecture" in Chapter 2 for a discussion of autonomous systems.

- If you're in the Asia and Pacific region, served by APNIC, you should use the application form at *http://ftp.apnic.net/apnic/docs/asn-request* and mail the completed form to *hostmaster@apnic.net*.

- If you're in the Americas, served by ARIN, you should use the application form at *http://www.arin.net/templates/asntemplate.txt* and mail the completed form to *hostmaster@arin.net*.

- If you're in Europe, served by RIPE, you should use the application form at *ftp://ftp.ripe.net/ripe/docs/ripe-147.txt* and mail the completed form to *hostmaster@ripe.net*.

If you submit an application, you are asked to explain why you need a unique autonomous system number. Unless you are an ISP, probably the only reason to obtain an ASN is that you are a *multi-homed site*. A multi-homed site is any site that connects to more than one ISP. Reachability information for the site may be advertised by both ISPs, confusing the routing policy. Assigning the site an ASN gives it direct responsibility for setting its own routing policy and advertising its own reachability information. This doesn't prevent the site from advertising bad routes, but it makes the advertisement traceable back to one site and ultimately to one technical contact. (Once you submit an ASN application, you have no one to blame but yourself!)

Registering in a Routing Database

If you obtain an official ASN, you must decide whether you need to register in a routing database. If you got your ASN because you're multi-homed, you should register with a routing database. The section "Internet Routing Architecture" in Chapter 2 explains that routing databases are used to validate routing in the new Internet because there is no longer a central core that can be relied on to determine "best" routes. When you obtain an official ASN, you become part of the structure of co-equal routing domains. You assume responsibility for a small portion of the routing burden and you declare that responsibility by registering in a routing database.

There are several different databases that make up the Internet Routing Registry (IRR). In addition to the Routing Arbiter Database (RADB) mentioned in Chapter 2, RIPE, ANS, Bell Canada, and Cable & Wireless all maintain databases. RIPE serves customers in the RIPE region. ANS, Bell Canada, and Cable & Wireless register only their paying customers. RADB is available to anyone.

To register in the RADB, first register a maintainer object. Maintainer objects identify the person who will be responsible for maintaining your database entries. Provide the required information, and pay the $200 fee. You must then register the autonomous system as an AS object. Finally, you create a Route object for each route your system will advertise. See *http://www.radb.net* for detailed information about registering these database objects.

All of the items discussed so far (addressing, subnetting, and routing) are required to configure the basic physical network on top of which the applications and services run. Now we begin planning the services that make the network useful and usable.

Planning Naming Service

To make your network user-friendly, you need to provide a service to convert hostnames into IP addresses. The Domain Name System (DNS) and the host table, explained in Chapter 3, perform this function. You should plan to use both.

To configure a computer, a network user needs to know the domain name, the system's hostname, and the hostname and address of at least one name server. The network administrator provides this information.

Obtaining a Domain Name

The first item you need for name service is a domain name. Your ISP may be willing to get one for you or to assign you a name within its domain; however, it is likely that you will have to apply for a domain name yourself. You can buy an official domain name from a domain name registrar.

Your domain is not part of the official domain name space until it is registered. Only certain organizations are permitted to officially register a domain name. You need to locate an official registrar and obtain its services to register your domain. The place to start is either *http://www.icann.org* or *http://www.internic.net*. Both of these sites provide listings of official registrars.

ICANN is the Internet Corporation for Assigned Names and Numbers, a nonprofit organization created to take over management of some functions previously managed through U.S. government contractors. ICANN oversees the domain name registrars. The ICANN web site provides pointers to various international registrars.

http://www.internic.net is a U.S. government web site designed to point users to official gTLD registrars and to answer any questions Internet users might have about the domain registration process. The imaginary domain used in this book is registered in *.com*. For *.org*, *.com*, or *.net* domains, this is a good place to start. Figure 4-2 shows part of the alphabetical list of accredited registrars found at *http://www.internic.net*.

There is not much that differentiates registrars. Domain registration is very inexpensive, usually less than $50 a year, so cost is not much of a factor. Service is also difficult to determine because once a domain is registered, it doesn't usually require any maintenance. Some administrators like to choose a registrar located close to home, but even this is not really significant in a wired world. Use your own judgment. I frankly can't find anything to recommend any individual registrar. In the following examples, I used Network Solutions as the registrar, in part because they are located a stone's throw away from my home. You, however, should choose your own registrar.

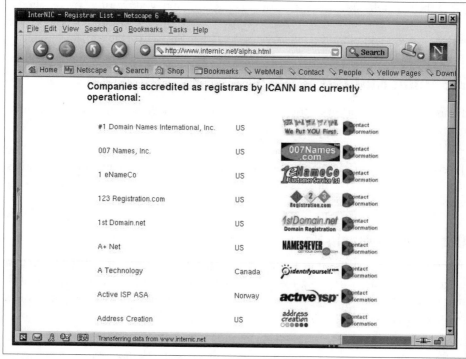

Figure 4-2. The registrar listing

Registering a Domain

Once you select a registrar, go to its web site for instructions on registering a domain. At *http://www.internic.net*, simply clicking the symbol of the registrar should take you to its web site. Most registrars provide an online web form for registering your domain name.

For example, if you select Network Solutions from the list at *http://www.internic.net*, you go to *http://www.netsol.com*. There, you are asked to select a domain name. This first step searches the existing domain database system to make sure that the name you want is available. If it isn't, you're asked to choose another name. If the name is available, you must provide information about the servers that will be authoritative for the new domain. Some registrars, including Network Solutions, will provide DNS service for your new domain as an optional, extra-cost service. Because we plan to create our own server for the *wrotethebook.com* domain, we will provide our own server information.

First, you're asked to provide the name of the person legally responsible for this domain. This information is used by the registrar for billing purposes and is included in the whois database that provides contact information about the people responsible for domains. If you're already in the whois database, you're asked to provide your NIC handle, which is a unique identifier linked to your whois database record. For example, my NIC handle is cwh3.

If you are a new customer, you're asked to provide the names and addresses of the people who will be the administrative, technical, and billing contacts. These can be three different people or the same person, depending on how your business is organized.

Next, the system prompts for the names and IP addresses of two servers that will be authoritative for this domain. Enter the names of the master and slave servers you have configured for your domain. The servers should already be operational when you fill in this form. If they aren't, you can pay a little extra and have Network Solutions host your domain until your servers are ready. You shouldn't enter the names of servers that aren't yet ready to run because that will cause a lame delegation when the root servers use this information to put pointers into the top-level domain to servers that are not really authoritative. Either preconfigure your servers, even with only minimal information, or pay the somewhat higher fee to reserve your domain name until your servers are ready.

Check the information. Pay the bill. Now you're ready to run your own domain.

Choosing a Hostname

Once you have a domain name, you are responsible for assigning hostnames within that domain. You must ensure that hostnames are unique within your domain or subdomain, in the same way that host addresses must be unique within a network or subnet. But there is more to choosing a hostname than just making sure the name is unique; it can be a surprisingly emotional issue. Many people feel very strongly about the name of their computer because they identify their computer with themselves or their work.

RFC 1178 provides excellent guidelines on how to choose a hostname. Some key suggestions from these guidelines are:

- Use real words that are short, easy to spell, and easy to remember. The point of using hostnames instead of IP addresses is that they are easier to use. If hostnames are difficult to spell and remember, they defeat their own purpose.
- Use theme names. For example, all hosts in a group could be named after human movements: fall, jump, hop, skip, walk, run, stagger, wiggle, stumble, trip, limp, lurch, hobble, etc. Theme names are often easier to choose than unrestricted names and increase the sense of community among network users.
- Avoid using project names, personal names, acronyms, numeric names, and technical jargon. Projects and users change over time. If you name a computer after the person who is currently using it or the project it is currently assigned to,

you will probably have to rename the computer in the future. Use nicknames to identify the server function of a system, e.g., *www*, *ftp*, *ns*, etc. Nicknames can easily move between systems if the server function moves. See the description of CNAME records in Chapter 8 for information on creating nicknames.

The only requirement for a hostname is that it be unique within its domain. But a well-chosen hostname can save future work and make the user happier.

Name service is the most basic network service, and it is one service that you will certainly run on your network. There are, however, other services that you should also include in your network planning process.

Other Services

Three services that are used on many networks are file servers, print servers, and mail servers. The purpose of these services and the protocols they are built on was discussed in Chapter 3. In this section we investigate what information must be passed to the users so that the client systems can be successfully configured and how the network administrator determines that information.

File Servers

At a minimum, the user needs to know the hostnames of the network file servers. Using the names and the showmount command, the user can determine what filesystems are being offered by the servers and who is permitted to use those filesystems.[*] Without at least the hostname, the user would have to guess which system offered file service.

A better approach is to give users information that includes what filesystems are being offered and who should use those filesystems. For example, if the Unix manpages are made available from a central server, the users should be informed not to install the man pages on their local disk drives and should be told exactly how to access the centrally supported files.

Print Servers

Whether printers are shared using lp, lpd, or Samba, the basic information needed to configure the print server's clients is the same: the hostname and IP address of the print server and the name of the printer. The printer make and model may be needed for non-PostScript printers. Printer security may also require that the user be given a username and password to access the printer.

---

[*] See the showmount command in Chapter 9.

This is the only information needed to configure the client. However, you will want to provide your users with additional information about the featu, tion, and administration of shared printers.

Planning Your Mail System

TCP/IP provides the tools you need to create a reliable, flexible electronic mail system. Servers are one of the tools that improve reliability. It is possible to create a peer-to-peer email network in which every end system directly sends and receives its own mail. However, relying on every system to deliver and collect the mail requires that every system be properly administered and consistently up and running. This isn't practical because many small systems are offline for large portions of the day. Most networks use servers so that only a few systems need to be properly configured and operational for the mail to go through.

The terminology that describes email servers is confusing because all the server functions usually occur in one computer, and all the terms are used interchangeably to refer to that system. This text differentiates between these functions, but it is expected that you will do all of these tasks on one Unix system running sendmail. The terms are used in the following manner:

Mail server
> The mail server collects incoming mail for other computers on the network. It supports interactive logins as well as POP and IMAP so that users can manage their mail as they see fit.

Mail relay
> A mail relay is a host that forwards mail between internal systems and from internal systems to remote hosts. Mail relays allow internal systems to have simple mail configurations because only the relay host needs to have software to handle special mail-addressing schemes and aliases.

Mail gateway
> A mail gateway is a system that forwards email between dissimilar systems. You don't need a gateway to go from one Internet host to another because both systems use SMTP. You do need a gateway to go from SMTP to X.400 or to a proprietary mailer. In a pure TCP/IP network, this function is not needed.

The mail server is the most important component of a reliable system because it eliminates reliance on the user's system. A centrally controlled, professionally operated server collects the mail regardless of whether or not the end system is operational.

The relay host also contributes to the reliability of the email system. If mail cannot be immediately delivered by the relay host, it is queued and processed later. An end system also queues mail, but if it is shut down no attempts can be made to deliver queued mail until the system is back online. The mail server and the mail relay are operated 24 hours a day.

The design of most TCP/IP email networks is based on the following guidelines:

- Use a mail server to collect mail, and POP or IMAP to deliver the mail to the client.

- Use a mail relay host to forward mail. Implement a simplified email address scheme on the relay host.

- Standardize on TCP/IP and SMTP. Users who insist on using a proprietary email system should be responsible for obtaining and configuring an SMTP mail gateway for that system in order to connect to your TCP/IP email network.

- Standardize on MIME for binary attachments. Avoid proprietary attachment schemes; they just cause confusion when the users of Brand X email cannot read attachments received from Brand Y.

For their client configurations, provide the users with the hostname and IP address of the mail server and the mail relay. The mail server will also require a username and password for each person.

Informing the Users

All of the configuration information that you gather or develop through the planning process must be given to the end users to configure their systems. You can use several techniques to help your users configure their systems.

First, you want to relieve end users of as much of the burden of configuration as possible. In Chapter 3 we discussed NIS, NFS, and configuration servers. All of these play a role in simplifying the configuration process, with DHCP having the most important role. DHCP configuration servers provide every parameter needed to configure a TCP/IP client. Everything covered in this chapter—IP address, subnet mask, hostname, domain name, default gateways, and server addresses—can all be provided by DHCP without involving the end user in the process.

One important thing that DHCP does is point clients to the other network servers. The servers require that the client is configured to be a client. For NIS and NFS, the client must have a full basic configuration. Once the client is running, NIS and NFS can provide additional levels of configuration support. NIS provides several system administration databases that include many of the basic configuration values. With NIS, you maintain these databases centrally so that users do not have to maintain them on their Unix desktop systems. NFS can distribute preconfigured system files and documentation files to client systems.

However, even DHCP combined with other servers is not the complete solution. Even DHCP requires that the users know that DHCP is being used so that they do not enter any incorrect values during the initial system installation. Therefore, the network administrator must directly communicate configuration instructions to the administrator of the end system, usually through written documentation or the Web.

To communicate this information, the network administrator will often create a short list of information for the user. When DHCP is used, the information given to the user is often the same for all Unix clients and for all Windows clients. For example, Unix clients might be told to use DHCP to configure the interface, to run NIS, and to run NFS. They might be further directed to mount specific NFS filesystems. Windows clients might be told to run DHCP to configure the interface and to use specific workgroup and NetBIOS names.

Building a TCP/IP network requires careful planning on your part. Once you have made your plans, you must document them and communicate your decisions to the people who will be using your network.

Summary

Planning is the first step in configuring TCP/IP. We began this chapter by deciding whether our network will connect to the Internet and exploring how that decision impacts the rest of our planning. We also looked at the basic information needed to configure a physical network: an IP address, a subnet mask, and a hostname. We discussed how to plan routing, which is essential for communicating between TCP/IP networks. We outlined the basic network services, starting with DNS, and discussed file, print, and email servers. Finally, we looked at the different ways that this planning information is communicated from the network administrator to the system administrators and users.

In the chapters that follow, we put these plans into action, starting with the configuration of the network interface in Chapter 6. First, however, we will go inside the Unix kernel to see how TCP/IP is built into the operating system.

CHAPTER 5

Basic Configuration

In this chapter:

• Kernel Configuration
• Startup Files
• The Internet Daemon
• The Extended Internet Daemon

Every Unix computer that runs TCP/IP has a technique for incorporating the basic transport and IP datagram services into its operating system. This chapter discusses two techniques for incorporating the basic TCP/IP configuration into a Unix system: recompiling the kernel, and loading dynamically linked kernel modules. We'll study these techniques and the role they play in linking TCP/IP and Unix. With this information, you should be able to understand how the vendor builds the basic configuration and how to modify it to create your own custom configuration.

The transport and datagram services installed in the operating system are used by the application services described in Chapter 3. There are two different techniques for starting application services: they are either run at boot time or launched on an on-demand basis. This chapter covers both of these techniques and shows you how to configure and control this startup process. But first let's look at how TCP/IP is incorporated into the Unix operating system.

Kernel Configuration

Kernel configuration is not really a network administration task—rather, it is a basic part of Unix system administration, whether or not the computer is connected to a network. But TCP/IP networking, like other system functions, is integrated into the kernel.

There are two very different approaches to kernel configuration. Some systems are designed to eliminate the need for you to recompile the kernel, while others encourage you to compile your own custom kernel. Linux is an example of the latter philosophy: its documentation encourages you to create your own configuration. Solaris is an example of the former.

The Solaris system comes with a generic kernel that supports all basic system services. When a Solaris system boots, it detects all system hardware and uses dynamically loadable modules to support that hardware. Solaris can rely on this technique because Sun is primarily a hardware vendor. Sun designs its hardware to work with the Solaris kernel, and has a well-defined device driver interface so that third-party hardware vendors can design hardware that clearly identifies itself to the kernel.

Using Dynamically Loadable Modules

Most versions of Unix support dynamically loadable modules, which are kernel modules that can be dynamically linked into the kernel at runtime. These modules provide the system with a great deal of flexibility because the kernel is able to load support for new hardware when the hardware is detected. Dynamically loadable modules are used to add new features to the system without requiring the system administrator to perform a manual reconfiguration.

Solaris depends on dynamically loadable modules. Solaris does have a kernel configuration file, defined in the */etc/system* file, but this file is very small, has only limited applicability, and is not directly edited by the system administrator. When a new software package is added to the system, the script that installs that package makes any changes it requires to the */etc/system* file. But even that is rare. Most drivers that are delivered with third-party hardware carry their own configuration files.

On a Solaris system, optional device drivers are installed using the pkgadd command. The syntax of the command is:

```
pkgadd -d device packagename
```

device is the device name. *packagename* is the name of the driver software package provided by the vendor.

The device driver installation creates the proper entry in the */dev* directory as well as in the */kernel/drv* directory. As an example, look at the Ethernet device driver for adapters that use the DEC 21140 chipset. The name of the driver is dnet.[*] There is a device named */dev/dnet* defined in the device directory. There is a dynamically loadable module named */kernel/drv/dnet* in the kernel driver directory, and there is a configuration file for the driver named */kernel/drv/dnet.conf*. dnet is a standard driver, but the installation of an optional driver will create similar files.

After installing a new device driver, create an empty file named */reconfigure*. Shut down the system and install the new hardware. Then restart the system. The */reconfigure* file is a flag to the system to check for new hardware. When the Solaris system reboots, it will detect the new hardware and load the dynamic module that provides the device driver for that hardware.

---

[*] dnet is not an optional device. It is a standard part of Solaris and it is the Ethernet device we use in all of our Solaris examples.

The Solaris `ifconfig` command, which is covered in extensive detail in Chapter 6, provides the `modlist` option to let you see the kernel modules that are associated with a TCP/IP network interface. For example:

```
# ifconfig dnet0 modlist
0 arp
1 ip
2 dnet
```

The purpose of each kernel module in this list is clear. arp provides the ARP protocol for the Ethernet interface. ip provides the TCP/IP protocols used for this network. Each of these modules has a configuration file in the */kernel/drv* directory. There is an *arp.conf* file, an *ip.conf* file, and a *dnet.conf* file. However, these files provide very limited capacity for controlling the function of the modules. On Solaris systems, use the ndd command to control the module.

To see what configuration options are available for a module, use the ndd command with a ? as an argument. For example, use the following command to see the variables available for the arp module:

```
# ndd /dev/arp ?
?                       (read only)
arp_cache_report        (read only)
arp_debug               (read and write)
arp_cleanup_interval    (read and write)
arp_publish_interval    (read and write)
arp_publish_count       (read and write)
```

The arp module offers six values:

?

>A read-only value that displays this list.

arp_cache_report

>A read-only value that displays the permanent values in the ARP cache. The arp command gives a better display of the cache. See the description of the arp command in Chapter 2.

arp_debug

>A variable that enables ARP protocol debugging. By default, it is set to 0 and debugging is disabled. Setting it to 1 enables debugging. The ARP protocol is very old and very reliable. ARP debugging is never needed.

arp_cleanup_interval

>A variable that defines how long temporary entries are kept in the cache.

arp_publish_interval

>A variable that defines how long the system waits between broadcasts of an Ethernet address that it is configured to publish.

arp_publish_count
> A variable that defines how many ARP broadcasts are sent in response to a query for an address that this system publishes.

The default configuration values set for the arp module have worked well for every Solaris system I have ever worked with. I have never had a need to change any of these settings. The second module displayed by modlist provides a slightly more interesting example.

Use the ndd /dev/ip ? command to list the configuration options for the ip module. There are almost 60 of them! Of all of these, there is only one that I have ever needed to adjust: ip_forwarding.

The ip_forwarding variable specifies whether the ip module should act as if the system is a router and forward packets to other hosts. By default, systems with one network interface are hosts that do not forward packets, and systems with more than one interface are routers that do forward packets. Setting ip_forwarding to 0 turns off packet forwarding, even if the system has more than one network interface. Setting ip_forwarding to 1 turns on packet forwarding, even if the system has only one network interface.

On occasion you will have a multi-homed host, which is a host connected to more than one network. Despite multiple network connections, the system is a host, not a router. To prevent that system from acting as a router and potentially interfering with the real routing configuration, disable IP forwarding as follows:

```
# ndd /dev/ip ip_forwarding
1
# ndd -set /dev/ip ip_forwarding 0
# ndd /dev/ip ip_forwarding
0
```

The first ndd command in this example queries the ip module for the value set in ip_forwarding. In this example it is set to 1, which enables forwarding. The second ndd command uses the -set option to write the value 0 into the ip_forwarding variable. The last command in the example redisplays the variable to show that it has indeed been changed.

The pkgadd command, the ifconfig modlist option, and the ndd command are all specific to Solaris. Other systems use dynamically loadable modules but use a different set of commands to control them.

Linux also uses loadable modules. Linux derives the same benefit from loadable modules as Solaris does, and like Solaris usually you have very little involvement with loadable modules. Generally the Linux system detects the hardware and determines the correct modules needed during the initial installation without any input from the system administrator. But not always. Sometimes hardware is not detected during the installation, and other times new hardware is added to a running system. To handle these situations, you need to know the Linux commands used to work with loadable modules.

Use the lsmod command to check which modules are installed in a Linux system. Here's an example from a Red Hat system:

```
# lsmod
Module                 Size   Used by
ide-cd                26848    0  (autoclean)
cdrom                 27232    0  (autoclean) [ide-cd]
autofs                11264    1  (autoclean)
smc-ultra              6048    1  (autoclean)
8390                   6816    0  (autoclean) [smc-ultra]
ipchains              38976    0  (unused)
nls_iso8859-1          2880    1  (autoclean)
nls_cp437              4384    1  (autoclean)
vfat                   9392    1  (autoclean)
fat                   32672    0  (autoclean) [vfat]
```

Loadable modules perform a variety of tasks. Some modules are hardware device drivers, such as the smc-ultra module for the SMC Ultra Ethernet card. Other modules provide support for the wide array of filesystems available in Linux, such as the ISO8859 filesystem used on CD-ROMs or the DOS FAT filesystem with long filename support (vfat).

Each entry in the listing produced by the lsmod command begins with the name of the module followed by the size of the module. As the size field indicates, modules are small. Often modules depend on other modules to get the task done. The interrelationships of modules are called *module dependencies*, which are shown in the listing. In the sample, the smc-ultra driver depends on the 8390 module, as indicated by the 8390 entry ending with the string "[smc-ultra]". The 8390 entry lists the modules that depend on it under the heading *Used by*. The listing shows other dependencies, including that vfat depends on fat and cdrom depends on ide-cd.

Most of the lines in the sample include the string "(autoclean)". This indicates that the specified module can be removed from memory automatically if it is unused. autoclean is an option. You can select different options by manually loading modules with the insmod command.

Modules can be manually loaded using the insmod command. This command is very straightforward—it's just the command and the module name. For example, to load the 3c509 device driver, enter insmod 3c509. This does not install the module with the autoclean option. If you want this driver removed from memory when it is not in use, add the -k option to the insmod command: insmod -k 3c509.

A critical limitation with the insmod command is that it does not understand module dependencies. If you used it to load the smc-ultra module, it would not automatically load the required 8390 module. For this reason, modprobe is a better command for manually loading modules. As with the insmod command, the syntax is simple. To load the smc-ultra module, simply enter modprobe smc-ultra.

modprobe reads the module dependencies file that is produced by the depmod command. Whenever the kernel or the module libraries are updated, run depmod to produce a new file containing the module dependencies. The command depmod -a searches all of the standard module libraries and creates the necessary file. After it is run, you can use modprobe to install any modules and have the other modules it depends on automatically installed.

Use the rmmod command to remove unneeded modules. Again, the syntax is simple: rmmod appletalk removes the appletalk driver from your system. There is rarely any need to remove unneeded modules because, as noted in the discussion of autoclean, the system automatically removes unused modules.

The smc-ultra module is an Ethernet device driver. It is in fact the device driver used for the network interface on our sample Linux system. Device drivers can be compiled into the kernel, as described later, or they can be dynamically loaded from a module. Most Ethernet device drivers are handled as dynamically loadable modules. The Ethernet driver modules are found in the */lib/modules* directory. On a Red Hat 7.2 system, Ethernet device drivers are in the */lib/modules/2.4.7-10/kernel/drivers/net* directory, as the following listing shows:

```
# ls /lib/modules/2.4.7-10/kernel/drivers/net
3c501.o             atp.o          eexpress.o   ni5010.o      smc-ultra.o
3c503.o             bcm            epic100.o    ni52.o        starfire.o
3c505.o             bonding.o      eql.o        ni65.o        strip.o
3c507.o             bsd_comp.o     es3210.o     pcmcia        sundance.o
3c509.o             cipe           eth16i.o     pcnet32.o     sunhme.o
3c515.o             cs89x0.o       ethertap.o   plip.o        tlan.o
3c59x.o             de4x5.o        ewrk3.o      ppp_async.o   tokenring
8139too.o           de600.o        fc           ppp_deflate.o tulip
82596.o             de620.o        hamachi.o    ppp_generic.o tun.o
8390.o              defxx.o        hp100.o      ppp_synctty.o via-rhine.o
ac3200.o            depca.o        hp.o         rcpci.o       wan
acenic.o            dgrs.o         hp-plus.o    sb1000.o      wavelan.o
aironet4500_card.o  dmfe.o         irda         shaper.o      wd.o
aironet4500_core.o  dummy.o        lance.o      sis900.o      winbond-840.o
aironet4500_proc.o  e1000.o        lne390.o     sk98lin       yellowfin.o
appletalk           e100.o         natsemi.o    skfp
arlan.o             e2100.o        ne2k-pci.o   sk_g16.o
arlan-proc.o        eepro100.o     ne3210.o     slip.o
at1700.o            eepro.o        ne.o         smc-ultra32.o
```

All loadable network device drivers are listed here. Some, such as *plip.o*, are not for Ethernet devices. Most are easily identifiable as Ethernet drivers, such as the 3COM drivers, the SMC drivers, the NE2000 drivers, and the Ethernet Express drivers.

The Linux system detects the Ethernet hardware during the initial installation, and if Linux has the correct driver for that hardware, it installs the appropriate driver. If the

Ethernet adapter is not detected during the operating system installation or if it is added after the system is installed, use the modprobe command to load the device driver manually. If the correct driver for the adapter is not included with your Linux system, you may need to compile the module yourself.

For a device driver to operate correctly, it must be compiled with the correct libraries for your kernel. Sometimes this means downloading the driver source code and compiling it yourself on your system. Ethernet driver source code is available for many adapters from *http://www.scyld.com*, which has a great repository of Linux network driver software. The comments in the driver source code includes the correct compiler command to compile the module.

After compiling, copy the object file to the correct */lib/modules* directory. Then use modprobe to load and test the driver. Alternatively, most device drivers are now available in RPM format, eliminating the need for compilation.

Linux frequently uses dynamically loadable modules for device drivers. But most other components of TCP/IP are not loaded at runtime; they are compiled into the kernel. Next we look at how Unix kernels are recompiled.

Recompiling the Kernel

This text uses Linux and FreeBSD as examples of systems that encourage you to compile a custom kernel.* This chapter's examples of kernel configuration statements come from these two Unix systems. While kernel configuration involves all aspects of system configuration, we include only statements that directly affect TCP/IP configuration.

Both of the Unix systems used in the examples come with a kernel configuration file preconfigured for TCP/IP. During the initial installation, you may need to select a preconfigured kernel that includes network support, but you probably won't need to modify the kernel configuration for networking. The kernel configuration file is normally changed only when you wish to:

- Produce a smaller, more efficient kernel by removing unneeded items
- Add a new device
- Modify a system parameter

While there is rarely any need to modify the kernel network statements, it is useful to understand what these statements do. Looking into the kernel configuration file shows how Unix is tied to the hardware and software of the network.

---

* The kernel configuration process of other BSD systems, such as SunOS 4.1.3, is similar to the FreeBSD example.

The procedures and files used for kernel configuration vary dramatically depending on Unix implementation. These variations make it essential that you refer to your system documentation before trying to configure the kernel on your system. Only your system documentation can provide you with the accurate, detailed instructions required to successfully complete this task.

Linux Kernel Configuration

The source code for the Linux kernel is normally delivered with a Linux distribution. If your system does not have the source code or you want a newer version of the Linux kernel, it can be downloaded from *http://www.kernel.org* as a compressed tar file. If you already have a directory named */usr/src/linux*, rename it before you unpack the tarball:

```
# cd /usr/src
# tar -zxvf linux-2.1.14.tar.gz
```

The Linux kernel is a C program compiled and installed by make. The make command customizes the kernel configuration and generates the files (including the Makefile) needed to compile and link the kernel. There are three variations of the command:

make config
> This form of the make command is entirely text-based. It takes you through a very long sequence of questions that ask about every aspect of the kernel configuration. Because it asks every question in a sequential manner, this can be the most cumbersome way to reconfigure the kernel, particularly if you wish to change only a few items.

make menuconfig
> This form of the make command uses curses to present a menu of configuration choices. It provides all of the capabilities of the make config command but is much easier to use because it allows you to jump to specific areas of interest. The make menuconfig command works from any terminal and on any system, even one that does not support X Windows.

make xconfig
> This form of the make command uses X Windows to provide a "point and click" interface for kernel configuration. It has all the power of the other commands and is very easy to use.

Choose the form of the command you like best. In this example we use make xconfig.

On Linux systems, the kernel source is found in */usr/src/linux*. To start the configuration process, change to the source directory and run make xconfig:

```
# cd /usr/src/linux
# make xconfig
```

The make xconfig command displays the screen shown in Figure 5-1.

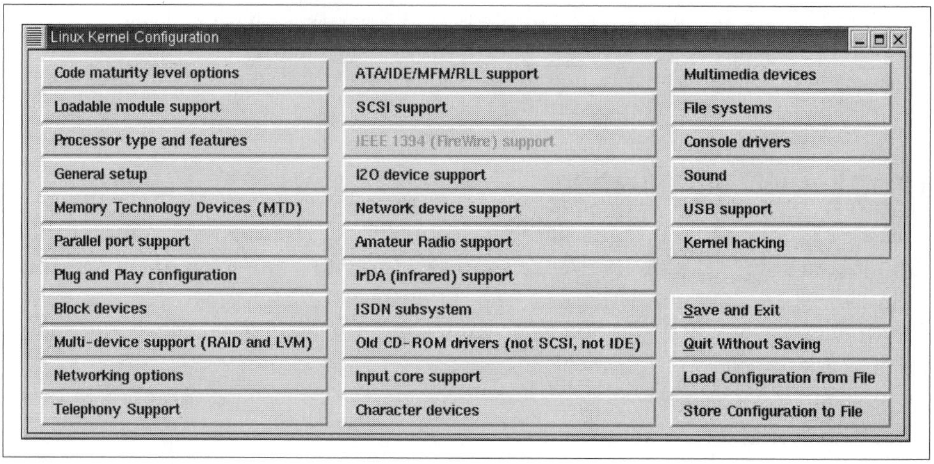

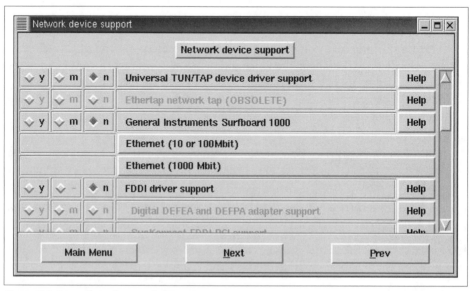

Figure 5-1. Linux xconfig main menu

The menu displays more than 30 buttons that represent different configuration categories. Click on a button to view and set the configuration options in that category. Because our focus is on the kernel configuration options that affect TCP/IP, the two menu items we're interested in are *Networking options* and *Network device support*. Figure 5-2 shows the window that appears if the *Network device support* button is selected.

Figure 5-2. Linux kernel network device support

This window lists the network device drivers that can be compiled into or loaded by the kernel and shows the three choices for most configuration options:

y   Selecting *y* compiles the option into the new kernel.

m   Selecting *m* causes the option to be loaded as a dynamically loadable module by the kernel. Not every option is available as a loadable module. When a configuration question must be answered yes or no, the module selection is not available. Notice the *FDDI driver support* option. Choosing *y* for that option enables FDDI driver support and highlights a selection of possible FDDI interface adapters, which are "grayed-out" in Figure 5-2. Frequently, interface support must be selected before an individual adapter can be selected.

n   Selecting *n* tells the kernel not to use the configuration option.

Each configuration option also has a *Help* button. Clicking on the *Help* button provides additional information about the option and advice about when the option should be set. Even if you think you know what the option is about, you should read the description displayed by the *Help* button before you change the default setting.

Two items shown in Figure 5-2, *Ethernet (10 or 100 Mbit)* and *Ethernet (1000 Mbit)*, open separate windows with extensive menu selections because Linux supports a very large number of Ethernet adapters. The Ethernet adapters available through those windows are selected using the same *y*, *m*, and *n* settings described above.

The *Network device support* window and the *Ethernet adapter* windows show that it is possible to compile specific adapter support into the kernel, but it is not necessary. As we saw in the previous section on dynamically loadable modules, network interfaces are usually controlled by loadable modules. All Linux systems need a network interface to run TCP/IP, but that interface does not need to be compiled into the kernel.

Selecting *Networking options* from the main menu in Figure 5-1 opens the *Network options* window, which contains over 60 menu selections because Linux supports a wide range of network services. Some of these are experimental and some relate to protocols other than IPv4. Here we limit ourselves to those options that directly relate to IPv4. Yet there are still a substantial number of options. They are:

Packet socket
>   This service allows applications to communicate directly with the network device. It is required for applications such as tcpdump that do packet capture and packet filtering. If *Packet socket* is enabled, *Packet socket: mmapped IO* can be selected to use memory-mapped I/O for the packet socket service. Packet socket service is usually enabled while packet socket memory mapped I/O is usually disabled.

Kernel/User netlink socket
>   This service provides communication between the kernel and user space programs. If enabled, *Routing messages* and *Netlink device emulation* can also be selected. Netlink sockets permit user space programs to interface with IPv4 routing and ARP tables and with kernel firewall code.

Network packet filtering

This service provides the IP packet filtering services that are required to make the system function as a firewall or a network address translation box. If *Network packet filtering* is enabled, *Network packet filtering debugging* can also be selected. Network packet filtering is normally enabled on routers and disabled on hosts, although it can be used to improve server security as described in the iptables section of Chapter 12.

TCP/IP networking

This selection installs kernel support for TCP/IP. It provides all basic TCP/IP transport and datagram protocols. Once TCP/IP networking is selected, many other optional TCP/IP services become available, listed below:

IP: multicasting

This provides IP multicasting support. Multicasting is described in Chapter 2.

IP: advanced router

This menu selection highlights several options that configure the kernel for advanced routing protocols. Advanced routing does not need to be enabled for basic routing to work, and is not needed for a host or a small interior router. Advanced routing is used only if the Linux system is configured as the primary router or an exterior router between autonomous systems. Chapter 7 describes how gated is used to run advanced routing protocols on Unix systems. The kernel configuration advanced routing options are:

IP: policy routing enables kernel-level policy-based routing, which is discussed in Chapter 7 in relationship to the BGP routing protocol, and in Chapter 2 in relationship to the Policy Routing Database (PRDB). This option is not needed by gated, which implements policy-based routing at the user level.

IP: equal cost multipath enables kernel support for multiple routes to the same destination. Multipath routing is described in Chapter 7 in relationship to the OSPF routing protocol.

IP use TOS value as routing key enables a type of tag switching (also called label switching) that uses the Type of Service (TOS) field of the IP header to hold the tag. Both OSPF and RIP version 2 can use a tag field. Appendix B touches upon the gated syntax used for tag fields.

IP: verbose route monitoring increases the number and length of the routing table update messages.

IP: large routing tables increases the memory reserved for the routing table.

IP: kernel level autoconfiguration

This service is used on diskless clients. When selected, two additional selections become available, *IP: BOOTP support* and *IP: RARP support,* that are used to specify whether the configuration comes from BOOTP or RARP. See Chapter 3 for a description of BOOTP and RARP.

IP: tunneling

This service encapsulates IPv4 datagrams within an IP tunnel, which makes a host appear to be on a different network than the one to which it is physically connected. This service is occasionally used on laptop machines to facilitate mobility.

IP: GRE tunnels over IP

This enables the Generic Routing Encapsulation (GRE) protocol that is used to encapsulate IPv4 or IPv6 datagrams in an IPv4 tunnel. Selecting this option makes the *IP: broadcast GRE over IP* option available, which provides support for multicasting with the tunnel. GRE is the preferred encapsulation protocol when dealing with Cisco routers.

IP: multicast routing

This selection provides support for multicast routing. It is needed only if your system acts as a multicast router, i.e., runs mrouted. When selected, you are given the options *IP: PIM-SM version 1 support* and *IP: PIM-SM version 2 support* that set the level of the PIM-SM protocol used by your system.

IP: TCP Explicit Congestion Notification support

This enables Explicit Congestion Notification (ECN). ECN messages are sent from a router to a client to alert the client of congestion. This would be enabled only if the Linux system is a router. Because many firewalls are incompatible with ECN, it is recommended that ECN not be enabled.

IP: TCP syncookie support

This enables support for *SYN cookies*, which are used to counteract *SYN flooding* denial-of-service attacks.

IP: Netfilter Configuration

Selecting this menu item opens a window that allows you to select a range of services for the kernel's Netfilter firewall. The iptables discussion in Chapter 12 describes how the Netfilter service is used.

QoS and/or fair queueing

This specifies options that change the way network packets are handled by the server. Because it is experimental, this option should be set to n for an operational server. The optional packet handlers require special software to administer them.

After completing the network configuration, run make dep; make clean to build the dependencies and clean up the odds and ends. When the makes are complete, compile the kernel. The make bzImage command builds a compressed kernel and puts it into the */usr/src/linux/i386/boot* directory.* When you're sure that the new kernel is

---

* Most Linux systems use a compressed kernel that is automatically decompressed during the system boot.

ready to run, simply copy the new kernel file, *bzImage*, to the *vmlinuz* file your system uses to boot.

Linux's list of network configuration options is long.* Linux is yin to the Solaris yang: Linux permits the system administrator to configure everything while Solaris configures everything for the administrator. BSD kernel configuration lies somewhere between these two extremes.

The BSD Kernel Configuration File

Like Linux, the BSD Unix kernel is a C program compiled and installed by make. The config command reads the kernel configuration file and generates the files (including the Makefile) needed to compile and link the kernel. On FreeBSD systems, the kernel configuration file is located in the directory */usr/src/sys/i386/conf*.†

A large kernel configuration file named *GENERIC* is delivered with the FreeBSD system. The *GENERIC* kernel file configures all of the standard devices for your system—including everything necessary for TCP/IP. In this section, we look at just those items found in the *GENERIC* file that relate to TCP/IP. No modifications are necessary for the *GENERIC* kernel to run basic TCP/IP services. The reasons for modifying the BSD kernel are the same as those discussed for the Linux kernel: to make a smaller, more efficient kernel, or to add new features.

There is no standard name for a BSD kernel configuration file. When you create a configuration file, choose any name you wish. By convention, BSD kernel configuration filenames use uppercase letters. To create a new configuration, copy *GENERIC* to the new file and then edit the newly created file. The following creates a new configuration file called *FILBERT*:

```
# cd /usr/src/sys/i386/conf
# cp GENERIC FILBERT
```

If the kernel has been modified on your system, the system administrator will have created a new configuration file in the */usr/src/sys/i386/conf* directory. The kernel configuration file contains many configuration commands that cover all aspects of the system configuration. This text discusses only those parameters that directly affect TCP/IP configuration. See the documentation that comes with the FreeBSD system for information about the other configuration commands.‡

---

* Not only is this list long, it is bound to change. Always check the system documentation before starting a kernel reconfiguration.

† */usr/src/sys* is symbolically linked to */sys*. We use */usr/src/sys* only as an example. Your system may use another directory.

‡ The book *The Complete FreeBSD* by Greg Lehey (published by Walnut Creek CDROM Books) is a good source for information on recompiling a BSD kernel.

TCP/IP in the BSD Kernel

For a network administrator, it is more important to understand which kernel statements are necessary to configure TCP/IP than to understand the detailed structure of each statement. Three types of statements are used to configure TCP/IP in the BSD kernel: options, pseudo-device, and device statements.

The options statement

The options statement tells the kernel to compile a software option into the system. The options statement that is most important to TCP/IP is:

```
options INET # basic networking support--mandatory
```

Every BSD-based system running TCP/IP has an options INET statement in its kernel configuration file. The statement produces a -DINET argument for the C compiler, which in turn causes the IP, ICMP, TCP, UDP, and ARP modules to be compiled into the kernel. This single statement incorporates the basic transport and IP datagram services into the system. Never remove this statement from the configuration file.

```
options ICMP_BANDLIM #Rate limit bad replies
```

This option limits the amount of bandwidth that can be consumed by ICMP error messages. Use it to protect your system from denial-of-service attacks that deliberately cause errors to overload your network.

```
options "TCP_COMPAT_43" # Compatible with BSD 4.3 [KEEP THIS!]
```

This option prevents connections between BSD 4.3 and FreeBSD systems from hanging by adjusting FreeBSD to ignore mistakes made by 4.3. In addition, setting this parameter prevents some applications from malfunctioning. For these reasons, keep this parameter as is.

The pseudo-device statement

The second statement type required by TCP/IP in all BSD configurations is a pseudo-device statement. A *pseudo-device* is a device driver not directly associated with an actual piece of hardware. The pseudo-device statement creates a header (*.h*) file that is identified by the pseudo-device name in the kernel directory. For example, the statement shown below creates the file *loop.h*:

```
pseudo-device    loop           # loopback network--mandatory
```

The loop pseudo-device is necessary to create the loopback device (lo0). This device is associated with the loopback address 127.0.0.1; it is defined as a pseudo-device because it is not really a piece of hardware.

Another pseudo-device that is used on many FreeBSD TCP/IP systems is:

```
pseudo-device    ether          # basic Ethernet support
```

This statement is necessary to support Ethernet. The ether pseudo-device is required for full support of ARP and other Ethernet specific functions. While it is possible that a system that does not have Ethernet may not require this statement, it is usually configured and should remain in your kernel configuration.

Other commonly configured pseudo-devices used by TCP/IP are those that support SLIP and PPP.

```
pseudo-device    sl      2    # Serial Line IP
```

This statement defines the interface for the Serial Line IP protocol. The number, 2 in the example, defines the number of SLIP pseudo-devices created by the kernel. The two devices created here would be addressed as devices sl0 and sl1.

```
pseudo-device    ppp     2    # Point-to-point protocol
```

The ppp pseudo-device is the interface for the Point-to-Point Protocol. The number, 2 in the example, defines the number of PPP pseudo-devices created by the kernel. The two devices created here would be addressed as devices ppp0 and ppp1. One other pseudo-device is directly related to PPP.

```
pseudo-device    tun     1    # Tunnel driver(user process ppp)
```

The tun pseudo-device is a tunnel driver used by user-level PPP software. *Tunneling* is when a system passes one protocol through another protocol; tun is a FreeBSD feature for doing this over PPP links. The number, 1 in the example, is the number of tunnels that will be supported by this kernel.

One pseudo-device is used for troubleshooting and testing.

```
pseudo-device    bpfilter    4    # Berkeley packet filter
```

The bpfilter statement adds the support necessary for capturing packets. Capturing packets is an essential part of protocol analyzers such as tcpdump; see Chapter 13. When the bpfilter statement is included in the BSD kernel, the Ethernet interface can be placed into *promiscuous mode.** An interface in promiscuous mode passes all packets, not just those addressed to the local system, up to the software at the next layer. This feature is useful for a system administrator troubleshooting a network. But it can also be used by intruders to steal passwords and compromise security. Use the bpfilter pseudo-device only if you really need it. The number, 4 in the example, indicates the maximum number of Ethernet interfaces that can be monitored by bpfilter.

The device statement

Real hardware devices are defined using the device statement. Every host connected to a TCP/IP network requires some physical hardware for that attachment. The hardware is declared with a device statement in the kernel configuration file. There are

---

* This assumes that the Ethernet hardware is capable of functioning in promiscuous mode. Not all Ethernet boards support this feature.

many possible network interfaces for TCP/IP, but the most common are Ethernet interfaces. The device statements for Ethernet interfaces found in the GENERIC kernel are listed below:

```
device de     # DEC/Intel DC21x4x (``Tulip'')
device fxp    # Intel EtherExpress PRO/100B (82557, 82558)
device tx     # SMC 9432TX (83c170 ``EPIC'')
device vx     # 3Com 3c590, 3c595 (``Vortex'')
device wx     # Intel Gigabit Ethernet Card (``Wiseman'')
device dc     # DEC/Intel 21143 and various workalikes
device rl     # RealTek 8129/8139
device sf     # Adaptec AIC-6915 (``Starfire'')
device sis    # Silicon Integrated Systems SiS 900/SiS 7016
device ste    # Sundance ST201 (D-Link DFE-550TX)
device tl     # Texas Instruments ThunderLAN
device vr     # VIA Rhine, Rhine II
device wb     # Winbond W89C840F
device xl     # 3Com 3c90x (``Boomerang'', ``Cyclone'')
device ed0 at isa? port 0x280 irq 10 iomem 0xd8000
device ex
device ep
device wi      # WaveLAN/IEEE 802.11 wireless NIC
device an      # Aironet 4500/4800 802.11 wireless NICs
device ie0 at isa? port 0x300 irq 10 iomem 0xd0000
device fe0 at isa? port 0x300
device le0 at isa? port 0x300 irq 5 iomem 0xd0000
device lnc0 at isa? port 0x280 irq 10 drq 0
device cs0 at isa? port 0x300
device sn0 at isa? port 0x300 irq 10
```

The device statement used to configure an Ethernet interface in the FreeBSD kernel comes in two general formats:

```
device ed0 at isa? port 0x280 net irq 10 iomem 0xd8000
device de0
```

The format varies depending on whether the device is an ISA device or a PCI device. The ed0 device statement defines the bus type (isa), the I/O base address (port 0x280), the interrupt number (irq 10) and the memory address (iomem 0xd8000). These values should match the values configured on the adapter card. All of these are standard items for configuring PC ISA hardware. On the other hand, the de0 device statement requires very little configuration because it configures a card attached to the PCI bus. The PCI is an intelligent bus that can determine the configuration directly from the hardware.

Ethernet is not the only TCP/IP network interface supported by FreeBSD. It supports several other interfaces. The serial line interfaces necessary for SLIP and PPP are shown below:

```
device sio0 at isa? port IO_COM1 flags 0x10 irq 4
device sio1 at isa? port IO_COM2 irq 3
device sio2 at isa? disable port IO_COM3 irq 5
device sio3 at isa? disable port IO_COM4 irq 9
```

The four serial interfaces, sio0 through sio3, correspond to the MS-DOS interfaces COM1 to COM4. These are needed for SLIP and PPP. Chapter 6 covers other aspects of configuring PPP.

The device statement varies according to the interface being configured. But how do you know which hardware interfaces are installed in your system? Remember that the *GENERIC* kernel that comes with your FreeBSD system is configured for a large number of devices. A simple way to tell which hardware interfaces are installed in your system is to look at the messages displayed on the console at boot time. These messages show all of the devices, including network devices, that the kernel found during initialization. Look at the output of the dmesg command. It displays a copy of the console messages generated during the last boot. Customizing the kernel for your network device more often than not means removing unneeded devices from the kernel configuration.

The options, pseudo-device, and device statements found in the kernel configuration file tell the system to include the TCP/IP hardware and software in the kernel. The statements in your configuration may vary somewhat from those shown in the previous examples. But you have the same basic statements in your kernel configuration file. With these basic statements, FreeBSD Unix is ready to run TCP/IP.

You may never change any of the variables discussed in this section. Like everything else in the kernel configuration file, they usually come correctly configured to run TCP/IP. You will, however, frequently be called upon to control the network services your server runs over TCP/IP. We'll now look at how network services are started and how you control which ones are started.

Startup Files

The kernel configuration brings the basic transport and IP datagram services of TCP/IP into Unix. But there is much more to the TCP/IP suite than just the basic services. How are these other protocols included in the Unix configuration?

Some protocols are explicitly started by including them in the boot files. This technique is used, for example, to start the Routing Information Protocol (RIP) and the Domain Name System (DNS). Network services that either have a long startup procedure or are in constant demand are normally started by a script at boot time, and run as daemon processes the entire time the system is running.

Anything that can be run from a shell prompt can be stored in a file and run as a shell script. Systems use this capability to automate the startup of system services. There are two basic Unix startup models that control how startup files are invoked: the BSD model and the System V model.

The BSD model is the simplest: a limited number of startup scripts are executed in order every time the system boots. At its simplest, there are three basic scripts, */etc/rc*, */etc/rc.boot*, and */etc/rc.local*, executed in that order for system initialization, service initialization, and local customization. On BSD Unix systems, network services are usually started by the */etc/rc.boot* file or the */etc/rc.local* file.

On systems that use the BSD startup model, place customized network configuration commands in the *rc.local* script. *rc.local* executes at the end of the startup process. Any configuration values set in this file override the earlier configuration commands.

The BSD startup model is used on BSD systems and SunOS systems. Linux and Solaris systems use the System V startup model. The System V startup model employs a much more complex set of startup files.* This model uses whole directories of scripts executed by the init process, with different directories being used depending on the runlevel of the system.

Startup Runlevels

To understand System V startup, you need to understand *runlevels*, which are used to indicate the state of the system when the init process is complete. There is nothing inherent in the system hardware that recognizes runlevels; they are purely a software construct. init and */etc/inittab*—the file used to configure init—are the only reasons why the runlevels affect the state of the system. We use Red Hat Linux as an example of how runlevels are used.

Linux defines several runlevels that run the full gamut of possible system states from not-running (halted) to running multiple processes for multiple users:

- Runlevel 0 shuts down all running processes and halts the system.
- Runlevel 1 places the system in single-user mode. Single-user mode is used by the system administrator to perform maintenance that cannot be done when users are logged in. This runlevel may also be indicated by the letter S instead of the number 1. Solaris uses S for single-user mode.
- Runlevel 2 is a special multiuser mode that does not support file sharing.
- Runlevel 3 provides full multiuser support with the full range of services, including NFS file sharing. It is the default mode used on Solaris systems.
- Runlevel 4 is unused. You can design your own system state and implement it through runlevel 4.
- Runlevel 5 initializes the system as a dedicated X Windows terminal. Linux systems use this to provide an X Windows console login. When Linux systems boot at runlevel 3, they provide a text-based console login. Solaris does not use this runlevel. Entering runlevel 5 on a Solaris system causes a system shutdown.
- Runlevel 6 shuts down all running processes and reboots the system.

---

* A good description of the maze of System V initialization files is provided in *Essential System Administration* by Æleen Frisch (O'Reilly & Associates).

As these notes make clear, different systems use the same runlevels in different ways. That is because runlevels are software. They are boot command arguments that tell init which startup scripts should be run. The scripts that are run can contain any valid commands. init maps runlevels to startup scripts using the *inittab* file.

Understanding /etc/inittab

All of the lines in the *inittab* file that begin with a sharp sign (#) are comments. A liberal dose of comments is needed because the syntax of *inittab* configuration lines is terse and arcane. An *inittab* entry has this general format:

```
label:runlevel:action:process
```

The *label* is a one- to four-character tag that identifies the entry. Because some systems support only two-character labels, most configurations limit all labels to two characters. The labels can be any arbitrary character string; they have no intrinsic meaning.

The *runlevel* field indicates the runlevels to which the entry applies. For example, if the field contains a 3, the process identified by the entry must be run for the system to initialize runlevel 3. More than one runlevel can be specified. Entries that have an empty runlevel field are not involved in initializing specific runlevels. For example, Linux systems have an *inittab* entry to handle the three-finger salute (Ctrl+Alt+Del); it does not have a value in the runlevel field.

The *action* field defines the conditions under which the process is run. Table 5-1 lists the action values used on Red Hat, Mandrake, and Caldera Linux systems.

Table 5-1. Linux inittab action values

Action	Meaning
Boot	Runs when the system boots. Runlevels are ignored.
Bootwait	Runs when the system boots, and init waits for the process to complete. Runlevels are ignored.
Ctrlaltdel	Runs when Ctrl+Alt+Del is pressed, which passes the SIGINT signal to init. Runlevels are ignored.
Initdefault	Doesn't execute a process. It sets the default runlevel.
Kbrequest	Runs when init receives a signal from the keyboard. This requires that a key combination be mapped to KeyBoardSignal.
Off	Disables the entry so the process is not run.
Once	Runs one time for every runlevel.
Ondemand	Runs when the system enters one of the special runlevels A, B, or C.
Powerfail	Runs when init receives the SIGPWR signal.
Powerokwait	Runs when init receives the SIGPWR signal and the file /etc/powerstatus contains the word OK.
Powerwait	Runs when init receives the SIGPWR signal, and init waits for the process to complete.
Respawn	Restarts the process whenever it terminates.
sysinit	Runs before any boot or bootwait processes.
wait	Runs the process upon entering the run mode, and init waits for the process to complete.

The last field in an *inittab* entry is *process*. It contains the process that init executes. The process appears in the exact format that it is executed from the command line. Therefore the *process* field starts with the name of the program that is to be executed followed by the arguments that will be passed to that process. For example, /sbin/ shutdown -t3 -r now, which is the process executed by some Linux systems when Ctrl+Alt+Del is pressed, is the same command that could be typed at the shell prompt to reboot the system. On most *inittab* entries, the *process* field contains the name of a startup script. Two main types of startup scripts are used: the system initialization script and the runlevel initialization scripts. These sample lines from a Red Hat Linux system show both:

```
# System initialization.
si::sysinit:/etc/rc.d/rc.sysinit

l0:0:wait:/etc/rc.d/rc 0
l1:1:wait:/etc/rc.d/rc 1
l2:2:wait:/etc/rc.d/rc 2
l3:3:wait:/etc/rc.d/rc 3
l4:4:wait:/etc/rc.d/rc 4
l5:5:wait:/etc/rc.d/rc 5
l6:6:wait:/etc/rc.d/rc 6
```

These seven lines are the real heart of the *inittab* file—they invoke the startup scripts. The first line tells init to run the boot script located at */etc/rc.d/rc.sysinit* to initialize the system. This entry has no runlevel value. It is run every time the system starts. The system initialization script performs certain essential tasks. For example, the Red Hat *rc.sysinit* script:

- Initializes the swap space
- Runs the filesystem check
- Mounts the */proc* filesystem
- Mounts the root filesystem as read-write after the fsck completes
- Loads the loadable kernel modules

Other initialization scripts may look different than Red Hat's, but they perform very similar functions. For example, a Caldera system begins by loading the loadable modules. It then activates the swap space, does the filesystem check, and remounts the root filesystem as read-write. The order is different, but the major functions are the same.

After the system initialization script is run, init runs a script for the specific runlevel. The remaining six lines in the sample are used to invoke the startup scripts for individual runlevels. Except for the runlevel involved, each line is identical.

Let's use the line with label l3 as an example. This line starts all of the processes and services needed to provide the full multiuser support. The runlevel is 3. The action wait directs init to wait until the startup script terminates before going on to any other entries in the *inittab* file that relate to runlevel 3. init executes the script */etc/rc.d/rc* and passes that script the command-line argument 3.

The control script, */etc/rc.d/rc*, then runs all the scripts that are appropriate for the runlevel. It does this by running the scripts that are stored in the directory /etc/rc*n*.d, where *n* is the specified runlevel. In our example, the *rc* script is passed a 3, so it runs the scripts found in the directory */etc/rc.d/rc3.d*. A listing of that directory from a Red Hat system shows that there are lots of scripts:

```
$ ls /etc/rc.d
init.d  rc0.d  rc2.d  rc4.d  rc6.d     rc.sysinit
rc      rc1.d  rc3.d  rc5.d  rc.local
$ ls /etc/rc.d/rc3.d
K03rhnsd      K35smb        K74ntpd    S05kudzu     S25netfs      S85httpd
K16rarpd      K45arpwatch   K74ypserv  S06reconfig  S26apmd       S90crond
K20nfs        K45named      K74ypxfrd  S08ipchains  S28autofs     S90xfs
K20rstatd     K50snmpd      K75gated   S09isdn      S40atd        S95anacron
K20rusersd    K50tux        K84bgpd    S10network   S55sshd       S99linuxconf
K20rwalld     K55routed     K84ospf6d  S12syslog    S56rawdevices S99local
K20rwhod      K61ldap       K84ospfd   S13portmap   S56xinetd
K28amd        K65identd     K84ripd    S14nfslock   S60lpd
K34yppasswdd  K73ypbind     K84ripngd  S17keytable  S80sendmail
K35dhcpd      K74nscd       K85zebra   S20random    S85gpm
```

The scripts that begin with a K are used to kill processes when exiting a specific runlevel. In the listing above, the K scripts would be used when terminating runlevel 3. The scripts that start with an S are used when starting runlevel 3. None of the items in *rc3.d*, however, is really a startup script. They are logical links to the real scripts, which are located in the */etc/rc.d/init.d* directory. For example, *S80sendmail* is linked to *init.d/sendmail*. This raises the question of why the scripts are executed from the directory *rc3.d* instead of directly from *init.d* where they actually reside. The reasons are simple. The same scripts are needed for several different runlevels. Using logical links, the scripts can be stored in one place and still be accessed by every runlevel from the directory used by that runlevel.

Scripts are executed in alphabetical order. Thus *S10network* is executed before *S80sendmail*. This allows the system to control the order in which scripts are executed through simple naming conventions. Different runlevels can execute the scripts in different orders while still allowing the real scripts in *init.d* to have simple, descriptive names. A listing of the *init.d* directory shows these descriptive names:

```
$ ls /etc/rc.d/init.d
amd       functions  kdcrotate  network   rarpd      rwalld    xfs
anacron   gated      keytable   nfs       rawdevices rwhod     xinetd
apmd      gpm        killall    nfslock   reconfig   sendmail  ypbind
arpwatch  halt       kudzu      nscd      rhnsd      single    yppasswdd
atd       httpd      ldap       ntpd      ripd       smb       ypserv
autofs    identd     linuxconf  ospf6d    ripngd     snmpd     ypxfrd
bgpd      ipchains   lpd        ospfd     routed     sshd      zebra
crond     iptables   named      portmap   rstatd     syslog
dhcpd     isdn       netfs      random    rusersd    tux
```

It is possible to place a customized configuration command directly in the applicable script in the *init.d* directory. A better alternative on a Red Hat system is to place any local changes in *rc.local*.

Like BSD systems, Linux systems provide an *rc.local* script for local customization. In general, you do not directly edit boot scripts. The exception to this rule is the *rc.local* script located in the */etc/rc.d* directory. It is the one customizable startup file, and it is reserved for your use; you can put anything you want in there. After the system initialization script executes, the runlevel scripts execute in alphabetical order. The last of these is *S99local*, which is a link to *rc.local*. Since it is executed last, the values set in the *rc.local* script override other configuration values.

Solaris also uses the System V startup model, but it makes things a little more difficult than Linux does. First off, it does not provide an *rc.local* script. If you want to use one, you need to add your own to the runlevel directories. Secondly, Solaris does not use many logical links in the runlevel directories. Therefore, there is no guarantee of a central place to modify scripts that are used for all runlevels. Additionally, each runlevel has a separate controlling script that can introduce differences in the startup process for each runlevel. For example, */sbin/rc2* is the controlling script for runlevel 2 and */sbin/rc3* is the controlling script for runlevel 3. All of these differences make the Solaris startup process more complex to analyze.

On a Solaris 8 system, runlevel 3 is the default runlevel for a multiuser system offering network services. The */sbin/rc3* controlling script runs the scripts in */etc/rc2.d* and then those in */etc/rc3.d*. Basic network configuration is handled in */etc/rc2.d* by the *S69inet* script and the *S72inetsvc* script. Several other scripts in both */etc/rc2.d* and */etc/rc3.d* are involved in launching network services.

For troubleshooting purposes it is important to understand where and how things happen during the system startup. When the network fails to initialize properly, it is good to know where to look. However, when you configure the network you should stick with the standard tools and procedures provided with your system. Directly modifying startup scripts can cause problems during the startup and can lead to lots of confusion for the other people who help you maintain your systems.

Of course, not all network services are started by a boot script. Most network services are started on demand. The most widely used tool for starting network services on demand is inetd, the Internet Daemon.

The Internet Daemon

The internet daemon, inetd (pronounced "i net d"), is started at boot time from an initialization file such as */etc/rc2.d/S72inetsvc*. When it is started, inetd reads its configuration from the */etc/inetd.conf* file. This file contains the names of the services that inetd listens for and starts. You can add or delete services by making changes to the *inetd.conf* file.

An example of a file entry from a Solaris 8 system is:

```
ftp stream tcp6 nowait root /usr/sbin/in.ftpd  in.ftpd
```

The fields in the *inetd.conf* entry are, from left to right:

name

> The name of a service, as listed in the */etc/services* file. In the sample entry, the value in this field is ftp.

type

> The type of data delivery service used, also called *socket type*. The commonly used socket types are:

> *stream*

> > The stream delivery service provided by TCP, i.e., TCP byte stream.[*]

> *dgram*

> > The packet (datagram) delivery service provided by UDP.

> *raw*

> > Direct IP datagram service.

> The sample shows that FTP uses a stream socket.

protocol

> The name of a protocol, as given in the */etc/protocols* file. Its value is usually either "tcp" or "udp". To indicate that a service can run over both IPv4 and IPv6, Solaris uses "tcp6" or "udp6" in this field. The FTP protocol uses TCP as its transport layer protocol, so the sample entry contains tcp6 in this field.

wait-status

> The value for this field is either "wait" or "nowait." Generally, but not always, datagram type servers require "wait," and stream type servers allow "nowait." If the status is "wait," inetd must wait for the server to release the socket before it begins to listen for more requests on that socket. If the status is "nowait," inetd can immediately begin to listen for more connection requests on the socket. Servers with "nowait" status use sockets other than the connection request socket for processing; i.e., they use dynamically allocated sockets.

uid

> The uid is the username under which the server runs. This can be any valid username, but it is normally *root*. There are several exceptions. For example, in the default Solaris 8 configuration, the finger service and the Sun Font Server (fs) both run as the user *nobody* for security reasons.

server

> This is the full pathname of the server program started by inetd. Because our example is from a Solaris system, the path is */usr/sbin/in.ftpd*. On your system

---

[*] Here the reference is to TCP/IP sockets and TCP streams, not to AT&T streams I/O or BSD socket I/O.

the path may be different. It is more efficient for inetd to provide some small services directly than it is for inetd to start separate servers for these functions. For these small services, the value of the server field is the keyword "internal," which means that this service is an internal inetd service.

arguments

These are any command-line arguments that should be passed to the server program when it is invoked. This list always starts with argv[0] (the name of the program being executed). The program's manpage documents the valid command-line arguments for each program. In the example, only in.ftpd, the name of the program, is provided.

There are a few situations in which you need to modify the *inetd.conf* file. For example, you may wish to disable a service. The default configuration provides a full array of servers. Not all of them are required on every system, and for security reasons you may want to disable non-essential services on some computers. To disable a service, place a # at the beginning of its entry (which turns the line into a comment) and pass a hang-up signal to the inetd server. When inetd receives a hang-up signal, it re-reads the configuration file, and the new configuration takes effect immediately.

You may also need to add new services. We'll see some examples of that in later chapters. Let's look in detail at an example of restoring a service that has been previously disabled. We'll begin by looking at some entries and comments from the Solaris */etc/inetd.conf* file:

```
# Tftp service is provided primarily for booting.  Most sites run this
# only on machines acting as "boot servers."
#
#tftp  dgram  udp6 wait    root    /usr/sbin/in.tftpd  in.tftpd -s /tftpboot
#
# Finger, systat and netstat give out user information which may be
# valuable to potential "system crackers."  Many sites choose to disable
# some or all of these services to improve security.
#
finger stream tcp6 nowait nobody /usr/sbin/in.fingerd  in.fingerd
```

This part of the file shows two TCP/IP services. One of these, tftp, is commented out. The TFTP protocol is a special version of FTP that allows file transfers without username/password verification. Because of this, it is a possible security hole and is often disabled in the *inetd.conf* file. The other is finger, which the comments suggest we might want to comment out.

As an example of modifying the *inetd.conf* file, we'll reconfigure the system to provide tftp service, which is sometimes necessary for supporting diskless devices. First, use your favorite editor to remove the comment (#) from the tftp entry in *inetd.conf*. (The example uses sed, everyone's favorite editor!) Then find out the process ID for inetd and pass it the SIGHUP signal. The following steps show how this is done:

```
# cd /etc
# mv inetd.conf inetd.conf.org
```

```
# cat inetd.conf.org | sed s/#tftp/tftp/ > inetd.conf
# ps -acx | grep inetd
  144 ?  I      0:12 inetd
# kill -HUP 144
```

In some situations, you may also need to modify the pathname of a server or the arguments passed to a particular server when it is invoked. For example, look again at the tftp entry. This line contains command-line arguments that are passed to the tftp server when it is started. The -s /tftpboot option addresses the most obvious tftp security hole. It prevents tftp users from retrieving files that are not located in the directory specified after the -s option. If you want to use another directory for tftp, you must change the *inetd.conf* file. The only command-line arguments passed to servers started by inetd are those defined in the *inetd.conf* file.

The Extended Internet Daemon

An alternative to inetd is the Extended Internet Daemon (xinetd). xinetd is configured in the */etc/xinetd.conf* file, which provides the same information to xinetd as *inetd.conf* provides to inetd. But instead of using positional parameters with meanings determined by location on a configuration line (as *inetd.conf* does), *xinetd.conf* uses attribute and value pairs. The attribute name clearly identifies the purpose of each parameter. The value configures the parameter. For example, the third field in an *inetd.conf* entry contains the name of the transport protocol. In an *xinetd.conf* file, the name of the transport protocol is defined using the protocol attribute, e.g., protocol = tcp. Here is an example of an *xinetd.conf* tftp entry:

```
# default: off
# description: The tftp server uses the trivial file transfer \
#        protocol.  The tftp protocol is often used to boot diskless \
#        workstations, download configuration files to network printers, \
#        and to start the installation process for some operating systems.
service tftp
{
        socket_type            = dgram
        protocol               = udp
        wait                   = yes
        user                   = root
        server                 = /usr/sbin/in.tftpd
        server_args            = -s /tftpboot
        disable                = yes
}
```

Lines that start with # are comments. The actual entry begins with the service command. The attributes enclosed in the curly braces ({}) define the characteristics of the specified service.

The service, socket_type, protocol, wait, user, server, and server_args values all parallel values shown in the tftp example from the Solaris *inetd.conf* file. These attributes perform exactly the same functions for xinetd that their positional counterparts did for inetd.

One item, disable = yes, needs a little explanation. disable = yes prevents xinetd from starting tftp on demand. disable = yes is equivalent to commenting tftp out of the *inetd.conf* file. To enable tftp, edit this file and change it to disable = no.

Red Hat 7 uses xinetd. However, you won't find the network services listed in the */etc/xinetd.conf* file on a Red Hat system. In the Red Hat configuration, *xinetd.conf* includes by reference all of the files defined in the directory */etc/xinetd.d*. The listing shown above is actually the contents of the */etc/xinetd.d/tftp* file from our sample Red Hat system. Each service has its own configuration file.

xinetd is used because it has enhanced security features. Security is one of the most important reasons for understanding the *inetd.conf* file or the *xinetd.conf* file. How to use the access control features of xinetd and inetd is covered in Chapter 12.

Summary

The basic configuration files, the kernel configuration file, the startup files, and the */etc/inetd.conf* or */etc/xinetd.conf* file are necessary for installing the TCP/IP software on a Unix system. The kernel comes configured to run TCP/IP on most systems. Some systems, such as Solaris, are designed to eliminate kernel configuration. Others, such as Linux, encourage it as a way to produce a more efficient kernel. In either case, a network administrator needs to be aware of the kernel configuration commands required for TCP/IP so that they are not accidentally removed from the kernel when it is rebuilt.

Network services are either started at boot time from a startup script or are started on demand using xinetd or inetd. BSD systems have a few startup scripts that are run in sequence for every boot. System V Unix runs a different set of startup scripts for each runlevel. Runlevels are used to start the system in different modes, e.g., single user mode or multi-user mode. Both Solaris and Linux use the System V startup scheme.

inetd and xinetd start essential network services. Most Unix systems use inetd, although some, such as Red Hat Linux, use xinetd. Reconfigure inetd or xinetd to add new services and to improve security. Security can be improved by removing unneeded services or by adding access control. Chapter 12 provides additional information on how inetd and xinetd are used to improve system security.

The kernel configuration defines the network interface. In the next chapter we configure it, calling upon the planning we did in Chapter 4.

CHAPTER 6

Configuring the Interface

In this chapter:
- The ifconfig Command
- TCP/IP Over a Serial Line
- Installing PPP

When networking protocols work only with a single kind of physical network, there is no need to identify the network interface to the software. The software knows what the interface *must* be; no configuration issues are left for the administrator. However, one important strength of TCP/IP is its flexible use of different physical networks. This flexibility adds complexity to the system administrator's task, because you must tell TCP/IP which interfaces to use, and you must define the characteristics of each interface.

Because TCP/IP is independent of the underlying physical network, IP addresses are implemented in the network software—not in the network hardware. Unlike Ethernet addresses, which are determined by the Ethernet hardware, the system administrator assigns an IP address to each network interface.

In this chapter, we use the ifconfig (interface configure) command to identify the network interface to TCP/IP and to assign the IP address, subnet mask, and broadcast address to the interface. We also configure a network interface to run Point-to-Point Protocol (PPP), which is the standard Network Access Layer protocol used to run TCP/IP over modem connections.

During a real installation the system administrator is isolated from most of the details of the network configuration. The installation program prompts the administrator for information, places that information in script files, and then uses the scripts to configure the interface at every boot. In this chapter we look beyond the superficial to see how things actually work by examining the details of the ifconfig command and the scripts that invoke the command. Let's begin with a discussion of ifconfig.

The ifconfig Command

The ifconfig command sets, or checks, configuration values for network interfaces. Regardless of the vendor or version of Unix, the ifconfig command sets the IP address, the subnet mask, and the broadcast address for each interface. Its most basic function is assigning the IP address.

Here is the ifconfig command that configures the Ethernet interface on a Solaris system:

```
# ifconfig dnet0 172.16.12.2 netmask 255.255.255.0 broadcast 172.16.12.255
```

Many other arguments can be used with the ifconfig command; we discuss several of these later. But a few important arguments provide the basic information required by TCP/IP for every network interface. These are:

interface

> The name of the network interface that you want to configure for TCP/IP. In the example above, this is the Ethernet interface dnet0.

address

> The IP address assigned to this interface. Enter the address as either an IP address (in dotted decimal form) or as a hostname. If you use a hostname, place the hostname and its address in the */etc/hosts* file. Your system must be able to find the hostname in */etc/hosts* because ifconfig usually executes before DNS starts. The example uses the numeric IP address 172.16.12.2 as the address value.

netmask mask

> The address mask for this interface. Ignore this argument only if you're using the default mask derived from the traditional address class structure. The address mask chosen for our imaginary network is 255.255.255.0, so that is the value assigned to interface dnet0. See Chapters 2 and 4 for information on address masks.

broadcast address

> The broadcast address for the network. Most systems default to the standard broadcast address, which is an IP address with all host bits set to 1. In the ifconfig example we explicitly set the broadcast address to 172.16.12.255 to avoid any confusion, despite the fact that a Solaris 8 system will set the correct broadcast address by default. Every system on the subnet must agree on the broadcast address.

In the example above, we use keyword/value pairs because this makes explaining and understanding the syntax easier. However, Solaris does not require that syntax. The following (much shorter) command does exactly the same thing as the previous one:

```
# ifconfig dnet0 172.16.12.2/24
```

In this command the network mask is defined with an address prefix and the broadcast address is allowed to default. A prefix length of 24 is the same as 255.255.255.0. The default broadcast address given that prefix length is 172.16.12.255.

The network administrator provides the values for the address, subnet mask, and broadcast address. The values in our example are taken directly from the plans we developed in Chapter 4. But the name of the interface, the first argument on every ifconfig command line, is determined by the system during startup.

The Interface Name

In Chapter 5, we saw that Ethernet network interfaces come in many varieties and that different Ethernet cards usually have different interface names. You can usually determine which interface is used on a system from the messages displayed on the console during a boot. On many systems these messages can be examined with the dmesg command. The following example shows the output of the dmesg command on two different systems:

```
$ dmesg | grep ether
Oct  1 13:07:23 crab gld: [ID 944156 kern.info] dnet0: DNET 21x4x:
 type "ether" mac address 00:00:c0:dd:d4:da
```

```
$ dmesg | grep eth
eth0: SMC EtherEZ at 0x240, 00 00 C0 9A 72 CA,assigned  IRQ 5 programmed-I/O mode.
```

The first dmesg command in the example shows the message displayed when an Ethernet interface is detected during the boot of a Solaris 8 system. The string type "ether" makes it clear that dnet0 is an Ethernet interface. The Ethernet address (00: 00:c0:dd:d4:da) is also displayed.

The second dmesg example, which comes from a PC running Linux, provides even more information. On Linux systems, the Ethernet interface name starts with the string "eth", so we look for a message containing that string. The message from the Linux system displays the Ethernet address (00:00:c0:9a:72:ca) and the make and model (SMC EtherEZ) of the network adapter card.

It is not always easy to determine all available interfaces on your system by looking at the output of dmesg. These messages show only the physical hardware interfaces. In the TCP/IP protocol architecture, the Network Access Layer encompasses all functions that fall below the Internet Layer. This can include all three lower layers of the OSI Reference Model: the Physical Layer, the Data Link Layer, and the Network Layer. IP needs to know the specific interface in the Network Access Layer where packets should be passed for delivery to a particular network. This interface is not limited to a physical hardware driver. It could be a software interface into the network layer of another protocol suite. So what other methods can help you determine the network interfaces available on a system? Use the netstat and the ifconfig commands. For example, to see all network interfaces that are already configured, enter:

```
# netstat -in
Name  Mtu  Net/Dest    Address      Ipkts Ierrs Opkts Oerrs Collis Queue
lo0   8232 127.0.0.0   127.0.0.1    4504  0     4504  0     0      0
dnet0 1500 172.16.12.0 172.16.12.1  366   0     130   0     0      0
```

The `-i` option tells `netstat` to display the status of all configured network interfaces, and the `-n` tells `netstat` to display its output in numeric form. In the Solaris 8 example shown above, the `netstat -in` command displays the following fields:

Name
> The Interface Name field shows the actual name assigned to the interface. This is the name you give to `ifconfig` to identify the interface. An asterisk (*) in this field indicates that the interface is not enabled; i.e., the interface is not "up."

Mtu
> The Maximum Transmission Unit shows the longest frame (packet) that can be transmitted by this interface without fragmentation. The MTU is displayed in bytes and is discussed in more detail later in this chapter.

Net/Dest
> The Network/Destination field shows the network or the destination host to which the interface provides access. In our Ethernet examples, this field contains a network address. The network address is derived from the IP address of the interface and the subnet mask. This field contains a host address if the interface is configured for a point-to-point (host-specific) link. The destination address is the address of the remote host at the other end of the point-to-point link.* A point-to-point link is a direct connection between two computers. You can create a point-to-point link with the `ifconfig` command. How this is done is covered later in this chapter.

Address
> The IP Address field shows the Internet address assigned to this interface.

Ipkts
> The Input Packets field shows how many packets this interface has received.

Ierrs
> The Input Errors field shows how many damaged packets the interface has received.

Opkts
> The Output Packets field shows how many packets were sent out by this interface.

Oerrs
> The Output Errors field shows how many of the packets caused an error condition.

Collis
> The Collisions field shows how many Ethernet collisions were detected by this interface. Ethernet collisions are a normal condition caused by Ethernet traffic contention. This field is not applicable to non-Ethernet interfaces.

---

* See the description of the H flag in the section "The Routing Table" in Chapter 2.

Queue

The Packets Queued field shows how many packets are in the queue, awaiting transmission via this interface. Normally this is zero.

The output of a `netstat -in` command on a Linux system appears quite different:

```
$ netstat -in
Kernel Interface table
Iface MTU Met RX-OK RX-ERR RX-DRP RX-OVR  TX-OK TX-ERR TX-DRP TX-OVR Flg
eth0 1500   0  2234    280      0      0   1829      0      0      0 BRU
lo  16436   0    10      0      0      0     10      0      0      0 LRU
```

This output appears different, but as is often the case, appearances can fool you. Again we have the interface name, the MTU, and the packet statistics.[*] Here RX-OK is the total number of input packets, while RX-ERR (errors), RX-DRP (drops), and RX-OVR (overruns) added together give the total number of input errors. The total number of output packets is TX-OK, and the TX-ERR, TX-DRP, and TX-OVR counters provide the total number of output errors. Only two fields, Net/Dest and Address, that are provided in the Solaris output are not provided here. On the other hand, this display has two fields not used in the Solaris output. The Met field contains the routing metric assigned to this interface. The Flg field shows the interface flags:

- R means the interface is running.
- U means the interface is up.
- B means it is a broadcast-capable interface.
- L means it is a loopback interface.

This display shows that this workstation has only two network interfaces. In this case it is easy to identify each network interface. The lo0 interface is the loopback interface, which every TCP/IP system has. It is the same loopback device discussed in Chapter 5. eth0 is the Ethernet interface, also discussed previously.

On most systems, the loopback interface is part of the default configuration, so you won't need to configure it. If you do need to configure lo0 on a Solaris system, use the following command:

```
# ifconfig lo0 plumb 127.0.0.1 up
```

This example is specific to Solaris because it contains the plumb option. This option literally creates the "plumbing" required by the network interface the first time it is configured. Subsequent reconfigurations of this interface do not require the plumb option, and other systems, such as Linux, do not use this option.

The configuration of the Ethernet interface requires more attention than the loopback interface. Many systems use an installation script to install Unix. This script

---

[*] The packet statistics displayed by netstat are used in Chapter 13.

requests the host address, which it then uses to configure the interface. Later we'll look at these scripts and what to do when the user does not successfully set up the interface with the installation script.

The ifconfig command can also be used to find out what network interfaces are available on a system. The netstat command shows only interfaces that are configured. On some systems the ifconfig command can be used to show all interfaces, even those that have not yet been configured. On Solaris 8 systems, ifconfig -a does this; on a Linux 2.0.0 system, entering ifconfig without any arguments will list all of the network interfaces.

While most hosts have only one real network interface, some hosts and all gateways have multiple interfaces. Sometimes all interfaces are the same type; e.g., a gateway between two Ethernets may have two Ethernet interfaces. netstat on a gateway like this might display lo0, eth0, and eth1. Deciphering a netstat display with multiple interfaces of the same type is still very simple. But deciphering a system with many different types of network interfaces is more difficult. You must rely on documentation that comes with optional software to choose the correct interface. When installing new network software, always read documentation carefully.

This long discussion about determining the network interface is not meant to overshadow the important ifconfig functions of assigning the IP address, subnet mask, and broadcast address. So let's return to these important topics.

Checking the Interface with ifconfig

As noted previously, the Unix installation script configures the network interface. However, this configuration may not be exactly what you want. Check the configuration of an interface with ifconfig. To display the current values assigned to the interface, enter ifconfig with an interface name and no other arguments. For example, to check interface dnet0:

```
% ifconfig dnet0
dnet0: flags=1000843<UP,BROADCAST,NOTRAILERS,RUNNING,MULTICAST,IPv4> mtu 1500 index 2
    inet 172.16.12.2 netmask ffff0000 broadcast 172.16.255.255
```

When used to check the status of an interface on a Solaris system, the ifconfig command displays two lines of output. The first line shows the interface name, the flags that define the interface's characteristics, and the Maximum Transmission Unit (MTU) of this interface.* In our example the interface name is dnet0, and the MTU is 1500 bytes. The flags are displayed as both a numeric value and a set of keywords.

The interface's flags have the numeric value 1000843, which corresponds to:

---

* index is an interface characteristic that is specific to Solaris. It is an internal number used to uniquely identify the interface. The number does not have meaning to TCP/IP.

UP

The interface is enabled for use.

BROADCAST

The interface supports broadcasts, which means it is connected to a network that supports broadcasts, such as an Ethernet.

NOTRAILERS

This interface does not support trailer encapsulation.

RUNNING

This interface is operational.

MULTICAST

This interface supports multicasting.

IPv4

This interface supports TCP/IP version 4, which is the standard version of TCP/IP used on the Internet and described in this book.

The second line of ifconfig output displays information that directly relates to TCP/IP. The keyword inet is followed by the Internet address assigned to this interface. Next comes the keyword netmask, followed by the address mask written in hexadecimal. Finally, the keyword broadcast and the broadcast address are displayed.

On a Linux system the ifconfig command displays up to seven lines of information for each interface instead of the two lines displayed by the Solaris system. The additional information includes the Ethernet address, the PC IRQ, I/O Base Address and memory address, and packet statistics. The basic TCP/IP configuration information is the same on both systems.

```
> ifconfig eth0
eth0   Link encap:Ethernet  HWaddr 00:00:C0:9A:D0:DB
       inet addr:172.16.55.106  Bcast:172.16.55.255  Mask:255.255.255.0
       UP BROADCAST RUNNING MULTICAST  MTU:1500  Metric:1
       RX packets:844886 errors:0 dropped:0 overruns:0 frame:0
       TX packets:7668 errors:0 dropped:0 overruns:0 carrier:0
       collisions:0 txqueuelen:100
       Interrupt:11 Base address:0x7c80 Memory:c0000-c2000
```

Refer to the Solaris ifconfig dnet0 example at the beginning of this section, and check the information displayed in that example against the subnet configuration planned for our imaginary network. You'll see that the interface needs to be reconfigured. The configuration done by the user during the Unix installation did not provide all of the values we planned. The address (172.16.12.2) is correct, but the address mask (ffff0000 or 255.255.0.0) and the broadcast address (172.16.0.0) are incorrect. Let's look at the various ways values are assigned, and how to correct them.

Assigning an Address

The IP address can be assigned directly on the `ifconfig` command line or indirectly from a file. The `ifconfig` examples seen earlier in this chapter had an IP address written in standard dotted decimal notation directly on the command line. An alternative is to use a hostname from the */etc/hosts* file on the `ifconfig` command line to provide the address. For example:

```
# ifconfig dnet0 crab netmask 255.255.255.0
```

Most administrators are very comfortable with using hostnames in place of addresses. Vendor configurations, however, tend to take address assignment to another level of indirection. The `ifconfig` command in the startup script references a file. The file contains a hostname and the hostname maps to an address. Solaris systems place the hostname in a file named /etc/hostname.*interface*, where *interface* is the name of the interface being configured. On our sample system the file is called */etc/hostname.dnet0*. The *hostname.dnet0* file created by a standard Solaris installation contains only a simple hostname:

```
$ cat /etc/hostname.dnet0
crab
$ grep crab /etc/hosts
172.16.12.1    crab    crab.wrotethebook.com        loghost
```

The example shows that the Solaris configuration created the *hostname.dnet0* file and the necessary entry in the */etc/hosts* file to map the name from *hostname.dnet0* to an IP address. The Solaris boot first gets the hostname from a file and then gets the address associated with that hostname from a second file. Both of these entries are required for the configuration.

Linux also uses indirection for the `ifconfig` configuration. Several Linux systems, including Red Hat, Mandrake, and Caldera, place the values used to configure the network interface in a file named ifcfg.*interface*, where *interface* is the name of the interface.[*] For example, *ifcfg.eth0* contains the configuration values for the Ethernet interface eth0.

```
$ cat /etc/sysconfig/network-scripts/ifcfg-eth0
DEVICE=eth0
ONBOOT=yes
BOOTPROTO=none
BROADCAST=172.16.12.255
NETWORK=172.16.12.0
NETMASK=255.255.255.0
IPADDR=172.16.12.2
USERCTL=no
```

This file makes the configuration very easy to see.

---

[*] Our sample Red Hat system places the file *ifcfg.eth0* in the directory */etc/sysconfig/network-scripts*.

- DEVICE defines the device name, in this case eth0.

- ONBOOT specifies whether the interface is initialized when the system boots. Normally an Ethernet interface is brought up and running every time the system boots.

- BOOTPROTO identifies the configuration service used to configure the interface. In this case it is none, meaning that the interface is configured locally. Alternates are bootp if an old-fashioned BootP server is used, or dhcp if a DHCP server is used. If either DHCP or BootP is used, the specific configuration values listed below are not found in this file.

- BROADCAST defines the broadcast address used by ifconfig.

- NETWORK defines the network address.

- NETMASK defines the address mask used by ifconfig.

- IPADDR defines the IP address used by ifconfig.

- USERCTL specifies whether users can run usernetctl to bring the interface up or down. The usernetctl command is found on only a few versions of Linux. In this case, the value no prevents the user from downing the interface.

Most systems take advantage of the fact that the IP address, subnet mask, and broadcast address can be set indirectly to reduce the extent that startup files need to be customized. Reducing customization lessens the chance that a system might hang while booting because a startup file was improperly edited, and it makes it possible to preconfigure these files for all of the systems on the network. Solaris systems have the added advantage that the *hosts*, *networks*, and *netmasks* files, which provide input to the ifconfig command, all produce NIS maps that can be centrally managed at sites using NIS.

A disadvantage of setting the ifconfig values indirectly is that it can make troubleshooting more cumbersome. If all values are set in the boot file, you only need to check the values there. When network configuration information is supplied indirectly, you may need to check several files to find the problem. An error in any of these files could cause an incorrect configuration. To make debugging easier, a few operating systems set the configuration values directly on the ifconfig command line in the boot file.

My advice is that you follow the standard model used on your system. If you use a Solaris system, set the address in */etc/hostname.dnet0* and */etc/hosts*. If you use a Red Hat system, set the address in the */etc/sysconfig/network-scripts/ifcfg.eth0* file. If you use a Slackware system, set the address directly in the *rc.inet* boot file. Following the standard procedure for your system makes it easier for others to troubleshoot your computer. We'll see more of these alternatives as we assign the remaining interface configuration values.

Assigning a Subnet Mask

In order to function properly, every interface on a specific physical network segment must have the same address mask. For *crab* and *rodent*, the netmask value is 255.255.255.0 because both systems are attached to the same subnet. However, although *crab*'s local network interface and its external network interface are parts of the same computer, they use different netmasks because they are on different networks.

To assign an address mask, write the mask value after the keyword netmask on the ifconfig command line or as a prefix attached to the address. When written as a prefix, the address mask is a decimal number that defines the number of bits in the address mask. For example, 172.16.12.2/24 defines a 24-bit address mask. When the subnet mask follows the keyword netmask, it is usually written in the dotted decimal form used for IP addresses.* For example, the following command assigns the correct subnet mask to the dnet0 interface on *rodent*:

```
# ifconfig le0 172.16.12.2 netmask 255.255.255.0
```

Putting the netmask value directly on the ifconfig command line is the most common, the simplest, and the best way to assign the mask to an interface manually. But it is rare for the mask to be assigned manually. Like addresses, address masks are made part of the configuration during the initial installation. To simplify configuration, ifconfig is able to take the netmask value from a file instead of from the command line. Conceptually, this is similar to using a hostname in place of an IP address. The administrator can place the mask value in either the *hosts* file or the *networks* file and then reference it by name. For example, the *books-net* administrator might add the following entry to */etc/networks*:

```
books-mask 255.255.255.0
```

Once this entry has been added, you can use the name *books-mask* on the ifconfig command line instead of the actual mask. For example:

```
# ifconfig dnet0 172.16.5.2 netmask books-mask
```

The name *books-mask* resolves to 255.255.255.0, which is the correct netmask value for our sample systems.

Personally, I avoid setting the address mask value indirectly from a file that is not primarily intended for this use. The *hosts* file is a particularly bad choice for storing mask values. The *hosts* file is heavily used by other programs, and placing a mask value in this file might confuse one of these programs. Setting the address mask directly on the command line or from a file that is dedicated to this purpose is probably the best approach.

---

* Hexadecimal notation can also be used for the address mask. To enter a netmask in hexadecimal form, write the value as a single hex number starting with a leading 0x. For example, the hexadecimal form of 255.255.255.0 is 0xffffff00. Choose the form that is easier for you to understand.

On Solaris systems, the /etc/inet/netmasks file is specifically designed to set the subnet mask.* The /etc/inet/netmasks file is a table of one-line entries, each containing a network address separated from a mask by whitespace.† If a Solaris system on *books-net* (172.16.0.0) has an /etc/inet/netmasks file that contains the entry:

```
172.16.0.0 255.255.255.0
```

then the following ifconfig command can be used to set the address mask:

```
# ifconfig dnet0 172.16.5.1 netmask +
```

The plus sign after the keyword netmask causes ifconfig to take the mask value from /etc/inet/netmasks. ifconfig searches the file for a network address that matches the network address of the interface being configured. It then extracts the mask associated with that address and applies it to the interface.

Most Linux systems also set the address mask indirectly from a file. The *ifcfg-eth0* file shown in the previous section contains the following line:

```
NETMASK=255.255.255.0
```

This line clearly defines the netmask value that is used by the ifconfig command. To modify the address mask on this Red Hat system, edit this line in the *ifcfg-eth0* file.

Setting the Broadcast Address

RFC 919, *Broadcasting Internet Datagrams*, clearly defines the format of a broadcast address as an address with all host bits set to 1. Since the broadcast address is so precisely defined, ifconfig is able to compute it automatically, and you should always be able to use the default. Unfortunately, the user in the example under "Checking the Interface with ifconfig" used a broadcast address with all host bits set to 0 and didn't allow the broadcast address to be set by default.

Correct this mistake by defining a broadcast address for the network device with the ifconfig command. Set the broadcast address in the ifconfig command using the keyword broadcast followed by the correct broadcast address. For example, the ifconfig command to set the broadcast address for *crab*'s dnet0 interface is:

```
# ifconfig dnet0 172.16.12.1 netmask 255.255.255.0 broadcast 172.16.12.255
```

Note that the broadcast address is relative to the local subnet. *crab* views this interface as connected to network 172.16.12.0; therefore, its broadcast address is 172.16.12.255. Depending on the implementation, a Unix system could interpret the address 172.16.255.255 as host address 255 on subnet 255 of network 172.16.0.0, or as the broadcast address for *books-net* as a whole. In neither case would it consider 172.16.255.255 the broadcast address for subnet 172.16.12.0.

---

* /etc/netmasks is symbolically linked to /etc/inet/netmasks.

† Use the official network address, not a subnet address.

Solaris systems can indirectly set the broadcast address from the netmask value defined in */etc/inet/netmasks*, if that file is used. The previous section showed that netmask + takes the netmask value from a file. Likewise, the broadcast + syntax calculates the correct broadcast value using the netmask value from the *netmasks* file:

```
# ifconfig dnet0 172.16.12.1 netmask + broadcast +
```

Assume that the netmask defined in *netmasks* is 255.255.255.0. This tells the Solaris system that the first three bytes are network bytes and that the fourth byte contains the host portion of the address. Since the standard broadcast address consists of the network bits plus host bits of all 1s, Solaris can easily calculate that the broadcast address in this case is 172.16.12.255.

Linux makes it even easier. The *ifcfg-eth0* file on our sample Red Hat system clearly defines the broadcast address with the line:

```
BROADCAST=172.16.12.255
```

Modify the broadcast address by modifying this line in the *ifcfg-eth0* file.

The Other Command Options

We've used ifconfig to set the interface address, the subnet mask, and the broadcast address. These are certainly the most important functions of ifconfig, but it has other functions as well. It can enable or disable the address resolution protocol and the interface itself. ifconfig can set the routing metric used by the Routing Information Protocol (RIP) and the maximum transmission unit (MTU) used by the interface. We'll look at examples of each of these functions.

Enabling and disabling the interface

The ifconfig command has two arguments, up and down, for enabling and disabling the network interface. The up argument enables the network interface and marks it ready for use. The down argument disables the interface so that it cannot be used for network traffic.

Use the down argument when interactively reconfiguring an interface. Some configuration parameters—for example, the IP address—cannot be changed unless the interface is down. First, the interface is brought down. Then, the reconfiguration is done, and the interface is brought back up. For example, the following steps change the address for an interface:

```
# ifconfig eth0 down
# ifconfig eth0 172.16.1.2 up
```

After these commands execute, the interface operates with the new configuration values. The up argument in the second ifconfig command is not always required because it is the default on some systems. However, an explicit up is commonly used after the interface has been disabled, or when an ifconfig command is used in a script file to avoid problems because up is not the default on all systems.

ARP

Chapter 2 discusses the Address Resolution Protocol (ARP), an important protocol that maps IP addresses to physical Ethernet addresses. Enable ARP with the ifconfig keyword arp and disable it with the keyword -arp. It is possible (though very unlikely) that a host attached to your network cannot handle ARP. This would only happen on a network using specialized equipment or developmental hardware. In these very rare circumstances, it may be necessary to disable ARP in order to interoperate with the nonstandard systems. By default, ifconfig enables ARP. Leave ARP enabled on all your systems.

Promiscuous mode

In Chapter 13, promiscuous mode is used to examine the packets traveling on a local Ethernet. By default, an Ethernet interface passes only frames that are addressed to the local host up to the higher layer protocols. Promiscuous mode passes all frames up without regard to the address in those frames.

On a Linux system, promiscuous mode is enabled using the promisc option of the ifconfig command. For example:

```
$ ifconfig eth0 promisc
```

Promiscuous mode is disabled by using -promisc.* By default promiscuous mode is disabled. When it is enabled, the local system is forced to process many packets that are normally discarded by the Ethernet interface hardware. Promiscuous mode is enabled only for certain troubleshooting applications.

Metric

On some systems, the ifconfig command creates an entry in the routing table for every interface that is assigned an IP address. Each interface is the route to a network. Even if a host isn't a gateway, its interface is still its "route" to the local network. ifconfig determines the route's destination network by applying the interface's address mask to the interface's IP address. For example, the dnet0 interface on *crab* has an address of 172.16.12.1 and a mask of 255.255.255.0. Applying this mask to the address provides the destination network, which is 172.16.12.0. The netstat -in display shows the destination address:

```
% netstat -in
Name Mtu  Net/Dest     Address      Ipkts   Ierrs Opkts  Oerrs Collis Queue
le0  1500 172.16.12.0 172.16.12.1 1125826 16    569786 0     8914   0
lo0  1536 127.0.0.0   127.0.0.1   94280   0     94280  0     0      0
```

---

* On Solaris systems, promiscuous mode is enabled by programs that need it. It is not set by the ifconfig command.

The Routing Information Protocol (RIP) is a routing protocol sometimes used by Unix. RIP does two things: it distributes routing information to other hosts, and it uses incoming routing information to build routing tables dynamically. The routes created by ifconfig are one source of the routing information distributed by RIP, and the ifconfig metric argument can be used to control how RIP uses this routing information.

RIP makes routing decisions based on the cost of a route. The route's cost is determined by a routing metric associated with the route. A routing metric is just a number. The lower the number, the lower the cost of the route; the higher the number, the higher the cost. When building a routing table, RIP favors low-cost routes over high-cost routes. Directly connected networks are given a very low cost. Therefore, the default metric is 0 for a route through an interface to a directly attached network. However, you can use the metric argument to supply a different routing metric for an interface.

To increase the cost of an interface to 3, so that RIP prefers routes with values of 0, 1, or 2, use metric 3 on the ifconfig command line:

```
# ifconfig std0 10.104.0.19 metric 3
```

Use the metric option only if there is another route to the same destination and you want to use it as the primary route. We did not use this command on *crab* because it has only one interface connected to the outside world. If it had a second connection, say, through a higher-speed link, then the command shown above could be used to direct traffic through the higher-performance interface.

A related ifconfig parameter is available on Solaris systems. RIP builds the routing table by choosing the most economical routes, and it distributes the routing table information to other hosts. The metric parameter controls which routes RIP selects as the lowest cost. The private argument, available on Solaris systems, controls the routes that RIP distributes. If private is specified on the ifconfig command line, the route created by that ifconfig command is not distributed by RIP. The default value is -private, which permits the route to be distributed. The private parameter is not universally supported.

Additionally, not all systems make use of the metric argument. A Linux system doesn't create a routing table entry when it processes the ifconfig command. When configuring a Linux system, you add an explicit route command for each interface. (The route command is covered in the next chapter.) Linux systems reject the metric argument, as this example shows:

```
# ifconfig eth0 192.168.0.4 metric 3
SIOCSIFMETRIC: Operation not supported
```

Set the routing metric in a routing configuration file instead of on the ifconfig command line. This is the preferred method of providing routing information for newer routing software. We discuss the format of routing configuration files in the next chapter.

Maximum transmission unit

A network has a maximum transmission unit (MTU), which is the largest packet that can be transported over that physical network. On Ethernet, the maximum size is 1500 bytes, which is defined as part of the Ethernet standard. There is rarely any need to change the MTU on the ifconfig command line. By default, ifconfig chooses the optimum MTU, which is usually the largest legal MTU for a given type of network hardware. A large MTU is the default because it normally provides the best performance. However, a smaller MTU is helpful to achieve the following goals:

- To avoid fragmentation. If the traffic travels from a network with a large MTU (such as an FDDI network with an MTU of 4500 bytes) through a network with a smaller MTU (like an Ethernet), the smaller MTU size may be best in order to avoid packet fragmentation. It is possible that specifying an MTU of 1500 on the interface connected to the FDDI may actually improve performance by avoiding fragmentation in the routers. This would be done only if fragmentation actually appeared to be the cause of a performance problem.

- To reduce buffer overruns or similar problems. On serial line connections, it is possible to have equipment of such low performance that it cannot keep up with standard 1006-byte packets. In this case, it is possible to avoid buffer overruns or SILO overflows by using a smaller MTU. However, such solutions are temporary fixes. The real fix is to purchase the correct hardware for the application.

To change the MTU, use the mtu command-line argument:

```
# ifconfig fddi0 172.16.16.1 netmask 255.255.255.0 mtu 1500
```

This forces the FDDI interface on 172.16.16.1 to use an MTU of 1500 bytes.

Point-to-point

There are probably several more ifconfig command-line arguments available on your system. Linux has parameters to define the PC interrupt of the Ethernet hardware (irq) and the Ethernet hardware address (hw), and to enable multicasting (multicast) and promiscuous mode (promisc). Solaris has arguments to set up or tear down the streams for an interface (plumb/unplumb) and to use Reverse ARP (RARP) to obtain the IP address for an interface (auto-revarp). But most of these parameters are not standardized between versions of Unix.

One last feature that is available on most versions of Unix is the ability to define point-to-point connections with the ifconfig command. Point-to-point connections are network links that directly connect only two computers. Of course the computers at either end of the link could be gateways to the world, but only two computers are directly connected to the link. Examples of a point-to-point connection are two computers linked together by a leased telephone line, or two computers in an office linked together by a null modem cable.

To define a point-to-point link on a Solaris system:

```
# ifconfig zs0 172.16.62.1 172.16.62.2
```

This `ifconfig` command has two addresses immediately following the interface name. The first is the address of the local host. The second address, called the destination address, is the address of the remote host at the other end of the point-to-point link. The second address shows up as the Net/Dest value in a `netstat -ni` display.

On a Linux system, this same configuration looks slightly different:

```
$ ifconfig sl0 172.16.62.1 point-to-point 172.16.62.2
```

The syntax is different but the effect is the same. This enables the interface to run in point-to-point mode and identifies the hosts at both ends of the link.

Does this set up the Point-to-Point Protocol (PPP) used for TCP/IP serial line communication? No, it does not. These `ifconfig` parameters sometimes confuse people about how to set up PPP. There is much more to configuring PPP, which we cover later in this chapter.

Before moving on to PPP, you should note that the configuration entered on an `ifconfig` command line will not survive a system boot. For a permanent configuration, put `ifconfig` in a startup file.

Putting ifconfig in the startup scripts

The `ifconfig` command is normally executed at boot time by a startup file. The two basic Unix startup models, the BSD model and the System V model, were explained in Chapter 5. On BSD Unix systems, the `ifconfig` commands are usually located in */etc/rc.boot* or */etc/rc.local*.

To override a BSD system's default configuration, place a full `ifconfig` command in the *rc.local* script. *rc.local* executes at the end of the startup process. Any interface configuration values set in this file override the earlier interface configuration. For example, the following line placed in that file configures eth0 without regard to any earlier configuration:

```
ifconfig eth0 172.16.12.1 broadcast 172.16.12.255 netmask 255.255.255.0
```

The BSD startup model is used on BSD systems and SunOS systems. Linux and Solaris systems use the System V startup model. However, Red Hat Linux systems have an *rc.local* script in the */etc/rc.d* directory. On a Red Hat system, place the custom `ifconfig` command in the *rc.local* file to override the default configuration.

Solaris does not have an *rc.local* script or a central directory of scripts for all runlevels. If you want to use an *rc.local* script on a Solaris system, you need to create your own and add it to the runlevel 3 directory. You need to name it properly to ensure it executes at the end of the Solaris startup process. For example, the file */etc/*

rc3.d/S99local would execute at the end of the standard Solaris runlevel 3 startup. Commands placed in this file would override the previous configuration.

If possible, however, configure the network with the standard tools and procedures provided with your system. Directly modifying startup scripts or adding nonstandard scripts can lead to lots of confusion for the people who help you maintain your systems.

TCP/IP Over a Serial Line

TCP/IP runs over a wide variety of physical media. The media can be Ethernet cables, as in your local Ethernet, or telephone circuits, as in a wide area network. In the first half of this chapter, we used `ifconfig` to configure a local Ethernet interface. In this section, we use other commands to configure a network interface to use a telephone circuit.

Almost all data communication takes place via serial interfaces. A *serial interface* is just an interface that sends the data as a series of bits over a single wire, as opposed to a parallel interface that sends the data bits in parallel over several wires simultaneously. This description of a serial interface would fit almost any communications interface (including Ethernet itself), but the term is usually applied to an interface that connects to a telephone circuit via a modem or similar device. Likewise, a telephone circuit is often called a serial line.

In the TCP/IP world, serial lines are used to create wide area networks (WANs). Unfortunately, TCP/IP has not always had a standard physical layer protocol for serial lines. Because of the lack of a standard, network designers were forced to use a single brand of routers within their WANs to ensure successful physical layer communication. The growth of TCP/IP WANs led to a strong interest in standardizing serial line communications to provide vendor independence.

Other forces that increased interest in serial line communications were the advent of small, affordable systems that run TCP/IP, and the advent of high-speed, dial-up modems that provide "reasonable" TCP/IP performance. When the ARPAnet was formed, computers were very expensive and dial-up modems were very slow. At that time, if you could afford a computer, you could afford a leased telephone line. In recent years, however, it has become possible to own a Unix system at home. In this new environment, there is a strong demand for services that allow TCP/IP access over dial-up modems. Currently, approximately 7% of home users have a high-speed Digital Subscriber Line (DSL) connection or a cable modem. Most DSL and cable modems connect to the host via Ethernet, meaning that no special host configuration is required to use those services. But most home users still use dial-up serial lines. Dial-up serial lines require special protocols and special configurations.

These two forces—the need for standardized wide area communications and the need for dial-up TCP/IP access—led to the creation of two serial line protocols: Serial Line IP (SLIP) and Point-to-Point Protocol (PPP).*

The Serial Protocols

Serial Line IP was created first. It is a minimal protocol that allows isolated hosts to link via TCP/IP over the telephone network. The SLIP protocol defines a simple mechanism for framing datagrams for transmission across serial lines. SLIP sends the datagram across the serial line as a series of bytes, and it uses special characters to mark when a series of bytes should be grouped together as a datagram. SLIP defines two special characters for this purpose:

- The SLIP END character, a single byte with the decimal value 192, is the character that marks the end of a datagram. When the receiving SLIP encounters the END character, it knows that it has a complete datagram that can be sent up to IP.

- The SLIP ESC character, a single byte with the decimal value of 219, is used to "escape" the SLIP control characters. If the sending SLIP encounters a byte value equivalent to either a SLIP END character or a SLIP ESC character in the datagram it is sending, it converts that character to a sequence of two characters. The two-character sequences are ESC 220 for the END character, and ESC 221 for the ESC character itself.† When the receiving SLIP encounters these two-byte sequences, it converts them back to single-byte values. This procedure prevents the receiving SLIP from incorrectly interpreting a data byte as the end of the datagram.

SLIP is described in RFC 1055, *A Nonstandard for Transmission of IP Datagrams Over Serial Lines: SLIP*. As the name of the RFC makes clear, SLIP is not an Internet standard. The RFC does not propose a standard; it documents an existing protocol. The RFC identifies the deficiencies in SLIP, which fall into two categories:

- The SLIP protocol does not define any link control information that could be used to dynamically control the characteristics of a connection. Therefore, SLIP systems must assume certain link characteristics. Because of this limitation, SLIP can be used only when both hosts know each other's addresses, and only when IP datagrams are being transmitted.

- SLIP does not compensate for noisy, low-speed telephone lines. The protocol does not provide error correction or data compression.

---

* Dial-up modems are usually asynchronous. Both PPP and SLIP support asynchronous dial-up service as well as synchronous leased-line service.

† Here ESC refers to the SLIP escape character, not the ASCII escape character.

To address SLIP's weaknesses, Point-to-Point Protocol (PPP) was developed as an Internet standard. There are several RFCs that document Point-to-Point Protocol.* Two key documents are RFC 1661, *The Point-to-Point Protocol (PPP)*, and RFC 1172, *The Point-to-Point Protocol (PPP) Initial Configuration Options*.

PPP addresses the weaknesses of SLIP with a three-layered protocol:

Data Link Layer Protocol
> The Data Link Layer Protocol used by PPP is a slightly modified version of High-level Data Link Control (HDLC). PPP modifies HDLC by adding a Protocol field that allows PPP to pass traffic for multiple Network Layer protocols. HDLC is an international standard protocol for reliably sending data over synchronous, serial communications lines. PPP also uses a proposed international standard for transmitting HDLC over asynchronous lines, so PPP can guarantee reliable delivery over any type of serial line.

Link Control Protocol
> The Link Control Protocol (LCP) provides control information for the serial link. It is used to establish the connection, negotiate configuration parameters, check link quality, and close the connection. LCP was developed specifically for PPP.

Network Control protocols
> The Network Control protocols are individual protocols that provide configuration and control information for the Network Layer protocols. Remember, PPP is designed to pass data for a wide variety of network protocols. NCP allows PPP to be customized to do just that. Each network protocol (DECNET, IP, OSI, etc.) has its own Network Control protocol. The Network Control protocol defined in RFCs 1661 and 1332 is the Internet Control Protocol (IPCP), which supports Internet Protocol.

Point-to-Point Protocol is the best TCP/IP serial protocol. PPP is preferred because it is an Internet standard, which ensures interoperability between systems from a wide variety of vendors. It has more features than SLIP and is more robust. These benefits make PPP the best choice as an open protocol for connecting routers over serial lines and for connecting remote computers via dial-up lines.

Some Linux systems include both SLIP and PPP. However, on most Unix systems, such as Solaris, PPP is included and SLIP is not. This is fine, as you should avoid using SLIP and use PPP instead.

---

* If you want to make sure you have the very latest version of a standard, obtain the latest list of RFCs as described in Appendix G.

Installing PPP

The procedures for installing and configuring PPP vary from implementation to implementation.* In this section, we use the PPP daemon implementation (pppd) included with Linux and the supporting configuration commands that come with it. PPP is an Internet standard, and most Unix systems include support for it in the kernel as part of the standard operating system installation. Usually this does not require any action on your part. Refer to Chapter 5 for examples of how PPP is configured in the Linux kernel. The Linux system installs the PPP physical and data link layer software (the HDLC protocol) in the kernel.

Installing PPP in the kernel is only the beginning. In this section, we look at how pppd is used to provide PPP services on a Linux system.

The PPP Daemon

Point-to-Point Protocol is implemented on the Linux system in the PPP daemon (pppd), which was derived from a freeware PPP implementation for BSD systems. pppd can be configured to run in all modes: as a client, as a server, over dial-up connections, and over dedicated connections. (Clients and servers are familiar concepts from Chapter 3.) A dedicated connection is a direct cable connection or a leased line, neither of which requires a telephone to establish the connection. A dial-up connection is a modem link established by dialing a telephone number.

Configuring pppd for a dedicated line is the simplest configuration. A dial-up script is not needed for a leased line or direct connection. There is no point in dynamically assigning addresses because a dedicated line always connects the same two systems. Authentication is of limited use because the dedicated line physically runs between two points. There is no way for an intruder to access the link, short of "breaking and entering" or a wiretap. A single pppd command placed in a startup file configures a dedicated PPP link for our Linux system:

```
pppd /dev/cua3 56000 crtscts defaultroute
```

The /dev/cua3 argument selects the device to which PPP is attached. It is, of course, the same port to which the dedicated line is attached. Next, the line speed is specified in bits per second (56000). The remainder of the command line is a series of keyword options. The crtscts option turns on hardware flow control. The final option, defaultroute, creates a default route using the remote server as the default gateway.†

PPP exchanges IP addresses during the initial link connection process. If no address is specified on the pppd command line, the daemon sends the address of the local

---

* Check your system documentation to find out exactly how to configure PPP on your system.

† If a default route already exists in the routing table, the defaultroute option is ignored.

host, which it learns from DNS or the host table, to the remote host. Likewise, the remote system sends its address to the local host. The addresses are then used as the source and destination addresses of the link. You can override this by specifying the addresses on the command line in the form *local-address*:*remote-address*. For example:

```
pppd /dev/cua3 56000 crtscts defaultroute 172.16.24.1:
```

Here we define the local address as 172.16.24.1 and leave the remote address blank. In this case *pppd* sends the address from the command line and waits for the remote server to send its address. The local address is specified on the command line when it is different from the address associated with the local hostname in the host table or the DNS server. For example, the system might have an Ethernet interface that already has an address assigned. If we want to use a different address for the PPP connection, we must specify it on the *pppd* command line; otherwise, the PPP link will be assigned the same address as the Ethernet interface.

The *pppd* command has many more options than those used in these examples (see Appendix A for a full list of options). In fact, there are so many *pppd* command-line options that it is sometimes easier to put them in a file than to enter them all on the command line. *pppd* reads its options from the */etc/ppp/options* file, then the *~/.ppprc* file, then the */etc/ppp/options.device* file (where *device* is a device name like cua3), and finally from the command line. The order in which they are processed creates a hierarchy such that options on the command line can override those in the *~/.ppprc* file, which can in turn override those in the */etc/ppp/options* file. This permits the system administrator to establish certain systemwide defaults in the */etc/ppp/options* file while still permitting the end user to customize the PPP configuration. The */etc/ppp/ options* file is a convenient and flexible way to pass parameters to *pppd*.

A single *pppd* command is all that is needed to set up and configure the software for a dedicated PPP link. Dial-up connections are more challenging.

Dial-Up PPP

A direct-connect cable can connect just two systems. When a third system is purchased, it cannot be added to the network. For that reason, most people use expandable network technologies, such as Ethernet, for connecting systems in a local area. Additionally, leased lines are expensive. They are primarily used by large organizations to connect networks of systems. For these reasons, using PPP for dedicated network connections is less common than using it for dial-up connections.

Several different utilities provide dial-up support for PPP. Dial-up IP (dip) is a popular package for simplifying the process of dialing the remote server, performing the login, and attaching PPP to the resulting connection. We discuss dip in this section because it is popular and freely available for a wide variety of Unix systems, and because it comes with Red Hat Linux, which is the system we have been using for our PPP examples.

One of the most important features of dip is a scripting language that lets you automate all the steps necessary to set up an operational PPP link. Appendix A covers all the scripting commands supported by the 3.3.7o-uri version of dip, which is the version included with Red Hat. You can list the commands supported by your system by running dip in test mode (-t) and then entering the help command:

```
> dip -t
DIP: Dialup IP Protocol Driver version 3.3.7o-uri (8 Feb 96)
Written by Fred N. van Kempen, MicroWalt Corporation.

DIP> help
DIP knows about the following commands:

        beep      bootp    break     chatkey   config
        databits  dec      default   dial      echo
        flush     get      goto      help      if
        inc       init     mode      modem     netmask
        onexit    parity   password  proxyarp  print
        psend     port     quit      reset     send
        shell     sleep    speed     stopbits  term
        timeout   wait
DIP> quit
```

These commands can configure the interface, control the execution of the script, and process errors. Only a subset of the commands is required for a minimal script:

```
# Ask PPP to provide the local IP address
get $local 0.0.0.0
# Select the port and set the line speed
port cua1
speed 38400
# Reset the modem and flush the terminal
reset
flush
# Dial the PPP server and wait for the CONNECT response
dial *70,301-555-1234
wait CONNECT
# Give the server 2 seconds to get ready
sleep 2
# Send a carriage-return to wake up the server
send \r
# Wait for the Login> prompt and send the username
wait ogin>
send kristin\r
# Wait for the Password> prompt and send the password
wait word>
password
# Wait for the PPP server's command-line prompt
wait >
# Send the command required by the PPP server
```

```
send ppp enabled\r
# Set the interface to PPP mode
mode PPP
# Exit the script
exit
```

The get command at the beginning of the script allows PPP to provide the local and remote addresses. $local is a script variable. There are several available script variables, all of which are covered in Appendix A. $local normally stores the local address, which can be set statically in the script. A PPP server, however, is capable of assigning an address to the local system dynamically. We take advantage of this capability by giving a local address of all 0s. This peculiar syntax tells dip to let pppd handle the address assignments. A pppd client can get addresses in three ways:

- The PPP systems can exchange their local addresses as determined from DNS. This was discussed previously for the dedicated line configuration.

- The addresses can be specified on the pppd command line, also discussed previously.

- The client can allow the server to assign both addresses. This feature is most commonly used on dial-up lines. It is very popular with servers that must handle a large number of short-lived connections. A dial-up Internet Service Provider (ISP) is a good example.

The next two lines select the physical device to which the modem is connected, and set the speed at which the device operates. The port command assumes the path /dev, so the full device path is not used. On most PC Unix systems, the value provided to the port command is cua0, cua1, cua2, or cua3. These values correspond to MS-DOS ports COM1 to COM4. The speed command sets the maximum speed used to send data to the modem on this port. The default speed is 38400. Change it if your modem accepts data at a different speed.

The reset command resets the modem by sending it the Hayes modem interrupt (+++) followed by the Hayes modem reset command (ATZ). This version of dip uses the Hayes modem AT command set and works only with Hayes-compatible modems.* Fortunately, that includes most brands of modems. After being reset, the modem responds with a message indicating that the modem is ready to accept input. The flush command removes this message, and any others that might have been displayed by the modem, from the input queue. Use flush to avoid the problems that can be caused by unexpected data in the queue.

The next command dials the remote server. The dial command sends a standard Hayes ATD dial command to the modem. It passes the entire string provided on the

---

* If your modem doesn't use the full Hayes modem command set, avoid using dip commands, such as rest and dial, that generate Hayes commands. Use send instead. This allows you to send any string you want to the modem.

---

command line to the modem as part of the ATD command. The sample dial command generates ATD*70,301-555-1234. This causes the modem to dial *70 (which turns off call waiting*), and then area code 301, exchange 555, and number 1234. When this modem successfully connects to the remote modem, it displays the message CONNECT. The wait command waits for that message from the modem.

The sleep 2 command inserts a two-second delay into the script. It is often useful to delay at the beginning of the connection to allow the remote server to initialize. Remember that the CONNECT message is displayed by the modem, not by the remote server. The remote server may have several steps to execute before it is ready to accept input. A small delay can sometimes avoid unexplained intermittent problems.

The send command sends a carriage return (\r) to the remote system. Once the modems are connected, anything sent from the local system goes all the way to the remote system. The send command can send any string. In the sample script, the remote server requires a carriage return before it issues its first prompt. The carriage return is entered as \r and the newline is entered as \n.

The remote server then prompts for the username with Login>. The wait ogin> command detects this prompt, and the send kristin command sends the username kristin as a response. The server then prompts for the password with Password>. The password command causes the script to prompt the local user to manually enter the password. It is possible to store the password in a send command inside the script. However, this is a potential security problem if an unauthorized person gains access to the script and reads the password. The password command improves security.

If the password is accepted, our remote server prompts for input with the greater-than symbol (>). Many servers require a command to set the correct protocol mode. The server in our example supports several different protocols. We must tell it to use PPP by using send to pass it the correct command.

The script finishes with a few commands that set the correct environment on the local host. The mode command tells the local host to use the PPP protocol on this link. The protocol selected must match the protocol running on the remote server. Protocol values that are valid for the dip mode command are SLIP, CSLIP, PPP, and TERM. SLIP and CSLIP are variations of the SLIP protocol, which was discussed earlier. TERM is terminal emulation mode. PPP is the Point-to-Point Protocol. Finally, the exit command ends the script, while dip keeps running in the background servicing the link.

This simple script does work and it should give you a good idea of the wait/send structure of a dip script. However, your scripts will probably be more complicated. The sample script is not robust because it does not do any error checking. If an

---

* If you have call waiting, turn it off before you attempt to make a PPP connection. Different local telephone companies may use different codes to disable call waiting.

expected response does not materialize, the sample script hangs. To address this problem, use a timeout on each wait command. For example, the wait OK 10 command tells the system to wait 10 seconds for the OK response. When the OK response is detected, the $errlvl script variable is set to zero and the script falls through to the next command. If the OK response is not returned before the 10-second timer expires, $errlvl is set to a nonzero value and the script continues on to the next command. The $errlvl variable is combined with the if and goto commands to provide error handling in dip scripts. Refer to Appendix A for more details.

Once the script is created, it is executed with the dip command. Assume that the sample script shown above was saved to a file named *start-ppp.dip*. The following command executes the script, creating a PPP link between the local system and the remote server:

> **dip start-ppp**

Terminate the PPP connection with the command dip -k. This closes the connection and kills the background dip process.

pppd options are not configured in the dip script. dip creates the PPP connection; it doesn't customize pppd. pppd options are stored in the */etc/ppp/options* file.

Assuming the dip script shown above, we might use the following pppd options:

```
noipdefault
ipcp-accept-local
ipcp-accept-remote defaultroute
```

The noipdefault option tells the client not to look up the local address. ipcp-accept-local tells the client to obtain its local address from the remote server. The ipcp-accept-remote option tells the system to accept the remote address from the remote server. Finally, pppd sets the PPP link as the default route. This is the same defaultroute option we saw on the pppd command line in an earlier example. Any pppd option that can be invoked on the command line can be put in the */etc/ppp/options* file and thus be invoked when pppd is started by a dip script.

I use dip on my home computer to set up my dial-up PPP connection.* Personally, I find dip simple and straightforward to use, in part because I am familiar with the dip scripting language. You may prefer to use the chat command that comes with the pppd software package.

chat

A chat script is a simple expect/send script consisting of the strings the system expects and the strings it sends in response. The script is organized as a list of

---

* For me, the PPP dial-up is just a backup; like many other people I use a high-speed connection. However, DSL and cable modem connections do not require a special configuration because the interface to most DSL and cable modems is Ethernet.

expect/send pairs. chat does not really have a scripting language, but it does have some special characters that can be used to create more complex scripts. The chat script to perform the same dial-up and login functions as the sample dip script would contain:

```
'' ATZ
OK ATDT*70,301-555-1234
CONNECT \d\d\r
ogin> kristin
word> Wats?Wat?
> 'set port ppp enabled'
```

Each line in the script begins with an expected string and ends with the string sent as a response. The modem does not send a string until it receives a command. The first line in the script says, in effect, "expect nothing and send the modem a reset command." The pair of single quotes ('') at the beginning of the line tells chat to expect nothing. The script then waits for the modem's OK prompt and dials the remote server. When the modem displays the CONNECT message, the script delays two seconds (\d\d) and then sends a carriage return (\r). Each \d special character causes a one-second delay. The \r special character is the carriage return. chat has many special characters that can be used in the expect strings and the send strings.* Finally, the script ends by sending the username, password, and remote server configuration command in response to the server's prompts.

Create the script with your favorite editor and save it in a file such as *dial-server*. Test the script using chat with the -V option, which logs the script execution through stderr:

```
% chat -V -f dial-server
```

Invoking the chat script is not sufficient to configure the PPP line. It must be combined with pppd to do the whole job. The connect command-line option allows you to start pppd and invoke a dial-up script all in one command:

```
# pppd /dev/cua1 56700 connect "chat -V -f dial-server" \
    nodetach crtscts modem defaultroute
```

The chat command following the connect option is used to perform the dial-up and login. Any package capable of doing the job could be called here; it doesn't have to be chat.

The pppd command has some other options that are used when PPP is run as a dial-up client. The modem option causes pppd to monitor the carrier-detect (DCD) indicator of the modem. This indicator tells pppd when the connection is made and when the connection is broken. pppd monitors DCD to know when the remote server hangs up the line. The nodetach option prevents pppd from detaching from the terminal to run as a background process. This is necessary only when running chat with the -V

---

* See Appendix A for more details.

option. When you are done debugging the chat script, you can remove the -V option from the chat subcommand and the nodetach option from the pppd command. An alternative is to use -v on the chat command. -v does not require pppd to remain attached to a terminal because it sends the chat logging information to syslogd instead of to stderr. We have seen all of the other options on this command line before.

PPP Daemon Security

A major benefit of PPP over SLIP is the enhanced security PPP provides. Put the following pppd options in the */etc/ppp/options* file to enhance security:

```
lock
auth
usehostname domain wrotethebook.com
```

The first option, lock, makes pppd use UUCP-style lock files. This prevents other applications, such as UUCP or a terminal emulator, from interfering with the PPP connection. The auth option requires the remote system to be authenticated before the PPP link is established. This option causes the local system to request authentication data from the remote system. It does not cause the remote system to request similar data from the local system. If the remote system administrator wants to authenticate your system before allowing a connection, she must put the auth keyword in the configuration of her system. The usehostname option requires that the hostname is used in the authentication process and prevents the user from setting an arbitrary name for the local system with the name option. (More on authentication in a minute.) The final option makes sure that the local hostname is fully qualified with the specified domain before it is used in any authentication procedure.

Recall that the ~/.ppprc file and the pppd command-line options can override options set in the */etc/ppp/options* file, which could be a security problem. For this reason, several options, once configured in the */etc/ppp/options* file, cannot be overridden. That includes the options just listed.

pppd supports two authentication protocols: Challenge Handshake Authentication Protocol (CHAP) and Password Authentication Protocol (PAP). PAP is a simple password security system that is vulnerable to all of the attacks of any reusable password system. CHAP, however, is an advanced authentication system that does not use reusable passwords and that repeatedly reauthenticates the remote system.

Two files are used in the authentication process, the */etc/ppp/chap-secrets* file and the */etc/ppp/pap-secrets* file. Given the options file shown above, pppd first attempts to authenticate the remote system with CHAP. To do this, there must be data in the *chap-secrets* file, and the remote system must respond to the CHAP challenge. If either of these conditions is not true, pppd attempts to authenticate the remote system with PAP. If there is no applicable entry in the *pap-secrets* file or the remote system does not respond to the PAP challenge, the PPP connection is not established. This process allows you to authenticate remote systems with CHAP (the preferred protocol), if they support it, and to fall back to PAP for systems that support only PAP. For this to work, however, you must have the correct entries in both files.

Each entry in the *chap-secrets* file contains up to four fields:

client
> The name of the computer that must answer the challenge, i.e., the computer that must be authenticated before the connection is made. This is not necessarily a client that is seeking access to a PPP server; although *client* is the term used in most of the documentation, it is really the respondent—the system that responds to the challenge. Both ends of a PPP link can be forced to undergo authentication. In your *chap-secrets* file you will probably have two entries for each remote system: one entry to authenticate the remote system, and a corresponding entry to authenticate your system when it is challenged by the remote system.

server
> The name of the system that issues the CHAP challenge, i.e., the computer that requires the authentication before the PPP link is established. This is not necessarily a PPP server. The client system can require the server to authenticate itself. *Server* is the term used in most documentation, but really this is the authenticator—the system that authenticates the response.

secret
> The secret key that is used to encrypt the challenge string before it is sent back to the system that issued the challenge.

address
> An address, written as a hostname or an IP address, that is acceptable for the host named in the first field. If the host listed in the first field attempts to use an address other than the address listed here, the connection is terminated even if the remote host properly encrypts the challenge response. This field is optional.

A sample *chap-secrets* file for the host *ring* might contain:

```
limulus    ring       Peopledon'tknowyou    172.16.15.3
ring       limulus    andtrustisajoke.      172.16.15.1
```

The first entry is used to validate *limulus*, the remote PPP server. *limulus* is being authenticated and the system performing the authentication is *ring*. The secret key is "Peopledon'tknowyou". The allowable address is 172.16.15.3, which is the address assigned to *limulus* in the host table. The second entry is used to validate *ring* when *limulus* issues the challenge. The secret key is "andtrustisajoke.". The only address *ring* is allowed to use is 172.16.15.1. A pair of entries, one for each end of the link, is normal. The *chap-secret* file usually contains two entries for every PPP link: one for validating the remote system and one for answering the challenge of that remote system.

Use PAP only when you must. If you deal with a system that does not support CHAP, make an entry for that system in the *pap-secrets* file. The format of *pap-secrets* entries is the same as those used in the *chap-secrets* file. A system that does not support CHAP might have the following entry in the *pap-secrets* file:

```
24seven  ring      Whorearethestrong?  24seven.wrotethebook.com
ring     24seven   Whoarethetrusted?   ring.wrotethebook.com
```

Again we have a pair of entries: one for the remote system and one for our system. We support CHAP but the remote system does not. Thus we must be able to respond using the PAP protocol in case the remote system requests authentication.

PPP authentication improves security in a dial-up environment. It is most important when you run the PPP server into which remote systems dial. In the next section, we look at PPP server configuration.

PPP Server Configuration

The PPP server can be started in several different ways. One way is to use pppd as a login shell for dial-in PPP users. Replace the login shell entry in the */etc/passwd* file with the path of pppd to start the server. A modified */etc/passwd* entry might contain:

```
craig:wJxX.iPuPzg:101:100:Craig Hunt:/etc/ppp:/usr/sbin/pppd
```

The fields are exactly the same as in any */etc/passwd* entry: username, password, uid, gid, gcos information, home directory, and login shell. For a remote PPP user, the home directory is */etc/ppp* and the login shell is the full path of the pppd program. The encrypted password must be set using the passwd program, just as for any user, and the login process is the same as it is for any user. When getty detects incoming traffic on the serial port it invokes login to authenticate the user. login verifies the username and the password entered by the user and starts the login shell. In this case, the login shell is actually the PPP daemon.

When the server is started in this manner, server options are generally placed in the */etc/ppp/.ppprc* file. login validates the user, and pppd authenticates the client. Therefore the *chap-secrets* or *pap-secrets* file must be set up to handle the client system from which this user logs in.

A traditional alternative to using pppd as the login script is to create a real script in which pppd is only one of the commands. For example, you might create an */etc/ppp/ppplogin* script such as the following:

```
#!/bin/sh
mesg -n
stty -echo
exec /sbin/pppd auth passive crtscts modem
```

You can see that the script can contain more than just the pppd command. The mesg -n command makes sure that other users cannot write to this terminal with talk, write, or similar programs. The stty command turns off character echoing. On some systems, characters typed at the terminal are echoed from the remote host instead of being locally echoed by the terminal; this behavior is called *full duplex*. We don't want to echo anything back on a PPP link, so we turn full duplex off. Controlling the characteristics of the physical line is the main reason that pppd is often placed inside a script file.

The key line in the script is, of course, the line that starts pppd. We start the daemon with several options, but one thing that is not included on the command line is the *tty* device name. In all of the previous pppd examples, we provided a device name. When it is not provided, as is this case, pppd uses the controlling terminal as its device and doesn't put itself in background mode. This is just what we want. We want to use the device that login was servicing when it invoked the *ppplogin* script.

The auth command-line option tells pppd to authenticate the remote system, which of course requires us to place an entry for that system in the *chap-secrets* or the *pap-secrets* file. The crtscts option turns on hardware flow control, and the modem option tells PPP to monitor the modem's DCD indicator so that it can detect when the remote system drops the line. We have seen all of these options before. The one new option is passive. With passive set, the local system waits until it receives a valid LCP packet from the remote system, even if the remote system fails to respond to its first packet. Normally, the local system would drop the connection if the remote system fails to respond in a timely manner. This option gives the remote system time to initialize its own PPP daemon.

A final option for running PPP as a server is to allow the user to start the server from the shell prompt. To do this, pppd must be installed as setuid root, which is not the default installation. Once pppd is setuid root, a user with a standard login account can log in and then issue the following command:

```
$ pppd proxyarp
```

This command starts the PPP daemon. Assuming that the auth parameter is set in the */etc/ppp/options* file, pppd authenticates the remote client using CHAP or PAP. Once the client is authenticated, a proxy ARP entry for the client is placed in the server's ARP table so that the client appears to other systems to be located on the local network.

Of these three approaches, I prefer to create a shell script that is invoked by login as the user's login shell. With this approach, I don't have to install pppd setuid root. I don't have to place the burden of running pppd on the user. And I get all the power of the pppd command plus all the power of a shell script.

Solaris PPP

dip and pppd are available for Linux, BSD, AIX, Ultrix, OSF/1, and SunOS. If you have a different operating system, you probably won't use these packages. Solaris is a good example of a system that uses a different set of commands to configure PPP.

PPP is implemented under Solaris as the Asynchronous PPP Daemon (aspppd). aspppd is configured by the */etc/asppp.cf* file. The *asppp.cf* file is divided into two sections: an ifconfig section and a path section.

```
ifconfig ipdptp0 plumb ring limulus up

path
    interface ipdptp0
    peer_system_name limulus    inactivity_timeout 300
```

The ifconfig command configures the PPP interface (ipdptp0) as a point-to-point link with a local address of *ring* and a destination address of *limulus*. The ifconfig command does not have to define the destination address of the link. However, if you always connect to the same remote server, it will probably be defined here as the destination address. We saw all of these options in the discussion of the ifconfig command earlier in this chapter.

The more interesting part of this file is the path section, which defines the PPP environment. The interface statement identifies the interface used for the connection. It must be one of the PPP interfaces defined in the ifconfig section. In the example, only one is defined, so it must be ipdptp0. The peer_system_name statement identifies the system at the remote end of the connection. This may be the same address as the destination address from the ifconfig statement, but it doesn't have to be. It is possible to have no destination address on the ifconfig command and several path sections if you connect to several different remote hosts. The hostname on the peer_system_name statement is used in the dialing process, as described later.

The path section ends with an inactivity_timeout statement. The command in the sample sets the timeout to 300 seconds. This points out a nice feature of the Solaris system. Solaris automatically dials the remote system when it detects data that needs to be delivered through that system. Further, it automatically disconnects the PPP link when it is inactive for the specified time. With this feature you can use a PPP link without manually initiating the dial program and without tying up phone lines when the link is not in use.

Like pppd, aspppd does not have a built-in dial facility. It relies on an external program to do the dialing. In the case of aspppd, it utilizes the dial-up facility that comes with UUCP. Here's how.

First, the serial port, the modem attached to it, and the speed at which they operate are defined in the */etc/uucp/Devices* file. For example, here we define an Automatic Call Unit (ACU is another name for a modem) attached to serial port B (cua/b) that operates at any speed defined in the *Systems* file, and that has the modem characteristics defined by the "hayes" entry in the *Dialers* file:

```
ACU cua/b - Any hayes
```

Next, the modem characteristics, such as its initialization setting and dial command, are defined in the */etc/uucp/Dialers* file. The initialization and dial commands are defined as a chat script using the standard expect/send format and the standard set of chat special characters. For example:

```
hayes =,-, "" \dA\pTE1V1X1Q0S2=255S12=255\r\c OK\r \EATDT\T\r\c CONNECT
```

The system comes with *Devices* and *Dialers* preconfigured. The preconfigured entries are probably compatible with the modem on your system. The */etc/uucp/Systems* file may be the only configuration file that you modify. In the *Systems* file, you need to enter the name of the remote system, select the modem you'll use, enter the telephone number, and enter a chat script to handle the login. For example:

```
limulus Any ACU 56700 5551234 "" \r ogin> kristin word> Wats?Watt? >     set ppp on
```

In this one line, we identify *limulus* as the remote system, declare that we allow connections to and from that host at any time of the day (Any), select the ACU entry in the *Devices* file to specify the port and modem, set the line speed to 56700, send the dialer the telephone number, and define the login chat script.

This is not a book about UUCP, so we won't go into further details about these files. I'd suggest looking at the Solaris AnswerBook and the Solaris *TCP/IP Network Administration Guide* (where did they come up with such a great name?) for more information about UUCP and aspppd.

Troubleshooting Serial Connections

There are several layers of complexity that make PPP connections difficult to debug. To set up PPP, we must set up the serial port, configure the modem, configure PPP, and configure TCP/IP. A mistake in any one of these layers can cause a problem in another layer. All of these layers can obscure the true cause of a problem. The best way to approach troubleshooting on a serial line is by debugging each layer, one layer at a time. It is usually best to troubleshoot each layer before you move on to configure the next layer.

The physical serial ports should be configured by the system during the system boot. Check the */dev* directory to make sure they are configured. On a Linux system with four serial ports, the inbound serial ports are */dev/ttyS0* through */dev/ttyS3* and the outbound serial ports are */dev/cua0* through */dev/cua3*. There are many more tty and cua device names. However, the other devices are associated with real physical devices only if you have a multi-port serial card installed in your Linux system. Most Unix systems use the names tty and cua, even if those names are just symbolic links to the real devices. Solaris is a good example:

```
% ls -l /dev/tty?
lrwxrwxrwx 1 root root 6 Sep 23  2001 /dev/ttya -> term/a
lrwxrwxrwx 1 root root 6 Sep 23  2001 /dev/ttyb -> term/b
% ls -l /dev/cua/*
lrwxrwxrwx 1 root root 35 Sep 23 2001 /dev/cua/a ->
```

```
    /devices/obio/zs@0,100000:a,cu
lrwxrwxrwx 1 root root 35 Sep 23 2001 /dev/cua/b ->    /devices/obio/zs@0,100000:b,cu
```

If the serial devices do not show up in the *dev* directory, they can be manually added with a mknod command. For example, the following commands create the serial devices for the first serial port on a Linux system:

```
# mknod -m 666 /dev/cua0 c 5 64
# mknod -m 666 /dev/ttyS0 c 4 64
```

However, if you need to add the serial devices manually, there may be a problem with the kernel configuration. The serial devices should be installed in your system by default during the boot when the hardware is detected. The following boot message shows the detection of a single serial interface on a Linux system:

```
$ dmesg | grep tty
ttyS00 at 0x03f8 (irq = 4) is a 16550
```

You should see similar messages from your system boot for each interface that is detected. If you don't, you may have a hardware problem with the serial interface board.

The modem used for the connection is attached to one of the serial ports. Before attempting to build a dial-up script, make sure the modem works and that you can communicate with it through the port. Use a simple serial communications package, such as minicom, kermit, or seyon. First, make sure the program is configured to use your modem. It must be set to the correct port, speed, parity, number of databits, etc. Check your modem's documentation to determine these settings.

We'll use minicom on a Linux system for our examples. To configure minicom, su to *root* and run it with the -s option, which displays a configuration menu. Walk through the menu and make sure everything is properly set. One thing you might notice is that the port is set to */dev/modem*. That device name is sometimes symbolically linked to the port to which the modem is connected. If you're not sure that the link exists on your system, enter the correct port name in the minicom configuration, e.g., */dev/cua1*. After checking the configuration, exit the menu and use the minicom terminal emulator to make sure you can communicate with the modem:

```
Welcome to minicom 1.83.1

OPTIONS: History Buffer, F-key Macros, Search History Buffer, I18n
Compiled on Feb 23 2001, 07:31:40.

Press CTRL-A Z for help on special keys

AT S7=45 S0=0 L1 V1 X4 &c1 E1 Q0
OK
atz
OK
atdt555-1234
CONNECT 26400/LAPM-V
^M
```

```
Enter login> kristin
Enter user password> Wats?Watt?

    Welcome to the PPP MODEM POOL

PORT-9> set port ppp enabled
+++
OK
ath
OK
atz
OK
^A
CTRL-A Z for help | 57600 8N1 | NOR | Minicom 1.83.1 | VT102 | Offline
X
```

In the sample, minicom displays a few header lines and then sends a Hayes command (AT) to the modem. We didn't set this command; it was part of the default minicom configuration. (If it causes problems, edit it out of the configuration using the menus discussed previously.) We then reset the modem (atz) and dial the remote server (atdt). When the modems connect, we log into the server and configure it. (The login process is different for every remote server; this is just an example.) Everything appears to be running fine, so we end the connection by getting the modem's attention (+++), hanging up the line (ath), and resetting the modem. Exit minicom by pressing Ctrl-A followed by X. On our sample system the port and modem are working. If you cannot send simple commands to your modem, ensure that:

- The modem is properly connected to the port
- You have the correct cables
- The modem is powered up
- The modem is properly configured for dial-out and for echoing commands

When the modem responds to simple commands, use it to dial the remote server as we did in the example above. If the modem fails to dial the number or displays the message NO DIALTONE, check that the telephone line is connected to the correct port of the modem and to the wall jack. You may need to use an analog phone to test the telephone wall jack and replace the line between the modem and the wall to make sure that the cable is good. If the modem dials but fails to successfully connect to the remote modem, check that the local modem configuration matches the configuration required by the remote system. You must know the requirements of that remote system to successfully debug a connection. See the following list of script debugging tips for some hints on what to check. If you can successfully connect to the remote system, note everything you entered to do so, and note everything that the modem and the remote server display. Then set the remote server to PPP or SLIP mode and note how you accomplished this. You will need to duplicate all of these steps in your dip script.

Start with a bare-bones script, like the sample *start-ppp.dip* script, so that you can debug the basic connection before adding the complexity of error processing to the script. Run the script through dip using the verbose option (-v) option. This displays each line of the script as it is processed. Look for the following problems:

- The modem does not respond to the script. Check that you are using the correct device on the port command. Make sure that if the script contains databits, parity, speed, or stopbits commands, they are set to values compatible with your modem. Double-check that the modem is Hayes-compatible, particularly if you attempt to do modem configuration using dip keywords instead of using send.

- The modem fails to connect to the remote host. Make sure the modem is configured exactly as it was during the manual login. The modem's databits, parity, and other options need to match the configuration of the remote system. It is possible that you will need a special configuration, for example, 7-bit/even-parity, to perform the login before you can switch to the 8-bit/no-parity configuration required by PPP and SLIP. Don't forget to check that the phone number entered in the dial command is correct, particularly if the modem displays VOICE, RING - NO ANSWER, or BUSY when you expect to see CONNECT.

- The script hangs. It is probably waiting for a response. Make sure that the string in each wait command is correct. Remember that the string only needs to be a subset of the response. It is better to use the string ">" than it is to use "Port9>" if you are not sure whether the remote system always displays the same port number. Use a substring from the end of the expected response so that the script does not send to the server before the server is ready for input. Also try putting a delay into the script just before the script sends the first command to the server, e.g., sleep 2 to delay two seconds. A delay is sometimes needed to allow the server to initialize the port after the modems connect.

- The remote server displays an error message. The script probably sent an incorrect value. Check the string in each send command. Make sure they terminate with the correct carriage-return or line-feed combination expected by the remote server.

If you have trouble with the script, try running dip in test mode (-t), which allows you to enter each command manually one at a time. Do this repeatedly until you are positive that you know all the commands needed to log into the remote server. Then go back to debugging the script. You'll probably have fresh insight into the login process that will help you find the flaw in the script.

Once the script is running and the connection is successfully made, things should run smoothly. You should be able to ping the remote server without difficulty. If you have problems, they may be in the IP interface configuration or in the default route. The script should have created the serial interface. The netstat -ni command shows which interfaces have been configured:

```
# netstat -ni
Name  Mtu  Net/Dest       Address        Ipkts Ierrs Opkts Oerrs Collis Queue
dnet0 1500 172.16.15.0    172.16.15.1       1     0    4     0      0     0
lo0   1536 127.0.0.0      127.0.0.1      1712     0 1712     0      0     0
ppp0  1006 172.16.15.26   172.16.15.3       0     0    0     0      0     0
```

The interface, ppp0 in the example, has been installed. The default command in the script creates a default route. Use netstat to see the contents of the routing table:

```
# netstat -nr
Routing tables
Destination     Gateway        Flags  Refcnt  Use  Interface
127.0.0.1       127.0.0.1       UH      1      28      lo0
default         172.16.25.3     U       0       0      ppp0
172.16.15.0     172.16.15.1     U      21    1687      le0
```

The contents of routing tables are explained in detail in the next chapter. For now, just notice that the interface used for the default route is ppp0 and that the default route is a route to the remote PPP server (172.16.25.3 in the example).

If the script creates the connection, the interface is installed, and the routing table contains the default route, everything should work fine. If you still have problems they may be related to other parts of the TCP/IP installation. Refer to Chapter 13 for more troubleshooting information.

Summary

TCP/IP works with a wide variety of networks. TCP/IP cannot make assumptions about the network it runs on—the network interface and its characteristics must be identified to TCP/IP. In this chapter we looked at several examples of how to configure the physical network interface over which TCP/IP runs.

ifconfig is the most commonly used interface configuration command. It assigns the interface its IP address, sets the subnet mask, sets the broadcast address, and performs several other functions.

TCP/IP can also run over telephone lines using dial-up connections. Two protocols are available to do this: Serial Line IP (SLIP) and Point-to-Point Protocol (PPP). PPP is the preferred choice. It is an Internet standard and offers better reliability, performance, and security.

There are several steps to setting up a PPP connection: configuring the serial protocol, configuring the port and modem, making the dial-up connection, and completing the remote login. Some programs, such as dip, combine all of these steps into one program. Other programs, such as pppd and chat, separate the functions.

Configuring the network interface allows us to talk to the local network, while configuring routing allows us to talk to the world. We touched on routing in Chapter 2 and again in this chapter in our discussion of routing metrics for ifconfig and default routes for PPP. In the next chapter we look at routing in much greater detail.

CHAPTER 7
Configuring Routing

In this chapter:
- Common Routing Configurations
- The Minimal Routing Table
- Building a Static Routing Table
- Interior Routing Protocols
- Exterior Routing Protocols
- Gateway Routing Daemon
- Configuring gated

Routing is the glue that binds the Internet together. Without it, TCP/IP traffic is limited to a single physical network. Routing allows traffic from your local network to reach its destination somewhere else in the world—perhaps after passing through many intermediate networks.

The important role of routing and the complex interconnection of Internet networks make the design of routing protocols a major challenge to network software developers. Consequently, most discussions of routing concern protocol design. Very little is written about the important task of properly configuring routing protocols. However, more day-to-day problems are caused by improperly configured routers than by improperly designed routing algorithms. As system administrators, we need to ensure that the routing on our systems is properly configured. This is the task we tackle in this chapter.

Common Routing Configurations

First, we must make a distinction between *routing* and *routing protocols*. All systems route data, but not all systems run routing protocols. *Routing* is the act of forwarding datagrams based on the information contained in the routing table. *Routing protocols* are programs that exchange the information used to build routing tables.

A network's routing configuration does not always require a routing protocol. In situations where the routing information does not change—for example, when there is only one possible route—the system administrator usually builds the routing table manually. Some networks have no access to any other TCP/IP networks and therefore do not require that the system administrator build the routing table at all. The three most common routing configurations* are the following.

---

* Chapter 4 presents guidelines for choosing the correct routing configuration for your network.

Minimal routing

A network completely isolated from all other TCP/IP networks requires only minimal routing. A minimal routing table usually is built when the network interface is configured by adding a route for each interface. If your network doesn't have direct access to other TCP/IP networks and you are not using subnetting, this may be the only routing table you'll require.

Static routing

A network with a limited number of gateways to other TCP/IP networks can be configured with static routing. When a network has only one gateway, a static route is the best choice. A static routing table is constructed manually by the system administrator using the route command. Static routing tables do not adjust to network changes, so they work best where routes do not change.

Dynamic routing

A network with more than one possible route to the same destination should use dynamic routing. A dynamic routing table is built from the information exchanged by routing protocols. The protocols are designed to distribute information that dynamically adjusts routes to reflect changing network conditions. Routing protocols handle complex routing situations more quickly and accurately than the system administrator can. Routing protocols are designed not only to switch to a backup route when the primary route becomes inoperable, but also to decide which is the "best" route to a destination. On any network where there are multiple paths to the same destination, a routing protocol should be used.

Routes are built manually by the system administrator or dynamically by routing protocols. But no matter how routes are entered, they all end up in the routing table.

The Minimal Routing Table

Let's look at the contents of the routing table constructed when ifconfig is used to configure the network interfaces on a Solaris 8 system:

```
% netstat -rn
Routing Table: IPv4
  Destination          Gateway          Flags  Ref   Use   Interface
-------------------- -------------------- ----- ----- ------ ---------
172.16.12.0          172.16.12.15         U      1      8   dnet0
224.0.0.0            172.16.12.15         U      1      0   dnet0
127.0.0.1            127.0.0.1            UH     20   3577   lo0
```

The first entry is the route to network 172.16.12.0 through interface dnet0. Address 172.16.12.15 is not a remote gateway address; it is the address assigned to the dnet0 interface on this host. The other two entries do not define routes to real physical networks; both are special software conventions. 224.0.0.0 is the multicast address. This entry tells Solaris to send multicast addresses to interface 172.16.12.15 for delivery. The last entry is the loopback route to *localhost* created when lo0 was configured.

Look at the Flags field for these entries. All entries have the U (up) flag set, indicating that they are ready to be used, but no entry has the G (gateway) flag set. The G flag indicates that an external gateway is used. The G flag is not set because all of these routes are direct routes through local interfaces, not through external gateways.

The loopback route also has the H (host) flag set. This indicates that only one host can be reached through this route. The meaning of this flag becomes clear when you look at the Destination field for the loopback entry. It shows that the destination is a host address, not a network address. The loopback network address is 127.0.0.0. The destination address shown (127.0.0.1) is the address of *localhost*, an individual host. Some systems use a route to the loopback network and others use a route to the localhost, but all systems have some route for the loopback interface in the routing table.

Although this routing table has a host-specific route, most routes lead to networks. One reason network routes are used is to reduce the size of the routing table. An organization may have only one network but hundreds of hosts. The Internet has thousands of networks but millions of hosts. A routing table with a route for every host would be unmanageable.

Our sample table contains only one route to a physical network, 172.16.12.0. Therefore, this system can communicate only with hosts located on that network. The limited capability of this routing table is easily verified with the ping command. ping uses the ICMP Echo Message to force a remote host to echo a packet back to the local host. If packets can travel to and from a remote host, it indicates that the two hosts can successfully communicate.

To check the routing table on this system, first ping another host on the local network:

```
% ping -s crab
PING crab.wrotethebook.com: 56 data bytes
64 bytes from crab.wrotethebook.com (172.16.12.1): icmp_seq=0. time=11. ms
64 bytes from crab.wrotethebook.com (172.16.12.1): icmp_seq=1. time=10. ms
^C
----crab.wrotethebook.com PING Statistics----
2 packets transmitted, 2 packets received, 0% packet loss
round-trip (ms)  min/avg/max = 10/10/11
```

ping displays a line of output for each ICMP ECHO_RESPONSE received.[*] When ping is interrupted, it displays some summary statistics. All of this indicates successful communication with *crab*. But if we check a host that is not on network 172.16.12.0, say a host at O'Reilly, the results are different.

```
% ping 207.25.98.2
sendto: Network is unreachable
```

---

[*] Sun's ping would display only the message "*crab* is alive" if the -s option was not used. Most ping implementations do not require the -s option.

Here the message "sendto: Network is unreachable" indicates that this host does not know how to send data to the network that host 207.25.98.2 is on. There are only three routes in this system's routing table, and none is a route to 207.25.98.0.

Even other subnets on *books-net* cannot be reached using this routing table. To demonstrate this, ping a host on another subnet. For example:

```
% ping 172.16.1.2
sendto: Network is unreachable
```

These ping tests show that the minimal routing table created when the network interfaces were configured allows communication only with other hosts on the local network. If your network does not require access to any other TCP/IP networks, this may be all you need. However, if it does require access to other networks, you must add more routes to the routing table.

Building a Static Routing Table

As we have seen, the minimal routing table works to reach hosts only on the directly connected physical networks. To reach remote hosts, routes through external gateways must be added to the routing table. One way to do this is by constructing a static routing table with route commands.

Use the Unix route command to add or delete entries manually in the routing table. For example, to add the route 207.25.98.0 to a Solaris system's routing table, enter:

```
# route add 207.25.98.0 172.16.12.1 1
add net 207.25.98.0: gateway crab
```

The first argument after the route command in this sample is the keyword add. The first keyword on a route command line is either add or delete, telling route either to add a new route or delete an existing one. There is no default; if neither keyword is used, route displays the routing table.

The next value is the destination address, which is the address reached via this route. The destination address can be specified as an IP address, a network name from the */etc/networks* file, a hostname from the */etc/hosts* file, or the keyword default. Because most routes are added early in the startup process, numeric IP addresses are used more than names. This is done so that the routing configuration is not dependent on the state of the name server software. Always use the complete numeric address (all four bytes). route expands the address if it contains fewer than four bytes, and the expanded address may not be what you intended.[*]

If the keyword default is used for the destination address, route creates a *default route*.[†] The default route is used whenever there is no specific route to a destination,

---

[*] Some implementations of route expand "26" to 0.0.0.26, even though "26" could mean Milnet (26.0.0.0).

[†] The network address associated with the default route is 0.0.0.0.

and it is often the only route you need. If your network has only one gateway, use a default route to direct all traffic bound for remote networks through that gateway.

Next on the route command line is the gateway address.[*] This is the IP address of the external gateway through which data is sent to the destination address. The address must be the address of a gateway on a directly connected network. TCP/IP routes specify the next hop in the path to a remote destination. That next hop must be directly accessible to the local host; therefore, it must be on a directly connected network.

The last argument on the command line is the routing metric. The metric argument is not used when routes are deleted, but some older systems require it when a route is added; for Solaris 8, the metric is optional. Systems that require a metric value for the route command use it only to decide if this is a route through a directly attached interface or a route through an external gateway. If the metric is 0, the route is installed as a route through a local interface, and the G flag, which we saw in the netstat -i display, is not set. If the metric value is greater than 0, the route is installed with the G flag set, and the gateway address is assumed to be the address of an external gateway. Static routing makes no real use of the metric. Dynamic routing is required to make real use of varying metric values.

Adding Static Routes

As an example, let's configure static routing on the imaginary workstation *rodent*. Figure 7-1 shows the subnet 172.16.12.0. There are two gateways on this subnet, *crab* and *horseshoe*. *crab* is the gateway to thousands of networks on the Internet; *horseshoe* provides access to the other subnets on *books-net*. We'll use *crab* as our default gateway because it is used by thousands of routes. The smaller number of routes through *horseshoe* can easily be entered individually. The number of routes through a gateway, not the amount of traffic it handles, decides which gateway to select as the default. Even if most of *rodent*'s network traffic goes through *horseshoe* to other hosts on *books-net*, the default gateway should be *crab*.

To install the default route on *rodent*, we enter:

```
# route add default gw 172.16.12.1
```

The destination is default, and the gateway address (172.16.12.1) is *crab*'s address. Now *crab* is *rodent*'s default gateway. Notice that the command syntax is slightly different from the Solaris route example shown earlier. *rodent* is a Linux system. Most values on the Linux route command line are preceded by keywords. In this case, the gateway address is preceded by the keyword gw.

---

[*] Linux precedes the values on the route command line with keywords; e.g., route add -net 207.25.98.0 netmask 255.255.255.0 gw 172.16.12.1. Check your system's documentation for the details.

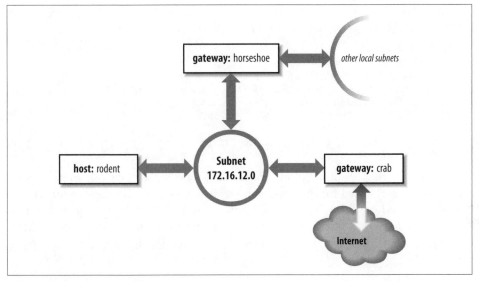

Figure 7-1. Routing on a subnet

After installing the default route, examine the routing table to make sure the route has been added:*

```
# route -n
Kernel IP routing table
Destination   Gateway       Genmask         Flags Metric Ref Use Iface
172.16.12.0   0.0.0.0       255.255.255.0   U     0      0   0 eth0
127.0.0.0     0.0.0.0       255.0.0.0       U     0      0   0 lo
0.0.0.0       172.16.12.1   0.0.0.0         UG    0      0   0 eth0
```

Try ping again to see whether *rodent* can now communicate with remote hosts. If we're lucky,† the remote host responds and we see:

```
% ping 207.25.98.2
PING 207.25.98.2: 56 data bytes
64 bytes from ruby.ora.com (207.25.98.2): icmp_seq=0. time=110. ms
64 bytes from ruby.ora.com (207.25.98.2): icmp_seq=1. time=100. ms
^C
----207.25.98.2 PING Statistics----
2 packets transmitted, 2 packets received, 0% packet loss
round-trip (ms)  min/avg/max = 100/105/110
```

This display indicates successful communication with the remote host, which means that we now have a good route to hosts on the Internet.

---

* Solaris always uses netstat to examine the routing table. Linux can use either netstat or route, but route is more common.

† It is possible that the remote host is down. If it is, ping receives no answer. Don't give up; try another host.

However, we still haven't installed routes to the rest of *books-net*. If we ping a host on another subnet, something interesting happens:

```
% ping 172.16.1.2
PING 172.16.1.2: 56 data bytes
ICMP Host redirect from gateway crab.wrotethebook.com (172.16.12.1)
 to horseshoe.wrotethebook.com (172.16.12.3) for ora.wrotethebook.com (172.16.1.2)
64 bytes from ora.wrotethebook.com (172.16.1.2): icmp_seq=1. time=30. ms
^C
----172.16.1.2 PING Statistics----
1 packets transmitted, 1 packets received, 0% packet loss round-trip (ms)  min/avg/
max = 30/30/30
```

rodent believes that all destinations are reachable through its default route. Therefore, even data destined for the other subnets is sent to *crab*. If *rodent* sends data to *crab* that should go through *horseshoe*, *crab* sends an ICMP Redirect to *rodent* telling it to use *horseshoe*. (See Chapter 1 for a description of the ICMP Redirect Message.) ping shows the ICMP Redirect in action. The redirect has a direct effect on the routing table:

```
# route -n
Kernel IP routing table
Destination    Gateway        Genmask         Flags Metric Ref Use Iface
172.16.12.0    0.0.0.0        255.255.255.0   U     0      0     0 eth0
127.0.0.0      0.0.0.0        255.0.0.0       U     0      0     0 lo
0.0.0.0        172.16.12.1    0.0.0.0         UG    0      0     0 eth0
172.16.1.2     172.16.12.3    255.255.255.0   UGHD  0      0   514 eth0
```

The route with the D flag set was installed by the ICMP Redirect.

Some network managers take advantage of ICMP Redirects when designing a network. All hosts are configured with a default route, even those on networks with more than one gateway. The gateways exchange routing information through routing protocols and redirect hosts to the best gateway for a specific route. This type of routing, which is dependent on ICMP Redirects, became popular because of personal computers (PCs). Many PCs cannot run a routing protocol; some early models did not have a route command and were limited to a single default route. ICMP Redirects were one way to support these clients. Also, this type of routing is simple to configure and well suited for implementation through a configuration server, as the same default route is used on every host. For these reasons, some network managers encourage repeated ICMP Redirects.

Other network administrators prefer to avoid ICMP Redirects and to maintain direct control over the contents of the routing table. To avoid redirects, specific routes can be installed for each subnet using individual route statements:

```
# route add -net 172.16.1.0 netmask 255.255.255.0 gw 172.16.12.3
# route add -net 172.16.6.0 netmask 255.255.255.0 gw 172.16.12.3
# route add -net 172.16.3.0 netmask 255.255.255.0 gw 172.16.12.3
# route add -net 172.16.9.0 netmask 255.255.255.0 gw 172.16.12.3
```

rodent is directly connected only to 172.16.12.0, so all gateways in its routing table have addresses that begin with 172.16.12. The finished routing table is shown below:

```
# route -n
Kernel IP routing table
Destination    Gateway       Genmask         Flags Metric Ref Use Iface
172.16.6.0     172.16.12.3   255.255.255.0   UG    0      0     0 eth0
172.16.3.0     172.16.12.3   255.255.255.0   UG    0      0     0 eth0
172.16.12.0    0.0.0.0       255.255.255.0   U     0      0     0 eth0
172.16.1.0     172.16.12.3   255.255.255.0   UG    0      0     0 eth0
172.16.9.0     172.16.12.3   255.255.255.0   UG    0      0     0 eth0
127.0.0.0      0.0.0.0       255.0.0.0       U     0      0     0 lo
0.0.0.0        172.16.12.1   0.0.0.0         UG    0      0     0 eth0
172.16.1.2     172.16.12.3   255.255.255.0   UGHD  0      0   514 eth0
```

The routing table we have constructed uses the default route (through *crab*) to reach external networks, and specific routes (through *horseshoe*) to reach other subnets within *books-net*. Rerunning the ping tests produces consistently successful results. However, if any subnets are added to the network, the routes to these new subnets must be manually added to the routing table. Additionally, if the system is rebooted, all static routing table entries are lost. Therefore, to use static routing, you must ensure that the routes are re-installed each time your system boots.

Installing static routes at startup

If you decide to use static routing, you need to make two modifications to your startup files:

1. Add the desired route statements to a startup file.
2. Remove any statements from the startup file that run a routing protocol.

To add static routing to a startup script, you must first select an appropriate script. On BSD and Linux systems, the script *rc.local* is set aside for local modifications to the boot process. *rc.local* runs at the end of the boot process so it is a good place to put in changes that will modify the default boot process. On our sample Red Hat Linux system, the full path of the *rc.local* file is */etc/rc.d/rc.local*. On a Solaris system, edit */etc/init.d/inetinit* to add the route statements:

```
route -n add default 172.16.12.1 > /dev/console
route -n add 172.16.1.0 172.16.12.3 > /dev/console
route -n add 172.16.6.0 172.16.12.3 > /dev/console
route -n add 172.16.3.0 172.16.12.3 > /dev/console
route -n add 172.16.9.0 172.16.12.3 > /dev/console
```

The -n option tells route to display numeric addresses in its informational messages. When you add route commands to a Solaris startup file, use the -n option to prevent route from wasting time querying name server software that may not be running. The -n option is not required on a Linux system because Linux does not display informational messages when installing a route.

After adding the route commands, check whether the script starts a routing protocol. If it does, comment out the lines that start it. You don't want a routing protocol running when you are using static routing. On our Solaris sample system, the routing software is started only if the system has more than one network interface (i.e., is a router) or the *letc/gateways* file has been created. (More on this file later.) Neither of these things is true; therefore, the routing daemon won't be run by the startup process and we don't have to do anything except add the route statements.

Before making changes to your real system, check your system's documentation. You may need to modify a different boot script, and the execution path of the routing daemon may be different. Only the documentation can provide the exact details you need.

Although the startup filename may be different on your system, the procedure should be basically the same. These simple steps are all you need to set up static routing. The problem with static routing is not setting it up, but maintaining it if you have a changeable networking environment. Routing protocols are flexible enough to handle simple and complex routing environments. That is why some startup procedures run routing protocols by default. However, most Unix systems need only a static default route. Routing protocols are usually needed only by routers.

Interior Routing Protocols

Routing protocols are divided into two general groups: *interior* and *exterior* protocols. An interior protocol is a routing protocol used inside—interior to—an independent network system. In TCP/IP terminology, these independent network systems are called autonomous systems.* Within an autonomous system (AS), routing information is exchanged using an interior protocol chosen by the autonomous system's administration.

All interior routing protocols perform the same basic functions. They determine the "best" route to each destination and distribute routing information among the systems on a network. How they perform these functions (in particular, how they decide which routes are best) is what makes routing protocols different from each other. There are several interior protocols:

- The *Routing Information Protocol* (RIP) is the interior protocol most commonly used on Unix systems. RIP is included as part of the Unix software delivered with most systems. It is adequate for local area networks and is simple to configure. RIP selects the route with the lowest "hop count" (*metric*) as the best route. The RIP hop count represents the number of gateways through which data must pass to reach its destination. RIP assumes the best route is the one that uses the fewest gateways. This approach to route choice is called a *distance-vector algorithm*.

* Autonomous systems are described in Chapter 2.

- *Hello* is a protocol that uses delay as the deciding factor when choosing the best route. *Delay* is the length of time it takes a datagram to make the round trip between its source and destination. A Hello packet contains a timestamp indicating when it was sent. When the packet arrives at its destination, the receiving system subtracts the timestamp from the current time to estimate how long it took the packet to arrive. Hello is not widely used. It was the interior protocol of the original 56 Kbps NSFNET backbone and has had very little use otherwise.

- *Intermediate System to Intermediate System* (IS-IS) is an interior routing protocol from the OSI protocol suite. It is a *Shortest Path First* (SPF) *link-state* protocol. It was the interior routing protocol used on the T1 NSFNET backbone, and it is still used by some large service providers.

- *Open Shortest Path First* (OSPF) is another link-state protocol developed for TCP/IP. It is suitable for very large networks and provides several advantages over RIP.

Of these protocols, we will discuss RIP and OSPF in detail. OSPF is widely used on routers. RIP is widely used on Unix systems. We will start the discussion with RIP.

Routing Information Protocol

As delivered with many Unix systems, Routing Information Protocol (RIP) is run by the routing daemon routed (pronounced "route" "d"). When routed starts, it issues a request for routing updates and then listens for responses to its request. When a system configured to supply RIP information hears the request, it responds with an update packet based on the information in its routing table. The update packet contains the destination addresses from the routing table and the routing metric associated with each destination. Update packets are issued in response to requests as well as periodically to keep routing information accurate.

To build the routing table, routed uses the information in the update packets. If the routing update contains a route to a destination that does not exist in the local routing table, the new route is added. If the update describes a route whose destination is already in the local table, the new route is used only if it is a better route. As noted previously, RIP considers a route with a lower "hop count" to be a better route. In RIP terminology, the hop count is called the *cost* of the route or the routing *metric*. We saw earlier that the routing metric in the local routing table can be manually controlled using the metric argument of the route command. To select the best route, RIP must first determine the cost of the route. The cost of a route is determined by adding the cost of reaching the gateway that sent the update to the metric contained in the RIP update packet. If the total cost is less than the cost of the current route, the new route is used.

RIP also deletes routes from the routing table. It accomplishes this in two ways. First, if the gateway to a destination says the cost of the route is greater than 15, the route is deleted. Second, RIP assumes that a gateway that doesn't send updates is dead. All routes through a gateway are deleted if no updates are received from that gateway for a specified time period. In general, RIP issues routing updates every 30 seconds. In many implementations, if a gateway does not issue routing updates for 180 seconds, all routes through that gateway are deleted from the routing table.

Running RIP with routed

To run RIP using the routing daemon (routed),[*] enter the following command:

```
# routed
```

The routed statement is often used without any command-line arguments, but you may want to use the -q option. The -q option prevents routed from advertising routes. It just listens to the routes advertised by other systems. If your computer is not a gateway, you should probably use the -q option.

In the section on static routing, we did not need to comment out the routed statement found in the *inetinit* startup file because Solaris runs routed only if the system has two network interfaces or if the */etc/gateways* file is found. If your Unix system starts routed unconditionally, no action is required to run RIP; just boot your system and RIP will run. Otherwise, you need to make sure the routed command is in your startup and the conditions required by your system are met. The easiest way to get Solaris to run routed is to create a *gateways* file—even an empty one will do.

routed reads */etc/gateways* at startup and adds its information to the routing table. routed can build a functioning routing table simply by using the RIP updates received from the RIP suppliers. However, it is sometimes useful to supplement this information with, for example, an initial default route or information about a gateway that does not announce its routes. The */etc/gateways* file stores this additional routing information.

The most common use of the */etc/gateways* file is to define an active default route, so we'll use that as an example. This one example is sufficient because all entries in the */etc/gateways* file have the same basic format. The following entry specifies *crab* as the default gateway:

```
net 0.0.0.0 gateway 172.16.12.1 metric 1 active
```

The entry starts with the keyword net. All entries start with either the keyword net or the keyword host to indicate whether the address that follows is a network address or a host address. The destination address 0.0.0.0 is the address used for the default route. In the route command we used the keyword default to indicate this route, but in */etc/gateways* the default route is indicated by network address 0.0.0.0.

Next is the keyword gateway followed by the gateway's IP address. In this case it is the address of *crab* (172.16.12.1).

---

[*] On some systems the routing daemon is in.routed.

Then comes the keyword `metric` followed by a numeric metric value. The metric is the cost of the route. The metric was almost meaningless when used with static routing, but now that we are running RIP, the metric is used to make routing decisions. The RIP metric represents the number of gateways through which data must pass to reach its final destination. But as we saw with `ifconfig`, the metric is really an arbitrary value used by the administrator to prefer one route over another. (The system administrator is free to assign any metric value.) However, it is useful to vary the metric only if you have more than one route to the same destination. With only one gateway to the Internet, the correct metric to use for *crab* is 1.

All */etc/gateways* entries end with either the keyword `passive` or the keyword `active`. "Passive" means the gateway listed in the entry is not required to provide RIP updates. Use `passive` to prevent RIP from deleting the route if no updates are expected from the gateway. A passive route is placed in the routing table and kept there as long as the system is up. In effect, it becomes a permanent static route.

The keyword `active`, on the other hand, creates a route that can be updated by RIP. An active gateway is expected to supply routing information and will be removed from the routing table if, over a period of time, it does not provide routing updates. Active routes are used to "prime the pump" during the RIP startup phase, with the expectation that the routes will be updated by RIP when the protocol is up and running.

Our sample entry ends with the keyword `active`, which means that this default route will be deleted if no routing updates are received from *crab*. Default routes are convenient; this is especially true when you use static routing. But when you use dynamic routing, default routes should be used with caution, especially if you have multiple gateways that can reach the same destination. A passive default route prevents the routing protocol from dynamically updating the route to reflect changing network conditions. Use an active default route that can be updated by the routing protocol.

RIP is easy to implement and simple to configure. Perfect! Well, not quite. RIP has three serious shortcomings:

Limited network diameter
> The longest RIP route is 15 hops. A RIP router cannot maintain a complete routing table for a network that has destinations more than 15 hops away. The hop count cannot be increased because of the second shortcoming.

Slow convergence
> Deleting a bad route sometimes requires the exchange of multiple routing update packets until the route's cost reaches 16. This is called "counting to infinity" because RIP keeps incrementing the route's cost until it becomes greater than the largest valid RIP metric. (In this case, 16 is infinity.) Additionally, RIP may wait 180 seconds before deleting the invalid routes. In network-speak, we say that these conditions delay the "convergence of routing," i.e., it takes a long time for the routing table to reflect the current state of the network.

Classful routing

RIP interprets all addresses using the class rules described in Chapter 2. For RIP, all addresses are class A, B, or C, which makes RIP incompatible with the current practice of interpreting an address based on the address bit mask.

Nothing can be done to change the limited network diameter. A small metric is essential to reduce the impact of counting to infinity. However, limited network size is the least important of RIP's shortcomings. The real work of improving RIP concentrates on the other two problems, slow convergence and classful routing.

Features have been added to RIP to address slow convergence. Before discussing them we must understand how the "counting-to-infinity" problem occurs. Figure 7-2 illustrates a network where a counting-to-infinity problem might happen.

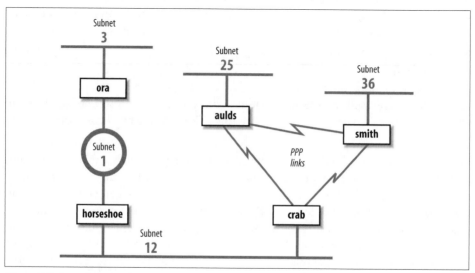

Figure 7-2. Sample network

Figure 7-2 shows that *crab* reaches subnet 3 through *horseshoe* and then through *ora*. Subnet 3 is two hops away from *crab* and one hop away from *horseshoe*. Therefore *horseshoe* advertises a cost of 1 for subnet 3 and *crab* advertises a cost of 2, and traffic continues to be routed through *horseshoe*. That is, until something goes wrong. If *ora* crashes, *horseshoe* waits for an update from *ora* for 180 seconds. While waiting, *horseshoe* continues to send updates to *crab* that keep the route to subnet 3 in *crab*'s routing table. When *horseshoe*'s timer finally expires, it removes all routes through *ora* from its routing table, including the route to subnet 3. It then receives an update from *crab* advertising that *crab* is two hops away from subnet 3. *horseshoe* installs this route and announces that it is three hops away from subnet 3. *crab* receives this update, installs the route, and announces that it is four hops away from subnet 3. Things continue on in this manner until the cost of the route to subnet 3 reaches 16 in both routing tables. If the update interval is 30 seconds, this could take a long time!

Split horizon and *poison reverse* are two features that attempt to avoid counting to infinity. Here's how:

Split horizon
> With this feature, a router does not advertise routes on the link from which those routes were obtained. This would solve the count-to-infinity problem described above. Using the split horizon rule, *crab* would not announce the route to subnet 3 on subnet 12 because it learned that route from the updates it received from *horseshoe* on subnet 12. While this feature works for the previous example described, it does not work for all count-to-infinity configurations. (More on this later.)

Poison reverse
> This feature is an enhancement of split horizon. It uses the same idea: "Don't advertise routes on the link from which those routes were obtained." But it adds a positive action to that essentially negative rule. Poison reverse says that a router should advertise an infinite distance for routes on this link. With poison reverse, *crab* would advertise subnet 3 with a cost of 16 to all systems on subnet 12. The cost of 16 means that subnet 3 cannot be reached through *crab*.

Split horizon and poison reverse solve the problem described above. But what happens if *crab* crashes? Refer to Figure 7-2. With split horizon, *aulds* and *smith* do not advertise to *crab* the route to subnet 12 because they learned the route from *crab*. They do, however, advertise the route to subnet 12 to each other. When *crab* goes down, *aulds* and *smith* perform their own count to infinity before they remove the route to subnet 12. Triggered updates address this problem.

Triggered updates are a big improvement. Instead of waiting the normal 30-second update interval, a triggered update is sent immediately. Therefore, when an upstream router crashes or a local link goes down, the router sends the changes to its neighbors immediately after it updates its local routing table. Without triggered updates, counting to infinity can take almost eight minutes! With triggered updates, neighbors are informed in a few seconds. Triggered updates also use network bandwidth efficiently. They don't include the full routing table; they include only the routes that have changed.

Triggered updates take positive action to eliminate bad routes. Using triggered updates, a router advertises the routes deleted from its routing table with an infinite cost to force downstream routers to also remove them. Again, look at Figure 7-2. If *crab* crashes, *smith* and *aulds* wait 180 seconds and remove the routes to subnets 1, 3, and 12 from their routing tables. They then send each other triggered updates with a metric of 16 for subnets 1, 3, and 12. Thus they tell each other that they cannot reach these networks and no count to infinity occurs. Split horizon, poison reverse, and triggered updates go a long way toward eliminating counting to infinity.

It is the final shortcoming—the fact that RIP is incompatible with CIDR supernets and variable-length subnets—that caused the RIP protocol to be moved to "historical" status in 1996. RIP is not compatible with current and future plans for the TCP/IP protocol stack. A new version of RIP had to be created to address this final problem.

RIP Version 2

RIP version 2 (RIP-2), defined in RFC 2453, is a new version of RIP. It is not a completely new protocol; it simply defines extensions to the RIP packet format. RIP-2 adds a network mask and a next-hop address to the destination address and metric found in the original RIP packet.

The network mask frees the RIP-2 router from the limitation of interpreting addresses based on outdated address class rules. The mask is applied to the destination address to determine how the address should be interpreted. Using the mask, RIP-2 routers support variable-length subnets and CIDR supernets.

The next-hop address is the IP address of the gateway that handles the route. If the address is 0.0.0.0, the source of the update packet is the gateway for the route. The next-hop route permits a RIP-2 supplier to provide routing information about gateways that do not speak RIP-2. Its function is similar to an ICMP Redirect, pointing to the best gateway for a route and eliminating extra routing hops.

RIP-2 adds other new features to RIP. It transmits updates via the multicast address 224.0.0.9 to reduce the load on systems that are not capable of processing a RIP-2 packet. RIP-2 also introduces a packet authentication scheme to reduce the possibility of accepting erroneous updates from misconfigured systems.

Despite these changes, RIP-2 is compatible with RIP. The original RIP specification allowed for future versions of RIP. RIP has a version number in the packet header, and several empty fields for extending the packet. The new values used by RIP-2 did not require any changes to the structure of the packet. The new values are simply placed in the empty fields that the original protocol reserved for future use. Properly implemented RIP routers can receive RIP-2 packets and extract the data that they need from the packet without becoming confused by the new data.

Split horizon, poison reverse, triggered updates, and RIP-2 eliminate most of the problems with the original RIP protocol. But RIP-2 is still a distance-vector protocol. There are other, newer routing technologies that are considered superior for large networks. In particular, *link-state* routing protocols are favored because they provide rapid routing convergence and reduce the possibility of routing loops.

Open Shortest Path First

Open Shortest Path First (OSPF), defined by RFC 2328, is a *link-state* protocol. As such, it is very different from RIP. A router running RIP shares information about the entire network with its neighbors. Conversely, a router running OSPF shares information about its neighbors with the entire network. The "entire network" means, at most, a single autonomous system. RIP doesn't try to learn about the entire Internet, and OSPF doesn't try to advertise to the entire Internet. That's not their job. These are interior routing protocols, so their job is to construct the routing inside an autonomous system. OSPF further refines this task by defining a hierarchy of routing areas within an autonomous system:

Areas

> An *area* is an arbitrary collection of interconnected networks, hosts, and routers. Areas exchange routing information with other areas within the autonomous system through *area border routers*.

Backbone

> A *backbone* is a special area that interconnects all of the other areas within an autonomous system. Every area must connect to the backbone because the backbone is responsible for distributing routing information between the areas.

Stub area

> A *stub area* has only one area border router, which means that there is only one route out of the area. In this case, the area border router does not need to advertise external routes to the other routers within the stub area. It can simply advertise itself as the default route.

Only a large autonomous system needs to be subdivided into areas. The sample network shown in Figure 7-2 is small and would not need to be divided. We can, however, use it to illustrate the different areas. We could divide this autonomous system into any areas we wish. Assume we divide it into three areas: area 1 contains subnet 3; area 2 contains subnet 1 and subnet 12; and area 3 contains subnet 25, subnet 36, and the PPP links. Furthermore, we could define area 1 as a stub area because *ora* is that area's only area border router. We also could define area 2 as the backbone area because it interconnects the other two areas and all routing information between areas 1 and 3 must be distributed by area 2. Area 2 contains two area border routers, *crab* and *ora*, and one interior router, *horseshoe*. Area 3 contains three routers: *crab*, *smith*, and *aulds*.

Clearly OSPF provides lots of flexibility for subdividing an autonomous system. But why is it necessary? One problem for a link-state protocol is the large quantity of data that can be collected in the *link-state database* and the amount of time it can take to calculate the routes from that data. A look at the protocol shows why this is true.

Every OSPF router builds a *directed graph* of the entire network using the Dijkstra Shortest Path First (SPF) algorithm. A directed graph is a map of the network from the perspective of the router; that is, the root of the graph is the router. The graph is built from the link-state database, which includes information about every router on the network and all the neighbors of every router. The link-state database for the autonomous system in Figure 7-2 contains 5 routers and 10 neighbors: *ora* has 1 neighbor, *horseshoe*; *horseshoe* has 2 neighbors, *ora* and *crab*; *crab* has 3 neighbors, *horseshoe*, *aulds*, and *smith*; *aulds* has 2 neighbors, *crab* and *smith*; and *smith* has 2 neighbors, *aulds* and *crab*. Figure 7-3 shows the graph of this autonomous system from the perspective of *ora*.

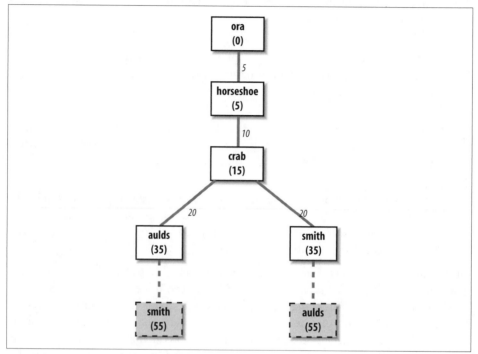

Figure 7-3. A network graph

The Dijkstra algorithm builds the map in this manner:

1. Install the local system as the root of the map with a cost of 0.

2. Locate the neighbors of the system just installed and add them to the map. The cost of reaching the neighbors is calculated as the sum of the cost of reaching the system just installed plus the cost it advertises for reaching each neighbor. For example, assume that *crab* advertises a cost of 20 for *aulds* and that the cost of reaching *crab* is 15. Then the cost for *aulds* in *ora*'s map is 35.

3. Walk through the map and select the lowest-cost path for each destination. For example, when *aulds* is added to the map, its neighbors include *smith*. The path to *smith* through *aulds* is temporarily added to the map. In this third phase of the algorithm, the cost of reaching *smith* through *crab* is compared to the cost of reaching it through *aulds*. The lowest-cost path is selected. Figure 7-3 shows the deleted paths in dotted lines. Steps 2 and 3 of the algorithm are repeated for every system in the link-state database.

The information in the link-state database is gathered and distributed in a simple and efficient manner. An OSPF router discovers its neighbors through the use of Hello packets.* It sends Hello packets and listens for Hello packets from adjacent routers. The Hello packet identifies the local router and lists the adjacent routers from which it has received packets. When a router receives a Hello packet that lists it as an adjacent router, it knows it has found a neighbor. It knows this because it can hear packets from that neighbor and, because the neighbor lists it as an adjacent router, the neighbor must be able to hear packets from it. The newly discovered neighbor is added to the local system's neighbor list.

The OSPF router then advertises all of its neighbors. It does this by *flooding* a Link-State Advertisement (LSA) to the entire network. The LSA contains the address of every neighbor and the cost of reaching that neighbor from the local system. Flooding means that the router sends the LSA out of every interface and that every router that receives the LSA sends it out of every interface except the one from which it was received. To avoid flooding duplicate LSAs, the routers store a copy of the LSAs they receive and discard duplicates.

Figure 7-2 provides an example. When OSPF starts on *horseshoe* it sends a Hello packet on subnet 1 and one on subnet 12. *ora* and *crab* hear the Hello and respond with Hello packets that list *horseshoe* as an adjacent router. *horseshoe* hears their Hello packets and adds them to its neighbor list. *horseshoe* then creates an LSA that lists *ora* and *crab* as neighbors with appropriate costs assigned to each. For instance, *horseshoe* might assign a cost of 5 to *ora* and a cost of 10 to *crab*. *horseshoe* then floods the LSA on subnet 1 and subnet 12. *ora* hears the LSA and floods it on subnet 3. *crab* receives the LSA and floods it on both of its PPP links. *aulds* floods the LSA on the link toward *smith*, and *smith* floods it on the same link to *aulds*. When *aulds* and *smith* received the second copy of the LSA, they discarded it because it duplicated one that they had already received from *crab*. In this manner, every router in the entire network receives every other router's link-state advertisement.

OSPF routers track the state of their neighbors by listening for Hello packets. Hello packets are issued by all routers on a periodic basis. When a router stops issuing packets, it or the link it is attached to is assumed to be down. Its neighbors update their LSA and flood them through the network. The new LSAs are included into the link-state database on every router on the network, and every router recalculates its network map based on this new information. Clearly, limiting the number of routers by limiting the size of the network reduces the burden of recalculating the map. For many networks, the entire autonomous system is small enough. For others, dividing the autonomous system into areas improves efficiency.

Another feature of OSPF that improves efficiency is the *designated router*. The designated router is one router on the network that treats all other routers on the network as its neighbors, while all other routers treat only the designated router as their neighbor. This helps reduce the size of the link-state database and thus improves the

---

* Don't confuse Hello packets with the Hello protocol. These are OSPF Hello packets.

speed of the Shortest-Path-First calculation. Imagine a broadcast network with 5 routers. Five routers each with 4 neighbors produce a link-state database with 20 entries. But if one of those routers is the designated router, then that router has 4 neighbors and all other routers have only 1 neighbor, for a total of 10 link-state database entries. While there is no need for a designated router on such a small network, the larger the network, the more dramatic the gains. For example, a broadcast network with 25 routers has a link-state database of 50 entries when a designated router is used, versus a database of 600 entries without one.

OSPF provides the router with an end-to-end view of the route between two systems instead of the limited next-hop view provided by RIP. Flooding quickly disseminates routing information throughout the network. Limiting the size of the link-state database through areas and designated routers speeds the SPF calculation. Taken altogether, OSPF is an efficient link-state routing protocol.

OSPF also offers additional features that RIP doesn't. It provides simple password authentication to ensure that the update comes from a valid router using an eight-character, clear-text password. It provides Message Digest 5 (MD5) crypto-checksum for stronger authentication.

OSPF also supports *equal-cost multi-path routing*. This mouthful means that OSPF routers can maintain more than one path to a single destination. Given the proper conditions, this feature can be used for load balancing across multiple network links. However, many systems are not designed to take advantage of this feature. Refer to your router's documentation to see if it supports load balancing across equal-cost OSPF routes.

With all of these features, OSPF is the preferred TCP/IP interior routing protocol for dedicated routers.

Exterior Routing Protocols

Exterior routing protocols are used to exchange routing information between autonomous systems. The routing information passed between autonomous systems is called *reachability information*. Reachability information is simply information about which networks can be reached through a specific autonomous system.

RFC 1771 defines Border Gateway Protocol (BGP), the leading exterior routing protocol, and provides the following description of the routing function of an autonomous system:

> The classic definition of an Autonomous System is a set of routers under a single technical administration, using an interior gateway protocol and common metrics to route packets within the AS, and using an exterior gateway protocol to route packets to other ASs.... The administration of an AS appears to other ASs to have a single coherent interior routing plan and presents a consistent picture of what networks are reachable through it. From the standpoint of exterior routing, an AS can be viewed as monolithic...

Moving routing information into and out of these monoliths is the function of exterior routing protocols. Exterior routing protocols are also called exterior gateway protocols. Don't confuse *an* exterior gateway protocol with *the* Exterior Gateway Protocol (EGP). EGP is not a generic term; it is a particular exterior routing protocol, and an old one at that.

Exterior Gateway Protocol

A gateway running EGP announces that it can reach networks that are part of its autonomous system. It does not announce that it can reach networks outside its autonomous system. For example, the exterior gateway for our imaginary autonomous system *book-as* can reach the entire Internet through its external connection, but only one network is contained in its autonomous system. Therefore, it would announce only one network (172.16.0.0) if it ran EGP.

Before sending routing information, the systems exchange EGP *Hello* and *I-Heard-You* (I-H-U) messages. These messages establish a dialogue between two EGP gateways. Computers communicating via EGP are called *EGP neighbors*, and the exchange of Hello and I-H-U messages is called *acquiring a neighbor*.

Once a neighbor is acquired, routing information is requested via a *poll*. The neighbor responds by sending a packet of reachability information called an *update*. The local system includes the routes from the update into its local routing table. If the neighbor fails to respond to three consecutive polls, the system assumes that the neighbor is down and removes the neighbor's routes from its table. If the system receives a poll from its EGP neighbor, it responds with its own update packet.

Unlike the interior protocols discussed above, EGP does not attempt to choose the "best" route. EGP updates contain distance-vector information, but EGP does not evaluate this information. The routing metrics from different autonomous systems are not directly comparable. Each AS may use different criteria for developing these values. Therefore, EGP leaves the choice of a "best" route to someone else.

When EGP was designed, the network relied upon a group of trusted core gateways to process and distribute the routes received from all of the autonomous systems. These core gateways were expected to have the information necessary to choose the best external routes. EGP reachability information was passed into the core gateways, where the information was combined and passed back out to the autonomous systems.

A routing structure that depends on a centrally controlled group of gateways does not scale well and is therefore inadequate for the rapidly growing Internet. As the number of autonomous systems and networks connected to the Internet grew, it became difficult for the core gateways to keep up with the expanding workload. This is one reason why the Internet moved to a more distributed architecture that places a share of the burden of processing routes on each autonomous system. Another reason is that no central authority controls the commercialized Internet. The Internet is composed of many equal networks. In a distributed architecture, the autonomous systems require routing protocols, both interior and exterior, that can make intelligent routing choices. Because of this, EGP is no longer popular.

Border Gateway Protocol

Border Gateway Protocol (BGP) is the leading exterior routing protocol of the Internet. It is based on the OSI *InterDomain Routing Protocol* (IDRP). BGP supports *policy-based routing*, which uses non-technical reasons (for example, political, organizational, or security considerations) to make routing decisions. Thus BGP enhances an autonomous system's ability to choose between routes and to implement routing policies without relying on a central routing authority. This feature is important in the absence of core gateways to perform these tasks.

Routing policies are not part of the BGP protocol. Policies are provided externally as configuration information. As described in Chapter 2, the National Science Foundation provides Routing Arbiters (RAs) at the Network Access Points (NAPs) where large Internet Service Providers (ISPs) interconnect. The RAs can be queried for routing policy information. Most ISPs also develop private policies based on the bilateral agreements they have with other ISPs. BGP can be used to implement these policies by controlling the routes it announces to others and the routes it accepts from others. In the gated section later in this chapter, we discuss the import command and the export command, which control what routes are accepted (import) and what routes are announced (export). The network administrator enforces the routing policy through configuring the router.

BGP is implemented on top of TCP, which provides BGP with a reliable delivery service. BGP uses well-known TCP port 179. It acquires its neighbors through the standard TCP three-way handshake. BGP neighbors are called *peers*. Once connected, BGP peers exchange OPEN messages to negotiate session parameters, such as the version of BGP that is to be used.

The UPDATE message lists the destinations that can be reached through a specific path and the attributes of the path. BGP is a *path-vector protocol*. It is called a path-vector protocol because it provides the entire end-to-end path of a route in the form of a sequence of autonomous system numbers. Having the complete AS path eliminates the possibility of routing loops and count-to-infinity problems. A BGP UPDATE contains a single path vector and all of the destinations reachable through that path. Multiple UPDATE packets may be sent to build a routing table.

BGP peers send each other complete routing table updates when the connection is first established. After that, only changes are sent. If there are no changes, just a small (19-byte) KEEPALIVE message is sent to indicate that the peer and the link are still operational. BGP is very efficient in its use of network bandwidth and system resources.

By far the most important thing to remember about exterior protocols is that most systems never run them. Exterior protocols are required only when an AS must exchange routing information with another AS. Most routers within an AS run an interior protocol such as OSPF. Only those gateways that connect the AS to another AS need to run an exterior routing protocol. Your network is probably an independent part of an AS run by someone else. ISPs are good examples of autonomous systems made up of many independent networks. Unless you provide a similar level of service, you probably don't need to run an exterior routing protocol.

Choosing a Routing Protocol

Although there are many routing protocols, choosing one is usually easy. Most of the interior routing protocols mentioned above were developed to handle the special routing problems of very large networks. Some of the protocols have been used only by large national and regional networks. For local area networks, RIP is still a common choice. For larger networks, OSPF is the choice.

If you must run an exterior routing protocol, the protocol that you use is often not a matter of choice. For two autonomous systems to exchange routing information, they must use the same exterior protocol. If the other AS is already in operation, its administrators have probably decided which protocol to use, and you will be expected to conform to their choice. Most often this choice is BGP.

The type of equipment affects the choice of protocols. Routers support a wide range of protocols, though individual vendors may have a preferred protocol. Hosts don't usually run routing protocols at all, and most Unix systems are delivered with only RIP. Allowing host systems to participate in dynamic routing could limit your choices. gated, however, gives you the option to run many different routing protocols on a Unix system. While the performance of hardware designed specifically to be a router is generally better, gated gives you the option of using a Unix system as a router.

In the following sections we discuss the Gateway Routing Daemon (gated) software that combines interior and exterior routing protocols into one software package. We look at examples of running RIP, RIPv2, OSPF, and BGP with gated.

Gateway Routing Daemon

Routing software development for general-purpose Unix systems is limited. Most sites use Unix systems only for simple routing tasks for which RIP is usually adequate. Large and complex routing applications, which require advanced routing protocols, are handled by dedicated router hardware that is optimized specifically for routing. Many of the advanced routing protocols are only available for Unix systems in gated. gated combines several different routing protocols in a single software package.

Additionally, gated provides other features that are usually associated only with dedicated routers:

- Systems can run more than one routing protocol. gated combines the routing information learned from different protocols and selects the "best" routes.

- Routes learned through an interior routing protocol can be announced via an exterior routing protocol, which allows the reachability information announced externally to adjust dynamically to changing interior routes.

- Routing policies can be implemented to control what routes are accepted and what routes are advertised.

- All protocols are configured from a single file (*/etc/gated.conf*) using a single consistent syntax for the configuration commands.

- gated is constantly being upgraded. Using gated ensures that you're running the most up-to-date routing software.

gated's Preference Value

There are two sides to every routing protocol implementation. One side, the external side, exchanges routing information with remote systems. The other side, the internal side, uses the information received from the remote systems to update the routing table. For example, when OSPF exchanges Hello packets to discover a neighbor, it is an external protocol function. When OSPF adds a route to the routing table, it is an internal function.

The external protocol functions implemented in gated are the same as those in other implementations of the protocols. However, the internal side of gated is unique for Unix systems. Internally, gated processes routing information from different routing protocols, each of which has its own metric for determining the best route, and combines that information to update the routing table. Before gated was written, if a Unix system ran multiple routing protocols, each would write routes into the routing table without knowledge of the others' actions. The route found in the table was the last one written—not necessarily the best route.

With multiple routing protocols and multiple network interfaces, it is possible for a system to receive routes to the same destination from different protocols. gated compares these routes and attempts to select the best one. However, the metrics used by different protocols are not directly comparable. Each routing protocol has its own metric. It might be a hop count, the delay on the route, or an arbitrary value set by the administrator. gated needs more than that protocol's metric to select the best route. It uses its own value to prefer routes from one protocol or interface over another. This value is called *preference*.

Preference values help gated combine routing information from several different sources into a single routing table. Table 7-1 lists the sources from which gated receives routes and the default preference given to each source. Preference values range from 0 to 255, with the lowest number indicating the most preferred route. From this table you can see that gated prefers a route learned from OSPF over the same route learned from BGP.

Table 7-1. Default preference values

Route type	Default preference
direct route	0
OSPF	10
IS-IS Level 1	15
IS-IS Level 2	18
Internally generated default	20
ICMP redirect	30
Routes learned from the route socket	40
static route	60
SLSP routes	70
RIP	100
Point-to-Point interface routes	110
Routes through a downed interface	120
Aggregate and generate routes	130
OSPF ASE routes	150
BGP	170
EGP	200

Preference can be set in several different configuration statements. It can be used to prefer routes from one network interface over another, from one protocol over another, or from one remote gateway over another. Preference values are not transmitted or modified by the protocols. Preference is used only in the configuration file. In the next section we'll look at the gated configuration file (*/etc/gated.conf*) and the configuration commands it contains.

Configuring gated

gated is available from *http://www.gated.org*. Appendix B provides information about downloading and compiling the software. In this section, we use gated release 3.6, the version of gated that is currently available without restrictions. There are other versions of gated available to members of the Gated Consortium. If you plan to build products based on gated or do research on routing protocols using gated, you should join the consortium. For the purposes of this book, release 3.6 is fine.

gated reads its configuration from the */etc/gated.conf* file. The configuration commands in the file resemble C code. All statements end with a semicolon, and associated statements are grouped together by curly braces. This structure makes it simple to see what parts of the configuration are associated with each other, which is important when multiple protocols are configured in the same file. In addition to structure in the language, the /etc/gated.conf file also has a structure.

The different configuration statements, and the order in which these statements must appear, divide gated.conf into sections: *option statements*, *interface statements*, *definition statements*, *unicast* and *multicast protocol statements*, *static statements*, *control statements*, and *aggregate statements*. Entering a statement out of order causes an error when parsing the file.

Two other types of statements do not fall into any of these categories. They are *directive statements* and *trace statements*. These can occur anywhere in the gated.conf file and do not directly relate to the configuration of any protocol. These statements provide instructions to the parser and instructions to control tracing from within the configuration file.

The gated configuration commands are summarized in Table 7-2. The table lists each command by name, identifies the statement type, and provides a very short synopsis of each command's function. The entire command language is covered in detail in Appendix B.

Table 7-2. gated configuration statements

Statement	Type	Function
%directory	directive	Sets the directory for include files
%include	directive	Includes a file into *gated.conf*
traceoptions	trace	Specifies which events are traced
options	option	Defines gated options
interfaces	interface	Defines interface options
autonomoussystem	definition	Defines the AS number
routerid	definition	Defines the originating router for BGP or OSPF
martians	definition	Defines invalid destination addresses
multicast	protocol	Defines multicast protocol options
snmp	protocol	Enables reporting to SNMP
rip	protocol	Enables RIP
isis	protocol	Enables IS-IS protocol
kernel	protocol	Configures kernel interface options
ospf	protocol	Enables OSPF protocol
redirect	protocol	Removes routes installed by ICMP
egp	protocol	Enables EGP
bgp	protocol	Enables BGP
icmp	protocol	Configures the processing of general ICMP packets

Table 7-2. gated configuration statements (continued)

Statement	Type	Function
pim	protocol	Enables the PIM multicast protocol
dvmrp	protocol	Enables the DVMRP multicast protocol
msdp	protocol	Enables the MSDP multicast protocol
static	static	Defines static routes
import	control	Defines what routes are accepted
export	control	Defines what routes are advertised
aggregate	aggregate	Controls route aggregation
generate	aggregate	Controls creation of a default route

You can see that the gated configuration language has many commands. The language provides configuration control for several different protocols and additional commands to configure the added features of gated itself. All of this can be confusing.

To avoid confusion, don't try to understand the details of everything offered by gated. Your routing environment will not use all of these protocols and features. Even if you are providing the gateway at the border between two anonymous systems, you will probably run only two routing protocols: one interior protocol and one exterior protocol. Only those commands that relate to your actual configuration need to be included in your configuration file. As you read this section, skip the things you don't need. For example, if you don't use the BGP protocol, don't study the bgp statement. When you do need more details about a specific statement, look it up in Appendix B. With this in mind, let's look at some sample configurations.

Sample gated.conf Configurations

The details in Appendix B may make gated configuration appear more complex than it is. gated's rich command language can be confusing, as can its support for multiple protocols and the fact that it often provides a few ways to do the same thing. But some realistic examples will show that individual configurations do not need to be complex.

The basis for the sample configurations is the network in Figure 7-4. We have installed a new router that provides our backbone with direct access to the Internet, and we have decided to install new routing protocols. We'll configure a host to listen to RIP-2 updates, an interior gateway to run RIP-2 and OSPF, and an exterior gateway to run OSPF and BGP.

Gateway *limulus* interconnects subnet 172.16.9.0 and subnet 172.16.1.0. To hosts on subnet 9, it advertises itself as the default gateway because it is the gateway to the outside world. It uses RIP-2 to advertise routes on subnet 9. On subnet 1, gateway *limulus* advertises itself as the gateway to subnet 9 using OSPF.

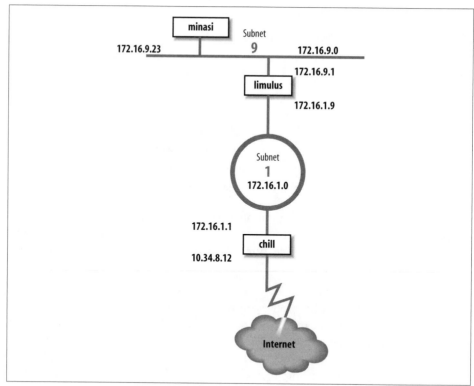

Figure 7-4. Sample routing topology

Gateway *chill* provides subnet 1 with access to the Internet through autonomous system 164. Because gateway *chill* provides access to the Internet, it announces itself as the default gateway to the other systems on subnet 1 using OSPF. To the external autonomous system, it uses BGP to announce itself as the path to the internal networks it learns about through OSPF.

Let's look at the routing configuration of host *minasi*, gateway *limulus*, and gateway *chill*.

A host configuration

The host routing configuration is very simple. The rip yes statement enables RIP, and that's all that is really required to run RIP. That basic configuration should work for any system that runs RIP. The additional clauses enclosed in curly braces modify the basic RIP configuration. We use a few clauses to create a more interesting example. Here is the RIP-2 configuration for host *minasi*:

```
#
#  enable rip, don't broadcast updates,
#  listen for RIP-2 updates on the multicast address,
#  check that the updates are authentic.
#
```

```
rip yes {
        nobroadcast ;
        interface 172.16.9.23
              version 2
              multicast
              authentication simple "REAL stuff" ;
} ;
```

This sample file shows the basic structure of *gated.conf* configuration statements. Lines beginning with a sharp sign (#) are comments.* All statements end with semicolons. Clauses associated with a configuration statement can span multiple lines and are enclosed in curly braces ({}). In the example, the nobroadcast and interface clauses apply directly to the rip statement. The version, multicast, and authentication keywords are part of the interface clause.

The keyword nobroadcast prevents the host from broadcasting its own RIP updates. The default is nobroadcast when the system has one network interface, and broadcast when it has more than one. The nobroadcast keyword performs the same function as the -q command-line option does for routed. However, gated can do much more than routed, as the next clause shows.

The interface clause defines interface parameters for RIP. The parameters associated with this clause say that RIP-2 updates will be received via the RIP-2 multicast address on interface 172.16.9.23 and that authentic updates will contain the password REAL^stuff. For RIP-2, simple authentication is a clear-text password up to 16 bytes long. This is not intended to protect the system from malicious actions; it is intended only to protect the routers from a configuration accident. If a user mistakenly sets his system up as a RIP supplier, he is very unlikely to accidentally enter the correct password into his configuration. Stronger authentication is available in the form of a Message Digest 5 (MD5) cryptographic checksum by specifying md5 in the authentication clause.

Interior gateway configurations

Gateway configurations are more complicated than the simple host configuration shown above. Gateways always have multiple interfaces and occasionally run multiple routing protocols. Our first sample configuration is for the interior gateway between subnet 9 and the central backbone, subnet 1. It uses RIP-2 on subnet 9 to announce routes to the Unix hosts. It uses OSPF on subnet 1 to exchange routes with the other gateways. Here's the configuration of gateway *limulus*:

```
# Don't time-out subnet 9
interfaces {
    interface 172.16.9.1 passive ;
} ;
# Define the OSPF router id
```

---

* Comments can also be enclosed between * and *\.

```
routerid 172.16.1.9 ;
# Enable RIP-2; announce OSPF routes to
# subnet 9 with a cost of 5.
rip yes {
    broadcast ;
    defaultmetric 5 ;
    interface 172.16.9.1
        version 2
        multicast
        authentication simple "REAL stuff" ;
} ;
# Enable OSPF; subnet 1 is the backbone area;
# use password authentication.
ospf yes {
    backbone {
        interface 172.16.1.9 {
            priority 5 ;
            auth simple "It'sREAL" ;
            } ;
        } ;
} ;
```

The interfaces statement defines routing characteristics for the network interfaces. The keyword passive in the interface clause is used here, just as we have seen it used before, to create a permanent static route that will not be removed from the routing table. In this case, the permanent route is through a directly attached network interface. Normally when gated thinks an interface is malfunctioning, it increases the cost of the interface by giving it a high-cost preference value (120) to reduce the probability of a gateway routing data through a non-operational interface. gated determines that an interface is malfunctioning when it does not receive routing updates on that interface. We don't want gated to downgrade the 172.16.9.1 interface, even if it does think the interface is malfunctioning, because our router is the only path to subnet 9. That's why this configuration includes the clause interface 172.16.9.1 passive.

The routerid statement defines the router identifier for OSPF. Unless it is explicitly defined in the configuration file, gated uses the address of the first interface it encounters as the default router identifier address. Here we specify the address of the interface that actually speaks OSPF as the OSPF router identifier.

In the previous example we discussed all the clauses on the rip statement except one—the defaultmetric clause. The defaultmetric clause defines the RIP metric used to advertise routes learned from other routing protocols. This gateway runs both OSPF and RIP-2. We wish to advertise the routes learned via OSPF to our RIP clients, and to do that, a metric is required. We choose a RIP cost of 5. If the defaultmetric clause is not used, routes learned from OSPF are not advertised to the RIP clients.[*] This statement is required for our configuration.

---

[*] This is not strictly true. The routes are advertised with a cost of 16, meaning that the destinations are unreachable.

The ospf yes statement enables OSPF. The first clause associated with this statement is backbone. It states that the router is part of the OSPF backbone area. Every ospf yes statement must have at least one associated area clause. It can define a specific area, e.g., area 2, but at least one router must be in the backbone area. While the OSPF backbone is area 0, it cannot be specified as area 0; it must be specified with the keyword backbone. In our sample configuration, subnet 1 is the backbone, and all routers attached to it are in the backbone area. It is possible for a single router to attach to multiple areas with a different set of configuration parameters for each area. Notice how the nested curly braces group the clauses together. The remaining clauses in the configuration file are directly associated with the backbone area clause.

The interface that connects this router to the backbone area is defined by the interface clause. It has two associated subclauses, the priority clause and the auth clause.

The priority 5 ; clause defines the priority used by this router when the backbone is electing a designated router. The higher the priority number, the less likely a router will be elected as the designated router. Use priority to steer the election toward the most capable routers.

The auth simple "It'sREAL" ; clause says that simple, password-based authentication is used in the backbone area and defines the password used for simple authentication. Three choices, none, simple, and md5, are available for authentication in GateD 3.6. none means no authentication is used. simple means that the correct eight-character password must be used or the update will be rejected. Password authentication is used only to protect against accidents; it is not intended to protect against malicious actions. Stronger authentication based on MD5 is used when md5 is selected.

Exterior gateway configuration

The configuration for gateway *chill* is the most complex because it runs both OSPF and BGP. Here's the configuration file for gateway *chill*:

```
# Defines our AS number for BGP
autonomoussystem 249;

# Defines the OSPF router id
routerid 172.16.1.1;

# Disable RIP
rip no;

# Enable BGP
bgp yes {
    group type external peeras 164 {
        peer 10.6.0.103 ;
        peer 10.20.0.72 ;
        };
```

```
};

# Enable OSPF; subnet 1 is the backbone area;
# use password authentication.
ospf yes {
    backbone {
        interface 172.16.1.1 {
            priority 10 ;
            auth simple "It'sREAL" ;
            } ;
        } ;
};

# Announce routes learned from OSPF and route
# to directly connected network via BGP to AS 164
export proto bgp as 164 {
    proto direct ;
    proto ospf ;
};

# Announce routes learned via BGP from
# AS number 164 to our OSPF area.
export proto ospfase type 2  {
    proto bgp autonomoussystem 164  {
        all ;
        };
};
```

This configuration enables both BGP and OSPF and sets certain protocol-specific parameters. BGP needs to know the AS number, which is 249 for *books-net*. OSPF needs to know the router identifier address. We set it to the address of the router interface that runs OSPF. The AS number and the router identifier are defined early in the configuration because autonomoussystem and routerid are definition statements and therefore must occur before the first protocol statement. Refer back to Table 7-2 for the various statement types.

The first protocol statement is the one that turns RIP off. We don't want to run RIP, but the default for gated is to turn RIP on. Therefore we explicitly disable RIP with the rip no ; statement.

BGP is enabled by the bgp yes statement, which also defines a few additional BGP parameters. The group clause sets parameters for all of the BGP peers in the group. The clause defines the type of BGP connection being created. The example is a classic external routing protocol connection, and the external autonomous system we are connecting to is AS number 164. gated can create five different types of BGP sessions, but only one, type external, is used to directly communicate with an external autonomous system. The other four group types are used for *internal BGP* (IBGP).[*]

---

[*] See Appendix B for information on all group types.

IBGP is simply an acronym for BGP when it is used to move routing information around inside an autonomous system. In our example we use it to move routing information between autonomous systems.

The BGP neighbors from which updates are accepted are indicated by the peer clauses. Each peer is a member of the group. Everything related to the group, such as the AS number, applies to every system in the group. To accept updates from any system with ASN 164, use allow in place of the list of peers.

The OSPF protocol is enabled by the ospf yes statement. The configuration of OSPF on this router is the same as it is for other routers in the backbone area. The only parameter that has been changed from the previous example is the priority number. Because this route has a particularly heavy load, we have decided to make it slightly less preferred for the designated router election.

The export statements control the routes that gated advertises to other routers. The first export statement directs gated to use BGP (proto bgp) to advertise to autonomous system 164 (as 164) any directly connected networks (proto direct) and any routes learned from OSPF (proto ospf). Notice that the AS number specified in this statement is not the AS number of *books-net*; it is the AS number of the external system. The first line of the export statement defines to whom we are advertising. The proto clauses within the curly braces define what we are advertising.

The second export statement announces the routes learned from the external autonomous system. The routes are received via BGP and are advertised via OSPF. Because these are routes from an external autonomous system, they are advertised as *autonomous system external* (ASE) routes. That's why the export statement specifies ospfase as the protocol through which the routes are announced. The type 2 parameter defines the type of external routes that are being advertised. There are two types supported by gated. Type 2 routes are those learned from an exterior gateway protocol that does not provide a routing metric comparable to the OSPF metric. These routes are advertised with the cost of reaching the border router. In this case, the routes are advertised with the OSPF cost of reaching gateway *chill*. Type 1 routes are those learned from an external protocol that does provide a metric directly comparable to the OSPF metric. In that case, the metric from the external protocol is added to the cost of reaching the border router when routes are advertised.

The source of the routes advertised in the second export statement is the BGP connection (proto bgp) to autonomous system 164 (autonomoussystem 164). The proto clause is qualified with an optional *route filter*. A route filter is used to select the routes from a specific source. The filter can list networks with associated netmasks to select an individual destination. In the example, the keyword all is used to select all routes received via BGP, which is, in fact, the default. As the default, the keyword all does not need to be specified. However, it does no harm, and it provides clear documentation of our intentions.

All of the routes received from an external autonomous system could produce a very large routing table. Individual routes are useful when you have multiple border routers that can reach the outside world. However, if you have only one border router, a default route may be all that is needed. To export a default route, insert an options gendefault ; statement at the beginning of the configuration file.* This tells gated to generate a default route when the system peers with a BGP neighbor. Next, replace the second export statement in the sample file with the following export statement:

```
# Announce a default route when peering
# with a BGP neighbor.
export proto ospfase type 2  {
    proto default ;
};
```

This export statement tells gated to advertise the border router as the default gateway, but only when it has an active connection to the external system.

These few examples show that *gated.conf* files are usually small and easy to read. Use gated if you need to run a routing protocol on your computer. It allows you to use the same software and the same configuration language on all of your hosts, interior gateways, and exterior gateways.

Testing the Configuration

Test the configuration file before you try to use it; the gated configuration syntax is complex and it is easy to make a mistake. Create your new configuration in a test file, test the new configuration, and then move the test configuration to */etc/gated.conf*. Here's how.

Assume that a configuration file called *test.conf* has already been created. It is tested using -f and -c on the command line:

```
% gated -c -f test.conf trace.test
```

The -f option tells gated to read the configuration from the named file instead of from */etc/gated.conf*. In the sample it reads the configuration from *test.conf*. The -c option tells gated to read the configuration file and check for syntax errors. When gated finishes reading the file, it terminates; it does not modify the routing table. The -c option turns on tracing, so specify a trace file or the trace data will be displayed on your terminal. In the sample we specified *trace.test* as the trace file. The -c option also produces a snapshot of the state of gated after reading the configuration file, and writes the snapshot to */usr/tmp/gated_dump*.† You don't need to be superuser or to terminate the active gated process to run gated when the -c option is used.

---

* The generate statement is an alternative way to create a default route. See Appendix B for details.

† */usr/tmp* is the default for this file and for the *gated_parse* file described later; however, some systems place these files in */var/tmp*.

The dump and the trace file (*trace.test*) can then be examined for errors and other information. When you're confident that the configuration is correct, become super-user and move your new configuration (*test.conf*) to */etc/gated.conf*.

An alternative command for testing the configuration file is gdc, though it must be run by the root user or as a setuid root program. It includes features for checking and installing a new configuration. gdc uses three different configuration files. The current configuration is */etc/gated.conf*. The previous configuration is stored in */etc/gated.conf-*. The "next" configuration is stored in */etc/gated.conf+*, which is normally the configuration that needs to be tested. Here's how gdc tests a configuration:

```
# cp test.conf /etc/gated.conf+
# gdc checknew
configuration file /etc/gated.conf+ checks out okay
# gdc newconf
# gdc restart
gated not currently running
gdc: /etc/gated was started
```

In this sample, the test configuration is copied to */etc/gated.conf+* and tested with the gdc checknew command. If syntax problems are found in the file, a warning message is displayed and detailed error messages are written to */usr/tmp/gated_parse*. There are no syntax errors in the example, so we make the test file the current configuration with the gdc newconf command. This command moves the current configuration to *gated.conf-* and moves the new configuration (*gated.conf+*) to the current configuration. The gdc restart command terminates gated if it is currently running—it was not in the example—and starts a new copy of gated using the new configuration.

Running gated at startup

As with any routing software, gated should be included in your startup file. Some systems come with the code to start gated included in the startup file. If your system doesn't, you'll need to add it. If you already have code in your startup file that runs routed, replace it with code to run gated. gated and routed should not be running at the same time.

Our imaginary gateway, *crab*, is a Solaris system with code in the */etc/init.d/inetinit* file that starts routed. We comment out those lines, and add these lines:

```
if [ -f /usr/sbin/gated -a -f /etc/gated.conf ]; then
    /usr/sbin/gated;      echo -n 'gated' > /dev/console
fi
```

This code assumes that gated is installed in */usr/sbin* and that the configuration file is named */etc/gated.conf*. The code checks that gated is present and that the configuration file */etc/gated.conf* exists. If both files are found, gated begins.

The code checks for a configuration file because gated usually runs with one. If gated is started without a configuration file, it checks the routing table for a default route. If it doesn't find one, it starts RIP; otherwise, it just uses the default route. Create an

/etc/gated.conf file even if you only want to run RIP. The configuration file documents your routing configuration and protects you if the default configuration of gated changes in the future.

Summary

Routing is the glue that binds networks together to build internets. Without it, networks cannot communicate with each other. Configuring routing is an important task for the network administrator.

Minimal routing is required to communicate through the network interface to the directly attached network. These routes can be seen in the routing table where they show up as entries that do not have the G (gateway) flag set. On some systems, minimal routes are created by the ifconfig command when an interface is installed. On Linux systems, the route through the interface must be explicitly installed with a route command.

The route command is used to build a static routing table. Static routing is routing that is manually maintained by the network administrator. Routes are added to or removed from the routing table with the route command. The most common use for static routing is to install a default route.

Dynamic routing uses routing protocols to select the best routes and to update the routing table. There are many different dynamic routing protocols. The one that is available on most Unix systems is Routing Information Protocol (RIP). RIP is run by routed. routed builds the routing table from information received on the network and from information read from */etc/gateway*.

gated is a software package that provides several more routing protocols for Unix systems, including advanced protocols such as Open Shortest Path First (OSPF) and Border Gateway Protocol (BGP). gated is configured through the */etc/gated.conf* file. The gated configuration commands are covered in Appendix B.

This is the last chapter on how to create the physical network connection. Once routing is installed, the system is capable of basic communication. In the next chapter, we begin the discussion of the various applications and services that are necessary to make the network truly useful.

In this chapter:
- BIND: Unix Name Service
- Configuring the Resolver
- Configuring named
- Using nslookup

CHAPTER 8

Configuring DNS

Congratulations! You have installed TCP/IP in the kernel, configured the network interface, and configured routing. At this point, you have completed all of the configuration tasks required to run TCP/IP on a Unix system. While none of the remaining tasks is *required* for TCP/IP software to operate, they are necessary for making the network more friendly and useful. In the next two chapters, we look at how to configure basic TCP/IP network services. Perhaps the most important of these is name service.

It is, as the name implies, a service—specifically, a service intended to make the network more user-friendly. Computers are perfectly happy with IP addresses, but people prefer names. The importance of name service is indicated by the amount of coverage it has in this book. Chapter 3 discusses *why* name service is needed; this chapter covers *how* it is configured; and Appendix C covers the *details* of the name server configuration commands. This chapter provides sufficient information to show you how to configure the BIND software to run on your system.* But if you want to know more about why something is done or details on how to do it, don't hesitate to refer to Chapter 3 and Appendix C.

BIND: Unix Name Service

In Unix, DNS is implemented by the *Berkeley Internet Name Domain* (BIND) software. BIND is a client/server software system. The client side of BIND is called the *resolver*. It generates the queries for domain name information and sends them to the server. The DNS server software answers the resolver's queries. The server side of BIND is a daemon called named (pronounced "name" "d").

This chapter covers three basic BIND configuration tasks:

---

* BIND 8 is the version of domain name software that comes with most versions of Linux and with Solaris 8. A newer version of DNS software—BIND 9—is also available. BIND 8 and BIND 9 use essentially the same configuration file syntax. The examples presented here should work with both BIND 8 and BIND 9.

- Configuring the BIND resolver
- Configuring the BIND name server (named)
- Constructing the name server database files, called the *zone files*

A *zone* is a piece of the domain namespace over which a name server holds authority. A zone cannot contain a domain that is delegated to another server. Here we use "zone" to refer to the DNS database file, while the term "domain" is used in more general contexts. In this book, a domain is part of the domain hierarchy identified by a domain name. A zone is a collection of domain information contained in a DNS database file. The file that contains the domain information is called a zone file.

RFC 1033, the *Domain Administrators Operations Guide*, defines the basic set of standard records used to construct zone files. Many RFCs propose new DNS records that are not widely implemented. In this chapter and in Appendix C, we stick to the basic resource records that you are most likely to use. We'll use these records to construct the zone files used in this chapter. But how, or even if, you need to construct zone files on your system is controlled by the type of BIND configuration you decide to use.

BIND Configurations

BIND configurations are described by the type of service the software is configured to provide. The four levels of service that can be defined in a BIND configuration are *resolver-only systems*, *caching-only servers*, *master servers*, and *slave servers*.

The resolver is the code that asks name servers for domain information. On Unix systems, it is implemented as a library rather than as a separate client program. Some systems, called resolver-only systems, use only the resolver; they don't run a name server. Resolver-only systems are very easy to configure: you just need to set up the */etc/resolv.conf* file.

The three other BIND configurations all require that the local system run the named server software. They are:

Master
> The master name server is the authoritative source for all information about a specific zone. It loads the domain information from a locally maintained disk file that is built by the domain administrator. This file (the zone file) contains the most accurate information about a piece of the domain hierarchy over which this name server has authority. The master server is an authoritative server because it can answer any query about its zone with full authority.
>
> Configuring a master server requires creating a complete set of configuration files: zone files for the forward-mapping zone and the reverse-mapping zone, the conf file, the root hints file, and the loopback file. No other configuration requires creating this complete set of files.

Slave

A slave server transfers a complete set of zone information from the master server. The zone data is transferred from the master server and stored on the slave server as a local disk file. This transfer is aptly called a *zone transfer*. A slave server keeps a complete copy of all zone information and can answer queries about that zone with authority. Therefore, a slave server is also considered an authoritative server.

Configuring a slave server does not require creating local zone files because the zone files are downloaded from the master server. However, other files (a boot file, a cache file, and a loopback file) are required.

Caching-only

A caching-only server runs the name server software but keeps no zone files. It learns the answer to every name server query from some remote server. Once it learns an answer, the server caches the answer and uses it to answer future queries for the same information. All name servers use cached information in this manner, but a caching-only server depends on this technique for all of its name server information. It is not considered an authoritative server because all of the information it provides is secondhand. Only a boot file and a cache file are required for a caching-only configuration, but the most common configuration also includes a loopback file. This is probably the most common name server configuration, and apart from the resolver-only configuration, it is the easiest to configure.

A name server may use any one of these configurations or, as is often the case, it may combine elements of more than one type of configuration. However, all systems run the resolver, so let's begin by examining the configuration of the client side of the DNS software.

Configuring the Resolver

The resolver is configured in the */etc/resolv.conf* file. The resolver is not a separate and distinct process; it is a library of routines called by network processes. The *resolv.conf* file is read when a process using the resolver starts, and is cached for the life of that process. If the configuration file is not found, the resolver attempts to connect to the named server running on the local host. While this may work, I don't recommend it. By allowing the resolver configuration to default, you give up control over your system and become vulnerable to variations in the techniques used by different systems to determine the default configuration. For these reasons, the resolver configuration file should be created on every system running BIND.

The Resolver Configuration File

The configuration file clearly documents the resolver configuration. It allows you to identify up to three name servers, two of which provide backup if the first server doesn't respond. It defines the default domain and various other processing options. The *resolv.conf* file is a critical part of configuring name service.

resolv.conf is a simple, human-readable file. There are system-specific variations in the commands used in the file, but the entries supported by most systems are:

nameserver *address*

> The nameserver entries identify, by IP address, the servers that the resolver is to query for domain information. The name servers are queried in the order that they appear in the file. If no response is received from a server, the next server in the list is tried until the maximum number of servers are tried.[*] If no nameserver entries are contained in the *resolv.conf* file or if no *resolv.conf* file exists, all queries are sent to the local host. However, if there is a *resolv.conf* file and it contains nameserver entries, the local host is *not* queried unless an entry points to it. Specify the local host with its official IP address or with 0.0.0.0, not with the loopback address. The official address avoids problems seen on some versions of Unix when the loopback address is used. A resolver-only configuration never contains a nameserver entry that points to the local host.

domain *name*

> The domain entry defines the default domain name. The resolver appends the default domain name to any hostname that does not contain a dot.[†] It then uses the expanded hostname in the query it sends to the name server. For example, if the hostname *crab* (which does not contain a dot) is received by the resolver, the default domain name is appended to *crab* to construct the query. If the value for *name* in the domain entry is wrotethebook.com, the resolver queries for *crab.wrotethebook.com*. If the environment variable LOCALDOMAIN is set, it overrides the domain entry, and the value of LOCALDOMAIN is used to expand the hostname.

search *domain* ...

> The search entry defines a series of domains that is searched when a hostname does not contain a dot. Assume the entry search essex.wrotethebook.com butler.wrotethebook.com. A query for the hostname *cookbook* is first tried as *cookbook.essex.wrotethebook.com*. If that fails to provide a successful match, the resolver queries for *cookbook.butler.wrotethebook.com*. If that query fails, no other attempts are made to resolve the hostname. Use either a search statement or a domain statement. (The search command is preferred.) Never use both in the same configuration. If the environment variable LOCALDOMAIN is set, it overrides the search entry.

sortlist *network*[*/netmask*] ...

> Addresses from the networks listed on the sortlist command are preferred over other addresses. If the resolver receives multiple addresses in response to a query

---

[*] Three is the maximum number of servers tried by most BIND implementations.

[†] This is the most common way that default domain names are used, but this is configurable.

about a multi-homed host or a router, it reorders the addresses so that an address from a network listed in the sortlist statement is placed in front of the other addresses. Normally addresses are returned to the application by the resolver in the order in which they are received.

The sortlist command is rarely used because it interferes with the servers' ability to reorder addresses for load balancing and other purposes. The primary exception to this is that sometimes sortlist is configured to prefer addresses on a shared network over other addresses. Using this configuration, if the computer running the resolver is connected to network 172.16.0.0/16 and one of the addresses returned in a multiple address response is from that network, the address from 172.16.0.0 is placed in front of the other addresses.

options *option* ...

The options entry is used to select optional settings for the resolver. There are several possible options:[*]

debug

Turns on debugging, which prints debugging messages to standard output. debug works only if the resolver was compiled with the –DDEBUG option, and most weren't.

ndots:*n*

Sets the number of dots in a hostname used to determine whether or not the search list is applied before sending the query to the name server. The default is 1. Therefore a hostname with one dot does not have a domain appended before it is sent to the name server. If options ndots:2 is specified, a hostname with one dot does have the search list domain added before the query is sent out, but a hostname with two or more dots does not have a domain added.

ndots may be useful for you if some component of your domain could be confused with a top-level domain and your users consistently truncate hostnames at that domain. In that case, the queries would first be sent to the root servers for resolution in the top-level domain before eventually getting back to your local server. It is very bad form to bother the root servers over nothing. Use ndots to force the resolver to extend the troublesome hostnames with your local domain name so that they will be resolved before reaching the root servers.

timeout:*n*

Sets the initial query timeout for the resolver. By default, the timeout is 5 seconds for the first query to every server. Under the Solaris 8 version of BIND, the syntax of this option is retrans:*n*.

---

[*] This list shows the options on Linux systems that run BIND 8. The Solaris version of BIND 8 does not provide the rotate, no-check-names, or inet6 options.

attempts:*n*

> Defines the number of times the resolver will retry a query. The default value is 2, which means the resolver will retry a query two times with every server in its server list before returning an error to the application. Under the Solaris 8 version of BIND, the syntax of this option is retry:*n*, and the default is 4.

rotate

> Turns on round-robin selection of name servers. Normally, the resolver sends the query to the first server in the name server list, sending it to another server only if the first server does not respond. The rotate option tells the resolver to share the name server workload evenly among all of the servers.

no-check-names

> Disables checking of domain names for compliance with RFC 952, *DOD Internet Host Table Specification*. By default, domain names that contain an underscore (_), non-ASCII characters, or ASCII control characters are considered to be in error. Use this option if you must work with hostnames that contain an underscore.

inet6

> Causes the resolver to query for IPv6 addresses. The version of the Internet Protocol (IP) used in today's Internet is IPv4. IPv4 uses 32-bit addresses. IPv6 expands those to 128-bit addresses.

The most common *resolv.conf* configuration defines the local domain name as the search list, the local host as the first name server, and one or two backup name servers. An example of this configuration is:

```
# Domain name resolver configuration file
#
search wrotethebook.com
# try yourself first
nameserver 172.16.12.2
# try crab next
nameserver 172.16.12.1
# finally try ora
nameserver 172.16.1.2
```

The example is based on our imaginary network, so the default domain name is *wrotethebook.com*. The configuration is for *rodent,* and it specifies itself as the first name server. The backup servers are *crab* and *ora*. The configuration does not contain a sort list or any options, as these are infrequently used. This is an example of an average resolver configuration.

A resolver-only configuration

The resolver-only configuration is very simple. It is identical to the average configuration except that it does not contain a nameserver entry for the local system. A sample *resolv.conf* file for a resolver-only system is shown here:

```
# Domain name resolver configuration file
#
search wrotethebook.com
# try crab
nameserver 172.16.12.1
# next try ora
nameserver 172.16.1.2
```

The configuration tells the resolver to pass all queries to *crab*; if that fails, try *ora*. Queries are never resolved locally. This simple *resolv.conf* file is all that is required for a resolver-only configuration.

Configuring named

While the resolver configuration requires, at most, one configuration file, several files are used to configure named. The complete set of named files is:

The configuration file
> Sets general named parameters and points to the sources of DNS database information used by this server. These sources can be local disk files or remote servers. This file is usually called *named.conf*.

The root hints file
> Points to the root zone servers. Some common names for this file are *named.ca*, *db.cache*, *named.root*, or *root.ca*.

The localhost file
> Used to locally resolve the loopback address. The filename *named.local* is generally used for this file.

The forward-mapping zone file
> The zone file that maps hostnames to IP addresses. This is the file that contains the bulk of the information about the zone. To make it easier to discuss this file, this text generally refers to it as the *zone file*, dropping the "forward-mapping" qualifier. The zone file is generally given a descriptive name, such as *wrotethebook.com.hosts*, that identifies which zone's data is contained in the file.

The reverse-mapping zone file
> The zone file that maps IP addresses to hostnames. To make it easier to discuss this file, this text generally refers to it as the *reverse zone file*. The reverse zone file is generally given a descriptive name, such as *172.16.rev*, that identifies which IP address is mapped by the file.

All of these files can have any names you wish. However, you should use descriptive names for your zone files, the filenames *named.conf* and *named.local* for the boot file and the loopback address file, and one of the well-known names for the root hints file to make it easier for others to maintain your system. In the following sections, we'll look at how each of these files is used, starting with *named.conf*.

The named.conf File

The *named.conf* file points named to sources of DNS information. Some of these sources are local files; others are remote servers. You need to create only the files referenced in the master and cache statements. We'll look at an example of each type of file you may need to create.

The structure of the configuration commands in *named.conf* is similar to the structure of the C programming language. A statement ends with a semicolon (;), literals are enclosed in quotes (""), and related items are grouped together inside curly braces ({}). A comment can be enclosed between /* and */, like a C language comment; it can begin with //, like a C++ comment, or with #, like a shell comment. These examples use C++ style comments, but, of course, you can use any of the three valid styles you like.

Table 8-1 summarizes the basic *named.conf* configuration statements. It provides just enough information to help you understand the examples. Not all of the *named.conf* configuration commands are used in the examples, and you probably won't use all of the commands in your configuration. The commands are designed to cover the full spectrum of configurations, even the configurations of root servers. If you want more details about the *named.conf* configuration statements, Appendix C contains a full explanation of each command.

Table 8-1. named.conf configuration commands

Command	Function
acl	Defines an access control list of IP addresses
include	Includes another file into the configuration file
key	Defines security keys for authentication
logging	Defines what will be logged and where it will be stored
options	Defines global configuration options and defaults
server	Defines a remote server's characteristics
zone	Defines a zone

The way you configure the *named.conf* file controls whether the name server acts as a zone's master server, a zone's slave server, or a caching-only server. The best way to understand these different configurations is to look at sample *named.conf* files. The next sections show examples of each type of configuration.

A caching-only server configuration

A caching-only server configuration is simple. A *named.conf* file and a *named.ca* file are all that you need, though the *named.local* file is usually also used. A possible *named.conf* file for a caching-only server is:

```
$ cat /etc/named.conf
options {
        directory "/var/named";
};

//
// a caching only name server config
//
zone "." {
        type hint;
        file "named.ca";
};

zone "0.0.127.in-addr.arpa" {
        type master;
        file "named.local";
};
```

The options statement defines the default directory for named. In the sample file, this is */var/named*. All subsequent file references in the *named.conf* file are relative to this directory.

The two zone statements in this caching-only configuration are found in all server configurations. The first zone statement defines the hints file that is used to help the name server locate the root servers during startup. The second zone statement makes the server the master for its own loopback address, and says that the information for the loopback domain is stored in the file *named.local*. The loopback domain is an *in-addr.arpa* domain* that maps the address 127.0.0.1 to the name *localhost*. The idea of resolving your own loopback address makes sense to most people, and *named.conf* files should contain this entry. The hints file and the local host file, along with the *named.conf* file, are used for every server configuration.†

These zone and options statements are the only statements used in most caching-only server configurations, but the options statement used can be more complex. A forwarders option and a forward only option are sometimes used. The forwarders option causes the caching-only server to send all of the queries that it cannot resolve from its own cache to specific servers. For example:

```
options {
        directory "/var/named";
        forwarders { 172.16.12.1; 172.16.1.2; };
};
```

This forwarders option forwards every query that cannot be answered from the local cache to 172.16.12.1 and 172.16.1.2. The forwarders option builds a rich DNS cache on selected servers located on the local network. This reduces the number of times

---

* See Chapter 4 for a description of *in-addr.arpa* domains.

† BIND 8 requires the root hints file, but BIND 9 has hints compiled in that are used if no root hints file is provided.

that queries must be sent out on the wide area network, which is particularly useful if you have limited bandwidth to the wide area network or if you are charged for usage.

When network access to the outside world is severely limited, use the `forward only` option to force the local server to always use the forwarder:

```
options {
        directory "/var/named";
        forwarders { 172.16.12.1; 172.16.1.2; };
        forward only;
};
```

With this option in the configuration file, the local server will not attempt to resolve a query itself even if it cannot get an answer to that query from the forwarders.

Adding options to the `options` statements does not change this from being a caching-only server configuration. Only the addition of master and slave zone commands will do that.

Master and slave server configurations

The imaginary *wrotethebook.com* domain is the basis for our sample master and slave server configurations. Here is the *named.conf* file to define *crab* as the master server for the *wrotethebook.com* domain:

```
options {
        directory "/var/named";
};

// a master name server configuration
//
zone "." {
        type hint;
        file "named.ca";
};

zone "0.0.127.in-addr.arpa" {
        type master;
        file "named.local";
};

zone "wrotethebook.com" {
        type master;
        file "wrotethebook.com.hosts";
};

zone "16.172.in-addr.arpa" {
        type master;
        file "172.16.rev";
};
```

The directory option saves keystrokes on the subsequent filenames. It tells named that all relative filenames (i.e., filenames that don't begin with a /), no matter where they occur in the named configuration, are relative to the directory /var/named. This option also tells named where to write various files, such as the dump file.

The first two zone statements in the sample configuration are the zone statements for the loopback address and the hints file. These statements were discussed earlier in reference to caching-only configurations. They always have the same function and are found in almost every configuration.

The first new zone statement declares that this is the master server for the *wrotethe-book.com* domain and that the data for that domain is loaded from the file *wrotethe-book.com.hosts*.

The second new zone statement points to the file that maps IP addresses from 172. 16.0.0 to hostnames. This statement says that the local server is the master server for the reverse domain *16.172.in-addr.arpa* and that the data for that domain is loaded from the file *172.16.rev*.

A slave server's configuration differs from a master's only in the structure of the zone statements. Slave server zone statements point to remote servers as the source of the domain information instead of local disk files, and they define the zone as type slave. Unlike the file clause in a master zone statement, the file clause in a slave zone statement contains the name of a local file where information received from the remote server will be stored—not a file from which the domain is loaded. The following *named.conf* file configures *ora* as a slave server for the *wrotethebook.com* domain:

```
options {
        directory "/var/named";
};

// a slave server configuration
//
zone "." {
        type hint;
        file "named.ca";
};

zone "0.0.127.in-addr.arpa" {
        type master;
        file "named.local";
};

zone "wrotethebook.com" {
        type slave;
        file "wrotethebook.hosts";
        masters { 172.16.12.1; };
};
```

```
zone "16.172.in-addr.arpa" {
        type slave;
        file "172.16.rev";
        masters { 172.16.12.1; };
};
```

The first zone statement with its type set to slave makes this a slave server for the *wrotethebook.com* domain. The statement tells named to download the data for the *wrotethebook.com* domain from the server at IP address 172.16.12.1 and to store that data in the file */var/named/wrotethebook.hosts*. If the *wrotethebook.hosts* file does not exist, named creates it, gets the zone data from the remote server, and writes the data in the newly created file. If the file does exist, named checks with the remote server to see if the remote server's data is newer than the data in the file. If the data has changed, named downloads the updated data and overwrites the file's contents with the new data. If the data has not changed, named loads the contents of the disk file and doesn't bother with a zone transfer.* Keeping a copy of the database on a local disk file makes it unnecessary to transfer the zone file every time the local host is rebooted. It's necessary to transfer the zone only when the data changes.

The last zone statement in this configuration says that the local server is also a slave server for the reverse domain *16.172.in-addr.arpa*, and that the data for that domain should also be downloaded from 172.16.12.1. The reverse domain data is stored locally in a file named *172.16.rev*, following the same rules discussed previously for creating and overwriting *wrotethebook.hosts*.

Standard Resource Records

The configuration commands discussed above and listed in Table 8-1 are used only in the *named.conf* file. All other files used to configure named (the zone file, the reverse zone file, *named.local*, and *named.ca*) store DNS database information. These files all have the same basic format and use the same type of database records. They use standard resource records, called RRs. These are defined in RFC 1033, the *Domain Administrators Operations Guide*, and in other RFCs. Table 8-2 summarizes all of the standard resource records used in this chapter. These records are covered in detail in Appendix C.

Table 8-2. Standard resource records

Resource record text name	Record type	Function
Start of Authority	SOA	Marks the beginning of a zone's data and defines parameters that affect the entire zone.
Nameserver	NS	Identifies a domain's name server.

---

* Appendix C (in the "Start of Authority record" section) discusses how named determines if data has been updated.

Table 8-2. Standard resource records (continued)

Resource record text name	Record type	Function
Address	A	Converts a hostname to an address.
Pointer	PTR	Converts an address to a hostname.
Mail Exchange	MX	Identifies where to deliver mail for a given domain name.
Canonical Name	CNAME	Defines an alias hostname.
Text	TXT	Stores arbitrary text strings.

The resource record syntax is described in Appendix C, but a little understanding of the structure of these records is necessary to read the sample configuration files used in this chapter.

The format of DNS resource records is:

```
[name] [ttl] IN type data
```

name

> The name of the domain object that the resource record references. It can be an individual host or an entire domain. The string entered for the *name* field is relative to the current domain unless it ends with a dot. If the *name* field is blank, i.e., contains only whitespace, the record applies to the domain object that was named last. For example, if the A record for *rodent* is followed by an MX record with a blank *name* field, both the A record and the MX record apply to *rodent*.

ttl

> Time-to-live defines the length of time, in seconds, that the information in this resource record should be kept in a remote system's cache. Usually this field is left blank and the default *ttl*, set for the entire zone by the $TTL directive, is used.[*]

IN

> Identifies the record as an Internet DNS resource record. There are other classes of records, but they are rarely used. Curious? See Appendix C for the other, non-Internet, classes.

type

> Identifies the kind of resource record. Table 8-2 lists the record types under the heading *Record type*. Specify one of these values in the *type* field.

data

> The information specific to this type of resource record. For example, in an A record, this is the field that contains the actual IP address.

---

[*] See the description of the $TTL directive later in this chapter.

Later in this chapter we look at each of the remaining configuration files. As you look at the files, remember that all of the standard resource records in these files follow the format described above.

The bulk of a zone file is composed of standard resource records. In addition, BIND provides some zone file directives that are used to build a DNS database.

Zone File Directives

BIND provides four directives that simplify the construction of a zone file or define a value used by the resource records in the file. The four directives are evenly divided into two commands that simplify the construction of a zone file, $INCLUDE and $GENERATE, and two that define values used by the resource records, $ORIGIN and $TTL.

The $TTL directive

The $TTL directive defines the default TTL for resource records that do not specify an explicit time to live. The time value can be specified as a number of seconds or as a combination of numbers and letters. Defining one week as the default TTL using the numeric format is:

```
$TTL 604800
```

One week is equal to 604800 seconds. Using the alphanumeric format, one week can be defined simply as:

```
$TTL 1w
```

The possible values that can be used with the alphanumeric format are:

- w for week
- d for day
- h for hour
- m for minute
- s for second

The $ORIGIN directive

The $ORIGIN directive sets the current origin, which is the domain name used to complete any relative domain names. A relative domain name is any name that does not end with a dot. By default, $ORIGIN starts out as the domain name defined on the zone statement. Use the $ORIGIN directive to change the setting.

The $INCLUDE directive

The $INCLUDE directive reads in an external file and includes it as part of the zone file. The external file is included in the zone file at the point where the $INCLUDE directive occurs.

The $GENERATE directive

The $GENERATE directive is used to create a series of resource records. The resource records created by the $GENERATE directive are almost identical, varying only by a numeric iterator. For example:

```
$ORIGIN 20.16.172.in-addr.arpa.
$GENERATE 1-4 $ CNAME $.1to4
```

The $GENERATE keyword is followed by the range of records to be created. In the example the range is 1 through 4. The range is followed by the template of the resource records to be generated. In this case, the template is $ CNAME $.1to4. A $ sign in the template is replaced by the current iterator value. In the example, the value iterates from 1 to 4. This $GENERATE directive produces the following resource records:

```
1 CNAME 1.1to4
2 CNAME 2.1to4
3 CNAME 3.1to4
4 CNAME 4.1to4
```

Given that *20.16.172.in-addr.arpa.* is the value defined for the current origin, these resource records are the same as:

```
1.20.16.172.in-addr.arpa. CNAME 1.1to4.20.16.172.in-addr.arpa.
2.20.16.172.in-addr.arpa. CNAME 2.1to4.20.16.172.in-addr.arpa.
3.20.16.172.in-addr.arpa. CNAME 3.1to4.20.16.172.in-addr.arpa.
4.20.16.172.in-addr.arpa. CNAME 4.1to4.20.16.172.in-addr.arpa.
```

These odd-looking records are helpful for delegating reverse subdomains. Delegating domains is described later in this chapter.

Except for *named.conf*, all of the BIND configuration files are composed of standard records and directives. All four of the remaining configuration files are database files. Two of these files, *named.ca* and *named.local,* are used on all servers, regardless of server type.

The Cache Initialization File

The zone statement in *named.conf* that has its type set to hints points to the cache initialization file. Each server that maintains a cache has such a file. It contains the information needed to begin building a cache of domain data when the name server starts. The root domain is indicated on the zone statement by a single dot in the domain name field because the cache initialization file contains the names and addresses of the root servers.

The *named.ca* file is called a "hints" file because it contains hints that named uses to initialize the cache. The hints it contains are the names and addresses of the root servers. The hints file is used to help the local server locate a root server during startup. Once a root server is found, an authoritative list of root servers is downloaded from that server. The hints are not referred to again until the local server is forced to restart. The information in the *named.ca* file is not referred to often, but it is critical for booting a named server.

The basic *named.ca* file contains NS records that name the root servers and A records that provide the addresses of the root servers. A sample *named.ca* file is shown here:

```
;
.                     3600000  IN  NS   A.ROOT-SERVERS.NET.
A.ROOT-SERVERS.NET.   3600000  IN  A    198.41.0.4
;
.                     3600000      NS   B.ROOT-SERVERS.NET.
B.ROOT-SERVERS.NET.   3600000  IN  A    128.9.0.107
;
.                     3600000      NS   C.ROOT-SERVERS.NET.
C.ROOT-SERVERS.NET.   3600000  IN  A    192.33.4.12
;
.                     3600000      NS   D.ROOT-SERVERS.NET.
D.ROOT-SERVERS.NET.   3600000  IN  A    128.8.10.90
;
.                     3600000      NS   E.ROOT-SERVERS.NET.
E.ROOT-SERVERS.NET.   3600000  IN  A    192.203.230.10
;
.                     3600000      NS   F.ROOT-SERVERS.NET.
F.ROOT-SERVERS.NET.   3600000  IN  A    192.5.5.241
;
.                     3600000      NS   G.ROOT-SERVERS.NET.
G.ROOT-SERVERS.NET.   3600000  IN  A    192.112.36.4
;
.                     3600000      NS   H.ROOT-SERVERS.NET.
H.ROOT-SERVERS.NET.   3600000  IN  A    128.63.2.53
;
.                     3600000      NS   I.ROOT-SERVERS.NET.
I.ROOT-SERVERS.NET.   3600000  IN  A    192.36.148.17
;
.                     3600000      NS   J.ROOT-SERVERS.NET.
J.ROOT-SERVERS.NET.   3600000  IN  A    198.41.0.10
;
.                     3600000      NS   K.ROOT-SERVERS.NET.
K.ROOT-SERVERS.NET.   3600000  IN  A    193.0.14.129
;
.                     3600000      NS   L.ROOT-SERVERS.NET.
L.ROOT-SERVERS.NET.   3600000  IN  A    198.32.64.12
;
.                     3600000      NS   M.ROOT-SERVERS.NET.
M.ROOT-SERVERS.NET.   3600000  IN  A    202.12.27.33
```

This file contains only name server and address records. Each NS record identifies a name server for the root (.) domain. The associated A record gives the address of each root server. The TTL value for all of these records is 3600000—a very large value that is approximately 42 days.

Create the *named.ca* file by downloading the file *domain/named.root* from *ftp.rs.internic.net* via anonymous ftp. The file stored there is in the correct format for a Unix system. The following example shows the superuser downloading the *named.root* file directly into the local system's *named.ca* file. The file doesn't even need to be edited; it is ready to run.

```
# ftp ftp.rs.internic.net
Connected to rs.internic.net.
220-*****Welcome to the InterNIC Registration Host  *****
      *****Login with username "anonymous"
      *****You may change directories to the following:
          policy          - Registration Policies
          templates       - Registration Templates
          netinfo         - NIC Information Files
          domain          - Root Domain Zone Files
220 And more!
Name (ftp.rs.internic.net:craig): anonymous
331 Guest login ok, send your complete e-mail address as password.
Password: craig@wrotethebook.com
230 Guest login ok, access restrictions apply.
Remote system type is Unix.
Using binary mode to transfer files.
ftp> get /domain/named.root /var/named/named.ca
local: /var/named/named.ca remote: /domain/named.root
200 PORT command successful.
150 Opening BINARY mode data connection for /domain/named.root (2769 bytes).
226 Transfer complete.
2769 bytes received in 0.998 secs (2.7 Kbytes/sec)
ftp> quit
221 Goodbye.
```

Download the *named.root* file every few months to keep accurate root server information in your cache. A bogus root server entry could cause problems with your local server. The data given above is correct as of publication, but could change at any time.

If your system is not connected to the Internet, it won't be able to communicate with the root servers. Initializing your hints file with the servers listed above would be useless. In this case, initialize your hints with entries that point to the major name servers on your local network. Those servers must also be configured to answer queries for the "root" domain. However, this root domain contains only NS records pointing to the domain servers on your local network. For example, assume that *wrotethebook.com* is not connected to the Internet and that *crab* and *horseshoe* are going to act as root servers for this isolated domain. *crab* is declared the master server for the root domain in its *named.conf* file. *horseshoe* is configured as the slave server for the root domain. They load the root from a zone file that starts with an SOA record identifying *crab* as the server and providing an in-house point of contact. Following the SOA record, the file contains NS records and A records, stating that *crab* and *horseshoe* are authoritative for the root and delegating the *wrotethebook.com* and *16.172.in-addr.arpa* domains to the local name servers that service those domains. (How domains are delegated is covered later in the chapter.) Details of this type of configuration are provided in *DNS and BIND* by Liu and Albitz (O'Reilly & Associates).

The named.local File

The *named.local* file is used to convert the address 127.0.0.1 (the "loopback address") into the name *localhost*. It's the zone file for the reverse domain *0.0.127. IN-ADDR.ARPA*. Because all systems use 127.0.0.1 as the "loopback" address, this file is virtually identical on every server. Here's a sample *named.local* file:

```
$TTL    86400
@       IN  SOA     crab.wrotethebook.com. alana.crab.wrotethebook.com. (
                    1                   ; serial
                    360000              ; refresh every 100 hours
                    3600                ; retry after 1 hour
                    3600000             ; expire after 1000 hours
                    3600                ; negative cache is 1 hour
                    )
        IN  NS      crab.wrotethebook.com.
0       IN  PTR     loopback.
1       IN  PTR     localhost.
```

Most zone files start as this one does, with a $TTL directive. This directive sets the default TTL for all resource records in this zone. It can be overridden on any individual record by defining a specific TTL on that record.

The SOA record and the NS record identify the zone and the name server for the zone. The first PTR record maps the network 127.0.0.0 to the name *loopback*, which is an alternative to mapping the network name in the */etc/networks* file. The second PTR record is the heart of this file. It maps host address 1 on network 127.0.0 to the name *localhost*.

The SOA record's data fields and the NS record that contains the computer's hostname vary from system to system. The sample SOA record identifies *crab.wrotethebook.com.* as the server originating this zone, and the email address *alana.crab. wrotethebook.com.* as the point of contact for any questions about the zone. (Note that in an SOA record, the email address is written with a dot separating the recipient's name from the hostname: *alana* is the user and *crab.wrotethebook.com* is the host. The domain names end in a dot, indicating that they are fully qualified and no default domain name should be appended.) The NS record also contains the computer's hostname. Change these three data fields and you can use this identical file on any host.

The files discussed so far, *named.conf*, *named.ca*, and *named.local*, are the only files required to configure caching-only servers and slave servers. Most of your servers will use only these files, and the files used will contain almost identical information on every server. The simplest way to create these three files is to copy a sample file and modify it for your system. Most systems come with sample files. If your system doesn't, get sample configuration files from a running server.

The remaining named configuration files are more complex, but the relative number of systems that require these files is small. Only the master server needs all of the configuration files, and there should be only one master server per zone.

The Reverse Zone File

The reverse zone file is very similar in structure to the *named.local* file. Both of these files translate IP addresses into hostnames, so both files contain PTR records.

The *172.16.rev* file in our example is the reverse zone file for the *16.172.in-addr.arpa* domain. The domain administrator creates this file on *crab*, and every other host that needs this information gets it from there.

```
$TTL 86400
;
;               Address to hostname mappings.
;
@       IN      SOA     crab.wrotethebook.com. jan.crab.wrotethebook.com. (
                                2001061401   ;   Serial
                                21600        ;   Refresh
                                1800         ;   Retry
                                604800       ;   Expire
                                900 )        ;   Negative cache TTL
                IN      NS      crab.wrotethebook.com.
                IN      NS      ora.wrotethebook.com.
                IN      NS      bigserver.isp.com.
1.12            IN      PTR     crab.wrotethebook.com.
2.12            IN      PTR     rodent.wrotethebook.com.
3.12            IN      PTR     horseshoe.wrotethebook.com.
4.12            IN      PTR     jerboas.wrotethebook.com.
2.1             IN      PTR     ora.wrotethebook.com.
6               IN      NS      linuxuser.articles.wrotethebook.com.
                IN      NS      horseshoe.wrotethebook.com.
```

Like all zone files, the first resource record in the reverse zone file is an SOA record. The @ in the name field of the SOA record references the current origin. Because this zone file does not contain an $ORIGIN directive to explicitly define the origin, the current origin is the domain *16.172.in-addr.arpa* defined by the zone statement for this file in our sample *named.conf* file:

```
zone "16.172.in-addr.arpa" {
        type master;
        file "172.16.rev";
};
```

The @ in the SOA record allows the zone statement to define the zone file domain. This same SOA record is used on every zone; it always references the correct domain name because it references the domain defined for that particular zone file in *named.conf*. Change the hostname (*crab.wrotethebook.com.*) and the manager's mail address (*jan.crab.wrotethebook.com.*), and use this SOA record in any of your zone files.

The NS records that follow the SOA record define the name servers for the domain. Generally the name servers are listed immediately after the SOA and have a blank name field. Recall that a blank name field means that the last domain name is still in force. This means that the NS records apply to the same domain as the SOA's.

PTR records dominate the reverse zone file because they are used to translate addresses to hostnames. The PTR records in our example provide address-to-name conversions for hosts 12.1, 12.2, 12.3, 12.4, and 2.1 on network 172.16. Because they don't end in dots, the values in the name fields of these PTR records are relative to the current domain. For example, the value 3.12 is interpreted as *3.12.16.172.in-addr.arpa*. The hostname in the data field of the PTR record is fully qualified to prevent it from being relative to the current domain name (and therefore it ends with a dot). Using the information in this PTR, named will translate *3.12.16.172.in-addr.arpa* into *horseshoe.wrotethebook.com*.

The last two lines of this file are additional NS records. As with any domain, subdomains can be created in an *in-addr.arpa* domain. This is what the last two NS records do. These NS records point to *horseshoe* and *linuxuser* as name servers for the subdomain *6.16.172.in-addr.arpa*. Any query for information in the *6.16.172.in-addr. arpa* subdomain is referred to them. NS records that point to the servers for a subdomain must be placed in the higher-level domain before you can use that subdomain.

Domain names and IP addresses are not the same thing and do not have the same structure. When an IP address is turned into an *in-addr.arpa* domain name, the four bytes of the address are treated as four distinct pieces of a name. In reality, the IP address is 32 contiguous bits, not four distinct bytes. Subnets divide up the IP address space and subnet masks are bit-oriented, which does not limit them to byte boundaries. Limiting subdomains to byte boundaries makes them less flexible than the subnets they must support. Our example *in-addr.arpa* domain delegates the subdomain at a full byte boundary, which treats each byte of the address as a distinct "name." This is the simplest reverse subdomain delegation, but it might not be flexible enough for your situation.

The $GENERATE example shown earlier in this chapter helps create more flexible reverse domain delegations. The $GENERATE directive created CNAME records to map a range of addresses in an *in-addr.arpa* domain to a different domain that has more flexible domain name rules. Real *in-addr.arpa* domain names *must* be four numeric fields, corresponding to the four bytes of the IP address, followed by the string *in-addr.arpa*. In the $GENERATE example, we mapped these names to longer names that give us more flexibility. Here is a larger example of the $GENERATE command:

```
$ORIGIN 30.168.192.in-addr.arpa.
$GENERATE 0-63    $ CNAME $.1ST64
$GENERATE 63-127  $ CNAME $.2ND64
$GENERATE 128-191 $ CNAME $.3RD64
$GENERATE 192-255 $ CNAME $.4TH64
```

These four $GENERATE commands map the 256 numeric names in the *30.168.192. in-addr.arpa* domain into four other domains, each composed of 64 numeric names. When a remote server seeks the PTR record for *52.30.168.192.in-addr.arpa*, it is told that the canonical name for that host is *52.1st64.30.168.192.in-addr.arpa* and that the server must seek the pointer record for that host from the server for the *1st64.30.168.192.in-addr.arpa* domain. In effect, the $GENERATE directive lets us divide the single *30.168.192.in-addr.arpa* domain into multiple domains. Once it is divided, each piece can be delegated to a different server.

Subdomain delegation can make reverse domains complex.[*] In most cases, however, reverse zone files are simpler than the forward-mapping zone file.

The Forward-Mapping Zone File

The forward-mapping zone file contains most of the domain information. This file converts hostnames to IP addresses, so A records predominate, but it also contains MX, CNAME, and other records. The zone file, like the reverse zone file, is created only on the master server; all other servers get this information from the master server.

```
$TTL 86400
;
;          Addresses and other host information.
;
@       IN      SOA     crab.wrotethebook.com. jan.crab.wrotethebook.com. (
                                2001061401   ;   Serial
                                21600        ;   Refresh
                                1800         ;   Retry
                                604800       ;   Expire
                                900 )        ;   Negative cache TTL
;          Define the name servers and the mail servers
                IN      NS      crab.wrotethebook.com.
                IN      NS      ora.wrotethebook.com.
                IN      NS      bigserver.isp.com.
                IN      MX      10 crab.wrotethebook.com.
                IN      MX      20 horseshoe.wrotethebook.com.

;
;          Define localhost
;
localhost       IN      A       127.0.0.1
;
;          Define the hosts in this zone
;
crab            IN      A       172.16.12.1
loghost         IN      CNAME   crab.wrotethebook.com.
rodent          IN      A       172.16.12.2
                IN      MX      5 crab.wrotethebook.com.
mouse           IN      CNAME   rodent.wrotethebook.com.
horseshoe       IN      A       172.16.12.3
jerboas         IN      A       172.16.12.4
ora             IN      A       172.16.1.2
;          host table has BOTH host and gateway entries for 10.104.0.19
wtb-gw          IN      A       10.104.0.19
;
```

[*] For even more complex examples, see *DNS and BIND* by Albitz and Liu.

```
;       Glue records for servers within this domain
;
linuxmag.articles   IN      A       172.16.18.15
24seven.events      IN      A       172.16.6.1
;
;       Define sub-domains
;
articles            IN      NS      linuxmag.articles.wrotethebook.com.
                    IN      NS      horseshoe.wrotethebook.com.
events              IN      NS      24seven.events.wrotethebook.com.
                    IN      NS      linuxmag.articles.wrotethebook.com.
```

Like the reverse zone file, the zone file begins with an SOA record and a few NS records that define the domain and its servers, but the zone file contains a wider variety of resource records than a reverse zone file does. We'll look at each of these records in the order they occur in the sample file, so you can follow along using the sample file as your reference.

The first MX record identifies a mail server for the entire domain. This record says that *crab* is the mail server for *wrotethebook.com* with a preference of 10. Mail addressed to *user@wrotethebook.com* is redirected to *crab* for delivery. Of course, for *crab* to successfully deliver the mail, it must be properly configured as a mail server. The MX record is only part of the story. We look at configuring sendmail in Chapter 10.

The second MX record identifies *horseshoe* as a mail server for *wrotethebook.com* with a preference of 20. Preference numbers let you define alternate mail servers. The lower the preference number, the more desirable the server. Therefore, our two sample MX records say "send mail for the *wrotethebook.com* domain to *crab* first; if *crab* is unavailable, try sending the mail to *horseshoe*." Rather than relying on a single mail server, preference numbers allow you to create backup servers. If the main mail server is unreachable, the domain's mail is sent to one of the backups instead.

These sample MX records redirect mail addressed to *wrotethebook.com*, but mail addressed to *user@jerboas.wrotethebook.com* will still be sent directly to *jerboas. wrotethebook.com*—not to *crab* or *horseshoe*. This configuration allows simplified mail addressing in the form *user@wrotethebook.com* for those who want to take advantage of it, but it continues to allow direct mail delivery to individual hosts for those who wish to take advantage of that.

The first A record in this example defines the address for *localhost*. This is the opposite of the PTR entry in the *named.local* file. It allows users within the *wrotethebook. com* domain to enter the name *localhost* and have it resolved to the address 127.0.0.1 by the local name server.

The next A record defines the IP address for *crab*, which is the master server for this domain. This A record is followed by a CNAME record that defines *loghost* as an alias for *crab*.

rodent's A record is followed by an MX record and a CNAME record. (Note that the records that relate to a single host are grouped together, which is the most common structure used in zone file.) *rodent*'s MX record directs all mail addressed to *user@rodent.wrotethebook.com* to *crab*. This MX record is required because the MX records at the beginning of the zone file redirect mail only if it is addressed to *user@wrotethebook.com*. If you also want to redirect mail addressed to *rodent*, you need a "rodent-specific" MX record.

The name field of the CNAME record contains an alias for the official hostname. The official name, called the *canonical name*, is provided in the data field of the record. Because of these records, *crab* can be referred to by the name *loghost*, and *rodent* can be referred to as *mouse*. The *loghost* alias is a generic hostname used to direct syslogd output to *crab*.* Hostname aliases should *not* be used in other resource records.† For example, don't use an alias as the name of a mail server in an MX record. Use *only* the canonical (official) name that's defined in an A record.

Your zone file could be much larger than the sample file we've discussed, but it will contain essentially the same records. If you know the names and addresses of the hosts in your domain, you have most of the information necessary to create the named configuration.

Controlling the named Process

After you construct the *named.conf* file and the required zone files, start named. named is usually started at boot time from a startup script. On a Solaris 8 system, named is started by the */etc/init.d/inetsvc* script. On a Red Hat Linux system, the script that starts named is */etc/rc.d/init.d/named*. The Red Hat script can be run from the command prompt with optional arguments. For example, on a Red Hat system, the following command can be used to stop the name server:

    # /etc/rc.d/init.d/named stop

To resume name service, use the command:

    # /etc/rc.d/init.d/named start

Startup scripts work, but the named control (ndc) program is a more effective tool for managing the named process. It comes with BIND 8 and provides a variety of functions designed to help you manage named. BIND 9 has a similar tool named rndc. Table 8-3 lists the ndc options and the purpose of each.‡

---

* See Chapter 3 for a further discussion of generic hostnames.

† See Appendix C for additional information about using CNAME records in the zone data file.

‡ At this writing, the status, trace, and restart commands are not yet implemented for rndc.

Table 8-3. ndc options

Option	Function
status	Displays the process status of named.
dumpdb	Dumps the cache to *named_dump.db*.[a]
reload	Reloads the name server.
stats	Dumps statistics to *named.stats*.
trace	Turns on tracing to *named.run*.
notrace	Turns off tracing and closes *named.run*.
querylog	Toggles query logging, which logs each incoming query to syslogd.
start	Starts named.
stop	Stops named.
restart	Stops the current named process and starts a new one.

[a] This file is stored in the directory defined by the directory option in the *named.conf* file.

ndc options are simple to understand and easy to use. The following commands would stop, then restart the named process:

```
# ndc stop
# ndc start
new pid is 795
```

This command sequence assumes that there is some length of time between stopping the old named process and starting a new one. If you really want to quickly kill and restart the named process, use the restart option:

```
# ndc restart
new pid is 798
```

The first time you run named, watch for error messages. named logs errors to the *messages* file.[*] Once named is running to your satisfaction, use nslookup to query the name server to make sure it is providing the correct information.

Using nslookup

nslookup is a debugging tool provided as part of the BIND software package. It allows anyone to query a name server directly and retrieve any of the information known to the DNS system. It is helpful for determining if the server is running correctly and is properly configured, or for querying for information provided by remote servers.

---

[*] This file is found in */usr/adm/messages* on our Solaris system and in */var/log/messages* on our Red Hat system. It might be located somewhere else on your system; check your documentation.

The nslookup program is used to resolve queries either interactively or directly from the command line. Here is a command-line example of using nslookup to query for the IP address of a host:

```
% nslookup crab.wrotethebook.com
Server:   rodent.wrotethebook.com
Address:  172.16.12.2

Name:     crab.wrotethebook.com
Address:  172.16.12.1
```

Here, a user asks nslookup to provide the address of *crab.wrotethebook.com*. nslookup displays the name and address of the server used to resolve the query, and then it displays the answer to the query. This is useful, but nslookup is more often used interactively.

The real power of nslookup is seen in interactive mode. To enter interactive mode, type nslookup on the command line without any arguments. Terminate an interactive session by typing Ctrl-D (^D) or entering the exit command at the nslookup prompt. As an interactive session, the previous query shown is:

```
% nslookup
Default Server:  rodent.wrotethebook.com
Address:  172.16.12.2

> crab.wrotethebook.com
Server:   rodent.wrotethebook.com
Address:  172.16.12.2

Name:     crab.wrotethebook.com
Address:  172.16.12.1
> ^D
```

By default, nslookup queries for A records, but you can use the set type command to change the query to another resource record type or to the special query type ANY. ANY is used to retrieve all available resource records for the specified host.*

The following example checks MX records for *crab* and *rodent*. Note that once the query type is set to MX, it stays MX. It doesn't revert to the default A-type query. Another set type command is required to reset the query type.

```
% nslookup
Default Server:  rodent.wrotethebook.com
Address:  172.16.12.2

> set type=MX
> crab.wrotethebook.com
```

---

* "All available" records can vary based on the server answering the question. A server that is authoritative for the zone that contains the host's records responds with all records. A nonauthoritative server that has cached information about the host provides all of the records it has cached, which might not be every record the host owns.

```
Server:  rodent.wrotethebook.com
Address:  172.16.12.2

crab.wrotethebook.com      preference = 5, mail exchanger = crab.wrotethebook.com
crab.wrotethebook.com      inet address = 172.16.12.1

> rodent.wrotethebook.com
Server:  rodent.wrotethebook.com
Address:  172.16.12.2

rodent.wrotethebook.com     preference = 5, mail exchanger = rodent.wrotethebook.com
rodent.wrotethebook.com     inet address = 172.16.12.2
> exit
```

You can use the `server` command to control the server used to resolve queries. This is particularly useful for going directly to an authoritative server to check some information. The following example does just that. In fact, this example contains several interesting commands:

- First we set type=NS and get the NS records for the *zoo.edu* domain.

- From the information returned by this query, we select a server and use the `server` command to direct `nslookup` to use that server.

- Next, using the `set domain` command, we set the default domain to *zoo.edu*. `nslookup` uses this default domain name to expand the hostnames in its queries in the same way that the resolver uses the default domain name defined in *resolv. conf*.

- We reset the query type to ANY. If the query type is not reset, `nslookup` still queries for NS records.

- Finally, we query for information about the host *tiger.zoo.edu*. Because the default domain is set to *zoo.edu*, we simply enter *tiger* at the prompt.

Here's the example:

```
% nslookup
Default Server:  rodent.wrotethebook.com
Address:  172.16.12.2

> set type=NS
> zoo.edu
Server:  rodent.wrotethebook.com
Address:  172.16.12.2

Non-authoritative answer:
zoo.edu nameserver = NOC.ZOO.EDU
zoo.edu nameserver = NI.ZOO.EDU
zoo.edu nameserver = NAMESERVER.AGENCY.GOV
Authoritative answers can be found from:
NOC.ZOO.EDU     inet address = 172.28.2.200
NI.ZOO.EDU      inet address = 172.28.2.240
NAMESERVER.AGENCY.GOV inet address = 172.21.18.31
```

```
> server NOC.ZOO.EDU
Default Server:  NOC.ZOO.EDU
Address:  172.28.2.200

> set domain=zoo.edu
> set type=any
> tiger
Server:  NOC.ZOO.EDU
Address:  172.28.2.200

tiger.zoo.edu    inet address = 172.28.172.8
tiger.zoo.edu    preference = 10, mail exchanger = tiger.ZOO.EDU
tiger.zoo.edu    CPU=ALPHA OS=Unix
tiger.zoo.edu    inet address = 172.28.172.8, protocol = 6
         7 21 23 25 79
tiger.ZOO.EDU    inet address = 172.28.172.8
> exit
```

The final example shows how to download an entire domain from an authoritative server and examine it on your local system. The ls command requests a zone transfer and displays the contents of the zone it receives.* If the zone file is more than a few lines long, redirect the output to a file and use the view command to examine the contents of the file. (view sorts a file and displays it using the Unix more command.) The combination of ls and view is helpful when tracking down a remote hostname. In this example, the ls command retrieves the *big.com* zone and stores the information in *temp.file*. Then view is used to examine *temp.file*.

```
rodent% nslookup
Default Server:  rodent.wrotethebook.com
Address:  172.16.12.2

> server minerals.big.com
Default Server:  minerals.big.com
Address:  192.168.20.1

> ls big.com > temp.file
[minerals.big.com]
########
Received 406 records.
> view temp.file
 acmite                         192.168.20.28
 adamite                        192.168.20.29
 adelite                        192.168.20.11
 agate                          192.168.20.30
 alabaster                      192.168.20.31
 albite                         192.168.20.32
 allanite                       192.168.20.20
 altaite                        192.168.20.33
```

---

* For security reasons, many name servers do not respond to the ls command. See the allow-transfer option in Appendix C for information on how to limit access to zone transfers.

```
alum                        192.168.20.35
aluminum                    192.168.20.8
amaranth                    192.168.20.85
amethyst                    192.168.20.36
andorite                    192.168.20.37
apatite                     192.168.20.38
beryl                       192.168.20.23
--More--q
> exit
```

These examples show that nslookup allows you to:

- Query for any specific type of standard resource record
- Directly query the authoritative servers for a domain
- Get the entire contents of a domain into a file so you can view it

Use nslookup's help command to see its other features. Turn on debugging (with set debug) and examine the additional information this provides. As you play with this tool, you'll find many helpful features.

Summary

The Domain Name System (DNS) provides an important user service that should be used on every system connected to the Internet. The vast majority of Unix implementations of DNS are based on the Berkeley Internet Name Domain (BIND) software. BIND provides both a DNS client and a DNS server.

The BIND client issues name queries and is implemented as library routines. It is called the resolver. The resolver is configured in the *resolv.conf* file. All systems run the resolver.

The BIND server answers name queries and runs as a daemon. It is called named. named is configured by the *named.conf* file, which defines where the server gets the DNS database information and the type of server being configured. The server types are master, slave, and caching servers. Because all servers are caching servers, a single configuration often encompasses more than one server type.

The original DNS database source files are found on the master server. The DNS database file is called a zone file. The zone file is constructed from standard resource records (RRs) that are defined in RFCs. The RRs share a common structure and are used to define all DNS database information.

The DNS server can be tested using nslookup. This test tool is included with the BIND release.

In this chapter we have seen how to configure and test DNS. In the next chapter, we configure several other services.

## CHAPTER 9

In this chapter:

- The Network File System
- Sharing Unix Printers
- Using Samba to Share Resources with Windows
- Network Information Service
- DHCP
- Managing Distributed Servers
- Post Office Servers

Local Network Services

Now our attention turns to configuring local network servers. As with name service, these servers are not strictly required for the network to operate, but they provide services that are central to the network's purpose.

There are many network services—many more than can be covered in this chapter. Here we concentrate on servers that provide essential services for local clients. The services covered in this chapter are:

- The Network File System (NFS)
- The Line Printer Daemon (LPD) and the Line Printer (LP) service
- Windows file and print services (Samba)
- The Network Information Service (NIS)
- Dynamic Host Configuration Protocol (DHCP)
- The Post Office Protocol (POP)
- Internet Message Access Protocol (IMAP)

All of these software packages are designed to provide service to systems within your organization and are not intended to service outsiders. Essential services that are as important to external users as they are to in-house users, such as email, web service, and name service, are covered in separate chapters.

We begin our discussion of local network services with NFS, which is the server that provides file sharing on Unix networks.

The Network File System

The Network File System (NFS) allows directories and files to be shared across a network. It was originally developed by Sun Microsystems but is now supported by virtually all Unix and many non-Unix operating systems. Through NFS, users and programs can access files located on remote systems as if they were local files. In a perfect NFS environment, the user neither knows nor cares where files are actually stored.

NFS has several benefits:

- It reduces local disk storage requirements because a server can store a single copy of a directory that is fully accessible to everyone on the network.

- It simplifies central support tasks—files can be updated centrally yet be available throughout the network.

- It allows users to use familiar Unix commands to manipulate remote files instead of learning new commands. There is no need to use ftp or rcp to copy a file between hosts on the network; cp works fine.

There are two sides to NFS: a client side and a server side. The client is the system that uses the remote directories as if they were part of its local filesystem. The server is the system that makes the directories available for use. Attaching a remote directory to the local filesystem (a client function) is called *mounting* a directory. Offering a directory for remote access (a server function) is called *sharing* or *exporting* a directory.* Frequently, a system runs both the client and the server NFS software. In this section we'll look at how to configure a system to export and mount directories using NFS.

If you're responsible for an NFS server for a large site, you should take care in planning and implementing the NFS environment. This chapter describes how NFS is configured to run on a client and a server, but you may want more details to design an optimal NFS environment. For a comprehensive treatment, see *Managing NFS and NIS* by Hal Stern (O'Reilly & Associates).

NFS Daemons

The Network File System is run by several daemons, some performing client functions and some performing server functions. Before we discuss the NFS configuration, let's look at the function of the daemons that run NFS on a Solaris 8 system:

nfsd [*nservers*]

> The NFS daemon, nfsd, runs on NFS servers. This daemon services the client's NFS requests. The *nservers* option specifies how many daemons should be started.

mountd

> The NFS mount daemon, mountd, processes the clients' mount requests. NFS servers run the mount daemon.

nfslogd

> The NFS logging daemon, nfslogd, logs activity for exported filesystems. NFS servers run the logging daemon.

---

* Solaris uses the term *sharing*. Most other systems use the term *exporting*.

---

rquotad

> The remote quota server, rquotad, provides information about user quotas on remote filesystems that is then displayed by the quota command. The remote quota server is run on both clients and servers.

lockd

> The lock daemon, lockd, handles file lock requests. Both clients and servers run the lock daemon. Clients request file locks, and servers grant them.

statd

> The network status monitor daemon, statd, is required by lockd to provide monitoring services. In particular, it allows locks to be reset properly after a crash. Both clients and servers run statd.

On a Solaris 8 system, the daemons necessary to run NFS are found in the */usr/lib/nfs* directory. Most of these daemons are started at boot time by two scripts located in the */etc/init.d* directory, *nfs.client* and *nfs.server*. The *nfs.client* script starts the statd and lockd programs.[*] NFS server systems run those two daemons, plus the NFS server daemon (nfsd), the NFS logging daemon (nfslogd), and the mount server daemon (mountd). On Solaris systems, the *nfs.server* script starts mountd, nfslogd, and 16 copies of nfsd. Solaris systems do not normally start rquotad at boot time. Instead, rquotad is started by inetd, as this grep of the */etc/inetd.conf* file shows:

```
$ grep rquotad /etc/inetd.conf
rquotad/1   tli   rpc/datagram_v  wait root /usr/lib/nfs/rquotad  rquotad
```

Each system has its own technique for starting these daemons. If some of the daemons aren't starting, ensure your startup scripts and your *inetd.conf* file are correct.

Sharing Unix Filesystems

The first step in configuring a server is deciding which filesystems will be shared and what restrictions will be placed on them. Only filesystems that provide a benefit to the client should be shared. Before you share a filesystem, think about what purpose it will serve. Some common reasons for sharing filesystems are:

- To provide disk space to diskless clients
- To prevent unnecessary duplication of the same data on multiple systems
- To provide centrally supported programs and data
- To share data among users in a group

Once you've selected the filesystems you'll share, you must configure them for sharing using the appropriate commands for your system. The following section emphasizes the way this is done on Solaris systems. It is very different on Linux systems,

---

[*] Alternatively, the prefix *rpc.* may be used on the daemon names. For example, the Slackware Linux system uses the filename *rpc.nfsd* for the NFS daemon. Check your system's documentation.

which are covered later. Check your system's documentation to find out exactly how it implements NFS file sharing.

The share command

On Solaris systems, directories are exported using the share command.

A simplified syntax for the share command is:

```
share -F nfs [-o options] pathname
```

where *pathname* is the path of the directory the server is offering to share with its clients, and *options* are the access controls for that directory. The options are:

rw

The rw option grants read and write access to the shared filesystem. It can be specified in the form rw=*accesslist* to identify the systems that are granted this access. When used in this way, only the systems identified in the list are given access to the filesystem. If the access list is not provided with the rw option, all hosts are given read/write access to the filesystem.

ro

This option limits access to read-only. It also can be specified with an access list, e.g., ro=*accesslist*. When the access list is included, only the systems on the list have access and that access is limited to read-only. If the access list is not provided with the ro option, all hosts are given read-only access to the filesystem, which is the default if no options are specified.

aclok

This option grants full access to all clients, which could open up a security hole. This option is documented on the Solaris system, but it should never be used. It is intended to provide backward compatibility with a version of NFS that no longer exists.

anon=*uid*

Defines the UID used for users who do not provide a valid user ID.

index=*file*

Tells NFS to use a web-style index file instead of a directory listing for this filesystem.

log[=*tag*]

Enable logging. If an optional tag is specified, it must match a tag defined in the */etc/nfs/nfslog.conf* file.

nosub

Do not allow clients to mount subdirectories. The default is sub, which allows subdirectories to be mounted.

nosuid

> Do not allow clients to create setuid or setgid files on this filesystem. The default is suid, which allows clients to create setuid and setgid files.

public

> Use the public file handle for this filesystem.

root=*accesslist*

> This option allows the root users from the systems specified by the access list to have root access to the filesystem.

sec=*type*

> Defines the type of authentication used for accessing this filesystem. *type* is a colon-separated list of NFS security modes. For access to be successful, the client must support at least one of the security modes identified in the *type* list. The possible *type* values are:

> sys

>> Use clear-text user IDs and group IDs to control access to the filesystem. This is the same as traditional Unix file permissions, which are granted based on UID and GID, with the exception that the UID and GID are passed over the network and the server must trust the remote source.

> dh

>> Use Diffie-Hellman public key cryptography for authentication.

> krb4

>> Use the Kerberos Version 4 for authentication.

> none

>> Do not use authentication. When no authentication is used, all users access the filesystem as user *nobody*.

window=*seconds*

> Defines the maximum lifetime in seconds that the NFS server will permit for a dh or krb4 authentication. The server rejects any security credentials that have a longer lifetime value. *seconds* defaults to 30000.

A few of the options contain an access list. The access list is a colon-separated list that identifies computers by individual hostnames, individual IP addresses, or by the domain, network, or NIS netgroup to which the hosts belong. The syntax of these list elements is:

hostname

> This is any hostname that resolves to an IP address. It can be a fully qualified name or just the hostname as long as the name as written will resolve to an IP address. If the hostname can be found in the local host table, the short name can be used. If the name must be resolved by DNS, the fully qualified hostname, with its domain name attached, should be specified. However, fully qualified

names should not be used if your system does not use DNS, i.e., if your system relies exclusively on NIS.

address

An IP address in dotted decimal format can be used.

netgroup

If an NIS netgroup name is used, the option applies to every system within that netgroup. Netgroup names look identical to unqualified hostnames and are easy to confuse with hostnames. Netgroup names should only be used if your system uses NIS.

.domain

A domain name is used to apply the option to every system within that domain. When a domain name is used, it is preceded by a dot (.). Thus *.wrotethebook. com* applies to every system in the *wrotethebook.com* domain. Domain names should be used only if your server uses DNS.

@network[/prefix]

A network address is used to apply an option to every system within the network. When a network address is used, it must be preceded by an at-sign (@). An optional network prefix can be used with the address to clearly define the network mask.

The rw and ro options can be combined to grant different levels of access to different clients. For example:

```
share -F nfs -o rw=crab:horseshoe ro   /usr/man
share -F nfs -o rw=rodent:crab:horseshoe:jerboas   /export/home/research
```

The first share command grants read and write access to *crab* and *rodent,* and read-only access to all other clients. On the other hand, the second share command grants read/write access to *rodent*, *crab*, *horseshoe*, and *jerboas*, and no access of any kind to any other client.

The share command does not survive a boot. Put the share commands in the */etc/dfs/ dfstab* file to make sure that the filesystems continue to be offered to your clients even if the system reboots. Here is a sample *dfstab* file containing our two share commands:

```
% cat /etc/dfs/dfstab
#    place share(1M) commands here for automatic execution
#    on entering init state 3.
#
#    share [-F fstype] [ -o options] [-d "<text>"] <pathname> [resource]
#    .e.g.,
#    share  -F nfs  -o rw=engineering  -d "home dirs"  /export/home2
share -F nfs -o rw=crab:horseshoe ro  /usr/man
share -F nfs -o rw=rodent:crab:horseshoe:jerboas  /export/home/research
```

The share command, the *dfstab* file, and even the terminology "share" are Solaris-specific. Most Unix systems say that they are *exporting* files, instead of *sharing* files, when they are offering files to NFS clients. Furthermore, they do not use the *share* command or the *dfstab* file; instead, they offer filesystems through the */etc/exports* file. Linux is an example of such a system.

The /etc/exports file

The */etc/exports* file is the NFS server configuration file for Linux systems. It controls which files and directories are exported, which hosts can access them, and what kinds of access are allowed. A sample */etc/exports* file might contain these entries:

```
/usr/man        crab(rw) horseshoe(rw)  (ro)
/usr/local      (ro)
/home/research  rodent(rw) crab(rw) horseshoe(rw) jerboas(rw)
```

This sample file says that:

- */usr/man* can be mounted by any client, but it can be written to only by *crab* and *horseshoe*. Other clients have read-only access.

- */usr/local* can be mounted by any client, with read-only access.

- */home/research* can be mounted only by the hosts *rodent*, *crab*, *horseshoe*, and *jerboas*. These four hosts have read/write access.

The options used in each of the entries in the */etc/exports* file determine what kinds of access are allowed. The information derived from the sample file is based on the options specified on each line in the file. The general format of the entries is as follows:

```
directory [host(option)]...
```

directory names the directory or file that is available for export. The *host* is the name of the client granted access to the exported directory, while the *option* specifies the type of access being granted.

In the sample */etc/exports* file shown above, the *host* value is either the name of a single client or it is blank. When a single hostname is used, access is granted to the individual client. If no host value is specified, the directory is exported to everyone. Like Solaris, Linux also accepts values for domains, networks, and netgroups, although the syntax is slightly different. Valid host values are:

- Individual hostnames such as *crab* or *crab.wrotethebook.com*.

- Domain wildcards such as **wrotethebook.com* for every host in the *wrotethebook.com* domain.

- IP address/address mask pairs such as 172.16.12.0/255.255.255.0 for every host with an address that begins with 172.16.12.

- Net groups such as *@group1*.

Notice that in Linux, domain names begin with an asterisk (*), instead of the dot used in Solaris. Also note that the at-sign begins a netgroup name, whereas in Solaris the at-sign is used at the beginning of a network address.

The options used in the sample */etc/exports* file are:

ro

> Read-only prevents NFS clients from writing to this directory. Attempts by clients to write to a read-only directory fail with the message "Read-only filesystem" or "Permission denied." If ro is specified without a client hostname, all clients are granted read-only access.

rw

> Read/write permits clients to read and write to this directory. When specified without hostname, all clients are granted read/write access. If a hostname is specified, only the named host is given read/write permission.

Although specific hosts are granted read/write access to some of these directories, the access granted to individual users of those systems is controlled by standard Unix user, group, and world file permissions based on the user's user ID (UID) and group ID (GID). NFS trusts that a remote host has authenticated its users and assigned them valid UIDs and GIDs. Exporting files grants the client system's users the same access to the files they would have if they directly logged into the server. This assumes, of course, that both the client and the server have assigned exactly the same UIDs and GIDs to the same users, which is not always the case. If both the client and the server assign the same UID to a given user, for example, if Craig is assigned 501 on both systems, then both systems properly identify Craig and grant him appropriate access to his files. On the other hand, if the client assigns Craig a UID of 501 and the server has assigned that UID to Michael, the server will grant Craig access to Michael's files as if Craig owned those files. NFS provides several tools to deal with the problems that arise because of mismatched UIDs and GIDs.

One obvious problem is dealing with the root account. It is very unlikely that you want people with root access to your clients to also have root access to your server. By default, NFS prevents this with the root_squash setting, which maps requests that contain the root UID and GID to the *nobody* UID and GID. Thus if someone is logged into a client as root, they are only granted world permissions on the server. You can undo this with the no_root_squash setting, but no_root_squash opens a potential security hole.

Map other UIDs and GIDs to *nobody* with the squash_uids, squash_gids, and all_squash options. all_squash maps every user of a client system to the user *nobody*. squash_uids and squash_gids map specific UIDs and GIDs. For example:

```
/pub          (ro,all_squash)
/usr/local/pub (squash_uids=0-50,squash_gids=0-50)
```

The first entry exports the */pub* directory with read-only access to every client. It limits every user of those clients to the world permissions granted to *nobody*, meaning that the only files the users can read are those that have world read permission.

The second entry exports */usr/local/pub* to every client with default read/write permission. The squash_uid and squash_gid options in the example show that a range of

UIDs and GIDs can be specified in some options.* A single UID or GID can be defined with these options, but it is frequently useful to affect a range of values with a single command. In the example we prevent users from accessing the directory with a UID or GID that is 50 or less. These low numbers are usually assigned to non-user accounts. For example, on our Linux system, UID 10 is assigned to *uucp*. Attempting to write a file as *uucp* would cause the file to be written with the owner mapped to *nobody*. Thus the user *uucp* would be able to write to the */usr/local/pub* directory only if that directory had world write permission.

It is also possible to map every user from a client to a specific user ID or group ID. The anonuid and anongid options provide this capability. These options are most useful when the client has only one user and does not assign that user a UID or GID, for example, in the case of a Microsoft Windows PC running NFS. PCs generally have only one user and they don't use UIDs or GIDs. To map the user of a PC to a valid user ID and group ID, enter a line like this in the */etc/exports* file:

```
/home/alana  giant(all_squash,anonuid=1001,anongid=1001)
```

In this example, the hostname of Alana's PC is *giant*. The entry grants that client read/write access to the directory */home/alana*. The all_squash option maps every request from that client to a specific UID, but this time, instead of *nobody*, it maps to the UID and the GID defined by the anonuid and anongid options. Of course, for this to work correctly, 1001:1001 should be the UID and GID pair assigned to *alana* in the */etc/passwd* file.

A single mapping is sufficient for a PC, but it might not handle all of the mapping needed for a Unix client. Unix clients assign their users UIDs and GIDs. Problems occur if those differ from the UIDs and GIDs assigned to those same users on the NFS server. Use the map_static option to point to a file that maps the UIDs and GIDs for a specific client. For example:

```
/export/oscon oscon(map_static=/etc/nfs/oscon.map)
```

This entry says that the */export/oscon* directory is exported to the client *oscon* with read/write permission. The map_static option points to a file on the server named */etc/nfs/oscon.map* that maps the UIDs and GIDs used on *oscon* to those used on the server. The *oscon.map* file might contain the following entries:

```
# UID/GID mapping for client oscon
# remote    local    comment
uid 0-50     -      #squash these
gid 0-50     -      #squash these
uid 100-200   1000    #map 100-200 to 1000-1100
gid 100-200   1000    #map 100-200 to 1000-1100
uid 501     2001    #map individual user
gid 501     2001    #map individual user
```

---

* Of the eight options discussed in this section, three, squash_uid, squash_gid, and map_static, map a range of UIDs and GIDs. These three options are not available in the kernel-level NFS (knfsd) used on some Linux systems. Mapping for knfsd must be done with the other options.

The first two lines map the UIDs and GIDs from 0 to 50 to the user *nobody*. The next two lines map all of the client UIDs and GIDs in the range of 100 to 200 to corresponding numbers in the range of 1000 to 1100 on the server. In other words, 105 on the client maps to 1005 on the server. This is the most common type of entry. On most systems, existing UIDs and GIDs have been assigned sequentially. Often, several systems have assigned the UIDs and GIDs sequentially from 101 to different users in a completely uncoordinated manner. This entry maps the users on *oscon* to UIDs and GIDs starting at 1000. Another file might map the 100 to 200 entries of another client to UIDs and GIDs starting at 2000. A third file might map yet another client to 3000. This type of entry allows the server to coordinate UIDs and GIDs where no coordination exists. The last two lines map an individual user's UID and GID. This is less commonly required, but it is possible.

The exportfs command

After defining the directories in the */etc/exports* file, run the exportfs command to process the *exports* file and to build */var/lib/nfs/xtab*. The *xtab* file contains information about the currently exported directories, and it is the file that mountd reads when processing client mount requests. To process all of the entries in the */etc/exports* file, run exportfs with the -a command-line option:

```
# exportfs -a
```

This command, which exports everything in the *exports* file, is normally run during the boot from a startup script. To force changes in the */etc/exports* file to take effect without rebooting the system, use the -r argument:

```
# exportfs -r
```

The -r switch synchronizes the contents of the *exports* file and the *xtab* file. Items that have been added to the *exports* file are added to the *xtab* file, and items that have been deleted are removed from *xtab*.

The exportfs command can export a directory that is not listed in the */etc/exports* file. For example, to temporarily export */usr/local* to the client *fox* with read/write permission, enter this command:

```
# exportfs fox:/usr/local -o rw
```

After the client has completed its work with the temporarily exported filesystem, the directory is removed from the export list with the -u option, as shown:

```
# exportfs -u fox:/usr/local
```

The -u option can be combined with the -a option to completely shut down all exports without terminating the NFS daemon:

```
# exportfs -ua
```

Once the server exports or shares the appropriate filesystems, the clients can mount and use those filesystems. The next section looks at how an NFS client system is configured.

Mounting Remote Filesystems

Some basic information is required before you can decide which NFS directories to mount on your system. You need to know which servers are connected to your network and which directories are available from those servers. A directory cannot be mounted unless it is first exported by a server.

Your network administrator is a good source for this information. The administrator can tell you what systems are providing NFS service, what directories they are exporting, and what these directories contain. If you are the administrator of an NFS server, you should develop this type of information for your users. See Chapter 4 for advice on planning and distributing network information.

On Solaris and Linux systems, you can also obtain information about the shared directories directly from the servers by using the showmount command. The NFS servers are usually the same centrally supported systems that provide other services such as mail and DNS. Select a likely server and query it with the command showmount -e *hostname*. In response to this command, the server lists the directories that it exports and the conditions applied to their export.

For example, a showmount -e query to *jerboas* produces the following output:

```
% showmount -e jerboas
export list for jerboas:
/usr/man            (everyone)
/home/research      rodent,crab,limulus,horseshoe
/usr/local          (everyone)
```

The export list shows the NFS directories exported by *jerboas* as well as who is allowed to access those directories. From this list, *rodent*'s administrator may decide to mount any of the directories offered by *jerboas*. Our imaginary administrator decides to:

1. Mount */usr/man* from *jerboas* instead of maintaining the manpages locally.
2. Mount */home/research* to more easily share files with other systems in the research group.
3. Mount the centrally maintained programs in */usr/local*.

These selections represent some of the most common motivations for mounting NFS directories:

- Saving disk space
- Sharing files with other systems
- Maintaining common files centrally

The extent to which you use NFS is a personal choice. Some people prefer the greater personal control you get from keeping files locally, while others prefer the convenience offered by NFS. Your site may have guidelines for how NFS should be used, which directories should be mounted, and which files should be centrally maintained. Check with your network administrator if you're unsure about how NFS is used at your site.

The mount command

A client must mount a shared directory before using it. "Mounting" the directory attaches it to the client's filesystem hierarchy. Only directories offered by the servers can be mounted, but any part of the offered directory, such as a subdirectory or a file, can be mounted.

NFS directories are mounted using the mount command. The general structure of the mount command is:

```
mount hostname:remote-directory local-directory
```

The *hostname* identifies an NFS server, and the *remote-directory* identifies all or part of a directory offered by that server. The mount command attaches that remote directory to the client's filesystem using the directory name provided for *local-directory*. The client's local directory, called the mount point, must be created before mount is executed. Once the mount is completed, files located in the remote directory can be accessed through the local directory exactly as if they were local files.

For example, assume that *jerboas.wrotethebook.com* is an NFS server and that it shares the files shown in the previous section. Further assume that the administrator of *rodent* wants to access the */home/research* directory. The administrator simply creates a local */home/research* directory and mounts the remote */home/research* directory offered by *jerboas* on this newly created mount point:

```
# mkdir /home/research
# mount jerboas:/home/research /home/research
```

In this example, the local system knows to mount an NFS filesystem because the remote directory is preceded by a hostname and NFS is the default network filesystem for this client. NFS is the most common default network filesystem. If your client system does not default to NFS, specify NFS directly on the mount command line. On a Solaris 8 system, the -F switch is used to identify the filesystem type:

```
# mount -F nfs jerboas:/home/research /home/research
```

On a Linux system the -t switch is used:

```
# mount -t nfs jerboas:/home/research /home/research
```

Once a remote directory is mounted, it stays attached to the local filesystem until it is explicitly dismounted or the local system reboots. To dismount a directory, use the umount command. On the umount command line, specify either the local or remote name of the directory that is to be dismounted. For example, the administrator of *rodent* can dismount the remote *jerboas:/home/research* filesystem from the local */home/research* mount point, with either:

```
# umount /home/research
```

or:

```
# umount jerboas:/home/research
```

Booting also dismounts NFS directories. Because systems frequently wish to mount the same filesystems every time they boot, Unix provides a system for automatically remounting after a boot.

The vfstab and fstab files

Unix systems use the information provided in a special table to remount all types of filesystems, including NFS directories, after a system reboot. The table is a critical part of providing users consistent access to software and files, so care should be taken whenever it is modified. Two different files with two different formats are used for this purpose by the different flavors of Unix. Linux and BSD systems use the */etc/fstab* file, and Solaris, our System V example, uses the */etc/vfstab* file.

The format of the NFS entries in the Solaris *vfstab* file is:

```
filesystem - mountpoint nfs - yes options
```

The various fields in the entry must appear in the order shown and be separated by whitespace. The items not in italics (both dashes and the words nfs and yes) are keywords that must appear exactly as shown. *filesystem* is the name of the directory offered by the server, *mountpoint* is the pathname of the local mount point, and *options* are the mount options discussed below. A sample NFS *vfstab* entry is:

```
jerboas:/home/research - /home/research nfs - yes rw,soft
```

This entry mounts the NFS filesystem *jerboas:/home/research* on the local mount point */home/research*. The filesystem is mounted with the rw and soft options set. We previously discussed the commonly used read/write (rw) and read-only (ro) options, and there are many more NFS options. The NFS mount options available on Solaris systems are:

remount
:   If the filesystem is already mounted read-only, remount the filesystem as read/write.

soft
:   If the server fails to respond, return an error and don't retry the request.

timeo=*n*
:   Defines the number of seconds to wait for a timeout before issuing an error.

hard

> If the server fails to respond, retry until it does respond. This is the default.

bg

> Do the retries in background mode, which allows the boot to proceed.

fg

> Do the retries in foreground mode. This option could hang the boot process while the mount is being retried. For this reason, fg is used primarily for debugging.

intr

> Allow a keyboard interrupt to kill a process that is hung waiting for the server to respond. Hard-mounted filesystems can become hung because the client retries forever, even if the server is down. This is a default.

nointr

> Don't allow keyboard interrupts. In general, this is a bad idea.

nosuid

> Do not allow an executable stored on the mounted filesystem to run setuid. This improves security but may limit utility.

acdirmax=*n*

> Cache directory attributes for no more than *n* seconds. The default is to hold cache values for a maximum of 60 seconds. Repeated requests for filesystem attributes is one of the leading contributors to NFS traffic. Caching this information helps to reduce the traffic.

acdirmin=*n*

> Cache directory attributes for at least *n* seconds. The default is 30 seconds.

acregmax=*n*

> Cache file attributes for no more than *n* seconds. The default is 60 seconds.

acregmin=*n*

> Cache file attributes for at least *n* seconds. The default is 3 seconds.

actimeo=*n*

> Sets a single value for acdirmax, acdirmin, acregmax, and acregmin.

grpid

> Use the group ID of the parent directory when creating new files. If this option is not set, the effective GID of the calling process is used.

noac

> Do not cache information. The default is to use caching, which can be specified with the ac option.

port=*n*

> Identifies the IP port number used by the server.

`posix`

> Use POSIX standards for the filesystem. POSIX is a wide-ranging Unix interoper-ability standard that includes many standards for filesystems, such as the maximum length of filenames and how file locks are set.

`proto=protocol`

> Specifies the transport protocol that will be used by NFS.

`public`

> Use the public file handle when connecting to the NFS server.

`quota`

> Use quota to enforce user quotas on this filesystem.

`noquota`

> Do not use quota to enforce user quotas on this filesystem.

`retrans=n`

> Defines the number of times NFS will retransmit when a connectionless transport protocol is used.

`retry=n`

> Defines the number of times a mount attempt will be retried. The default is to retry 10,000 times.

`rsize=n`

> Defines the size of the read buffer as *n* bytes. The default for NFS version 3 is 32,768 bytes.

`sec=type`

> Specifies the type of security used for NFS transactions. The type values supported on the Solaris 8 mount command are the same as those listed for the share command: sys, dh, krb4, or none.

`wsize=n`

> Sets the size of the write buffer to *n* bytes. The default is 32768 bytes for NFS version 3.

`vers=version`

> Specifies the version of NFS that should be used for this mount. By default, the system automatically selects the latest version supported by both the client and the server.

On the Solaris system, the filesystems defined in the *vfstab* file are mounted by a `mountall` command located in a startup file. On Linux systems, the startup file contains a `mount` command with the -a flag set, which causes Linux to mount all filesystems listed in *fstab*.[*] The format of NFS entries in the */etc/fstab* file is:

```
filesystem mountpoint nfs options
```

---

[*] Red Hat Linux uses a special script, */etc/init.d/netfs*, just for mounting all of the different networked filesystems, which include NFS.

The fields must appear in the order shown and must be separated by whitespace. The keyword nfs is required for NFS filesystems. *filesystem* is the name of the directory being mounted. *mountpoint* is the pathname of the local mount point. *options* are any of the Linux mount options.

Linux uses most of the same NFS mount options as Solaris. rsize, wsize, timeo, retrans, acregmin, acregmax, acdirmin, acdirmax, actimeo, retry, port, bg, fg, soft, hard, intr, nointr, ac, noac, and posix are all options that Linux has in common with Solaris. In addition to these, Linux uses:

mountport=*n*
> Defines the port to be used by mountd.

mounthost=*name*
> Identifies the server running mountd.

mountprog=*n*
> Defines the RPC program number used by mountd on the remote host.

mountvers=*n*
> Defines the RPC version number used by mountd on the remote host.

nfsprog=*n*
> Defines the RPC program number used by nfsd on the remote host.

nfsvers=*n*
> Defines the RPC version number used by nfsd on the remote host.

namlen=*n*
> Defines the maximum length of the filenames supported by the remote server.

nocto
> Do not retrieve attributes when creating a file. The default is to retrieve the attributes, which can be specified with the cto option.

tcp
> Specifies that NFS should use TCP as its transport protocol.

udp
> Specifies that NFS should use UDP as its transport protocol.

nolock
> Prevents the system from starting lockd. The default is to run lockd, which can be requested with the lock option.

Finally, there are several options that are not specific to NFS and can be used on the mount command for any type of filesystem. Table 9-1 lists the common mount options used on Linux systems.

Table 9-1. Common mount options

Option	Function
async	Use asynchronous file I/O, which acknowledges writes as soon as they are received to improve performance.
auto	Mount when the -a option is used.
dev	Allow character and block special devices on the filesystem.
exec	Permit execution of files from the filesystem.
noauto	Don't mount with the -a option.
nodev	Don't allow character and block special devices on the filesystem.
noexec	Don't allow execution of files from the filesystem.
nosuid	Don't allow programs stored on the filesystem to run setuid or setgid.
nouser	Only root can mount the filesystem.
remount	Remount a mounted filesystem with new options.
ro	Mount the filesystem read-only.
rw	Mount the filesystem read/write.
suid	Allow programs to run setuid or setgid.
sync	Use synchronous filesystem I/O, which acknowledges writes only after they are written to disk to improve reliability.
user	Permit ordinary users to mount the filesystem.
atime	Update inode access time for every access.
noatime	Do not update inode access time.
defaults	Set the rw, suid, dev, exec, auto, nouser, and async options.

A grep of *fstab* shows sample NFS entries.[*]

```
% grep nfs /etc/fstab
jerboas:/usr/spool/mail   /usr/spool/mail   nfs rw   0 0
jerboas:/usr/man          /usr/man          nfs rw   0 0
jerboas:/home/research    /home/research    nfs rw   0 0
```

The grep shows that there are three NFS filesystems contained in the */etc/fstab* file. The mount -a command in the boot script remounts these three directories every time the system boots.

The *vfstab* and *fstab* files are the most common methods used for mounting filesystems at boot time. There is another technique that automatically mounts NFS filesystems, but only when they are actually needed. It is called automounter.

NFS Automounter

An *automounter* is a feature available on most NFS clients. Two varieties of automounters are in widespread use: autofs and amd. The Automounter Filesystem

---

[*] grep is used because the *fstab* file contains other information not related to NFS.

(autofs) is the automounter implementation that comes with Solaris and Linux, and it is the implementation we cover in this section. Automounter Daemon (amd) is available for many Unix versions and is included with Linux but not with Solaris. To find out more about amd, see *Linux NFS and Automounter Administration* written by Erez Zadok, the amd maintainer. In this section, automounter and automounter daemon refer to the version of autofs that comes with Solaris 8.

The automounter configuration files are called *maps*. Three basic map types are used to define the automounter filesystem:

Master map

> The configuration file read by automount. It lists all of the other maps that are used to define the autofs filesystem.

Direct map

> A configuration file that lists the mount points, pathnames, and options of filesystems that are to be mounted by the automounter daemon (automountd).

Indirect map

> A configuration file that contains pathnames and "relative" mount points. The mount points are relative to a directory path declared in the master map. How indirect maps are used will become clear in the examples.

On Solaris systems the automounter daemon (automountd) and the automount command are started by the */etc/init.d/autofs* script. The script is run with the start option to start automounter, i.e., autofs start. It is run with the stop option to shut down automounter. automount and automountd are two distinct, separate programs. automountd runs as a daemon and dynamically mounts filesystems when they are needed. automount processes the *auto_master* file to determine the filesystems that can be dynamically mounted.

To use automounter, first configure the */etc/auto_master* file. Entries in the *auto_master* file have this format:

```
mount-point     map-name        options
```

The Solaris system comes with a default *auto_master* file preconfigured. Customize the file for your configuration. Comment out the +auto_master entry unless you run NIS+ or NIS and your servers offer a centrally maintained *auto_master* map. Also ignore the /xfn entry, which is for creating a federated (composite) name service. Add an entry for your direct map. In the example, this is called auto_direct. Here is */etc/auto_master* after our modifications:

```
# Master map for automounter
#
#+auto_master
#/xfn           -xfn
/net            -hosts          -nosuid
/home           auto_home
/-              auto_direct
```

All lines that begin with a sharp sign (#) are comments, including the +auto_master and /xfn lines we commented out. The first real entry in the file specifies that the shared filesystems offered by every NFS server listed in the /etc/hosts file are automatically mounted under the /net directory. A subdirectory is created for each server under /net using the server's hostname. For example, assume that *jerboas* is listed in the *hosts* file and that it exports the /usr/local directory. This auto_master entry automatically makes that remote directory available on the local host as /net/jerboas/usr/local.

The second entry automatically mounts the home directories listed in the /etc/auto_home map under the /home directory. A default /etc/auto_home file is provided with the Solaris system. Comment out the +auto_home entry found in the default file. It is used only if you run NIS+ or NIS and your servers offer a centrally maintained *auto_home* map. Add entries for individual user home directories or for all home directories from specific servers. Here is a modified *auto_home* map:

```
# Home directory map for automounter
#
#+auto_home
craig           crab:/export/home/craig
*               horseshoe:/export/home/&
```

The first entry mounts the /export/home/craig filesystem shared by *crab* on the local mount point /home/craig. The *auto_home* map is an indirect map, so the mount point specified in the map (craig) is relative to the /home mount point defined in the *auto_master* map. The second entry mounts every home directory found in the /export/home filesystem offered by *horseshoe* to a "like-named" mount point on the local host. For example, assume that *horseshoe* has two home directories, /export/home/daniel and /export/home/kristin. Automounter makes them both available on the local host as /home/daniel and /home/kristin. The asterisk (*) and the ampersand (&) are wildcard characters used specifically for this purpose in autofs maps.

That's it for the *auto_home* map. Refer back to the *auto_master* map. The third and final entry in the /etc/auto_master file is:

```
/-              auto_direct
```

We added this entry for our direct map. The special mount point /- means that the map name refers to a direct map. Therefore the real mount points are found in the direct map file. We named our direct map file /etc/auto_direct. There is no default direct map file; you must create it from scratch. The file we created is:

```
# Direct map for automounter
#
/home/research  -rw         jerboas:/home/research
/usr/man        -ro,soft  horseshoe,crab,jerboas:/usr/share/man
```

The format of entries in a direct map file is:

```
mount-point     options     remote filesystem
```

Our sample file contains two typical entries. The first entry mounts the remote file-system */home/research* offered by the server *jerboas* on the local mount point */home/research*. It is mounted read/write. The second entry mounts the manpages read-only with a "soft" timeout.* Note that three servers are specified for the manpages in a comma-separated list. If a server is unavailable or fails to respond within the soft timeout period, the client asks the next server in the list. This is one of the nice features of automounter.

Automounter has four key features: the -hosts map, wildcarding, automounting, and multiple servers. The -hosts map makes every exported filesystem from every server listed in the */etc/hosts* file available to the local user. The wildcard characters make it very easy to mount every directory from a remote server to a like-named directory on the local system. Automounting goes hand-in-glove with these two features because only the filesystems that are actually used are mounted. While -hosts and wildcards make a very large number of filesystems available to the local host, automounting limits the filesystems that are actually mounted to those that are needed. The last feature, multiple servers, improves the reliability of NFS by removing the dependence on a single server.

Sharing Unix Printers

Unix uses NFS to share files; it uses two different tools, the *Line Printer Daemon* (lpd) and the *Line Printer* (lp) printer service, to provide printer services for local and remote users. lpd is used on BSD systems and most Linux systems. lp is used on System V systems, including Solaris 8. In the following sections we discuss both tools.

Line Printer Daemon

lpd manages the printer spool area and the print queues. lpd is started at boot time from a startup script. It is generally included in the startup of Linux and BSD systems by default, so you might not need to add it to your startup script. For example, it is started by the */etc/init.d/lpd* script on a Red Hat Linux system.

The printcap file

When lpd starts, it reads the */etc/printcap* file to find out about the printers available for its use. The *printcap* file defines the printers and their characteristics. Configuring a *printcap* file is the scariest part of setting up a Unix print server. (Don't worry. As we'll see later with the Solaris admintool, most systems provide a GUI tool for configuring printers.) The *printcap* file scares system administrators because the

---

* See the description of NFS mount options earlier in this chapter.

parser that reads the file is very finicky, and the syntax of the parameters in the file is terse and arcane. Most parser problems can be avoided by following these rules:

- Start each entry with a printer name that begins in the first column. No white-space should precede the first printer name. Multiple printer names can be used if they are separated by pipe characters (|). One entry must have the printer name *lp*. If you have more than one printer on the server, assign *lp* to the "default" printer.

- Continue printer entries across multiple lines by escaping the newline character at the end of the line with a backslash (\) and beginning the following line with a tab. Take care that no blank space comes after the backslash. The character after the backslash must be the newline character.

- Every field, other than the printer name, begins and ends with a colon (:). The character before the backslash on a continued line is a colon and the first charac-ter after the tab on the continuation line is a colon.

- Begin comments with a sharp sign (#).

The configuration parameters used in a *printcap* file describe the characteristics of the printer. These characteristics are called "capabilities" in the *printcap* documenta-tion, but really they are the printer characteristics that lpd needs to know in order to communicate with the printer. Parameters are identified by names that are two char-acters long and are usually assigned a value. The syntax of the parameters varies slightly depending on the type of value they are assigned. Parameters come in three different flavors:

Boolean
> All *printcap* Boolean values default to "false." Specifying a Boolean enables its function. Booleans are specified simply by entering the two-character parameter name in the file. For example, :rs: enables security for remote users.

Numeric
> Some parameters are assigned numeric values. For example, :br#9600: sets the baud rate for a serial printer.

String
> Some parameters use string values. For example, :rp=laser: defines the name of a remote printer.

A glance at the manpage shows that there are many *printcap* parameters. Thank-fully, you'll never need to use most of them. Most printer definitions are fairly sim-ple, and most *printcap* files are small.

Print servers usually have only one or two directly attached printers; any other print-ers defined in *printcap* are probably remote printers. Most, if not all, of the printers defined in a client's *printcap* are remote printers.

```
#
# Remote LaserWriter
```

```
#
lw:\
    :lf=/var/adm/lpd-errs:\
    :lp=:rm=horseshoe:rp=lw:\
    :sd=/var/spool/lpd-lw:
```

The *lw* printer in this sample *printcap* file is a remote printer. The lf parameter points to the log file used to log status and error messages. The remote machine to which the printer is attached is defined by the :rm=horseshoe: parameter, and the name of the remote printer on that machine is defined by the :rp=lw: parameter. Multiple printers can use the same log file. The final parameter, sd, defines the spool directory. Each printer has its own unique spool directory. Defining the remote printer in the client's *printcap* file is all that is needed to configure an LPD client.

Writing a *printcap* from scratch is unnecessary. At most, you will need to tweak the *printcap* configuration for your own special needs. All modern Unix systems have printer configuration tools that will build the basic *printcap* for you. The Red Hat printconf-gui tool is an example.

Launch the printer configuration tool on a Red Hat 7.2 system running the Gnome desktop by selecting Printer Configuration from the System menu. When the printconf-gui window opens, click the New button to add a printer to the *printcap* file. The New button launches a printer configuration wizard. Use the first page of the wizard to define the printer name and the queue type. Enter the printer name, for example *lw*, in the Queue Name box. Then select the Queue Type. Red Hat 7.2 offers five choices:

Local Printer
> Use this type to define a directly attached printer. When Local Printer is selected, the wizard asks you to select the printer port to which the printer is attached. The default is */dev/lp0*.

Unix Printer
> Use this type to define a printer located on a remote server that is accessed via the LPD protocol. When Unix Printer is selected, the wizard asks for the name of the remote server and the name of the printer on the remote server.

Windows Printer
> Use this type to define a remote printer that is accessed via the SMB protocol. When Windows Printer is selected, the wizard asks for the IP address of the remote server, the SMB workgroup, and the name of the remote printer, which it calls a *share name*. The wizard also allows a username and password to be input in case they are required for access to the printer. Printer sharing through SMB is is covered in detail later in this chapter.

Novell Printer
> Use this type to define a remote printer accessed via the NetWare protocols. When Novell Printer is selected, the wizard asks for the name of the server and the printer on that server. A username and password can also be entered if they

---

are required for printer access. To communicate with a Novell printer you must have the NetWare protocols installed on your system.

JetDirect Printer

Use this type to define a network-attached printer that uses the JetDirect protocol. Primarily, this protocol is used on HP printers that contain a built-in Ethernet interface and that connect directly to the Ethernet cable without going through a server. When JetDirect is selected, the wizard asks for the IP address of the printer and gives you a chance to enter a port number in case the printer is not configured to use the standard JetDirect port.

Finally, the wizard presents you with a selection of hundreds of printer drivers. Most Unix systems use standard PostScript printers. Linux systems, however, are built on commodity PC hardware. PCs use a hodgepodge of different printers. The wizard lets you select the correct driver for your printer by selecting the printer make and then the printer model. Once you select the drive, the configuration is finished and the new printer is installed.

The Red Hat tool is just an example. Future versions of Red Hat will have a newer tool, and other Unix systems have their own tools. The point is not the details of the tool, but the fact that the *printcap* file is not usually written by hand. It is created by a configuration tool.

Using LPD

Once the printer is configured, print jobs are sent to the line printer daemon using the *Line Printer Remote* (lpr) program. The lpr program creates a control file and sends it and the print file to lpd. There are many possible lpr command-line arguments, but in general the command simply identifies the printer and the file to be printed, as in:

```
% lpr -Plj ch09
```

This command sends a file called *ch09* to a printer called *lj*. The printer can be local or remote. It doesn't matter as long as the printer is defined in the *printcap* file and therefore known to lpd.

The client software provides commands to allow the user to check the status of the print job. Table 9-2 lists these commands, their syntax, and their meaning.

Table 9-2. Line printer commands

Command	Function
lpc start [*printer*]	Starts a new printer daemon.
lpc status [*printer*]	Displays printer and queue status.
lpq -P*printer* [*user*] [*job*]	Lists the jobs in the printer's queue.
lprm -P*printer job*	Removes a print job from the queue.

In this syntax, *printer* is the name of the printer as defined in the */etc/printcap* file, *user* is the username of the owner of a print job, and *job* is the job number associated with the print job while it is waiting in the queue. The keyword all can be used in place of a printer name in any lpc command to refer to all printers.

While lpc is primarily for the system administrator, the status and start commands can be used by anyone. All the commands shown in Table 9-2 are available to users.

The lpq command displays a list of jobs queued for a printer. Command-line arguments permit the user to select which printer queue is displayed and to limit the display from that queue to a specific user's jobs or even to a specific job. Here's an example of displaying the queue for the printer *lp*:

```
$ lpq -Plp
Printer: lp@crab 'Canon'
Queue: 4 printable jobs
Server: pid 1459 active
Unspooler: pid 1460 active
Status: waiting for subserver to exit at 14:17:47.120
Rank    Owner/ID              Class Job Files                      Size Time
active alana@crab+458          A    458 /usr/share/printconf 18043 14:16:53
2       micheal@crab+477        A    477 /usr/share/printconf/t 193 14:17:38
3       james@crab+479          A    479 /usr/share/printconf 18259 14:17:43
4       daniel@crab+481         A    481 /usr/share/printconf 18043 14:17:46
```

A queued print job can be removed by the owner of the job with the lprm command. Assume that *daniel* wants to remove print job number 481. He enters the following command:

```
$ lprm -Plp 481
Printer lp@crab:
  checking perms 'daniel@crab+481'
  dequeued 'daniel@crab+481'
```

lpd and lpr were among the first commands created for Unix to exploit the power of TCP/IP networking. Managing printers is primarily a system administration task. Only those aspects of lpd related to remote printing are covered here.

Line Printer Service

The Line Printer (LP) print service is used by most System V Unix systems. LP offers the same type of service as LPD.

Traditionally on System V Unix systems, the LP configuration files are located in the */etc/lp* directory. These files perform the same basic function that the */etc/printcap* file does for LPD. However, the */etc/lp* files are not directly edited by the system administrator. The files are created and modified using the System V lpadmin and lpsystem commands.

The lpadmin command adds local printers to the */etc/lp/printers* directory, which makes the printers available to LP. The basic syntax of adding a new printer is simple.

The -p switch defines the local name of the printer. The -p switch is used with either the -v switch that defines the interface for a local printer or the -s switch that defines the server and printer name for a remote printer. For example, the following command adds a local printer named *lp* connected to the parallel printer port */dev/lp1*:

```
# lpadmin -plp -v /dev/lp1
```

This command adds a printer locally known as *laser* that is the *lj* printer on the remote server *crab*:

```
# lpadmin -llaser -s crab!lj
```

The specific characteristics of a printer added by lpadmin are controlled by the *terminfo* file. *terminfo* is a file that is almost identical to the *printcap* file. Like *printcap*, it has a great many possible parameters. For more information on *terminfo*, see the manpage.

The lpsystem command manages printer access on System V systems. By default, most System V systems share all local printers. Remote printer access settings are defined in the */etc/lp/Systems* file, which comes preconfigured with the following entry:

```
+:x:-:s5:-:n:10:-:-:Allow all connections
```

As the comment at its end makes clear, this entry grants all remote systems access to the local printers. The first field defines the name of the host being granted access. When a plus sign (+) is used in this field, it means all hosts.

The fields in an */etc/lp/Systems* entry are separated by colons (:). The field containing an x and all of the fields containing a dash (-) can be ignored. These fields are unused.

The fourth field identifies the type of operating system used on the remote client. It contains either s5 for System V computers that use LP to print jobs, or bsd for BSD systems that use LPD.

The n in the sixth field indicates that this "connection" should never be timed out and removed from the system. A timeout period in minutes could be entered in this field, but this is not usually done. Keep the connection available as long as the local server is up. The 10 is a related value. It indicates that if a connection to a remote system fails, it should be retried after 10 minutes. This is a good value: it is long enough to give the remote system a chance to restart after a crash. Both n and 10 are the defaults and don't usually need to be changed.

Don't directly edit the */etc/lp/Systems* file. Modify it with the lpsystem command. To remove a system from the *Systems* file, use lpsystem with the -r *hostname* command-line argument, where *hostname* is the value in the first field of the entry you wish to delete. For example, to remove the plus sign (+) entry from the default */etc/lp/Systems* file, type:

```
# lpsystem -r +
```

To add an entry to the *Systems* file, use the lpsystem command without the -r option. For example, to add a BSD system named *clock*, enter:

```
# lpsystem -t bsd -y "Linux PC in room 820" clock
```

The command adds the following entry to the *Systems* file:

```
clock:x:-:bsd:-:n:10:-:-:Linux PC in room 820
```

The -t command-line option defines the operating system type. The -y option defines the comment; *clock* is, of course, the hostname. We accepted the default values for the timeout and the retry intervals. These could have been modified from the command line using the -T *timeout* and the -R *retry* options. See the manpage for lpsystem for more information.

The lpadmin and lpsystem commands are found on most System V systems, including Solaris. Solaris 8, however, does not rely solely on these commands and the */etc/lp* directory to configure LP. On a Solaris system, printers are configured through the */etc/printers.conf* file. The lpadmin command will add new printers to the */etc/printers.conf* file, but printers are usually configured through the Printer Manager window of the admintool. Figure 9-1 shows the Printer Manager window.

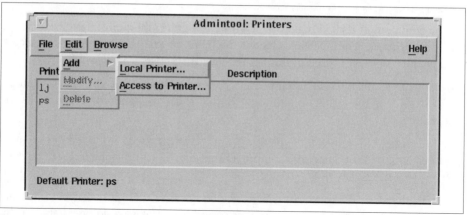

Figure 9-1. Printer Manager

Clients select Add, then Access to Printer from the Edit menu, and enter the name of the remote printer and its server in the window that appears. Servers share printers simply by selecting Add, then Local Printer in the same menu and configuring a local printer.

All Unix systems provide some technique for sharing printers. The network administrator's task is to ensure that the printers are accessible via the network and that they are properly secured.

Using Samba to Share Resources with Windows

NFS and lpd are file and print sharing services for Unix systems, and are both native TCP/IP applications. Microsoft Windows printer and file sharing applications are based on NetBIOS (Network Basic Input Output System). *Samba* bridges these two worlds, providing file and print sharing for Unix and Windows systems. Samba is the key to integrating Unix and Windows because it allows a Unix system to be a file and print server for Windows clients, or to be a client of a Windows server.

The protocol used between NetBIOS clients and servers is Server Message Block Protocol (SMB). Originally, NetBIOS was a monolithic protocol that took data all the way from the application to the physical network. Today, NetBIOS runs over TCP/IP, which allows NetBIOS applications to run on Unix systems that use TCP/IP.

Two things are needed to run NetBIOS on a TCP/IP network: a protocol to carry NetBIOS data over TCP/IP and a technique to map NetBIOS addresses to TCP/IP addresses. The protocol that transports NetBIOS is *NetBIOS over TCP/IP* (NBT), which is defined by RFCs 1001 and 1002. Address mapping is handled by a special NetBIOS name server. Samba provides both of these services.

Samba services are implemented as two daemons. The SMB daemon (smbd), the heart of Samba, provides the file and printer sharing services. The NetBIOS name server daemon (nmbd) provides NetBIOS-to-IP-address name service. NBT requires some method for mapping NetBIOS computer names, which are the addresses of a NetBIOS network, to the IP addresses of a TCP/IP network.

Samba is included in most Linux distributions and is installed during the initial system installation. On a Red Hat system, the */etc/rc.d/init.d/smb* script runs at boot time, and starts both smbd and nmbd. Samba is not included in Solaris 8, but the software is available for download from the Internet. Go to *http://www.samba.org* to select your nearest download site.

Configuring a Samba Server

The Samba server is configured by the *smb.conf* file. Look in the startup script to see where smbd expects to find the configuration file. On a Red Hat system, it is */etc/samba/smb.conf*. On a Caldera system, it is */etc/samba.d/smb.conf*. The default used in most Samba documentation is */usr/local/samba/lib/smb.conf*. Use find or check the startup script so you know where it is on your system.

The *smb.conf* file is divided into sections. Except for the global section, which defines configuration parameters for the entire server, the sections are named after *shares*. A share is a resource offered by the server to the clients. It can be either a filesystem or a shared printer.

The best way to learn about the *smb.conf* file is to look at one. Minus the printers share, which is covered later, the Red Hat *smb.conf* file contains these active lines:

```
[global]
    workgroup = MYGROUP
    server string = Samba Server
    printcap name = /etc/printcap
    load printers = yes
    printing = lprng
    log file = /var/log/samba/%m.log
    max log size = 0
    security = user
    encrypt passwords = yes
    smb passwd file = /etc/samba/smbpasswd
    socket options = TCP_NODELAY SO_RCVBUF=8192 SO_SNDBUF=8192
    dns proxy = no
[homes]
    comment = Home Directories
    browseable = no
    writable = yes
    valid users = %S
    create mode = 0664
    directory mode = 0775
```

Two sections of the Red Hat configuration file, *global* and *homes*, are listed above. The global section defines parameters that affect the entire server:

workgroup

> Defines the hierarchical grouping of hosts, called a workgroup, of which this server is a member. Replace the MYGROUP name in the example with a meaningful workgroup name of 15 characters or less. Make sure you use a meaningful name. Never use the name MYGROUP or WORKGROUP.

server string

> Defines the descriptive comment for this server that is displayed by the net view command on DOS clients. Change the string in the example to something meaningful for your system.

printcap name

> Defines the location of the *printcap* file. The *printcap* file is used to identify the printers that are available to share. The default path is */etc/printcap*.

load printers

> Specifies whether or not all the printers in the *printcap* file are to be shared. The default is yes, use all the printers defined in the *printcap* file. no means don't read the *printcap* file at all. If no is specified, all shared printers must be defined individually.

printing

> Identifies the Unix printing system used by the server. In the example, it is LPR Next Generation (lprng), which is an implementation of the standard LPR/LPD system described earlier in this chapter.

log file

Defines the location of the log file. The example contains the %m variable,* which varies according to the client's NetBIOS name. This creates a different log file for each client with a file extension that is the client's NetBIOS name. If the Net-BIOS name of the client is *crab*, the log file is named */var/log/samba/log.crab*. If the client's NetBIOS name is *rodent*, the log file is */var/log/samba/log.rodent*.

max log size

Defines the maximum size of a log file in kilobytes. The default is 5 MB, or 5000 KB. (If the maximum size is exceeded, smbd closes the log and renames it with the extension *.old*.) In the sample configuration, this is set to 0, which means that no maximum size is set for log files.

security

Defines the type of security used. There are four possible settings:

share

Requests share-level security. This is the lowest level of security. The resource is shared with everyone. It is possible to associate a password with a share, but the password is the same for everyone.

user

Requests user-level security. Every user is required to enter a username and an associated password. By default, this is the username and password defined in */etc/passwd*. The default values for passwords can be changed. See the discussion of passwords later in this section.

server

Defines server-level security. This is similar to user-level security, but an external server is used to authenticate the username and password. The external server must be defined by the password server option.

domain

Defines domain-level security. In this scheme, the Linux server joins a Windows NT/2000 domain and uses the Windows NT/2000 domain controller as the server that approves usernames and passwords. Use the password server option to point to the Windows NT/2000 Primary Domain Controller (PDC). Log into the PDC and create an account for the Linux system. Finally, add these lines to the global section on the Linux system:

```
domain master = no
local master = no
preferred master = no
os level = 0
```

---

* Samba has about 20 different variables. See the manpage for a full list.

encrypt passwords

Setting this option to yes causes Samba to encrypt passwords before they are sent across the network. This makes the server more compatible with Windows clients from Windows 98 on, which default to encrypted passwords, and makes it harder for intruders to sniff passwords from the network. By default, Samba uses clear-text Unix passwords.

smb passwd file

This option points to the location of the *smbpasswd* file, where encrypted Samba passwords are stored. When encrypted passwords are used, the Samba server must maintain two password files: *passwd* and *smbpasswd*. Use the *mksmbpasswd.sh* script to build the initial *smbpasswd* file from the *passwd* file.

socket options

Defines performance tuning parameters. This option is not required, although setting the send and receive buffers to 8 KB may slightly increase performance. In the case of this sample Red Hat configuration, the TCP_NODELAY setting, which causes Samba to send multiple packets with each transfer, has no effect because it is the default for versions of Samba 2.0.4 or higher. See Appendix B of *Using Samba*, by Kelly, Eckstein, and Collier-Brown (O'Reilly) for a good discussion of Samba performance tuning.

dns proxy

Specifies whether or not nmbd should forward unresolved NBNS queries to DNS.

In addition to the options described above, several other parameters are commonly used in the global section; they are shown in Table 9-3.

Table 9-3. Other global section parameters

Option	Function
deadtime	Defines the timeout for inactive connections.
debug level	Sets the level of messages written to the log.
keepalive	Uses keepalives to check on the state of the clients.
lock directory	Defines the path of the directory where *wins.dat*, status files, and lock files are stored.
message command	Defines how smbd handles WinPopup messages.
name resolve order	Defines the order in which services are queried to resolve NetBIOS names. Possible values are: lmhosts, hosts, wins, and bcast.
netbios aliases	Defines other names the server will answer to.
netbios name	Defines the server's NetBIOS name.
syslog	Maps debug levels to syslog levels.
syslog only	Uses syslog instead of Samba log files.
time server	Tells the server to advertise itself as a Windows time server.
wins support	Enables the WINS name server.

As the Red Hat sample configuration demonstrates, many servers come preconfig-ured with reasonable global parameters to begin running a simple server system. In addition to a preconfigured *global* section, the Red Hat configuration comes with a preconfigured *homes* section.

The smb.conf homes section

The *homes* section is a special share section. It tells smbd to permit users to access their home directories through SMB. Unlike other share sections, which we cover later, this section does not tell smbd the specific path of the directory being shared. Instead, smbd uses the home directory from the */etc/passwd* file based on the user-name of the user requesting the share. The configuration parameters in the Red Hat *homes* section are:

comment
> Provides a description of the share that is displayed in the comment field of the Network Neighborhood window when this share is viewed on a Windows PC.

browseable
> Specifies whether or not all users may browse the contents of this share. no means that only users with the correct user ID are allowed to browse this share. yes means all users, regardless of UID, can browse the share. This parameter controls only browsing; actual access to the contents of the share is controlled by standard Linux file permissions.

writable
> Specifies whether or not files can be written to this share. If yes, the share can be written to. If no, the share is read-only. This parameter defines the actions per-mitted by Samba. Actual permission to write to the directory defined by the share is still controlled by standard Linux file permissions.

valid users
> This option lists the users who are allowed to use this share. In this example, %S contains the name of the user allowed to access this share.

create mode
> This option defines the file permissions used when a client creates a file within the *homes* share.

directory mode
> This option defines the permissions used when a client creates a directory within the *homes* share.

Sharing directories through Samba

To share a directory through Samba, create a share section in *smb.conf* that describes the directory and the conditions under which it will be shared. To share a new directory named *lusr/doc/pcdocs* and the */home/research* directory used in the NFS examples, add the following two share sections to the sample *smb.conf* file:

```
[pcdocs]
      comment = PC Documentation
      path = /usr/doc/pcdocs
      browseable = yes
      writable = no
      public = yes

[research]
      comment = Research Deptment Shared Directory
      path = /home/research
      browseable = no
      writable = yes
      create mode = 0750
      hosts allow = horseshoe,jerboas,crab,rodent
```

Each share section is labeled with a meaningful name. This name is displayed as a folder in the Network Neighborhood window on client PCs. The example contains some commands we have already covered and a few new commands. The first new command is path, which defines the path of the directory being offered by this share.

The *pcdocs* share also contains the command public, which grants everyone access, even if they don't have a valid username or password. These public users are granted "guest account" access to the share. On a Linux system, this means they run as user *nobody* and group *nobody* and are limited to world permissions.

Files may be written to the research share. The create mode command controls the Unix permissions used when a client writes a file to the share. In the example, the permission 0750 specifies that files will be created as read/write/execute for the owner, read/execute for the group, and no permissions for the world. A related command, directory mode, defines the permission used when a client creates a directory within a share. For example:

```
directory mode = 0744
```

This sets the permissions for new directories to read/write/execute for the owner, read/execute for the group, and read/execute for the world. This is a reasonable setting that allows cd and ls to work as expected.

The *research* share section also contains a hosts allow command, which defines the clients that are allowed to access this share. Even if a user has the correct username and password, that user is allowed to access this share only from the specified hosts. By default, all hosts are granted access, and specific access is controlled by the username and password.

In addition to the hosts allow command, there is a hosts deny command that defines computers that are explicitly denied access to the share. Its syntax is similar to that of the hosts allow command.

Combining these two new share sections with the section that came with the Red Hat configuration creates a server that provides access to user home directories, to public directories, and to private directories limited to members of a group. This provides the same services as NFS in a manner that is simpler for Microsoft Windows clients to use. Samba can also be used to share printers with Windows clients.

Sharing printers through Samba

Shared printers are configured through the *smb.conf* file. The Red Hat system comes with a *smb.conf* file that is preconfigured for sharing printers. The following lines occur right after the *global* and *homes* sections in the Red Hat *smb.conf* file:

```
[printers]
    comment = All Printers
    path = /var/spool/samba
    browseable = no
    guest ok = no
    writable = no
    printable = yes
```

The printcap and load printers lines in the global section prepare the server to share the printers defined in the *printcap* file. This *printers* section makes those printers available to the clients in a manner similar to the way the *homes* section makes every home directory available to the appropriate user. The Red Hat *printers* share section contains five parameters.

Three of the parameters, comment, browseable, and path, were explained previously. Here, however, path does not define the path of a shared file. Instead, it defines the path of the spool directory for the SMB printers.

We introduce two new parameters in this configuration, the first of which is printable, which identifies this share as a printer. The default for this option is no, meaning that by default, shares are considered to be file shares instead of printer shares. To create a printer share, set this option to yes. Setting printable = yes permits clients to write printer files to the spool directory defined by the path option. Use a create mode command to limit the permissions of the files created by clients in the spool directory. For example, create mode = 0700.

The other new line, guest ok, defines whether or not guest accounts are permitted access to the resource. This is exactly the same as the public option discussed earlier, so these two options are used interchangeably. no means that the user *nobody* cannot send a print job to the printer. A user must have a valid user account to use the printer. This is designed to prevent guest users from abusing the printer, but it is also useful to have a valid username for sorting out print jobs if you use banner pages and accounting on the server.

Generally, a print server offers all of its printers to all of its clients. However, individual share sections can be created for each printer in the same way that they are created for file sharing. If you don't want to share every printer, remove the printers section, set the load printers option to no, and add individual share sections for just those printers that you want to share.

An *smb.conf* file with a share section for a specific printer might contain:

```
[global]
    workgroup = BOOKS
    server string = Print Server
    load printers = no
    security = user
[homes]
    comment = Home Directories
    browseable = no
    writable = yes
[hp5m]
    comment = PostScript Laser Printer
    path = /var/spool/samba
    browseable = no
    public = no
    create mode = 0700
    printable = yes
    printer = lp
```

This sample file has no printers section. Instead, a share section named *hp5m* is added that shares a printer named *lp*. The printer name must be found in the *printcap* file for this to work. The printcap option is allowed to default to */etc/printcap*.

smbd is the component of Samba that provides file and printer sharing. The other component of Samba is nmbd.

NetBIOS Name Service

The NetBIOS name server daemon (nmbd) is the part of the basic Samba software distribution that turns a Unix server into a NetBIOS name server (NBNS). nmbd can handle queries from LanManager clients, and it can be configured to act as a Windows Internet Name Server (WINS).

nmbd is configured in the global section of the *smb.conf* file. The options that relate to running WINS are:

wins support

> Set to yes or no. This option determines whether or not nmbd runs as a WINS server. no is the default, so by default, nmbd provides browsing controls but does not provide WINS service.

dns proxy

> Set to yes or no. This option tells nmbd to use DNS to resolve WINS queries that it cannot resolve any other way. This is significant only if nmbd is running as a

WINS server. The default is yes. DNS can help with NetBIOS name resolution only if NetBIOS names and DNS hostnames are the same.

wins server

Set to the IP address of an external WINS server. This option is useful only if you're not running a WINS server on your Linux system. This option tells Samba the address of the external WINS server to which it should send Net-BIOS name queries.

wins proxy

Set to yes or no. The default is no. When set to yes, nmbd resolves broadcast Net-BIOS name queries by turning them into unicast queries and sending them directly to the WINS server. If wins support = yes is set, these queries are handled by nmbd itself. If instead wins server is set, these queries are sent to the external server. The wins proxy option is needed only if clients don't know the address of the server or don't understand the WINS protocol.

The NetBIOS name server is generally started at boot time with the following command:

```
nmbd -D
```

When started with the -D option, nmbd runs continuously as a daemon listening for NetBIOS name service requests on port 137. The server answers requests using registration data collected from its clients and the NetBIOS name-to-address mappings it has learned from other servers.

The *lmhosts* file is used to manually map addresses when that is necessary. Most WINS servers do not need an *lmhosts* file because the servers learn address mappings dynamically from clients and other servers. NetBIOS names are self-registered; clients register their NetBIOS names with the server when they boot. The addresses and names are stored in the WINS database, *wins.dat*. The *lmhosts* file is only a small part of the total database.

The *lmhosts* file is similar to the *hosts* file described in Chapter 4. Each entry begins with an IP address that is followed by a hostname. However, this time, the hostname is the NetBIOS name. Here is a sample *lmhosts* file:

```
$ cat /etc/lmhosts
172.16.12.3      horseshoe
172.16.12.1      crab
172.16.12.2      rodent
172.16.12.4      jerboas
```

Given this *lmhosts* file, the NetBIOS name *rodent* maps to IP address 172.16.12.2. Notice that these NetBIOS names are the same as the TCP/IP hostnames assigned to these clients. Use the same hostnames for both NetBIOS and TCP/IP. Doing otherwise limits configuration choices and creates confusion.

Network Information Service

The *Network Information Service* (NIS)[*] is an administrative database that provides central control and automatic dissemination of important administrative files. NIS converts several standard Unix files into databases that can be queried over the network. The databases are called *NIS maps*. Some maps are created from files that you're familiar with from system administration, such as the password file (*/etc/passwd*) and the groups file (*/etc/group*). Others are derived from files related to network administration:

/etc/ethers
> Creates the NIS maps *ethers.byaddr* and *ethers.byname*. The */etc/ethers* file is used by RARP (see Chapter 2).

/etc/hosts
> Creates the maps *hosts.byname* and *hosts.byaddr* (see Chapter 3).

/etc/networks
> Creates the maps *networks.byname* and *networks.byaddr* (see Chapter 3).

/etc/protocols
> Creates the maps *protocols.byname* and *protocols.byaddr* (see Chapter 2).

/etc/services
> Creates a single map called *services.byname* (see Chapter 2).

/etc/aliases
> Defines electronic mail aliases and creates the maps *mail.aliases* and *mail.byaddr* (see Chapter 10).

Check the maps available on your server with the ypcat -x command. This command produced the same map list on both our Solaris and Linux sample systems. Your server may display a longer list. Here is the list from a Linux system:

```
% ypcat -x
Use "passwd"    for map "passwd.byname"
Use "group"     for map "group.byname"
Use "networks"  for map "networks.byaddr"
Use "hosts"     for map "hosts.byname"
Use "protocols" for map "protocols.bynumber"
Use "services"  for map "services.byname"
Use "aliases"   for map "mail.aliases"
Use "ethers"    for map "ethers.byname"
```

NIS allows these important administrative files to be maintained on a central server yet remain completely accessible to every workstation on the network. All of the maps are stored on a master server that runs the NIS server process ypserv. The maps are queried remotely by client systems. Clients run ypbind to locate the server.

---

[*] NIS was formerly called the "Yellow Pages," or *yp*. Although the name has changed, the abbreviation *yp* is still used.

The NIS server and its clients are a *NIS domain*, a term NIS shares with DNS. The NIS domain is identified by a NIS domain name. The only requirement for the name is that different NIS domains accessible through the same local network must have different names. Although NIS domains and DNS domains are distinct entities, Sun recommends using the DNS domain name as the NIS domain name to simplify administration and reduce confusion.

NIS uses its domain name to create a directory within */var/yp* where the NIS maps are stored. For example, the DNS domain of our imaginary network is *wrotethebook.com*, so we also use this as our NIS domain name. NIS creates a directory named */var/yp/ wrotethebook.com* and stores the NIS maps in it.

While the NIS protocols and commands were originally defined by Sun Microsystems, the service is now widely implemented. To illustrate this, the majority of examples in this section come from Linux, not from Solaris. The syntax of the commands is very similar from system to system.

The command domainname checks or sets the NIS domain name. The superuser can make *wrotethebook.com* the NIS domain name by entering:

```
# domainname wrotethebook.com
```

The NIS domain name is normally configured at startup by placing the domainname command in one of the startup files. On many systems, the NIS domain name that is used as input to a domainname command is placed in a second file. For example, on Solaris systems, the value for the NIS domain name is taken from the */etc/default-domain* file. As shown here, *defaultdomain* contains only the name of the NIS domain:

```
% cat /etc/defaultdomain
wrotethebook.com
```

On Red Hat Linux systems, the NIS domain name is just one of the values in the */etc/ sysconfig/network* file:

```
$ cat /etc/sysconfig/network
NETWORKING=yes
HOSTNAME=jerboas.wrotethebook.com
NISDOMAIN=wrotethebook.com
```

Initialize the NIS server and build the initial maps with make. The */var/yp/Makefile* contains the instructions needed to build the maps. As noted above, it creates a directory using the NIS domain name. The Makefile reads the files in the */etc* directory and places maps created from them in the new directory. To initialize a Linux system as a NIS server:

```
# domainname wrotethebook.com
# cd /var/yp
# make
make[1]: Entering directory '/var/yp/wrotethebook.com'
Updating hosts.byname...
Updating hosts.byaddr...
Updating networks.byaddr...
```

```
Updating networks.byname...
Updating protocols.bynumber...
Updating protocols.byname...
Updating rpc.byname...
Updating rpc.bynumber...
Updating services.byname...
Updating passwd.byname...
Updating passwd.byuid...
Updating group.byname...
Updating group.bygid...
Updating netid.byname...
make[1]: Leaving directory '/var/yp/wrotethebook.com'
```

After initializing the maps, start the NIS server process ypserv and the NIS binder process ypbind:[*]

```
# ypserv
# ypbind
```

Our system is now running as both a NIS server and a NIS client. A quick test with ypwhich shows that we are bound to the correct server. Use ypcat or ypmatch to test that you can retrieve data from the server. We use ypcat in the following example:

```
# ypwhich
localhost
# ypcat hosts
172.16.55.105           cow cow.wrotethebook.com
172.16.55.106           pig pig.wrotethebook.com
172.16.26.36            island.wrotethebook.com island
127.0.0.1               localhost
```

The clients need only to define the correct domain name and to run the binder software ypbind:

```
# domainname wrotethebook.com
# ypbind
```

Most NIS clients use ypbind to locate the server. Using the NIS domain name, ypbind broadcasts a request for a server for that domain. The first server that responds is the server to which the client "binds." The theory is that the server that responds quickest is the server with the least workload. Generally this works well. However, it is possible for the client to bind to an inappropriate system, e.g., a system that was accidentally configured to run ypserv or one that was maliciously configured to be a false server. Because of this possibility, some systems allow you to explicitly configure the server to which the client binds. Linux provides the */etc/yp.conf* file for this purpose. The syntax of the entries in different versions of this file varies, so see your system documentation before attempting to use it.

---

[*] If, during the initial build of the NIS maps, make complains that ypserv is not registered, run ypserv before running make.

Place the NIS domain name in the appropriate startup file so that the NIS setup survives the boot. The ypbind and ypserv commands are probably already in a startup file. On a Red Hat Linux NIS system, ypbind and ypserv have their own scripts in the */etc/init.d* directory. In addition to putting a value for NISDOMAIN in */etc/sysconfig/network*, use the chkconfig command to make sure the ypbind and the ypserv scripts run at boot time.

NIS is a possible alternative to DNS, but most systems use both NIS and DNS. Hostnames can be converted to IP addresses by DNS, NIS, and the host file. The order in which the various sources are queried is defined in the *nsswitch.conf* file.

The nsswitch.conf file

The Name Service Switch file (*nsswitch.conf*) defines the order in which the sources of information are searched. Despite its name, it applies to more than just name service. All of the databases handled by NIS are covered by the *nsswitch.conf* file, as shown in this example:

```
hosts:      dns  nis  files
networks:   nis  [NOTFOUND=return]  files
services:   nis  files
protocols:  nis  files
```

The first entry in the file says that a hostname lookup is first passed to DNS for resolution; if DNS fails to find a match, the lookup is then passed to NIS and finally looked up in the *hosts* file. The second entry says that network names are looked up through NIS. The [NOTFOUND=return] string says to use the *networks* file only if NIS fails to respond, that is, if NIS is down. In this case, if NIS answers that it cannot find the requested network name, terminate the search. The last two entries search for services port and protocol numbers through NIS and then in the files in the */etc* directory.

NIS+

Before leaving the topic of NIS, I should say a word about NIS+. It will be a short discussion, because I do not use NIS+ and do not know much about it.

NIS+ replaces NIS on Sun systems. It is not a new version of NIS, but a completely new software product that provides all the functionality of NIS and some new features. The new features are:

- Improved security. NIS does not authenticate servers (as noted in the ypbind discussion) or clients. NIS+ provides authentication of users with a secure DES-encrypted authentication scheme. NIS+ also provides various levels of access so that different users have authority to look at different levels of data. NIS can only provide the same access to everyone in the NIS domain.

- A hierarchical, decentralized architecture. NIS+, like DNS, is a distributed, hierarchical database system. This allows for a very large namespace. It also allows distributed management of the information structure while maintaining consistent access to the data. NIS is a flat structure. All information about a NIS domain comes from a single master server, and NIS domains are not interrelated.

- Enhanced data structures. NIS converts ASCII files into simple keyed files that the NIS+ documentation calls "two-column maps." NIS+ builds multicolumn database *tables*. Tables can be searched in a variety of ways to retrieve information about an entry. In addition, NIS+ tables can be linked together to provide related information about an entry.

Clearly, NIS+ has some excellent new features and advantages over NIS. So why don't I use it? Good question! The hierarchical architecture and enhanced data structures are important if you have a very large network and lots of data in your namespace. However, many sites evolved using NIS on local subnets and do not see the need to move the entire enterprise under NIS+. Improved security seems like a real winner, but sites with low security requirements don't see the need for additional security, and sites with high security requirements may already be behind a firewall that blocks external NIS queries. Additionally, NIS+ is not available for as many operating systems as NIS. And finally, other directory services, such as LDAP, that provide similar services and are more widely available have overtaken NIS+. Taken together, these reasons have slowed the move to NIS+.

To learn more about NIS+ and how to install it on your system, read the *NIS+ Transition Guide*, the *Name Service Configuration Guide*, and the *Name Service Administration Guide*. All of these are available from Sun as part of the Solaris System and Network Administration manual set.

NIS and NIS+ provide a wide range of system configuration information to their clients. However, they cannot provide all the information needed to configure a TCP/IP system. In the next two sections, we look at configuration servers that can do the entire job.

DHCP

Bootstrap Protocol (BOOTP) was the first comprehensive configuration protocol. It provides all of the information commonly used to configure TCP/IP, from the client's IP address to what print server the client should use. BOOTP was simple and effective; so effective, in fact, that it became the basis for Dynamic Host Configuration Protocol (DHCP). DHCP operates over the same UDP ports, 67 and 68, as BOOTP. It provides all of the services of BOOTP as well as some important extensions. Dynamic Host Configuration Protocol provides three important features:

Backward compatibility with Bootstrap Protocol
>   A DHCP server can support BOOTP clients. Properly configured, a DHCP server
>   can support all of your clients.

Full configurations
>   A DHCP server provides a complete set of TCP/IP configuration parameters.
>   (See Appendix D for a full list.) The network administrator can handle the entire
>   configuration for the users.

Dynamic address assignments
>   A DHCP server can provide permanent addresses manually, permanent
>   addresses automatically, and temporary addresses dynamically. The network
>   administrator can tailor the type of address to the needs of the network and the
>   client system.

In this section we configure a DHCP server that supports BOOTP clients, performs
dynamic address allocation, and provides a wide range of configuration parameters
for its clients.

Several implementations of DHCP are available for Unix systems. Some are commercial packages and some run on a specific version of Unix. We use the Internet Software Consortium (ISC) Dynamic Host Configuration Protocol Daemon (dhcpd). It is
freely available over the Internet and runs on a wide variety of Unix systems, including both our Linux and Solaris sample systems. (See Appendix D for information on
downloading and compiling dhcpd.) If you use different DHCP server software, it will
have different configuration commands, but it will probably perform the same basic
functions.

dhcpd.conf

dhcpd reads its configuration from the */etc/dhcpd.conf* file. The configuration file contains the instructions that tell the server what subnets and hosts it services and what
configuration information it should provide them. *dhcpd.conf* is an ASCII text file
that is similar to a C language source file. The easiest way to learn about the *dhcpd.
conf* file is to look at a sample:

```
# Define global values that apply to all systems.

default-lease-time 86400;
max-lease-time 604800;
get-lease-hostnames true;
option subnet-mask 255.255.255.0;
option domain-name "wrotethebook.com";
option domain-name-servers 172.16.12.1, 172.16.3.5;
option lpr-servers 172.16.12.1;
option interface-mtu 1500;

# Identify the subnet served, the options related
# to the subnet, and the range of addresses that
# are available for dynamic allocation.
```

```
subnet 172.16.3.0 netmask 255.255.255.0 {
    option routers 172.16.3.25;
    option broadcast-address 172.16.3.255;
    range 172.16.3.50 172.16.3.250;
}

subnet 172.16.12.0 netmask 255.255.255.0 {
    option routers 172.16.12.1;
    option broadcast-address 172.16.12.255;
    range 172.16.12.64 172.16.12.192;
    range 172.16.12.200 172.16.12.250;
}

# Identify each BOOTP client with a host statement

group {
    use-host-decl-names true;
    host 24seven {
        hardware ethernet 00:80:c7:aa:a8:04;
        fixed-address 172.16.3.4;
    }
    host rodent {
        hardware ethernet 08:80:20:01:59:c3;
        fixed-address 172.16.12.2;
    }
    host ring {
        hardware ethernet 00:00:c0:a1:5e:10;
        fixed-address 172.16.3.16;
    }
}
```

This sample configuration file defines a server that is connecting to and serving two separate subnets. It assigns IP addresses dynamically to the DHCP clients on each subnet and supports a few BOOTP clients. All of the lines that begin with a sharp sign (#) are comments. The first few real configuration lines in the file specify a set of parameters and options that apply to all of the subnets and clients served. The first three lines are parameters, which provide direction to the server. All three of the sample parameters define some aspect of how dhcpd should handle dynamic address assignments.

default-lease-time
  Tells the server how many seconds long a default address lease should be. The client can request that the address be leased for a specific period of time. If it does, it is assigned the address for that period of time, given some restrictions. Frequently, clients do not request a specific lifetime for an address lease. When that happens, the default-lease-time is used. In the example, the default lease is set to one day (86400 seconds).

max-lease-time
  Sets the upper limit for how long an address can be leased. Regardless of the length of time requested by the client, this is the longest address lease that dhcpd

will grant. The life of the lease is specified in seconds. In the example here, it is one week.

get-lease-hostnames

Directs dhcpd to provide a hostname to each client that is assigned a dynamic address. Further, the hostname is to be obtained from DNS. This parameter is a Boolean. If it is set to false, which is the default, the client receives an address but no hostname. Looking up the hostname for every possible dynamic address adds substantial time to the startup. Set this to false. Set it to true only if the server handles a very small number of dynamic addresses.

The configuration file uses a few more parameters that will be explained as we go. For a complete list of all DHCP parameters, see Appendix D.

The next four lines are options. The options all start with the keyword option. The keyword is followed by the name of the option and the value assigned to the option. Options define configuration values that are used by the client.

The meanings of the sample options are easy to deduce. The option names are very descriptive. We are providing the clients with the subnet mask, domain name, domain name server addresses, and print server address. These values are similar to those that could have been provided with the old BOOTP service.

DHCP, however, can do more than BOOTP. For sake of illustration, we also define the maximum transmission unit (MTU). The sample interface-mtu option tells the client that the MTU is 1500 bytes. In this case, the option is not needed because 1500 bytes is the default for Ethernet. However, it illustrates the point that DHCP can provide a very complete set of configuration information.

The subnet statements define the networks that dhcpd serves. The identity of each network is determined from the address and the address mask, both of which are required by the subnet statement. dhcpd provides configuration services only to clients that are attached to one of these networks. There must be a subnet statement for every subnet to which the server physically connects, even if some subnets do not contain any clients. dhcpd requires the subnet information to complete its startup.

The options and parameters defined in a subnet statement apply only to the subnet and its clients. The meanings of the sample options are clear. They tell the clients what router and what broadcast address to use. The range parameter is more interesting, as it goes to the heart of one of DHCP's key features.

The range parameter defines the scope of addresses that are available for dynamic address allocation. It always occurs in association with a subnet statement, and the range of addresses must fall within the address space of the subnet. The scope of the range parameter is defined by the two addresses it contains. The first address is the lowest address that can be automatically assigned, and the second is the highest address that can be assigned. The first range parameter in the example identifies a contiguous group of addresses from 172.16.12.50 to 172.16.12.250 that are available for dynamic assignment. Notice that the second subnet statement has two range parameters. This creates two separate groups of dynamic addresses. The reason for this might be that some addresses were already manually assigned before the DHCP server was installed. Regardless of the reason, the point is that we can define a non-contiguous dynamic address space with multiple range statements.

If a range parameter is defined in a subnet statement, any DHCP client on the subnet that requests an address is granted one as long as addresses are available. If a range parameter is not defined, dynamic addressing is not enabled.

To provide automatic address assignment for BOOTP clients, add the `dynamic-bootp` argument to the range parameter. For example:

```
range dynamic-bootp 172.16.8.10 172.16.8.50;
```

By default, BOOTP clients are assigned permanent addresses. It is possible to override this default behavior with either the `dynamic-bootp-lease-cutoff` or the `dynamic-bootp-lease-length` parameter. However, BOOTP clients do not understand address leases and do not know that they should renew an address. Therefore the `dynamic-bootp-lease-cutoff` and the `dynamic-bootp-lease-length` parameters are used only in special circumstances. If you're interested in these parameters, see Appendix D.

Each BOOTP client should have an associated host statement that is used to assign the client configuration parameters and options. It can be used to manually assign the client a permanent, fixed address. The sample configuration file ends with three host statements: one for *24seven*, one for *rodent*, and one for *ring*. Each host statement contains a hardware parameter that defines the type of network hardware (ethernet) and the physical network address (e.g., `08:80:20:01:59:c3`) used by the client. The hardware parameter is required in host statements for BOOTP clients. The Ethernet address is used by `dhcpd` to identify the BOOTP client. DHCP clients can also have associated host statements. For DHCP clients, the hardware parameter is optional because a DHCP client can be identified by the `dhcp-client-identifier` option. However, it is simpler for a DHCP client connected via Ethernet to be identified by its Ethernet address.

A wide variety of parameters and options can be defined in the host statement. For example, adding to each host statement an option similar to the following assigns each client a hostname:

```
option host-name 24seven;
```

It is often easier, however, to define options and parameters at a higher level. Global options apply to all systems. Subnet options apply to every client on the subnet, but the options defined inside a host statement apply to only a single host. The host-name option shown above would need to be repeated with a different hostname in every host statement. An easier way to define a parameter or option for a group of hosts is to use a group statement.

A group statement groups together any other statements. The sole purpose of the group statement is to apply parameters and options to all members of the group. That is exactly what we do in the example. The group statement groups all of the host statements together. The use-host-decl-names parameter in the group statement applies to every host in the group. This particular parameter tells dhcpd to assign each client the hostname that is declared on the host statement associated with that client, which makes the host-name option unnecessary for this configuration.

Given the sample *dhcpd.conf* file shown earlier, when dhcpd receives a request packet from a client with the Ethernet address 08:80:20:01:59:c3, it sends that client:

- The address 172.16.12.2
- The hostname *rodent*
- The default router address 172.16.12.1
- The broadcast address 172.16.12.255
- The subnet mask 255.255.255.0
- The domain name *wrotethebook.com*
- The domain name server addresses 172.16.12.1 and 172.16.3.5
- The print server address 172.16.12.1
- The MTU for an Ethernet interface

The client receives all global values, all subnet values, and all host values that are appropriate. Clearly, DHCP can provide a complete configuration.

Your DHCP configuration, though larger in the number of systems supported, probably is simpler than the example. Some commands appear in the sample primarily for the purpose of illustration. The biggest difference is that most sites do not serve more than one subnet with a single configuration server. Servers are normally placed on each subnet. This reduces the burden on the server, particularly the burden that can be caused by a network-wide power outage. It eliminates the need to move boot packets through routers. Also, the fact that addresses are assigned at the subnet level makes placing the assigning system at the subnet level as well somehow more logical. DHCP servers are not the only servers that work best when located close to the clients. In the next section we look at how to keep distributed servers updated.

Managing Distributed Servers

Large networks have multiple servers. As noted earlier, the servers are often distributed around the network with a server on every subnet. This improves network efficiency, but it conflicts with the goal of central configuration control. The more servers you have, the more dispersed the control, and the more likely that a configuration error will occur. Implementing distributed servers requires a technique for maintaining central control and coordinating configuration information among the servers. TCP/IP offers several techniques for doing this.

Any file transfer protocol can be used to move configuration data or any other kind of data from a central system to a group of distributed systems. Either FTP or TFTP will work, but both present difficulties when used in this way. FTP and TFTP are *interactive* protocols, and require multiple commands to retrieve a file, making them difficult to script. Additionally, FTP requires password authentication before it grants access to a file, and most security experts frown on storing passwords in scripts. For these reasons, we don't concentrate on using these protocols to distribute the configuration file. Besides, if you know how to use FTP (and you should!), you know how to use it to send a configuration file.

Another possibility is to use NFS to distribute the information. NFS allows files on the server to be used by clients as if they are local files. It is a powerful tool, but it does have limitations when used to distribute configuration information to boot servers. The same power outage that affects the distributed servers can cause the central server to crash. The distributed servers and their clients can be delayed in booting while waiting for the central server to come back online. Sharing a single copy of the configuration file conflicts with the effort to distribute boot services because it puts too much reliance on the central server.

One way to avoid this problem is for the distributed servers to periodically copy the configuration file from the mounted filesystem to a local disk. This is very simple to script, but it creates the possibility that the servers will be "out of sync" at certain times—the distributed servers copy the configuration file on a periodic schedule without knowing if, in the interim, the master file has been updated. Of course, it is possible for all of the remote servers to export filesystems that the central server mounts. The central server can then copy the configuration file directly to the remote filesystems whenever the master file is updated. However, there are easier ways to do this.

The Unix r-commands rcp and rdist provide the most popular methods for distributing the configuration file.

rcp

Remote copy (rcp) is simply a file transfer protocol. It has two advantages over FTP for this particular application: it is easy to script and it does not require a password. rcp is easy to script because only a single line is needed to complete a transfer. An example of transferring the file *dhcpd.conf* from the master server to a remote server named *arthropod.wrotethebook.com* is:

```
# rcp /etc/dhcpd.conf arthropod.wrotethebook.com:/etc/dhcpd.conf
```

For every remote server that the file is sent to, add a line like this one to the procedure that updates the master configuration file.

rcp is only one choice for distributing the central configuration file. rdist, while a little harder to use, is often a better choice because it has several features that make it particularly well suited for this application.

rdist

The *Remote File Distribution Program* (rdist) is designed to maintain identical copies of files on multiple hosts. A single rdist command can distribute several different files to many different hosts. It does this by following the instructions stored in an rdist configuration file called a *Distfile*.

The function of a *Distfile* is similar to that of the Makefile used by the make command, and it has a similar syntax and structure. Now, don't panic! It's not that bad. The initial configuration of an rdist command is more difficult than the straightforward syntax of an rcp command, but the rdist command provides much more control and is much easier to maintain in the long run.

A *Distfile* is composed of *macros* and *primitives*. Macros can be assigned a single value or a list of values. If a list of values is used, the list is enclosed in parentheses, e.g., *macro* = (*value value*). Once assigned a value, the macro is referenced using the syntax ${*macro*}, where *macro* is the name of the macro. The other components of a *Distfile*, the primitives, are explained in Table 9-4.[*]

Table 9-4. rdist primitives

Primitive	Function
install	Recursively updates files and directories.
notify *address*	Sends error/status mail messages to *address*.
except *file*	Omits *file* from the update.
except_pat *pattern*	Omits filenames that match the pattern.
special *"command"*	Executes *command* after each file update.

The simplest way to understand how the primitives and macros are combined to make a functioning *Distfile* is to look at a sample. The following configuration file distributes the current version of dhcpd and the latest *dhcpd.conf* configuration file to the remote boot servers *horseshoe, arthropod,* and *limulus:*

```
HOSTS = ( horseshoe root@limulus arthropod )
FILES = ( /usr/sbin/dhcpd /etc/dhcpd.conf )

${FILES} -> ${HOSTS}
        install ;
        notify craig@crab.wrotethebook.com
```

---

[*] For more details, see the rdist manpage.

Let's look at each line of the file:

`HOSTS = ( horseshoe root@limulus arthropod )`

This line defines HOSTS, a macro that contains the hostname of each of the remote servers. Notice the entry for *limulus*. It tells rdist to log in as *root* on *limulus* to perform the update. On *horseshoe* and *arthropod*, rdist will run under the same username it has on the local host.

`FILES = ( /usr/sbin/dhcpd /etc/dhcpd.conf )`

This macro, FILES, defines the two files that will be sent.

`${FILES} -> ${HOSTS}`

The -> symbol has a special meaning to rdist. It tells rdist to copy the files named at the left of the symbol to the hosts named at the right. In this case, FILES is a macro that contains the file names */usr/sbin/dhcpd* and */etc/dhcpd.conf*, and HOSTS is a macro that contains the hostnames *horseshoe*, *limulus*, and *arthropod*. Therefore this command tells rdist to copy two files to three different hosts. Any primitives that follow apply to this file-to-host mapping.

`install ;`

The install primitive explicitly tells rdist to copy the specified files to the specified hosts if the corresponding file is out of date on the remote host. A file is considered out of date if the creation date or the size is not the same as the master file. The semicolon at the end of this line indicates that another primitive follows.

`notify craig@crab.wrotethebook.com`

Status and error messages are to be mailed to *craig@crab.wrotethebook.com*.

Additional files and hosts can be easily added to this file. In the long run, most people find rdist the simplest way to distribute multiple files to multiple hosts.

One final note: the configuration file does not have to be called *Distfile*. Any filename can be specified on the rdist command line using the -f option. For example, the *Distfile* shown above could be saved under the name *dhcp.dist* and invoked with the following command:

```
% rdist -f dhcp.dist
```

Post Office Servers

In this section we configure a system to act as a post office server. A *post office server*, or *mailbox server*, is a computer that holds mail for a client computer until the client is ready to download it for the mail reader. This service is essential to support mobile users and small systems that are frequently offline and thus not able to receive mail in real time. We look at two techniques for creating a post office server: Post Office Protocol (POP), which is the original protocol for this purpose, and Internet Message Access Protocol (IMAP), which is a popular alternative. We start with POP.

POP Server

A Unix host turns into a Post Office Protocol server when it runs a POP daemon. Check your system's documentation to see if a POP daemon is included in the system software. If it isn't clear from the documentation, check the *inetd.conf* or *xinetd. conf* file, or try the simple telnet test from Chapter 4. If the server responds to the telnet test, not only is the daemon available on your system, it is installed and ready to run.

```
% telnet localhost 110
Trying 127.0.0.1 ...
Connected to localhost.
Escape character is ' ]'.
+OK POP3 crab Server (Version 1.004) ready
quit
+OK POP3 crab Server (Version 1.001) shutdown
Connection closed by foreign host.
```

This example is from a system that comes with POP3 ready to run. The Red Hat Linux system includes POP3, although it must be enabled in the */etc/xinetd.d/pop3* file before it can be used. The Solaris system, on the other hand, does not ship with POP2 or POP3. Don't worry if your system doesn't include this software. POP3 software is available from several sites on the Internet where it is stored in both the *popper17.tar* and the *pop3d.tar* files. I have used them both, and both work fine.

If you don't have POP3 on your system, download the source code. Extract it using the Unix tar command. *pop3d.tar* creates a directory called *pop3d* under the current directory, but *popper17.tar* does not. If you decide to use popper, create a new directory before extracting it with tar. Edit the Makefile to configure it for your system and do a make to compile the POP3 daemon. If it compiles without errors, install the daemon in a system directory.

On a Solaris system, POP3 is started by the Internet daemon, inetd. Start POP3 from inetd by placing the following in the *inetd.conf* file:

```
pop3    stream tcp    nowait root    /usr/sbin/pop3d              pop3d
```

This entry assumes that you are using pop3d, that you placed the executable in the */usr/ sbin* directory, and that the port for this daemon is identified in the */etc/services* file by the name pop3. If these things aren't true, adjust the entry accordingly.

Make sure that POP3 is actually defined in */etc/services*. If it isn't, add the following line to that file:

```
pop3        110/tcp              # Post Office Version 3
```

Once the lines are added to the *services* file and the *inetd.conf* file, send a SIGHUP to inetd to force it to read the new configuration, as in this example:

```
# ps -ef | grep inetd
    root  109  1  0   Jun 09 ?    0:01 /usr/sbin/inetd -s
# kill -HUP 109
```

Now that POP3 is installed, rerun the test using telnet localhost pop3. If the POP3 daemon answers, you're in business. All users who have a valid user account on the system are now able to download mail via POP3 or read the mail directly on the server.

IMAP Server

Internet Message Access Protocol (IMAP) is an alternative to POP. It provides the same basic service as POP and adds features to support *mailbox synchronization*, which is the ability to read mail on a client or directly on the server while keeping the mailboxes on both systems completely up to date. On an average POP server, the entire contents of the mailbox are moved to the client and either deleted from the server or retained as if never read. Deletion of individual messages on the client is not reflected on the server because all the messages are treated as a single unit that is either deleted or retained after the initial transfer of data to the client. IMAP provides the ability to manipulate individual messages on either the client or the server and to have those changes reflected in the mailboxes of both systems.

IMAP is not a new protocol; it is about as old as POP3. There have been four distinct versions: IMAP, IMAP2, IMAP3, and the current version, IMAP4, which is defined in RFC 2060. IMAP is popular because of the importance of email as a means of communicating, even when people are out of the office, and the need for a mailbox that can be read and maintained from anywhere.

Solaris 8 does not include IMAP. IMAP binaries for Solaris are available from *http://sunfreeware.com*. IMAP source code can be obtained via anonymous FTP from *ftp.cac.washington.edu*. Download */mail/imap.tar.Z* from *ftp.cac.washington.edu* as a binary image. Uncompress and untar the file. This creates a directory containing the source code and Makefile needed to build IMAP.* Read the Makefile carefully. It supports many versions of Unix. If you find yours listed, use the three-character operating system type listed there. For a Solaris system using the gcc compiler, enter:

```
# make gso
```

If it compiles without error, as it does on our Solaris system, it produces three daemons: ipop2d, ipop3d, and imapd. We are familiar with installing POP3. The new one is imapd. Install it in */etc/services*:

```
imap        143/tcp      # IMAP version 4
```

Also add it to */etc/inetd*:

```
imap  stream  tcp  nowait  root  /usr/sbin/imapd  imapd
```

Now basic IMAP service is available to every user with an account on the server.

---

* The name of the directory tells you the current release level of the software. At this writing, it is *imap-2001*.

A nice feature of the University of Washington package is that it provides implementations of POP2 and POP3 as well as IMAP. This is important because many email clients run POP3. The IMAP server can be accessed only by an IMAP client. Installing POP3 along with IMAP gives you the chance to support the full range of clients.

Most Linux systems include IMAP, so compiling the source code is not a requirement. Simply make sure that the service is listed in the */etc/services* file and available through inetd or xinetd. On Red Hat Linux 7, the */etc/xinetd.d/imap* file is disabled by default and must be enabled to allow clients access to the service.

POP and IMAP are important components of a mail service. However, there is a great deal more to configuring a complete email system, as we will see in the next chapter.

Summary

This chapter covered several important TCP/IP network services.

Network File System (NFS) is the leading TCP/IP file-sharing protocol for Unix systems. It allows server systems to share directories with clients that are then used by the clients as if they were local disk drives. NFS uses trusted hosts and Unix UIDs and GIDs for authentication and authorization.

Unix printer sharing is available on a TCP/IP network through the use of the Line Printer Daemon (LPD) or the Line Printer (LP) server. The lpd software is originally from BSD Unix but is widely available. The lpd program reads the printer definitions from the *printcap* file. The LP software is originally from System V. It uses *terminfo* for printer capabilities and the */etc/lp* directory to configure individual printers. Solaris 8 printer sharing is based on the LP software but it configures printers in a single file, */etc/printers.conf*.

Windows PCs use NetBIOS and Server Message Block (SMB) protocol for file and printer sharing. Unix systems can act as SMB servers by using the Samba software package. Samba provides file and printer sharing in a single package that is configured through the *smb.conf* file.

Network Information Service (NIS) is a server that distributes several system administration databases. It allows central control and automatic distribution of important system configuration information.

Dynamic Host Configuration Protocol (DHCP) extends BOOTP to provide the full set of configuration parameters defined in the *Requirements for Internet Hosts* RFC. It also provides for *dynamic address* allocation, which allows a network to make maximum use of a limited set of addresses.

Large networks use distributed boot servers to avoid overloading a single server and to avoid sending boot parameters through IP routers. The configuration files on distributed boot servers are kept synchronized through file transfer, NFS file sharing, or the Remote File Distribution Program (rdist).

Post Office Protocol (POP) and Internet Message Access Protocol (IMAP) servers allow email to be stored on the mail server until the user is ready to read it. In the next chapter, we take a closer look at configuring an electronic mail system as we explore sendmail.

In this chapter:
- sendmail's Function
- Running sendmail as a Daemon
- sendmail Aliases
- The sendmail.cf File
- sendmail.cf Configuration Language
- Rewriting the Mail Address
- Modifying a sendmail.cf File
- Testing sendmail.cf

CHAPTER 10

sendmail

Users have a love-hate relationship with email: they love to use it, and hate when it doesn't work. It's the system administrator's job to make sure it does work. That is the job we tackle in this chapter.

sendmail is not the only mail transport program; smail and qmail are also popular, but plain sendmail is the most widely used mail transport program. This entire chapter is devoted to sendmail, and an entire book can easily be devoted to the subject.* In part, this is because of email's importance, but it is also because sendmail has a complex configuration.

Oddly enough, the complexity of sendmail springs in part from an attempt to reduce complexity by placing all email support in one program. At one time, a wide variety of programs and protocols were used for email. Multiple programs complicate configuration and support. Even today, a few distinct delivery schemes remain. SMTP sends email over TCP/IP networks; another program sends mail between users on the same system; still another sends mail between systems on UUCP networks. Each of these mail systems—SMTP, UUCP, and local mail—has its own delivery program and mail addressing scheme. All of this can cause confusion for mail users and for system administrators.

sendmail's Function

sendmail eliminates the confusion caused by multiple mail delivery programs. It does this by routing mail for the user to the proper delivery program based on the email address. It accepts mail from a user's mail program, interprets the mail address, rewrites the address into the proper form for the delivery program, and routes the mail to the correct delivery program. sendmail insulates the end user from these

---

* See *sendmail* by Costales and Allman (O'Reilly & Associates) and *Linux Sendmail Administration* by Craig Hunt (Sybex) for book-length treatments of sendmail.

details. If the mail is properly addressed, sendmail will see that it is properly passed on for delivery. Likewise, for incoming mail, sendmail interprets the address and either delivers the mail to a user's mail program or forwards it to another system.

Figure 10-1 illustrates sendmail's special role in routing mail between the various mail programs found on Unix systems.

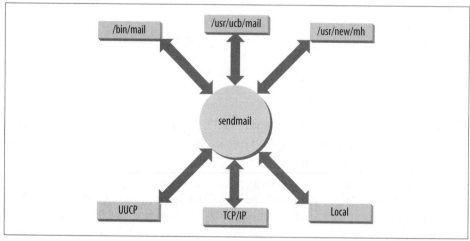

Figure 10-1. Mail routed through sendmail

In addition to routing mail between user programs and delivery programs, sendmail does the following:

- Receives and delivers SMTP (Internet) mail
- Provides systemwide mail aliases, which allow mailing lists

Configuring a system to perform all of these functions properly is a complex task. In this chapter we discuss each of these functions, look at how they are configured, and examine ways to simplify the task. First, we'll see how sendmail is run to receive SMTP mail. Then we'll see how mail aliases are used, and how sendmail is configured to route mail based on the mail's address.

Running sendmail as a Daemon

To receive SMTP mail from the network, run sendmail as a daemon during system startup. The sendmail daemon listens to TCP port 25 and processes incoming mail. In most cases, the code to start sendmail is already in one of your boot scripts. If it isn't, add it. The following command starts sendmail as a daemon:

```
# /usr/lib/sendmail -bd -q15m
```

This command runs sendmail with two command-line options. The -q option tells sendmail how often to process the mail queue. In the sample code, the queue is processed every 15 minutes (-q15m), which is a good setting to process the queue frequently. Don't set this time too low. Processing the queue too often can cause problems if the queue grows very large due to a delivery problem such as a network outage. For the average desktop system, every hour (-q1h) or half hour (-q30m) is an adequate setting.

The other option relates directly to receiving SMTP mail. The -bd option tells sendmail to run as a daemon and to listen to TCP port 25 for incoming mail. Use this option if you want your system to accept incoming TCP/IP mail.

The command-line example is a simple one. Most system startup scripts are more complex. These scripts generally do more than just start sendmail. Solaris 8 uses the */etc/init.d/sendmail* script to run sendmail. First the Solaris script checks for the existence of the mail queue directory. If a mail queue directory doesn't exist, it creates one. In the Solaris 8 script, the command-line options are set in script variables. The variable MODE holds the -bd option, and the variable QUEUEINTERVAL holds the queue processing interval. In the Solaris 8 script, QUEUEINTERVAL defaults to 15m; change the value stored in the QUEUEINTERVAL variable to change how often the queue is processed. Do not change the value in the MODE variable unless you don't want to accept inbound mail. The value must be -bd for sendmail to run as a daemon and collect inbound mail. If you want to add other options to the sendmail command line that is run by the Solaris 8 script file, store those options in the OPTIONS variable.

The Red Hat */etc/rc.d/init.d/sendmail* script is even more complex than the Solaris version. It accepts the arguments start, stop, restart, condrestart, and status so that the script can be used to effectively manage the sendmail daemon process. The start and stop arguments are self-explanatory. The restart argument first stops the sendmail process and then runs a new sendmail process. The condrestart argument is similar to restart except that it runs only if there is a current sendmail process running. If the sendmail daemon is not running when the script is run with the condrestart argument, the script does nothing. The status argument returns the status of the daemon, which is basically the process ID number if it is running or a message saying that sendmail is stopped if sendmail is not running.

When the Red Hat script is run with the start argument, it begins by rebuilding all of the sendmail database files. It then starts the sendmail daemon using the command-line options defined in the */etc/sysconfig/sendmail* file. Like the Solaris script, the Red Hat script uses variables to set the value of the command-line options, but the variables themselves are set indirectly by values from */etc/sysconfig/sendmail* file. The */etc/sysconfig/sendmail* file from a default Red Hat configuration contains only two lines:

```
$ cat /etc/sysconfig/sendmail
DAEMON=yes
QUEUE=1h
```

If DAEMON is set to yes, sendmail is run with the -bd option. How often the queue is processed is determined by the value set for QUEUE. In this example, the queue is processed every hour (1h). The additional code found in most startup scripts is helpful, but it is not required to run sendmail as a daemon. All you really need is the sendmail command with the -bd option.

sendmail Aliases

It is almost impossible to exaggerate the importance of mail aliases. Without them, a sendmail system could not act as a central mail server. Mail aliases provide for:

- Alternate names (nicknames) for individual users
- Forwarding of mail to other hosts
- Mailing lists

sendmail mail aliases are defined in the *aliases* file.[*] The basic format of entries in the *aliases* file is:

```
alias: recipient[, recipient,...]
```

alias is the name to which the mail is addressed, and *recipient* is the name to which the mail is delivered. *recipient* can be a username, the name of another alias, or a full email address containing both a username and a hostname. Including a hostname allows mail to be forwarded to a remote host. Additionally, there can be multiple recipients for a single alias. Mail addressed to that alias is delivered to all of the recipients, thus creating a mailing list.

Aliases that define nicknames for individual users can be used to handle frequently misspelled names. You can also use aliases to deliver mail addressed to special names, such as *postmaster* or *root*, to the real users that do those jobs. Aliases can also be used to implement simplified mail addressing, especially when used in conjunction with MX records.[†] This *aliases* file from *crab* shows all of these uses:

```
# special names
postmaster: clark
root: norman
# accept firstname.lastname@wrotethebook.com
rebecca.hunt: becky@rodent
jessie.mccafferty: jessie@jerboas
anthony.resnick: anthony@horseshoe
andy.wright: andy@ora
# a mailing list
admin: kathy, david@rodent, sara@horseshoe, becky@rodent, craig,
       anna@rodent, jane@rodent, christy@ora
owner-admin: admin-request
admin-request: craig
```

---

[*] The location of the file is defined in the ALIAS_FILE parameter in the sendmail m4 configuration.

[†] Chapter 8 discusses MX records.

The first two aliases are special names. Using these aliases, mail addressed to *post-master* is delivered to the local user *clark*, and mail addressed to *root* is delivered to *norman*.

The second set of aliases is in the form of *firstname* and *lastname*. The first alias in this group is *rebecca.hunt*. Mail addressed to *rebecca.hunt* is forwarded from *crab* and delivered to *becky@rodent*. Combine this alias with an MX record that names *crab* as the mail server for *wrotethebook.com*, and mail addressed to *rebecca.hunt@wrotethebook.com* is delivered to *becky@rodent.wrotethebook.com*. This type of addressing scheme allows each user to advertise a consistent mailing address that does not change just because the user's account moves to another host. Additionally, if a remote user knows that this *firstname.lastname* addressing scheme is used at *wrotethebook.com*, the remote user can address mail to Rebecca Hunt as *rebecca.hunt@wrotethebook.com* without knowing her real email address.

The last two aliases are for a mailing list. The alias *admin* defines the list itself. If mail is sent to *admin*, a copy of the mail is sent to each of the recipients (*kathy*, *david*, *sara*, *becky*, *craig*, *anna*, *jane*, and *christy*). Note that the mailing list continues across multiple lines. A line that starts with a blank or a tab is a continuation line.

The *owner-admin* alias is a special form used by sendmail. The format of this special alias is owner-*listname* where *listname* is the name of a mailing list. The person specified on this alias line is responsible for the list identified by *listname*. If sendmail has problems delivering mail to any of the recipients in the *admin* list, an error message is sent to *owner-admin*. The *owner-admin* alias points to *admin-request* as the person responsible for maintaining the mailing list *admin*. Aliases in the form of *listname-request* are commonly used for administrative requests, such as subscribing to a list, for manually maintained mailing lists. Notice that we point an alias to another alias, which is perfectly legal. The *admin-request* alias resolves to *craig*.

sendmail does not use the *aliases* file directly. The *aliases* file must first be processed by the newaliases command. newaliases is equivalent to sendmail with the -bi option, which causes sendmail to build the *aliases* database. newaliases creates the database files that are used by sendmail when it is searching for aliases. Invoke newaliases after updating the *aliases* file to make sure that sendmail is able to use the new aliases.*

Personal Mail Forwarding

In addition to the mail forwarding provided by *aliases*, sendmail allows individual users to define their own forwarding. The user defines personal forwarding in the *.forward* file in her home directory. sendmail checks for this file after using the *aliases* file

---

* The AutoRebuildAliases option causes sendmail to automatically rebuild the aliases database—even if newaliases is not run. See Appendix E.

and before making final delivery to the user. If the *.forward* file exists, sendmail delivers the mail as directed by that file. For example, say that user *kathy* has a *.forward* file in her home directory that contains *kathy@podunk.edu*. The mail that sendmail would normally deliver to the local user *kathy* is forwarded to *kathy*'s account at *podunk.edu*.

Use the *.forward* file for temporary forwarding. Modifying *aliases* and rebuilding the database takes more effort than modifying a *.forward* file, particularly if the forwarding change will be short-lived. Additionally, the *.forward* file puts users in charge of their own mail forwarding.

Mail aliases and mail forwarding are handled by the *aliases* file and the *.forward* file. Everything else about the sendmail configuration is handled in the *sendmail.cf* file.

The sendmail.cf File

The sendmail configuration file is *sendmail.cf*.* It contains most of the sendmail configuration, including the information required to route mail between the user mail programs and the mail delivery programs. The *sendmail.cf* file has three main functions:

- It defines the sendmail environment.
- It rewrites addresses into the appropriate syntax for the receiving mailer.
- It maps addresses into the instructions necessary to deliver the mail.

Several commands are necessary to perform all of these functions. Macro definitions and option commands define the environment. Rewrite rules rewrite email addresses. Mailer definitions define the instructions necessary to deliver the mail. The terse syntax of these commands makes most system administrators reluctant to read a *sendmail.cf* file, let alone write one! Fortunately, you can avoid writing your own *sendmail.cf* file, as we'll see next.

Locating a Sample sendmail.cf File

There is never any good reason to write a *sendmail.cf* file from scratch. Sample configuration files are delivered with most systems' software. Some system administrators use the *sendmail.cf* configuration file that comes with the system and make small modifications to it to handle site-specific configuration requirements. We cover this approach to sendmail configuration later in this chapter.

Most system administrators prefer to use the m4 source files to build a *sendmail.cf* file. Building the configuration with m4 is recommended by the sendmail developers and is the easiest way to build and maintain a configuration. Some systems, however, do not ship with the m4 source files, and even when m4 source files come with a system,

---

* The default location for the configuration file prior to sendmail 8.11 was the */etc* directory. Now the default is */etc/mail,* but the file is often placed in other directories, such as */usr/lib*.

they are adequate only if used with the sendmail executable that comes with that system. If you update sendmail, use the m4 source files that are compatible with the updated version of sendmail. If you want to use m4 or the latest version of sendmail, download the sendmail source code distribution from *http://www.sendmail.org*. See Appendix E for an example of installing the sendmail distribution.

The sendmail *cf/cf* directory contains several sample configuration files. Several of these are generic files preconfigured for different operating systems. The *cf/cf* directory in the *sendmail.8.11.3* directory contains generic configurations for BSD, Solaris, SunOS, HP Unix, Ultrix, OSF1, and Next Step. The directory also contains a few prototype files designed to be easily modified and used for other operating systems. We will modify the *tcpproto.mc* file, which is for systems that have direct TCP/IP network connections and no direct UUCP connections, to run on our Linux system.

Building a sendmail.cf with m4 macros

The prototype files that come with the sendmail tar are not "ready to run." They must be edited and then processed by the m4 macro processor to produce the actual configuration files. For example, the *tcpproto.mc* file contains the following macros:

```
divert(0)dnl
VERSIONID(`$Id: ch10,v 1.3 2002/03/01 21:02:23 sue Exp emily $')
OSTYPE(`unknown')
FEATURE(`nouucp', `reject')
MAILER(`local')
MAILER(`smtp')
```

These macros are not sendmail commands; they are input for the m4 macro processor. The few lines shown above are the active lines in the *tcpproto.mc* file. They are preceded by a section of comments, not shown here, that is discarded by m4 because it follows a divert(-1) command, which diverts the output to the "bit bucket." This section of the file begins with a divert(0) command, which means these commands should be processed and that the results should be directed to standard output.

The dnl command that appears at the end of the divert(0) line is used to prevent unwanted lines from appearing in the output file. dnl deletes everything up to the next newline. It affects the appearance, but not the function, of the output file. dnl can appear at the end of any macro command. It can also be used at the beginning of a line. When it is, the line is treated as a comment.

The VERSIONID macro is used for version control. Usually the value passed in the macro call is a version number in RCS (Release Control System) or SCCS (Source Code Control System) format. This macro is optional, and we can just ignore it.

The OSTYPE macro defines operating system–specific information for the configuration. The *cf/ostype* directory contains almost 50 predefined operating system macro files. The OSTYPE macro is required and the value passed in the OSTYPE macro call must match the name of one of the files in the directory. Examples of values are bsd4.4, solaris8, and linux.

The FEATURE macro defines optional features to be included in the *sendmail.cf* file. The nouucp feature in the example shown says that UUCP addresses are not used on this system. The argument reject says that local addresses that use the UUCP bang syntax (i.e., contain an ! in the local part) will be rejected. Recall that in the previous section we identified *tcpproto.mc* as the prototype file for systems that have no UUCP connections. Another prototype file would have different FEATURE values.

The prototype file ends with the mailer macros. These must be the last macros in the input file. The example shown above specifies the local mailer macro and the SMTP mailer macro.

The MAILER(local) macro includes the *local* mailer that delivers local mail between users of the system and the *prog* mailer that sends mail files to programs running on the system. All the generic macro configuration files include the MAILER(local) macro because the *local* and *prog* mailers provide essential local mail delivery services.

The MAILER(smtp) macro includes all of the mailers needed to send SMTP mail over a TCP/IP network. The mailers included in this set are:

smtp

> This mailer can handle traditional 7-bit ASCII SMTP mail. It is outmoded because most modern mail networks handle a variety of data types.

esmtp

> This mailer supports Extended SMTP (ESMTP). It understands the ESMTP protocol extensions and it can deal with the complex message bodies and enhanced data types of MIME mail. This is the default mailer used for SMTP mail.

smtp8

> This mailer sends 8-bit data to the remote server, even if the remote server does not indicate that it can support 8-bit data. Normally, a server that supports 8-bit data also supports ESMTP and thus can advertise its support for 8-bit data in the response to the EHLO command. (See Chapter 3 for a description of the SMTP protocol and the EHLO command.) It is possible, however, to have a connection to a remote server that can support 8-bit data but does not support ESMTP. In that rare circumstance, this mailer is available for use.

dsmtp

> This mailer allows the destination system to retrieve mail queued on the server. Normally, the source system sends mail to the destination in what might be called a "push" model, where the source pushes mail out to the destination. On demand, SMTP allows the destination to "pull" mail down from the mail server when it is ready to receive the mail. This mailer implements the ETRN command that permits on-demand delivery. (The ETRN protocol command is described in RFC 1985.)

relay

> This mailer is used when SMTP mail must be relayed through another mail server. Several different mail relay hosts can be defined.

Every server that is connected to or communicates with the Internet uses the MAILER(smtp) set of mailers, and most systems on isolated networks use these mailers because they use TCP/IP on their enterprise network. Despite the fact that the vast majority of sendmail systems require these mailers, installing them is not the default. To support SMTP mail, you must have the MAILER(smtp) macro in your configuration, which is why it is included in the prototype file.

In addition to these two important sets of mailers, there are nine other sets of mailers available with the MAILER command, all of which are covered in Appendix E. Most of them are of very little interest for an average configuration. The two sets of mailers included in the *tcpproto.mc* configuration are the only ones that most administrators ever use.

To create a sample *sendmail.cf* from the *tcpproto.mc* prototype file, copy the prototype file to a work file. Edit the work file to change the OSTYPE line from unknown to the correct value for your operating system, e.g., solaris8 or linux. In the example we use sed to change unknown to linux. We store the result in a file we call *linux.mc*:

```
# sed 's/unknown/linux/' < tcpproto.mc > linux.mc
```

Then enter the m4 command:

```
# m4 ../m4/cf.m4 linux.mc > sendmail.cf
```

The *sendmail.cf* file output by the m4 command is in the correct format to be read by the sendmail program. With the exception of how UUCP addresses are handled, the output file produced above is similar to the sample *generic-linux.cf* configuration file delivered with the sendmail distribution.

OSTYPE is not the only thing in the macro file that can be modified to create a custom configuration. There are a large number of configuration options, all of which are explained in Appendix E. As an example we modify a few options to create a custom configuration that converts *user@host* email addresses originating from our computer into *firstname.lastname@domain*. To do this, we create two new configuration files: a macro file with specific values for the domain that we name *wrotethebook.com.m4*, and a modified macro control file, *linux.mc*, that calls the new *wrotethebook.com.m4* file.

We create the new macro file *wrotethebook.com.m4* and place it in the *cf/domain* directory. The new file contains the following:

```
$ cat domain/wrotethebook.com.m4
MASQUERADE_AS(wrotethebook.com)
FEATURE(masquerade_envelope)
FEATURE(genericstable)
```

These lines say that we want to hide the real hostname and display the name *wrotethebook.com* in its place in outbound email addresses. Also, we want to do this on "envelope" addresses as well as message header addresses. The first two lines handle the conversion of the host part of the outbound email address. The last line says that we will use the generic address conversion database, which converts login usernames to any value we wish to convert the user part of the outbound address. We must build the database by creating a text file with the data we want and processing that file through the makemap command that comes with sendmail.

The format of the database can be very simple:

```
dan Dan.Scribner
tyler Tyler.McCafferty
pat Pat.Stover
willy Bill.Wright
craig Craig.Hunt
```

Each line in the file has two fields: the first field is the key, which is the login name, and the second field is the user's real first and last names separated by a dot. Fields are separated by spaces. Using this database, a query for dan will return the value Dan.Scribner. A small database such as this one can be easily built by hand. On a system with a large number of existing user accounts, you may want to automate this process by extracting the user's login name and first and last names from the */etc/passwd* file. The gcos field of the */etc/passwd* file often contains the user's real name.[*] Once the data is in a text file, convert it to a database with the makemap command. The makemap command is included in the sendmail distribution. The syntax of the makemap command is:

```
makemap type name
```

makemap reads the standard input and writes the database out to a file it creates using the value provided by *name* as the filename. The *type* field identifies the database type. The most commonly supported database types for sendmail are dbm, btree, and hash.[†] All of these types can be made with the makemap command.

Assume that the data shown above has been put in a file named *realnames*. The following command converts that file to a database:

```
# makemap hash genericstable < realnames
```

makemap reads the text file and produces a database file called *genericstable*. The database maps login names to real names, e.g., the key willy returns the value Bill. Wright.

Now that we have created the database, we create a new sendmail configuration file to use it. All of the m4 macros related to using the database are in the *wrotethebook. com.m4* file. We need to include that file in the configuration. To do that, add a DOMAIN(wrotethebook.com) line to the macro control file (*linux.mc*) and then process

---

[*] See Appendix E for a sample script that builds the *realnames* database from */etc/passwd*.

[†] On Solaris systems, NIS maps and NIS+ tables are built with standard commands that come with the operating system. The syntax for using those maps within sendmail is different (see Table 10-3).

the *linux.mc* through m4. The following grep command shows what the macros in the file look like after the change:

```
# grep '^[A-Z]' linux.mc
VERSIONID(`$Id: ch10,v 1.3 2002/03/01 21:02:23 sue Exp emily $')
OSTYPE(`linux')
DOMAIN(`wrotethebook.com')
FEATURE(`nouucp', `reject')
MAILER(`local')
MAILER(`smtp')
# m4 ../m4/cf.m4 linux.mc > sendmail.cf
```

Use a prototype *mc* file as the starting point of your configuration if you install sendmail from the tar file. To use the latest version of sendmail you must build a compatible *sendmail.cf* file using the m4 macros. Don't attempt to use an old *sendmail.cf* file with a new version of sendmail; you'll just cause yourself grief. As you can see from the sample above, m4 configuration files are very short and can be constructed from only a few macros. Use m4 to build a fresh configuration every time you upgrade sendmail.

Conversely, you should not use a *sendmail.cf* file created from the prototype files found in the sendmail distribution with an old version of sendmail. Features in these files require that you run a compatible version of sendmail, which means it is necessary to recompile sendmail to use the new configuration file.* This is not something every system administrator will choose to do, because some systems don't have the correct libraries; others don't even have a C compiler! If you choose not to recompile sendmail, you can use the sample *sendmail.cf* file provided with your system as a starting point. However, if you have major changes planned for your configuration, it is probably easier to recompile sendmail and build a new configuration with m4 than it is to make major changes directly to the *sendmail.cf*.

In the next part of this chapter, we use one of the sample *sendmail.cf* files provided with Linux. The specific file we start with is *generic-linux.cf* found in the *cf/cf* directory of the sendmail distribution. All of the things we discuss in the remainder of the chapter apply equally well to *sendmail.cf* files that are produced by m4. The structure of a *sendmail.cf* file, the commands that it contains, and the tools used to debug it are universal.

General sendmail.cf Structure

Most *sendmail.cf* files have more or less the same structure because most are built from the standard m4 macros. Therefore, the files provided with your system probably are similar to the ones used in our examples. Some systems use a different structure,

---

* See Appendix E for information about compiling sendmail.

but the functions of the sections described here will be found somewhere in most *sendmail.cf* files.

The Linux file, *generic-linux.cf*, is our example of *sendmail.cf* file structure. The section labels from the sample file are used here to provide an overview of the *sendmail.cf* structure. These sections will be described in greater detail when we modify a sample configuration. The sections are:

Local Information

Defines the information that is specific to the individual host. In the *generic-linux.cf* file, Local Information defines the hostname, the names of any mail relay hosts, and the mail domain. It also contains the name that sendmail uses to identify itself when it returns error messages, the message that sendmail displays during an SMTP login, and the version number of the *sendmail.cf* file. (Increase the version number each time you modify the configuration.) This section is usually customized during configuration.

Options

Defines the sendmail options. This section usually requires no modifications.

Message Precedence

Defines the various message precedence values used by sendmail. This section is not modified.

Trusted Users

Defines the users who are trusted to override the sender address when they are sending mail. This section is not modified. Adding users to this list is a potential security problem.

Format of Headers

Defines the format of the headers that sendmail inserts into mail. This section is not modified.

Rewriting Rules

Defines the rules used to rewrite mail addresses. Rewriting Rules contains the general rules called by sendmail or other rewrite rules. This section is not modified during the initial sendmail configuration. Rewrite rules are usually modified only to correct a problem or to add a new service.

Mailer Definitions

Defines the instructions used by sendmail to invoke the mail delivery programs. The specific rewrite rules associated with each individual mailer are also defined in this section. The mailer definitions are usually not modified. However, the rewrite rules associated with the mailers are sometimes modified to correct a problem or to add a new service.

The section labels in the sample file delivered with your system may be different from these. However, the structure of your sample file is probably similar to the structure discussed above in these ways:

- The information that is customized for each host is probably at the beginning of the file.

- Similar types of commands (option commands, header commands, etc.) are usually grouped together.

- The bulk of the file consists of rewrite rules.

- The last part of the file probably contains mailer definitions intermixed with the rewrite rules that are associated with the individual mailers.

Look at the comments in your *sendmail.cf* file. Sometimes these comments provide valuable insight into the file structure and the things that are necessary to configure a system.

It's important to realize how little of *sendmail.cf* needs to be modified for a typical system. If you pick the right sample file to work from, you may need to modify only a few lines in the first section. From this perspective, sendmail configuration appears to be a trivial task. So why are system administrators intimidated by it? It is largely because of the difficult syntax of the *sendmail.cf* configuration language.

sendmail.cf Configuration Language

Every time sendmail starts up, it reads *sendmail.cf*. For this reason, the syntax of the *sendmail.cf* commands is designed to be easy for sendmail to parse—not necessarily easy for humans to read. As a consequence, sendmail commands are very terse, even by Unix standards.

The configuration command is not separated from its variable or value by any spaces. This "run together" format makes the commands hard to read. Figure 10-2 illustrates the format of a command. In the figure, a define macro command assigns the value *wrotethebook.com* to the macro D.

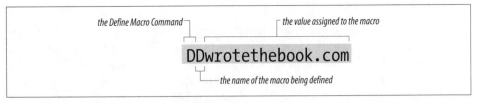

Figure 10-2. A sendmail.cf configuration command

Starting with version 8 of sendmail, variable names are no longer restricted to a single character. Long variable names, enclosed in braces, are now acceptable. For example, the define macro shown in Figure 10-2 could be written:

```
D{Domain}wrotethebook.com
```

Long variable names are easier to read and provide for more choices than the limited set provided by single character names. However, the old-fashioned, short variable names are still common. This terse syntax can be very hard to decipher, but it helps to remember that the first character on the line is always the command. From this single character you can determine what the command is and therefore its structure. Table 10-1 lists the *sendmail.cf* commands and their syntax.

Table 10-1. sendmail configuration commands

Command	Syntax	Function
Version Level	V*level*[/*vendor*]	Specify version level.
Define Macro	D*xvalue*	Set macro *x* to *value*.
Define Class	C*cword1*[*word2*] ...	Set class *c* to *word1 word2* ....
Define Class	F*cfile*	Load class *c* from *file*.
Set Option	O*option=value*	Set *option* to *value*.
Trusted Users	T*user1*[*user2* ...]	Trusted users are *user1 user2* ....
Set Precedence	P*name=number*	Set *name* to precedence *number*.
Define Mailer	M*name*, {*field=value*}	Define mailer *name*.
Define Header	H[?*mflag*?]*name:format*	Set header format.
Set Ruleset	S*n*	Start ruleset number *n*.
Define Rule	R*lhs rhs comment*	Rewrite *lhs* patterns to *rhs* format.
Key File	K*name type* [*argument*]	Define database *name*.

The following sections describe each configuration command in more detail.

The Version Level Command

The version level command is an optional command not found in all *sendmail.cf* files. You don't add a V command to the *sendmail.cf* file or change one if it is already there. The V command is inserted into the configuration file when it is first built from m4 macros or by the vendor.

The level number on the V command line indicates the version level of the configuration syntax. V1 is the oldest configuration syntax and V9 is the version supported by sendmail 8.11.3. Every level in between adds some feature extensions. The *vendor* part of the V command identifies if any vendor-specific syntax is supported. The default *vendor* value for the sendmail distribution is Berkeley.

The V command tells the sendmail executable the level of syntax and commands required to support this configuration. If the sendmail program cannot support the requested commands and syntax, it displays the following error message:

```
# /usr/lib/sendmail -Ctest.cf
Warning: .cf version level (9) exceeds sendmail version 8.9.3+Sun functionality (8):
Operation not permitted
```

This error message indicates that this sendmail program supports level 8 configuration files with Sun syntax extensions.* The example was produced on a Solaris 8 system running the sendmail program that came with the operating system. In the example we attempted to read a configuration file that was created by the m4 macros that came with sendmail 8.11.3. The syntax and functions needed by the configuration file are not available in the sendmail program. To use this configuration file, we would have to compile a newer version of the sendmail program. See Appendix E for an example of compiling sendmail.

You will never change the values on a V command. You might, however, need to customize some D commands.

The Define Macro Command

The define macro command (D) defines a macro and stores a value in it. Once the macro is defined, it is used to provide the stored value to other *sendmail.cf* commands and directly to sendmail itself. This allows sendmail configurations to be shared by many systems simply by modifying a few system-specific macros.

A macro name can be any single ASCII character or a word enclosed in curly braces. Use long names for user-created macros. sendmail's own internal macros use most of the available letters and special characters as names. Additionally, a large number of long macro names are already defined. This does not mean that you won't be called upon to name a macro, but it does mean you will have to be careful that your name doesn't conflict with a name that has already been used. Internal macros are sometimes defined in the *sendmail.cf* file. Appendix E provides a complete list of sendmail's internal macros. Refer to that list when creating a user-defined macro to avoid conflicting with an internal macro. To retrieve the value stored in a macro, reference it as $x, where x is the macro name. Macros are expanded when the *sendmail.cf* file is read. A special syntax, $&x, is used to expand macros when they are referenced. The $&x syntax is only used with certain internal macros that change at runtime.

The code below defines the macros {our-host}, M, and Q. After this code executes, ${our-host} returns *crab*, $M returns *wrotethebook.com*, and $Q returns *crab.wrotethebook.com*. This sample code defines Q as containing the value of {our-host} (which is ${our-host}), plus a literal dot, plus the value of M ($M).

```
D{our-host}crab
DMwrotethebook.com
DQ${our-host}.$M
```

---

* See Table 10-4 for Sun-specific syntax.

If you customize your *sendmail.cf* file, it will probably be necessary to modify some macro definitions. The macros that usually require modification define site-specific information, such as hostnames and domain names.

Conditionals

A macro definition can contain a conditional. Here's a conditional:

```
DX$g$?x ($x)$.
```

The D is the define macro command; X is the macro being defined; and $g says to use the value stored in macro g. But what does $?x ($x)$. mean? The construct $?x is a conditional. It tests whether macro x has a value set. If the macro has been set, the text following the conditional is interpreted. The $. construct ends the conditional.

Given this, the assignment of macro X is interpreted as follows: X is assigned the value of g; and if x is set, X is also assigned a literal blank, a literal left parenthesis, the value of x, and a literal right parenthesis.

So if g contains *chunt@wrotethebook.com* and x contains *Craig Hunt*, X will contain:

```
chunt@wrotethebook.com (Craig Hunt)
```

The conditional can be used with an "else" construct, which is $|. The full syntax of the conditional is:

```
$?x text1 $| text2 $.
```

This is interpreted as:

- if ($?) *x* is set;
- use *text1*;
- else ($|);
- use *text2*;
- end if ($.).

Defining Classes

Two commands, C and F, define sendmail classes. A class is similar to an array of values. Classes are used for anything with multiple values that are handled in the same way, such as multiple names for the local host or a list of uucp hostnames. Classes allow sendmail to compare against a list of values instead of against a single value. Special pattern matching symbols are used with classes. The $= symbol matches any value in a class, and the $~ symbol matches any value not in a class. (More on pattern matching later.)

Like macros, classes can have single-character names or long names enclosed in curly braces. User-created classes use long names that do not conflict with sendmail's internal names. (See Appendix E for a complete list of the names that sendmail uses for its internal class values.) Class values can be defined on a single line, on multiple lines, or loaded from a file. For example, class w is used to define all of the hostnames by which the local host is known. To assign class w the values *goober* and *pea*, you can enter the values on a single line:

```
Cwgoober pea
```

Or you can enter the values on multiple lines:

```
Cwgoober
Cwpea
```

You can also use the F command to load the class values from a file. The F command reads a file and stores the words found there in a class variable. For example, to define class w and assign it all of the strings found in */etc/mail/local-host-names*, use:[*]

```
Fw/etc/mail/local-host-names
```

You may need to modify a few class definitions when creating your *sendmail.cf* file. Frequently information relating to uucp, to alias hostnames, and to special domains for mail routing is defined in class statements. If your system has a uucp connection as well as a TCP/IP connection, pay particular attention to the class definitions. But in any case, check the class definitions carefully and make sure they apply to your configuration.

Here we grep the Linux sample configuration file for lines beginning with C or F:

```
% grep '^[CF]' generic-linux.cf
Cwlocalhost
Fw/etc/mail/local-host-names
CP.
CO @ % !
C..
C[[
FR-o /etc/mail/relay-domains
C{E}root
CPREDIRECT
```

This grep shows that *generic-linux.cf* defines classes w, P, O, ., [, R, and E. w contains the host's alias hostnames. Notice that values are stored in w with both a C command and an F command. Unlike a D command, which overwrites the value stored in a macro, the commands that store values in class arrays are additive. The C command and the F command at the start of this listing add values to class w. Another example of the additive nature of C commands is class P. P holds pseudo-domains

---

[*] sendmail 8.11 uses */etc/mail/local-host-names* to load class w. Earlier versions of sendmail used */etc/sendmail.cw*. Only the name has changed; the file still contains a list of hostnames.

used for mail routing. The first C command affecting class P stores a dot in the array. The last command in the list adds REDIRECT to class P.

Class O stores operators that cannot be part of a valid username. The classes . (dot) and [are primarily of interest because they show that variable names do not have to be alphabetic characters and that sometimes arrays have only one value. E lists the usernames that should always be associated with the local host's fully qualified domain name, even if simplified email addresses are being used for all other users. (More on simplified addresses later.) Notice that even a single character class name, in this case E, can be enclosed in curly braces.

Remember that your system will be different. These same class names may be assigned other values on your system, and are only presented here as an example. Carefully read the comments in your *sendmail.cf* file for guidance as to how classes and macros are used in your configuration.

Many class names are reserved for internal sendmail use. All internal classes defined in sendmail version 8.11 are shown in Appendix E. Only class w, which defines all of the hostnames the system will accept as its own, is commonly modified by system administrators who directly configure the *sendmail.cf* file.

Setting Options

The option (O) command is used to define the sendmail environment. Use the O command to set values appropriate for your installation. The value assigned to an option is a string, an integer, a Boolean, or a time interval, as appropriate for the individual option. All options define values used directly by sendmail.

There are no user-created options. The meaning of each sendmail option is defined within sendmail itself. Appendix E lists the meaning and use of each option, and there are plenty of them.

A few sample options from the *generic-linux.cf* file are shown below. The AliasFile option defines the name of the sendmail *aliases* file as */etc/mail/aliases*. If you want to put the *aliases* file elsewhere, change this option. The TempFileMode option defines the default file mode as 0600 for temporary files created by sendmail in */var/spool/mqueue*. The Timeout.queuereturn option sets the timeout interval for undeliverable mail, here set to five days (5d). These options show the kind of general configuration parameters set by the option command.

```
# location of alias file
O AliasFile=/etc/mail/aliases
# temporary file mode
O TempFileMode=0600
# default timeout interval
O Timeout.queuereturn=5d
```

The syntax of the option command shown in this example and in Appendix E was introduced in sendmail version 8.7.5. Prior to that, the option command used a syntax more like the other sendmail commands. The old syntax is: O*ovalue*, where O is the command, *o* is the single character option name, and *value* is the value assigned to the option. The options shown in the previous discussion, if written in the old syntax, would be:

```
# location of alias file
OA/etc/aliases
# temporary file mode
OF0600
# default timeout interval OT5d
```

If your configuration uses the old option format, it is dangerously out of date and should be upgraded. See Appendix E for information on downloading, compiling, and installing the latest version of sendmail.

Most of the options defined in the *sendmail.cf* file that comes with your system don't require modification. People change options settings because they want to change the sendmail environment, not because they have to. The options in your configuration file are almost certainly correct for your system.

Defining Trusted Users

The T command defines a list of users who are trusted to override the sender address using the mailer -f flag.[*] Normally the trusted users are defined as *root*, *uucp*, and *daemon*. Trusted users can be specified as a list of usernames on a single command line or on multiple command lines. The users must be valid usernames from the */etc/passwd* file.

The most commonly defined trusted users are:

```
Troot
Tdaemon
Tuucp
```

Do not modify this list. Additional trusted users increase the possibility of security problems.

Defining Mail Precedence

Precedence is one of the factors used by sendmail to assign priority to messages entering its queue. The P command defines the message precedence values available to sendmail users. The higher the precedence number, the greater the precedence of the message. The default precedence of a message is 0. Negative precedence numbers

---

[*] Mailer flags are listed in Appendix E.

indicate especially low-priority mail. Error messages are not generated for mail with a negative precedence number, making low priorities attractive for mass mailings. Some commonly used precedence values are:

```
Pfirst-class=0
Pspecial-delivery=100
Plist=-30
Pbulk=-60
Pjunk=-100
```

To specify a desired precedence, add a Precedence header to your outbound message. Use the text name from the P command in the Precedence header to set the specific precedence of the message. Given the precedence definitions shown above, a user who wanted to avoid receiving error messages for a large mailing could select a message precedence of –60 by including the following header line in the mail:

```
Precedence: bulk
```

The five precedence values shown are probably more than you'll ever need.

Defining Mail Headers

The H command defines the format of header lines that sendmail inserts into messages. The format of the header command is the H command, optional header flags enclosed in question marks, a header name, a colon, and a header template. The header template is a combination of literals and macros that are included in the header line. Macros in the header template are expanded before the header is inserted in a message. The same conditional syntax used in macro definitions can be used in header templates, and it functions in exactly the same way: it allows you to test whether a macro is set and to use another value if it is not set.

The header template field can contain the $>*name* syntax that is used in rewrite rules. When used in a header template, the $>*name* syntax allows you to call the ruleset identified by *name* to process an incoming header. This can be useful for filtering headers in order to reduce spam email. We discuss rulesets, rewrite rules, the $>*name* syntax, and how these things are used later in this chapter.

The header flags often arouse more questions than they merit. The function of the flags is very simple. The header flags control whether or not the header is inserted into mail bound for a specific mailer. If no flags are specified, the header is used for all mailers. If a flag is specified, the header is used only for a mailer that has the same flag set in the mailer's definition. (Mailer flags are listed in Appendix E.) Header flags control only header *insertion*. If a header is received in the input, it is passed to the output regardless of the flag settings.

Some sample header definitions from the *generic-linux.cf* sample file are:

```
H?P?Return-Path: <$g>
HReceived: $?sfrom $s $.$?_($?s$|from $.$_)
H?D?Resent-Date: $a
```

```
H?D?Date: $a
H?F?Resent-From: $?x$x <$g>$|$g$.
H?F?From: $?x$x <$g>$|$g$.
H?x?Full-Name: $x
H?M?Resent-Message-Id: <$t.$i@$j>
H?M?Message-Id: <$t.$i@$j>
```

The headers provided in your system's *sendmail.cf* are sufficient for most installations. It's unlikely you'll ever need to change them.

Defining Mailers

The M commands define the mail delivery programs used by sendmail. The syntax of the command is:

```
Mname, {field=value}
```

name is an arbitrary name used internally by sendmail to refer to this mailer. The name doesn't matter as long as it is used consistently within the *sendmail.cf* file to refer to this mailer. For example, the mailer used to deliver SMTP mail within the local domain might be called *smtp* on one system and *ether* on another system. The function of both mailers is the same; only the names are different.

There are a few exceptions to this freedom of choice. The mailer that delivers local mail to users on the same machine must be called *local*, and a mailer named *local* must be defined in the *sendmail.cf* file. Three other special mailer names are:

- *prog*
  Delivers mail to programs.
- **file**
  Sends mail to files.
- **include**

  Directs mail to :include: lists.

Of these, only the *prog* mailer is defined in the *sendmail.cf* file. The other two are defined internally by sendmail.

Despite the fact that the mailer name can be anything you want, it is usually the same on most systems because the mailers in the *sendmail.cf* file are built by standard m4 macros. In the *linux.mc* configuration created earlier, the MAILER(local) macro created the *prog* and *local* mailers, and the MAILER(smtp) macro created the *smtp, esmtp, smtp8, dsmtp,* and *relay* mailers. Every system you work with will probably have this same set of mailer names.

The mailer name is followed by a comma-separated list of *field=value* pairs that define the characteristics of the mailer. Table 10-2 shows the single-character *field* identifiers and the contents of the *value* field associated with each of them. Most mailers don't require all of these fields.

Table 10-2. Mailer definition fields

Field	Meaning	Contents	Example
P	Path	Path of the mailer	P=/bin/mail
F	Flags	sendmail flags for this mailer	F=lsDFMe
S	Sender	Rulesets for sender addresses	S=10
R	Recipient	Rulesets for recipient addresses	R=20
A	Argv	The mailer's argument vector	A=sh -c $u
E	Eol	End-of-line string for the mailer	E=\r\n
M	Maxsize	Maximum message length	M=100000
L	Linelimit	Maximum line length	L=990
D	Directory	*prog* mailer's execution directory	D=$z:/
U	Userid	User and group ID used to run mailer	U=uucp:wheel
N	Nice	nice value used to run mailer	N=10
C	Charset	Content-type for 8-bit MIME characters	C=iso8859-1
T	Type	Type information for MIME errors	T=dns/rfc822/smtp

The Path (P) fields contain either the path to the mail delivery program or the literal string [IPC]. Mailer definitions that specify P=[IPC] use sendmail to deliver mail via SMTP.* The path to a mail delivery program varies from system to system depending on where the systems store the programs. Make sure you know where the programs are stored before you modify the Path field. If you use a *sendmail.cf* file from another computer, make sure that the mailer paths are valid for your system. If you use m4 to build the configuration, the path will be correct.

The Flags (F) field contains the sendmail flags used for this mailer. These are the mailer flags referenced earlier in this chapter under "Defining Mail Headers," but mailer flags do more than just control header insertion. There are a large number of flags. Appendix E describes all of them and their functions.

The Sender (S) and the Recipient (R) fields identify the rulesets used to rewrite the sender and recipient addresses for this mailer. Each ruleset is identified by its number. We'll discuss rulesets more later in this chapter, and we will refer to the S and R values when troubleshooting the sendmail configuration.

The Argv (A) field defines the argument vector passed to the mailer. It contains, among other things, macro expansions that provide the recipient username (which is $u),† the recipient hostname ($h), and the sender's From address ($f). These macros are expanded before the argument vector is passed to the mailer.

---

* [TCP] and [IPC] are used interchangeably, both in the P field and in the A field.

† In the *prog* mailer definition, $u actually passes a program name in the argument vector.

The End-of-line (E) field defines the characters used to mark the end of a line. A carriage return and a line feed (CRLF) is the default for SMTP mailers.

Maxsize (M) defines, in bytes, the longest message that this mailer will handle. This field is used most frequently in definitions of UUCP mailers.

Linelimit (L) defines, in bytes, the maximum length of a line that can be contained in a message handled by this mailer. This mailer field was introduced in sendmail V8. Previous versions of sendmail limited lines to 80 characters because this was the limit for SMTP mail before MIME mail was introduced.

The Directory (D) field specifies the working directory for the *prog* mailer. More than one directory can be specified for the directory field by separating the directory paths with colons. The example in Table 10-2 tells *prog* to use the recipient's home directory, which is the value returned by the internal macro $z. If that directory is not available, it should use the root (/) directory.

The Userid (U) field is used to specify the default user and the group ID used to execute the mailer. The example U=uucp:wheel says that the mailer should be run under the user ID *uucp* and the group ID *wheel*. If no value is specified for the Userid field, the value defined by the DefaultUser option is used.

Use Nice (N) to change the nice value for the execution of the mailer. This allows you to change the scheduling priority of the mailer. This is rarely used. If you're interested, see the nice manpage for appropriate values.

The last two fields are used only for MIME mail. Charset (C) defines the character set used in the Content-type header when an 8-bit message is converted to MIME. If Charset is not defined, the value defined in the DefaultCharSet option is used. If that option is not defined, unknown-8bit is used as the default value.

The Type (T) field defines the type information used in MIME error messages. MIME-type information defines the mailer transfer agent type, the mail address type, and the error code type. The default is *dns/rfc822/smtp*.

Some common mailer definitions

The following mailer definitions are from *generic-linux.cf*:

```
Mlocal,    P=/usr/bin/procmail, F=lsDFMAw5:/|@qSPfhn9,
           S=EnvFromL/HdrFromL, R=EnvToL/HdrToL, T=DNS/RFC822/X-Unix,
           A=procmail -Y -a $h -d $u
Mprog,     P=/bin/sh, F=lsDFMoqeu9, S=EnvFromL/HdrFromL,
           R=EnvToL/HdrToL, D=$z:/, T=X-Unix/X-Unix/X-Unix,
           A=sh -c $u
Msmtp,     P=[IPC], F=mDFMuX, S=EnvFromSMTP/HdrFromSMTP, R=EnvToSMTP,
           E=\r\n, L=990, T=DNS/RFC822/SMTP, A=TCP $h
Mesmtp,    P=[IPC], F=mDFMuXa, S=EnvFromSMTP/HdrFromSMTP, R=EnvToSMTP,
           E=\r\n, L=990, T=DNS/RFC822/SMTP, A=TCP $h
Msmtp8,    P=[IPC], F=mDFMuX8, S=EnvFromSMTP/HdrFromSMTP, R=EnvToSMTP,
           E=\r\n, L=990, T=DNS/RFC822/SMTP, A=TCP $h
```

```
Mdsmtp,   P=[IPC], F=mDFMuXa%, S=EnvFromSMTP/HdrFromSMTP, R=EnvToSMTP,
          E=\r\n, L=990, T=DNS/RFC822/SMTP, A=TCP $h
Mrelay,   P=[IPC], F=mDFMuXa8, S=EnvFromSMTP/HdrFromSMTP, R=MasqSMTP,
          E=\r\n, L=2040, T=DNS/RFC822/SMTP,A=TCP $h
```

This example contains the following mailer definitions:

- A definition for local mail delivery, always called *local*. This definition is required by sendmail.

- A definition for delivering mail to programs, always called *prog*. This definition is found in most configurations.

- A definition for TCP/IP mail delivery, here called *smtp*.

- A definition for an Extended SMTP mailer, here called *esmtp*.

- A definition for an SMTP mailer that handles unencoded 8-bit data, here called *smtp8*.

- A definition for on-demand SMTP, here called *dsmtp*.

- A definition for a mailer that relays TCP/IP mail through an external mail relay host, here called *relay*.

A close examination of the fields in one of these mailer entries, for example the entry for the *smtp* mailer, shows the following:

Msmtp

A mailer, arbitrarily named *smtp*, is being defined.

P=[IPC]

The path to the program used for this mailer is [IPC], which means delivery of this mail is handled internally by sendmail.

F=mDFMuX

The sendmail flags for this mailer say that this mailer can send to multiple recipients at once; that Date, From, and Message-Id headers are needed; that uppercase should be preserved in hostnames and usernames; and that lines beginning with a dot have an extra dot prepended. Refer to Appendix E for more details.

S =EnvFromSMTP/HdrFromSMTP

The sender address in the mail "envelope" is processed through ruleset EnvFromSMTP, and the sender address in the message is processed through ruleset HdrFromSMTP. More on this later.

R= EnvToSMTP

All recipient addresses are processed through ruleset EnvToSMTP.

E=\r\n

Lines are terminated with a carriage return and a line feed.

L=990

This mailer will handle lines up to 990 bytes long.

T=DNS/RFC822/SMTP

> The MIME-type information for this mailer says that DNS is used for hostnames, RFC 822 email addresses are used, and SMTP error codes are used.

A=TCP $h

> The meaning of each option in an argument vector is exactly as defined on the manpage for the command; see the *local* mailer as an example. In the case of the *smtp* mailer, however, the argument refers to an internal sendmail process designed to deliver SMTP mail over a TCP connection. The macro $h is expanded to provide the recipient host ($h) address.

Despite this long discussion, don't worry about mailer definitions. The configuration file that is built by m4 for your operating system contains the correct mailer definitions to run sendmail in a TCP/IP network environment. You shouldn't need to modify any mailer definitions.

Rewriting the Mail Address

Rewrite rules are the heart of the *sendmail.cf* file. Rulesets are groups of individual rewrite rules used to parse email addresses from user mail programs and rewrite them into the form required by the mail delivery programs. Each rewrite rule is defined by an R command. The syntax of the R command is:

> Rpattern transformation comment

The fields in an R command are separated by tab characters. The comment field is ignored by the system, but good comments are vital if you want to have any hope of understanding what's going on. The pattern and transformation fields are the heart of this command.

Pattern Matching

Rewrite rules match the input address against the pattern, and if a match is found, they rewrite the address in a new format using the rules defined in the transformation. A rewrite rule may process the same address several times because, after being rewritten, the address is again compared against the pattern. If it still matches, it is rewritten again. The cycle of pattern matching and rewriting continues until the address no longer matches the pattern.

The pattern is defined using macros, classes, literals, and special metasymbols. The macros, classes, and literals provide the values against which the input is compared, and the metasymbols define the rules used in matching the pattern. Table 10-3 shows the metasymbols used for pattern matching.

Table 10-3. Pattern matching metasymbols

Symbol	Meaning
$@	Match exactly zero tokens.
$*	Match zero or more tokens.
$+	Match one or more tokens.
$-	Match exactly one token.
$=x	Match any token in class x.
$~x	Match any token not in class x.
$x	Match all tokens in macro x.
$%x	Match any token in the NIS map named in macro x.[a]
$!x	Match any token not in the NIS map named in macro x.
$%y	Match any token in the NIS *hosts.byname* map.

[a] This symbol is specific to Sun operating systems.

All of the metasymbols request a match for some number of tokens. A *token* is a string of characters in an email address delimited by an operator. The operators are the characters defined in the OperatorChars option. Operators are also counted as tokens when an address is parsed. For example:

    becky@rodent.wrotethebook.com

This email address contains seven tokens: becky, @, rodent, ., wrotethebook, ., and com. This address would match the pattern:

    $-@$+

The address matches the pattern because:

- It has exactly one token before the @ that matches the requirement of the $- symbol.
- It has an @ that matches the pattern's literal @.
- It has one or more tokens after the @ that match the requirement of the $+ symbol.

Many addresses, such as *hostmaster@apnic.net* and *craigh@ora.com*, match this pattern, but other addresses do not. For example, *rebecca.hunt@wrotethebook.com* does not match because it has three tokens: rebecca, ., and hunt, before the @. Therefore, it fails to meet the requirement of exactly one token specified by the $- symbol. Using the metasymbols, macros, and literals, patterns can be constructed to match any type of email address.

When an address matches a pattern, the strings from the address that match the metasymbols are assigned to *indefinite tokens*. The matching strings are called indefinite tokens because they may contain more than one token value. The indefinite tokens are identified numerically according to the relative position in the pattern of the metasymbol that the string matched. In other words, the indefinite token produced by the match of the first metasymbol is called $1; the match of the second symbol is called $2; the third is $3; and so on. When the address *becky@rodent. wrotethebook.com* matched the pattern $-@$+, two indefinite tokens were created. The first is identified as $1 and contains the single token, becky, that matched the $- symbol. The second indefinite token is $2 and contains the five tokens—rodent, ., wrotethebook, ., and com—that matched the $+ symbol. The indefinite tokens created by the pattern matching can then be referenced by name ($1, $2, etc.) when rewriting the address.

A few of the symbols in Table 10-3 are used only in special cases. The $@ symbol is normally used by itself to test for an empty, or null, address. The symbols that test against NIS maps can only be used on Sun systems that run the sendmail program that Sun provides with the operating system. We'll see in the next section that systems running basic sendmail can use NIS maps, but only for transformation—not for pattern matching.

Transforming the Address

The transformation field, from the right-hand side of the rewrite rule, defines the format used for rewriting the address. It is defined with the same things used to define the pattern: literals, macros, and special metasymbols. Literals in the transformation are written into the new address exactly as shown. Macros are expanded and then written. The metasymbols perform special functions. The transformation metasymbols and their functions are shown in Table 10-4.

Table 10-4. Transformation metasymbols

Symbol	Meaning
$n	Substitute indefinite token *n*.
$[*name$*]	Substitute the canonical form of *name*.
$map key$@argument $:default$)	Substitute a value from database *map* indexed by *key*.
$>n	Call ruleset *n*.
$@	Terminate ruleset.
$:	Terminate rewrite rule.

The $*n* symbol, where *n* is a number, is used for the indefinite token substitution discussed above. The indefinite token is expanded and written to the "new" address. Indefinite token substitution is essential for flexible address rewriting. Without it, values could not be easily moved from the input address to the rewritten address. The following example demonstrates this.

Addresses are always processed by several rewrite rules. No one rule tries to do everything. Assume the input address *mccafferty@rodent* has been through some preliminary processing and now is:

```
kathy.mccafferty<@rodent>
```

Assume the current rewrite rule is:

```
R$+<@$-> $1<@$2.$D> user@host -> user@host.domain
```

The address matches the pattern because it contains one or more tokens before the literal <@, exactly one token after the <@, and then the literal >. The pattern match produces two indefinite tokens that are used in the transformation to rewrite the address.

The transformation contains the indefinite token $1, a literal <@, indefinite token $2, a literal dot (.), the macro D, and the literal >. After the pattern matching, $1 contains *kathy.mccafferty* and $2 contains *rodent*. Assume that the macro D was defined elsewhere in the *sendmail.cf* file as *wrotethebook.com*. In this case the input address is rewritten as:

```
kathy.mccafferty<@rodent.wrotethebook.com>
```

Figure 10-3 illustrates this specific address rewrite. It shows the tokens derived from the input address and how those tokens are matched against the pattern. It also shows the indefinite tokens produced by the pattern matching and how the indefinite tokens and other values from the transformation are used to produce the rewritten address. After rewriting, the address is again compared to the pattern. This time it fails to match the pattern because it no longer contains exactly one token between the literal <@ and the literal >. So, no further processing is done by this rewrite rule and the address is passed to the next rule in line. Rules in a ruleset are processed sequentially, though a few metasymbols can be used to modify this flow.

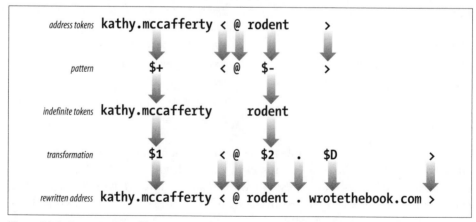

Figure 10-3. Rewriting an address

The $>n$ symbol calls ruleset *n* and passes the address defined by the remainder of the transformation to ruleset *n* for processing. For example:

```
$>9 $1 % $2
```

This transformation calls ruleset 9 ($>9), and passes the contents of $1, a literal %, and the contents of $2 to ruleset 9 for processing. When ruleset 9 finishes processing, it returns a rewritten address to the calling rule. The returned email address is then compared again to the pattern in the calling rule. If it still matches, ruleset 9 is called again.

The recursion built into rewrite rules creates the possibility for infinite loops. sendmail does its best to detect possible loops, but you should take responsibility for writing rules that don't loop. The $@ and the $: symbols are used to control processing and to prevent loops. If the transformation begins with the $@ symbol, the entire ruleset is terminated and the remainder of the transformation is the value returned by the ruleset. If the transformation begins with the $: symbol, the individual rule is executed only once. Use $: to prevent recursion and to prevent loops when calling other rulesets. Use $@ to exit a ruleset at a specific rule.

The $[*name*$] symbol converts a host's nickname or its IP address to its canonical name by passing the value *name* to the name server for resolution. For example, using the *wrotethebook.com* name servers, $[mouse$] returns *rodent.wrotethebook.com* and $[[172.16.12.1]$] returns *crab.wrotethebook.com*.

In the same way that a hostname or address is used to look up a canonical name in the name server database, the $(*map key*$) syntax uses the *key* to retrieve information from the database identified by *map*. This is a more generalized database retrieval syntax than the one that returns canonical hostnames, and it is more complex to use. Before we get into the details of setting up and using databases from within sendmail, let's finish describing the rest of the syntax of rewrite rules.

There is a special rewrite rule syntax that is used in ruleset 0. Ruleset 0 defines the triple (*mailer, host, user*) that specifies the mail delivery program, the recipient host, and the recipient user.

The special transformation syntax used to do this is:

```
$#mailer$@host$:user
```

An example of this syntax taken from the *generic-linux.cf* sample file is:

```
R$*<@$*>$*    $#esmtp $@ $2 $: $1 < @ $2 > $3 user@host.domain
```

Assume the email address *david<@ora.wrotethebook.com>* is processed by this rule. The address matches the pattern $*<@$+>$* because:

- The address has zero or more tokens (david) that match the first $* symbol.
- The address has a literal <@.

- The address has zero or more tokens (the five tokens in ora.wrotethebook.com) that match the requirement of the second $* symbol.

- The address has a literal >.

- The address has zero or more (in this case, zero) tokens that match the requirement of the last $* symbol.

This pattern match produces two indefinite tokens. Indefinite token $1 contains *david* and $2 contains *ora.wrotethebook.com*. No other matches occurred, so $3 is null. These indefinite tokens are used to rewrite the address into the following triple:

```
$#smtp$@ora.wrotethebook.com$:david<@ora.wrotethebook.com>
```

The components of this triple are:

$#smtp
> smtp is the internal name of the mailer that delivers the message.

$@ora.wrotethebook.com
> ora.wrotethebook.com is the recipient host.

$:david<@ora.wrotethebook.com>
> david<@ora.wrotethebook.com> is the recipient user.

There are a few variations on the mailer triple syntax that are also used in the templates of some rules. Two of these variations use only the "mailer" component.

$#OK
> Indicates that the input address passed a security test. For example, the address is permitted to relay mail.

$#discard
> Indicates that the input address failed some security test and that the email message should be discarded.

 Neither OK, discard, nor error (which is discussed in a second) is declared in M commands like real mailers. But the sendmail documentation refers to them as "mailers" and so do we.

The $#OK and $#discard mailers are used in relay control and security. The $#discard mailer silently discards the mail and does not return an error message to the sender. The $#error mailer also handles undeliverable mail, but unlike $#discard, it returns an error message to the sender. The template syntax used with the $#error mailer is more complex than the syntax of either $#OK or $#discard. That syntax is shown here:

```
$#error $@dsn-code $:message
```

The mailer value must be $#error. The $:*message* field contains the text of the error message that you wish to send. The $@*dsn-code* field is optional. If it is provided, it appears before the *message* and must contain a valid Delivery Status Notification (DSN) error code as defined by RFC 1893, *Mail System Status Codes*.

DSN codes are composed of three dot-separated components:

class
> Provides a broad classification of the status. Three values are defined for class in the RFC: 2 means success, 4 means temporary failure, and 5 means permanent failure.

subject
> Classifies the error messages as relating to one of eight categories:
>
> 0 *(Undefined)*
>> The specific category cannot be determined.
>
> 1 *(Addressing)*
>> A problem was encountered with the address.
>
> 2 *(Mailbox)*
>> A problem was encountered with the delivery mailbox.
>
> 3 *(Mail system)*
>> The destination mail delivery system is having a problem.
>
> 4 *(Network)*
>> The network infrastructure is having a problem.
>
> 5 *(Protocol)*
>> A protocol problem was encountered.
>
> 6 *(Content)*
>> The message content caused a translation error.
>
> 7 *(Security)*
>> A security problem was reported.

detail
> Provides the details of the specific error. The detail value is meaningful only in context of the subject code. For example, x.1.1 means a bad destination user address and x.1.2 means a bad destination host address, while x.2.1 means the mailbox is disabled and x.2.2 means the mailbox is full. There are far too many detail codes to list here. See RFC 1893 for a full list.

An error message written to use the DSN format might be:

```
R<@$+>    $#error$@5.1.1$:"user address required"
```

This rule returns the DSN code 5.1.1 and the message "user address required" when the address matches the pattern. The DSN code has a 5 in the class field, meaning it is a permanent failure; a 1 in the subject field, meaning it is an addressing failure; and a 1 in the detail field, meaning that, given the subject value of 1, it is a bad user address.

Error codes and the error syntax are part of the advanced configuration options used for relay control and security. These values are generated by the m4 macro used to select these advanced features. These values are very rarely placed in the *sendmail.cf* file by a system administrator directly.

Transforming with a database

External databases can be used to transform addresses in rewrite rules. The database is included in the transformation part of a rule by using the following syntax:

    $(map key [$@argument...] [$:default] $)

map is the name assigned to the database within the *sendmail.cf* file. The name assigned to *map* is not limited by the rules that govern macro names. Like mailer names, map names are used only inside of the *sendmail.cf* file and can be any name you choose. Select a simple descriptive name, such as "users" or "mailboxes". The map name is assigned with a K command. (More on the K command in a moment.)

key is the value used to index into the database. The value returned from the database for this key is used to rewrite the input address. If no value is returned, the input address is not changed unless a *default* value is provided.

An *argument* is an additional value passed to the database procedure along with the key. Multiple arguments can be used, but each argument must start with $@. The argument can be used by the database procedure to modify the value it returns to sendmail. It is referenced inside the database as %*n*, where *n* is a digit that indicates the order in which the argument appears in the rewrite rule—%1, %2, and so on—when multiple arguments are used. (Argument %0 is the *key*.)

An example will make the use of arguments clear. Assume the following input address:

    tom.martin<@sugar>

Further, assume the following database with the internal sendmail name of "relays":

    oil   %1<@relay.fats.com>
    sugar   %1<@relay.calories.com>
    salt   %1<@server.sodium.org>

Finally, assume the following rewrite rule:

    R$+<@$-> $(relays $2 $@ $1 $:$1<@$2> $)

The input address *tom.martin<@sugar>* matches the pattern because it has one or more tokens (tom.martin) before the literal <@ and exactly one token (sugar) after it. The pattern matching creates two indefinite tokens and passes them to the transformation. The transformation calls the database (relays) and passes it token $2 (sugar) as the key and token $1 (tom.martin) as the argument. If the key is not found in the database, the default ($1<@$2>) is used. In this case, the key is found in the database. The database program uses the key to retrieve "%1@relay.calories.com", expands the %1 argument, and returns "tom.martin@relay.calories.com" to sendmail, which uses the returned value to replace the input address.

Before a database can be used within sendmail, it must be defined. This is done with the K command. The syntax of the K command is:

```
Kname type [arguments]
```

name is the name used to reference this database within sendmail. In the example above, the *name* is "relays".

type is the class of database. The *type* specified in the K command must match the database support compiled into your sendmail. Most sendmail programs do not support all database types, but a few basic types are widely supported. Common types are hash, btree, and nis. There are many more, all of which are described in Appendix E.

arguments are optional. Generally, the only argument is the path of the database file. Occasionally the arguments include flags that are interpreted by the database program. The full list of K command flags that can be passed in the argument field is found in Appendix E.

To define the "relays" database file used in the example above, we might enter the following command in the *sendmail.cf* file:

```
Krelays hash /etc/mail/relays
```

The name *relays* is simply a name you chose because it is descriptive. The database type *hash* is a type supported by your version of sendmail and was used by you when you built the database file. Finally, the argument */etc/mail/relays* is the location of the database file you created.

Don't worry if you're confused about how to build and use database files within sendmail. We will revisit this topic later in the chapter and the examples will make the practical use of database files clear.

The Set Ruleset Command

Rulesets are groups of associated rewrite rules that can be referenced by a name or a number. The S command marks the beginning of a ruleset and names it. In the S*name* command syntax, *name* identifies the ruleset. Optionally a number can also be assigned to the ruleset using the full S*name=number* syntax. In that case, the ruleset can be referenced either by its name or its number. It is even possible to identify a ruleset with a number instead of a name by using the old S*number* syntax. This form of the syntax is primarily found in old configurations because old versions of sendmail used numbers to identify rulesets.

Rulesets can be thought of as subroutines, or functions, designed to process email addresses. They are called from mailer definitions, from individual rewrite rules, or directly by sendmail. Six rulesets have special functions and are called directly by sendmail. These are:

- Ruleset canonify (3) is the first ruleset applied to addresses. It converts an address to the canonical form: *local-part@host.domain*.
- Ruleset parse (0) is applied to the addresses used to deliver the mail. Ruleset parse is applied after ruleset canonify, and only to the recipient addresses actually used for mail delivery. It resolves the address to the triple (*mailer, host, user*) composed of the name of the mailer that will deliver the mail, the recipient hostname, and the recipient username.
- Ruleset sender (1) is applied to all sender addresses in the message.
- Ruleset recipient (2) is applied to all recipient addresses in the message.
- Ruleset final (4) is applied to all addresses in the message and is used to translate internal address formats into external address formats.
- Ruleset localaddr (5) is applied to local addresses after sendmail processes the address against the aliases file. Ruleset 5 is applied only to local addresses that do not have an alias.

Figure 10-4 shows the flow of the message and addresses through these rulesets. The S and R symbols stand for additional rulesets. They have names just like all normal rulesets, but the names are not fixed as is the case with the rulesets described above. The S and R ruleset names are identified in the S and R fields of the mailer definition. Each mailer may specify its own S and R rulesets for mailer-specific cleanup of the sender and recipient addresses just before the message is delivered.

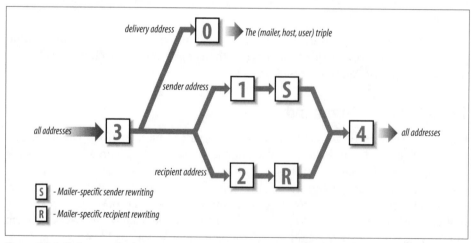

Figure 10-4. Sequence of rulesets

There are, of course, many more rulesets in most *sendmail.cf* files. The other rulesets provide additional address processing, and are called by existing rulesets using the

$>n$ construct. (See Table 10-5 later in this chapter.) The rulesets provided in any vendor's *sendmail.cf* file will be adequate for delivering SMTP mail. It's unlikely you'll have to add to these rulesets, unless you want to add new features to your mailer.

Modifying a sendmail.cf File

In this section we put into practice everything we discussed about sendmail configuration files—their structure and the commands used to build them. We'll modify the configuration file, *generic-linux.cf*, for use on *rodent.wrotethebook.com*. We'll modify this particular file because its configuration is closest to the configuration we need for *rodent.wrotethebook.com*. *rodent* is a Linux workstation on a TCP/IP Ethernet, and it uses SMTP mail and DNS.

The following sections are titled according to the sections of the file, and they describe the modifications we'll make to the file, section by section. Remember that other *sendmail.cf* files will probably use different section titles, but the basic information provided in the configuration will be the same.

Modifying Local Information

The first line in the local information section of the configuration file defines class w.* Class w is the full set of hostnames for which this system accepts mail. Use the C command or the F command to add hostnames to this set. sendmail initializes this class to the value in macro w ($w), which is the hostname of this computer. On many systems that is enough. However, sometimes a sendmail server acts as a mailbox server that must accept and store mail for clients that do not directly receive SMTP mail. The w class needs to identify systems that expect this host to accept mail for them. You'll need to add a hostname to class w for every mailbox client.

In our sample, we accept the Cw command as written, and let sendmail define the value for w internally. This is the most common method for desktop systems like *rodent*. On the system *crab*, which is also known by the name *wtb-gw*, we would add values to class w as follows:

```
Cwlocalhost wtb-gw wtb-gw.wrotethebook.com
```

Now mail addressed to *user@wtb-gw.wrotethebook.com* would be accepted by *crab* and not rejected as being addressed to the wrong host.

Some mail servers might need to be configured to accept mail for many different hostnames. In that case, you may want to load class w from a file containing all the hostnames. You can do that with the F command. The *generic-linux.cf* file already

---

* The C and F commands from *generic-linux.cf* are shown earlier in this chapter.

has an F command, so we could just place the client hostnames in the file */etc/mail/local-host-names*.

No modification is necessary for the j macro definition because, on this system, sendmail obtains a fully qualified domain name for the j macro from DNS. On most systems this is the case; on other systems sendmail obtains the hostname without the domain extension. If j doesn't contain the full name, initialize j with the hostname ($w) and the domain name. In the sample file, we would do this by "uncommenting" the Dj command and editing the domain string to be *wrotethebook.com*. However, there is no need to do this because j has the correct value.

To test if j is set to the correct value on your system, run sendmail with the -bt option and the debug level set to 0.4. In response to this, sendmail displays several lines of information, including the value of j. In the example below, sendmail displays the value *rodent.wrotethebook.com* for j. If it displayed only *rodent*, we would edit *sendmail.cf* to correct the value for j.

```
# sendmail -bt -d0.4
Version 8.11.3
 Compiled with: LOG MATCHGECOS MIME8TO7 NAMED_BIND NDBM
                NETINET NETUNIX NEWDB SCANF USERDB XDEBUG
canonical name: rodent.wrotethebook.com
 UUCP nodename: rodent
        a.k.a.: rodent.wrotethebook.com
        a.k.a.: [172.16.12.2]


============ SYSTEM IDENTITY (after readcf) ============
        (short domain name) $w = rodent
    (canonical domain name) $j = rodent.wrotethebook.com
          (subdomain name) $m = wrotethebook.com
                (node name) $k = rodent
========================================================

ADDRESS TEST MODE (ruleset 3 NOT automatically invoked)
Enter <ruleset> <address> > ^D
```

The next line in the local information section defines class P. In our sample configuration file, class P stores the names of two pseudo-domains. These pseudo-domain names are "." and REDIRECT. The pseudo-domain dot (.) is used to identify canonical domain names. The REDIRECT pseudo-domain is used by the redirect feature described in Appendix E. Other pseudo-domains can be added to class P to address users who are not on the Internet with Internet-style email addresses. For example, we could add UUCP to class P so that mail can be addressed using the old UUCP "bang" syntax, e.g., *ora!los!craig*, or it can be addressed in a pseudo-Internet format, e.g., *craig@los.ora.uucp*. These mail routing domains simplify the address that the user enters and route the mail to the correct mail relay host. However, additional pseudo-domains are rarely needed because most mailers now support standard Internet-style addresses. The class P definition in *generic-linux.cf* does not require any modification.

The configuration file has macro definitions for several mail relays. None of these are assigned a value in our sample file. You only need a relay host if your system cannot deliver the mail because it lacks capability or connectivity. Unix systems do not lack capability, but a firewall might limit connectivity. Some sites use a mail relay so that only one system needs a full *sendmail.cf* configuration. The other hosts at the site simply forward their mail to the smart host for delivery. If this is the configuration policy of your site, enter the name of the mail relay as the "smart" relay. For example:

```
DSrelay.wrotethebook.com
```

We don't enter anything in any of the relay settings on *rodent*. This desktop system will handle all its own mail. Hey, that's why we run Unix!

The local information section in the sample file also includes five key file definitions. Two of these K commands define pseudo-databases, which are internal sendmail routines used in rewrite rules as if they were true databases. The *arith* database is an internal routine used to perform certain arithmetic functions. The *dequote* database is an internal sendmail routine used to remove quotes from within email addresses. The other three K commands define real databases: *mailertable, virtuser,* and *access.* These are real databases, but the database files exist only if you create them. The *mailertable* database is used to send mail addressed to a specific domain through a particular mailer to a specific remote host. The *virtuser* database routes mail for virtual mail domains, which are mail domains that have no real existence beyond the sendmail server itself. The *access* database provides access controls for mail relaying and for spam control.

The version number doesn't *require* modification—but it's a good idea to keep track of the changes you make to your *sendmail.cf* file, and this is the place to do it. Each time you modify the configuration, change the version number by adding your own revision number. At the same time, enter a comment in the file describing the changes you made. Usually, this is the last change made to the files so the comments reflect all changes. For example, the original version number section in the *generic-linux.cf* file is:

```
#####################
#   Version Number   #
#####################
DZ8.11.3
```

After we have finished all of our modifications, it will contain:

```
#####################
#   Version Number   #
#####################
#  R1.0 - modified for rodent by Craig
#        - cleaned up the comments in the local info section
#  R1.1 - modified macro M to use wrotethebook.com instead of the
#          hostname in outgoing mail
#  R2.0 - added rule a to SEnvFromSMTP & S HdrFromSMTP to rewrite
#          the user in outgoing mail to firstname.lastname format
DZ8.11.3R2.0
```

Finally, we need to understand the purpose of a few other classes and macros found in this section. The M macro is used to rewrite the sender host address. Define a value for M to hide the name of the local host in outbound mail. Classes E and M are both related to macro M. Class E defines the usernames for which the hostname is not rewritten even if the M macro is defined. For example, *root@rodent.wrotethe-book.com* is not rewritten to *root@wrotethebook.com* even if M is defined as DMwrotethebook.com. Class M defines other hostnames, not just the local host-name, that should be rewritten to the value of macro M. This is used on mail servers that might need to rewrite sender addresses for their clients. For example:

```
# who I masquerade as (null for no masquerading) (see also $=M)
DMwrotethebook.com
```

```
# class M: domains that should be converted to $M CM24seven.wrotethebook.com brazil.
wrotethebook.com ora.wrotethebook.com
```

Given the macro M and class M definitions shown above, this host would rewrite mail from *user@brazil.wrotethebook.com* or *user@24seven.wrotethebook.com* to *user@wrotethebook.com*. *rodent* is not a server so we won't use class M. But we will use macro M later in the configuration.

We've spent lots of time looking at the local information section because almost everything you will need to do to configure a system can be done here. We will quickly discuss the other section before getting into the really challenging task of working with rewrite rules.

Modifying Options

The section "Options" defines the sendmail environment. For example, some of the options specify the file paths used by sendmail, as in these lines from the *generic-linux.cf* file:

```
# location of alias file
O AliasFile=/etc/mail/aliases
# location of help file
O HelpFile=/etc/mail/helpfile
# status file
O StatusFile=/etc/mail/statistics
# queue directory
O QueueDirectory=/var/spool/mqueue
```

If these paths are correct for your system, don't modify them. On *rodent* we want to keep the files just where they are, which is generally the case when you use a *send-mail.cf* file that was designed for your operating system. In fact, you will probably not need to change any of the options if you use a configuration file designed for your operating system. If you're really curious about sendmail options, see Appendix E.

The next few sections of the *generic-linux.cf* file define the messages' precedences, the trusted users, and the headers. None of these sections is modified. Following these sections are the rewrite rules and the mailers. This material is the bulk of the file and the heart of the configuration. The sample configuration file is designed to allow SMTP mail delivery on a Linux system running DNS, so we assume no modifications are required. We want to test the configuration before copying it into *sendmail.cf*. We'll save it in a temporary configuration file, *test.cf*, and use the troubleshooting features of sendmail to test it.

Testing sendmail.cf

sendmail provides powerful tools for configuration testing and debugging. These test tools are invoked on the sendmail command line using some of the many sendmail command-line arguments. Appendix E lists all of the command-line arguments; Table 10-5 summarizes those that relate to testing and debugging.

Table 10-5. sendmail arguments for testing and debugging

Argument	Function
-t	Send to everyone listed in To:, Cc:, and Bcc:.
-bt	Run in test mode.
-bv	Verify addresses; don't collect or deliver mail.
-bp	Print the mail queue.
-C*file*	Use *file* as the configuration file.
-d*level*	Set debugging level.
-O*option=value*	Set *option* to the specified *value*.
-e	Defines how errors are returned.
-v	Run in verbose mode.

Some command-line arguments are used to verify address processing and to gain confidence in the new configuration. Once you think your configuration will work, send mail to yourself at various sites—testing is a great reason to have several email accounts at various free services. Use the -C argument to read the test configuration file and the -v argument to display the details of the mail delivery. -v displays the complete SMTP exchange between the two hosts.

By observing whether your mailer properly connects to the remote mailer and formats the addresses correctly, you'll get a good idea of how the configuration is working. The following example is a test from *rodent* using the *test.cf* configuration file we just created:

```
rodent# sendmail -Ctest.cf -t -v
To: craigh@ora.com
From: craig
```

```
Subject: Sendmail Test
Ignore this test.
^D
craigh@ora.com... Connecting to ora.com. via esmtp...
220-ruby.ora.com ESMTP Sendmail 8.9.3+Sun/8.9.3; Wed, 23 May 2001
>>> EHLO rodent.wrotethebook.com
250-ruby.ora.com Hello craig@rodent.wrotethebook.com [172.16.12.2],
pleased to meet you
250-EXPN
250-VERB
250-8BITMIME
250-SIZE
250-DSN
250-ONEX
250-ETRN
250-XUSR
250 HELP
>>> MAIL From:<craig@rodent.wrotethebook.com> SIZE=64
250 <craig@rodent.wrotethebook.com>... Sender ok
>>> RCPT To:<craigh@ora.com>
250 <craigh@ora.com>... Recipient ok
>>> DATA
354 Enter mail, end with "." on a line by itself
>>> .
250 SAA27399 Message accepted for delivery
craigh@ora.com... Sent (SAA27399 Message accepted for delivery)
Closing connection to ora.com.
>>> QUIT
221 ruby.ora.com closing connection
```

We entered everything before the Ctrl-D (^D). Everything after the ^D was displayed by sendmail. Figure 10-5 highlights some of the important information in this display and notes the sendmail macros that relate to the highlighted material.

This test successfully transfers mail to a remote Internet site. The sendmail output shows that *rodent* sent the mail to *ora.com* via the *smtp* mail delivery program. The sendmail greeting shows that the remote host handling this SMTP connection is *ruby.ora.com*. Therefore, *ruby* must be the mail server for the *ora.com* domain; i.e., the MX record for *ora.com* points to *ruby.ora.com*.

The EHLO messages indicate that both *rodent* and *ruby* use Extended Simple Mail Transfer Protocol (ESMTP).

Everything worked just fine! We could quit right now and use this configuration. But like most computer people, we cannot stop ourselves from tinkering in order to make things "better."

The From: address, *craig@rodent.wrotethebook.com*, is clearly a valid address but is not quite what we want. We want to have people address us as *firstname.lastname@domain*—not as *user@host.domain*, which is exactly the configuration we created earlier in this chapter with a few lines of m4 code. We will create the same

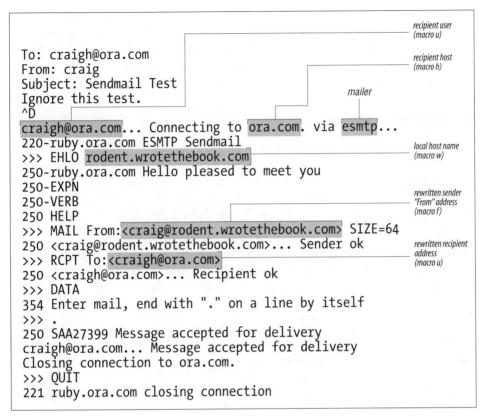

```
                                                        recipient user
                                                        (macro u)
To: craigh@ora.com
From: craig                                             recipient host
Subject: Sendmail Test                                  (macro h)
Ignore this test.                              mailer
^D
craigh@ora.com... Connecting to ora.com. via esmtp...
220-ruby.ora.com ESMTP Sendmail
>>> EHLO rodent.wrotethebook.com                        local host name
250-ruby.ora.com Hello pleased to meet you              (macro w)
250-EXPN
250-VERB                                                rewritten sender
250 HELP                                                "From" address
                                                        (macro f)
>>> MAIL From:<craig@rodent.wrotethebook.com> SIZE=64
250 <craig@rodent.wrotethebook.com>... Sender ok       rewritten recipient
>>> RCPT To:<craigh@ora.com>                            address
250 <craigh@ora.com>... Recipient ok                   (macro u)
>>> DATA
354 Enter mail, end with "." on a line by itself
>>> .
250 SAA27399 Message accepted for delivery
craigh@ora.com... Message accepted for delivery
Closing connection to ora.com.
>>> QUIT
221 ruby.ora.com closing connection
```

Figure 10-5. Verbose mail output

configuration here to provide an example of how to use the various troubleshooting tools that come with sendmail. However, if you really want to make major sendmail configuration changes, you should use m4 to build your configuration.

Most changes to *sendmail.cf* are small and are made near the beginning of the file in the *Local Information* section. Looking closely at that section provides the clues we need to solve part of our configuration problem.

Without knowing what "masquerading" means, the comments for class E, class M, and macro M lead us to guess that the value set for macro M will be used to rewrite the hostname.* In particular, the comment "names that should be exposed as from this host, even if we masquerade" led me to believe that masquerading hides the hostname. Based on this guess, we set a value for macro M as follows:

```
# who I masquerade as (null for no masquerading) (see also $=M) DMwrotethebook.com
```

---

* In the m4 source file we configured masquerading with the MASQUERADE_AS(wrotethebook.com) command.

Are we sure that setting a value for the M macro will hide the hostname? No, but changing the value in *test.cf* and running another test will do no harm. Running the test program with the test configuration has no effect on the running sendmail daemon started by the `sendmail -bd -q1h` command in the boot script. Only an instantiation of sendmail with the `-Ctest.cf` argument will use the *test.cf* test configuration.

Testing Rewrite Rules

In the initial test, the From: address went into sendmail as *craig*, and it came out as *craig@rodent.wrotethebook.com*. Obviously it has been rewritten. This time we test whether the change we made to the macro M in the configuration files modifies the rewrite process by directly testing the rewrite rulesets. First, we need to find out what rules were used to rewrite this address. To get more information, we run sendmail with the `-bt` option.

When sendmail is invoked with the `-bt` option, it prompts for input using the greater-than symbol (>). At the prompt, enter one of the test commands shown in Table 10-6.

Table 10-6. sendmail testing commands

Command	Function
ruleset[,*ruleset...*] *address*	Process *address* through *ruleset*(s).
.D*mvalue*	Assign *value* to macro *m*.
.C*cvalue*	Add *value* to class *c*.
=S*ruleset*	Display the rules in *ruleset*.
=M	Display the mailer definitions.
-d*value*	Set the debug flag to *value*.
$*m*	Display the value of macro *m*.
$=*c*	Display the contents of class *c*.
/mx *host*	Display the MX records for *host*.
/parse *address*	Return the mailer/host/user triple for *address*.
/try *mailer address*	Process *address* for *mailer*.
/tryflags *flags*	Set the address processed by /parse or /try to H (Header), E (Envelope), S (Sender), or R (Recipient).
/canon *hostname*	Canonify *hostname*.
/map *mapname key*	Display the value for *key* found in *mapname*.
/quit	Exit address test mode.

The most basic test is a ruleset name followed by an email address. The address is the test data, and the name is the ruleset to be tested. The address is easy to select; it is the one that was improperly rewritten. But how do you know which ruleset to specify?

Use Figure 10-4 to determine which rulesets to enter. The *canonify* ruleset is applied to all addresses. It is followed by different rulesets depending on whether the address is a delivery address, a sender address, or a recipient address. Furthermore, the rulesets used for sender and recipient addresses vary depending on the mailer that is used to deliver the mail. All addresses are then processed by ruleset *final*.

There are two variables in determining the rulesets used to process an address: the type of address and the mailer through which it is processed. The three address types are delivery address, recipient address, and sender address. You know the address type because you select the address being tested. In our test mail we were concerned about the sender address. Which mailer is used is determined by the delivery address. One way to find out which mailer delivered the test mail is to run sendmail with the -bv argument and the delivery address:

```
# sendmail -bv craigh@ora.com
craigh@ora.com... deliverable: mailer esmtp, host ora.com.,
        user craigh@ora.com
```

Knowing the mailer, we can use sendmail with the -bt option to process the sender From: address. There are two types of sender addresses: the sender address in the "envelope" and the sender address in the message header. The message header address is the one on the From: line sent with the message during the SMTP DATA transfer. You probably see it in the mail headers when you view the message with your mail reader. The "envelope" address is the address used during the SMTP protocol interactions. sendmail allows us to view the processing of both of these addresses:

```
# sendmail -bt -Ctest.cf
ADDRESS TEST MODE (ruleset 3 NOT automatically invoked)
Enter <ruleset> <address>
> /tryflags HS
> /try esmtp craig
Trying header sender address craig for mailer esmtp
canonify          input: craig
Canonify2         input: craig
Canonify2       returns: craig
canonify        returns: craig
1                 input: craig
1               returns: craig
HdrFromSMTP       input: craig
PseudoToReal      input: craig
PseudoToReal    returns: craig
MasqSMTP          input: craig
MasqSMTP        returns: craig < @ *LOCAL* >
MasqHdr           input: craig < @ *LOCAL* >
MasqHdr         returns: craig < @ wrotethebook . com . >
HdrFromSMTP     returns: craig < @ wrotethebook . com . >
final             input: craig < @ wrotethebook . com . >
final           returns: craig @ wrotethebook . com
Rcode = 0, addr = craig@wrotethebook.com
```

```
> /tryflags ES
> /try esmtp craig
Trying envelope sender address craig for mailer esmtp
canonify          input: craig
Canonify2         input: craig
Canonify2        returns: craig
canonify         returns: craig
1                 input: craig
1                returns: craig
EnvFromSMTP       input: craig
PseudoToReal      input: craig
PseudoToReal     returns: craig
MasqSMTP          input: craig
MasqSMTP         returns: craig < @ *LOCAL* >
MasqEnv           input: craig < @ *LOCAL* >
MasqEnv          returns: craig < @ rodent . wrotethebook . com . >
EnvFromSMTP      returns: craig < @ rodent . wrotethebook . com . >
final             input: craig < @ rodent . wrotethebook . com . >
final            returns: craig @ rodent . wrotethebook . com
Rcode = 0, addr = craig@rodent.wrotethebook.com
> /quit
```

The /tryflags command defines the type of address to be processed by a /try or a /parse command. Four flags are available for the /tryflags command: S for sender, R for recipient, H for header, and E for envelope. By combining two of these flags, the first /tryflags command says we will process a header sender (HS) address. The /try command tells sendmail to process the address through a specific mailer. In the example, we process the email address *craig* through the mailer *esmtp*. First, we process it as the header sender address, and then as the envelope sender address. From this test, we can tell that the value that we entered in the M macro is used to rewrite the sender address in the message header, but it is not used to rewrite the sender address in the envelope.

The results of these tests show that the value of the M macro rewrites the hostname in the message header sender address just as we wanted. The hostname in the envelope sender address is not rewritten. Usually this is acceptable. However, we want to create exactly the same configuration as in the m4 example. The FEATURE(masquerade_envelope) command used in the m4 example causes the envelope sender address to be rewritten. Therefore, we want this configuration to also rewrite it.

The only difference between how the message and envelope addresses are processed is that one goes through ruleset HdrFromSMTP and the other goes through ruleset EnvFromSMTP. The tests show that both rulesets call basically the same rulesets. They diverge where ruleset HdrFromSMTP calls ruleset MasqHdr and ruleset Env-FromSMTP calls ruleset MasqEnv. The tests also show that ruleset MasqHdr provides the address rewrite that we want for the message sender address, while the envelope sender address is not processed in the manner we desire by ruleset MasqEnv. The *test.cf* code for rulesets MasqEnv is shown here:

```
##################################################################
###   Ruleset 94 -- convert envelope names to masquerade form   ###
##################################################################
SMasqEnv=94
R$+                $: $>93 $1        do masquerading
R$* < @ *LOCAL* > $*      $: $1 < @ $j . > $2
```

Clearly, ruleset MasqEnv does not do what we want, and ruleset MasqHdr does. A quick inspection of ruleset MasqEnv shows that it does not contain a single reference to macro M. Yet the comment on the line at the start of the ruleset indicates it should "do masquerading." Our solution is to add a line to ruleset MasqEnv so that it now calls ruleset MasqHdr, which is the ruleset that really does the masquerade processing. The modified ruleset is shown here:

```
##################################################################
###   Ruleset 94 -- convert envelope names to masquerade form   ###
##################################################################
SMasqEnv=94
R$+                $: $>93 $1              do masquerading
R$* < @ *LOCAL* > $*      $: $1 < @ $j . > $2
```

Debugging a *sendmail.cf* file is more of an art than a science. Deciding to add the first line to ruleset MasqEnv to call ruleset MasqHdr is little more than a hunch. The only way to verify the hunch is through testing. We run sendmail -bt -Ctest.cf again to test the addresses *craig*, *craig@rodent*, and *craig@localhost* using the /try esmtp command. All tests run successfully, rewriting the various input addresses into *craig@wrotethebook.com*. We then retest by sending mail via sendmail -v -t -Ctest. cf. Only when all of these tests run successfully do we really believe in our hunch and move on to the next task, which is to rewrite the user part of the email address into the user's first and

last names.

Using Key Files in sendmail

The last feature we added to the m4 source file was FEATURE(genericstable), which adds a database process to the configuration that we use to convert the user portion of the email address from the user's login name to the user's first and last names. To do the same thing here, create a text file of login names and first and last names and build a database with makemap.[*]

```
# cd /etc/mail
# cat realnames
dan Dan.Scribner
tyler Tyler.McCafferty
pat Pat.Stover
willy Bill.Wright
```

---

[*] See the m4 section for more information about makemap.

```
craig Craig.Hunt
# makemap hash realnames < realnames
```

Once the database is created, define it for sendmail. Use the K command to do this. To use the database that we have just built, insert the following lines into the Local Information section of the *sendmail.cf* file:

```
# define a database to map login names to firstname.lastname
Krealnames hash /etc/mail/realnames
```

The K command defines *realnames* as the internal sendmail name of this database. Further, it identifies that this is a database of type *hash* and that the path to the database is */etc/realnames*. sendmail adds the correct filename extensions to the pathname depending on the type of the database, so you don't need to worry about it.

Finally, we add a new rule that uses the database to rewrite addresses. We add it to ruleset EnvFromSMTP and ruleset HdrFromSMTP immediately after the lines in those rulesets that call ruleset MasqHdr. This way, our new rule gets the address as soon as ruleset MasqHdr finishes processing it.

```
# when masquerading convert login name to firstname.lastname
R$-<@$M.>$*    $:$(realnames $1 $)<@$M.>$2    user=>first.last
```

This rule is designed to process the output of ruleset MasqHdr, which rewrites the hostname portion of the address. Addresses that meet the criteria to have the hostname part rewritten are also the addresses for which we want to rewrite the user part. Look at the output of ruleset MasqHdr from the earlier test. That address, *craig<@wrotethebook.com.>*, matches the pattern $-<@$M.>$*. The address has exactly one token (craig) before the literal <@, followed by the value of M (wrotethebook.com), the literal .>, and zero tokens.

The transformation part of this rule takes the first token ($1) from the input address and uses it as the key to the *realnames* database, as indicated by the $:$(realnames $1 $) syntax. For the sample address *craig<@wrotethebook.com>*, $1 is *craig*. When used as an index into the database *realnames* shown at the beginning of this section, it returns *Craig.Hunt*. This returned value is prepended to the literal <@, the value of macro M ($M), the literal .>, and the value of $2, as indicated by the <@$M.>$2 part of the transformation. The effect of this new rule is to convert the username to the user's real first and last names.

After adding the new rule to rulesets EnvFromSMTP and HdrFromSMTP, a test yields the following results:

```
# sendmail -bt -Ctest.cf
ADDRESS TEST MODE (ruleset 3 NOT automatically invoked)
Enter <ruleset> <address>
> /tryflags HS
> /try esmtp craig
Trying header sender address craig for mailer esmtp
canonify          input: craig
Canonify2         input: craig
```

```
Canonify2      returns: craig
canonify       returns: craig
1                input: craig
1              returns: craig
HdrFromSMTP      input: craig
PseudoToReal     input: craig
PseudoToReal   returns: craig
MasqSMTP         input: craig
MasqSMTP       returns: craig < @ *LOCAL* >
MasqHdr          input: craig < @ *LOCAL* >
MasqHdr        returns: craig < @ wrotethebook . com . >
HdrFromSMTP    returns: Craig . Hunt < @ wrotethebook . com . >
final            input: Craig . Hunt < @ wrotethebook . com . >
final          returns: Craig . Hunt @ wrotethebook . com
Rcode = 0, addr = Craig.Hunt@wrotethebook.com
> /tryflags ES
> /try esmtp craig
Trying envelope sender address craig for mailer esmtp
canonify         input: craig
Canonify2        input: craig
Canonify2      returns: craig
canonify       returns: craig
1                input: craig
1              returns: craig
EnvFromSMTP      input: craig
PseudoToReal     input: craig
PseudoToReal   returns: craig
MasqSMTP         input: craig
MasqSMTP       returns: craig < @ *LOCAL* >
MasqEnv          input: craig < @ *LOCAL* >
MasqHdr          input: craig < @ *LOCAL* >
MasqHdr        returns: craig < @ wrotethebook . com . >
MasqEnv        returns: craig < @ wrotethebook . com . >
EnvFromSMTP    returns: Craig . Hunt < @ wrotethebook . com . >
final            input: Craig . Hunt < @ wrotethebook . com . >
final          returns: Craig . Hunt @ wrotethebook . com
Rcode = 0, addr = Craig.Hunt@wrotethebook.com
> /quit
```

If the tests do not give the results you want, make sure that you have correctly entered the new rewrite rules and that you have correctly built the database. The following error message could also be displayed:

```
test.cf: line 116: readcf: map realnames: class hash not available
```

This indicates that your system does not support hash databases. You can try changing the database type on the K command line to hash and rerunning sendmail -bt until you find a type of database that your sendmail likes. When you do, rerun makemap using that database type. If your sendmail doesn't support any database type, see Appendix E for information on recompiling sendmail with database support.

Note that all of the changes made directly to the *sendmail.cf* file in the second half of this chapter (masquerading the sender address, masquerading the envelope address, and converting usernames) were handled by just three lines in the m4 source file. These examples demonstrated how to use the sendmail test tools. If you really need to make a new, custom configuration, use m4. It is easiest to maintain and enhance the sendmail configuration through the m4 source file.

Summary

sendmail sends and receives SMTP mail, processes mail aliases, and interfaces between user mail agents and mail delivery agents. sendmail is started as a daemon at boot time to process incoming SMTP mail. sendmail aliases are defined in the *aliases* file. The rules for interfacing between user agents and mail delivery agents can be complex; sendmail uses the *sendmail.cf* file to define these rules.

Configuring the *sendmail.cf* file is the most difficult part of setting up a sendmail server. The file uses a very terse command syntax that is hard to read. Sample *sendmail.cf* files are available to simplify this task. Most systems come with a vendor-supplied configuration file, and others are available with the sendmail software distribution. The sendmail sample files must first be processed by the m4 macro processor. Once the proper sample file is available, very little of it needs to be changed. Almost all of the changes needed to complete the configuration occur at the beginning of the file and are used to define information about the local system, such as the hostname and the name of the mail relay host. sendmail provides an interactive testing tool that is used to check the configuration before it is installed.

sendmail is a big, complex service that is important enough to deserve its own chapter. Web service is another important service, provided by Apache on most Unix systems. Apache's complex configuration syntax is the topic of the next chapter.

In this chapter:
- Installing Apache Software
- Configuring the Apache Server
- Understanding an httpd.conf File
- Web Server Security
- Managing Your Web Server

CHAPTER 11

Configuring Apache

Web servers provide the leading method for delivering information over an IP network. The Web is best known for providing information over the global Internet, yet it can just as effectively provide information to internal staff as it does to external customers. All but the smallest networks can benefit from a well-run web server, which can advertise products and offer support services to external customers, as well as coordinate and disseminate information to users within your organization. The Web is the single most effective tool for delivering on-demand information to end users.

Most Unix web servers are built with Apache software. Apache is freely available web server software with origins in the National Center for Supercomputer Applications (NCSA) web server, the first widely used web server. Because of these "ancient" roots, Apache has undergone years of testing and development. Because it is the most widely deployed web server software on the Internet, you will probably use Apache to build your Unix web server.

In this chapter, we focus on installing and configuring an Apache server. The large number of configuration options can make Apache configuration appear more complex than it really is. This chapter provides an example of a simple configuration to get Apache up and running quickly.

Our focus is configuration and administration of the service, not the design of the content provided by the service; web page design is beyond the scope of this book. If you're lucky, your organization has trained web designers; if you're not so lucky, you may be expected to take on this artistic task yourself. O'Reilly has books that can help you: try *HTML and XHTML: The Definitive Guide,* by Chuck Musciano and Bill Kennedy, or *Web Design in a Nutshell*, by Jennifer Niederst.

Installing Apache Software

The Apache server software is bundled with many Unix systems. Frequently, Apache is installed as part of the initial operating system installation. For example, the initial installation of a Red Hat system presents a screen that allows the user to select the Apache software by clicking on an icon labeled *Apache Web Server*.

Frequently, users select the Apache server software even when they don't plan to run a web server. You might be surprised to find an Apache server installed and running on client desktop workstations. Try a ps test:

```
$ ps ax | grep httpd
 321  ?  S    0:00 httpd
 324  ?  S    0:00 httpd
 325  ?  S    0:00 httpd
 326  ?  S    0:00 httpd
 329  ?  S    0:00 (httpd)
 330  ?  S    0:00 (httpd)
 331  ?  S    0:00 (httpd)
 332  ?  S    0:00 (httpd)
 333  ?  S    0:00 (httpd)
 334  ?  S    0:00 (httpd)
 335  ?  S    0:00 (httpd)
2539  p1 D    0:00 grep http
```

The daemon that Apache installs to provide web services is the Hypertext Transport Protocol daemon (httpd). Use the process status (ps) command to check for all processes in the system, and the grep command to display only those with the name httpd. Running this test on a freshly installed system will show you if Apache is installed and running.

If Apache is running, start the Netscape web browser and enter "localhost" in the search box. Figure 11-1 shows the result on a sample Red Hat 7 system. Not only is Apache installed and running, it is configured and responding with a web page. Users of desktop Linux systems are sometimes surprised to find out they are running a fully functional web server. Of course, if you're the administrator of a web server system, this is exactly what you want to see—Apache installed, up, and running.

If the Apache software is not installed on your system, you need to install the package. The easiest way to install optional software on a Linux system is to use a package manager. Several good ones are available. Most Linux systems support the Red Hat Package Manager (rpm), so we'll use that in the following example.

Using the Red Hat Package Manager

Use the Red Hat Package Manager to install needed software, remove unneeded software, and check what software is installed. rpm has many options for the developers

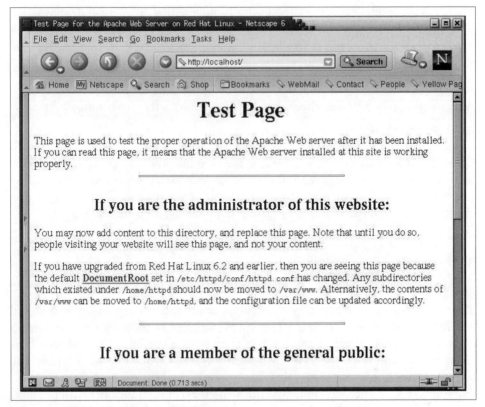

Figure 11-1. Default Apache server web page

who build the packages, but for a network administrator, rpm comes down to three basic commands:

rpm --install package
    The --install option installs software.

rpm --uninstall package
    The --uninstall option removes software.

rpm --query
    The --query option lists a software package that is already installed. Use --all with the --query option to list all installed packages.

You must know the name of a package to install it with rpm. To find the full name of the Apache package, mount the Linux CD-ROM and look in the *RPMS* directory. Here is an example from a Red Hat 7.2 system:

```
$ cd /mnt/cdrom/RedHat/RPMS
$ ls *apache*
apache-1.3.20-16.i386.rpm
apacheconf-0.8.1-1.noarch.rpm
```

This example assumes that the CD-ROM was mounted on * /mnt/cdrom*. It shows that two Apache software packages are included in the Red Hat distribution: the web server software and a Red Hat configuration tool. Install *apache-1.3.20-16.i386.rpm* with this command to get the web server software:

```
# rpm --install apache-1.3.20-16.i386.rpm
```

After installing the package, check that it is installed with this rpm command:

```
$ rpm --query apache
apache-1.3.20-16
```

Once the Apache package is installed, make sure the httpd daemons are started at boot time. On a Red Hat system, the script */etc/init.d/httpd* starts the daemons. Use chkconfig or a similar command to add the script to the boot process. The following example adds the *httpd* startup script to the boot process for runlevels 3 and 5:

```
# chkconfig --list httpd
httpd            0:off  1:off  2:off  3:off  4:off  5:off  6:off
# chkconfig --level 35  httpd on
# chkconfig --list httpd
httpd            0:off  1:off  2:off  3:on   4:off  5:on   6:off
```

The first chkconfig command lists the status of the *httpd* script for every runlevel. The response shows that *httpd* is off for all seven runlevels, meaning that the script is not run. We want to start the web server at runlevel 3, which is the multiuser runlevel, and at runlevel 5, which is the default runlevel for this Red Hat system. The second chkconfig command does this. The --level argument specifies that runlevel 3 and runlevel 5 are affected—note that the 3 and the 5 are run together with no intervening spaces. The httpd on argument says that the *httpd* script should be executed for those two runlevels. The last chkconfig command again lists the status of the *httpd* script for all runlevels. This time it shows that *httpd* will be executed for runlevel 3 and runlevel 5.

The next time this Red Hat system reboots, the web server will be running. To start the web server without rebooting, invoke the *httpd* script from the command line:

```
# /etc/init.d/httpd start
Starting httpd:                                      [  OK  ]
```

Installing Apache on a Linux system is straightforward. It is often installed during the initial system setup; if not, it can usually be installed from the CDs that came with the system. Installing Apache on a Solaris system is just as simple because Solaris 8 also includes Apache as part of the operating system. If your Unix system does not include Apache, download it from the Internet.

Downloading Apache

Apache is available from *http://www.apache.org* in both source and binary forms. The Apache source is available for Unix systems in both compressed and zipped tarballs. You can download and compile the source, but the easiest way to get Apache is as a precompiled binary. Figure 11-2 shows just some of the versions of Unix for which precompiled httpd server daemons are available.

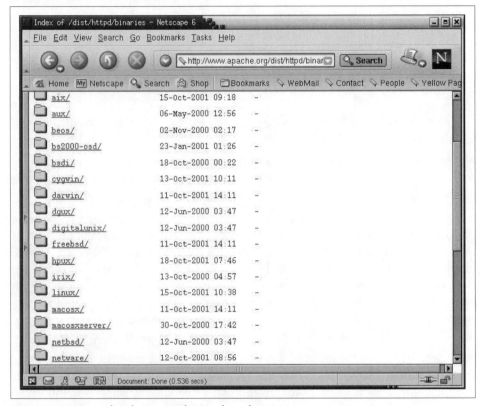

Figure 11-2. Binary distributions at the Apache web site

The binaries are listed by operating system. Assume you have a FreeBSD system. Click on the *freebsd* link, and you're presented with a long list of zipped tarballs. Each tarball relates to a different version of FreeBSD and contains an Apache binary distribution. Select the binary that is appropriate for your version of FreeBSD and download it to a working directory. Make a backup copy of the current daemon and extract the new daemon with tar. The software should now be installed and ready to run with the configuration files from your current configuration.

Configuring the Apache Server

Apache configuration traditionally involves three files:

httpd.conf
> This is the primary configuration file. It traditionally contains configuration settings for the HTTP protocol and for the operation of the server. This file is processed first.

srm.conf
> This file traditionally contains configuration settings to help the server respond to client requests. The settings include how to handle different MIME types, how to format output, and the location of HTTP documents and Common Gateway Interface (CGI) scripts. This file is processed second.

access.conf
> This file traditionally defines access control for the server and the information the server provides. This file is processed last.

All three files have a similar structure: they are all written as ASCII text files, comments begin with a #, and the files are well commented. Most of the directives in the files are written in the form of an option followed by a value.

We say that these three files *traditionally* handle Apache configuration, but common practice today has diverged from that approach. There is overlap in the function of the three files. You may think you know where a certain value should be set, only to be surprised to find it in another file. In fact, any Apache configuration directive can be used in any of the configuration files—the traditional division of the files into server, data, and security functions was essentially arbitrary. Some administrators still follow tradition, but it is most common for the entire configuration to be defined in the *httpd.conf* file. This is the recommended approach, and the one we use in this chapter.

Different systems put the *httpd.conf* file in different directories. On a Solaris system, the file is stored in the */etc/apache* directory; on a Red Hat system, it is found in the */etc/httpd/conf* directory; and on Caldera systems, in the */etc/httpd/apache/conf* directory. The Apache manpage should tell you where *httpd.conf* is located on your system; if it doesn't, look in the script that starts httpd at boot time. The location of the *httpd.conf* file will either be defined by a script variable or by the -f argument on the httpd command line. Of course, a very simple way to locate the file is with the find command, as in this Caldera Linux example:

```
# find / -name httpd.conf -print
/etc/httpd/apache/conf/httpd.conf
```

Once you find *httpd.conf*, customize it for your system. The Apache configuration file is large and complex; however, it is preconfigured, so your server will run with only a little input from you. Edit the *httpd.conf* file to set the web administrator's

---

email address in ServerAdmin and the server's hostname in ServerName. With those small changes, the httpd configuration provided with your Unix system will probably be ready to run. Let's look at a Solaris 8 example.

Configuring Apache on Solaris

The first step to configure Apache on a Solaris system is to copy the file *httpd.conf-example* to *httpd.conf*:

```
# cd /etc/apache
# cp httpd.conf-example httpd.conf
```

Use an editor to put valid ServerAdmin and ServerName values into the configuration. In the Solaris example, we change ServerAdmin from:

```
ServerAdmin you@your.address
```

to:

```
ServerAdmin webmaster@www.wrotethebook.com
```

We change ServerName from:

```
#ServerName new.host.name
```

to:

```
ServerName www.wrotethebook.com
```

Once these minimal changes are made, the server can be started. The easiest way to do this on a Solaris system is to run the */etc/init.d/apache* script file. The script accepts three possible arguments: start, restart, and stop. Since httpd is not yet running, there is no daemon to stop or restart, so we use the start command:

```
# /etc/init.d/apache start
httpd starting.
# ps -ef | grep '/httpd'
  nobody   474   473  0 12:57:27 ?         0:00 /usr/apache/bin/httpd
  nobody   475   473  0 12:57:27 ?         0:00 /usr/apache/bin/httpd
  nobody   476   473  0 12:57:27 ?         0:00 /usr/apache/bin/httpd
    root   473     1  0 12:57:26 ?         0:00 /usr/apache/bin/httpd
  nobody   477   473  0 12:57:27 ?         0:00 /usr/apache/bin/httpd
  nobody   478   473  0 12:57:27 ?         0:00 /usr/apache/bin/httpd
    root   501   358  0 13:10:04 pts/2     0:00 grep /httpd
```

After running the *apache* startup script, run ps to verify that the httpd daemon is running.* In this example, several copies of the daemon are running, just as we saw earlier in the Linux example. This group of daemons is called the *swarm*, and we'll examine the Apache configuration directives that control the size of the swarm later.

---

* The DynaWeb (dwhttpd) daemon, which is used to display the *AnswerBook*, may also appear in the ps list on Solaris systems that run an *AnswerBook2* server.

Now that the daemons are running, run Netscape. Enter "localhost" in the location box, and you should see something like Figure 11-3.

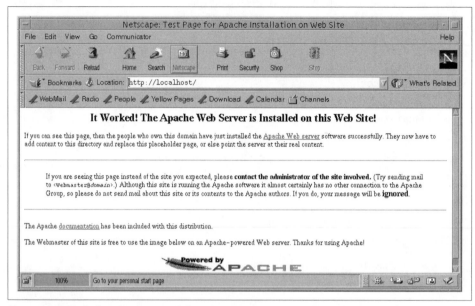

Figure 11-3. Default web page on a Solaris server

Our Solaris Apache server is now up, running, and serving data. Of course, this is not really the data we want to serve our clients. There are two solutions to this problem: either put the correct data in the directory that the server is using, or configure the server to use the directory in which the correct data is located.

The DocumentRoot directive points the server to the directory that contains web page information. By default, the Solaris server gets web pages from the */var/apache/ htdocs* directory, as you can see by checking the value for DocumentRoot in the *httpd.conf* file:

```
# grep '^DocumentRoot' httpd.conf
DocumentRoot "/var/apache/htdocs"
# ls /var/apache/htdocs
apache_pb.gif  index.html
```

The */var/apache/htdocs* directory contains only two files. The GIF file is the Apache feather graphic seen at the bottom of the web page in Figure 11-3. The *index.html* file is the HTML document that creates this web page. By default, Apache looks for a file named *index.html* and uses it as the home page if a specific page has not been requested. You can put your own *index.html* file in this directory, along with any other supporting files and directories you need, and Apache will start serving your data. Alternately, you can edit the *httpd.conf* file to change the value in the Document-Root directive to point to the directory where you store your data. The choice is yours. Either way, you need to create HTML documents for the web server to display.

Although the Solaris server can run after modifying only two or three configuration directives, you still need to understand the full range of Apache configuration. Given the importance of web services for most networks, Apache is too essential for you to ignore. To properly debug a misconfigured web server, you need to understand the entire *httpd.conf* file. The following sections examine this file in detail.

Understanding an httpd.conf File

It's helpful to know the default configuration when you're called upon to correct the configuration of someone else's system. In this section we examine the values set in the default configuration on a Solaris 8 system. (The default Solaris 8 configuration file is listed in Appendix F.)

Here we focus on the directives that are actually used in the Solaris 8 configuration, and a few others that show important Apache features. There are some other directives that we don't discuss. If you need additional information about any directive, there are many places to look. The full *httpd.conf* file contains many comments, which explain the purpose of each directive and are an excellent source of information. The Apache web site (*http://www.apache.org*) provides online documentation. Two excellent books on Apache configuration are *Apache: The Definitive Guide*, by Ben and Peter Laurie (O'Reilly), and *Linux Apache Web Server Administration*, by Charles Aulds (Sybex). However, you'll probably find more information about the *httpd.conf* file than you need for an average configuration right here in this chapter.

The *httpd.conf* file that comes with Solaris has 160 active configuration lines. To tackle that much information, the following sections organize the configuration directives into different groups. Note that the configuration file itself organizes directives by scope: global environment directives, main server directives, and virtual host directives. (Virtual hosts are explained later in this chapter.) Although that organization is great for httpd when it is processing the file, it's not so great for a human reading the file. Here, related directives are grouped by function to make the individual directives more understandable. Once you understand the individual directives, you will understand the entire configuration.

We start our look at the *httpd.conf* file with the directives that load dynamically loadable modules. These modules must be loaded before the directives they provide can be used in the configuration, so it makes sense to discuss loading the modules before we discuss the features they provide. Understanding dynamically loadable modules is a good place to start understanding Apache configuration.

Loading Dynamic Shared Objects

The two directives that appear most in the Solaris *httpd.conf* file are LoadModule and AddModule. Together, they make up more than 60 of the 160 active lines in the *httpd.conf* file. All 60 of these lines configure the Dynamic Shared Object (DSO) modules used by the Apache web server.

Apache is composed of many software modules. Like kernel modules, DSO modules can be compiled into Apache or loaded at runtime. Running httpd with the -l command-line option lists all the modules compiled into Apache. The following example is from a Solaris 8 system:

```
$ /usr/apache/bin/httpd -l
Compiled-in modules:
  http_core.c
  mod_so.c
```

Some systems may have many modules compiled into the Apache daemon. Solaris and Red Hat systems are delivered with only the following two modules compiled in:

http_core.c
> This is the core module. It is always statically linked into the Apache kernel, and it provides the basic functions that must be found in every Apache web server. This module is required; all other modules are optional.

mod_so.c
> This module provides runtime support for Dynamic Shared Object modules. It is required if you plan to dynamically link in other modules at runtime. If modules are loaded through the *httpd.conf* file, this module must be installed in Apache to support those modules. For this reason it is often statically linked into the Apache kernel.

In addition to these statically linked modules, Solaris uses many dynamically loadable modules. The LoadModule and AddModule directives are used in the *httpd.conf* file to load DSOs. First, each module is identified by a LoadModule directive. For example, this line in the Solaris *httpd.conf* file identifies the module that tracks users through the use of cookies:

```
LoadModule usertrack_module /usr/apache/libexec/mod_usertrack.so
```

The LoadModule directive is followed by the module name and the path of the shared object file.

Before a module can be used, it must be added to the list of modules that are available to Apache. The first step in building the new module list is to clear the old one. This is done with the ClearModuleList directive. ClearModuleList has no arguments or options. It occurs in the *httpd.conf* file after the last LoadModule directive and before the first AddModule directive.

The AddModule directive adds a module name to the module list. The module list must include all optional modules, both those compiled into the server and those that are dynamically loaded. On our sample Solaris system, that means that there is one more AddModule directive in the *httpd.conf* file than there are LoadModule directives. The extra AddModule directive handles *mod_so.c*, which is the only optional module compiled into Apache on our sample system.[*] Mostly, however, LoadModule and AddModule directives occur in pairs: there is one AddModule directive for every LoadModule directive. For example, the following AddModule directive in the Solaris *httpd.conf* file adds the usertrack_module defined by the LoadModule directive shown previously to the module list:

```
AddModule mod_usertrack.c
```

The AddModule directive is followed by the name of the source file for the module being loaded. Notice that this is the name of the source file that produced the object module, not the module name seen in the LoadModule directive. This name is identical to the object filename except for the extension. In the LoadModule directive, which uses the shared object extension *.so*, the object filename is *mod_usertrack.so*. AddModule uses the source filename extension *.c*, so the module name is *mod_usertrack.c*.

Table 11-1 lists all the modules referenced by AddModule directives in the Solaris 8 *httpd.conf* file.

Table 11-1. DSO modules loaded in the Solaris configuration

Module	Function
mod_access	Enables allow/deny type access controls.
mod_actions	Enables the use of user-defined handlers for specific MIME types or access methods.
mod_alias	Allows references to documents and scripts outside the document root.
mod_asis	Defines file types returned without headers.
mod_auth	Enables user authentication.
mod_auth_anon	Enables anonymous logins.
mod_auth_dbm	Enables use of a DBM authentication file.
mod_autoindex	Enables automatic index generation.
mod_cern_meta	Enables compatibility with old CERN web servers.
mod_cgi	Enables execution of CGI programs.
mod_digest	Enables MD5 authentication.
mod_dir	Controls formatting of directory listings.
mod_env	Allows CGI scripts and server-side includes (SSI) to inherit all shell environment variables.

[*] The *http_core.c* module is an integrated part of Apache. It is not installed with LoadModule and AddModule commands.

Table 11-1. DSO modules loaded in the Solaris configuration (continued)

Module	Function
mod_expires	Set the date for the Expires: header.
mod_headers	Enables customized response headers.
mod_imap	Processes image map files.
mod_include	Processes SSI files.
mod_info	Enables use of the server-info handler.
mod_log_config	Enables use of custom log formats.
mod_mime	Provides support for MIME files.
mod_mime_magic	Determines the MIME type of a file from its content.
mod_negotiation	Enables MIME content negotiation.
mod_perl	Provides support for the Perl language.
mod_proxy	Enables web caching.
mod_rewrite	Enables URI-to-filename mapping.
mod_setenvif	Sets environment variables from client information.
mod_so	Provides runtime support for dynamic shared objects (DSOs).
mod_speling	Automatically corrects minor spelling errors.
mod_status	Provides web-based access to the server-info report.
mod_unique_id	Generates a unique request identifier for each request.
mod_userdir	Defines where users can create public web pages.
mod_usertrack	Provides user tracking through a unique identifier called a cookie.
mod_vhost_alias	Provides support for name-based virtual hosts.

If you decide to add modules to your configuration, do so very carefully. The order of the LoadModule and AddModule directives in the *httpd.conf* file is critical. Don't change things without knowing what you're doing. Before proceeding with a new installation, read the documentation that comes with your new module and the modules documentation found in the *manual/mod* directory of the Apache distribution. See the previously mentioned book *Linux Apache Web Server Administration* for detailed advice about adding new modules.

Once the DSOs are loaded, the directives that they provide can be used in the configuration file. Let's continue looking at the Solaris *httpd.conf* file by examining some of the basic configuration directives.

Basic Configuration Directives

This section covers six different directives. The directives as they appear in the sample configuration we created for our Solaris system are:

```
ServerAdmin webmaster@www.wrotethebook.com
ServerName www.wrotethebook.com
```

```
UseCanonicalName On
ServerRoot "/var/apache"
ServerType standalone
Port 80
```

Two of the basic directives, ServerAdmin and ServerName, were touched upon earlier in the chapter. ServerAdmin defines the email address of the web server administrator. This is set to a bogus value, *you@your.host*, in the default Solaris configuration. You should change this to the full email address of the real web administrator before starting the server.

ServerName defines the hostname returned to clients when they read data from this server. In the default Solaris configuration, the ServerName directive is commented out, which means that the "real" hostname is sent to clients. Thus, if the name assigned to the first network interface is *crab.wrotethebook.com*, then that is the name sent to clients. Many Apache experts suggest defining an explicit value for ServerName in order to document your configuration and to ensure that you get exactly the value you want. Earlier, we set ServerName to *www.wrotethebook.com*, so that even though the web server is running on *crab*, the server will be known as *www.wrotethebook.com* during web interactions. Of course, *www.wrotethebook.com* must be a valid hostname configured in DNS. (See Chapter 8, where *www* is defined as a nickname for *crab* in the *wrotethebook.com* zone file.)

A configuration directive related to ServerName is UseCanonicalName, which defines how httpd builds "self-referencing" URLs. A self-referencing URL contains the name of the server itself in the hostname portion of the URL. For example, on the server *www.wrotethebook.com*, a URL that starts with *http://www.wrotethebook.com* would be a self-referencing URL. The hostname in the URL should be a *canonical name*, which is a name that DNS can resolve to a valid IP address. When UseCanonicalName is set to on, as it is in the default Solaris configuration, the value in ServerName is used to identify the server in self-referencing URLs. For most configurations, leave it set to on. If it is set to off, the value that came in the query from the client is used.

The ServerRoot option defines the directory that contains important files used by httpd, including error files, log files, and the three configuration files: *httpd.conf*, *srm.conf*, and *access.conf*. In the Solaris configuration, ServerRoot points to */var/apache*. This is surprising in that the Solaris httpd configuration files are actually located in */etc/apache*, so clearly something else is at work.

Solaris uses the -f option on the httpd command line to override the location of the *httpd.conf* file at runtime. httpd is started at boot time using the script */etc/init.d/apache*. That script defines a variable named CONF_FILE that contains the value */etc/apache/httpd.conf*. This variable is used with the httpd command that launches the web server, and it is this variable that defines the location of the configuration file on a Solaris system.

The ServerType option defines how the server is started. If the server starts from a startup script at boot time, the option is set to standalone. If the server is run on demand by inetd, the option is set to inetd. The default Solaris configuration sets ServerType to standalone, which is the best value; web servers are usually in high demand, so it is best to start them at boot time. It is possible, of course, for a user to set up a small, rarely used web site on a desktop workstation, in which case running the server from inetd may be desirable. But the web server you create for your network should be standalone.

Port defines the TCP port number used by the server. The standard port number is 80. On occasion, private web servers run on other port numbers. For example, Solaris runs the *AnswerBook2* server on port 8888. Other popular alternative ports for special-purpose web sites are 8080 and 8000. If you change the port number, you must then tell your users the nonstandard port number. For example, *http://jerboas. wrotethebook.com:8080* is a URL for a web site running on TCP port 8080 on host *jerboas.wrotethebook.com*.

When ServerType is set to inetd, it is usually desirable to set Port to something other than 80. The reason for this is that the ports under 1024 are "privileged" ports. If 80 is used, httpd must be run from inetd with the userid root. This is a potential security problem, as an intruder might be able to exploit the web site to get root access. Using port 80 is okay when ServerType is standalone because the initial httpd process does not provide direct client service. Instead it starts several other HTTP daemons, called the *swarm*, to provide client services. The daemons in the swarm do not run with root privilege.

Managing the Swarm

In the original web server design, the server would create separate processes to handle individual requests. This placed a heavy load on the CPU when the server was busy and had a major negative impact on responsiveness. It was possible for the entire system to be overwhelmed by httpd processes.

Apache uses a different approach. A swarm of server processes starts at boot time (the ps command earlier in the chapter shows several httpd processes running on the Solaris system), and all the processes in the swarm share the workload. If all the persistent httpd processes become busy, spare processes are started to share the work. Five directives in the Apache configuration control how the swarm of server child processes is managed. They are:

MinSpareServers
> This directive sets the minimum number of idle server processes that must be maintained. In the Solaris configuration, this is set to 5, which is the default value used in the Apache distribution. When the number of idle processes drops below 5, another process is created to maintain the correct number of idle processes.

Five is a good value for an average server; it allows a burst of up to five quick requests to be handled without making the client wait for a child process to start. A lightly used server might have a lower number, and a heavily used server could benefit from a higher number. However, you don't want too many idle servers waiting around for requests that may never come.

MaxSpareServers

This directive sets the maximum number of idle server processes that may be maintained. It prevents too many idle servers from sitting around with nothing to do. If the number of idle servers exceeds MaxSpareServers, the excess idle servers are killed. In the Solaris configuration, MaxSpareServers is set to 10, which is the default value that ships with the Apache distribution. Set this value to about twice the value set for MinSpareServers.

StartServers

This directive defines the number of httpd daemons started at boot time. In the Solaris configuration, it is set to 5. The effect of this directive can be seen in the output of the ps command earlier in this chapter, which showed that six httpd daemons were running. One of these is the parent process that manages the swarm; the other five are the child processes that actually handle client requests for data.

MaxClients

This directive sets the maximum number of client connections that can be serviced simultaneously. HTTP connection requests beyond the number set by MaxClients are rejected. Solaris sets this to 150, which is the most commonly used value. MaxClients prevents the server from consuming all system resources when it receives an overwhelming number of client requests. MaxClients should be increased only if you have an extremely powerful system with fast disks and a large amount of memory. It is generally best to handle additional clients by adding additional servers. The upper limit for MaxClients is set by HARD_SERVER_LIMIT, which is compiled into Apache. The default for HARD_SERVER_LIMIT is 256.

MaxRequestsPerChild

This directive defines the number of client requests a child process can handle before it must terminate. Solaris sets MaxRequestsPerChild to 0, which means "unlimited"—a child process can keep handling client requests for as long as the system is up and running. This directive should always be set to 0, unless you know for a fact that the library you used to compile Apache has a memory leak.

The User and Group directives define the UID and GID under which the swarm of httpd processes are run. When httpd starts at boot time, it runs as a root process, binds to port 80, and then starts a group of child processes that provide the actual web services. These child processes are the ones given the UID and GID defined in the file. The UID and GID should provide the least possible system privileges to the web server. On the Solaris system, this is the user *nobody* and the group *nobody*. The previous ps command output shows this clearly. One httpd process belongs to *root* and five other httpd processes belong to the user *nobody*. An alternative to using *nobody* is to create a userid and groupid just for httpd. If you do this, create the file permissions granted to the new user account very carefully. The advantage of creating a special user and group for httpd is that you can use group permissions for added protection, and you won't be completely dependent on the world permissions granted to *nobody*.

Defining Where Things Are Stored

The DocumentRoot directive defines the directory that contains the web server documents. For security reasons, this is not the same directory that holds the configuration files. As we saw earlier, the Solaris setting for DocumentRoot is:

```
DocumentRoot "/var/apache/htdocs"
```

To apply directives to a specific directory, create a *container* for those directives. Three of the *httpd.conf* directives used to create containers are:

<Directory *pathname*>

> The Directory directive creates a container for directives that apply to the directory identified by *pathname*. Any configuration directives that occur after the Directory directive and before the next </Directory> statement apply only to the specified directory.

<Location *document*>

> The Location directive creates a container for directives that apply to a specific *document*. Any configuration directives that occur after the Location directive and before the next </Location> statement apply only to the specified document.

<Files *filename*>

> The Files directive creates a container for directives that apply to the file identified by *filename*. Any configuration directives that occur after the Files directive and before the next </Files> statement apply only to the specified file. *filename* can refer to more than one file if it contains the Unix wildcard character * or ?. Additionally, if the Files directive is followed by an optional ~ (tilde), the *filename* field is interpreted as a regular expression.

Directories and files are easy to understand: they are parts of the Unix filesystem that every system administrator knows. Documents, on the other hand, are specific to the web server. The screenful of information that appears in response to a web query is a document; it can be made up of many files from different directories. The Location container provides an easy way to refer to a complex document as a single entity. We will see examples of Location and Files containers later in this chapter. Here we look at Directory containers.

The Solaris configuration defines a Directory container for the server's root directory and for the DocumentRoot:

```
<Directory />
    Options FollowSymLinks
    AllowOverride None
</Directory>
<Directory "/var/apache/htdocs">
    Options Indexes FollowSymLinks
    AllowOverride None
    Order allow,deny
    Allow from all
</Directory>
```

Each Directory container starts with a Directory directive and ends with a </Directory> tag. Both containers shown here enclose configuration statements that apply to only a single directory. The purpose of the directives inside these containers is covered later in the section "Web Server Security." For now, it is sufficient to understand that containers are used inside the *httpd.conf* file to limit the scope of various configuration directives.

The Alias directive and the ScriptAlias directive both map a URL path to a directory on the server. For example, the Solaris configuration contains the following three directives:

```
Alias /icons/ "/var/apache/icons/"
Alias /manuals/ "/usr/apache/htdocs/manual/"
ScriptAlias /cgi-bin/ "/var/apache/cgi-bin/"
```

The first line maps the URL path */icons/* to the directory */var/apache/icons/*. Thus a request for *www.wrotethebook.com/icons/* is mapped to *www.wrotethebook.com/var/apache/icons/*. The second directive maps the URL path */manuals/* to *www.wrotethebook.com/usr/apache/htdocs/manual/*.

You may have several Alias directives to handle several different mappings, but you will have only one ScriptAlias directive. The ScriptAlias directive functions in exactly the same ways as the Alias directive, except that the directory it points to contains executable CGI programs. Therefore, httpd grants this directory execution privileges. ScriptAlias is particularly important because it allows you to maintain executable web scripts in a directory separate from the DocumentRoot. CGI scripts are the single biggest security threat to your server; maintaining them separately allows you to have tighter control over who has access to the scripts.

The Solaris configuration has containers for the */var/apache/icons* directory and the */var/apache/cgi-bin* directory, but none for the */usr/apache/htdocs/manual* directory. Just because a directory is defined inside the *httpd.conf* file does not mean that a Directory container must be created for that directory. The */var/apache/icons* and the */var/apache/cgi-bin* containers are shown here:

```
<Directory "/var/apache/icons">
    Options Indexes MultiViews
    AllowOverride None
    Order allow,deny
    Allow from all
</Directory>
```

```
<Directory "/var/apache/cgi-bin">
    AllowOverride None
    Options None
    Order allow,deny
    Allow from all
</Directory>
```

These containers enclose AllowOverride, Options, Order, and Allow statements—all of which relate to security. Most of the directives found in containers have security implications, and have been placed in containers to provide special security settings for a file, document, or directory. All of the directives used in the containers shown above are covered in the "Web Server Security" section later in this chapter.

The UserDir directive enables personal user web pages and points to the directory that contains the user pages. UserDir usually points to *public_html*, and it does in the Solaris configuration. With this default setting, users create a directory named *public_html* in their home directories to hold their personal web pages. When a request comes in for *www.wrotethebook.com/~sara*, for example, it is mapped to *www.wrotethebook.com/export/home/sara/public_html*. An alternative is to define a full pathname on the UserDir directive line such as */export/home/userpages*. Then the administrator creates the directory and allows each user to store personal pages in subdirectories of this directory, so that a request for *www.wrotethebook.com/~sara* will map to *www.wrotethebook.com/export/home/userpages/sara*. The advantage of this approach is that it makes it easier for you to monitor the content of user pages. The disadvantage is that a separate user web directory tree must be created and protected separately, whereas a web folder within the user's home directory will inherit the protection of that user's home.

The PidFile and ScoreBoardFile directives define the paths of files that relate to process status. The PidFile is the file in which httpd stores its process ID, and the ScoreBoardFile is the file where httpd writes process status information.

The DirectoryIndex option defines the name of the file retrieved if the client's request does not include a filename. Our Solaris system has the following value for this option:

```
DirectoryIndex index.html
```

Given the value defined for DocumentRoot and this value, if the server gets a request for *http://www.wrotethebook.com*, it gives the client the file */var/apache/htdocs/index.html*. If it gets a request for *http://www.wrotethebook.com/books/*, it gives the client the file */var/apache/htdocs/books/index.html*. The DocumentRoot is prepended to every request, and the DirectoryIndex is appended to any request that doesn't end in a filename.

Earlier in this chapter, we saw from an ls of */var/apache/htdocs* that the directory contains a file named *index.html*. But what if it didn't? What would Apache send to the client? If the file *index.html* is not found in the directory, httpd sends the client a listing of the directory, if the configuration permits it. A directory listing is allowed if the Options directive in the Directory container for the directory contains the key-word Indexes. (More on Options later.) If a directory index is allowed, several differ-ent directives control how that directory listing is formatted.

Creating a Fancy Index

The keyword FancyIndexing is used on the IndexOptions directive line to enable a "fancy index" of the directory when Apache is forced to send the client a directory listing. When fancy indexing is enabled, httpd creates a directory list that includes graphics, links, and other advanced features. The Solaris configuration enables fancy indexing with the IndexOptions directive, and it contains about 20 extra lines to help configure the fancy index. Solaris uses the following directives to define the graphics and features used in the fancy directory listing:

IndexIgnore
> Identifies the files that should not be included in the directory listing. Files can be specified by name, partial name, extension, or by standard wildcard characters.

HeaderName
> Specifies the name of a file that contains information to be displayed at the top of the directory listing.

ReadmeName
> Specifies the name of a file that contains information to be displayed at the bottom of the directory listing.

AddIconByEncoding
> Points to the icon used to represent a file based on its MIME encoding type.

AddIconByType
> Points to the icon used to represent a file based on its MIME file type.

AddIcon
> Points to the icon used to represent a file based on its extension.

DefaultIcon
> Points to the icon file used to represent a file that has not been given an icon by any other option.

Defining File Types

MIME file types and file extensions play a major role in helping the server determine how a file should be handled. Specifying MIME options is also a major part of the Solaris *httpd.conf* file. The directives involved are:

DefaultType
> Defines the MIME type that is used when the server cannot determine the type of a file. In the Solaris configuration this is set to text/plain. Thus, when a file has no file extension, the server assumes it is a plain-text file.

AddEncoding

Maps a MIME encoding type to a file extension. The Solaris configuration contains two AddEncoding directives:

```
AddEncoding x-compress Z
AddEncoding x-gzip gz tgz
```

The first directive maps the extension Z to the MIME encoding type x-compress. The second line maps the extensions gz and tgz to MIME encoding type x-gzip.

AddLanguage

Maps a MIME language type to a file extension. The Solaris configuration contains mappings for six languages, e.g., .en for English and .fr for French.

LanguagePriority

Sets the priority of the language encoding used when preparing multiviews, and the language used when the client does not specify a preference. In the Solaris configuration, the priority is English (en), French (fr), and German (de). This means that English, French, and German views will be prepared if multiviews are used. The client will be sent the English version if no language preference is specified.

AddType

Maps a MIME file type to a file extension. The Solaris configuration has only one AddType directive; it maps MIME type application/x-tar to the extension .tgz. A configuration can have several AddType directives.

Another directive that is commonly used to process files based on the filename extension is the AddHandler directive. This directive maps a file handler to a file extension. A file handler is a program that knows how to process a specific file type. For example, the handler cgi-script is able to execute CGI files. The Solaris configuration does not define any optional handlers, so all the AddHandler directives are commented out.

Performance Tuning Directives

The KeepAlive directive enables the use of persistent connections. Without persistent connections, the client must make a new connection to the server for every link the user selects. Because HTTP runs over TCP, every connection requires a connection setup, adding time to every file retrieval. With persistent connections, the server waits to see if the client has additional requests before it closes the connection. Therefore, the client does not need to create a new connection to request a new document. The KeepAliveTimeout defines the number of seconds the server holds a persistent connection open waiting to see if the client has additional requests. The Solaris configuration turns KeepAlive on and sets KeepAliveTimeout to 15 seconds.

MaxKeepAliveRequests defines the maximum number of requests that will be accepted on a "kept-alive" connection before a new TCP connection is required.

Solaris sets this value to 100, which is the Apache default. Setting MaxKeepAlive-Requests to 0 allows unlimited requests. 100 is a good value for this parameter: few users request 100 document transfers, so the value essentially creates a persistent connection for all reasonable cases. If the client does request more than 100 document transfers, it might indicate a problem with the client system, so requiring another connection request is probably a good idea.

Timeout defines the number of seconds the server waits for a transfer to complete. The value needs to be large enough to handle the size of the files your site sends as well as the low performance of the modem connections of your clients. But if it is set too high, the server will hold open connections for clients that may have gone offline. The Solaris configuration has the Timeout set to 5 minutes (300 seconds), which is a very common setting.

BrowserMatch is a different type of tuning parameter: it reduces performance for compatibility's sake. The Solaris configuration contains the following five Browser-Match directives:

```
BrowserMatch "Mozilla/2" nokeepalive
BrowserMatch "MSIE 4\.0b2;" nokeepalive downgrade-1.0 force-response-1.0
BrowserMatch "RealPlayer 4\.0" force-response-1.0
BrowserMatch "Java/1\.0" force-response-1.0
BrowserMatch "JDK/1\.0" force-response-1.0
```

The BrowserMatch statements are used to present information in ways that are compatible with the capabilities of different web browsers. For example, a browser may be able to handle only HTTP 1.0, not HTTP 1.1. In this case, downgrade-1.0 is used on the BrowserMatch line to ensure that the server uses only HTTP 1.0 when dealing with that browser.

In the Solaris configuration, keepalives are disabled for two browsers. One browser is offered only HTTP 1.0 during the connection, and responses are formatted to be compatible with HTTP 1.0 for four different browsers.

Don't fiddle with the BrowserMatch directives. These settings are shipped as defaults in the Apache distribution, and are set to handle the limitations of different browsers. These are tuning parameters, but they are used by the Apache developers to adjust to the limitations of older browsers.

HostnameLookups tells httpd whether or not it should log hostnames as well as IP addresses. The advantage of enabling hostname logging is that you get a more readable log. The disadvantage is that httpd has the added overhead of DNS name lookups. Setting this to off, as in the Solaris configuration, enhances server performance. The HostnameLookups directive affects what is logged, but its major impact is on system performance, which is why we cover it under tuning parameters instead of logging directives.

Logging Configuration Directives

Log files provide a great deal of information about the web server. The following seven lines define the Apache logging configuration in the default Solaris 8 *httpd.conf* file:

```
ErrorLog /var/apache/logs/error_log
LogLevel warn
LogFormat "%h %l %u %t \"%r\" %>s %b \"%{Referer}i\" \"%{User-Agent}i\"" combined
LogFormat "%h %l %u %t \"%r\" %>s %b" common
LogFormat "%{Referer}i -> %U" referer
LogFormat "%{User-agent}i" agent
CustomLog /var/apache/logs/access_log common
```

ErrorLog defines the path of the error log file. Use the error log to track and correct failures. You should review the log at least once a day to check for problems. To keep a close eye on the file while you're logged in, use the `tail` command with the `-f` option:

```
$ tail -l 1 -f /var/log/httpd/apache/error_log
```

The `tail` command prints the tail end of a file; in the example, the file is */var/log/ httpd/apache/error_log*. The `-l` option is the lines option. It tells `tail` how many lines from the end of the file to print. In this case, `-l 1` directs `tail` to print the (one) last line in the file. The `-f` option keeps the `tail` process running so that you will see each record as it is written to the file. This allows you to monitor the file in real time.

The LogLevel directive defines the type of events written to the error log. The Solaris configuration sets LogLevel to `warn`, which specifies that warnings and other more critical errors are to be written to the log. This is a safe setting for an error log because it logs a wide variety of operational errors. LogLevel has eight possible settings: `debug`, `info`, `notice`, `warn`, `error`, `crit`, `alert`, and `emerg`. The log levels are cumulative. For example, `warn` provides warnings, errors, critical messages, alerts, and emergency messages; `debug` provides all types of logging, which causes the file to grow at a very rapid rate; `emerg` keeps the file small but notifies you only of disasters. `warn` is a good compromise between not enough detail and too much detail.

Just as important as reporting errors, the logs provide information about who is using the server, how much it is being used, and how well it is servicing the users. Web servers are used to distribute information; if no one wants or uses the information, you need to know it. The LogFormat and CustomLog directives do not configure the error log, but rather *how* server activity is logged.

Defining the log file format

The LogFormat directives define the format of log file entries. A LogFormat directive contains two things: the layout of a file entry and a label used in the *httpd.conf* file to identify the log entry. The layout of the entry is placed directly after the LogFormat keyword and is enclosed in quotes. The layout is defined using literals and variables.

Examining a sample LogFormat directive shows how the variables are used. The basic Apache log file conforms to the Common Log Format (CLF). CLF is a standard used by all web server vendors, and using this format means that the logs generated by Apache servers can be processed by any log analysis tool that conforms to the standard. The format of a standard CLF entry is clearly defined by the second LogFormat directive in the Solaris *httpd.conf* file:

```
LogFormat "%h %l %u %t \"%r\" %>s %b" common
```

This LogFormat directive specifies exactly the information required for a CLF log entry. It does this using seven different LogFormat variables:

%h

> Logs the IP address of the client. If HostnameLookups is set to on, this is the client's fully qualified hostname. On the sample Solaris system, this would be the client's IP address because HostnameLookups is turned off to enhance server performance.

%l

> Logs the username used to log in to the client, if available. The name is retrieved using the identd protocol; however, most clients do not run identd and thus do not provide this information. Therefore, this field usually contains a hyphen to indicate a missing value. Likewise, if the server does not have a value for a field, the log contains a hyphen in the field.

%u

> Logs the username used to access a password-protected web page. This should match a name you defined in the AuthUser file or the AuthDBMUser database you created on the server. (AuthUser and AuthDBMUser are covered in the "Web Server Security" section of this chapter.) Most documents are not password protected, and therefore this field contains a hyphen in most log entries.

%t

> Logs the date and time the log entry was made.

%r

> Logs the first line of the client's request. This often contains the URL of the requested document. The \" characters in the LogFormat directive indicate that quotes should be inserted in the output. In the log file, the client's request will be enclosed in quotes.

%>s

> Logs the status of the last request. This is the three-digit response code that the server returned to the client.

%b

> Logs the number of bytes contained in the document sent to the client.

Apache log entries are not limited to the CLF format. The LogFormat directive lets you define what information is logged. A wide variety of information can be logged.

The Solaris configuration contains three additional LogFormat directives that demonstrate some optional log formats. The three directives are:

```
LogFormat "%{User-agent}i" agent
LogFormat "%{Referer}i -> %U" referer
LogFormat "%h %l %u %t \"%r\" %>s %b \"%{Referer}i\" \"%{User-Agent}i\"" combined
```

All of these directives log the contents of HTTP headers. For example, the first directive logs the value received from the client in the User-agent header. User-agent is the user program that generates the document request; generally this is the name of a browser. The format that logs the header is:

```
%{User-agent}i
```

This format works for any header: simply replace User-agent with the name of the header. The i indicates that this is an input header; output headers are indicated by an o. Apache can log the contents of any header records received or sent.

The second LogFormat directive logs the contents of the Referer header received from the client (%{Referer}i), the literal characters dash and greater-than sign (->), and the requested URL (%U). Referer is the name of the remote site that referred the client to your web site; %U is the document to which the site referred the client.

The last LogFormat directive starts with the CLF (%h %l %u %t \"%r\" %>s %b \") and adds to that the values from the Referer header and the User-agent header. This format is labeled combined because it combines the CLF with other information; the other two formats are also aptly labeled as agent and referer. Yet none of these formats is actually used in the Solaris configuration. Simply creating a LogFormat is not enough to generate a log file; you must also add a matching CustomLog directive to map the format to a file, as explained later.

In the LogFormat directive, the layout of the log entry is enclosed in quotes. The label that occurs after the closing quote is not part of the format. In the LogFormat directive that defines the CLF format, the label common is an arbitrary string used to tie the LogFormat directive to a CustomLog directive. In the Solaris configuration, that particular LogFormat is tied to the file */var/apache/logs/access_log* defined by this line:

```
CustomLog /var/apache/logs/access_log common
```

The label common binds the two directives together. Thus the CLF entries defined by this LogFormat directive are written to the file defined by this CustomLog directive.

In the Solaris configuration, the other CustomLog directives that create the agent, referer, and combined log files are commented out:

```
#CustomLog /var/apache/logs/referer_log referer
#CustomLog /var/apache/logs/agent_log agent
#CustomLog /var/apache/logs/access_log combined
```

The *referer_log* stores the URL of the source page that linked to your web server. This helps you determine what sites are pointing to your web pages. Entries in the *referer_log* are defined by this line:

```
LogFormat "%{Referer}i -> %U" referer
```

To create the log, uncomment this line:

```
CustomLog /var/apache/logs/referer_log referer
```

The *agent_log* identifies the browsers that are used to access your site, and is defined by this LogFormat statement:

```
LogFormat "%{User-agent}i" agent
```

To create the log, uncomment this line:

```
CustomLog /var/apache/logs/agent_log agent
```

Lastly, the format for the expanded CLF log is defined by this line:

```
LogFormat "%h %l %u %t \"%r\" %>s %b \"%{Referer}i\" \"%{User-Agent}i\"" combined
```

To create a combined log, uncomment this line:

```
CustomLog /var/apache/logs/access_log combined
```

and comment this line:

```
#CustomLog /var/apache/logs/access_log common
```

These changes cause the combined log format to be used to build a log file named */var/apache/logs/access_log*. This is the same log file that is used by the default common log format. To avoid duplicate log entries, turn off common logging when you turn on combined logging. In effect, these changes switch the *access_log* file from using the common log format to logging the combined log entry.

Each LogFormat statement and its associated CustomLog statement end with the same label. The label is an arbitrary name used to bind the format and the file together.

Using conditional logging

Apache also supports conditional logging to identify fields that are logged only when certain status codes are returned by the server. The status codes are listed in Table 11-2.

Table 11-2. Apache server status codes

Status code	Meaning
200: OK	A valid request
302: Found	The document was found
304: Not Modified	The requested document has not been modified
400: Bad Request	An invalid request

Table 11-2. Apache server status codes (continued)

Status code	Meaning
401: Unauthorized	The client or user is denied access
403: Forbidden	The requested access is not allowed
404: Not Found	The requested document does not exist
500 Server Error	An unspecified server error occurred
503: Out of Resources (Service Unavailable)	The server has insufficient resources to honor the request
501: Not Implemented	The requested server feature is not available
502: Bad Gateway	The client specified an invalid gateway

To make a field conditional, put one or more status codes on the field in the Log-Format entry. If multiple status codes are used, separate them with commas. Assume that you want to log the browser name only if the browser requests a service that is not implemented in your server. Combine the Not Implemented (501) status code with User-agent header in this manner:

```
%501{User-agent}i
```

If this value appears in the LogFormat statement, the name of the browser is logged only when the status code is 501.

Place an exclamation mark in front of the status codes to specify that you want to log a field only when the status code does not contain the specified values. For example, to log the address of the site that referred the user to your web page only if the status code is not one of the good status codes, add the following to a LogFormat:

```
%!200,302,304{Referer}i
```

This particular conditional log entry is very useful, as it tells you when a remote page has a stale link pointing to your web site.

Combine these features with the common log format to create a more useful log entry. Here we modify the Solaris combined format to include conditional logging:

```
LogFormat "%h %l %u %t \"%r\" %>s %b \"%!200,302,304{Referer}i\" \"%{User-Agent}i\""
combined
```

This entry provides all the data of the CLF and thus can be analyzed by standard tools. But it also provides the browser name and, when the user requests a stale link, it provides the address of the remote site that references that link.

Despite the fact that the Solaris configuration file contains over 160 active lines, there are some interesting Apache features that the Solaris configuration does *not* exploit. Before we move on to the important ongoing tasks of server security and server monitoring, the following sections provide a quick overview of three features not included in the default Solaris configuration: proxies and caching, multi-homed server configuration, and virtual hosts.

Proxy Servers and Caching

Servers that act as intermediaries between clients and web servers are called *proxy servers*. When firewalls are used, direct web access is often blocked. Instead, users connect to the proxy server through the local network, and the proxy server is trusted to connect to the remote web server. Proxy servers can maintain cached copies of remote servers' web pages to improve performance by reducing the amount of traffic sent over the wide area network and by reducing the contention for popular web sites. The options that control caching behavior are:

CacheNegotiatedDocs
> Allows proxy servers to cache web pages from your server. By default, Apache asks proxy servers not to cache your server's web pages. This option takes no command-line arguments.

ProxyRequests
> Setting this option to on turns your server into a proxy server. By default, this is set to off.

ProxyVia
> Enables or disables the use of Via: headers, which aid in tracking where cached pages actually came from.

CacheRoot
> Specifies the directory path where cached web pages are written when this server is configured as a proxy server. To avoid making the directory writable by the user *nobody*, create a special userid for httpd when you run a proxy server.

CacheSize
> Sets the maximum size of the cache in kilobytes. The default is 5.

CacheGcInterval
> Sets the time interval (in hours) at which the server prunes the cache. The default is 4. Given the defaults, the server prunes the cache down to 5 kilobytes every 4 hours.

CacheMaxExpire
> Sets the maximum number of hours a document can be held in the cache without requesting a fresh copy from the remote server. The default is 24 hours. With the default, a cached document can be up to a day out of date.

CacheLastModifiedFactor
> Sets the length of time a document is cached based on when it was last modified. The default factor is 0.1. Therefore, if a document that was modified 10 hours ago is retrieved, it is held in the cache for only 1 hour before a fresh copy is requested. The assumption is that if a document changes frequently, the time of its last modification will be recent; thus, documents that change frequently are cached for only a short period of time. Regardless, nothing is cached longer than CacheMaxExpire.

CacheDefaultExpire

Sets a default cache expiration value for protocols that do not provide the value. The default is 1 hour.

NoCache

Defines a list of servers whose pages you do not want to cache. If you know that a server has constantly changing information, you won't want to cache information from that server because your cache will always be out of date. Listing the name of that server on the NoCache command line means that queries are sent directly to the server, and responses from the server are not saved in the cache.

All of these directives are commented out in the Solaris configuration. By default, the Solaris Apache server is not configured to be a proxy server. If you need to create a proxy server, refer to a book dedicated to Apache configuration such as *Linux Apache Web Server Administration*.

Multi-Homed Server Options

Web servers with more than one IP address are said to be *multi-homed*. A multi-homed web server needs to know what address it should listen to for incoming server requests. There are two configuration options to handle this:

BindAddress

Specifies the address used for server interactions. The default value is *, which means that the server should respond to web service requests addressed to any of its valid IP addresses. If a specific address is used on the BindAddress line, only requests for that address are honored.

Listen

Specifies addresses and ports to monitor for web service requests in addition to the default port and address. Address and port pairs are separated by a colon. For example, to monitor port 8080 on IP address 172.16.12.5, enter Listen 172.16.12.5:8080. If a port is entered with no address, the address of the server is used. If the Listen directive is not used, httpd monitors only the port defined by the Port directive.

The BindAddress and Listen directives are commented out of the Solaris configuration.

Defining Virtual Hosts

Some of the options commented out of the sample *httpd.conf* file are used if your server hosts multiple web sites. For example, to host web sites for *fish.edu* and *mammals.com* on the *crab.wrotethebook.com* server, add these lines to the *httpd.conf* file:

```
<VirtualHost "www.fish.edu">
DocumentRoot /var/apache/fish
ServerName www.fish.edu
</VirtualHost>
```

```
<VirtualHost "www.mammals.com">
DocumentRoot /var/apache/mammals
ServerName www.mammals.com
</VirtualHost>
```

Each VirtualHost option defines a hostname alias that your server responds to. For this to be valid, DNS must define the alias with a CNAME record. Our example requires CNAME records that assign *crab.wrotethebook.com* the aliases of *www.fish. edu* and *www.mammals.com*. When *crab* receives a server request addressed to one of these aliases, it uses the configuration parameters defined here to override its normal settings. Therefore, when it gets a request for *www.fish.edu*, it uses *www.fish.edu* as its ServerName value instead of its own server name, and */var/apache/fish* as the DocumentRoot.

Web Server Security

Web servers are vulnerable to all of the normal security problems discussed in Chapter 12, but they also have their own special security considerations. In addition to guarding against the usual threats, web servers should be set up to protect the integrity of the information they disseminate as well as the information they receive from the client.

Access to the information on the server is protected by access controls. You can control access to the server at the host level and at the user level in the *httpd.conf* configuration file. Access control is important for protecting internal and private web pages, but most web information is intended for dissemination to the world at large. For these global web pages, you don't want to limit access in any way, but you still want to protect the integrity of the information on the pages.

One of the unique security risks for a web server is the possibility of an intruder changing the information on your web pages. We have all heard of high-profile incidents in which intruders alter the home page of some government agency to include comical or pornographic material. Although these attacks are not intended to do long-term harm to the server, they can certainly embarrass the organization that runs the web site.

Unix file permissions protect the files and directories where web documents are stored. The server does not need write permissions, but it does need to read and execute these files. Executable files, if they are poorly designed, are always a potential security threat.

The CGI and SSI Threat

Apache itself is reliable and reasonably secure. The biggest threat to the security of your server is the code that you write for your server to execute, most commonly Common Gateway Interface programs and Server Side Includes.

CGI programs can be written in C, Perl, Python, or other programming languages. Badly written CGI programs represent one of the biggest threats to server security: intruders can exploit poor code by forcing buffer overflows or passing shell commands through the program to the system. To avoid this, you must be very careful about the code that you make available on your system. You should personally review all programs included in the *cgi-bin* directory. Try to write programs that do not allow free-form user input; use pull-down menus instead of keyboard input where possible. Limit and validate what comes in from the user to your system.

To make it easier to review your CGI scripts, keep them all in the ScriptAlias directory. Don't allow scripts to be executed from any other directory unless you're positive no one can place a script there that you have not personally reviewed. In the next section, we'll see how to control which directories allow CGI execution when we discuss the Options directive.

Server Side Includes (SSI) are also a potential problem for the same reason as CGI programs. Server Side Includes are also called Server Parsed HTML, and the files often have the *.shtml* file extension. These files are processed by the server before they are sent to the client, and they can include other files or execute code from script files. If user input is used to dynamically modify an SSI file, the file is vulnerable to the same type of attacks as CGI scripts.

SSI commands are embedded inside HTML comments, and therefore begin with <!-- and conclude with -->. The SSI commands are listed in Table 11-3.

Table 11-3. Server Side Include commands

Command	Function
#config	Formats the display of file size and time.
#echo	Displays variables.
#exec	Executes a CGI script or a shell command.
#flastmod	Displays the date a document was last modified.
#fsize	Displays the size of a document.
#include	Inserts another file into the current document.

The most secure way to operate is to disallow all SSI processing. This is the default unless All or Includes is specified by an Options directive in the *httpd.conf* file. A compromise setting is to allow SSI processing but disallow the #include and #exec commands. These are the greatest security threats because #include writes data to the document from an external file, and #exec enables script and command execution. Use IncludesNOEXEC on the Options directive for this setting. Let's now look at how Options are set for individual directories.

Controlling Server Options

The *httpd.conf* file can define server controls for all web documents or for documents in individual directories. The Options directive specifies what server options are permitted for documents. Placing the Options directive inside a Directory container limits the scope of the directive to that specific directory. The Solaris configuration provides an example:

```
<Directory />
    Options FollowSymLinks
    AllowOverride None
</Directory>
<Directory "/var/apache/htdocs">
    Options Indexes FollowSymLinks
    AllowOverride None
    Order allow,deny
    Allow from all
</Directory>
<Directory "/var/apache/icons">
    Options Indexes MultiViews
    AllowOverride None
    Order allow,deny
    Allow from all
</Directory>
<Directory "/var/apache/cgi-bin">
    AllowOverride None
    Options None
    Order allow,deny
    Allow from all
</Directory>
```

This configuration defines server option controls for four directories: the root (/), */var/apache/htdocs*, */var/apache/icons*, and */var/apache/cgi-bin*. The example shows four possible values for the Options directive: FollowSymLinks, Indexes, None, and MultiViews. The Options directive has several possible settings:

All
> Permits the use of all server options.

ExecCGI
> Permits the execution of CGI scripts from this directory. The ExecCGI option allows CGI scripts to be executed from directories other than the directory pointed to by the ScriptAlias directive. Many administrators set this option for the ScriptAlias directory, but doing so is somewhat redundant: the ScriptAlias directive already defines */var/apache/cgi-bin* as the script directory. In the example, Options is set to None for the */var/apache/cgi-bin* directory without undoing the effect of the ScriptAlias directive.

FollowSymLinks
> Permits the use of symbolic links. If this is allowed, the server treats a symbolic link as if it were a document in the directory.

Includes

>Permits the use of Server Side Includes (SSI).

IncludesNOEXEC

>Permits Server Side Includes (SSI) files that do not contain #exec and #include commands.

Indexes

>Permits a server-generated listing of the directory if an *index.html* file is not found.

MultiViews

>Permits the document language to be negotiated. See the AddLanguage and LanguagePriority directives discussed earlier in "Defining File Types."

None

>Disallows all server options. My personal favorite!

SymLinksIfOwnerMatch

>Permits the use of symbolic links if the target file of the link is owned by the same userid as the link itself.

Use server options with care. The None and MultiViews options used in the Solaris configuration should not cause security problems, although MultiViews consumes server resources. The Indexes option poses a slight security risk, as it exposes a listing of the directory contents if no *index.html* file is found, which may be more information than you want to share with the world. FollowSymLinks has the potential for security problems because symbolic links can increase the number of directories in which documents are stored. The more directories you have, the more difficult it is to secure them, because each must have the proper permissions set and be monitored for possible file corruption. (See Chapter 12 for information on Tripwire, a tool that helps monitor files.)

The Directory containers in the previous example also contain AllowOverride directives. These directives limit the amount of configuration control given to the individual directories.

Directory-Level Configuration Controls

The statement AccessFileName .htaccess enables directory-level configuration control and states that the name of the directory configuration file is *.htaccess*. If the server finds a file with this name in a directory from which it is retrieving information, it applies the configuration lines defined in the file before it releases the data. The AccessFileName directive delegates configuration control to the people who create and manage the individual web pages, giving them a file in which they can write configuration directives. The configuration directives in the *.htaccess* file are the same as those in the *httpd.conf* file that defines systemwide configuration. The Solaris configuration contains the AccessFileName .htaccess line, so directory-level configuration is allowed on Solaris systems by default.

The AllowOverride directive can be used to limit the amount of configuration control given to individual directories. It defines when the *.htaccess* file is allowed to override the configuration values set in *httpd.conf*. Placing the AllowOverride directives inside a Directory container limits the scope of AllowOverride to that specific directory, as we saw in the previous example.

The AllowOverride directive has many possible settings. In addition to the keywords All, which permits the *.htaccess* file to override everything defined in the configuration files, and None, which allows no overrides, individual directives can be permitted through this directive. For example, to allow an *.htaccess* file to define file extension mappings, specify AllowOverride AddType. When this value is used on an AllowOverride directive, AddType directives can be used in the directory's *.htaccess* file to define file extension mappings. AllowOverride can be used to permit just about anything in the configuration to be overridden by the *.htaccess* file.

The Options and AllowOverride directives limit access to server features and configuration controls, and can help keep information safe from corruption. Sometimes, however, you have information you want to keep safe from widespread distribution. Access controls limit the distribution of information.

Defining Access Controls

Use the *httpd.conf* file to define host and user access controls. A few examples will make this capability clear. Let's start with an example of host access controls:

```
<Directory "/var/apache/htdocs/internal">
Order deny,allow
Deny from all
Allow from wrotethebook.com
</Directory>
```

This shows access controls for the directory */var/apache/htdocs/internal*. The access controls are designed to grant access only to those hosts within the *wrotethebook. com* domain. The Directory container encloses three access control directives:

Order
> Defines the order in which the access control rules are evaluated. deny,allow tells httpd to apply the deny rule first, and then permit exceptions to that rule based on the allow rule. In the example, we block access from everyone with the deny rule and then permit exceptions for systems that are part of the *wrotethebook. com* domain with the allow rule. This is an example of access rules that might be used to protect an internal web site.

Deny from
> Identifies the hosts not allowed to access web documents found in the */var/ apache/htdocs/internal* directory. The hosts can be identified by full or partial hostnames or IP addresses. Each Deny from directive can identify only one source; to specify multiple sources, use multiple Deny from directives. However, if a domain

name or a network address is used, the source can encompass every host in an entire domain or network. The keyword all blocks all hosts.

Allow from

Identifies hosts that are granted access to documents in the directory. The hosts can be identified by full or partial hostnames or IP addresses. Each Allow from directive can identify only one source; to specify multiple sources, use multiple Allow from directives. However, if a domain name or a network address is used, the source can encompass every host in an entire domain or network. The keyword all allows all hosts.

The example here controls access on a host-by-host basis. This type of control is commonly used to segregate information for internal users from information for external customers. It is also possible to control file access at the user and group level.

Requiring user authentication

User authentication can be required before granting access to a document or directory. It is generally used to limit information to a small group. An example of user access control is:

```
<Directory "/var/apache/htdocs/internal/accounting">
AuthName "Accounting"
AuthType Basic
AuthUserFile /etc/apache/http.passwords
AuthGroupFile /etc/apache/http.groups
Require hdqtrs rec bill pay
Order deny,allow
Deny from all
Allow from Limit>
</Directory>
```

The first two directives in this Directory container are AuthName and AuthType. AuthName provides the value for the *authentication realm*—a value that is placed on the WWW-Authenticate header sent to the client. A realm is a group of server resources that share the same authentication. In the example, the directory */var/apache/htdocs/internal/accounting* is the only item in the Accounting realm. But it would be possible to have other password-protected directories or documents in the Accounting realm. If we did, a user that was authenticated for any resource in the Accounting realm would be authenticated for all resources in that realm.

The AuthType directive specifies the type of password authentication that will be used. This can be either Basic or Digest. When Basic is specified, a plain clear-text password is used for authentication. When Digest is specified, Message Digest 5 (MD5) is used for authentication. Digest is rarely used, partly because it is not completely implemented in all browsers, but more importantly because data that requires strong authentication is better protected using Secure Sockets Layer (SSL) security. SSL is covered later in the "Using Encryption" section.

In this example, access is granted if the user belongs to a valid group and has a valid password. These groups and passwords have nothing to do with the groups and passwords used by login. The groups and passwords used here are specifically defined by you for use with the web server. The files you create for this purpose are the ones pointed to by the AuthUserFile and AuthGroupFile entries. Add passwords to the web server password file with the htpasswd command that comes with the Apache system; add groups to the group file by editing the file with any text editor. The entries in the group file start with the group name followed by a colon and a list of users that belong to the group. For example:

```
hdqtrs: amanda pat craig kathy
```

The Require directive requires the user to enter the web username and password. The example limits access to users who belong to one of the groups hdqtrs, rec, bill, or pay, and who also enter a valid password. Alternatively, placing the keyword valid-user on the Require line instead of a list of groups grants access to any user with a valid password and ignores the group file.

Even if you do not use web server groups, specify the AuthGroupFile entry when using password authentication. If you don't want to create a dummy group file, simply point the entry to /dev/null.

The Order, Deny, and Allow directives perform the same function in this example as they did in the previous one. Here we are adding password authentication to host authentication. That's not required. If the Order, Deny, and Allow directives were not in the example, any system on the Internet would be allowed to access the documents if the user on that system had the correct username and password.

Improved user authentication

The standard authentication module, mod_auth, stores user authentication data in flat files that are searched sequentially. A sequential search of even a few hundred entries can be time consuming. Use an indexed database to improve performance if you have more than a few password entries.

Two modules, mod_auth_db, which uses Berkeley DB databases, and mod_auth_dbm, which uses Unix DBM databases, provide support for password databases. The basic Solaris configuration dynamically loads mod_auth_dbm, so we can use a password database on a Solaris system with very little effort.

The password database is used in much the same way as the sequential database. Using the authentication example shown previously, we can change to a password database simply by changing the AuthUserFile directive to an AuthDBMUserFile directive and the AuthGroupFile directive to an AuthDBMGroupFile directive. Here is an example:

```
<Directory "/var/apache/htdocs/internal/accounting">
AuthName "Accounting"
```

```
AuthType Basic
AuthDBMUserFile /etc/apache/passwords
AuthDBMGroupFile /etc/apache/groups
Require hdqtrs rec bill pay
Order deny,allow
Deny from all
Allow from Limit>
</Directory>
```

These two small changes are all that is needed in the *httpd.conf* file. The biggest change when using a password database is that passwords are no longer defined with the htpassword command. Instead, the dbmmanage command is used to create password and group database entries. The syntax of the dbmmanage command is:

```
dbmmanage filename command username password
```

The items on a dbmmanage command line are largely self-explanatory. *filename* is the name of the database file. *username* and *password* are just what you would expect for a password database. *command* is a keyword that defines the function of the dbmmanage command. The possible *command* keywords are:

add

> Adds a username and password to the database. The password must already be encrypted because dbmmanage does not encrypt the password for you when you use the add keyword. See the adduser keyword.

adduser

> Adds a username and password to the database. The password is provided in clear text and then encrypted by dbmmanage.

check

> Checks if the username and password match those in the database.

delete

> Removes a username and password from the database.

import

> Copies *username:password* entries from stdin. The passwords must already be encrypted.

update

> Changes the password for a username that is already in the database.

view

> Displays the contents of the database.

In the following example, the */etc/apache/passwords* file is created and two new users are added to the database:

```
# dbmmanage /etc/apache/passwords adduser sara
New password:
Re-type new password:
User sara added with password encrypted to XsH4aRiQbEzp2
```

```
# dbmmanage /etc/apache/passwords adduser alana
New password:
Re-type new password:
User alana added with password encrypted to AslrgF/FPQvF6
# dbmmanage /etc/apache/passwords view
alana:AslrgF/FPQvF6
sara:XsH4aRiQbEzp2
```

Notice that dbmmanage prompts for the password if it is not provided on the command line.

All of the access control examples shown so far define access controls for a directory. It is also possible to define access control for all directories on a server or for individual documents. To apply access controls to every document provided by the server, simply place the access control directives outside a Directory container; the access controls here apply only to a single directory because they are located within a Directory container. To apply access controls to a single file or document, place the directives inside a Files or Document container.

Setting file-level access controls

The Solaris configuration provides an example of applying access controls to individual files. In order to prevent the *.htaccess* file from being downloaded by a curious client, the Solaris configuration contains the following Files container:

```
<Files ~ "^\.ht">
    Order allow,deny
    Deny from all
</Files>
```

The Order and Deny directives are somewhat different from previous examples. Here the Order directive tells Apache to process the Allow directive first and then the Deny directive. This enables the Deny directive to override anything done by the Allow directive. In this case there is no Allow directive, and the Deny directive denies all remote access to the *.htaccess* file.

In fact, this Deny directive applies to more than just the *.htaccess* file. The tilde (~) on the Files line tells Apache to interpret the filename as a regular expression. The regular expression ^\.ht matches any filename that begins with .ht. This was done because users and administrators often start httpd configuration files with the string .ht, e.g., a user password file might be named *.htpassword*. Using a regular expression as a filename on the Files line applies the access controls to a wide range of possible files.

Setting document-level access controls

Use the Location directive to apply access controls at the document level. Where the Directory line has a directory name, the Location directive has a document name from a URL. The directives defined inside a Location container apply only to that document. In the following example, access controls are applied to the *server-status* document:

```
<Location /server-status>
SetHandler server-status
Order deny,allow
Deny from all
Allow from wrotethebook.com
</Location>
```

If the Apache server gets a request for *www.wrotethebook.com/server-status*, it applies these access controls. */server-status* is the name of a document, not the name of a directory. In fact, this is a special document that shows the server status and is constructed by a special handler. The access controls make the server status available to everyone in our domain but deny it to all outsiders. The last section in this chapter shows how the server-status page is used to monitor a web server. But before we move on to that topic, we need to look at one final aspect of security—protecting the information the client sends to the server.

Using Encryption

The security features described in the previous sections are all designed to protect information provided by the server. However, you are also responsible for protecting the security of your client's data. If you want to run an electronic commerce business, you must use a secure server that protects your customers' personal information, such as credit card numbers. Secure Apache servers use Secure Sockets Layer (SSL) to encrypt protected sessions.

SSL is both more powerful and more complex than the security features discussed so far. It is more powerful because it uses public key cryptography for strong authentication and to negotiate session encryption. When SSL is used, the exchange of data between the client and server is encrypted and protected.

SSL is also more complex because it uses public key cryptography. All encryption is complex, and public key encryption is particularly so. Chapter 12 describes how public key encryption works and, in particular, how the SSL protocol works. If you want this background information, read Chapter 12 before adding SSL to your Apache server.

The mod_ssl package adds SSL support to Apache. In turn, mod_ssl depends on OpenSSL for encryption libraries, tools, and the underlying SSL protocols. Many Linux systems and some Unix systems include OpenSSL. Before installing mod_ssl, make sure OpenSSL is installed on your system; if it isn't, download the source code from *http://www.openssl.org*. Run the config utility that comes with the source code and then run make to compile OpenSSL. Run make test and make install to install it.

Once OpenSSL is installed, mod_ssl can be installed. Many Linux systems and some Unix systems include mod_ssl as part of the basic Apache system. If your system doesn't, download the mod_ssl package from *http://www.modssl.org*. Recompile Apache using the --with-ssl option to incorporate the SSL extensions into Apache.*

The mod_ssl installation inserts various SSL configuration lines into the sample Apache configuration, usually called *httpd.conf.default*. These new lines are placed inside IfDefine containers so that SSL support is an option that can be invoked from the httpd command line. Red Hat, which bundles mod_ssl into the basic system, provides a good example of how this is done. Here are the IfDefine containers for the mod_ssl LoadModule and AddModule directives from a Red Hat system:

```
<IfDefine HAVE_SSL>
LoadModule ssl_module          modules/libssl.so
</IfDefine>
<IfDefine HAVE_SSL>
AddModule mod_ssl.c
</IfDefine>
```

The LoadModule and AddModule directives are used only if HAVE_SSL is defined on the httpd command line. The string "HAVE_SSL" is arbitrary; on another system, the string might be "SSL". All that matters is that the string matches a value defined on the httpd command line. For example:

```
# httpd -DHAVE_SSL
```

This command attempts to start an SSL Apache server on a Red Hat 7.2 system.

In addition to the containers for the LoadModule and AddModule directives, there is an IfDefine container that defines a special SSL server configuration. The container from the Red Hat configuration is shown here:

```
<IfDefine HAVE_SSL>
Listen 80
Listen 443
</IfDefine>
<IfDefine HAVE_SSL>
AddType application/x-x509-ca-cert .crt
AddType application/x-pkcs7-crl    .crl
</IfDefine>
<IfDefine HAVE_SSL>
<VirtualHost _default_:443>
ErrorLog logs/error_log
TransferLog logs/access_log
SSLEngine on
SSLCertificateFile /etc/httpd/conf/ssl.crt/server.crt
SSLCertificateKeyFile /etc/httpd/conf/ssl.key/server.key
<Files ~ "·(cgi|shtml|phtml|php3?)$">
    SSLOptions +StdEnvVars
</Files>
<Directory "/var/www/cgi-bin">
    SSLOptions +StdEnvVars
```

---

* *Linux Apache Web Server Administration* is an excellent reference on compiling Apache.

```
        </Directory>
        SetEnvIf User-Agent ".*MSIE.*" \
                nokeepalive ssl-unclean-shutdown \
                downgrade-1.0 force-response-1.0
        CustomLog logs/ssl_request_log \
                "%t %h %{SSL_PROTOCOL}x %{SSL_CIPHER}x '%r' %b"
        </VirtualHost>
        </IfDefine>
```

The two lines in the first IfDefine container tell the server to listen to port 443, as well as to the standard port 80. Port 443 is the port used by SSL. The two lines in the second IfDefine container map the file extensions *.crt* and *.crl* to specific MIME file types. The extensions *.crt* and *.crl* are both related to SSL certificates. More on certificates in a moment.

The bulk of the SSL server configuration is defined in a VirtualHost container. This virtual host configuration is invoked when a connection comes into the default server on port 443—the SSL port. A special log file is created to track SSL requests. Error-Log, TransferLog, and CustomLog are directives we have seen before. Most of the other configuration directives are valid only when SSL is running:

SSLEngine
> Turns on SSL processing for this virtual host.

SetEnvIf
> Performs essentially the same function as the BrowserMatch directives described earlier. In this case, the SetEnvIf directive checks to see if the User-Agent (the browser) is Microsoft Internet Explorer. If it is, the ssl-unclean-shutdown option lets Apache know that this browser will not properly shut down the connection and that keepalives should not be used with Internet Explorer.

SSLOptions
> Sets special SSL protocol options. In the example, StdEnvVars are enabled for the */var/www/cgi-bin* directory and for all CGI and SSI files. StdEnvVars are environment variables sent over the connection to the client. Retrieving these variables is time consuming for the server, so they are sent only when it is possible that the client could use them, as is the case when CGI scripts or SSI files are involved.

SSLCertificateFile
> Points to the file that contains the server's public key.

SSLCertificateKeyFile
> Points to the file that contains the server's private key.

Public key cryptography requires two encryption keys: a public key that is made available to all clients, and a private key that is kept secret. The public key is in a special format called a *certificate*. Before you can start SSL on your server, you must create these two keys.

OpenSSL provides the tools to create the public and private keys required for SSL. The simplest of these is the Makefile found in the *ssl/certs* directory,[*] which allows you to create certificates and keys with a make command. Two different types of arguments can be used with the make command to create an SSL certificate or key. One type of argument uses the file extension to determine the type of certificate or key created:

make *name*.key
> Creates a private key and stores it in the file *name*.key.

make *name*.crt
> Creates a certificate containing a public key and stores it in the file *name*.crt.

make *name*.pem
> Creates a certificate and a key in the Privacy Enhanced Mail (PEM) format and stores it in the file *name*.pem. In Chapter 12, this make command is used to create the keys required for the stunnel program.

make *name*.csr
> Creates a certificate signature request. A certificate can be digitally signed by a trusted agent, called a *certificate authority* (CA), who vouches for the authenticity of the public key contained in the certificate. More about this later in this section.

Keywords are the other type of argument that can be used with this Makefile. The keywords create certificates and keys that are intended solely for use with Apache:

make genkey
> Creates a private key for the Apache server. The key is stored in the file pointed to by the KEY variable in the Makefile.

make certreq
> Creates a certificate signature request for the Apache server. The certificate signature request is stored in the file pointed to by the CSR variable in the Makefile.

make testcert
> Creates a certificate for the Apache server. This certificate can be used to boot and test the SSL server. However, the certificate is not signed by a recognized CA and therefore is not acceptable for use on the Internet. The certificate is stored in the file pointed to by the CRT variable in the Makefile.

The */etc/httpd/conf* directory on the Red Hat system has a link to the Makefile to make it easy to build the keys in the place where the *httpd.conf* file expects to find them. A look at the */etc/httpd/conf* directory on a Red Hat system shows that the keys pointed to by SSLCertificateFile and SSLCertificateKeyFile already exist, even though you did not create them.

The Makefile uses the openssl command to create the certificates and keys. The openssl command has a large and complex syntax, so using the Makefile provides real

---

[*] *ssl/certs* is relative to the path where OpenSSL is installed on your system. On our Red Hat system, the full path is */usr/share/ssl/certs*.

benefit. However, you can use the openssl command directly to do things that are not available through the Makefile. For example, to look at the contents of the certificate that Red Hat has placed in the /etc/httpd/conf directory, enter the following command:

```
# openssl x509 -noout -text -in ssl.crt/server.crt
Certificate:
    Data:
        Version: 3 (0x2)
        Serial Number: 0 (0x0)
        Signature Algorithm: md5WithRSAEncryption
        Issuer: C=--, ST=SomeState, L=SomeCity, O=SomeOrganization,
                OU=SomeOrganizationalUnit,
                CN=localhost.localdomain/Email=root@localhost.localdomain
        Validity
            Not Before: Jul 27 12:58:42 2001 GMT
            Not After : Jul 27 12:58:42 2002 GMT
        Subject: C=--, ST=SomeState, L=SomeCity, O=SomeOrganization,
                OU=SomeOrganizationalUnit,
                CN=localhost.localdomain/Email=root@localhost.localdomain
        Subject Public Key Info:
            Public Key Algorithm: rsaEncryption
            RSA Public Key: (1024 bit)
                Modulus (1024 bit):
                    00:a3:e7:ef:ba:71:2a:52:ff:d9:df:da:94:75:59:
                    07:f9:49:4b:1c:d0:67:b2:da:bd:7b:0b:64:63:93:
                    50:3d:a1:02:e3:05:3b:8e:e6:25:06:a3:d2:0f:75:
                    0a:85:71:66:d0:ce:f9:8b:b0:73:2f:fe:90:75:ad:
                    d6:28:77:b0:27:54:81:ce:3b:88:38:88:e7:eb:d6:
                    e9:a0:dd:26:79:aa:43:31:29:08:fe:f8:fa:90:d9:
                    90:ed:80:96:91:53:9d:88:a4:24:0a:d0:21:7d:5d:
                    53:9f:77:a1:2b:4f:62:26:13:57:7f:de:9b:40:33:
                    c3:9c:33:d4:25:1d:a3:e2:47
                Exponent: 65537 (0x10001)
        X509v3 extensions:
            X509v3 Subject Key Identifier:
                55:E9:ED:C1:BF:1A:D4:F8:C2:78:6E:7A:2C:D4:9C:AC:7B:CD:D2
            X509v3 Authority Key Identifier:
                keyid:55:E9:ED:C1:BF:1A:D4:6E:7A:2C:D4:DD:9C:AC:7B:CD:D2
                DirName:/C=-/ST=SomeState/L=SomeCity/O=SomeOrganization/
                        OU=SomeOrganizationalUnit/CN=localhost.localdomain/
                        Email=root@localhost.localdomain
                serial:00
            X509v3 Basic Constraints:
                CA:TRUE
    Signature Algorithm: md5WithRSAEncryption
        76:78:77:f0:a2:19:3b:39:5f:2a:bd:d0:42:da:85:6e:c2:0c:
        5e:80:40:9c:a8:65:da:bf:38:2b:f0:d6:aa:30:72:fb:d3:1d:
        ce:cd:19:22:fb:b3:cc:07:ce:cc:9b:b6:38:02:7a:21:72:7c:
        26:07:cc:c9:e0:36:4f:2f:23:c9:08:f7:d4:c1:57:2f:3e:5c:
        d5:74:70:c6:02:df:1a:62:72:97:74:0a:a6:db:e0:9d:c9:3d:
        8e:6b:18:b1:88:93:68:48:c3:a3:27:99:67:6f:f7:89:09:52:
        3a:a3:fb:20:52:b0:03:06:22:dd:2f:d2:46:4e:42:f2:1c:f0:
        f1:1a
```

As you can see, there is a lot of information in a certificate. But only a few pieces of it are needed to determine whether this is a valid certificate for our server:

Issuer

> The Issuer is the *distinguished name* of the CA that issued and signed this certificate. A distinguished name is a name format designed to uniquely identify an organization. It's clear in this certificate that the name of the Issuer is just an example, not a real organization.

Subject

> The Subject is the distinguished name of the organization to which this certificate was issued. In our case, it should be the name of our organization. Again, the Subject in this certificate is just an example.

Validity

> The Validity is the time frame in which this certificate is valid. Here, the certificate is valid for a year. Because the dates are valid, this certificate can be used to test SSL.

To test that the SSL server is indeed running, use a browser to attach to the local server. However, instead of starting the URL with http://, start it with https://. https connects to port 443, which is the SSL port. The browser responds by warning you that the server has an invalid certificate, as shown in Figure 11-4.

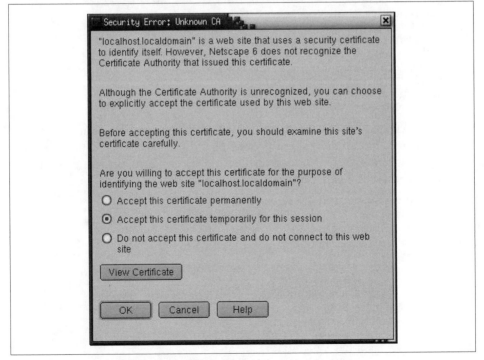

Figure 11-4. A warning about an invalid certificate

Clicking on View Certificate shows some of the same certificate information we just saw. You can accept the certificate for this session and connect to the "secure document." In this case, the secure document is just a test page because we have not yet stored any real secure documents on the system.

The server is up and running, but it can't be used by external customers until we get a valid signed certificate. Use make certreq to create a certificate signature request specific to your server. Here is an example:

```
# cd /etc/httpd/conf
# make certreq
umask 77 ; \
/usr/bin/openssl req -new -key /etc/httpd/conf/ssl.key/server.key -out /etc/http
d/conf/ssl.csr/server.csr
Using configuration from /usr/share/ssl/openssl.cnf
You are about to be asked to enter information that will be incorporated
into your certificate request.
What you are about to enter is what is called a Distinguished Name or a DN.
There are quite a few fields but you can leave some blank.
For some fields there will be a default value.
If you enter '.', the field will be left blank.
-----
Country Name (2 letter code) [AU]:US
State or Province Name (full name) [Some-State]:Maryland
Locality Name (eg, city) []:Gaithersburg
Organization Name (eg, company) [Internet Widgits Ltd]:WroteThebook.com
Organizational Unit Name (eg, section) []:Headquarters
Common Name (eg, your name or hostname)[]:crab.wrotethebook.com
Email Address []:alana@wrotethebook.com

Please enter the following 'extra' attributes
to be sent with your certificate request
A challenge password []:
An optional company name []:
```

The freshly created request can be examined using the openssl command. Notice that this request has a valid Subject containing a distinguished name that identifies our server. However, there is no Issuer. This request needs to be signed by a recognized CA to become a useful certificate.

```
# openssl req -noout -text -in server.csr
Using configuration from /usr/share/ssl/openssl.cnf
Certificate Request:
    Data:
        Version: 0 (0x0)
        Subject: C=US, ST=Maryland, L=Gaithersburg, O=WroteThebook.com,
                OU=Headquarters,
                CN=crab.wrotethebook.com/Email=alana@wrotethebook.com
        Subject Public Key Info:
            Public Key Algorithm: rsaEncryption
            RSA Public Key: (1024 bit)
                Modulus (1024 bit):
                    00:a3:e7:ef:ba:71:2a:52:ff:d9:df:da:94:75:59:
                    07:f9:49:4b:1c:d0:67:b2:da:bd:7b:0b:64:63:93:
```

```
            50:3d:a1:02:e3:05:3b:8e:e6:25:06:a3:d2:0f:75:
            0a:85:71:66:d0:ce:f9:8b:b0:73:2f:fe:90:75:ad:
            d6:28:77:b0:27:54:81:ce:3b:88:38:88:e7:eb:d6:
            e9:a0:dd:26:79:aa:43:31:29:08:fe:f8:fa:90:d9:
            90:ed:80:96:91:53:9d:88:a4:24:0a:d0:21:7d:5d:
            53:9f:77:a1:2b:4f:62:26:13:57:7f:de:9b:40:33:
            c3:9c:33:d4:25:1d:a3:e2:47
        Exponent: 65537 (0x10001)
    Attributes:
        a0:00
Signature Algorithm: md5WithRSAEncryption
    3f:c2:34:c1:1f:21:d7:93:5b:c0:90:c5:c9:5d:10:cd:68:1c:
    7d:90:7c:6a:6a:99:2f:f8:51:51:69:9b:a4:6c:80:b9:02:91:
    f7:bd:29:5e:a6:4d:a7:fc:c2:e2:39:45:1d:6a:36:1f:91:93:
    77:5b:51:ad:59:e1:75:63:4e:84:7b:be:1d:ae:cb:52:1a:7c:
    90:e3:76:76:1e:52:fa:b9:86:ab:59:b7:17:08:68:26:e6:d4:
    ef:e6:17:30:b6:1c:95:c9:fc:bf:21:ec:63:81:be:47:09:c7:
    67:fc:73:66:98:26:5e:53:ed:41:c5:97:a5:55:1d:95:8f:0b:
    22:0b
```

CAs are commercial, for-profit businesses. Fees and forms, as well as the CSR, are required before you can get your certificate signed. Your web browser contains a list of recognized CAs. On a Netscape 6.1 browser, you can view this list in the Certificate Manager in the Preferences, as shown in Figure 11-5. All CAs have web sites that provide the details of the cost and the application process.

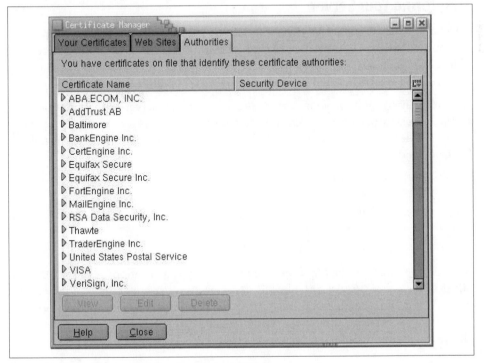

Figure 11-5. The Netscape 6.1 list of recognized CAs

Although certificates signed by a recognized CA are the most widely used, it is possible to create a self-signed certificate. However, this has limited utility. As we saw in Figure 11-4, a certificate that is not signed by a recognized CA must be manually accepted by the client. Therefore, self-signed certificates can be used only if you have a small client base. Use the openssl command to sign the certificate yourself:

```
# openssl req -x509 -key ssl.key/server.key \
> -in ssl.csr/server.csr -out ssl.crt/server.crt
```

Examining the newly created *server.crt* file with openssl shows that the Issuer and the Subject contain the same distinguished name. But this time, the name is the valid name of our server.

Managing Your Web Server

Despite the enormous number of options found in the *httpd.conf* configuration file, configuration is not the biggest task you undertake when you run a web server. Configuration usually requires no more than adjusting a few options when the server is first installed; however, monitoring your server's usage and performance and ensuring its reliability and security are daily tasks. The Apache server provides some tools to simplify these tasks.

Monitoring Your Server

Apache provides tools to monitor the status of the server, and logs that keep a history of how the system is used and how it performs over time. The earlier discussion of logging configuration touched on these issues. We even looked at a technique for observing log entries in real time.

A better way to monitor your server in real time is the server-status monitor. This monitor must either be compiled in to httpd or installed as a dynamically loadable module. These two lines from the Solaris *httpd.conf* configuration file install the loadable module:

```
LoadModule status_module      modules/mod_status.so
AddModule mod_status.c
```

To get the maximum information from the server-status display, add the Extended-Status option to your *httpd.conf* file:

```
ExtendedStatus on
```

Enable the monitor in the *httpd.conf* file by inserting the Location /server-status container. The Solaris *httpd.conf* file has the Location /server-status container predefined, but it is commented out of the configuration. To enable the monitor, uncomment the lines and edit the Allow directive to specify the hosts that will be allowed to monitor the server. For example:

```
<Location /server-status>
SetHandler server-status
Order deny,allow
Deny from all
Allow from wrotethebook.com
</Location>
```

Once the monitor is installed and enabled, access it from your browser. For our sample system, we use the URL *http://www.wrotethebook.com/server-status/?refresh=20*. The refresh value is not required, but using it will cause the status display to update automatically. In this example, we are asking for a status update every 20 seconds. Figure 11-6 shows the status screen for our test server.

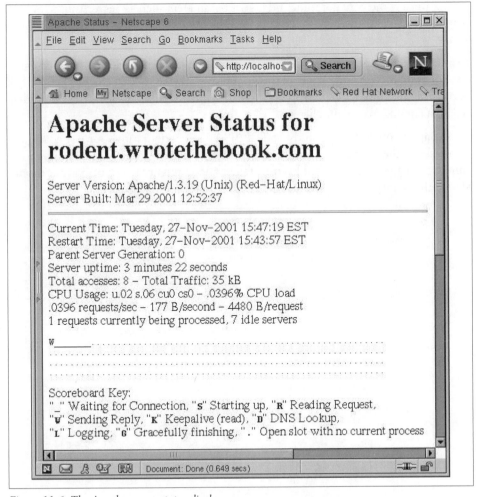

Figure 11-6. The Apache server status display

Monitoring tells you about the real-time status of your server. Logging provides information about how your server is used over time. Together, logging and monitoring can help you maintain a healthy, useful web service.

Summary

Web servers are an essential part of any organization's network, and the Apache web server is an excellent choice. It runs as the HTTP daemon (httpd), which is configured in the *httpd.conf* file.

The Apache software on Linux and Solaris systems comes preconfigured and ready to run. Review the configuration and adjust parameters such as ServerAdmin, ServerName, and DocumentRoot to make sure they are exactly what you want for your server.

Use the monitoring tools and log files to closely observe the usage and performance of your system. Keep tight control on Common Gateway Interface (CGI) scripts and Server Side Includes (SSI) to keep your server secure. Use SSL to secure the confidential data coming from your clients.

This chapter concludes our study of TCP/IP server configuration, our last configuration task. In the next chapter, we begin to look at the ongoing tasks that are part of running a network once it has been installed and configured. We begin that discussion with security.

## CHAPTER 12

Network Security

In this chapter:
- Security Planning
- User Authentication
- Application Security
- Security Monitoring
- Access Control
- Encryption
- Firewalls
- Words to the Wise

Hosts attached to a network—particularly the worldwide Internet—are exposed to a wider range of security threats than are unconnected hosts. Network security reduces the risks of connecting to a network. But by nature, network access and computer security work at cross-purposes. A network is a data highway designed to increase access to computer systems, while security is designed to control access to those systems. Providing network security is a balancing act between open access and security.

The highway analogy is very appropriate. Like a highway, the network provides equal access for all—welcome visitors as well as unwelcome intruders. At home, you provide security for your possessions by locking your house, not by blocking the streets. Likewise, network security requires adequate security on individual host computers. Simply securing the network with a firewall is not enough.

In very small towns where people know each other, doors are often left unlocked. But in big cities, doors have deadbolts and chains. The Internet has grown from a small town of a few thousand users into a big city of millions of users. Just as the anonymity of a big city turns neighbors into strangers, the growth of the Internet has reduced the level of trust between network neighbors. The ever-increasing need for computer security is an unfortunate side effect. Growth, however, is not all bad. In the same way that a big city offers more choices and more services, the expanded network provides increased services. For most of us, security consciousness is a small price to pay for network access.

Network break-ins have increased as the network has grown and become more impersonal, but it is easy to exaggerate the extent of these security breaches. Overreacting to the threat of break-ins may hinder the way you use the network. Don't make the cure worse than the disease. The best advice about network security is to use common sense. RFC 1244, now replaced by RFC 2196, stated this principle very well:

> Common sense is the most appropriate tool that can be used to establish your security policy. Elaborate security schemes and mechanisms are impressive, and they do have their place, yet there is little point in investing money and time on an elaborate implementation scheme if the simple controls are forgotten.

This chapter emphasizes the simple controls that can be used to increase your network's security. A reasonable approach to security, based on the level of security required by your system, is the most cost-effective—both in terms of actual expense and in terms of productivity.

Security Planning

One of the most important network security tasks, and probably one of the least enjoyable, is developing a network security policy. Most computer people want a technical solution to every problem. We want to find a program that "fixes" the network security problem. Few of us want to write a paper on network security policies and procedures. However, a well-thought-out security plan will help you decide what needs to be protected, how much you are willing to invest in protecting it, and who will be responsible for carrying out the steps to protect it.

Assessing the Threat

The first step toward developing an effective network security plan is to assess the threat that connection presents to your systems. RFC 2196, *Site Security Handbook*, identifies three distinct types of security threats usually associated with network connectivity:

Unauthorized access
   A break-in by an unauthorized person.

Disclosure of information
   Any problem that causes the disclosure of valuable or sensitive information to people who should not have access to the information.

Denial of service (DoS)
   Any problem that makes it difficult or impossible for the system to continue to perform productive work.

Assess these threats in relation to the number of users who would be affected, as well as to the sensitivity of the information that might be compromised. For some organizations, break-ins are an embarrassment that can undermine the confidence that others have in the organization. Intruders tend to target government and academic organizations that will be embarrassed by the break-in. But for most organizations, unauthorized access is not a major problem unless it involves one of the other threats: disclosure of information or denial of service.

Assessing the threat of information disclosure depends on the type of information that could be compromised. While no system with highly classified information should ever be directly connected to the Internet, systems with other types of sensitive information might be connected without undue hazard. In most cases, files such as personnel and medical records, corporate plans, and credit reports can be adequately protected by network access controls and standard Unix file security procedures. However, if the risk of liability in case of disclosure is great, the host may choose not to be connected to the Internet.

Denial of service can be a severe problem if it impacts many users or a major mission of your organization. Some systems can be connected to the network with little concern. The benefit of connecting individual workstations and small servers to the Internet generally outweighs the chance of having service interrupted for the individuals and small groups served by these systems. Other systems may be vital to the survival of your organization. The threat of losing the services of a mission-critical system must be evaluated seriously before connecting such a system to the network.

An insidious aspect of DoS appears when your system becomes an unwitting tool of the attackers. Through unauthorized access, intruders can place malicious software on your system in order to use your system as a launching pad for attacks on others. This is most often associated with Microsoft systems, but any type of computer system can be a victim. Preventing your system from becoming a tool of evil is an important reason for protecting it.

In his class on computer security, Brent Chapman classifies information security threats into three categories: threats to the secrecy, to the availability, and to the integrity of data. Secrecy is the need to prevent the disclosure of sensitive information. Availability means that you want information and information processing resources available when they are needed; a denial-of-service attack disrupts availability. The need for the integrity of information is equally obvious, but its link to computer security is more subtle. Once someone has gained unauthorized access to a system, the integrity of the information on that system is in doubt. Some intruders just want to compromise the integrity of data; we are all familiar with cases where web vandals gain access to a web server and change the data on the server in order to embarrass the organization that runs the web site. Thinking about the impact network threats have on your data can make it easier to assess the threat.

Network threats are not, of course, the only threats to computer security, or the only reasons for denial of service. Natural disasters and internal threats (threats from people who have legitimate access to a system) are also serious. Network security has had a lot of publicity, so it's a fashionable thing to worry about, but more computer time has probably been lost because of fires and power outages than has ever been lost because of network security problems. Similarly, more data has probably been improperly disclosed by authorized users than by unauthorized break-ins. This book naturally emphasizes network security, but network security is only part of a larger security plan that includes physical security and disaster recovery plans.

Many traditional (non-network) security threats are handled, in part, by physical security. Don't forget to provide an adequate level of physical security for your network equipment and cables. Again, the investment in physical security should be based on your realistic assessment of the threat.

Distributed Control

One approach to network security is to distribute the responsibility for and control over different segments of a large network to small groups within the organization. This approach involves a large number of people in security and runs counter to the school of thought that seeks to increase security by centralizing control. However, distributing responsibility and control to small groups can create an environment of small, easily monitored networks composed of a known user community. Using the analogy of small towns and big cities, it is similar to creating a neighborhood watch to reduce risks by giving people connections with their neighbors, mutual responsibility for one another, and control over their own fates.

Additionally, distributing security responsibilities formally recognizes one of the realities of network security—most security actions take place on individual systems. The managers of these systems must know that they are responsible for security and that their contribution to network security is recognized and appreciated. If people are expected to do a job, they must be empowered to do it.

Use subnets to distribute control

Subnets are a possible tool for distributing network control. A subnet administrator should be appointed when a subnet is created. The administrator is then responsible for the security of the network and for assigning IP addresses to the devices connected to the networks. Assigning IP addresses gives the subnet administrator some control over who connects to the subnet. It also helps to ensure that the administrator knows each system that is connected and who is responsible for that system. When the subnet administrator gives a system an IP address, he also delegates certain security responsibilities to the system's administrator. Likewise, when the system administrator grants a user an account, the user takes on certain security responsibilities.

The hierarchy of responsibility flows from the network administrator to the subnet administrator to the system administrator and finally to the user. At each point in this hierarchy the individuals are given responsibilities and the power to carry them out. To support this structure, it is important for users to know what they are responsible for and how to carry out that responsibility. The network security policy described in the next section provides this information.

Use the network to distribute information

If your site adopts distributed control, you must develop a system for disseminating security information to each group. Mailing lists for each administrative level can be used for alerts and other real-time information. An internal web site can be used to provide policy, background, and archival information as well as links to important security sites.

The network administrator receives security information from outside authorities, filters out irrelevant material, and forwards the relevant material to the subnet administrators. Subnet administrators forward the relevant parts to their system administrators, who in turn forward what they consider important to the individual users. The filtering of information at each level ensures that individuals get the information they need without receiving too much. If too much unnecessary material is distributed, users begin to ignore everything they receive.

At the top of this information structure is the information that the network administrator receives from outside authorities. In order to receive this, the network administrator should join the appropriate mailing lists and newsgroups and browse the appropriate web sites. A few places to start looking for computer security information are the following:

Your Unix vendor
> Many vendors have their own security information mailing lists. Most vendors also have a security page on their web sites. Place a link on your internal web site to the vendor information that you find important and useful.

The Bugtraq archive
> Bugtraq reports on software bugs, some of which are exploited by intruders. Knowing about these bugs and the fixes for them is the single most important thing you can do to improve system security. Bugtraq is widely available on the Web. Two sites I use are *http://www.geek-girl.com/bugtraq* and *http://www.securityfocus.com*, which provide access to a wide range of security information.

Security newsgroups
> The *comp.security* newsgroups—*comp.security.unix*, *comp.security.firewalls*, *comp.security.announce*, and *comp.security.misc*—contain some useful information. Like most newsgroups, they also contain lots of unimportant and uninteresting material. But they do contain an occasional gem.

FIRST web site
> The Forum of Incident Response and Security Teams (FIRST) is a worldwide organization of computer security response teams. FIRST provides a public web site for computer security information.

NIST Computer Security Alerts
> The National Institute of Standards and Technology's Computer Security Division maintains a web site with pointers to security-related web pages all over the world. Follow the Alerts link from *http://csrc.nist.gov*.

CERT advisories
> The Computer Emergency Response Team (CERT) advisories provide information about known security problems and the fixes to these problems. You can retrieve these advisories from the CERT web site at *http://www.cert.org*.

SANS Institute

The System Administration, Networking and Security (SANS) Institute offers informative security newsletters that are delivered weekly via email. They also have a useful online reading room. These resources are available from their web site, *http://www.sans.org*.

Exploit sites

Most intruders use canned attack scripts that are available from the Web. Sites that provide the scripts often provide discussions of the current security vulnerabilities that might affect your system. *http://www.insecure.org* is a good site because it provides descriptions of current exploits as well as plenty of other useful information.

Writing a Security Policy

Security is largely a "people problem." People, not computers, are responsible for implementing security procedures, and people are responsible when security is breached. Therefore, network security is ineffective unless people know their responsibilities. It is important to write a security policy that clearly states what is expected and from whom. A network security policy should define:

The network user's security responsibilities

The policy may require users to change their passwords at certain intervals, to use passwords that meet certain guidelines, or to perform certain checks to see if their accounts have been accessed by someone else. Whatever is expected from users, it is important that it be clearly defined.

The system administrator's security responsibilities

The policy may require that every host use specific security measures, login banner messages, or monitoring and accounting procedures. It might list applications that should not be run on any host attached to the network.

The proper use of network resources

Define who can use network resources, what things they can do, and what things they should not do. If your organization takes the position that email, files, and histories of computer activity are subject to security monitoring, tell the users very clearly that this is the policy.

The actions taken when a security problem is detected

What should be done when a security problem is detected? Who should be notified? It is easy to overlook things during a crisis, so you should have a detailed list of the exact steps that a system administrator or user should take when a security breach is detected. This could be as simple as telling the users to "touch nothing, and call the network security officer." But even these simple actions should be in the written policy so that they are readily available.

Connecting to the Internet brings with it certain security responsibilities. RFC 1281, *A Guideline for the Secure Operation of the Internet*, provides guidance for users and network administrators on how to use the Internet in a secure and responsible manner. Reading this RFC will provide insight into the information that should be in your security policy.

A great deal of thought is necessary to produce a complete network security policy. The outline shown above describes the contents of a network policy document, but if you are personally responsible for writing a policy, you may want more detailed guidance. I recommend that you read RFC 2196, which is a very good guide for developing a security plan.

Security planning (assessing the threat, assigning security responsibilities, and writing a security policy) is the basic building block of network security, but the plan must be implemented before it can have any effect. In the remainder of this chapter, we'll turn our attention to implementing basic security procedures.

User Authentication

Good passwords are one of the simplest parts of good network security. Passwords are used to log into systems that use password authentication. Popular mythology says that all network security breaches are caused by sophisticated crackers who discover software security holes. In reality, some of the most famous intruders entered systems simply by guessing or stealing passwords or by exploiting well-known security problems in outdated software. Later in this chapter, we look at guidelines for keeping software up to date and ways to prevent a thief from stealing your password. First, let's see what we can do to prevent it from being guessed.

These are a few things that make it easy to guess passwords:

- Accounts that use the account name as the password. Accounts with this type of trivial password are called *joe accounts*.
- Guest or demonstration accounts that require no password or use a well-publicized password.
- System accounts with default passwords.
- User who tell their passwords to others.

Guessing these kinds of passwords requires no skill, just lots of spare time! Changing your password frequently is a deterrent to password guessing. However, if you choose good passwords, don't change them so often that it is hard to remember them. Many security experts recommend that passwords should be changed about every 3 to 6 months.

A more sophisticated form of password guessing is *dictionary guessing*. Dictionary guessing uses a program that encrypts each word in a dictionary (e.g., */usr/dict/words*) and compares each encrypted word to the encrypted password in the */etc/passwd* file. Dictionary guessing is not limited to words from a dictionary. Things known about you (your name, initials, telephone number, etc.) are also run through the guessing program. Because of dictionary guessing, you must protect the */etc/passwd* file.

Some systems provide a *shadow password file* to hide the encrypted passwords from potential intruders. If your system has a shadow password facility, use it. Hiding encrypted passwords greatly reduces the risk of password guessing.

The Shadow Password File

Shadow password files have restricted permissions that prevent them from being read by intruders. The encrypted password is stored only in the shadow password file, */etc/shadow*, and not in the */etc/passwd* file. The *passwd* file is maintained as a world-readable file because it contains information that various programs use. The *shadow* file can be read only by root and it does not duplicate the information in the *passwd* file. It contains only passwords and the information needed to manage them. The format of a *shadow* file entry on a Solaris system is:

```
username:password:lastchg:min:max:warn:inactive:expire:flag
```

username is the login username. *password* is the encrypted password or, on Solaris systems, one of the keyword values NP or *LK*. *lastchg* is the date that the password was last changed, written as the number of days from January 1, 1970 to the date of the change. *min* is the minimum number of days that must elapse before the password can be changed. *max* is the maximum number of days the user can keep the password before it must be changed. *warn* is the number of days before the password expires that the user is warned. *inactive* is the number of days the account can be inactive before it is locked. *expire* is the date on which the account will be closed. *flag* is unused.

The encrypted password appears only in this file. Every password field in the */etc/passwd* file contains an x, which tells the system to look in the *shadow* file for the real password. Every password field in the */etc/shadow* file contains either an encrypted password, NP, or *LK*. If it contains the keyword NP, it means that there is no password because this is not a login account. System accounts, such as *daemon* or *uucp*, are not login accounts, so they have NP in the password field. *LK* in the password field means that this account has been locked and is therefore disabled from any further use. Other systems use different symbols in the password field to indicate these conditions; some Linux systems use * and !!. However, all systems have some technique for differentiating active login accounts from other types of user IDs.

While the most important purpose of the *shadow* file is to protect the password, the additional fields in the shadow entry provide other useful security services. One of these is *password aging*. A password aging mechanism defines a lifetime for each password. When a password reaches the end of its lifetime, the password aging mechanism notifies the user to change the password. If it is not changed within some specified period, the password is removed from the system and the user is blocked from using his account.

The lastchg, max, and warn fields all play a role in password aging. They allow the system to know when the password was changed and how long it should be kept, as well as when the user should be warned about his impending doom. Another nice feature of the shadow file is the min field. This is a more subtle aspect of password aging. It prevents the user from changing her favorite password to a dummy password and then immediately back to the favorite. When the password is changed it must be used for the number of days defined by min before it can be changed again. This reduces one of the common tricks used to avoid really changing passwords.

The inactive and expire fields help eliminate unused accounts. Here, "inactivity" is determined by the number of days the account continues with an expired password. Once the password expires, the user is given some number of days to log in and set a new password. If the user does not log in before the specified number of days has elapsed, the account is locked and the user cannot log in.

The expire field lets you create a user account that has a specified "life." When the date stored in the expire field is reached, the user account is disabled even if it is still active. The expiration date is stored as the number of days since January 1, 1970.

On a Solaris system the /etc/shadow file is not edited directly. It is modified through the Users window of the admintool or special options on the passwd command line. This window is shown in Figure 12-1. The username, password, min, max, warn, inactive, and expire fields are clearly shown.

The passwd command on Solaris systems has -n *min*, -w *warn*, and -x *max* options to set the min, max, and warn fields in the /etc/shadow file. Only the root user can invoke these options. Here, root sets the maximum life of Tyler's password to 180 days:

```
# passwd -x 180 tyler
```

The Solaris system permits the system administrator to set default values for all of these options so that they do not have to be set every time a user is added through the admintool or the passwd command line. The default values are set in the /etc/default/passwd file.

```
% cat /etc/default/passwd
#ident  "@(#)passwd.dfl 1.3     92/07/14 SMI"
MAXWEEKS=
MINWEEKS=
PASSLENGTH=6
```

The default values that can be set in the /etc/default/passwd file are:

MAXWEEKS

> The maximum life of a password defined in weeks, not days. The 180-day period used in the example above would be defined with this parameter as MAXWEEKS=26.

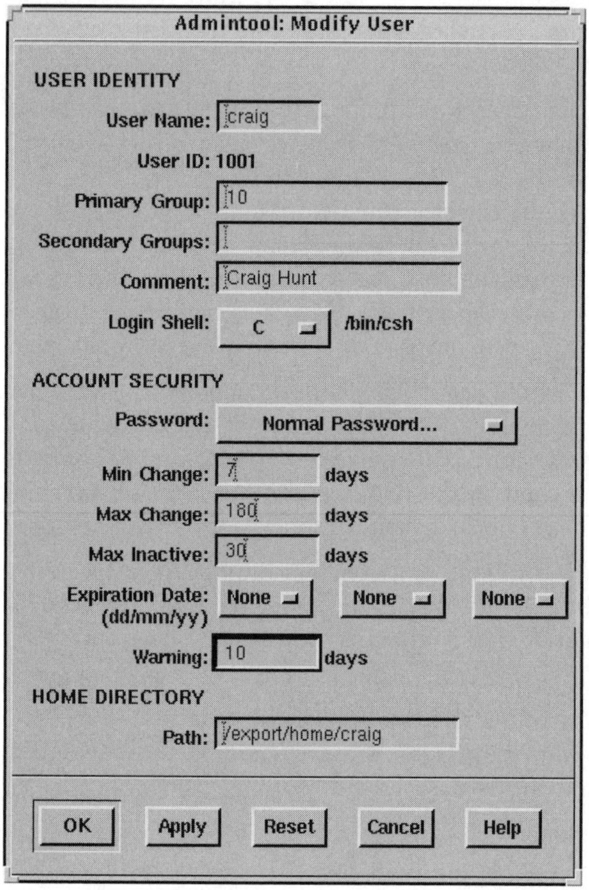

Figure 12-1. Admintool password maintenance

MINWEEKS

   The minimum number of weeks a password must be used before it can be changed.

PASSLENGTH

   The minimum number of characters that a password must contain. This is set to 6 in the sample file. Only the first eight characters are significant on a Solaris system; setting the value above 8 does not change that fact.

WARNWEEKS

   The number of weeks before a password expires that the user is warned.

This section uses Solaris as an example. The shadow password system is provided as part of the Solaris operating system. It is also included with Linux systems. The *shadow* file described here is exactly the same format as used on Linux systems, and it functions in the same way.

It is very difficult to take the encrypted password and decrypt it back to its original form, but encrypted passwords can be compared against encrypted dictionaries. If bad passwords are used, they can be easily guessed. Take care to protect the /etc/passwd file and choose good passwords.

Choosing a Password

A good password is an essential part of security. We usually think of the password used for a traditional login; however, passwords, passphrases, and keys are also needed for more advanced authentication systems. For all of these purposes, you want to choose a good password. Choosing a good password boils down to not choosing a password that can be guessed using the techniques described above. Some guidelines for choosing a good password are:

- Don't use your login name.
- Don't use the name of anyone or anything.
- Don't use any English or foreign-language word or abbreviation.
- Don't use any personal information associated with the owner of the account. For example, don't use your initials, phone number, social security number, job title, organizational unit, etc.
- Don't use keyboard sequences, e.g., qwerty.
- Don't use any of the above spelled backwards, or in caps, or otherwise disguised.
- Don't use an all-numeric password.
- Don't use a sample password, no matter how good, that you've gotten from a book that discusses computer security.
- *Do* use a mixture of numbers, special characters, and mixed-case letters.
- *Do* use at least six characters.
- *Do* use a seemingly random selection of letters and numbers.

Common suggestions for constructing seemingly random passwords are:

- Use the first letter of each word from a line in a book, song, or poem. For example, "People don't know you and trust is a joke."* would produce Pd'ky&tiaj.
- Use the output from a random password generator. Select a random string that can be pronounced and is easy to remember. For example, the random string "adazac" can be pronounced a-da-zac, and you can remember it by thinking of it as "A-to-Z." Add uppercase letters to create your own emphasis, e.g., aDAzac.†

---

* Toad the Wet Sprocket, "Walk on the Ocean."
† A password generator created this password.

- Use two short words connected by punctuation, e.g., wRen%Rug.
- Use numbers and letters to create an imaginary vanity license plate password, e.g., 2hot4U?.

A common theme of these suggestions is that the password should be easy to remember. Avoid passwords that must be written down to be remembered. If unreliable people gain access to your office and find the password you have written down, the security of your system will be compromised.

However, don't assume that you can't remember a random password. It may be difficult the first few times you use the password, but any password that is used often enough is easy to remember. If you have an account on a system that you rarely use, you may have trouble remembering a random password. But in that case, the best solution is to get rid of the account. Unused and underutilized accounts are prime targets for intruders. They like to attack unused accounts because there is no user to notice changes to the files or strange *Last login:* messages. Remove all unused accounts from your systems.

How do you ensure that the guidance for creating new passwords is followed? The most important step is to make sure that every user knows these suggestions and the importance of following them. Cover this topic in your network security plan, and periodically reinforce it through newsletter articles and online system bulletins.

It is also possible to use programs that force users to follow specific password selection guidelines. The web page *http://csrc.nist.gov/tools/tools.htm* lists several programs that do exactly that.

One-Time Passwords

Sometimes good passwords are not enough. Passwords are transmitted across the network as clear text. Intruders can use protocol-analyzer software to spy on network traffic and steal passwords. If a thief steals your password, it does not matter how good the password was.

The thief can be on any network that handles your TCP/IP packets. If you log in through your local network, you have to worry only about local snoops. But if you log in over the Internet, you must worry about unseen listeners from any number of unknown networks.

Commands that use encrypted passwords are not vulnerable to this type of attack. Because of this, telnet has been largely supplanted by secure shell (ssh). However, the secure shell client may not be available at a remote site. Use one-time passwords for remote logins when you cannot use secure shell. Because a one-time password can be used only once, a thief who steals the password cannot use it.

Naturally, one-time password systems are a hassle. You must carry with you a list of one-time passwords, or something that can generate them, any time you want to log in. If you forget the password list, you cannot log in. However, this may not be as big a problem as it seems. You usually log in from your office where your primary login host is probably on your desktop or your local area network. When you log into your desktop system from its keyboard, the password does not traverse the network, so you can use a reusable password. And ssh can be used any time you control both ends of the connection, for example, when logging in with your laptop. One-time passwords are needed only for the occasions when you log in from a remote location that does not offer ssh. For this reason, some one-time password systems are designed to allow reusable passwords when they are appropriate.

There are several one-time password systems. Some use specialized hardware such as "smart cards." OPIE is a free software system that requires no special hardware.

OPIE

One-time Passwords In Everything (OPIE) is free software from the U.S. Naval Research Laboratory (NRL) that modifies a Unix system to use one-time passwords. OPIE is directly derived from Skey, which is a one-time password system created by Bell Communications Research (Bellcore).

Download OPIE from the Internet from *http://inner.net/opie*. The current version of OPIE is *opie-2.4.tar.gz*. It is a binary file. gunzip the file and extract it using tar. The directory this produces contains the source files, Makefiles, and scripts necessary to compile and install OPIE.

OPIE comes with configure, an auto-configuration script that detects your system's configuration and modifies the Makefile accordingly. It does a good job, but you still should manually edit the Makefile to make sure it is correct. For example, my Linux system uses the Washington University FTP daemon wu.ftpd. OPIE replaces login, su, and ftpd with its own version of these programs. Using an earlier version of OPIE on my Linux system, configure did not find ftpd, and I did not notice the problem when I checked the Makefile. make ran without errors, but make install failed during the install of the OPIE FTP daemon. The Makefile was easily corrected and the rerun of make install was successful.

The effects of OPIE are evident as soon as the install completes. Run su and you're prompted with root's response: instead of Password:. login prompts with Response or Password: instead of just Password:. The response requested by these programs is the OPIE equivalent of a password. Programs that prompt with Response or Password accept either the OPIE response or the traditional password from the */etc/passwd* file. This feature permits users to migrate gracefully from traditional passwords to OPIE. It also allows local console logins with reusable passwords while permitting remote logins with one-time passwords. The best of both worlds—convenient local logins without creating separate local and remote login accounts!

To use OPIE you must first select a secret password that is used to generate the one-time password list, and then run the program that generates the list. To select a secret password, run opiepasswd as shown:

```
$ opiepasswd -c
Updating kristin:
Reminder  -  Only use this method from the console; NEVER from remote.
 If you are using telnet, xterm, or a dial-in, type ^C now or exit with
 no password. Then run opiepasswd without the -c parameter.
Using MD5 to compute responses.
Enter old secret pass phrase: 3J5Wd6PaWP
Enter new secret pass phrase: 9WA11WSfW95/NT
Again new secret pass phrase: 9WA11WSfW95/NT
```

This example shows the user *kristin* updating her secret password. She runs opiepasswd from the computer's console, as indicated by the -c command option. Running opiepasswd from the console is the most secure. If it is not run from the console, you must have a copy of the opiekey software with you to generate the correct responses needed to enter your old and new secret passwords, because clear text passwords are accepted only from the console. Kristin is prompted to enter her old password and to select a new one. OPIE passwords must be at least 10 characters long. Since the new password is long enough, opiepasswd accepts it and displays the following two lines:

```
ID kristin OPIE key is 499 be93564
CITE JAN GORY BELA GET ABED
```

These lines tell Kristin the information she needs to generate OPIE login responses and the first response she will need to log into the system. The one-time password needed for Kristin's next login response is the second line of this display: a group of six short, uppercase character strings. The first line of the display contains the initial sequence number (499) and the seed (be93564) she needs, along with her secret password, to generate OPIE login responses. The software used to generate those responses is opiekey.

opiekey takes the login sequence number, the user's seed, and the user's secret password as input and outputs the correct one-time password. If you have opiekey software on the system from which you are initiating the login, you can produce one-time passwords one at a time. If, however, you will not have access to opiekey when you are away from your login host, you can use the -n option to request several passwords. Write the passwords down, put them in your wallet, and you're ready to go! [*] In the following example we request five (-n 5) responses from opiekey:

```
$ opiekey -n 5 495 wi01309
Using MD5 algorithm to compute response.
```

---

[*] Security experts will cringe when they read this suggestion. Writing down passwords is a "no-no." Frankly, I think the people who steal wallets are more interested in my money and credit cards than in the password to my system. But you should consider this suggestion in light of the level of protection your system needs.

```
Reminder: Don't use  opiekey  from  telnet  or dial-in sessions.
Enter secret pass phrase: UUaX26CPaU
491: HOST VET FOWL SEEK IOWA YAP
492: JOB ARTS WERE FEAT TILE IBIS
493: TRUE BRED JOEL USER HALT EBEN
494: HOOD WED MOLT PAN FED RUBY
495: SUB YAW BILE GLEE OWE NOR
```

First opiekey tells us that it is using the MD5 algorithm to produce the responses, which is the default for OPIE. For compatibility with older Skey or OPIE implementations, force opiekey to use the MD4 algorithm by using the -4 command-line option. opiekey prompts for your secret password. This is the password you defined with the opiepasswd command. It then prints out the number of responses requested and lists them in sequence number order. The login sequence numbers in the example are 495 to 491. When the sequence number gets down to 10, rerun opiepasswd and select a new secret password. Selecting a new secret password resets the sequence number to 499.

The OPIE login prompt displays a sequence number, and you must provide the response that goes with that sequence number. For example:

```
login: tyler
otp-md5 492 wi01309 Response or Password:
JOB ARTS WERE FEAT TILE IBIS
```

At the login: prompt, Tyler enters her username. The system then displays a single line that tells her that one-time passwords are being generated with the MD5 algorithm (otp-md5), that this is login sequence number 492, and that the seed used for her one-time passwords is wi01309. She looks up the response for login number 492 and enters the six short strings. She then marks that response off her list because it cannot be used again to log into the system. A response from the list must be used any time she is not sitting at the console of her system. Reusable passwords can be used only at the console.

Secure shell is used for remote logins whenever it is available on the client. Because of this, one-time passwords are needed only in special cases. Generally, it is sufficient to have one small OPIE server on your network. Remote users who are forced to use one-time passwords log into that server and then use a preferred mechanism, such as ssh, to log into your real servers.

Secure the r Commands

Some applications use their own security mechanisms. Make sure that the security for these applications is configured properly. In particular, check the Unix r commands, which are a set of Unix networking applications comparable to ftp and telnet. Care must be taken to ensure that the r commands don't compromise system security. Improperly configured r commands can open access to your computer facilities to virtually everyone in the world. For this reason, use of the r commands is discouraged.

In place of password authentication, the r commands use a security system based on trusted hosts and users. Trusted users on trusted hosts are allowed to access the local system without providing a password. Trusted hosts are also called "equivalent hosts" because the system assumes that users given access to a trusted host should be given equivalent access to the local host. The system assumes that user accounts with the same name on both hosts are "owned" by the same user. For example, a user logged in as *becky* on a trusted system is granted the same access as the user logged in as *becky* on the local system.

This authentication system requires databases that define the trusted hosts and the trusted users. The databases used to configure the r commands are */etc/hosts.equiv* and *.rhosts*.

The */etc/hosts.equiv* file defines the hosts and users that are granted "trusted" r command access to your system. This file can also define hosts and users that are explicitly denied trusted access. Not having trusted access doesn't mean that the user is denied access; it just means that he is required to supply a password.

The basic format of entries in the */etc/hosts.equiv* file is:

    [+ | -][hostname] [+ | -][username]

The *hostname* is the name of a "trusted" host, which may optionally be preceded by a plus sign (+). The plus sign has no real significance, except when used alone. A plus sign without a hostname following it is a wildcard character that means "any host."

If a host is granted equivalence, users logged into that host are allowed access to like-named user accounts on your system without providing a password. (This is one reason for administrators to observe uniform rules in handing out login names.) The optional *username* is the name of a user on the trusted host who is granted access to all user accounts. If *username* is specified, that user is not limited to like-named accounts, but is given access to all user accounts without being required to provide a password.*

The *hostname* may also be preceded by a minus sign (-). This explicitly says that the host is *not* an equivalent system. Users from that host must always supply a password when they use an r command to interact with your system. A *username* can also be preceded by a minus sign. This says that, whatever else may be true about that host, the user is not trusted and must always supply a password.

The following examples show how entries in the *hosts.equiv* file are interpreted:

---

* The *root* account is not included.

`rodent`

Allows password-free access from any user on *rodent* to a like-named user account on your local system.

`-rodent`

Denies password-free access from any user on *rodent* to accounts on your system.

`rodent -david`

Denies password-free access to the user *david* if he attempts to access your system from *rodent*.

`rodent +becky`

Allows the user *becky* to access any account (except *root*) on your system, without supplying a password, if she logs in from *rodent*.

`+ becky`

Allows the user *becky* to access any account (except *root*) on your system without supplying a password, no matter what host she logs in from.

This last entry is an example of something that should never be used in your configuration. Don't use a standalone plus sign in place of a hostname. It allows access from any host anywhere and can open up a big security hole. For example, if the entry shown above was in your *hosts.equiv* file, an intruder could create an account named *becky* on his system and gain access to every account on your system. Check */etc/hosts.equiv*, *~/.rhosts*, and */etc/hosts.lpd* to make sure that none of them contains a + entry. Remember to check the *.rhosts* file in every user's home directory.

A simple typographical error could give you a standalone plus sign. For example, consider the entry:

    + rodent becky

The system administrator probably meant "give *becky* password-free access to all accounts when she logs in from *rodent*." However, with an extraneous space after the + sign, it means "allow users named *rodent* and *becky* password-free access from any host in the world." Don't use a plus sign in front of a hostname, and always use care when working with the */etc/hosts.equiv* file to avoid security problems.

When configuring the */etc/hosts.equiv* file, grant trusted access only to the systems and users you actually trust. Don't grant trusted access to every system attached to your local network. In fact, it is best not to use the r commands at all. If you must use them, only trust hosts from your local network when you know the person responsible for that host, when you know that the host is not available for public use, and when the local network is protected by a firewall. Don't grant trusted access by default—have some reason for conferring trusted status. Never grant trust to remotely located systems. It is too easy for an intruder to corrupt routing or DNS in order to fool your system when you grant trust to a remote system. Also, never begin your *hosts.equiv* file with a minus sign as the first character. This confuses some systems, causing them to improperly grant access. Always err on the side of caution when creating a *hosts.equiv* file. Adding trusted hosts as they are requested is much easier than recovering from a malicious intruder.

The *.rhosts* file grants or denies password-free r command access to a specific user's account. It is placed in the user's home directory and contains entries that define the trusted hosts and users. Entries in the *.rhosts* file use the same format as entries in the *hosts.equiv* file and function in almost the same way. The difference is the scope of access granted by entries in these two files. In the *.rhosts* file, the entries grant or deny access to a single user account; the entries in *hosts.equiv* control access to an entire system.

This functional difference can be shown in a simple example. Assume the following entry:

```
horseshoe anthony
```

In *crab*'s *hosts.equiv* file, this entry means that the user *anthony* on *horseshoe* can access any account on *crab* without entering a password. In an *.rhosts* file in the home directory of user *resnick*, the exact same entry allows *anthony* to rlogin from *horseshoe* as *resnick* without entering a password, but it does not grant password-free access to any other accounts on *crab*.

Individuals use the *.rhosts* file to establish equivalence among the different accounts they own. The entry shown above would probably be made only if *anthony* and *resnick* are the same person. For example, I have accounts on several different systems. Sometimes my username is *hunt*, and sometimes it is *craig*. It would be nice if I had the same account name everywhere, but that is not always possible; the names *craig* and *hunt* are used by two other people on my local network. I want to be able to rlogin to my workstation from any host that I have an account on, but I don't want mistaken logins from the other *craig* and the other *hunt*. The *.rhosts* file gives me a way to control this problem.

For example, assume my username on *crab* is *craig*, but my username on *filbert* is *hunt*. Another user on *filbert* is *craig*. To allow myself password-free access to my *crab* account from *filbert*, and to make sure that the other user doesn't have password-free access, I put the following *.rhosts* file in my home directory:

```
filbert hunt
filbert -craig
```

Normally the *hosts.equiv* file is searched first, followed by the user's *.rhosts* file, if it exists. The first explicit match determines whether or not password-free access is allowed. Therefore, the *.rhosts* file cannot override the *hosts.equiv* file. The exception to this is root user access. When a root user attempts to access a system via the r commands, the *hosts.equiv* file is not checked; only *.rhosts* in the root user's home directory is consulted. This allows root access to be more tightly controlled. If the *hosts.equiv* file were used for root access, entries that grant trusted access to hosts

---

would give root users on those hosts root privileges. You can add trusted hosts to *hosts.equiv* without granting remote root users root access to your system.

You should remember that the user can provide access with the *.rhosts* file even when the *hosts.equiv* file doesn't exist. The only way to prevent users from doing this is to periodically check for and remove the *.rhosts* files. As long as you have the r commands on your system, it is possible for a user to accidentally compromise the security of your system.

Secure Shell

The weak security of the r commands poses a security threat. You cannot use these commands to provide secure remote access, even if you use all the techniques given in the previous section. At best, only trusted local systems on a secured local network can be given access via the r commands. The reason for this is that the r commands grant trust based on a belief that the IP address uniquely identifies the correct computer. Normally it does. But an intruder can corrupt DNS to provide the wrong IP address or corrupt routing to deliver to the wrong network, thus undermining the authentication scheme used by the r commands.

An alternative to the remote shell is the *secure shell*. Secure shell replaces the standard r commands with secure commands that include encryption and authentication. Secure shell uses a strong authentication scheme to ensure that the trusted host really is the host it claims to be. Secure shell provides a number of public-key encryption schemes to ensure that every packet in the stream of packets is from the source it claims to be from. Secure shell is secure and easy to use.

There are currently two versions of secure shell in widespread use: SSH Secure Shell, which is a commercial product, and OpenSSH, which is an open source product. OpenSSH is included with various versions of Unix and Linux, and both the open source and the commercial secure shell products are available for download from the Internet if your system does not include secure shell. The examples used in this section are based on OpenSSH, but the basic functions of both versions of secure shell are essentially the same.

The basic components of secure shell are:

sshd

> The secure shell daemon handles incoming SSH connections. sshd should be started at boot time from one of the boot scripts; don't start it from *inetd.conf*. sshd generates an encryption key every time it starts. This can cause it to be slow to start, which makes it unsuitable for *inetd.conf*. A system serving SSH connections must run sshd.

ssh

> The secure shell user command. The ssh command replaces rsh and rlogin. It is used to securely pass a command to a remote system or to securely log into a

remote system. This command creates the outgoing connections that are handled by the remote secure shell daemon. A client system that wants to use an SSH connection must have the ssh command.

scp

Secure copy (scp) is the secure shell version of rcp.

ssh-keygen

Generates the public and private encryption keys used to secure the transmission for the secure shell.

sftp

A version of FTP that operates over a secure shell connection.

When an ssh client connects to an sshd server, they exchange public keys. The systems compare the keys they receive to the known keys they have stored in the */etc/ssh_known_hosts* file and in the *.ssh/known_hosts* file in the user's home directory.* If the key is not found or has changed, the user is asked to verify that the new key should be accepted:

```
> ssh horseshoe
Host key not found from the list of known hosts.
Are you sure you want to continue connecting (yes/no)? yes
Host 'horseshoe' added to the list of known hosts.
craig's password: Watts.Watt.
Last login: Thu Sep 25 15:01:32 1997 from rodent
Linux 2.0.0.
/usr/X11/bin/xauth:  creating new authority file /home/craig/.Xauthority
```

If the key is found in one of the files or is accepted by the user, the client uses it to encrypt a randomly generated session key. The session key is then sent to the server, and both systems use the key to encrypt the remainder of the SSH session.

The client is authenticated if it is listed in the *hosts.equiv* file, the *shost.equiv* file, the user's *.rhosts* file, or the *.shosts* file. This type of authentication is similar to the type used by the r commands, and the format of the *shost.equiv* and the *.shosts* files is the same as their r command equivalents. Notice that in the sample above, the user is prompted for a password. If the client is not listed in one of the files, password authentication is used. As you can see, the password appears in plain text. However, there is no need to worry about password thieves because SSH encrypts the password before it is sent across the link.

Users can employ a public-key challenge/response protocol for authentication. First generate your public and private encryption keys:

```
> ssh-keygen
Initializing random number generator...
Generating p:  ....................................++ (distance 616)
```

---

* The system administrator can initialize the *ssh_known_hosts* file by running make-ssh-known-hosts, which gets the key from every host within a selected domain.

```
Generating q:  ...................++ (distance 244)
Computing the keys...
Testing the keys...
Key generation complete.
Enter file in which to save the key (/home/craig/.ssh/identity):
Enter passphrase: Pdky&tiaj.
Enter the same passphrase again: Pdky&tiaj.
Your identification has been saved in /home/craig/.ssh/identity.
Your public key is:
1024 35 15856482348402585532090170200505710302394819717085015955921815522
craig@horseshoe
Your public key has been saved in /home/craig/.ssh/identity.pub
```

The ssh-keygen command creates your keys. Enter a password (or "passphrase") of at least 10 characters. Use the rules described earlier for picking a good password to choose a good passphrase that is easy to remember. If you forget the passphrase, no one will be able to recover it for you.

Once you have created your keys on the client system, copy the public key to your account on the server. The public key is stored in your home directory on the client in *.ssh/identity.pub*. Copy it to *.ssh/authorized_keys* in your home directory on the server. Now when you log in using ssh, you are prompted for the passphrase:

```
> ssh horseshoe
Enter passphrase for RSA key 'craig@horseshoe': Pdky&tiaj.
Last login: Thu Sep 25 17:11:51 2001
```

To improve system security, the r commands should be disabled after SSH is installed. Comment rshd, rlogind, rexcd, and rexd out of the *inetd.conf* file to disable inbound connections to the r commands. To ensure that SSH is used for outbound connections, replace rlogin and rsh with ssh. To do this, store copies of the original rlogin and rsh in a safe place, rerun configure with the special options shown here, and run make install:

```
# whereis rlogin
/usr/bin/rlogin
# whereis rsh
/usr/bin/rsh
# cp /usr/bin/rlogin /usr/lib/rlogin
# cp /usr/bin/rsh /usr/lib/rsh
# ./configure --with-rsh=/usr/bin --program-transform-name='s/ s/r/'
# make install
```

The example assumes that the path to the original rlogin and rsh commands is */usr/bin*. Use whatever is correct for your system.

After replacing rlogin and rsh, you can still log into systems that don't support SSH. You will, however, be warned that it is not a secure connection:

```
> rlogin cow
Secure connection to cow refused; reverting to insecure method.
Using rsh.  WARNING: Connection will not be encrypted.
Last login: Wed Sep 24 22:15:28 from rodent
```

SSH is an excellent way to have secure communications between systems across the Internet. However, it does require that both systems have SSH installed. When you control both ends of the link, this is not a problem. But there are times when you must log in from a system that is not under your control. For those occasions, one-time passwords, such as those provided by OPIE, are still essential.

Application Security

Having authentication is an important security measure. However, it isn't the only thing you can do to improve the security of your computer and your network. Most break-ins occur when bugs in applications are exploited or when applications are misconfigured. In this section we'll look at some things you can do to improve application security.

Remove Unnecessary Software

Any software that allows an incoming connection from a remote site has the potential of being exploited by an intruder. Some security experts recommend you remove every daemon from the */etc/inetd.conf* file that you don't absolutely need. (Configuring the *inetd.conf* file and the */etc/xinetd.conf* file is discussed in Chapter 5, with explicit examples of removing `tftp` from service.)

Server systems may require several daemons, but most desktop systems require very few, if any. Removing the daemons from *inetd.conf* prevents only inbound connections. It does not prevent out-bound connections. A user can still initiate a `telnet` to a remote site even after the `telnet` daemon is removed from her system's *inetd.conf*. A simple approach used by some people is to remove everything from *inetd.conf* and then add back to the file only those daemons that you decide you really need.

Keep Software Updated

Vendors frequently release new versions of network software for the express purpose of improving network security. Use the latest version of the network software offered by your vendor. Track the security alerts, CERT advisories, and bulletins to know what programs are particularly important to keep updated.

If you fail to keep the software on your system up to date, you open a big security hole for intruders. Most intruders don't discover new problems—they exploit well-known problems. Keep track of the known security problems so you can keep your system up to date.

Stay informed about all the latest fixes for your system. The computer security advisories are a good way to do this. Contact your vendor and find out what services they provide for distributing security fixes. Make sure that the vendor knows that security is important to you.

Figure 12-2 shows a software update list at the Red Hat web site. Clicking on any of the updates listed here provides a detailed description of the problem as well as a link to the fix for that problem.

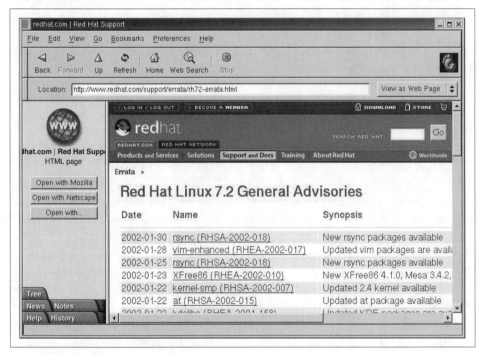

Figure 12-2. Vendor-provided updates

Vendor resources such as the one shown in Figure 12-2 are essential for keeping software up to date. However, you must use these resources for them to be effective. Frequently, administrators complain that vendors do not fix problems, and of course sometimes that is true. But a far more common problem is that system administrators do not install the fixes that are available. Set aside some time every month to apply the latest updates.

Software update services, such as the Red Hat Network, have the potential of lessening the burden of keeping software up to date. With a software update service, the vendor is responsible for periodically updating the system software via the network. Whether or not these services will be a success remains to be seen. They have the potential to improve security and reduce the administrative burden, but many administrators fear the loss of control that comes with giving update privileges to an outside organization.

Security Monitoring

A key element of effective network security is security monitoring. Good security is an ongoing process, and following the security guidelines discussed above is just the beginning. You must also monitor the systems to detect unauthorized user activity and to locate and close security holes. Over time, a system will change—active accounts become inactive and file permissions are changed. You need to detect and fix these problems as they arise.

Know Your System

Network security is monitored by examining the files and logs of individual systems on the network. To detect unusual activity on a system, you must know what activity is normal. What processes are normally running? Who is usually logged in? Who commonly logs in after hours? You need to know this, and more, about your system in order to develop a "feel" for how things should be. Some common Unix commands—ps and who—can help you learn what normal activity is for your system.

The ps command displays the status of currently running processes. Run ps regularly to gain a clear picture of what processes run on the system at different times of the day and who runs them. The Linux ps -au command and the Solaris ps -ef command display the user and the command that initiated each process. This should be sufficient information to learn who runs what and when they run it. If you notice something unusual, investigate it. Make sure you understand how your system is being used.

The who command provides information about who is currently logged into your system. It displays who is logged in, what device they are using, when they logged in and, if applicable, what remote host they logged in from. (The w command, a variation of who available on some systems, also displays the currently active process started by each user.) The who command helps you learn who is usually logged in as well as what remote hosts they normally log in from. Investigate any variations from the norm.

If any of these routine checks gives you reason to suspect a security problem, examine the system for unusual or modified files, for files that you know should be there but aren't, and for unusual login activity. This close examination of the system can also be made using everyday Unix commands. Not every command or file we discuss will be available on every system. But every system will have some tools that help you keep a close eye on how your system is being used.

Looking for Trouble

Intruders often leave behind files or shell scripts to help them re-enter the system or gain root access. Use the ls -a | grep '^\'. command to check for files with names that begin with a dot (.). Intruders particularly favor names such as *.mail*, *.xx*, ... (dot, dot, dot), .. (dot, dot, space), or ..^G (dot, dot, Ctl-G).

If any files with names like these are found, suspect a break-in. (Remember that one directory named . and one directory named .. are in every directory except the root directory.) Examine the contents of any suspicious files and follow your normal incident-reporting procedures.

You should also examine certain key files if you suspect a security problem:

/etc/inetd.conf and /etc/xinetd.conf
Check the names of the programs started from the */etc/inetd.conf* file or the */etc/xinetd.conf* file if your system uses xinetd. In particular, make sure that it does not start any shell programs (e.g., */bin/csh*). Also check the programs that are started by inetd or by xinetd to make sure the programs have not been modified. */etc/inetd.conf* and */etc/xinetd.conf* should not be world-writable.

r command security files
Check */etc/hosts.equiv*, */etc/hosts.lpd*, and the *.rhosts* file in each user's home directory to make sure they have not been improperly modified. In particular, look for any plus sign (+) entries and any entries for hosts outside of your local trusted network. These files should not be world-writable. Better yet, remove the r commands from your system and make sure no one reinstalls them.

/etc/passwd
Make sure that the */etc/passwd* file has not been modified. Look for new usernames and changes to the UID or GID of any account. */etc/passwd* should not be world-writable.

Files run by cron *or* at
Check all of the files run by cron or at, looking for new files or unexplained changes. Sometimes intruders use procedures run by cron or at to readmit themselves to the system, even after they have been kicked off.

Executable files
Check all executable files, binaries, and shell files to make sure they have not been modified by the intruder. Executable files should not be world-writable.

If you find or even suspect a problem, follow your reporting procedure and let people know about the problem. This is particularly important if you are connected to a local area network. A problem on your system could spread to other systems on the network.

Checking files

The find command is a powerful tool for detecting potential filesystem security problems because it can search the entire filesystem for files based on file permissions. Intruders often leave behind setuid programs to grant themselves root access.

The following command searches for these files recursively, starting from the root directory:

```
# find / -user root -perm -4000 -print
```

This find command starts searching at the root (/) for files owned by the user root (-user root) that have the setuid permission bit set (-perm -4000). All matches found are displayed at the terminal (-print). If any filenames are displayed by find, closely examine the individual files to make sure that these permissions are correct. As a general rule, shell scripts should not have setuid permission.

You can use the find command to check for other problems that might open security holes for intruders. The other common problems that find checks for are world-writable files (-perm -2), setgid files (-perm -2000), and unowned files (-nouser -o -nogroup). World-writable and setgid files should be checked to make sure that these permissions are appropriate. As a general rule, files with names beginning with a dot (.) should not be world-writable, and setgid permission, like setuid, should be avoided for shell scripts.

The process of scanning the filesystem can be automated with the Tripwire program. A commercially supported version of Tripwire is available from *http://www. tripwiresecurity.com,* and an open source version for Linux is available from *http:// www.tripwire.org.* This package not only scans the filesystem for problems, it computes digital signatures to ensure that if any files are changed, the changes will be detected.

Checking login activity

Strange login activity (at odd times of the day or from unfamiliar locations) can indicate attempts by intruders to gain access to your system. We have already used the who command to check who is currently logged into the system. To check who has logged into the system in the past, use the last command.

The last command displays the contents of the *wtmp* file.* It is useful for learning normal login patterns and detecting abnormal login activity. The *wtmp* file keeps a historical record of who logged into the system, when they logged in, what remote site they logged in from, and when they logged out.

Figure 12-3 shows a single line of last command output. The figure highlights the fields that show the user who logged in, the device, the remote location from which the login originated (if applicable), the day, the date, the time logged in, the time logged out (if applicable), and the elapsed time.

Simply typing last produces a large amount of output because every login stored in *wtmp* is displayed. To limit the output, specify a username or tty device on the

---

* This file is frequently stored in */usr/adm, /var/log,* or */etc.*

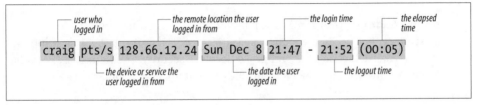

Figure 12-3. Last command output

command line. This limits the display to entries for the specified username or terminal. It is also useful to use grep to search last's output for certain conditions. For example, the command below checks for logins that occur on Saturday or Sunday:

```
% last | grep 'S[au]' | more
craig    console      :0              Sun Dec 15 10:33    still logged in
reboot   system boot                  Sat Dec 14 18:12
root     console                      Sat Dec 14 18:14
craig    pts/5        jerboas         Sat Dec 14 17:11 - 17:43  (00:32)
craig    pts/2        172.16.12.24    Sun Dec  8 21:47 - 21:52  (00:05)
         .
         .
--More--
```

The next example searches for root logins not originating from the console. If you don't know who made the two logins reported in this example, be suspicious:

```
% last root | grep -v console
root    pts/5    rodent.wrotethebook.com    Tue Oct 29 13:12 - down   (00:03)
root    ftp      crab.wrotethebook.com      Tue Sep 10 16:37 - 16:38  (00:00)
```

The last command is a major source of information about previous login activity. User logins at odd times or from odd places are suspicious. Remote root logins should always be discouraged. Use last to check for these problems.

Report any security problems that you detect, or even suspect. Don't be embarrassed to report a problem because it might turn out to be a false alarm. Don't keep quiet because you might get "blamed" for the security breach. Your silence will only help the intruder.

Automated Monitoring

Manually monitoring your system is time consuming and prone to errors and omissions. Fortunately, several automated monitoring tools are available. At this writing, the web site *http://www.insecure.com* lists the monitoring tools that are currently most popular. Tripwire (mentioned earlier) is one of them. Some other currently popular tools are:

Nessus

Nessus is a network-based security scanner that uses a client/server architecture. Nessus scans target systems for a wide range of known security problems.

SATAN

Security Auditing Tool for Analyzing Networks is the first network-based security scanner that became widely distributed. Somewhat outdated, it is still popular and can detect a wide range of known security problems. SATAN has spawned some children, SAINT and SARA, that are also popular.

SAINT

System Administrator's Integrated Network Tool scans systems for a wide range of known security problems. SAINT is based on SATAN.

SARA

Security Auditor's Research Assistant is the third-generation security scanner based on SATAN and SAINT. SARA detects a wide range of known security problems.

Whisker

Whisker is a security scanner that is particularly effective at detecting certain CGI script problems that threaten web site security.

ISS

Internet Security Scanner is a commercial security scanner for those who prefer a commercial product.

Cybercop

Cybercop is another commercial security scanner for those who prefer commercial products.

Snort

Snort provides a rule-based system for logging packets. Snort attempts to detect intrusions and report them to the administrator in real time.

PortSentry

PortSentry detects port scans and can, in real time, block the system initiating the scan. Port scans often precede a full-blown security attack.

The biggest problem with security scanners and intrusion detection tools is that they rapidly become outdated. New attacks emerge that the tools are not equipped to detect. For this reason, this book does not spend time describing the details of any specific scanner. These are the currently popular scanners. By the time you read this, new security tools or new versions of these tools may have taken their place. Use this list as a starting point to search the Web for the latest security tools.

Well-informed users and administrators, good password security, and good system monitoring are the foundation of network security. But more is needed. That "more" is some technique for controlling access to the systems connected to the network, or for controlling access to the data the network carries. In the remainder of this chapter, we look at various security techniques that control access.

Access Control

Access control is a technique for limiting access. Routers and hosts that use access control check the address of a host requesting a service against an *access control list*. If the list says that the remote host is permitted to use the requested service, the access is granted. If the list says that the remote host is not permitted to access the service, access is denied. Access control does not bypass any normal security checks. It adds a check to validate the source of a service request and retains all of the normal checks to validate the user.

Access control systems are common in terminal servers and routers. For example, Cisco routers have an access control facility. Access control software is also available for Unix hosts. Two such packages are xinetd and the TCP wrapper program. First we examine TCP wrapper (tcpd), which gets its name from the fact that you wrap it around a network service so that the service can be reached only by going through the wrapper.

wrapper

The wrapper package performs two basic functions: it logs requests for Internet services, and provides an access control mechanism for Unix systems. Logging requests for specific network services is a useful monitoring function, especially if you are looking for possible intruders. If this were all it did, wrapper would be a useful package. But the real power of wrapper is its ability to control access to network services.

The wrapper software is included with many versions of Linux and Unix. The wrapper tar file containing the C source code and Makefile necessary to build the wrapper daemon tcpd is also available from several sites on the Internet.

If your Unix system does not include wrapper, download the source, make tcpd, and then install it in the same directory as the other network daemons. Edit */etc/inetd.conf* and replace the path to each network service daemon that you wish to place under access control with the path to tcpd. The only field in the */etc/inetd.conf* entry affected by tcpd is the sixth field, which contains the path to the network daemon.

For example, the entry for the finger daemon in */etc/inetd.conf* on our Solaris 8 system is:

```
finger  stream  tcp6  nowait  nobody  /usr/sbin/in.fingerd  in.fingerd
```

The value in the sixth field is */usr/sbin/in.fingerd*. To monitor access to the finger daemon, replace this value with */usr/sbin/tcpd*, as in the following entry:

```
finger  stream  tcp6  nowait  nobody  /usr/sbin/tcpd  in.fingerd
```

Now when inetd receives a request for fingerd, it starts tcpd instead. tcpd then logs the fingerd request, checks the access control information, and, if permitted, starts the real finger daemon to handle the request. In this way, tcpd acts as a gatekeeper for other functions.

Make a similar change for every service you want to place under access control. Good candidates for access control are ftpd, tftpd, telnetd, and fingerd. Obviously, tcpd cannot directly control access for daemons that are not started by inetd, such as sendmail and NFS. However, other tools, such as portmapper, use the tcpd configuration files to enforce their own access controls. Thus the wrapper configuration can have a positive impact on the security of daemons that are not started by inetd.

Using the wrapper on most Linux systems is even easier. There is no need to download and install the tcpd software. It comes as an integral part of the Linux release. You don't even have to edit the */etc/inetd.conf* file because the sixth field of the entries in that file already points to the tcpd program, as shown below:

```
finger   stream tcp nowait nobody /usr/sbin/tcpd   in.fingerd -w
```

tcpd access control files

The information tcpd uses to control access is in two files, */etc/hosts.allow* and */etc/hosts.deny*. Each file's function is obvious from its name. *hosts.allow* contains the list of hosts that are allowed to access the network's services, and *hosts.deny* contains the list of hosts that are denied access. If the files are not found, tcpd permits every host to have access and simply logs the access request. Therefore, if you only want to monitor access, don't create these two files.

If the files are found, tcpd checks the *hosts.allow* file first, followed by the *hosts.deny* file. It stops as soon as it finds a match for the host and the service in question. Therefore, access granted by *hosts.allow* cannot be overridden by *hosts.deny*.

The format of entries in both files is the same:

```
service-list : host-list [: shell-command]
```

The *service-list* is a list of network services, separated by commas. These are the services to which access is being granted (*hosts.allow*) or denied (*hosts.deny*). Each service is identified by the process name used in the seventh field of the */etc/inetd.conf* entry. This is simply the name that immediately follows the path to tcpd in *inetd. conf*. (See Chapter 5 for a description of the arguments field in the */etc/inetd.conf* entry.)

Again, let's use finger as an example. We changed its *inetd.conf* entry to read:

```
finger   stream tcp nowait nobody /usr/etc/tcpd   in.fingerd
```

Given this entry, we would use in.fingerd as the service name in a *hosts.allow* or *hosts.deny* file.

The *host-list* is a comma-separated list of hostnames, domain names, Internet addresses, or network numbers. The systems listed in the host-list are granted access (*hosts.allow*) or denied access (*hosts.deny*) to the services specified in the service-list.

A hostname or an Internet address matches an individual host. For example, *rodent* is a hostname and 172.16.12.2 is an Internet address. Both match a particular host. A domain name matches every host within that domain; e.g., *.wrotethebook.com* matches *crab.wrotethebook.com*, *rodent.wrotethebook.com*, *horseshoe.wrotethebook.com*, and any other hosts in the domain. When specified in a tcpd access control list, domain names always start with a dot (.). A network number matches every IP address within that network's address space. For example, 172.16. matches 172.16.12.1, 172.16.12.2, 172.16.5.1, and any other address that begins with 172.16. Network addresses in a tcpd access control list always end with a dot (.).

A completed *hosts.allow* entry that grants FTP and Telnet access to all hosts in the *wrotethebook.com* domain is shown below:

```
ftpd,telnetd : .wrotethebook.com
```

Two special keywords can be used in *hosts.allow* and *hosts.deny* entries. The keyword ALL can be used in the service-list to match all network services, and in the host-list to match all hostnames and addresses. The second keyword, LOCAL, can be used only in the host-list. It matches all local hostnames. tcpd considers a hostname "local" if it contains no embedded dots. Therefore, the hostname *rodent* would match on LOCAL, but the hostname *rodent.wrotethebook.com* would not match. The following entry affects all services and all local hosts:

```
ALL : LOCAL
```

A more complete example of how tcpd is used will help you understand these entries. First, assume that you wish to allow every host in your local domain (*wrotethebook.com*) to have access to all services on your system, but you want to deny access to every service to all other hosts. Make an entry in */etc/hosts.allow* to permit access to everything by everyone in the local domain:

```
ALL : LOCAL, .wrotethebook.com
```

The keyword ALL in the services-list indicates that this rule applies to all network services. The colon (:) separates the services-list from the host-list. The keyword LOCAL indicates that all local hostnames without a domain extension are acceptable, and the *.wrotethebook.com* string indicates that all hostnames that have the *wrotethebook.com* domain name extensions are also acceptable.

After granting access to just those systems you want to service, explicitly deny access to all other systems using the *hosts.deny* file. To prevent access by everyone else, make this entry in the */etc/hosts.deny* file:

```
ALL : ALL
```

Every system that does not match the entry in */etc/hosts.allow* is passed on to */etc/hosts.deny*. Here the entry denies everyone access, regardless of what service they are asking for. Remember, even with ALL in the services-list field, only services started by inetd, and only those services whose entries in *inetd.conf* have been edited to invoke tcpd, are affected. This does not automatically provide security for any other service.

The syntax of a standard wrapper access control file can be a little more complicated than the examples above. A *hosts.allow* file might contain:

```
imapd, ipopd3 : 172.16.12.
ALL EXCEPT imapd, ipopd3 : ALL
```

The first entry says that every host whose IP address begins with 172.16.12 is granted access to the IMAP and POP services. The second line says that all services except IMAP and POP are granted to all hosts. These entries would limit mailbox service to a single subnet while providing all other services to anyone who requested them. The EXCEPT keyword is used to except items from an all-encompassing service list. It can also be used in the host-list of an access rule. For example:

```
ALL: .wrotethebook.com EXCEPT public.wrotethebook.com
```

If this appeared in a *hosts.allow* file it would permit every system in the *wrotethebook.com* domain to have access to all services except for the host *public.wrotethebook.com*. The assumption is that *public.wrotethebook.com* is untrusted for some reason—perhaps users outside of the domain are allowed to log into *public*.

The final syntax variation uses the at-sign (@) to narrow the definition of services or hosts. Here are two examples:

```
in.telnetd@172.16.12.2 : 172.16.12.0/255.255.255.0
in.rshd : KNOWN@robin.wrotethebook.com
```

When the @ appears in the services side of a rule it indicates that the server has more than one IP address and that the rule being defined applies only to one of those addresses. Examples of systems with more than one address are multi-homed hosts and routers. If your server is also the router that connects your local network to outside networks, you may want to provide services on the interface connected to the local network but not on the interface connected to the outside world. The @ syntax lets you do that. If the first line in this example appeared in a *hosts.allow* file, it would permit access to the Telnet daemon through the network interface that has the address 172.16.12.2 by any client with an address that begins with 172.16.12.

The purpose of the @ when it appears in the host-list of a rule is completely different. In the host-list, the @ indicates that a username is required from the client as part of the access control test. This means that the client must run an identd daemon. The host-list can test for a specific username, but it is more common to use one of three possible keywords:

KNOWN
> The result of the test is KNOWN when the remote system returns a username in response to the query.

UNKNOWN
> The result of the test is UNKNOWN when the remote host does not run identd and thus fails to respond to the query.

ALL

> This setting requires the remote host to return a username. It is equivalent to using KNOWN but is less commonly used.

The final field that can be used in these entries is the optional shell-command field. When a match occurs for an entry that has an optional shell command, tcpd logs the access, grants or denies access to the service, and then passes the shell command to the shell for execution.

Defining an optional shell command

The shell command allows you to define additional processing that is triggered by a match in the access control list. In all practical examples this feature is used in the *hosts.deny* file to gather more information about the intruder or to provide immediate notification to the system administrator about a potential security attack. For example:

```
ALL : ALL : (safe_finger -l @%h | /usr/sbin/mail -s %d - %h root) &
```

In this example from a *hosts.deny* file, all systems that are not explicitly granted access in the *hosts.allow* file are denied access to all services. After logging the attempted access and blocking it, tcpd sends the safe_finger command to the shell for execution. All versions of finger, including safe_finger, query the remote host to find out who is logged into that host. This information is useful when tracking down an attacker. The result of the safe_finger command is mailed to the root account. The ampersand (&) at the end of the line causes the shell commands to run in the background. This is important. Without it, tcpd would sit and wait for these programs to complete before returning to its own work.

The safe_finger program is provided with wrapper. It is specially modified to be less vulnerable to attack than the standard finger program.

There are some variables, such as %h and %d, used in the example above. These variables allow you to take values for the incoming connection and to use them in the shell process. Table 12-1 lists the variables you can use.

Table 12-1. Variables used with tcpd shell commands

Variable	Value
%a	The client's IP address.
%A	The server's IP address.
%c	All available client information, including the username when available.
%d	The network service daemon process name.
%h	The client's hostname. If the hostname is unavailable, the IP address is used.
%H	The server's hostname.
%n	The client's hostname. If the hostname is unavailable, the keyword UNKNOWN is used. If a DNS lookup of the client's hostname and IP address do not match, the keyword PARANOID is used.

Table 12-1. Variables used with tcpd shell commands (continued)

Variable	Value
%N	The server's hostname.
%p	The network service daemon process id (PID).
%s	All available server information, including the username when available.
%u	The client username or the keyword UNKNOWN if the username is unavailable.
%%	The percent character (%).

Table 12-1 shows that %h is the remote hostname and %d is the daemon being accessed. Refer back to the sample shell command. Assume that the attempted access to in.rshd came from the host *foo.bar.org*. The command passed to the shell would be:

```
safe_finger -l @foo.bar.org |
    /usr/sbin/mail -s in.rshd-foo.bar.org root
```

The standard wrapper access control syntax is a complete configuration language that should cover any reasonable need. Despite this, there is also an extended version of the wrapper access control language.

Optional access control language extensions

If wrapper is compiled with PROCESS_OPTIONS enabled in the Makefile, the syntax of the wrapper access control language is changed and extended. With PROCESS_OPTIONS enabled, the command syntax is not limited to three fields. The new syntax is:

```
service-list : host-list : option : option …
```

The *service-list* and the *host-list* are defined in exactly the same way they were in the original wrapper syntax. The options are new, and so is the fact that multiple options are allowed for each rule. There are several possible options:

allow
> Grants the requested service and must appear at the end of a rule.

deny
> Denies the requested service and must appear at the end of a rule.

spawn *shell-command*
> Executes the specified shell command as a child process.

twist *shell-command*
> Executes the shell command instead of the requested service.

keepalive
> Sends keepalive messages to the remote host. If the host does not respond, the connection is closed.

linger *seconds*

> Specifies how long to try to deliver data after the server closes the connection.

rfc931 [*timeout*]

> Uses the IDENT protocol to look up the user's name on the remote host. *timeout* defines how many seconds the server should wait for the remote host to respond.

banners *path*

> Sends the contents of a message file to the remote system. *path* is the name of a directory that contains the banner files. The file displayed is the file that has the same name as the network daemon process.

nice [*number*]

> Sets the nice value for the network service process. The default value is 10.

umask *mask*

> Sets a umask value for files used by the network service process.

user *user*[.*group*]

> Defines the user ID and group ID under which the network service process runs. This overrides what is defined in *inetd.conf*.

setenv *variable value*

> Sets an environment variable for the process runtime environment.

A few examples based on the samples shown earlier will illustrate the differences in the new syntax. Using the new syntax, a *hosts.allow* file might contain:

```
ALL : LOCAL, .wrotethebook.com : ALLOW
in.ftpd,in.telnetd : eds.oreilly.com : ALLOW
ALL : ALL : DENY
```

With the new syntax there is no need to have two files. The options ALLOW and DENY permit everything to be listed in a single file. The first line grants access to all services to every local host and every host in the *wrotethebook.com* domain. The second line gives the remote host *eds.oreilly.com* access through FTP and Telnet. The third line is the same as having the line ALL : ALL in the *hosts.deny* file; it denies all other hosts access to all of the services. Using the ALLOW and DENY options, the command:

```
ALL: .wrotethebook.com EXCEPT public.wrotethebook.com
```

can be rewritten as:

```
ALL: .wrotethebook.com : ALLOW
ALL: public.wrotethebook.com : DENY
```

The shell command example using the original syntax is almost identical in the new syntax:

```
in.rshd : ALL: spawn (safe_finger -l @%h | /usr/sbin/mail -s %d - %h root) & : DENY
```

A more interesting variation on the shell command theme comes from using the twist option. Instead of passing a command to the shell for execution, the twist command executes a program for the remote user, but not the program the user expects. For example:

```
in.ftpd : ALL: twist /bin/echo 421 FTP not allowed from %h : DENY
```

In this case, when the remote user attempts to start the FTP daemon, echo is started instead. The echo program then sends the message to the remote system and terminates the connection.

The extended wrapper syntax is rarely used because everything can be done with the traditional syntax. It is useful to understand the syntax so that you can read it when you encounter it, but it is unlikely that you will feel the need to use it. An alternative to wrapper that you will encounter is xinetd. It replaces inetd and adds access controls. The basics of xinetd are covered in Chapter 5. Here we focus on the access controls that it provides.

Controlling Access with xinetd

As noted in Chapter 5, most of the information in the *xinetd.conf* file parallels values found in the *inetd.conf* file. What xinetd adds are capabilities similar to those of wrapper. xinetd reads the */etc/hosts.allow* and */etc/hosts.deny* files and implements the access controls defined in those files. Additionally, xinetd provides its own logging and its own access controls. If your system uses xinetd, you will probably create *hosts.allow* and *hosts.deny* files to enhance the security of services, such as portmapper, that read those files, and you will use the security features of xinetd because those features provide improved access controls.

xinetd provides two logging parameters: log_on_success and log_on_failure. Use these parameters to customize the standard log entry made when a connection is successful or when a connection attempt fails. log_on_success and log_on_failure accept the following options:

USERID

Logs the user ID of the remote user. USERID can be logged for both successful and failed connection attempts.

HOST

Logs the address of the remote host. Like USERID, HOST can be used for both success and failure.

PID

Logs the process ID of the server started to handle the connection. PID applies only to log_on_success.

DURATION

Logs the length of time that the server handling this connection ran. DURATION applies only to log_on_success.

EXIT

Logs the exit status of the server when the connection terminates. EXIT applies only to log_on_success.

ATTEMPT

Logs unsuccessful connection attempts. ATTEMPT applies only to log_on_failure.

RECORD

Logs the connection information received from the remote server. RECORD applies only to log_on_failure.

In addition to logging, xinetd provides three parameters for access control. Use these parameters to configure xinetd to accept connections from certain hosts, paralleling the *hosts.allow* file, to reject connections from certain hosts, paralleling the *hosts.deny* file, and to accept connections only at certain times of the day. The three parameters are:

only_from

This parameter identifies the hosts that are allowed to connect to the service. Hosts can be defined using:

- a numeric address. For example, 172.16.12.5 defines a specific host, and 129.6.0.0 defines all hosts with an address that begins with 129.6. The address 0.0.0.0 matches all addresses.

- an address scope. For example, 172.16.12.{3,6,8,23} defines four different hosts: 172.16.12.3, 172.16.12.6, 172.16.12.8, and 172.16.12.23.

- a network name. The network name must be defined in the */etc/networks* file.

- a canonical hostname. The IP address provided by the remote system must reverse-map to this hostname.

- a domain name. The hostname returned by the reverse lookup must be in the specified domain. For example, the value .wrotethebook.com requires a host in the *wrotethebook.com* domain. Note that when a domain name is used, it starts with a dot.

- an IP address with an associated address mask. For example, 172.16.12.128/25 would match every address from 172.16.12.128 to 172.16.12.255.

no_access

This parameter defines the hosts that are denied access to the service. Hosts are defined using exactly the same methods as those described for the only_from attribute.

access_times

This parameter defines the time of day a service is available, in the form *hour:min-hour:min*. A 24-hour clock is used. Hours are 0 to 23 and minutes are 0 to 59.

If neither only_from nor no_access is specified, access is granted to everyone. If both are specified, the most exact match applies—for example:

```
no_access              = 172.16.12.250
only_from              = 172.16.12.0
```

The only_from command in this example permits every system on network 172.16.12.0 to have access to the service. The no_access command takes away that access for one system. It doesn't matter whether the no_access command comes before or after the only_from command. It always works the same way because the more exact match takes precedence.

A sample POP3 entry from *xinetd.conf* is shown below:

```
# default: on
# description: The POP3 service allows remote users to access their mail \
#              using an POP3 client such as Netscape Communicator, mutt, \
#              or fetchmail.

service login
{
        socket_type            = stream
        wait                   = no
        user                   = root
        log_on_success        += USERID
        log_on_failure        += USERID
        only_from              = 172.16.12.0
        no_access              = 172.16.12.231
        server                 = /usr/sbin/ipop3d
}
```

In the sample, the only_from command permits access from every system on network 172.16.12.0, which is the local network for this sample system, and blocks access from all other systems. Additionally, there is one system on subnet 17.16.12.0 (host 172.16.12.231) that is not trusted to have POP access. The no_access command denies access to anyone on the system 172.16.12.231.

Remember that wrapper and xinetd can only control access to services. These tools cannot limit access to data on the system or moving across the network. For that, you need encryption.

Encryption

Encryption is a technique for limiting access to the data carried on the network. Encryption encodes the data in a form that can be read only by systems that have the "key" to the encoding scheme. The original text, called the "clear text," is encrypted using an encryption device (hardware or software) and an encryption key. This produces encoded text, which is called the cipher. To recreate the clear text, the cipher must be decrypted using the same type of encryption device and an appropriate key.

Largely because of spy novels and World War II movies, encryption is one of the first things that people think of when they think of security. However, encryption has not always been applicable to network security. Traditionally, encrypting data for transmission across a network required that the same encryption key, called a *shared secret* or a *private key*, be used at both ends of the data exchange. Unless you controlled both ends of the network and could ensure that the same encryption key was available to all participants, it was difficult to use end-to-end data encryption. For this reason, encryption was most commonly used to exchange data where the facilities at both ends of the network were controlled by a single authority, such as military networks, private networks, individual systems, or when the individuals at both ends of the communication could reach personal agreement on the encryption technique and key. Encryption that requires prior agreement to share a secret key is called *symmetric encryption*.

Public-key encryption is the technology that makes encryption an important security technology for an open global network like the Internet. For example, an e-commerce web server and any customer's web browser can exchange encrypted data because they both use public-key cryptography. Public-key systems encode the clear text with a key that is widely known and publicly available, but the cipher can only be decoded back to clear text with a secret key. This means that Dan can look up Kristin's public key in a trusted database and use it to encode a message to her that no one else can read. Even though everyone on the Internet has access to the public key, only Kristin can decrypt the message using her secret key. This encrypted communication takes place without Kristin ever divulging her secret key.

Additionally, messages encrypted using the private key can only be decrypted by the public key. Thus the public key can be used to authenticate the source of a message since only the proper source should have access to the private key. Because public-key cryptography uses different keys for encryption and decryption, it is called *asymmetric encryption*.

One problem with asymmetric encryption is that it is computationally intensive and slow when compared to symmetric encryption. For this reason it is used for only a small portion of the data exchange. Public-key encryption is used for both encryption and authentication during the initial handshake of an encrypted connection. During the handshake, a shared secret key, protected by public-key encryption, is exchanged by the participants. The subsequent data exchange is encrypted with symmetric encryption using that shared key.

Another problem with public-key encryption in a global network is that it requires a universally recognized, trusted infrastructure to distribute public keys and to ensure that the keys have not been tampered with. The first step when Dan sent a message to Kristin was retrieving her public key. But where did it come from? The key probably came from one of two places: from a private exchange of public keys or from the network with verification from a trusted certificate authority. When the number of participants is limited, public keys can be exchanged through private agreements in the same manner that private keys used to be exchanged. That does not work, however, for global network applications where there is no prior knowledge of the participants. In that case the public key is obtained from the network and certified by a trusted third party called a *certificate authority* (CA). The CA provides the public key in a message called a *certificate* that contains the public key, the name of the organization whose key it is, and dates when the key became valid and when it will become invalid. This message is signed with the private key of the CA. Thus when the certificate is verified using the CA's public key, the recipient knows that the certificate came from the trusted CA. CA public keys are well known and widely distributed. For example, browser vendors provide the public keys of many CAs with every copy of their browser software.

The type of encryption used in the examples in the next section is symmetric encryption. It requires that the same encryption technique and the same secret key is used for both encrypting and decrypting the message. It does not rely on public keys, digital signatures, or a widely accepted infrastructure, but its usefulness is limited.

When Is Symmetric Encryption Useful?

Before using encryption, decide why you want to encrypt the data, whether the data should be protected with encryption, and whether the data should even be stored on a networked computer system.

A few valid reasons for encrypting data are:

- To prevent casual browsers from viewing sensitive data files
- To prevent accidental disclosure of sensitive data
- To prevent privileged users (e.g., system administrators) from viewing private data files
- To complicate matters for intruders who attempt to search through a system's files

There are several tools available for encrypting data files, many of which are commercial packages. Two open source filesystems that provide automatic file encryption are the Cryptographic File System (CFS) and the Practical Privacy Disk Driver (PPDD).* There are even a couple of file encryption tools included with Solaris and Linux.

Solaris includes the old Unix crypt command. crypt is easy to use, but it has limited value. The encryption provided by crypt is easily broken. At best, crypt protects files from casual browsing, nothing more.

---

* *Linux Security* by Ramon Hontanon (Sybex) covers the installation, configuration, and use of both CFS and PPDD.

The age of crypt and the fact that other, better, more recent symmetric encryption tools are not included with the operating system show that there is little demand for symmetric encryption tools. Public-key encryption is simply more flexible and can be used for a wider range of applications. In fact, the file encryption tool included with Linux is an asymmetric encryption tool.

Public-Key Encryption Tools

Public-key encryption is the type of encryption that has the greatest customer demand. The most popular Unix encryption tools, ssh and SSL, are public-key tools. Even for tasks such as encrypting files for local storage, public-key systems are popular because they do not require users to share their private keys.

Linux systems often include the GNU Privacy Guard (gpg). gpg, like the well-known tool PGP,* can be used to encrypt files or mail. It also provides digital signature services that can be used for email authentication. In the following example, gpg is used to encrypt and decrypt a file. We begin by creating our keys with the --gen-key option:

```
$ gpg --gen-key
gpg (GnuPG) 1.0.4; Copyright (C) 2000 Free Software Foundation, Inc.
This program comes with ABSOLUTELY NO WARRANTY.
This is free software, and you are welcome to redistribute it
under certain conditions. See the file COPYING for details.
gpg: Warning: using insecure memory!
gpg: /home/craig/.gnupg/secring.gpg: keyring created
gpg: /home/craig/.gnupg/pubring.gpg: keyring created
Please select what kind of key you want:
   (1) DSA and ElGamal (default)
   (2) DSA (sign only)
   (4) ElGamal (sign and encrypt)
Your selection? 1
DSA keypair will have 1024 bits.
About to generate a new ELG-E keypair.
              minimum keysize is   768 bits
              default keysize is 1024 bits
    highest suggested keysize is 2048 bits
What keysize do you want? (1024) 1024
Requested keysize is 1024 bits
Please specify how long the key should be valid.
        0 = key does not expire
      <n>  = key expires in n days
      <n>w = key expires in n weeks
      <n>m = key expires in n months
      <n>y = key expires in n years
Key is valid for? (0) 0
```

---

* *PGP: Pretty Good Privacy* by Simson Garfinkel (O'Reilly & Associates) provides a book-length treatment of PGP, an encryption program used for files and electronic mail.

```
Key does not expire at all
Is this correct (y/n)? y
A User-ID identifies your key; the software constructs the user id
from Real Name, Comment and Email Address in this form:
    "Heinrich Heine (Der Dichter) <heinrichh@duesseldorf.de>"
Real name: Craig Hunt
Email address: craig.hunt@wrotethebook.com
Comment:
You selected this USER-ID:
    "Craig Hunt <craig.hunt@wrotethebook.com>"
Change (N)ame, (C)omment, (E)mail or (O)kay/(Q)uit? o
You need a Passphrase to protect your secret key.
Type the passphrase: Fateful lightening
Repeat: Fateful lightening
We need to generate a lot of random bytes. It is a good idea to perform
some other action (type on the keyboard, move the mouse, utilize the
disks) during the prime generation; this gives the random number
generator a better chance to gain enough entropy.
+++++.+++++.+++++.+++++++++++++++++++++++.+++++.+++++++++++++++++++++++++++++.+++++++++++.
+++++++++++++++++++++++.++++++++++++++++++++++++++++++++++++++>.+++++.....................
........+++++^^^
public and secret key created and signed.
```

The --gen-key option asks several questions. However, the questions are simple and
the initial key generation needs to be done only once. First gpg asks what kind of key
you want. What it is really asking is whether you want to use the keys for digital signatures, for encryption, or for both digital signatures and encryption. Choose (1),
which is the default. This creates both types of keys so that you're prepared for any
encryption task. Next it asks how long the key should be; the longer the key, the
more difficult it is to generate and crack. The default is 1024 bits, which is plenty
long for any realistic gpg application. gpg asks for your name, email address, and,
optionally, a comment. It uses this information to identify your keys in the key databases. Finally, it asks for a passphrase that will be used to identify you when you
access your secret key.

gpg uses two key databases: one for secret keys and one for public keys. gpg calls
these databases "key rings." The database of secret keys is *secring.gpg* and the database of public keys is *pubring.gpg*. Both public and private keys are used when we
encrypt and then decrypt a file. The following example shows the encryption process:

```
$ cat test.txt
This is a test file.
$ gpg --recipient craig.hunt@wrotethebook.com --encrypt test.txt
gpg: Warning: using insecure memory!
$ cat test.txt.gpg
´¥→ºü¿  2J ë¥;Î¬[ Ø# LÏü" é ´ÉDÓ Sì P-EÜ ® ¸Õ!7 ñ6 ÍÓèî
¢Èó$2[9øÁÎ ï@E¬wY $2´6 $B«´6ÿk_¬ø1ÑOÔBî gíy¿[CyöU6®&V¯g TWn2¡Ó°ßx
ñÒñnT5ª ¥[uü¥ÊÀ2 ,hæq"?ºì´J\Põ ö/o?¨ÒTeBáâÛÛ»°5oNB= å}/Õ@Némstû
$ rm test.txt
```

The cat command shows that we have created a simple text file named *test.txt* that we wish to encrypt. It is clear what the --encrypt option on the gpg command line is doing, but the purpose of the --recipient argument is not as clear. The *pubring.gpg* database can contain many public keys. The --recipient argument identifies the public key used to encrypt the file. The word "recipient" is used because gpg is often used to encrypt mail, and therefore the public key of the mail recipient is used. For this same reason, it is common to identify the desired key with the email address provided when the key was created.

gpg produces a cipher file that has the same name as the clear-text file with the addition of the file extension *.gpg*. A cat of the cipher file shows that it is not readable. After checking that the cipher file exists, the clear-text file is deleted. It wouldn't do us much good to create an encrypted file if the unencrypted file was still around for everyone to read!

To read the cipher file, it must be decrypted. In the following example, the --decrypt option is used with the gpg command to decrypt the *test.txt.gpg* file:

```
$ gpg --output test.txt --decrypt test.txt.gpg
gpg: Warning: using insecure memory!
You need a passphrase to unlock the secret key for
user: "Craig Hunt <craig.hunt@wrotethebook.com>"
1024-bit ELG-E key, ID D99991BA, created 2001-09-18 (main key ID 9BE3B5AD)
Enter passphrase: Fateful lightening
$ cat test.txt
This is a test file.
```

The --output option tells gpg where to write the clear text after decrypting the cipher file. In the example we write it to *test.txt*. A cat of *test.txt* shows that the file is readable and that it contains the original test.

These gpg examples are reminiscent of the ssh examples seen earlier in this chapter and the openssl examples in Chapter 11. All of these programs have tools to generate public and private keys that are then used for a specific purpose. gpg secures files and email. ssh secures terminal connections. openssl secures web traffic. SSL, however, can be used to secure communications for a wide variety of applications.

stunnel

stunnel is a program that uses SSL to encrypt traffic for daemons that do not encrypt their own traffic. stunnel brings the benefit of public-key encryption to a wide variety of network applications. stunnel is included with OpenSSL and is installed when OpenSSL is installed.*

---

* OpenSSL is covered in Chapter 11.

Like all applications that use SSL, `stunnel` needs a certificate to function properly. The easiest way to create the `stunnel` certificate is to change to the SSL certificate directory and run make, as in the example below:

```
# cd /usr/share/ssl/certs
# make stunnel.pem
umask 77 ; \
PEM1=`/bin/mktemp /tmp/openssl.XXXXXX` ; \
PEM2=`/bin/mktemp /tmp/openssl.XXXXXX` ; \
/usr/bin/openssl req -newkey rsa:1024 -keyout $PEM1 -nodes -x509 -days 365 -out $PEM2
; \
cat $PEM1 >  stunnel.pem ; \
echo ""    >> stunnel.pem ; \
cat $PEM2 >> stunnel.pem ; \
rm -f $PEM1 $PEM2
Using configuration from /usr/share/ssl/openssl.cnf
Generating a 1024 bit RSA private key
....++++++
........++++++
writing new private key to '/tmp/openssl.3VVjex'
-----
You are about to be asked to enter information that will be incorporated
into your certificate request. What you are about to enter is what is
called a Distinguished Name or a DN. There are quite a few fields but you
can leave some blank. If you enter '.', the field will be left blank. For
some fields there will be a default value.
-----
Country Name (2 letter code) [AU]:US
State or Province Name (full name) [Some-State]:Maryland
Locality Name (eg, city) []:Gaithersburg
Organization Name (eg, company) [Internet Widgits Ltd]:WroteTheBook.com
Organizational Unit Name (eg, section) []:Books
Common Name (eg, your name or your server's hostname) []:Craig Hunt
Email Address []:craig.hunt@wrotethebook.com
```

By default the openssl installation creates the directory */usr/share/ssl/certs* to hold certificates, and by default `stunnel` looks for a certificate in that directory with the filename *stunnel.pem.** As with all new openssl certificates, you're prompted for the information needed to uniquely identify the certificate.

Once the certificate is created, `stunnel` is ready for use. POP and IMAP are excellent examples of services that can be run inside a secure connection using `stunnel`. The primary reason that POP and IMAP are run through `stunnel` is to ensure that the user's password cannot be stolen from a POP or IMAP session and then used by the thief to log into the server. `stunnel` encrypts everything: the login and the download of mail. This also guarantees that the contents of the mail cannot be surreptitiously read by a snooper during the download, although from the point of view of the system administrator, the password is really the piece of information you want to protect.

---

* The default certificate path can be changed on the `stunnel` command line with the -p option.

For secure POP and IMAP communication to work, both ends of the connection must be able to tunnel the data through SSL. This is not always the case. Some clients do not have stunnel; some do not even have SSL. For this reason, servers usually provide traditional POP and IMAP connections on the appropriate well-known ports, and SSL-secured POP and IMAP on other ports. When run over stunnel, POP is called *pops* and assigned TCP port 995, and IMAP is called *imaps* and assigned TCP port 993. *pops* and *imaps* are not special protocols. They are simply service names from the */etc/services* file that map to port numbers 995 and 993. The following command added to the system startup runs POP inside an SSL tunnel on port 995:

```
stunnel -d 995 -l /usr/sbin/ipop3d -- ipop3d
```

Alternatively, stunnel can be run by inetd using an entry in the *inetd.conf* file. For example, the following entry runs POP inside an SSL tunnel on a demand basis:

```
pops stream tcp nowait root /usr/sbin/stunnel -l /usr/sbin/ipop3d -- ipop3d
```

Systems that use xinetd can run stunnel from the *xinetd.conf* file. The following xinetd entry runs *imaps*:

```
service imaps
{
        socket_type             = stream
        wait                    = no
        user                    = root
        server                  = /usr/sbin/stunnel
        server_args             = -l /usr/sbin/imapd -- imapd
        log_on_failure          += USERID
}
```

stunnel has nothing specific to do with POP or IMAP. It can be used to secure a wide variety of daemons. When used to secure a daemon that is normally run by inetd or xinetd, the stunnel command is placed in the *inetd.conf* or *xinetd.conf* file, as appropriate. When used to secure a daemon that runs from a startup file, the stunnel command is placed in that startup file.

Despite the power of tools like stunnel and ssh, encryption is not a substitute for good computer security. Encryption can protect sensitive or personal information from snooping, but it should never be the sole means of protecting critical information. Encryption systems can be broken, and encrypted data can be deleted or corrupted just like any other data. So don't let encryption lull you into a false sense of security. Some information is so sensitive or critical that it should not be stored on a networked computer system, even if it is encrypted. Encryption is only a small part of a complete security system.

Firewalls

A firewall system is an essential component of network security. The term "firewall" implies protection from danger, and just as the firewall in your car protects the passengers' compartment from the car's engine, a firewall computer system protects your network from the outside world. A firewall computer system provides strict access control between your systems and the outside world.

The concept of a firewall is quite simple. A firewall is a choke point through which all traffic between a secured network and an unsecured network must pass. In practice, it is usually a choke point between an enterprise network and the Internet. Creating a single point through which all traffic must pass allows the traffic to be more easily monitored and controlled and allows security expertise to be concentrated on that single point.

Firewalls are implemented in many ways. In fact, there are so many different types of firewalls, the term is almost meaningless. When someone tells you they have a firewall, you really can't know exactly what they mean. Covering all of the different types of firewall architectures requires an entire book—see *Building Internet Firewalls* (O'Reilly & Associates). Here we cover the screened subnet architecture (probably the most popular firewall architecture) and the multi-homed host architecture, which is essentially a firewall-in-a-box.

The most common firewall architecture contains at least four hardware components: an exterior router, a secure server (called a *bastion host*), an exposed network (called a *perimeter network*), and an interior router. Each hardware component provides part of the complete security scheme. Figure 12-4 illustrates this architecture.

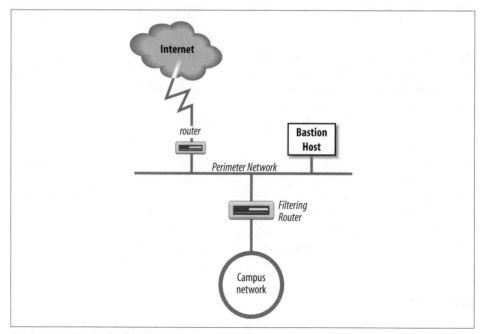

Figure 12-4. Screened subnet firewall

The exterior router is the only connection between the enterprise network and the outside world. This router is configured to do a minimal level of access control. It checks to make sure that no packet coming from the external world has a source address that matches the internal network. If our network number is 172.16, the exterior router discards any packets it receives on its exterior interface that contain the source address 172.16. That source address should be received by the router only on its interior interface. Security people call this type of access control *packet filtering*.

The interior router does the bulk of the access control work. It filters packets not only on address but also on protocol and port numbers to control the services that are accessible to and from the interior network. It's up to you which services this router blocks. If you plan to use a firewall, the services that will be allowed and those that will be denied should be defined in your security policy document. Almost every service can be a threat. These threats must be evaluated in light of your security needs. Services that are intended only for internal users (NIS, NFS, X-Windows, etc.) are almost always blocked. Services that allow writing to internal systems (Telnet, FTP, SMTP, etc.) are usually blocked. Services that provide information about internal systems (DNS, fingerd, etc.) are usually blocked. This doesn't leave much running! That is where the bastion host and perimeter network come in.

The bastion host is a secure server. It provides an interconnection point between the enterprise network and the outside world for the restricted services. Some of the services that are restricted by the interior gateway may be essential for a useful network. Those essential services are provided through the bastion host in a secure manner. The bastion host provides some services directly, such as DNS, SMTP mail services, and anonymous FTP. Other services are provided as *proxy services*. When the bastion host acts as a proxy server, internal clients connect to the outside through the bastion host, and external systems respond back to the internal clients through the host. The bastion host can therefore control the traffic flowing into and out of the site to any extent desired.

There can be more than one secure server, and there often is. The perimeter network connects the servers together and connects the exterior router to the interior router. The systems on the perimeter network are much more exposed to security threats than are the systems on the interior network. This is as it must be. After all, the secure servers are needed to provide service to the outside world as well as to the internal network. Isolating the systems that must be exposed on a separate network lessens the chance that a compromise of one of those systems will lead directly to the compromise of an internal system.

The multi-homed host architecture attempts to duplicate all of these firewall functions in a single box. It works by replacing an IP router with a multi-homed host that does not forward packets at the IP layer.* The multi-homed host effectively severs the

---

* The role of IP routers, also called gateways, in gluing the Internet together is covered extensively in earlier chapters.

connection between the interior and exterior networks. To provide the interior network with some level of network connectivity, it performs similar functions to the bastion hosts.

Figure 12-5 shows a comparison between an IP router and a multi-homed host firewall. A router handles packets up through the IP layer. The router forwards each packet based on the packet's destination address, and the route to that destination indicated in the routing table. A host, on the other hand, does not simply forward packets. A multi-homed host can process packets through the Application Layer, which provides it with complete control over how packets are handled.[*]

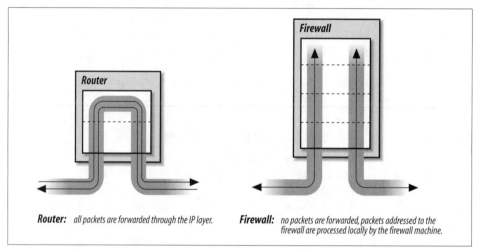

Figure 12-5. Firewalls versus routers

This definition of a firewall—as a device completely distinct from an IP router—is not universally accepted. Some people refer to routers with special security features as firewalls, but this is really just a matter of semantics. In this book, routers with special security features are called "secure routers" or "secure gateways." Firewalls, while they may include routers, do more than just filter packets.

Functions of the Firewall

Ideally, an intruder cannot mount a direct attack on any of the systems behind a firewall. Packets destined for hosts behind the firewall are simply delivered to the firewall. The intruder must instead mount an attack directly against the firewall machine. Because the firewall machine can be the target of break-in attacks, it employs very

---

[*] See Chapter 5 for information on how to prevent a multi-homed host from forwarding packets.

strict security guidelines. But because there is only one firewall versus many machines on the local network, it is easier to enforce strict security on the firewall.

The disadvantage of a firewall system is obvious. In the same manner that it restricts access from the outside world into the local network, it restricts access from the local network to the outside world. To minimize the inconvenience caused by the firewall, the system must do many more things than a router does. Some firewalls provide:

- DNS name service for the outside world
- Email forwarding
- Proxy services

Only the minimal services truly needed to communicate with external systems should be provided on a firewall system. Other common network services (NIS, NFS, X Windows, finger, etc.) should generally not be provided. Services are limited to decrease the number of holes through which an intruder can gain access. On firewall systems, security is more important than service.

The biggest problems for the firewall machine are ftp service and remote terminal service. To maintain a high level of security, user accounts are discouraged on the firewall machine; however, user data must pass through the firewall system for ftp and remote terminal services. This problem can be handled by creating special user accounts for ftp and telnet that are shared by all internal users. But group accounts are generally viewed as security problems. A better solution is to allow ssh services through the firewall. This encourages the use of ssh, which in turn provides strong authentication and encrypted data exchanges.

Because a firewall must be constructed with great care to be effective, and because there are many configuration variables for setting up a firewall machine, vendors offer special firewall software. Some vendors sell special-purpose machines designed specifically for use as firewall systems. There are several low-cost Linux firewall packages. Before setting up your own firewall, investigate the options available from software vendors and your hardware vendor.

The details of setting up a firewall system are beyond the scope of this book. Before you proceed, I recommend you read *Building Internet Firewalls* and *Firewalls and Internet Security*. Unless you have skilled Unix system administrators with adequate free time, a do-it-yourself firewall installation is a mistake. Hire a company that specializes in firewall design and installation. If your information is valuable enough to protect with a firewall, it should be valuable enough to protect with a professionally installed firewall.

Of course, not every site can afford a professionally installed firewall—you might be protecting a small office or even a home network. If you don't have money or time, you can buy a low-cost firewall router, sometimes referred to as a *firewall appliance*. These boxes are specifically designed for the small office and home office. They provide basic packet filtering, proxy services, and network address translation service, and they often cost only a few hundred dollars. In most cases, you simply buy the box and plug it in. At the very least, your network deserves this level of protection. If you have the time and the skill to build a firewall, you can use a firewall package or the firewall tools built into your operating systems. A firewall package increases initial cost, but it is easy to work with. The packet filtering tools built into the operating system cost nothing but are the most difficult to configure. The iptables tool provided with Linux is a good example of the type of firewall tools provided with some Unix operating systems.

Filtering Traffic with iptables

In its simplest incarnation, a firewall is a filtering router that screens out unwanted traffic. Use the routing capabilities of a multi-homed Linux host combined with the filtering features of iptables to create a filtering router.

The Linux kernel categorizes firewall traffic into three groups and applies different filter rules to each category of traffic. These are:

INPUT

> Incoming traffic bound for a process on the local system is tested against the INPUT filter rules before it is accepted.

OUTPUT

> Outbound traffic that initiated on the local system is tested against the OUTPUT filter rules before it is sent.

FORWARD

> Traffic from one external system bound for another external system is tested against the FORWARDING filter rules.

The INPUT and OUTPUT rules are used when the system acts as a host. The FORWARD rules are used when the system acts as a router. In addition to the three standard categories, iptables accepts user-defined categories.

Defining iptables filter rules

The Linux kernel maintains a list of rules for each of these categories. The lists of rules are maintained by the iptables command.* Use the options shown in Table 12-2 with the iptables command to create or delete user-defined chains, to add rules to a chain, to delete rules from a chain, and to change the order of the rules in the chain.

---

* iptables came into use with Linux kernel 2.4. Early kernels used the ipfwadm and the ipchains commands. See *Linux Firewalls* by Robert Ziegler (New Riders, 2000) for information on these older commands.

O'REILLY BOOK REGISTRATION

Register your book with O'Reilly by completing this card and receive a **FREE** copy of our latest catalog. Or register online at **register.oreilly.com** and, in addition to our catalog, we'll send you email notification of new editions of this book, information about new titles, and special offers available only to registered O'Reilly customers.

Which book(s) are you registering? Please include title and ISBN # (above bar code on back cover)

Title. _____ ISBN # _____

Title _____ ISBN # _____

Title _____ ISBN # _____

Name _____ Company/Organization _____

Address _____

City _____ State _____ Zip/Postal Code _____ Country _____

Telephone _____ Email address _____

Have you previously purchased online from O'Reilly? ☐ Yes, my account number is _____ ☐ No

www.oreilly.com

Table 12-2. iptables command-line options

Option	Function
-A	Appends rules to the end of a ruleset.
-D	Deletes rules from a ruleset.
-E	Renames a ruleset.
-F	Removes all of the rules from a ruleset.
-I	Inserts a rule into a specific location in a ruleset.
-L	Lists all rules in a ruleset.
-N	Creates a user-defined ruleset with the specified name.
-P	Sets the default policy for a chain.
-R	Replaces a rule in a chain.
-X	Deletes the specified user-defined ruleset.
-Z	Resets all packet and byte counters to zero.

Firewall rules are composed of a filter against which the packets are matched and the action taken when a packet matches the filter. The action can either be a standard policy or a jump to a user-defined ruleset for additional processing. The -j *target* command-line option identifies the user-defined ruleset or the standard policy to handle the packet. *target* is either the name of a ruleset or a keyword that identifies a standard policy. The keywords for the standard policies are:

ACCEPT
> Let the packet pass through the firewall.

DROP
> Discard the packet.

QUEUE
> Pass the packet up to user space for processing.

RETURN
> In a user-defined ruleset, this means to return to the ruleset that called this ruleset. In one of the three kernel rulesets, this means to exit the chain and use the default policy for the chain.

The iptables command constructs filters that match on the protocol used, the source or destination address, or the network interface used for the packet, using a variety of command-line parameters. The basic iptables parameters for building filters are:

-p *protocol*
> Defines the protocol to which the rule applies. *protocol* can be any numeric value from the */etc/protocols* file or one of the keywords: tcp, udp, or icmp.

-s *address*[*/mask*]

> Defines source address of the packets to which the rule applies. *address* can be a hostname, network name, or IP address.

--sport [*port*[*:port*]]

> Defines the source port of the packets to which the rule applies. *port* can be a name or number from the */etc/services* file. A range of ports can be specified using the format *port:port*. If no specific port value is specified, all ports are assumed.

-d *address*[*/mask*]

> Defines the destination address of the packets to which the rule applies. *address* can be a hostname, network name, or IP address.

--dport [*port*[*:port*]]

> Defines the destination port to which the rule applies. This filters all traffic bound for a specific port. The port is defined using the same rules as those used to define these values for the packet source.

--icmp-type *type*

> Defines the ICMP type to which the rule applies. *type* can be any valid ICMP message type number or name.

-i *name*

> Defines the name of the input network interface to which the rule applies. Only packets received on this interface are affected by the rule. Specify a partial interface name by ending it with a + (e.g., eth+ matches all Ethernet interfaces that begin with eth).

-o *name*

> Defines the name of the output network interface to which the rule applies. Only packets sent out this interface are affected by the rule. Specify a partial interface name by ending it with a + (e.g., eth+ matches all Ethernet interfaces that begin with eth).

-f

> Indicates that the rule refers only to second and subsequent fragments of fragmented packets.

Sample iptables commands

Putting this all together creates a firewall that can protect your network. Assume we have a Linux router attached to a perimeter network with the address 172.16.12.254 on interface eth0 and to an external network with the address 192.168.6.5 on interface eth1. Further assume that the perimeter network contains only a sendmail server and an Apache server. Here is an example of some iptables commands we might use on the Linux system to protect the perimeter network:

```
iptable -F INPUT
iptables -F FORWARD
iptables -A INPUT -i eth1 -j DROP
iptables -A FORWARD -i eth1 -s 172.16.0.0/16 -j DROP
iptables -A FORWARD -o eth1 -d 172.16.0.0/16 -j DROP
iptables -A FORWARD -d 172.16.12.1 25 -j ACCEPT
iptables -A FORWARD -d 172.16.12.6 80 -j ACCEPT
iptables -A FORWARD -j DROP
```

The first two commands use the -F option to clear the rulesets we plan to work with. The third line drops any packets from the external network that are bound for a process running locally on the Linux router. We do not allow any access to router processes from the external world.

The next two commands drop packets that are being routed to the external world using an internal address. If packets are received on the external interface with a source address from the internal network, they are dropped. Likewise, if packets are being sent out the external interface with a destination address from the internal network, they are dropped. These rules say that if packets on the external network interface (eth1) misuse addresses from the internal network (172.16), somebody is trying to spoof us and the packets should be discarded.

The next two rules are basically identical. They accept packets if the destination and port are the correct destination and port for a specific server. For example, port 25 is the SMTP port and 172.16.12.1 is the mail server, and port 80 is the HTTP port and 172.16.12.6 is the web server. We accept these inbound connections because they are destined for the correct systems. The last rule rejects all other traffic.

These examples illustrate the power of Linux's built-in filtering features and provide enough information to get you started. Clearly much more can and should be done to build a real firewall. If you want to know more about iptables, see *Building Internet Firewalls* and *Linux Security*, both mentioned in the reading list below, for many more detailed examples.

Words to the Wise

I am not a security expert; I am a network administrator. In my view, good security is good system administration and vice versa. Most of this chapter is just common-sense advice. It is probably sufficient for most circumstances, but certainly not for all.

Make sure you know whether there is an existing security policy that applies to your network or system. If there are policies, regulations, or laws governing your situation, make sure to obey them. Never do anything to undermine the security system established for your site.

No system is completely secure. No matter what you do, you will have problems. Realize this and prepare for it. Prepare a disaster recovery plan and do everything necessary so that when the worst does happen, you can recover from it with the minimum possible disruption.

If you want to read more about security, I recommend the following:

- RFC 2196, *Site Security Handbook*, B. Fraser, September 1997.
- RFC 1281, *Guidelines for the Secure Operation of the Internet*, R. Pethia, S. Crocker, and B. Fraser, November 1991.
- *Practical Unix and Internet Security*, Simson Garfinkel and Gene Spafford, O'Reilly & Associates, 1996.
- *Linux Security*, Ramon Hontanon, Sybex, 2001.
- *Building Internet Firewalls*, Elizabeth Zwicky, Simon Cooper, and Brent Chapman, O'Reilly & Associates, 2000.
- *Linux Firewalls*, Robert Ziegler, New Riders, 2000.
- *Firewalls and Internet Security*, William Cheswick and Steven Bellovin, Addison Wesley, 1994.

Summary

Network access and computer security work at cross-purposes. Attaching a computer to a network increases the security risks for that computer. Evaluate your security needs to determine what must be protected and how vigorously it must be protected. Develop a written site security policy that defines your procedures and documents the security duties and responsibilities of employees at all levels.

Network security is essentially good system security. Good user authentication, effective system monitoring, and well-trained system administrators provide the best security. Tools are available to help with these tasks. SSH, OPIE, Tripwire, OpenSSL, iptables, TCP wrappers, encryption, and firewalls are all tools that can help.

In this chapter:
- Approaching a Problem
- Diagnostic Tools
- Testing Basic Connectivity
- Troubleshooting Network Access
- Checking Routing
- Checking Name Service
- Analyzing Protocol Problems
- Protocol Case Study

## CHAPTER 13

Troubleshooting TCP/IP

Network administration tasks fall into two very different categories: configuration and troubleshooting. Configuration tasks prepare for the expected; they require detailed knowledge of command syntax, but are usually simple and predictable. Once a system is properly configured, there is rarely any reason to change it. The configuration process is repeated each time a new operating system release is installed, but with very few changes.

In contrast, network troubleshooting deals with the unexpected. Troubleshooting frequently requires knowledge that is conceptual rather than detailed. Network problems are usually unique and sometimes difficult to resolve. Troubleshooting is an important part of maintaining a stable, reliable network service.

In this chapter, we discuss the tools you will use to ensure that the network is in good running condition. However, good tools are not enough. No troubleshooting tool is effective if applied haphazardly. Effective troubleshooting requires a methodical approach to the problem, and a basic understanding of how the network works. We'll start our discussion by looking at ways to approach a network problem.

Approaching a Problem

To approach a problem properly, you need a basic understanding of TCP/IP. The first few chapters of this book discuss the basics of TCP/IP and provide enough background information to troubleshoot most network problems. Knowledge of how TCP/IP routes data through the network, between individual hosts, and between the layers in the protocol stack is important for understanding a network problem. But detailed knowledge of each protocol usually isn't necessary. When you need these details, look them up in a definitive reference—don't try to recall them from memory.

Not all TCP/IP problems are alike, and not all problems can be approached in the same manner. But the key to solving any problem is understanding what the problem is. This is not as easy as it may seem. The "surface" problem is sometimes misleading, and the "real" problem is frequently obscured by many layers of software.

Once you understand the true nature of the problem, the solution to the problem is often obvious.

First, gather detailed information about exactly what's happening. When a user reports a problem, talk to her. Find out which application failed. What is the remote host's name and IP address? What is the user's hostname and address? What error message was displayed? If possible, verify the problem by having the user run the application while you talk her through it. If possible, duplicate the problem on your own system.

Testing from the user's system, and other systems, find out:

- Does the problem occur in other applications on the user's host, or is only one application having trouble? If only one application is involved, the application may be misconfigured or disabled on the remote host. Because of security concerns, many systems disable some services.

- Does the problem occur with only one remote host, all remote hosts, or only certain "groups" of remote hosts? If only one remote host is involved, the problem could easily be with that host. If all remote hosts are involved, the problem is probably with the user's system (particularly if no other hosts on your local network are experiencing the same problem). If only hosts on certain subnets or external networks are involved, the problem may be related to routing.

- Does the problem occur on other local systems? Make sure you check other systems on the same subnet. If the problem occurs only on the user's host, concentrate testing on that system. If the problem affects every system on a subnet, concentrate on the router for that subnet.

Once you know the symptoms of the problem, visualize each protocol and device that handles the data. Visualizing the problem will help you avoid oversimplification, and keep you from assuming that you know the cause even before you start testing. Using your TCP/IP knowledge, narrow your attack to the most likely causes of the problem, but keep an open mind.

Troubleshooting Hints

Below are several useful troubleshooting hints. They are not part of a troubleshooting methodology—just good ideas to keep in mind.

- Approach problems methodically. Allow the information gathered from each test to guide your testing. Don't jump on a hunch into another test scenario without ensuring that you can pick up your original scenario where you left off.

- Work carefully through the problem, dividing it into manageable pieces. Test each piece before moving on to the next. For example, when testing a network connection, test each part of the network until you find the problem.

- Keep good records of the tests you have completed and their results. Keep a historical record of the problem in case it reappears.

- Keep an open mind. Don't assume too much about the cause of the problem. Some people believe their network is always at fault, while others assume the remote end is always the problem. Some are so sure they know the cause of a problem that they ignore the evidence of the tests. Don't fall into these traps. Test each possibility and base your actions on the evidence of the tests.

- Be aware of security barriers. Security firewalls sometimes block ping, traceroute, and even ICMP error messages. If problems seem to cluster around a specific remote site, find out if it has a firewall.

- Pay attention to error messages. Error messages are often vague, but they frequently contain important hints for solving the problem.

- Duplicate the reported problem yourself. Don't rely too heavily on the user's problem report. The user has probably seen this problem only from the application level. If necessary, obtain the user's data files to duplicate the problem. Even if you cannot duplicate the problem, log the details of the reported problem for your records.

- Most problems are caused by human error. You can prevent some of these errors by providing information and training on network configuration and usage.

- Keep your users informed. This reduces the number of duplicated trouble reports and the duplication of effort when several system administrators work on the same problem without knowing others are already working on it. If you're lucky, someone may have seen the problem before and have a helpful suggestion about how to resolve it.

- Don't speculate about the cause of the problem while talking to the user. Save your speculations for discussions with your networking colleagues. Your speculations may be accepted by the user as gospel, and become rumors. These rumors can cause users to avoid using legitimate network services and may undermine confidence in your network. Users want solutions to their problems; they're not interested in speculative techno-babble.

- Stick to a few simple troubleshooting tools. For most TCP/IP software problems, the tools discussed in this chapter are sufficient. Just learning how to use a new tool is often more time-consuming than solving the problem with an old, familiar tool.

- Thoroughly test the problem at your end of the network before locating the owners of the remote system to coordinate testing with them. The greatest difficulty of network troubleshooting is that you do not always control the systems at both ends of the network. In many cases, you may not even know who does control the remote system. The more information you have about your end, the simpler the job will be when you have to contact the remote administrator.

- Don't neglect the obvious. A loose or damaged cable is always a possible problem. Check plugs, connectors, cables, and switches. Small things can cause big problems.

Diagnostic Tools

Because most problems have simple causes, developing a clear idea of the problem often provides the solution. Unfortunately, this is not always true, so in this section we begin to discuss the tools that can help you attack the most intractable problems. Many diagnostic tools are available, ranging from commercial systems with specialized hardware and software that may cost thousands of dollars, to free software that is available from the Internet. Many software tools are provided with your Unix system. You should also keep some hardware tools handy.

To maintain the network's equipment and wiring, you need some simple hand tools. A pair of needle-nose pliers and a few screwdrivers may be sufficient, but you may also need specialized tools. For example, attaching RJ45 connectors to unshielded twisted pair (UTP) cable requires special crimping tools. It is usually easiest to buy a ready-made network maintenance toolkit from your cable vendor.

A full-featured cable tester is also useful. Modern cable testers are small hand-held units with a keypad and LCD display that test both thinnet and UTP cable. Tests are selected from the keyboard and results are displayed on the LCD screen. It is not necessary to interpret the results because the unit does that for you and displays the error condition in a simple text message. For example, a cable test might produce the message "Short at 74 feet." This tells you that the cable is shorted 74 feet away from the tester. What could be simpler? The proper test tools make it easier to locate, and therefore fix, cable problems.

A laptop computer can be a most useful piece of test equipment when properly configured. Install TCP/IP software on the laptop. Take it to the location where the user reports a network problem. Disconnect the Ethernet cable from the back of the user's system and attach it to the laptop. Configure the laptop with an appropriate address for the user's subnet and reboot it. Then ping various systems on the network and attach to one of the user's servers. If everything works, the fault is probably in the user's computer. Users trust this test because it demonstrates something they do every day. They have more confidence in the laptop than in an unidentifiable piece of test equipment displaying the message "No faults found." If the test fails, the fault is probably in the network equipment or wiring. That's the time to bring out the cable tester.

Another advantage of using a laptop as a piece of test equipment is its inherent versatility. It runs a wide variety of test, diagnostic, and management software. Install Unix on the laptop and run the software discussed in the rest of this chapter from your desktop or your laptop.

This book emphasizes free or "built-in" software diagnostic tools that run on Unix systems. The software tools used in this chapter, and many more, are described in RFC 1470, *FYI on a Network Management Tool Catalog: Tools for Monitoring and*

Debugging TCP/IP Internets and Interconnected Devices. A catchy title, and a useful RFC! The RFC is somewhat dated, but it does point out some very useful tools. The tools listed in that catalog and discussed in this book are:

ifconfig

Provides information about the basic configuration of the interface. It is useful for detecting bad IP addresses, incorrect subnet masks, and improper broadcast addresses. Chapter 6 covers ifconfig in detail. This tool is provided with the Unix operating system.

arp

Provides information about Ethernet/IP address translation. It can be used to detect systems on the local network that are configured with the wrong IP address. arp is covered in this chapter and is used in an example in Chapter 2. arp is delivered as part of Unix.

netstat

Provides a variety of information. It is commonly used to display detailed statistics about each network interface, the network sockets, and the network routing table. netstat is used repeatedly in this book, most extensively in Chapters 2, 6, and 7. netstat is delivered as part of Unix.

ping

Indicates whether a remote host can be reached. ping also displays statistics about packet loss and delivery time. ping is discussed in Chapter 1 and used in Chapter 7. ping also comes as part of Unix.

nslookup

Provides information about the DNS name service. nslookup is covered in detail in Chapter 8. It comes as part of the BIND software package.

dig

Also provides information about name service and is similar to nslookup.

traceroute

Prints information about each routing hop that packets take going from your system to a remote system.

snoop

Analyzes the individual packets exchanged between hosts on a network. snoop is a TCP/IP protocol analyzer included with Solaris 8 systems. It examines the contents of packets, including their headers, and is most useful for analyzing protocol problems. tcpdump is a tool similar to snoop that is provided with Linux systems.

This chapter discusses each of these tools, even those covered earlier in the text. We start with ping, which is used in more troubleshooting situations than any other diagnostic tool.

Testing Basic Connectivity

The ping command tests whether a remote host can be reached from your computer. This simple function is extremely useful for testing the network connection, independent of the application in which the original problem was detected. ping allows you to determine whether further testing should be directed toward the network connection (the lower layers) or the application (the upper layers). If ping shows that packets can travel to the remote system and back, the user's problem is probably in the upper layers. If packets can't make the round trip, lower protocol layers are probably at fault.

Frequently a user reports a network problem by stating that he can't telnet (or ftp, or send email, or whatever) to some remote host. He then immediately qualifies this statement with the announcement that it worked before. In cases like this, where the ability to connect to the remote host is in question, ping is a very useful tool.

Using the hostname provided by the user, ping the remote host. If your ping is successful, have the user ping the host. If the user's ping is also successful, concentrate your further analysis on the specific application that the user is having trouble with. Perhaps the user is attempting to telnet to a host that provides only anonymous ftp. Perhaps the host was down when the user tried his application. Have the user try it again, while you watch or listen to every detail of what he is doing. If he is doing everything right and the application still fails, detailed analysis of the application with snoop and coordination with the remote system administrator may be needed.

If your ping is successful and the user's ping fails, concentrate testing on the user's system configuration, and on those things that are different about the user's path to the remote host when compared to your path to the remote host.

If your ping fails, or the user's ping fails, pay close attention to any error messages. The error messages displayed by ping are helpful guides for planning further testing. The details of the messages may vary from implementation to implementation, but there are only a few basic types of errors:

Unknown host

> The remote host's name cannot be resolved by name service into an IP address. The name servers could be at fault (either your local server or the remote system's server), the name could be incorrect, or something could be wrong with the network between your system and the remote server. If you know the remote host's IP address, try to ping that. If you can reach the host using its IP address, the problem is with name service. Use nslookup or dig to test the local and remote servers, and to check the accuracy of the hostname the user gave you.

Network unreachable

> The local system does not have a route to the remote system. If the numeric IP address was used on the ping command line, re-enter the ping command using the hostname. This eliminates the possibility that the IP address was entered

incorrectly, or that you were given the wrong address. If a routing protocol is being used, make sure it is running and check the routing table with netstat. If a static default route is being used, reinstall it. If everything seems fine on the host, check its default gateway for routing problems.

No answer

The remote system did not respond. Most network utilities have some version of this message. Some ping implementations print the message "100% packet loss." telnet prints the message "Connection timed out" and sendmail returns the error "cannot connect." All of these errors mean the same thing. The local system has a route to the remote system, but it receives no response from the remote system to any of the packets it sends.

There are many possible causes of this problem. The remote host may be down. Either the local or the remote host may be configured incorrectly. A gateway or circuit between the local host and the remote host may be down. The remote host may have routing problems. Only additional testing can isolate the cause of the problem. Carefully check the local configuration using netstat and ifconfig. Check the route to the remote system with traceroute. Contact the administrator of the remote system and report the problem.

All of the tools mentioned here will be discussed later in this chapter. However, before leaving ping, let's look more closely at the command and the statistics it displays.

The ping Command

The basic format of the ping command on a Solaris system is:[*]

    ping host [packetsize] [count]

host

The hostname or IP address of the remote host being tested. Use the hostname or address provided by the user in the trouble report.

packetsize

Defines the size in bytes of the test packets. This field is required only if the *count* field is going to be used. Use the default *packetsize* of 56 bytes.

count

The number of packets to be sent in the test. Use the *count* field, and set the value low. Otherwise, the ping command may continue to send test packets until you interrupt it, usually by pressing Ctrl-C (^C). Sending excessive numbers of test packets is not a good use of network bandwidth and system resources. Usually five packets are sufficient for a test.

---

[*] Check your system's documentation. ping varies slightly from system to system. On Linux, the format shown above would be: ping [-c *count*] [-s *packetsize*] *host*.

To check that *ns.uu.net* can be reached from *crab*, we send five 56-byte packets with the following command:

```
% ping -s ns.uu.net 56 5
PING ns.uu.net: 56 data bytes
64 bytes from ns.uu.net (137.39.1.3): icmp_seq=0. time=32.8 ms
64 bytes from ns.uu.net (137.39.1.3): icmp_seq=1. time=15.3 ms
64 bytes from ns.uu.net (137.39.1.3): icmp_seq=2. time=13.1 ms
64 bytes from ns.uu.net (137.39.1.3): icmp_seq=3. time=32.4 ms
64 bytes from ns.uu.net (137.39.1.3): icmp_seq=4. time=28.1 ms

----ns.uu.net PING Statistics----
5 packets transmitted, 5 packets received, 0% packet loss
round trip (ms)  min/avg/max = 13.1/24.3/32.8
```

The -s option is included because *crab* is a Solaris workstation, and we want packet-by-packet statistics. Without the -s option, Sun's ping command prints only a summary line saying "ns.uu.net is alive." Other ping implementations do not require the -s option; they display the statistics by default, as the Linux example below shows:

```
$ ping -c5 ns.uu.net
PING ns.uu.net (137.39.1.3) from 172.16.12.3 : 56(84) bytes of data.
64 bytes from ns.UU.NET (137.39.1.3): icmp_seq=0 ttl=244 time=98.283 msec
64 bytes from ns.UU.NET (137.39.1.3): icmp_seq=1 ttl=244 time=94.114 msec
64 bytes from ns.UU.NET (137.39.1.3): icmp_seq=2 ttl=244 time=66.565 msec
64 bytes from ns.UU.NET (137.39.1.3): icmp_seq=3 ttl=244 time=24.301 msec
64 bytes from ns.UU.NET (137.39.1.3): icmp_seq=4 ttl=244 time=37.060 msec

--- ns.uu.net ping statistics ---
5 packets transmitted, 5 packets received, 0% packet loss
round trip min/avg/max/mdev = 24.301/64.064/98.283/29.634 ms
```

Both tests show a good wide area network link to *ns.uu.net* with no packet loss and a fast response. The round trip between *almond* and *ns.uu.net* took an average of only 24.3 milliseconds. A small packet loss, and a round trip time an order of magnitude higher, would not be abnormal for a connection made across a wide area network. The statistics displayed by the ping command can indicate low-level network problems. The key statistics are:

- The sequence in which the packets are arriving, as shown by the ICMP sequence number (icmp_seq) displayed for each packet.

- How long it takes a packet to make the round trip, displayed in milliseconds after the string time=.

- The percentage of packets lost, displayed in a summary line at the end of the ping output.

If the packet loss is high, the response time is very slow, or packets are arriving out of order, there could be a network hardware problem. If you see these conditions when communicating over great distances on a wide area network, there is nothing to worry about. TCP/IP was designed to deal with unreliable networks, and some wide area networks suffer a lot of packet loss. But if these problems are seen on a local area network, they indicate trouble.

On a local network cable segment, the round trip time should be near 0, there should be little or no packet loss, and the packets should arrive in order. If these things are not true, there is a problem with the network hardware. On an Ethernet, the problem could be improper cable termination, a bad cable segment, or a bad piece of "active" hardware, such as a hub, switch, or transceiver. Check the cable with a cable tester as described earlier. Good hubs and switches often have built-in diagnostic software that can be checked. Cheap hubs and transceivers may require the "brute force" method of disconnecting individual pieces of hardware until the problem goes away.

The results of a simple ping test, even if the ping is successful, can help you direct further testing toward the most likely causes of the problem. But other diagnostic tools are needed to examine the problem more closely and find the underlying cause.

Troubleshooting Network Access

The "no answer" and "cannot connect" errors indicate a problem in the lower layers of the network protocols. If the preliminary tests point to this type of problem, concentrate your testing on routing and on the network interface. Use the ifconfig, netstat, and arp commands to test the Network Access Layer.

Troubleshooting with the ifconfig Command

ifconfig checks the network interface configuration. Use this command to verify the user's configuration if the user's system has been recently configured or if the user's system cannot reach the remote host while other systems on the same network can.

When ifconfig is entered with an interface name and no other arguments, it displays the current values assigned to that interface. For example, checking interface dnet0 on a Solaris 8 system gives this report:

```
% ifconfig dnet0
dnet0: flags=1000843<UP,BROADCAST,RUNNING,MULTICAST,IPv4> mtu 1500 index 2
        inet 172.16.55.105 netmask ffffff00 broadcast 172.16.55.255
```

The ifconfig command displays two lines of output. The first line of the display shows the interface's name and its characteristics. Check for these characteristics:

UP

> The interface is enabled for use. If the interface is "down," have the system's superuser bring the interface "up" with the ifconfig command (e.g., ifconfig dnet0 up). If the interface won't come up, replace the interface cable and try again. If it still fails, have the interface hardware checked.

RUNNING

This interface is operational. If the interface is not "running," the driver for this interface may not be properly installed. The system administrator should review all of the steps necessary to install this interface, looking for errors or missed steps.

The second line of ifconfig output shows the IP address, the subnet mask (written in hexadecimal), and the broadcast address. Check these three fields to make sure the network interface is properly configured.

Two common interface configuration problems are misconfigured subnet masks and incorrect IP addresses. A bad subnet mask is indicated when the host can reach other hosts on its local subnet and remote hosts on distant networks, but it cannot reach hosts on other local subnets. ifconfig quickly reveals if a bad subnet mask is set.

An incorrectly set IP address can be a subtle problem. If the network part of the address is incorrect, every ping will fail with the "no answer" error. In this case, using ifconfig will reveal the incorrect address. However, if the host part of the address is wrong, the problem can be more difficult to detect. A small system, such as a PC that only connects out to other systems and never accepts incoming connections, can run for a long time with the wrong address without its user noticing the problem. Additionally, the system that suffers the ill effects may not be the one that is misconfigured. It is possible for someone to accidentally use your IP address on his system, and for his mistake to cause your system intermittent communications problems. An example of this problem is discussed later. This type of configuration error cannot be discovered by ifconfig because the error is on a remote host. The arp command is used for this type of problem.

Troubleshooting with the arp Command

The arp command is used to analyze problems with IP-to-Ethernet address translation. The arp command has three useful options for troubleshooting:

-a

Display all ARP entries in the table.

-d *hostname*

Delete an entry from the ARP table.

-s *hostname ether-address*

Add a new entry to the table.

With these three options you can view the contents of the ARP table, delete a problem entry, and install a corrected entry. The ability to install a corrected entry is useful in "buying time" while you look for the permanent fix.

Use arp if you suspect that incorrect entries are getting into the address resolution table. One clear indication of problems with the ARP table is a report that the "wrong" host responded to some command, like ftp or telnet. Intermittent problems that affect only certain hosts can also indicate that the ARP table has been corrupted. ARP table problems are usually caused by two systems using the same IP address. The problems appear intermittent because the entry that appears in the table is the address of the host that responded quickest to the last ARP request. Sometimes the "correct" host responds first, and sometimes the "wrong" host responds first.

If you suspect that two systems are using the same IP address, display the address resolution table with the arp -a command. Here's an example from a Solaris system:[*]

```
% arp -a
Net to Media Table: IPv4
Device   IP Address              Mask            Flags  Phys Addr
------   -------------------     ---------------  -----  ---------------
dnet0    pecan                   255.255.255.255         08:00:20:05:21:33
dnet0    horseshoe               255.255.255.255         00:00:0c:e0:80:b1
dnet0    crab                    255.255.255.255  SP     08:00:20:22:fd:51
dnet0    BASE-ADDRESS.MCAST.NET 240.0.0.0         SM     01:00:5e:00:00:00
```

It is easiest to verify that the IP and Ethernet address pairs are correct if you have a record of each host's correct Ethernet address. For this reason you should record each host's Ethernet and IP address when it is added to your network. If you have such a record, you'll quickly see if anything is wrong with the table.

If you don't have this type of record, the first three bytes of the Ethernet address can help you to detect a problem. The first three bytes of the address identify the equipment manufacturer. A list of these identifying prefixes is found at *http://ww.iana.org/ assignments/ethernet-numbers*.

From the vendor prefixes we see that two of the ARP entries displayed in our example are Sun systems (8:0:20). If *horseshoe* is also supposed to be a Sun, the 0:0:0c Cisco prefix indicates that a Cisco router has been mistakenly configured with *horseshoe*'s IP address.

If neither checking a record of correct assignments nor checking the manufacturer prefix helps you identify the source of the errant ARP, try using telnet to connect to the IP address shown in the ARP entry. If the device supports telnet, the login banner might help you identify the incorrectly configured host.

ARP problem case study

A user called in asking if the server was down, and reported the following problem. The user's workstation, called *limulus*, appeared to "lock up" for minutes at a time when certain commands were used, while other commands worked with no problems. The network commands that involved the NIS name server all caused the

---

[*] The format in which the ARP table is displayed may vary slightly between systems.

lock-up problem, but some unrelated commands also caused the problem. The user reported seeing the error message:

```
NFS getattr failed for server crab: RPC: Timed out
```

The server *crab* was providing *limulus* with NIS and NFS services. The commands that failed on *limulus* were commands that required NIS service, or that were stored in the centrally maintained */usr/local* directory exported from *crab*. The commands that ran correctly were installed locally on the user's workstation. No one else reported a problem with the server, and we were able to ping *limulus* from *crab* and get good responses.

We had the user check the *messages* file[*] for recent error messages, and she discovered this:

```
Mar  6 13:38:23 limulus vmunix: duplicate IP address!!
        sent from ethernet address: 0:0:c0:4:38:1a
```

This message indicates that the workstation detected another host on the Ethernet responding to its IP address. The "imposter" used the Ethernet address 0:0:c0:4:38:1a in its ARP response. The correct Ethernet address for *limulus* is 8:0:20:e:12:37.

We checked *crab*'s ARP table and found that it had the incorrect ARP entry for *limulus*. We deleted the bad *limulus* entry with the arp -d command, and installed the correct entry with the -s option, as shown below:

```
# arp -d limulus
limulus (172.16.180.130) deleted
# arp -s limulus 8:0:20:e:12:37
```

ARP entries received via the ARP protocol are temporary. The values are held in the table for a finite lifetime and are deleted when that lifetime expires. New values are then obtained via the ARP protocol. Therefore, if some remote interfaces change, the local table adjusts and communications continue. Usually this is a good idea, but if someone is using the wrong IP address, that bad address can keep reappearing in the ARP table even if it is deleted. However, manually entered values are permanent; they stay in the table and can only be deleted manually. This allowed us to install a correct entry in the table without worrying about it being overwritten by a bad address.

This quick fix resolved *limulus*'s immediate problem, but we still needed to find the culprit. We checked the */etc/ethers* file to see if we had an entry for Ethernet address 0:0:c0:4:38:1a, but we didn't. From the first three bytes of this address, 0:0:c0, we knew that the device was a Western Digital card. Since our network has only Unix workstations and PCs, we assumed the Western Digital card was installed in a PC. We also guessed that the problem address was recently installed because the user

---

[*] Check */etc/syslog.conf* for the full path of the *messages* file. Common locations are */var/adm/messages* and */var/log/messages*.

had never had the problem before. We sent out an urgent announcement to all users asking if anyone had recently installed a new PC, reconfigured a PC, or installed TCP/IP software on a PC. We got one response. When we checked his system, we found out that he had entered the address 172.16.180.130 when he should have entered 172.16.180.138. The address was corrected and the problem did not recur.

Nothing fancy was needed to solve this problem. Once we checked the error messages, we knew what the problem was and how to solve it. Involving the entire network user community allowed us to quickly locate the problem system and to avoid a room-to-room search for the PC. Reluctance to involve users and make them part of the solution is one of the costliest, and most common, mistakes made by network administrators.

Checking the Interface with netstat

If the preliminary tests lead you to suspect that the connection to the local area network is unreliable, the netstat -i command can provide useful information. The example below shows the output from the netstat -i command on a Solaris 8 system:[*]

```
% netstat -i
Name  Mtu   Net/Dest          Address    Ipkts  Ierrs Opkts  Oerrs Collis Queue
dnet0 1500  wrotethebook.com  crab        442697 2     633424 2     50679  0
lo0   1536  loopback          localhost  53040   0     53040  0     0      0
```

The line for the loopback interface, lo0, can be ignored. Only the line for the real network interface is significant, and only the last five fields on that line provide significant troubleshooting information.

Let's look at the last field first. There should be no packets queued (Queue) that cannot be transmitted. If the interface is up and running, and the system cannot deliver packets to the network, suspect a bad drop cable or a bad interface. Replace the cable and see if the problem goes away. If it doesn't, call the vendor for interface hardware repairs.

The input errors (Ierrs) and the output errors (Oerrs) should be close to 0. Regardless of how much traffic has passed through this interface, 100 errors in either of these fields is high. High output errors could indicate a saturated local network or a bad physical connection between the host and the network. High input errors could indicate that the network is saturated, the local host is overloaded, or there is a physical network problem. Tools, such as ping statistics or a cable tester, can help you determine if it is a physical network problem. Evaluating the collision rate can help you determine if the local Ethernet is saturated.

---

[*] The output on a Linux system is formatted differently, but the same statistics are provided.

A high value in the collision field (Collis) is normal, but if the percentage of output packets that result in a collision is too high, it indicates that the network is saturated. Collision rates greater than 5% bear watching. If high collision rates are seen consistently, and are seen among a broad sampling of systems on the network, you may need to subdivide the network to reduce traffic load.

Collision rates are a percentage of output packets. Don't use the total number of packets sent and received; use the values in the Opkts and Collis fields when determining the collision rate. For example, the output in the netstat example shows 50679 collisions out of 633424 outgoing packets. That's a collision rate of 8%. This sample network could be overworked; check the statistics on other hosts on this network. If the other systems also show a high collision rate, consider subdividing this network.

Subdividing an Ethernet

To reduce the collision rate, you must reduce the amount of traffic on the network segment. A simple way to do this is to create multiple segments out of the single segment. Each new segment will have fewer hosts and, therefore, less traffic. We'll see, however, that it's not quite this simple.

The most effective way to subdivide an Ethernet is to install an Ethernet switch. Each port on the switch is essentially a separate Ethernet. So a 16-port switch gives you 16 Ethernets to work with when balancing the load. On most switches the ports can be used in a variety of ways (see Figure 13-1). Lightly used systems can be attached to a hub that is then attached to one of the switch ports to allow the systems to share a single segment. Servers and demanding systems can be given dedicated ports so that they don't need to share a segment with anyone. Most switches provide both 10 Mbps Ethernet and Fast Ethernet 100 Mbps ports. These are called *asymmetric switches* because different ports operate at different speeds. Use the Fast Ethernet ports to connect heavily used servers or segments. Most 10/100 switches have auto-sensing ports. This allows every port to be used at either 100 Mbps or at 10 Mbps, which gives you the maximum configuration flexibility.

Gigabit Ethernet switches can also be used, but they have a unique place in the network topology. 10/100 switches connect servers and local networks. Gigabit switches are primarily used to create a "collapsed backbone" to interconnect other switches. Gigabit switches are used when designing a new corporate backbone network. 10/100 switches are used when subdividing an individual Ethernet segment.

Figure 13-1 shows an 8-port 10/100 Ethernet switch. Ports 1 and 2 are wired to Ethernet hubs. A few systems are connected to each hub. When new systems are added they are distributed evenly among the hubs to prevent any one segment from becoming overloaded. Additional hubs can be added to the available switch ports for future expansion. Port 4 attaches a demanding system with its own private segment.

Port 6 operates at 100 Mbps and attaches a heavily used server. A port can be reserved for a future 100 Mbps connection to a second 10/100 Ethernet switch for even more expansion.

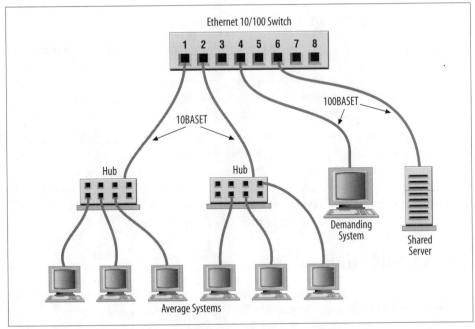

Figure 13-1. Subdividing an Ethernet with switches

Before allocating the ports on your switch, evaluate what services are in demand, and who talks to whom. Then develop a plan that reduces the amount of traffic flowing over any segment. For example, if the demanding system on Port 4 uses lots of bandwidth because it is constantly talking to one of the systems on Port 1, all of the systems on Port 1 will suffer because of this traffic. The computer that the demanding system communicates with should be moved to one of the vacant ports or to the same port (4) as the demanding system. Use your switch to the greatest advantage by balancing the load.

Should you segment an old coaxial cable Ethernet by cutting the cable and joining it back together through a router or a bridge? No. If you have an old network that is finally reaching saturation, it is time to install a new network built on a more robust technology. A *shared media* network, a network where everyone is on the same cable (in this example, a coaxial cable Ethernet) is an accident waiting to happen. Design a network that a user cannot bring down by merely disconnecting his system, or even by accidentally cutting a wire in his office. Use unshielded twisted pair (UTP) cable, ideally Category 5 cable, to create a 10BaseT Ethernet or 100BaseT Fast Ethernet that wires equipment located in the user's office to a hub securely stored in a wire closet. The network components in the user's office should be sufficiently isolated from the network so that damage to those components does not damage the entire network. The new network will solve your collision problem and reduce the amount of hardware troubleshooting you are called upon to do.

Network Hardware Problems

Some of the tests discussed in this section can show a network hardware problem. If a hardware problem is indicated, contact the people responsible for the hardware. If the problem appears to be in a leased telephone line, contact the telephone company. If the problem appears to be in a wide area network, contact the management of that network. Don't sit on a problem expecting it to go away. It could easily get worse.

If the problem is in your local area network, you will have to handle it yourself. Some tools, such as the cable tester, can help. But frequently the only way to approach a hardware problem is by brute force—disconnecting pieces of hardware until you find the one causing the problem. It is most convenient to do this at the switch or hub. If you identify a device causing the problem, repair or replace it. Remember that the problem can be the cable itself, rather than any particular device.

Checking Routing

The "network unreachable" error message clearly indicates a routing problem. If the problem is in the local host's routing table, it is easy to detect and resolve. First, use netstat -nr and grep to see whether or not a valid route to your destination is installed in the routing table.* This example checks for a specific route to network 128.8.0.0:

```
% netstat -nr | grep '^128\.8\.'
128.8.0.0      26.20.0.16     UG     0    37     dnet0
```

This same test, run on a system that did not have this route in its routing table, would return no response at all. For example, a user reports that the "network is down" because he cannot ftp to *helios.metalab.unc.edu*, and a ping test returns the following results:

```
% ping -s helios.metalab.unc.edu 56 2
PING helios.metalab.unc.edu: 56 data bytes
sendto: Network is unreachable
ping: wrote helios.metalab.unc.edu 64 chars, ret=-1
sendto: Network is unreachable
ping: wrote helios.metalab.unc.edu 64 chars, ret=-1

----helios.metalab.unc.edu PING Statistics----
2 packets transmitted, 0 packets received, 100% packet loss
```

---

* netstat -nr works on most systems, but Linux administrators prefer route -n.

Based on the "network unreachable" error message, check the user's routing table. In our example, we're looking for a route to *helios.metalab.unc.edu*. The IP address[*] of *helios.metalab.unc.edu* is 152.2.210.81. So we check for any route to a destination that begins with 152.2:

```
% netstat -nr | grep '^152\.2\.'
%
```

This test shows that there is no *specific* route to a destination that begins with 152.2. If a route was found, grep would display it. Since there's no specific route to the destination, remember to look for a default route. This example shows a successful check for a default route on a Solaris system:[†]

```
% netstat -nr | grep def
default       172.16.12.1    UG   0   101277   dnet0
```

If netstat shows the correct specific route or a valid default route, the problem is not in the routing table. In that case, use traceroute, as described in the next section, to trace the route all the way to its destination.

If the routing table doesn't contain the expected route, it's a local routing problem. There are two ways to approach local routing problems, depending on whether the system uses static or dynamic routing. If you're using static routing, install the missing route using the route add command. Remember, most systems that use static routing rely on a default route, so the missing route could be the default route. Make sure that the startup files add the needed route to the table whenever the system reboots. See Chapter 7 for details about the route add command.

If you're using dynamic routing, make sure that the routing program is running. For example, the command below makes sure that gated is running:

```
% ps 'cat /etc/gated.pid'
  PID TT STAT  TIME COMMAND
27711 ?  S   304:59 gated -tep /etc/log/gated.log
```

If the correct routing daemon is not running, restart it and specify tracing. Tracing allows you to check for problems that might be causing the daemon to terminate abnormally.

Tracing Routes

If the local routing table is correct, the problem may be occurring some distance away from the local host. Remote routing problems can cause the "no answer" error message, as well as the "network unreachable" error message. But the "network unreachable" message does not always signify a routing problem. It can mean that

---

[*] Use nslookup to find the IP address if you don't know it. nslookup is discussed later in this chapter.

[†] On a Linux system, grep for network 0.0.0.0, which Linux uses instead of the word "default" to indicate the default route.

the remote network cannot be reached because something is down between the local host and the remote destination. traceroute is the program that can help you locate these problems.

traceroute traces the route of UDP packets from the local host to a remote host. It prints the name (if it can be determined) and IP address of each gateway along the route to the remote host.

traceroute uses two techniques, small TTL (time-to-live) values and an invalid port number, to trace packets to their destination. traceroute sends out UDP packets with small TTL values to detect the intermediate gateways. The TTL values start at 1 and increase in increments of 1 for each group of three UDP packets sent. When a gateway receives a packet, it decrements the TTL. If the TTL is then 0, the packet is not forwarded and an ICMP "Time Exceeded" message is returned to the source of the packet. traceroute displays one line of output for each gateway from which it receives a "Time Exceeded" message. Figure 13-2 presents a sample of the single line of output that is displayed for a gateway, and shows the meaning of each field in the line.

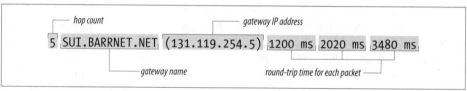

Figure 13-2. traceroute output

When the destination host receives a packet from traceroute, it returns an ICMP "Unreachable Port" message. This happens because traceroute intentionally uses an invalid port number (33434) to force this error. When traceroute receives the "Unreachable Port" message, it knows that it has reached the destination host, and it terminates the trace. So, traceroute is able to develop a list of the gateways, starting at one hop away and increasing one hop at a time until the remote host is reached. Figure 13-3 illustrates the flow of packets tracing to a host three hops away. The following shows a traceroute to *www.internic.net* from a Solaris system hanging off the Comcast network. traceroute sends out three packets at each TTL value. If no response is received to a packet, traceroute prints an asterisk (*). If a response is received, traceroute displays the name and address of the gateway that responded and the packet's round trip time in milliseconds.

```
$ traceroute www.internic.net
traceroute to www.internic.net (207.151.159.3), 30 hops max, 40 byte packets
 1 ani (192.168.0.1)  1.712 ms  1.40 ms  1.34 ms
 2 10.81.130.1 (10.81.130.1)  52.01 ms  34.38 ms  118.97 ms
 3 bb1-fe1-0.mtgmry1.md.home.net (24.11.248.1) 13.30 ms 100.92 ms 31.99 ms
 4 c2-se9-0-10.washdc1.home.net (24.7.73.25) 118.63 ms 94.92 ms 121.10 ms
 5 24.7.71.6 (24.7.71.6) 127.63 ms  26.29 ms  132.07 ms
 6 p4-6-1-0.r00.plalca01.us.bb.verio.net (129.250.2.245) 186.02 ms 164.81 ms 156.44
ms
```

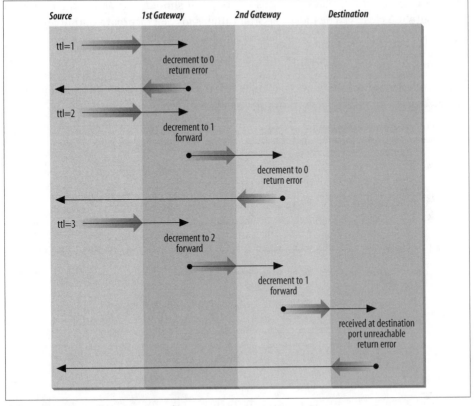

Source   1st Gateway   2nd Gateway   Destination

ttl=1

decrement to 0
return error

ttl=2

decrement to 1
forward

decrement to 0
return error

ttl=3

decrement to 2
forward

decrement to 1
forward

received at destination
port unreachable
return error

Figure 13-3. Flow of traceroute packets

```
     7 p16-0-0-0.r06.plalca01.us.bb.verio.net (129.250.2.161) 86.59 ms 130.28 ms 121.09
ms
     8 p16-0-0-0.r04.snjsca03.us.bb.verio.net (129.250.3.162) 84.594 ms 117.42 ms 174.59
ms
     9 p16-3-0-0.r01.snjsca03.us.bb.verio.net (129.250.2.63) 123.87 ms 91.39 ms 119.79 ms
    10 p4-2-0-0.r00.lsanca01.us.bb.verio.net (129.250.2.26) 142.38 ms 166.11 ms 95.32 ms
    11 ge-0-0-0.a02.lsanca02.us.ra.verio.net (129.250.29.116) 137.59 ms 98.28 ms 256.11
ms
    12 uscisi-pl.customer.ni.net (209.189.66.66) 98.64 ms 125.03 ms 231.11 ms
    13 207.151.151.2 (207.151.151.2) 192.06 ms 164.52 ms 103.30 ms
    14 icann-IWC.interworld.net (206.124.230.170) 113.33 ms 145.72 ms 107.39 ms
    15 * host159-3.icann.org (207.151.159.3) 99.67 ms 178.72 ms
```

This trace shows that 15 intermediate gateways are involved, that packets are making the trip, and that round trip travel time for packets from this host to *www.internic.net* is about 140 ms.

Variations and bugs in the implementation of ICMP on different types of gateways, as well as the unpredictable nature of the path a datagram can take through a network, can cause some odd displays. For this reason, you shouldn't examine the output of traceroute too closely. The most important things in the traceroute output are:

- Did the packet get to its remote destination?
- If not, where did it stop?

In the code below we show another trace of the path to *www.internic.net*. This time the trace does not go all the way through to the InterNIC.

```
$ traceroute www.internic.net
traceroute to www.internic.net (207.151.159.3), 30 hops max, 40 byte packets
 1 ani (192.168.0.1)  1.712 ms  1.40 ms  1.34 ms
 2 10.81.130.1 (10.81.130.1)  52.01 ms  34.38 ms  118.97 ms
 3 bb1-fe1-0.mtgmry1.md.home.net (24.11.248.1) 13.30 ms 100.92 ms 31.99 ms
 4 c2-se9-0-10.washdc1.home.net (24.7.73.25) 118.63 ms 94.92 ms 121.10 ms
 5 24.7.71.6 (24.7.71.6) 127.63 ms  26.29 ms  132.07 ms
 6 p4-6-1-0.r00.plalca01.us.bb.verio.net (129.250.2.245) 186.02 ms 164.81 ms 156.44
ms
 7 p16-0-0-0.r06.plalca01.us.bb.verio.net (129.250.2.161) 86.59 ms 130.28 ms 121.09
ms
 8 p16-0-0-0.r04.snjsca03.us.bb.verio.net (129.250.3.162) 84.594 ms 117.42 ms 174.59
ms
 9  * * *
10  * * *

     .
     .
     .
29  * * *
30  * * *
```

When traceroute fails to get packets through to the remote end system, the trace trails off, displaying a series of three asterisks at each hop count until the count reaches 30. If this happens, contact the administrator of the remote host you're trying to reach, and the administrator of the last gateway displayed in the trace. Describe the problem to them; they may be able to help. In our example, the last gateway that responded to our packets was *p16-0-0-0.r04.snjsca03.us.bb.verio.net*. We would therefore contact this system administrator and the administrator of *www.internic.net*.

Locating an Administrator

To contact a remote administrator, you must know who to contact. whois helps you locate important people. One of the most important pieces of information in a network is who is in charge at the other end. When troubleshooting a network problem, whois is a tool that helps you find this out.

whois obtains the requested information from the Internet white pages. The white pages is a database of information about responsible people that is maintained by the Internet registrars. When you request an official network number or domain name, you are asked to provide contact information, which becomes your personal record in the white pages database. Because of this, everyone who is responsible for an official network or domain is supposed to have an entry in the white pages, and that entry can be retrieved by anyone who needs to contact them.

Many Unix systems provide a whois command to query the white pages. The general form of this command is:

```
% whois [-h server] name
```

The *name* field is the information to be searched for in the white pages database. The *server* field is the name of a system containing the white pages.

In the following example, we search for contact information for the *verio.net* domain, which is the domain where the remote router from the traceroute example is located.

```
$ whois verio.net
[whois.crsnic.net]

Whois Server Version 1.3

Domain names in the .com, .net, and .org domains can now be registered
with many different competing registrars. Go to http://www.internic.net
for detailed information.

   Domain Name: VERIO.NET
   Registrar: MELBOURNE IT, LTD. D/B/A INTERNET NAMES WORLDWIDE
   Whois Server: whois.inww.com
   Referral URL: http://www.inww.com
   Name Server: NS0.VERIO.NET
   Name Server: NS1.VERIO.NET
   Name Server: NS2.VERIO.NET
   Updated Date: 13-jun-2001


>>> Last update of whois database: Tue, 17 Jul 2001 02:04:28 EDT <<<

The Registry database contains ONLY .COM, .NET, .ORG, .EDU domains and
Registrars.


[whois.inww.com]

Domain Name......... verio.net
   Creation Date....... 1996-12-07
   Registration Date.... 2000-05-10
   Expiry Date......... 2001-12-06
   Organisation Name.... Verio, Inc.
   Organisation Address. 8005 South Chester Street
   Organisation Address. Suite 200
   Organisation Address. Englewood
   Organisation Address. CO
   Organisation Address. 80112
   Organisation Address. UNITED STATES
```

```
Admin Name.......... Hostmaster Verio
   Admin Address........ 8005 South Chester Street
   Admin Address........ Suite 200
   Admin Address........ Englewood
   Admin Address........ 80112
   Admin Address........ CO
   Admin Address........ UNITED STATES
   Admin Email.......... DomainAdmin@verio.net
   Admin Phone.......... 214 290 8620
   Admin Fax............ .

Tech Name........... Hostmaster Verio
   Tech Address........ 8005 South Chester Street
   Tech Address........ Suite 200
   Tech Address........ Englewood
   Tech Address........ CO
   Tech Address........ 80112
   Tech Address........ UNITED STATES
   Tech Email.......... hostmaster@verio.net
   Tech Phone.......... 214 290 8620
   Tech Fax............ .
   Name Server......... NS0.VERIO.NET
   Name Server......... NS1.VERIO.NET
   Name Server......... NS2.VERIO.NET
```

The query displays the name, address, and telephone number of the contacts for the domain, as well as a list of hosts providing authoritative name service for the domain. This example shows how it is supposed to work, and for substantial, well-run networks such as *verio.net*, it usually does. Unfortunately, many whois queries return no useful information because the white pages database is poorly maintained. If whois provides no information, try checking DNS name service. The DNS SOA record should contain a mailing address for a domain contact who may be able to point you to the right system administrator.

Checking Name Service

Name server problems are indicated when the "unknown host" error message is returned by the user's application. Name server problems can usually be diagnosed with nslookup or dig. nslookup is discussed in detail in Chapter 8; dig is an alternative tool with similar functionality and is discussed in this chapter. Before looking at dig, let's take another look at nslookup and see how it is used to troubleshoot name service.

The three features of nslookup covered in Chapter 8 are particularly important for troubleshooting remote name server problems. These features are its ability to:

- Locate the authoritative servers for the remote domain using the NS query
- Obtain all records about the remote host using the ANY query
- Browse all entries in the remote zone using nslookup's ls and view commands

When troubleshooting a remote server problem, directly query the authoritative servers returned by the NS query. Don't rely on information returned by non-authoritative servers. If the problems that have been reported are intermittent, query all of the authoritative servers in turn and compare their answers. Intermittent name server problems are sometimes caused by the remote servers returning different answers to the same query.

The ANY query returns all records about a host, thus giving the broadest range of troubleshooting information. Simply knowing what information is (and isn't) available can solve a lot of problems. For example, if the query returns an MX record but no A record, it is easy to understand why the user couldn't telnet to that host! Many hosts are accessible to mail that are not accessible by other network services. In this case, the user is confused and is trying to use the remote host in an inappropriate manner.

If you are unable to locate any information about the hostname that the user gave you, perhaps the hostname is incorrect. Given that the hostname you have is wrong, looking for the correct name is like trying to find a needle in a haystack. However, nslookup can help. Use nslookup's ls command to dump the remote zone file, and redirect the listing to a file. Then use nslookup's view command to browse through the file, looking for names similar to the one the user supplied. Many problems are caused by a mistaken hostname.

All of the nslookup features and commands mentioned here are used in Chapter 8. However, some examples using these commands to solve real name server problems will be helpful. The three examples that follow are based on actual trouble reports.*

Some Systems Work, Others Don't

A user reported that she could resolve a certain hostname from her workstation, but could not resolve the same hostname from the central system. However, the central system could resolve other hostnames. We ran several tests and found that we could resolve the hostname on some systems and not on others. There seemed to be no predictable pattern to the failure. So we used nslookup to check the remote servers:

```
% nslookup
Default Server:  crab.wrotethebook.com
Address:  172.16.12.1

> set type=NS
> foo.edu.
Server:  crab.wrotethebook.com
Address:  172.16.12.1

foo.edu        nameserver = gerbil.foo.edu
```

---

* The host and server names are fictitious, but the problems were real.

```
foo.edu          nameserver = red.big.com
foo.edu          nameserver = shrew.foo.edu
gerbil.foo.edu   inet address = 198.97.99.2
red.big.com   inet address = 184.6.16.2
shrew.foo.edu    inet address = 198.97.99.1
> set type=ANY
> server gerbil.foo.edu
Default Server:  gerbil.foo.edu
Address:  198.97.99.2

> hamster.foo.edu
Server:  gerbil.foo.edu
Address:  198.97.99.2

hamster.foo.edu          inet address = 198.97.99.8
> server red.big.com
Default Server:  red.big.com
Address:  184.6.16.2
> hamster.foo.edu
Server:  red.big.com
Address:  184.6.16.2
*** red.big.com can't find hamster.foo.edu: Non-existent domain
```

This sample nslookup session contains several steps. The first step is to locate the authoritative servers for the hostname in question (*hamster.foo.edu*). We set the query type to NS to get the name server records, and query for the domain (*foo.edu*) in which the hostname is found. This returns three names of authoritative servers: *gerbil.foo.edu*, *red.big.com*, and *shrew.foo.edu*.

Next, we set the query type to ANY to look for any records related to the hostname in question. Then we set the server to the first server in the list, *gerbil.foo.edu*, and query for *hamster.foo.edu*. This returns an address record. So server *gerbil.foo.edu* works fine. We repeat the test using *red.big.com* as the server, and it fails. No records are returned.

The next step is to get SOA records from each server and see if they are the same:

```
> set type=SOA
> foo.edu.
Server:  red.big.com
Address:  184.6.16.2

foo.edu          origin = gerbil.foo.edu
   mail addr = amanda.gerbil.foo.edu
    serial=10164, refresh=43200, retry=3600, expire=3600000,
    min=2592000
> server gerbil.foo.edu
Default Server:  gerbil.foo.edu
Address:  198.97.99.2

> foo.edu.
Server:  gerbil.foo.edu
Address:  198.97.99.2
```

```
foo.edu        origin = gerbil.foo.edu
    mail addr = amanda.gerbil.foo.edu
    serial=10164, refresh=43200, retry=3600, expire=3600000,
    min=2592000
> exit
```

If the SOA records have different serial numbers, perhaps the zone file, and therefore the hostname, has not yet been downloaded to the slave server. If the serial numbers are the same and the data is different, as in this case, there is a definite problem. Contact the remote domain administrator and notify her of the problem. The administrator's mailing address is shown in the "mail addr" field of the SOA record. In our example, we would send mail to *amanda@gerbil.foo.edu* reporting the problem.

The Data Is Here and the Server Can't Find It!

This problem was reported by the administrator of one of our slave name servers. The administrator reported that his server could not resolve a certain hostname in a domain for which his server was a slave server. The master server was, however, able to resolve the name. The administrator dumped his cache (more on dumping the server cache in the next section), and he could see in the dump that his server had the correct entry for the host. But his server still would not resolve that hostname to an IP address!

The problem was replicated on several other slave servers. The master server would resolve the name; the slave servers wouldn't. All servers had the same SOA serial number, and a dump of the cache on each server showed that they all had the correct address records for the hostname in question. So why wouldn't they resolve the hostname to an address?

Visualizing the difference between the way master and slave servers load their data made us suspicious of the zone file transfer. Master servers load the data directly from local disk files. Slave servers transfer the data from the master server via a zone file transfer. Perhaps the zone files were getting corrupted. We displayed the zone file on one of the slave servers, and it showed the following data:

```
% cat /usr/etc/events.wrotethebook.com.hosts
PCpma    IN   A       172.16.64.159
         IN   HINFO   "pc" "n3/800eventsnutscom"
PCrkc    IN   A       172.16.64.155
         IN   HINFO   "pc" "n3/800eventsnutscom"
PCafc    IN   A       172.16.64.189
         IN   HINFO   "pc" "n3/800eventsnutscom"
accu     IN   A       172.16.65.27
cmgds1   IN   A       172.16.130.40
cmg      IN   A       172.16.130.30
PCgns    IN   A       172.16.64.167
         IN   HINFO   "pc" "(3/800eventsnutscom"
gw       IN   A       172.16.65.254
zephyr   IN   A       172.16.64.188
```

```
                  IN   HINFO   "Sun" "sparcstation"
       ejw        IN   A       172.16.65.17
       PCecp      IN   A       172.16.64.193
                  IN   HINFO   "pc" "n Lsparcstationstcom"
```

Notice the odd display in the last field of the HINFO statement for each PC.[*] This data might have been corrupted in the transfer or it might be bad on the master server. We used nslookup to check that:

```
% nslookup
Default Server:  crab.wrotethebook.com
Address:   172.16.12.1

> server 24seven.events.wrotethebook.com
Default Server:  24seven.events.wrotethebook.com
Address:   172.16.6.1

> set query=HINFO
> PCwlg.events.wrotethebook.com
Server:  24seven.events.wrotethebook.com
Address:   172.16.6.1

PCwlg.events.wrotethebook.com     CPU=pc  OS=ov
packet size error (0xf7fff590 != 0xf7fff528)
> exit
```

In this nslookup example, we set the server to *24seven.events.wrotethebook.com*, which is the master server for *events.wrotethebook.com*. Next we queried for the HINFO record for one of the hosts that appeared to have a corrupted record. The "packet size error" message clearly indicates that nslookup was even having trouble retrieving the HINFO record directly from the master server. We contacted the administrator of the master server and told him about the problem, pointing out the records that appeared to be in error. He discovered that he had forgotten to put an operating system entry on some of the HINFO records. He corrected this, and it fixed the problem.

Cache Corruption

The previous problem was caused by the name server cache being corrupted by bad data. Cache corruption can occur even if your system is not a slave server. All servers cache answers. If those answers are corrupted, entries in the cache may become corrupted. Dumping the cache can help diagnose these types of problems.

For example, a user reported intermittent name server failures. She had no trouble with any hostnames within the local domain or with some names outside the local domain, but names in several different remote domains would not resolve. nslookup tests produced no solid clues, so the name server cache was dumped and examined

---

[*] See Appendix C for a detailed description of the HINFO statement.

for problems. The root server entries were corrupted, so named was reloaded to clear the cache and reread the *named.ca* file. Here's how it was done.

The ndc dumpdb command or the SIGINT signal causes named to dump the name server cache to the file */var/tmp/named_dump.db*. The following example uses the signal:

```
# kill -INT 'cat /etc/named.pid'
```

The process ID of named can be obtained from */etc/named.pid*, as in the example above, because named writes its process ID in that file during startup.[*]

Once named writes its cache to the file, we can examine the file to see if the names and addresses servers are correct. The *named_dump.db* file is composed of three sections: the zone table section, the Cache & Data section, and the Hints section.

The zone table section

The first section of the dump file is the zone table, which shows the zones loaded when the server started. The zone table from the master server for zones *wrotethebook.com* and *16.172.in-addr.arpa* would show the following:

```
; Dumped at Tue Jul 17 16:08:18 2001
;; ++zone table++
; . (type 6, class 0, source Nil)
;       time=0, lastupdate=0, serial=0,
;       refresh=0, retry=0, expire=0, minimum=0
;       ftime=0, xaddrcnt=0, state=0000, pid=0
; . (type 3, class 1, source named.ca)
;       time=0, lastupdate=965723221, serial=0,
;       refresh=0, retry=0, expire=0, minimum=4294967295
;       ftime=965723221, xaddrcnt=0, state=0040, pid=0
; 0.0.127.in-addr.arpa (type 1, class 1, source named.local)
;       time=0, lastupdate=0, serial=1997022700,
;       refresh=0, retry=14400, expire=3600000, minimum=86400
;       ftime=965723221, xaddrcnt=0, state=0041, pid=0
; wrotethebook.com (type 1, class 1, source wrotethebook.com.hosts)
;       time=0, lastupdate=0, serial=2001070501,
;       refresh=0, retry=1800, expire=604800, minimum=900
;       ftime=982967703, xaddrcnt=0, state=0041, pid=0
; 16.172.in-addr.arpa (type 1, class 1, source 172.16.rev)
;       time=0, lastupdate=0, serial=2001071602,
;       refresh=0, retry=1800, expire=604800, minimum=900
;       ftime=982968091, xaddrcnt=0, state=0041, pid=0
;; --zone table--
```

The section begins by displaying the date and time that the dump was taken. Labels at the start and end of the section delimit the zone table. As indicated by the fact that each line begins with a semicolon, all of these lines are comments meant to provide information to the system administrator. None of these are real database entries used

---

[*] On our Linux system the process ID is written to */var/run/named.pid*.

by DNS. From the example above, you can tell that this server has a zone statement in its *named.conf* file for the following domains:

. (dot)
> The root domain that was loaded from a source file called *named.ca*. This is the hints file described in Chapter 8.

0.0.127.in-addr.arpa
> The loopback domain that was loaded from the source file *named.local*.

wrotethebook.com
> The *wrotethebook.com* domain that was loaded from the *wrotethebook.com.hosts* source file.

16.172.in-addr.arpa
> The reverse domain *16.172.in-addr.arpa* that was loaded from the *172.16.rev* source file.

The values from the SOA record of each zone are also printed. In the sample shown above, every zone except the root (.) has an SOA record.

The zone table section identifies every zone for which the server has authority. It tells you where the server obtained the information about the zone, and it tells you what defaults are set for the zone by the SOA record. If a zone is missing or is loading from the wrong source, correct the zone statement in the *named.conf* file.

The Cache & Data section

The second section of the dump file is by far the longest. This is the section that contains all of the DNS information known to the server. Because of the section's length, the Cache & Data information shown below is just an excerpt:

```
; Note: Cr=(auth,answer,addtnl,cache) tag only shown for non-auth RR's
; Note: NT=milliseconds for any A RR which we've used as a nameserver
; --- Cache & Data ---
$ORIGIN .
  .     513482    IN    NS    H.ROOT-SERVERS.NET.    ;Cr=auth
        513482    IN    NS    C.ROOT-SERVERS.NET.    ;Cr=auth
        513482    IN    NS    G.ROOT-SERVERS.NET.    ;Cr=auth
        513482    IN    NS    F.ROOT-SERVERS.NET.    ;Cr=auth
        513482    IN    NS    B.ROOT-SERVERS.NET.    ;Cr=auth
        513482    IN    NS    J.ROOT-SERVERS.NET.    ;Cr=auth
        513482    IN    NS    K.ROOT-SERVERS.NET.    ;Cr=auth
        513482    IN    NS    L.ROOT-SERVERS.NET.    ;Cr=auth
        513482    IN    NS    M.ROOT-SERVERS.NET.    ;Cr=auth
        513482    IN    NS    I.ROOT-SERVERS.NET.    ;Cr=auth
        513482    IN    NS    E.ROOT-SERVERS.NET.    ;Cr=auth
        513482    IN    NS    D.ROOT-SERVERS.NET.    ;Cr=auth
        513482    IN    NS    A.ROOT-SERVERS.NET.    ;Cr=auth
... Many Lines Deleted ...
$ORIGIN ROOT-SERVERS.NET.
K    599882    IN    A    193.0.14.129    ;NT=9 Cr=answer
A    599882    IN    A    198.41.0.4      ;NT=10 Cr=answer
```

```
L     599882  IN   A     198.32.64.12    ;NT=5 Cr=answer
M     599882  IN   A     202.12.27.33    ;NT=15 Cr=answer
B     599882  IN   A     128.9.0.107     ;NT=5 Cr=answer
C     599882  IN   A     192.33.4.12     ;NT=165 Cr=answer
D     599882  IN   A     128.8.10.90     ;NT=12 Cr=answer
E     599882  IN   A     192.203.230.10   ;NT=6 Cr=answer
F     599882  IN   A     192.5.5.241     ;NT=1021 Cr=answer
G     599882  IN   A     192.112.36.4 ;NT=1023 Cr=answer
H     599882  IN   A     128.63.2.53     ;NT=6 Cr=answer
I     599882  IN   A     192.36.148.17    ;NT=7 Cr=answer
J     599882  IN   A     198.41.0.10     ;NT=6 Cr=answer
... Many Lines Deleted ...
$ORIGIN com.
foobirds 86400 IN RP admin.foobirds.org. hotline.foobirds.org. ;Cl=2
      86400   IN   MX    10 wren.foobirds.org.     ;Cl=2
      86400   IN   MX    20 parrot.foobirds.org.     ;Cl=2
      86400   IN   NS    wren.foobirds.org.     ;Cl=2
      86400   IN   NS    parrot.foobirds.org.    ;Cl=2
      86400   IN   SOA   wren.foobirds.org. admin.wren.foobirds.org. (
              2000020501 21600 1800 604800 900 )     ;Cl=2
$ORIGIN foobirds.org.
ducks    86400   IN   NS    ruddy.ducks.foobirds.org.    ;Cl=2
         86400   IN   NS    wren.foobirds.org.    ;Cl=2
         86400   IN   NS    bear.mammals.org.    ;Cl=2
news     86400   IN   CNAME    parrot.foobirds.org.    ;Cl=2
robin    86400   IN   RP    admin.foobirds.org. hotline.foobirds.org.    ;Cl=2
         86400   IN   MX    5 wren.foobirds.org.    ;Cl=2
         86400   IN   A     172.16.5.2    ;Cl=2
puffin   86400   IN   RP    admin.foobirds.org. hotline.foobirds.org.    ;Cl=2
         86400   IN   MX    5 wren.foobirds.org.    ;Cl=2
         86400   IN   A     172.16.5.17    ;Cl=2
wren     86400   IN   RP    admin.foobirds.org. hotline.foobirds.org.    ;Cl=2
         86400   IN   A     172.16.5.1    ;Cl=2
parrot   86400   IN   RP    logan.parrot.foobirds.org. logan.foobirds.org.    ;Cl=2
         86400   IN   A     172.16.5.3    ;Cl=2
logan    86400   IN   TXT   "Logan Little (301)555-2021"    ;Cl=2
crow     86400   IN   RP    doris.crow.foobirds.org.foobirds.org. crowRP.foobirds.
org.  ;Cl=2
         86400   IN   A     172.16.5.5    ;Cl=2
localhost  86400   IN   A    127.0.0.1    ;Cl=2
terns    86400   IN   NS    sooty.terns.foobirds.org.    ;Cl=2
         86400   IN   NS    arctic.terns.foobirds.org.    ;Cl=2
www      86400   IN   CNAME    wren.foobirds.org.    ;Cl=2
hotline  86400   IN   TXT   "Support hotline (301)555-2000"    ;Cl=2
bob      86400   IN   CNAME    robin.foobirds.org.    ;Cl=2
redbreast  86400   IN   CNAME    robin.foobirds.org.    ;Cl=2
hawkRP   86400   IN   TXT   "Clark Smart (301)555-2099"    ;Cl=2
kestrel  86400   IN   RP    clark.foobirds.org.foobirds.org. hawkRP.foobirds.org.
;Cl=2
         86400   IN   A     172.16.5.20    ;Cl=2
crowRP   86400   IN   TXT   "Doris Nathan (301)555-2078"    ;Cl=2
kestral  86400   IN   CNAME    kestrel.foobirds.org.    ;Cl=2
hawk     86400   IN   RP    clark.foobirds.org.foobirds.org. hawkRP.foobirds.org.
;Cl=2
```

```
            86400    IN    A    172.16.5.4    ;Cl=2
foobirds-net    86400    IN    PTR    0.0.16.172.in-addr.arpa.    ;Cl=2
$ORIGIN terns.foobirds.org.
arctic   86400    IN    A    172.16.30.251    ;Cl=2
sooty    86400    IN    A    172.16.30.250    ;Cl=2
$ORIGIN 172.in-addr.arpa.
16       86400    IN    NS    wren.foobirds.org.    ;Cl=4
         86400    IN    SOA    wren.foobirds.org. admin.wren.foobirds.org. (
         2000021602 21600 1800 604800 900 )    ;Cl=4
$ORIGIN 6.16.172.in-addr.arpa.
1        86400    IN    PTR    arctic.terns.foobirds.org.    ;Cl=4
$ORIGIN 12.16.172.in-addr.arpa.
3        86400    IN    PTR    wren.foobirds.org.    ;Cl=4
$ORIGIN 5.16.172.in-addr.arpa.
20       86400    IN    PTR    kestrel.foobirds.org.    ;Cl=4
4        86400    IN    PTR    hawk.foobirds.org.    ;Cl=4
2        86400    IN    PTR    robin.foobirds.org.    ;Cl=4
17       86400    IN    PTR    puffin.foobirds.org.    ;Cl=4
5        86400    IN    PTR    crow.foobirds.org.    ;Cl=4
3        86400    IN    PTR    parrot.foobirds.org.    ;Cl=4
$ORIGIN 0.127.in-addr.arpa.
0        86400    IN    NS    localhost.    ;Cl=5
         86400    IN    SOA    localhost. root.localhost. (
         1997022700 28800 14400 3600000 86400 )    ;Cl=5
$ORIGIN 0.0.127.in-addr.arpa.
1        86400    IN    PTR    localhost.    ;Cl=5
```

The example is long even though the dump was taken shortly after the server started, and many lines have been deleted from the listing. The bulk of the data shown is information loaded from the local zone files, but a dump file also contains a good deal of cached information. Large chunks of the cache are the result of information provided in the authority and additional sections of the query responses. At least as much data enters the cache in this manner as enters as a result of specific answers to queries. The large number of NS entries and the A records for those NS entries make this clear.

The Cache & Data section is segmented by $ORIGIN directives. All of the other lines in this section are clearly identifiable DNS resource records. But some additional information is appended to the end of each record as a comment. Three comments that the server commonly adds to a record include the following:

Cl

> Identifies the number of fields in the current origin. Therefore, when the origin is *0.0.127.in-addr.arpa*, the Cl value is 5, and when the origin is *wrotethebook.com*, the Cl value is 2. The root (.) is assigned a Cl value of 0.

Nt

> The round trip time for queries to the specified name server. This comment is added only to the address records of name servers. The round trip time helps named select the best server for a given query.

Cr

The "credibility" tag identifies the authority level of the source of cached information. BIND has three authority levels:

auth

An authoritative answer.

answer

An answer from a non-authoritative source.

addtnl

A record learned from the authority or additional section of a query response.

The Cr value is used by named when a record is received that already exists in the name server's cache. If the record received has a higher credibility rating than the record in the cache, the new record replaces the cached record. If the new record has a lower credibility rating than the record in the cache, the cached record is retained. Of the Cr values, auth is the most credible and addtnl is the least credible.

The comments at the end of a record are not the only comments that you might see in the Cache & Data section of a dump file. Negative cached information also appears in the dump as a comment. There are no examples of this in our sample dump file, but if there were, you would see a normal resource record that starts with a semicolon. In other words, the negative cached information appears as a resource record that has been commented out of the file. Additionally, the tag NXDOMAIN is written near the end of the record.

Examine the Cache & Data section to discover if the data you entered in your zone file has been loaded as you expect. Also use this section to see if the information you have loaded from a remote server is what you expect. Local data can be corrected locally. Incorrect data from a remote server may require coordination with the administrator of a remote domain.

The Hints section

The last section in the dump file is the Hints section. This section contains the list of root name servers loaded from the hints file. (Defining and using the hints file is discussed in Chapter 8.) This hints file is used only when the name server starts. Once the server starts, one of the root servers is queried for an authoritative list of root servers. It is the authoritative list obtained from the root server that you see in the Cache & Data section following the $ORIGIN . statement.

The Hints section from our sample system is shown below. Notice that all of the name servers in the Hints section have an Nt number assigned. named queries each server to establish a round trip time to select the best root server to use.

```
; --- Hints ---
$ORIGIN .
```

```
.           3600000    IN    NS    A.ROOT-SERVERS.NET.      ;Cl=0
            3600000    IN    NS    B.ROOT-SERVERS.NET.      ;Cl=0
            3600000    IN    NS    C.ROOT-SERVERS.NET.      ;Cl=0
            3600000    IN    NS    D.ROOT-SERVERS.NET.      ;Cl=0
            3600000    IN    NS    E.ROOT-SERVERS.NET.      ;Cl=0
            3600000    IN    NS    F.ROOT-SERVERS.NET.      ;Cl=0
            3600000    IN    NS    G.ROOT-SERVERS.NET.      ;Cl=0
            3600000    IN    NS    H.ROOT-SERVERS.NET.      ;Cl=0
            3600000    IN    NS    I.ROOT-SERVERS.NET.      ;Cl=0
            3600000    IN    NS    J.ROOT-SERVERS.NET.      ;Cl=0
            3600000    IN    NS    K.ROOT-SERVERS.NET.      ;Cl=0
            3600000    IN    NS    L.ROOT-SERVERS.NET.      ;Cl=0
            3600000    IN    NS    M.ROOT-SERVERS.NET.      ;Cl=0
$ORIGIN ROOT-SERVERS.NET.
K       3600000    IN    A    193.0.14.129      ;NT=2 Cl=0
L       3600000    IN    A    198.32.64.12      ;NT=5 Cl=0
A       3600000    IN    A    198.41.0.4        ;NT=6 Cl=0
M       3600000    IN    A    202.12.27.33      ;NT=10 Cl=0
B       3600000    IN    A    128.9.0.107       ;NT=134 Cl=0
C       3600000    IN    A    192.33.4.12       ;NT=8 Cl=0
D       3600000    IN    A    128.8.10.90       ;NT=24 Cl=0
E       3600000    IN    A    192.203.230.10    ;NT=2 Cl=0
F       3600000    IN    A    192.5.5.241       ;NT=22 Cl=0
G       3600000    IN    A    192.112.36.4      ;NT=2 Cl=0
H       3600000    IN    A    128.63.2.53       ;NT=22 Cl=0
I       3600000    IN    A    192.36.148.17     ;NT=2 Cl=0
J       3600000    IN    A    198.41.0.10       ;Cl=0
```

The purpose of dumping the DNS cache is to examine what data is stored internally by DNS and how it is stored. Examining the authoritative information that you provide to the server in the zone files will give you insight into how that data is being stored. Examining the other data in the cache shows you how your users use DNS. Learning how DNS is normally used can help identify when usage patterns change.

If you see problems in the dump file, force named to reload its cache with the ndc reload command (on BIND 9, use rndc reload), or with the SIGHUP signal as shown below:

```
# kill -HUP 'cat /etc/named.pid'
```

This clears the cache and reloads the valid root server entries from your *named.ca* file.

If you know which system is corrupting your cache, instruct your system to ignore updates from the culprit by using a server statement in the */etc/named.conf* file with the bogus option set to yes. The server statement lists the IP address of a name server. Setting bogus to yes in the server statement tells named that information from that server cannot be trusted. For example, the previous section described a problem where *24seven.events.wrotethebook.com* (172.16.16.1) was causing cache corruption with improperly formatted HINFO records. The following entry in the *named.conf* file would reject answers from *24seven.events.wrotethebook.com* and thus prevent the cache corruption:

```
server 172.16.16.1 {
    bogus yes;
};
```

Setting bogus to yes is only a temporary measure, designed to keep things running while the remote domain administrator has a chance to diagnose and repair the problem. Once the remote system is fixed, remove the server statement from *named.conf*.

dig: An Alternative to nslookup

An alternative to nslookup for making name service queries is dig. dig queries are usually entered as single-line commands, while nslookup is usually run as an interactive session. But the dig command performs essentially the same function as nslookup. Which you use is mostly a matter of personal choice. They both work well.

As an example, we'll use dig to ask the root server *b.root-servers.net* for the NS records for the *mit.edu* domain. To do this, enter the following command:

```
% dig @b.root-servers.net mit.edu ns
```

In this example, *@b.root-servers.net* is the server that is being queried. The server can be identified by name or IP address. If you're troubleshooting a problem in a remote domain, specify an authoritative server for that domain. In this example we're asking for the names of servers for a top-level domain (*mit.edu*), so we ask a root server.

If you don't specify a server explicitly, dig uses the local name server or the name server defined in the */etc/resolv.conf* file. (Chapter 8 describes *resolv.conf*.) Optionally, you can set the environment variable LOCALRES to the name of an alternate *resolv.conf* file. This alternate file will then be used in place of */etc/resolv.conf* for dig queries. Setting the LOCALRES variable will affect only dig. Other programs that use name service will continue to use */etc/resolv.conf*.

The last item on our sample command line is *ns*. This is the query type. A query type is a value that requests a specific type of DNS information. It is similar to the value used in nslookup's set type command. Table 13-1 shows the possible dig query types and their meanings.

Table 13-1. dig query types

Query type	DNS record requested
a	Address records
any	Any type of record
mx	Mail Exchange records
ns	Name Server records
soa	Start of Authority records
hinfo	Host Info records
axfr	All records in the zone
txt	Text records

Notice that the function of nslookup's ls command is performed by the dig query type axfr.

dig also has an option that is useful for locating a hostname when you have only an IP address. If you have only the IP address of a host, you may want to find out the hostname because numeric addresses are more prone to typos. Having the hostname can reduce the user's problems. The *in-addr.arpa* domain converts addresses to hostnames, and dig provides a simple way to enter *in-addr.arpa* domain queries. Using the -x option, you can query for a number-to-name conversion without having to manually reverse the numbers and add "in-addr.arpa." For example, to query for the hostname of IP address 18.72.0.3, simply enter:

```
% dig -x 18.72.0.3

; <<>> DiG 2.2 <<>> -x
;; res options: init recurs defnam dnsrch
;; got answer:
;; ->>HEADER<<- opcode: QUERY, status: NOERROR, id: 4
;; flags: qr aa rd ra; QUERY: 1, ANSWER: 1, AUTHORITY: 3, ADDITIONAL: 3
;; QUERY SECTION:
;;      3.0.72.18.in-addr.arpa, type = ANY, class = IN

;; ANSWER SECTION:
3.0.72.18.in-addr.arpa.  6H IN PTR  BITSY.MIT.EDU.

;; AUTHORITY SECTION:
18.in-addr.arpa.      6H IN NS      W2ONS.MIT.EDU.
18.in-addr.arpa.      6H IN NS      BITSY.MIT.EDU.
18.in-addr.arpa.      6H IN NS      STRAWB.MIT.EDU.

;; ADDITIONAL SECTION:
W2ONS.MIT.EDU.        6H IN A       18.70.0.160
BITSY.MIT.EDU.        6H IN A       18.72.0.3
STRAWB.MIT.EDU.       6H IN A       18.71.0.151

;; Total query time: 367 msec
;; FROM: wren.foobirds.org to SERVER: default -- 0.0.0.0
;; WHEN: Thu Jul 19 16:00:39 2001
;; MSG SIZE  sent: 40  rcvd: 170
```

The answer to our query is BITSY.MIT.EDU, but dig displays lots of other output. For the purposes of this specific query, the only important information is the answer.* However, the additional information displayed by dig is useful for gaining an insight into the format of a DNS response packet and for learning where the various pieces of DNS information come from.

---

* To see a single-line answer to this query, pipe dig's output to grep; e.g., dig -x 18.72.0.3 | grep PTR.

The format of the DNS message is defined in RFC 1035, *Domain Names – Implementation and Specification*. The RFC defines a standard message format composed of up to five parts:

Header
Provides administrative information about the message, including information about what is contained in subsequent sections of the message.

Question
Defines the question being asked by a query. When the question section is returned in a response, it is used to help determine which question the response is answering.

Answer
The part of a response that contains the answer to the specific question sent in the query.

Authority
Contains pointers to the authoritative servers for the domain being queried.

Additional
Contains other resource records that provide additional, important information that supports the answer. This is not the answer to the query, but it helps in interpreting or utilizing the answer.

The core of the output of the dig command is found in the various sections from the DNS response packet. The header data from the example above is:

```
;; ->>HEADER<<- opcode: QUERY, status: NOERROR, id: 4
;; flags: qr aa rd ra; QUERY: 1, ANSWER: 1, AUTHORITY: 3, ADDITIONAL: 3
```

dig does not display the header data in the order in which it occurs in the header section, but it is easy to map the dig display to the header described in RFC 1035. The various values displayed in the example and their meanings are listed here:

opcode: QUERY
Indicates that this is a standard query.

status: NOERROR
Indicates that no error code was found in the RCODE field of the header, which means that the RCODE field contains a 0.

id: 6
Indicates that the identifier used for this message was the number 6.

flags: qr aa rd ra
flags groups together all of the one-bit fields from the header. In this case it covers four different fields in the header section and gives us information about three others. This flag group means that QR is set to 1, indicating this is a response. AA is set to 1 because this answer came from an authoritative server. RD is set to 1 to indicate that recursion was requested by the query. RA is set to

1, indicating that recursion is available on the server. TC is not listed, meaning it is set to 0 and that the response was not truncated. AD and CD are also set to 0 because DNSSEC is not in use.

QUERY: 1, ANSWER: 1, AUTHORITY: 3, ADDITIONAL: 3

These represent the header fields QDCOUNT, ANCOUNT, NSCOUNT, and ARCOUNT, which indicate the number of resource records in the remaining sections of the response. This display says that there is one entry in the question section, one resource record in the answer section, three records in the authority section, and three records in the additional section.

The sample dig command displays the following query data:

```
;; QUERY SECTION:
;;      3.0.72.18.in-addr.arpa, type = ANY, class = IN
```

The three fields of this query are clearly shown. The class field is IN because this is a query for Internet records. The query is asking for any record (type = any) associated with *3.0.72.18.in-addr.arpa*. Notice how dig reversed the address and created the proper reverse domain name for this query.

Next, the dig command displays the answer, authority, and additional sections:

```
;; ANSWER SECTION:
3.0.72.18.in-addr.arpa.  6H IN PTR  BITSY.MIT.EDU.

;; AUTHORITY SECTION:
18.in-addr.arpa.      6H IN NS      W20NS.MIT.EDU.
18.in-addr.arpa.      6H IN NS      BITSY.MIT.EDU.
18.in-addr.arpa.      6H IN NS      STRAWB.MIT.EDU.

;; ADDITIONAL SECTION:
W20NS.MIT.EDU.        6H IN A       18.70.0.160
BITSY.MIT.EDU.        6H IN A       18.72.0.3
STRAWB.MIT.EDU.       6H IN A       18.71.0.151
```

The answer is just what you would expect: the PTR record for *3.0.72.18.in-addr. arpa*. The record tells us that the hostname for the address 18.72.0.3 is *bitsy.mit.edu*.

The authority section lists the servers that are authoritative for the *18.in-addr.arpa* domain. There are three NS records, each providing the name of an authoritative server. From this, we know that *w20ns.mit.edu*, *bitsy.mit.edu*, and *strawb.mit.edu* are authoritative for the reverse domain *18.in-addr.arpa*.

The additional section completes the message by providing the address of each of the authoritative servers. The addresses are important because if the local server wants to send future queries directly to these authoritative servers, it needs to know the servers' addresses. In this case, the addresses are 18.70.0.160, 18.72.0.3, and 18.71.0.151.

In addition to the DNS response, dig provides status information in the first three lines and the last four lines of the display. The first line echoes the dig command-line options (-x in the example). The second line displays the resolver library settings, and the third line states whether or not an answer was found for the query. The last four lines show the query response time, the name and address of the server that answered the query, when the query was received, and the size of the query and response packets. All of this can be helpful information when debugging a DNS problem.

dig is useful because the format of the DNS message is clearly shown in the dig output. dig is included with Linux, but it is not found on all Unix systems. Don't worry if you don't have it on your system. nslookup can be used to attack the same problems as dig. nslookup and dig both test DNS very effectively.

Analyzing Protocol Problems

Problems caused by bad TCP/IP configurations are much more common than problems caused by bad TCP/IP protocol implementations. Most of the problems you encounter will succumb to analysis using the simple tools we have already discussed. But on occasion, you may need to analyze the protocol interaction between two systems. In the worst case, you may need to analyze the packets in the data stream bit by bit. Protocol analyzers help you do this.

snoop is the tool we'll use. It is provided with the Solaris operating system.[*] Although we use snoop in all of our examples, the concepts introduced in this section should be applicable to the analyzer that you use, since most protocol analyzers function in basically the same way. Protocol analyzers allow you to select, or filter, the packets you want to examine, and to examine those packets byte by byte. We'll discuss both of these functions.

Protocol analyzers watch all the packets on the network. Therefore, you only need one system that runs analyzer software on the affected part of the network. One Solaris system with snoop can monitor the network traffic and tell you what the other hosts are (or aren't) doing. This, of course, assumes a shared media network. If you use an Ethernet switch, only the traffic on an individual segment can be seen. Some switches provide a monitor port. For others you may need to take your monitor to the location of the problem.

Packet Filters

snoop reads all the packets on an Ethernet. It does this by placing the Ethernet interface into *promiscuous mode*.[†] Normally, an Ethernet interface only passes packets that are destined for the local host up to the higher layer protocols. In promiscuous mode,

---

[*] If you use Linux, try tcpdump. It is similar to snoop.

[†] This works only if the interface supports promiscuous mode; not all interfaces do.

all packets are accepted and passed to the higher layer. This allows snoop to view all packets and to select packets for analysis, based on a filter you define. Filters can be defined to capture packets from, or to, specific hosts, protocols, ports, or combinations of all these. As an example, let's look at a very simple snoop filter. The following snoop command displays all packets sent between the hosts *crab* and *rodent*:

```
# snoop host crab and host rodent
Using device /dev/le (promiscuous mode)
rodent.wrotethebook.com -> crab.wrotethebook.com ICMP Echo request
crab.wrotethebook.com -> rodent.wrotethebook.com ICMP Echo reply
rodent.wrotethebook.com -> crab.wrotethebook.com RLOGIN C port=1023
crab.wrotethebook.com -> rodent.wrotethebook.com RLOGIN R port=1023
^C
```

The filter "host crab and host rodent" selects only those packets that are from *rodent* to *crab*, or from *crab* to *rodent*. The filter is constructed from a set of primitives, and associated hostnames, protocol names, and port numbers. The primitives can be modified and combined with the operators and, or, and not. The filter may be omitted; this causes snoop to display all packets from the network.

Table 13-2 shows the primitives used to build snoop filters. There are a few additional primitives and some variations that perform the same functions, but these are the essential primitives. See the snoop manpage for additional details.

Table 13-2. Expression primitives

Primitive	Matches packets
dst host | net | port *destination*	To *destination* host, net, or port
src host | net | port *source*	From *source* host, net, or port
host *destination*	To or from *destination* host
net *destination*	To or from *destination* network
port *destination*	To or from *destination* port
ether *address*	To or from Ethernet *address*
protocol	Of *protocol* type (icmp, udp, or tcp)

Using these primitives with the operators and and or, complex filters can be constructed. However, filters are usually simple. Capturing the traffic between two hosts is probably the most common filter. You may further limit the data captured to a specific protocol, but often you're not sure which protocol will reveal the problem. Just because the user sees the problem in ftp or telnet does not mean that is where the problem actually occurs. Analysis must often start by capturing all packets, and can only be narrowed after test evidence points to some specific problem.

Modifying analyzer output

The example in the previous section shows that snoop displays a single line of summary information for each packet received. All lines show the source and destination addresses, and the protocol being used (ICMP and RLOGIN in the example). The lines that summarize the ICMP packets identify the packet types (Echo request and Echo reply in the example). The lines that summarize the application protocol packets display the source port and the first 20 characters of the packet data.

This summary information is sufficient to gain insight into how packets flow between two hosts and into potential problems. However, troubleshooting protocol problems requires more detailed information about each packet. snoop has options that give you control over what information is displayed. To display the data contained in a packet, use the -x option. It causes the entire contents of the packet to be dumped in hex and ASCII. In most cases, you don't need to see the entire packet; usually, the headers are sufficient to troubleshoot a protocol problem. The -v option displays the headers in a well-formatted and very detailed manner. Because of the large number of lines displayed for each packet, use -v only when you need it.

The following example shows an ICMP Echo Request packet displayed with the -v option. The same type of packet was summarized in the first line of the previous example.

```
# snoop -v host crab and host minasi
Using device /dev/le (promiscuous mode)
ETHER:  ----- Ether Header -----
ETHER:
ETHER:  Packet 3 arrived at 16:56:57.90
ETHER:  Packet size = 98 bytes
ETHER:  Destination = 8:0:20:22:fd:51, Sun
ETHER:  Source      = 0:0:c0:9a:d0:db, Western Digital
ETHER:  Ethertype = 0800 (IP)
ETHER:
IP:   ----- IP Header -----
IP:
IP:   Version = 4
IP:   Header length = 20 bytes
IP:   Type of service = 0x00
IP:         xxx. .... = 0 (precedence)
IP:         ...0 .... = normal delay
IP:         .... 0... = normal throughput
IP:         .... .0.. = normal reliability
IP:   Total length = 84 bytes
IP:   Identification = 3049
IP:   Flags = 0x0
IP:         .0.. .... = may fragment
IP:         ..0. .... = last fragment
IP:   Fragment offset = 0 bytes
IP:   Time to live = 64 seconds/hops
IP:   Protocol = 1 (ICMP)
IP:   Header checksum = fde0
IP:   Source address = 172.16.55.106, minasi.wrotethebook.com
IP:   Destination address = 172.16.12.1, crab.wrotethebook.com
IP:   No options
IP:
```

```
ICMP:   ----- ICMP Header -----
ICMP:
ICMP:   Type = 8 (Echo request)
ICMP:   Code = 0
ICMP:   Checksum = ac54 ICMP:
```

The detailed formatting done by snoop maps the bytes received from the network to the header structure. Look at the description of the various header fields in Chapter 1 and Appendix G for more information.

Protocol Case Study

This example is an actual case that was solved by protocol analysis. The problem was reported as an occasional ftp failure with the error message:

```
netout: Option not supported by protocol 421 Service not available, remote server has
closed connection
```

Only one user reported the problem, and it occurred only when transferring large files from a workstation to the central computer via our backbone network.

We obtained the user's data file and were able to duplicate the problem from other workstations, but only when we transferred the file to the same central system via the backbone network. Figure 13-4 graphically summarizes the tests we ran to duplicate the problem.

We notified all users of the problem. In response, we received reports that others had also experienced it, but again only when transferring to the central system, and only when transferring via the backbone. They had not reported it because they rarely saw it. But the additional reports gave us some evidence that the problem did not relate to any recent network changes.

Because the problem had been duplicated on other systems, it probably was not a configuration problem on the user's system. The ftp failure could also be avoided if the backbone routers and the central system did not interact. So we concentrated our attention on those systems. We checked the routing tables and ARP tables, and ran ping tests on the central system and the routers. No problems were observed.

Based on this preliminary analysis, the ftp failure appeared to be a possible protocol interaction problem between a certain brand of routers and a central computer. We made that assessment because the transfer routinely failed when these two brands of systems were involved, but never failed in any other circumstance. If the router or the central system were misconfigured, they should fail when transferring data to other hosts. If the problem was an intermittent physical problem, it should occur randomly, regardless of the hosts involved. Instead, this problem occurred predictably, and only between two specific brands of computers. Perhaps there was something incompatible in the way these two systems implemented TCP/IP.

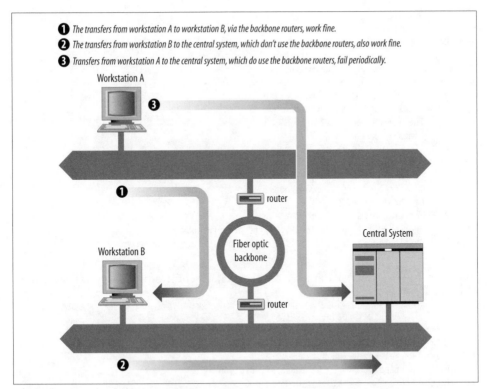

Figure 13-4. FTP test summary

Therefore, we used snoop to capture the TCP/IP headers during several ftp test runs. Reviewing the dumps showed that all transfers that failed with the "netout" error message had an ICMP Parameter Error packet near the end of the session, usually about 50 packets before the final close. No successful transfer had this ICMP packet. Note that the error did *not* occur in the last packet in the data stream, as you might expect. It is common for an error to be detected, and for the data stream to continue for some time before the connection is actually shut down. Don't assume that an error will always be at the end of a data stream.

Here are the headers from the key packets. First, the IP header of the packet from the backbone router that caused the central system to send the error:

```
ETHER:  ----- Ether Header -----
ETHER:
ETHER:  Packet 1 arrived at 16:56:36.39
ETHER:  Packet size = 60 bytes
ETHER:  Destination = 8:0:25:30:6:51, CDC
ETHER:  Source      = 0:0:93:e0:a0:bf, Proteon
ETHER:  Ethertype = 0800 (IP)
ETHER:
IP:   ----- IP Header -----
IP:
```

```
IP:   Version = 4
IP:   Header length = 20 bytes
IP:   Type of service = 0x00
IP:       xxx. .... = 0 (precedence)
IP:       ...0 .... = normal delay
IP:       .... 0... = normal throughput
IP:       .... .0.. = normal reliability
IP:   Total length = 552 bytes
IP:   Identification = 8a22
IP:   Flags = 0x0
IP:       .0.. .... = may fragment
IP:       ..0. .... = last fragment
IP:   Fragment offset = 0 bytes
IP:   Time to live = 57 seconds/hops
IP:   Protocol = 6 (TCP)
IP:   Header checksum = ffff
IP:   Source address = 172.16.55.106, fs.wrotethebook.com
IP:   Destination address = 172.16.51.252, bnos.wrotethebook.com
IP:   No options IP:
```

And this is the ICMP Parameter Error packet sent from the central system in response to that packet:

```
ETHER: ----- Ether Header -----
ETHER:
ETHER: Packet 3 arrived at 16:56:57.90
ETHER: Packet size = 98 bytes
ETHER: Destination = 0:0:93:e0:a0:bf, Proteon
ETHER: Source      = 8:0:25:30:6:51, CDC
ETHER: Ethertype = 0800 (IP)
ETHER:
IP:   ----- IP Header -----
IP:
IP:   Version = 4
IP:   Header length = 20 bytes
IP:   Type of service = 0x00
IP:       xxx. .... = 0 (precedence)
IP:       ...0 .... = normal delay
IP:       .... 0... = normal throughput
IP:       .... .0.. = normal reliability
IP:   Total length = 56 bytes
IP:   Identification = 000c
IP:   Flags = 0x0
IP:       .0.. .... = may fragment
IP:       ..0. .... = last fragment
IP:   Fragment offset = 0 bytes
IP:   Time to live = 59 seconds/hops
IP:   Protocol = 1 (ICMP)
IP:   Header checksum = 8a0b
IP:   Source address = 172.16.51.252, bnos.wrotethebook.com
IP:   Destination address = 172.16.55.106, fs.wrotethebook.com
IP:   No options
IP:
```

```
ICMP:  ----- ICMP Header -----
ICMP:
ICMP:  Type = 12 (Parameter problem)
ICMP:  Code = 0
ICMP:  Checksum = 0d9f ICMP:  Pointer = 10
```

Each packet header is broken out bit by bit and mapped to the appropriate TCP/IP header fields. From this detailed analysis of each packet, we see that the router issued an IP Header Checksum of 0xffff, and that the central system objected to this checksum. We know that the central system objected to the checksum because it returned an ICMP Parameter Error with a Pointer of 10. The Parameter Error indicates that there is something wrong with the data the system has just received, and the Pointer identifies the specific data that the system thinks is in error. The tenth byte of the router's IP header is the IP Header Checksum. The data field of the ICMP error message returns the header that it believes is in error. When we displayed that data we noticed that when the central system returned the header, the checksum field was "corrected" to 0000. Clearly the central system disagreed with the router's checksum calculation.

Occasional checksum errors will occur. They can be caused by transmission problems, and are intended to detect these types of problems. Every protocol suite has a mechanism for recovering from checksum errors. So how should they be handled in TCP/IP?

To determine the correct protocol action in this situation, we turned to the authoritative sources—the RFCs. RFC 791, *Internet Protocol*, provided information about the checksum calculation, but the best source for this particular problem was RFC 1122, *Requirements for Internet Hosts—Communication Layers*, by R. Braden. This RFC provided two specific references that define the action to be taken. These excerpts are from page 29 of RFC 1122:

> In the following, the action specified in certain cases is to "silently discard" a received datagram. This means that the datagram will be discarded without further processing and that the host will not send any ICMP error message (see Section 3.2.2) as a result....
>
> ... A host MUST verify the IP header checksum on every received datagram and silently discard every datagram that has a bad checksum.

Therefore, when a system receives a packet with a bad checksum, it is not supposed to do anything with it. The packet should be discarded, and the system should wait for the next packet to arrive. The system should not respond with an error message. A system cannot respond to a bad IP header checksum because it cannot really know where the packet came from. If the header checksum is in doubt, how do you know if the addresses in the header are correct? And if you don't know for sure where the packet came from, how can you respond to it?

IP relies on the upper-layer protocols to recover from these problems. If TCP is used (as it was in this case), the sending TCP eventually notices that the recipient has never acknowledged the segment, and it sends the segment again. If UDP is used, the sending application is responsible for recovering from the error. In neither case does recovery rely on an error message returned from the recipient.

Therefore, for an incorrect checksum, the central system should have simply discarded the bad packet. The vendor was informed of this problem and, much to their credit, they sent us a fix for the software within two weeks. Not only that, the fix worked perfectly!

Not all problems are resolved so cleanly. But the technique of analysis is the same no matter what the problem.

Summary

Every network will have problems. This chapter discusses the tools and techniques that can help you recover from these problems, and the planning and monitoring that can help avoid them. A solution is sometimes obvious if you can just gain enough information about the problem. Unix provides several built-in software tools that can help you gather information about system configuration, addressing, routing, name service, and other vital network components. Gather your tools and learn how to use them before a breakdown occurs.

Troubleshooting is an ongoing process. This book is just the beginning of another ongoing process—learning. As you explore your system and network, you'll see that there is much more to networking than can ever be covered in one book. This book has been your launching pad—helping you connect your system to the network. Now that your system is up and running, use it as a tool to expand your information horizons.

PPP Tools

This appendix is a reference for dip, pppd, and chat. These tools are used to create dial-up IP connections for the *Point-to-Point Protocol* (PPP). dip and chat are both scripting languages. Creating a script that initializes the modem, dials the remote server, logs in, and configures the remote server is the biggest task in configuring a PPP connection. Chapter 6 provides examples and tutorial information about all three of the programs covered here. This appendix provides a reference to the programs.

Dial-Up IP

dip is a scripting tool designed specifically for creating SLIP and PPP connections.[*] The syntax of the dip command is:

    dip [options] [scriptfile]

The dip command is invoked with an option set, a script file specified, or both. When *scriptfile* is specified, dip executes the commands contained in the script file to create a point-to-point connection. Examples of scripts and dip are shown in Chapter 6. The *options* valid with script files are:

-v

> Runs dip in verbose mode. In this mode, dip echoes each line of the script file as it is executed and displays enhanced status messages.

-m *mtu*

> Sets the maximum transmission unit (MTU) to the number of bytes specified by *mtu*. The default MTU is 296 bytes.

-p *proto*

> Selects the serial line protocol. Possible values for *proto* are: SLIP, CSLIP, PPP, or TERM.

---

[*] *Serial Line IP* (SLIP) predates PPP. Today most serial connections are PPP, which is what this appendix emphasizes.

The other dip command-line options are:

-k

Kills the last dip process you started. You can only kill a process you own, unless of course you're *root*.

-l *device*

Specifies that the process to be killed is the one that has locked the specified *device*. This option is valid only when used with the -k option.

-i [*username*]

Runs dip as a login shell to provide a PPP server. The diplogin command is equivalent to dip -i. These two forms of the command are used interchangeably, but diplogin is the most common form. diplogin is placed in the login shell field of the */etc/passwd* file entry for each PPP client. From there it is run by login. The username from the */etc/passwd* file is used to retrieve additional configuration information from */etc/diphosts*. If the optional *username* is specified with the diplogin command, that username is used to retrieve the information from the */etc/diphosts* file. Chapter 6 provides a tutorial and examples of creating a PPP server.

-a

Prompts for the username and password. The -a option is valid only when used with the -i option. The diplogini command is equivalent to dip -i -a. diplogini is used as a login shell in the */etc/passwd* file where it is run by login.

-t

Runs dip in test mode, which allows you to input individual script language commands directly from the keyboard. The -t option is frequently used in combination with -v so that the result of each command can be better observed. As shown in Chapter 6, this option is used to debug a dip script.

diplogin and diplogini are used only on servers and are not used with a script file. The script file is used on the PPP clients when dip is configured to dial into a remote server. The script file contains the instructions used to do this.

The dip Script File

The script file is made up of comments, labels, variables, and commands. Any line that begins with a sharp sign (#) is a comment. A label is a line that contains only a string ending in a colon. Labels are used to divide the script into separate procedures. For example, the section of the script that dials the remote host might begin with the label:

    Dial-in:

A variable stores a value. A variable name is a string that begins with a dollar sign ($). You might, for example, create a variable to hold a loop counter and give it the name $loopcntr. It is possible to create your own variables, but this is rarely done. The variables that are used in most scripts are the special variables defined by dip. Table A-1 lists the special variables and the value that each holds.

Table A-1. dip special variables

Variable	Value stored
$errlvl	The return code of the last command
$locip	The IP address of the local host
$local	The fully qualified domain name of the local host
$rmtip	The IP address of the remote host
$remote	The fully qualified domain name of the remote host
$mtu	The maximum transmission unit in bytes
$modem	The modem type; currently this must be HAYES
$port	The name of the serial device, e.g., cua0
$speed	The transmission speed of the port

The final component of the script file is the command list. There are many script commands. Because this appendix is a reference, we cover them all. However, most scripts are built using only a few of these commands. See the sample scripts in Chapter 6 and at the end of this section for realistic dip scripts. The complete list of script commands is:

beep [*n*]

Tells the system to beep the user. Repeat *n* times.

bootp

Tells the system to use the BOOTP protocol to obtain the local and remote IP addresses. This command applies only to SLIP. PPP has its own protocol for assigning addresses; SLIP does not. Usually SLIP addresses are statically set inside the script. However, some SLIP servers have evolved techniques for dynamic address assignment. The most common method is for the server to display the address as clear text immediately after the connection is made. Use the get $locip remote command to retrieve the address from this type of SLIP server. Other SLIP servers require you to send them a command before they will display the address. Put the required server command in the script and follow it with the get command. Finally, a few SLIP servers use BOOTP to distribute addresses. Use the bootp command in your script to enable BOOTP when it is required by your SLIP server.

break

Sends a BREAK. Some remote servers may require a BREAK as an attention character.

chatkey *keyword code*

> Maps a modem response *keyword* to a numeric *code*. The predefined mappings are:

0	OK
1	CONNECT
2	ERROR
3	BUSY
4	NO CARRIER
5	NO DIALTONE

config [interface|routing] [pre|up|down|post] *arguments...*

> Modifies interface characteristics (interface) or the routing table (routing) either before (pre) the link comes up, when it is up, when it goes down, or after (post) the link is shut down. For example:
>
> ```
> config up routing add canary gw ibis
> ```
>
> adds a route to *canary* using *ibis* as the gateway when the link is up. Allowing users to modify the routing table or interface characteristics is very dangerous. The config command is disabled in the DIP code and requires recompilation to be enabled.

databits 7|8

> Sets the number of data bits to 7 or 8. 8 bits is recommended for PPP and SLIP links.

dec *$variable* [*value*]

> Decrements *$variable* by *value*. The default *value* is 1.

default

> Sets the PPP connection as the default route.

dial *phonenumber* [*timeout*]

> Dials the *phonenumber*. If the remote modem does not answer within *timeout* seconds, the connection aborts. $errlvl is set to a numeric value based on the keyword returned by the local modem. Set chatkey for the keyword to numeric mappings.

echo on|off

> Enables or disables the display of modem commands.

exit [*n*]

> Exits the script, optionally returning the number *n* as the exit status. Clears the input buffer.

get *$variable* [ask | remote [*timeout*]] *value*

> Sets *$variable* to *value*, unless ask or remote is specified. When ask is specified, the user is prompted for the value. When remote is specified, the value is read from the remote machine, optionally waiting *timeout* seconds for the remote system to respond.

goto *label*
> Jumps to the section of the script identified by *label*.

help
> Lists the dip script commands.

if *expr* goto *label*
> A conditional statement that jumps to the section of the script identified by *label* if the *expression* evaluates to true. The expression must compare a variable to a constant using one of these operators: == (equal), != (not equal), < (less than), > (greater than), <= (less than or equal to), >= (greater than or equal to).

inc $variable [value]
> Increments $variable by value. The default value is 1.

init *command*
> Sets the command string used to initialize the modem. The default is ATE0 Q0 V1 X1.

mode SLIP|CSLIP|PPP|TERM
> Selects the serial protocol. The default is SLIP, so this should be set to PPP.

modem *type*
> Sets the modem type. Ignore this command. The only legal value is HAYES, and that is the default.

netmask *mask*
> Sets the address mask.

parity E|O|N
> Sets the parity to even (E), odd (O), or no (N). No parity (N) is recommended for SLIP and PPP links.

password
> Prompts the user for the password.

proxyarp
> Installs a proxy ARP entry for the remote system in the local host's ARP table.

print $variable
> Displays the contents of $variable.

psend *command*
> Executes *command* through the default shell passing the output to the serial device. The command runs using the user's real UID.

port *device*
> Identifies the serial device, such as cua0, that attaches the modem.

quit
> Exits the script with a nonzero exit status, aborting the connection.

reset
> Resets the modem.

send *string*

> Passes *string* to the serial device.

shell *command*

> Executes *command* through the default shell. The command runs using the user's real UID.

skey [*timeout*]

> Waits for an S/Key challenge from the remote terminal server, prompts the user for the secret key, and generates and sends the response. Waits *timeout* seconds for the challenge. If the timer expires, $errlvl is set to 1; otherwise, it is set to 0. S/Key must be compiled into dip.

sleep *time*

> Delays *time* seconds.

speed *bits-per-second*

> Sets the port speed. The default is 38400.

stopbits 1|2

> Sets the number of stop bits to 1 or 2. Enables terminal mode. In terminal mode, keyboard input is passed directly to the serial device.

timeout *time*

> Sets the *time* in seconds that the line is allowed to remain inactive. When this timer expires, the link is closed.

wait *text* [*timeout*]

> Waits *timeout* seconds for the *text* string to arrive from the remote system. If *timeout* is not specified, the script will wait forever.

In the next section we put some of these commands to work in a realistic script.

A sample dip script

This script is based on the PPP sample from Chapter 6. Labels and error detection have been added to create a more robust script.

```
# Select configuration settings
setup:
# Ask PPP to provide the addresses
get $local 0.0.0.0
# Select the port
port cua1
# Set the port speed
speed 57600
# Create a loop counter
get $loopcntr 0

# Dial the remote server
dialin:
# Reset the modem and clear the input buffer
reset
flush
```

```
# Dial the PPP server and check the modem response
dial *70,301-555-1234
# If BUSY, dial again
if $errlvl == 3 goto redial
# If some other error, abort
if $errlvl != 1 goto dial-error
# Otherwise rest loop counter
get $loopcntr 0
# Give the server 2 seconds to get ready
sleep 2

# Login to the remote server
login:
# Send a carriage-return to wake up the server
send \r
# Wait for the Username> prompt and send the username
wait name> 20
if $errlvl != 0 goto try-again
send kristin\r
# Wait for the Password> prompt and send the password
wait word> 10
if $errlvl != 0 goto server-failure
password
# Wait for the PPP server's command-line prompt
wait > 20
if $errlvl != 0 goto server-failure
# Send the command required by the PPP server
send ppp enabled\r

# Success! We're on-line
connected:
# Set the interface to PPP mode
mode PPP
# Exit the script
exit

# Error processing routines

# Try dialing 3 times.  Wait 5 seconds between attempts
redial:
inc $loopcntr
if $loopcntr > 3 goto busy-failure
sleep 5
goto dialin

# Try a second carriage return
try-again:
inc $loopcntr
if $loopcntr > 1 goto server-failure
goto login


dial-error:
print Dial up of $remote failed.
```

```
quit

server-failure:
print $remote failed to respond.
quit

busy-failure:
print $remote is busy.  Try again later.
quit
```

This script provides a realistic example of the commands used in most scripts. However, you may encounter a particularly tough scripting problem. If you do, the abundance of scripting commands available with dip should be able to handle it. If dip can't do the job, try expect. See *Exploring Expect* by Don Libes (O'Reilly & Associates) for a full description of the expect scripting language.

The PPP Daemon

The PPP Daemon (pppd) is a freely available implementation of the Point-to-Point Protocol (PPP) that runs on many Unix systems. Examples of configuring and using pppd are covered in Chapter 6. The syntax of the pppd command is:

```
pppd [device] [speed] [options]
```

device is the name of the serial port over which the PPP protocol operates and *speed* is the transmission speed of that port in bits per second. The complexity of this command comes not from these simple parameters but from the large number of *options* that it supports. There are so many options, in fact, that they are often stored in a file. There are three options files that can be used with pppd: the */etc/ppp/options* file, which is used to set systemwide pppd options; the *~/.ppprc* file, which is used by an individual to set personal pppd options; and the */etc/ppp/options.device* file, which sets options for a serial device, e.g., */etc/ppp/options.cua0* sets options for cua0. The order of precedence for options is that those specified in the */etc/ppp/options.device* file are the highest priority, followed by those defined on the command line, then those in the *~/.ppprc* file, and, finally, those defined in the */etc/ppp/options* file. Some options that relate to system security, once defined in the */etc/ppp/options* file, cannot be overridden by the user through the command line or the *~/.ppprc* file. The system administrator can override any option set by the user by setting the option in the */etc/ppp/options.device* file.

The following list contains all of the pppd options except those that do not relate to TCP/IP:

local_IP_address:*remote_IP_address*
> Defines static local and remote IP addresses. Either address may be omitted. For example, 172.16.25.3: defines only the local address, while :172.16.25.12 defines only the remote address. The default local address is the IP address associated with the local system's hostname.

active-filter *filter-expression*
> Defines a packet filter that determines which packets are regarded as link activity. Packets that pass through the filter reset the idle timer or cause the link to initialize when it is in demand-dial mode. The kernel and pppd must be compiled with PPP_FILTER defined.

allow-ip *address*
> Systems using the specified IP address, which can identify individual hosts or entire networks, do not need to be authenticated.

asyncmap *map*
> Defines the ASCII control characters that must be sent as two-character escape sequences. The first 32 ASCII characters are control characters. *map* is a 32-bit hex number with each bit representing a control character. Bit 0 (00000001) represents the character 0x00; bit 31 (80000000) represents the character 0x1f. If a bit is on in *map*, the character represented by that bit must be sent as an escape sequence. If no asyncmap option is specified, all control characters are sent as escape sequences.

auth
> Requires the use of an authentication protocol. See Chapter 6 for a discussion of the authentication protocols CHAP and PAP.

bsdcomp *receive,transmit*
> Enables the BSD-Compress scheme to compress packets. The maximum code word length used to compress packets accepted by this host is *receive* bits long. The maximum code word length used to compress packets sent by this host is *transmit* bits long. Acceptable code word length is 9 to 15 bits. Disable compression when receiving or transmitting by placing a 0 in *receive* or *transmit*, respectively.

call *name*
> Reads options from a file named */etc/ppp/peers/name*.

cdtrcts
> Tells pppd that the modem uses nonstandard hardware flow control based on the DTR and CTS signals.

chap-interval
> Tells the system to use the *Challenge Handshake Authentication Protocol* (CHAP) to reauthenticate the remote system every *n* seconds.

chap-max-challenge *n*
> Tells the system to send the CHAP challenge to the remote system a maximum of *n* times until the remote system responds. The default is 10.

chap-restart *n*
> Tells the system to wait *n* seconds before retransmitting a CHAP challenge when the remote system fails to respond. The default is 3 seconds.

connect *script*

> Invokes a *script* to create the serial connection. Any scripting language can be used, but chat is the most common. See Chapter 6 for an example of using connect to invoke an inline chat script.

connect-delay *n*

> Waits *n* milliseconds after the connect script finishes for a valid PPP packet from the remote system.

crtscts

> Enables hardware flow control (RTS/CTS).

debug

> Logs all control packets sent or received using syslogd with facility daemon and level debug. The debug option can also be written as -d.

default-asyncmap

> Disables asyncmap negotiation, forcing all control characters to be escaped.

default-mru

> Disables Maximum Receive Unit negotiation and uses a default MRU of 1500 bytes.

defaultroute

> Defines the PPP link as the default route. The route is removed when the connection is closed.

deflate *nr,nt*

> Tells pppd to request Deflate packet compression. *nr* is the maximum receive window size expressed as a power of 2; i.e., if *nr* is 8, the receive window is 2 to the 8 (or 256) bytes. *nt* defines the maximum transmit window size expressed as a power of 2. If *nt* is not specified, it defaults to the value given for *nr*.

demand

> Places the link in dial-on-demand mode. The network connection is made when network traffic is present.

disconnect *script*

> Invokes a *script* to gracefully shut down the serial connection. Any scripting language can be used, but chat is the most common.

domain *name*

> Defines the name of the local domain. Use this if hostname does not return a fully qualified name for the local system.

escape *x,x,...*

> Specifies characters that should be transmitted as two-character escape sequences. The characters are specified in a comma-separated list of hex numbers. Any character except 0x20 - 0x3f and 0x5e can be escaped.

endpoint *epdisc*

> Defines the endpoint discriminator sent to the remote system during multilink negotiation. The default endpoint discriminator is the MAC address of the first Ethernet interface or, if no Ethernet is found, the system's IP address. *epdisc* is defined in the form *type:value*, where *type* is one of the keywords local, IP, MAC, magic, or phone, and *value* is either an IP address in dotted-decimal notation for the IP type, the name of an Ethernet interface for the MAC type, or a string of colon-separated hexadecimal bytes for the other types. Multilink is available only on Linux systems.

file *file*

> Defines another options file, where *file* is the name of the new file. Options are normally read for */etc/ppp/options*, *~/.ppprc*, the command line, and */etc/ppp/options.device*. See the description of these files earlier in this section.

hide-password

> Hides the password string when logging the contents of *Password Authentication Protocol* (PAP) packets.

holdoff *n*

> Waits *n* seconds before restarting the link after the link terminates.

idle *n*

> Disconnects the link if no data packets are sent or received for *n* seconds.

init *script*

> Executes *script* to initialize the serial line.

ipcp-accept-local

> Tells the system to use the local IP address provided by the remote server even if it is defined locally.

ipcp-accept-remote

> Tells the system to use the remote IP address provided by the remote server even if it is defined locally.

ipcp-max-configure *n*

> Tells the system to send the IPCP configure-request packet a maximum of *n* times. The default is 10.

ipcp-max-failure *n*

> Tells the system to accept up to *n* IPCP configure-NAKs before sending a configure-reject. The default is 10.

ipcp-max-terminate *n*

> Tells the system to send no more than *n* IPCP terminate-request packets without receiving an acknowledgment. The default is 3.

ipcp-restart *n*

> Tells the system to wait *n* seconds before resending an IPCP configure-request packet. The default is 3.

ipparam *string*

> Passes *string* to the ip-up and ip-down scripts. */etc/ppp/ip-up* is a shell script executed by pppd when the link comes up. */etc/ppp/ip-down* is a shell script executed by pppd when the link is brought down.

ipv6 *local_interface_identifier,remote_interface_identifier*

> Sets the local and remote 64-bit interface identifier using standard IPv6 ASCII address notation. If no identifiers are defined, the system creates a random identifier. (See also the ipv6cp-use-ipaddr and the ipv6cp-use-persistent options.)

ipv6cp-max-configure *n*

> Send a maximum of *n* IPv6CP configure-request packets. The default is 10.

ipv6cp-max-failure *n*

> Accept a maximum of *n* IPv6CP configure-NAK packets. The default is 10.

ipv6cp-max-terminate *n*

> Send a maximum of *n* IPv6CP terminate-request packets. The default is 3.

ipv6cp-restart *n*

> Wait *n* seconds before resending an IPv6CP configure-request packet. The default is 3 seconds.

ipv6cp-use-ipaddr

> Use the system's IPv4 address as the IPv6 local interface identifier.

ipv6cp-use-persistent

> Use the system's unique persistent identifier as the IPv6 local interface identifier. Most systems do not support persistent identifiers.

kdebug *n*

> Enables kernel-level debugging. *n* is 1 to print general debugging messages, 2 to print received packets, and 4 to print transmitted packets.

ktune

> Tells the system to allow pppd to alter kernel settings. For example, on a Linux system, pppd could enable IP forwarding by setting */proc/sys/net/ipv4/ip_forward* to 1 if allowed to do so.

lcp-echo-failure *n*

> Tells the system to terminate the connection if no reply is received to *n* LCP echo-requests. Normally, echo-requests are not used for this purpose because "link down" conditions are determined by the modem hardware.

lcp-echo-interval *n*

> Tells the system to wait *n* seconds before sending another LCP echo-request when the remote system fails to reply.

lcp-max-configure *n*

> Tells the system to send the LCP configure-request packet a maximum of *n* times. The default is 10.

`lcp-max-failure` *n*

> Tells the system to accept up to *n* LCP configure-NAKs before sending a configure-reject. The default is 10.

`lcp-max-terminate` *n*

> Tells the system to send no more than *n* LCP terminate-request transmissions without receiving an acknowledgment. The default is 3.

`lcp-restart` *n*

> Tells the system to wait *n* seconds before resending an LCP configure-request packet. The default is 3.

`linkname` *name*

> Sets the logical name of the link to *name*. pppd writes its process ID into a file named ppp-*name*.pid in either */var/run* or */etc/ppp*. This maps each instantiation of pppd to a specific link.

`local`

> Tells the system to ignore the DCD (Data Carrier Detect) and DTR (Data Terminal Ready) modem control lines.

`lock`

> Tells the system to use a UUCP-style lock file to ensure that pppd has exclusive access to the serial device.

`logfd` *n*

> Logs messages to file descriptor *n*.

`logfile` *filename*

> Appends messages to the log file identified by *filename*.

`login`

> Tells the system to use the */etc/passwd* file to authenticate PAP users. Records the login in the *wtmp* file.

`maxconnect` *n*

> Sets the maximum connection time to *n* seconds. After *n* seconds, the connection is terminated even if it is active.

`maxfail` *n*

> Stop attempting to connect to the remote system after *n* consecutive connection attempt failures. The default value is 10 attempts.

`modem`

> Tells the system to use the DCD (Data Carrier Detect) and DTR (Data Terminal Ready) modem control lines; wait for the DCD signal before opening the serial device; and drop the DTR signal when terminating a connection.

`mp`

> This is an alias for the `multilink` option. See `multilink`.

mpshortseq

Use short, 12-bit sequence numbers in multilink headers instead of the standard 24-bit sequence numbers.

mrru *n*

Sets the Maximum Reconstructed Receive Unit (MRRU) to *n* bytes. The MRRU is the maximum packet size that can be received on a multilink bundle. The value is analogous to MRU on other media.

mru *n*

Sets the Maximum Receive Unit (MRU) to *n* bytes. MRU is used to tell the remote system the maximum packet size the local system can accept. The minimum is 128. The default is 1500.

ms-dns *address*

Supplies Domain Name System addresses to Microsoft Windows clients.

ms-wins *address*

Supplies Windows Internet Name Services (WINS) server addresses to Microsoft Windows clients.

mtu *n*

Sets the Maximum Transmission Unit (MTU) to *n* bytes. MTU defines the maximum length of a packet that can be sent. The smaller of the local MTU and the remote MRU is used to define the maximum packet length.

multilink

Enables the multilink protocol, which allows multiple physical connections to be bundled together as one logical link. This is used to increase the bandwidth to a remote system. For example, two modem connections to a single remote system could be viewed as a single multilink bundle to give twice the bandwidth of one modem connection. This option is currently available only with Linux.

name *name*

Tells the system to use *name* as the name of the local system for authentication purposes.

netmask *mask*

Defines the subnet mask.

noaccomp

Disables Address/Control compression negotiation.

noauth

Allows unauthenticated access.

nobsdcomp

Disables BSD-Compress compression.

noccp

Disables Compression Control Protocol (CCP) negotiation.

nocrtscts
    Disables all types of hardware flow control.

nodtrcts
    Disables all types of hardware flow control.

nodefaultroute
    Prevents users from creating a default route using the defaultroute option.

nodeflate
    Disables Deflate compression.

nodetach
    Prevents pppd from running as a background process. See the example in
    Chapter 6.

noendpoint
    Tells the system not to send or accept Multilink endpoint discriminators.

noip
    Disables the IPCP and IP protocols.

noipv6
    Disables IPv6CP negotiation and IPv6 communication.

noipdefault
    Instructs the system not to use hostname to determine the local IP address. The
    address must be obtained from the remote system or explicitly set by an option.

noktune
    Prevents pppd from changing kernel values.

nolog
    Disables logging.

nomagic
    Disables magic number negotiation.

nomp
    Disables the multilink protocol.

nompshortseq
    Disables the use of short, 12-bit sequence numbers in the multilink protocol.

nomultilink
    Disables the multilink protocol.

nopcomp
    Disables protocol field compression negotiation. By default, protocol field com-
    pression is not used. Setting this option means that even if the remote end
    requests it, it will not be used.

nopersist
    Terminates when the connection is made. This is the default.

nopredictor1

Tells the system not to use Predictor-1 compression.

noproxyarp

Disables the `proxyarp` option, preventing users from creating proxy ARP entries with `pppd`.

notty

Causes `pppd` to transmit characters to standard output and receive them on standard input. This option increases latency and overhead.

novj

Disables Van Jacobson header compression.

novjccomp

Disables the connection-ID compression option in Van Jacobson header compression.

papcrypt

Instructs the system not to accept passwords that are identical to those in the */etc/ppp/pap-secrets* file because the ones in the file are encrypted. Therefore the transmitted password should not match an entry in the *pap-secrets* file until it is also encrypted.

pap-max-authreq *n*

Tells the system to transmit no more than *n* PAP authenticate-requests if the remote system does not respond. The default is 10.

pap-restart *n*

Tells the system to wait *n* seconds before retransmitting a PAP authenticate-request. The default is 3 seconds.

pap-timeout *n*

Tells the system to wait no more than *n* seconds for the remote system to authenticate itself. When *n* is 0, there is no time limit.

pass-filter *filter-expression*

Defines a packet filter that determines which packets can be sent or received over the PPP link. Packets that do not pass through the filter are silently discarded. *filter-expression* is defined using the syntax of `tcpdump`.

passive

Tells the system to wait for a Link Control Protocol (LCP) packet from the remote system even if that system does not reply to the initial LCP packet sent by the local system. Without this option, the local system aborts the connection when it does not receive a reply. The `passive` option can also be written as -p.

persist

Tells the system to reopen the connection if it was terminated by a SIGHUP signal.

plugin *filename*

Loads a shared library object as a "plugin" to pppd.

predictor1

Tells the system to ask the remote system to use Predictor-1 compression.

privgroup *group-name*

Allows all members of the group *group-name* to use privileged options.

proxyarp

Tells the system to enable proxy ARP. This adds a proxy ARP entry for the remote system to the local system's ARP table.

pty *script*

Identifies a script that is run as a child process and used as the communications source in lieu of a terminal device. If used in conjunction with the record option, the child process will have pipes on its standard input and output.

receive-all

Tells the system to accept all control characters from the remote system, even those that should be discarded according to the standard asyncmap handling defined in RFC 1662.

record *filename*

Tells the system to log every character sent and received to *filename*.

remotename *name*

Tells the system to use *name* as the remote system's name for authentication purposes.

refuse-chap

Disables the use of CHAP. This is a bad idea.

refuse-pap

Disables the use of PAP.

require-chap

Requires the use of CHAP.

require-pap

Requires the use of PAP.

show-password

Shows the password when PAP packets are logged.

silent

Tells the system to wait for an LCP packet from the remote system. Do not send the first LCP packet.

sync

Tells the system to use synchronous HDLC physical layer protocols instead of the default asynchronous protocol.

updetach

Tells the system to detach from the controlling terminal after the connection is made.

usehostname

Disables the name option, forcing the local hostname to be used for authentication purposes.

usepeerdns

Asks the remote system to provide up to two DNS server addresses. The provided addresses are passed up to the */etc/ppp/ip-up* script in the environment variables DNS1 and DNS2. Additionally, pppd uses the addresses to create nameserver lines in a file named */etc/ppp/resolv.conf*.

user *username*

Tells the system to use *username* for PAP authentication when challenged by a remote host.

vj-max-slots *n*

Tells the system to use *n* connection slots for Van Jacobson header compression. *n* must be a number from 2 to 16.

welcome *script*

Execute *script* before initiating PPP negotiation.

xonxoff

Enables software flow control (XON/XOFF).

Several of the options listed above concern PPP security. One of the strengths of PPP is its security. The *Challenge Handshake Authentication Protocol* (CHAP) is the preferred PPP security protocol. The *Password Authentication Protocol* (PAP) is less secure and is only provided for compatibility with less capable systems. The usernames, IP addresses, and secret keys used for these protocols are defined in the */etc/ppp/chap-secrets* file and the */etc/ppp/pap-secrets* file. Chapter 6 shows the format of these files and describes their use.

It is very important that the directory */etc/ppp* and its contents not be world- or group-writable. Modifications to the *chap-secrets*, *pap-secrets*, or *options* files could compromise system security. In addition, the script files */etc/ppp/ip-up* and */etc/ppp/ip-down* may run with root privilege. If pppd finds a file with the name *ip-up* in the */etc/ppp* directory, it executes it as soon as the PPP connection is established. The *ip-up* script is used to modify the routing table, process the sendmail queue, or do other tasks that depend on the presence of the network connection. The *ip-down* script is executed by pppd after the PPP connection is closed and is used to terminate processes that depend on the link. Clearly these scripts and the */etc/ppp* directory must be protected.

Signal Processing

pppd handles the following signals:

SIGUSR1

> This signal toggles debugging on or off. The first SIGUSR1 signal received by pppd turns on debugging and begins logging diagnostic messages through syslogd with facility set to *daemon* and level set to *debug*. The second SIGUSR1 signal turns off debugging and closes the log file. See the debug option described previously.

SIGUSR2

> This signal causes pppd to renegotiate compression. It has limited applicability because it is needed only to restart compression after a fatal error has occurred. Most people close the PPP connection and open a new one after a fatal error.

SIGHUP

> This signal closes the PPP connection, returns the serial device to its normal operating mode, and terminates pppd. If the persist option is specified, pppd opens a new connection instead of terminating.

SIGINT

> This signal, or the SIGTERM signal, closes the PPP connection, returns the serial device to its normal operating mode, and terminates pppd. The persist option has no effect.

chat

chat is a general-purpose scripting language that is used to control the modem, dial the remote server, and perform the remote system login. chat is less powerful than dip but is widely used. The "expect/send" structure of a chat script is the fundamental structure used in most scripting languages.

A chat script is composed of expect/send pairs. These pairs consist of the string expected from the remote system, separated by whitespace from the response that is sent to the remote host when the expected string is received. If no string is expected from the remote system, two quotes ("") or two apostrophes (' ') are used to "expect nothing." A simple chat script is:

```
"" \r name> jane word> T0ga!toGA
```

The script expects nothing ("") until it sends the remote system a carriage return (\r). Then the script expects the remote system to send the string name>, which is part of the system's Username> prompt. In response to this prompt, the script sends the username jane. Finally the script waits for part of the Password> prompt and responds with T0ga!toGA. A script this simple can be defined directly on the chat command line:

```
% chat -v -t30 "" \r name> jane word> T0ga!toGA
```

This command runs chat in verbose mode, sets the length of time the script waits for an expected string to 30 seconds, and then executes the simple login script described above.

The syntax of the chat command is:

    chat [options] [script]

The chat command options are:

-e

> Echo all output from the modem to stderr. This has the same effect as using the ECHO keyword inside the chat script.

-E

> Enables the use of environment variables inside the chat script.

-s

> Send all log entries and all error messages to stderr.

-S

> Do not send log messages or error messages to the SYSLOG.

-T *phone-number*

> Replace the \T escape sequence in the chat script with the values specified for *phone-number*.

-U *phone-number-2*

> Replace the \U escape sequence in the chat script with the value specified for *phone-number-2*.

-v

> Runs the chat script in verbose mode. Verbose mode logs informational messages via syslogd.

-V

> Runs the chat script in stderr verbose mode. The stderr verbose mode displays informational messages on the stderr device. See Chapter 6 for an example of this being used with pppd.

-t *timeout*

> Sets the maximum time to wait for an expected string. If the expected string is not received in *timeout* seconds, the reply string is not sent and the script terminates—unless an alternate send is defined. If defined, the alternate send (more about this later) is sent and the remote system is given one more *timeout* period to respond. If this fails, the script is terminated with a nonzero error code. By default, the timeout period is 45 seconds.

-f *scriptfile*

> Reads the chat script from the *scriptfile* instead of from the command line. Multiple lines of expect/send pairs are permitted in the file.

-r *reportfile*

Writes the output generated by REPORT strings to the *reportfile*. By default, REPORT strings are written to stderr. The REPORT keyword is covered below.

In order to make the scripts more useful and robust, chat provides special keywords, escape sequences, and alternate send/expect pairs that can be used in the script. First let's look at the six basic chat keywords.

Two keywords transmit special signals to the remote system. The keyword EOT sends the End of Transmission character. On Unix systems, this is usually the End of File character, which is a Ctrl-D. The BREAK keyword sends a line break to the remote system. The five remaining keywords (TIMEOUT, ABORT, REPORT, CONNECT, and SAY) define processing characteristics for the script itself.

The TIMEOUT keyword defines the amount of time to wait for an expected string. Because it is defined inside the script, the timeout value can be changed for each expected string. For example, assume you want to allow the remote server 30 seconds to display the initial Username> prompt but only 5 seconds to display Password> once the username has been sent. Enter this script command:

```
TIMEOUT 30 name> karen TIMEOUT 5 word> beach%PARTY
```

The ABORT keyword and the REPORT keyword are similar. They both define strings that, when received, cause a special action to take place. The ABORT keyword defines strings that cause the script to abort if they are received when the system is expecting the string CONNECT from the modem. The REPORT keyword defines substrings that determine what messages received on the serial port should be written to stderr or the report file. A sample chat script file illustrates both of these keywords:

```
REPORT CONNECT
ABORT BUSY
ABORT 'NO CARRIER'
ABORT 'RING - NO ANSWER'
SAY "Dialing your PPP server..."
"" ATDT5551234
CONNECT \r
name> karen
word> beach%PARTY
```

The first line says that any message received by the script that contains the word CONNECT will be logged. If the -r command-line option was used when chat was started, the message is logged in the file defined by that option. Otherwise the message is displayed on stderr. The point of this command is to display the modem's connect message to the user. For example, the complete message might be CONNECT 28,800 LAPM/V, which tells the user the link speed and the transmission protocol used by the modems. The CONNECT message means success. The next three lines of the script begin with the keyword ABORT and define the modem messages that mean failure. If the modem responds with BUSY, NO CARRIER, or RING – NO ANSWER, the script aborts.

The SAY keyword sends the specified string to the user's terminal. In this case, we are telling the user that the dialing process has begun.

The last four lines are the basic expect/send pairs we have seen repeatedly in this section. We expect nothing ("") and send the dial command to the modem (ATDT). We expect CONNECT from the modem and send a carriage return (\r) to the remote server. We expect Username> from the remote server and send karen. Finally, we expect Password> from the server and send beach%PARTY.

chat extends the standard expect/send pair with an alternate send and an alternate expect to improve robustness. You may define an alternate send string and an alternate expect value to be used when the script times out waiting for the primary expected value. The alternate send and the alternate expect are indicated in the script by preceding them with dashes. For example:

    gin:-BREAK-gin: becca

In this sample we wait for the string gin: and send the string becca. The first string and the last string compose the standard expect/send pair. The alternate send/expect is used only if the timer expires and the expected gin: string has not been received. When this occurs, the script sends a line break, restarts the timer, and waits for gin: again, because that is what our alternate send/expect pair (-BREAK-gin:) tells the script to do. Note that unlike the standard expect/send pair, in the send/expect pair a value is transmitted before a string is expected, i.e., the send comes before the expect. Another example more in keeping with our other script examples is:

    name>--name> karen

Here the script expects the name> string. If it is not received, the script sends an empty line, which is simply a carriage return, and again waits for the name> string. This action is dictated by the alternate send/expect pair, --name>. The pair begins with a dash that signals the start of the send string, but the next character is the second dash that marks the beginning of the alternate expect string. There is no send string. It is this "empty string" that causes the script to send a single return character. This example is more common than the BREAK example shown above, though a little harder to explain.

The carriage return character is not the only special character that can be sent from a chat script. chat provides several escape sequences for sending and receiving special characters. Table A-2 lists these.

Table A-2. chat escape sequences

Escape sequence	Meaning
\b	The backspace character
\	Send without the terminating return character
\d	Delay sending for one second
\K	Send a BREAK
\n	Send a newline character
\N	Send a null character
\	Delay sending 1/10th of a second
\xd5	Send the string but don't log it
\r	The carriage return
\s	The space character
\T	Send the value provided on the chat command line by the -T argument
\t	The tab character
\U	Send the value provided on the chat command line by the -U argument
\\	The backslash character
\ddd	The ASCII character with the octal value ddd
^C	A control character

All of the escape sequences start with a backslash (\) except for the sequence used to enter a control character. Control characters are entered as a caret (^) followed by an uppercase letter. For example, control X is entered as ^X. The escape sequences that are described in Table A-2 with the words "send" or "sending" can be used only in a send string; all others can be used in either a send or expect string. Several escape sequences are used in the following example:

```
"" \d\d^G\p^G\p\p^GWake\sUp!\nSleepy\sHead!
```

Expect nothing (""). Wait two seconds (\d\d). Send three ASCII BELL characters, which is Ctrl-G on the keyboard, at intervals of 1/10 of a second (^G\p^G\p\p^G). Send the string Wake Up!. Go to a new line (\n) and send the string Sleepy Head!.

For security reasons, some servers call the client back before allowing the connection. This allows the server to verify that the client call is coming from an approved telephone number. It works this way:

- The client calls the server and provides an identifying string.
- The server hangs up after receiving the string.
- The server uses the identifying string to find out the valid phone number for the client and calls the client back.
- The client continues with the login process.

The fact that the server hangs up the connection could cause a problem for a chat script. Normally, a hangup unconditionally ends the connection. chat provides the HANGUP command to handle "callback" servers. The command HANGUP OFF prevents chat from ending the login script when the server breaks the connection. Place the HANGUP OFF command immediately after the command that sends the identifying script to the server. After the server calls back and the connection is established, use the HANGUP ON command to return to normal hangup processing. HANGUP ON is the default. With HANGUP ON, the script terminates when a hangup is detected.

When a chat script terminates, a termination code is set. A termination code is a numeric value that represents the state of the script when it exited. The basic numeric codes and what those codes mean is shown below:

0

> The script terminated normally.

1

> The script failed because of an invalid parameter or an expect string that overflowed the internal buffer.

2

> The script shut down because of an I/O error or a termination signal (SIGINT/SIGTERM).

3

> The program terminated because an expected string was not received before the timeout.

4 or more

> A condition defined by an ABORT command occurred. The numeric value indicates which condition occurred. The condition defined by the first ABORT command is assigned the value 4; the condition defined by the second ABORT command is assigned the value 5; the condition defined by the third ABORT command is assigned the value 6; and so on.

The termination codes 0 through 3 are self-explanatory. An example is useful for understanding the codes above 3.

The sample script shown earlier in this section contained three ABORT commands: the first one for the BUSY condition, the second one for the NO CARRIER condition, and the third one for the RING – NO ANSWER condition. If the modem returns the BUSY string, the script aborts and returns the termination code 4. If the modem returns the string RING – NO ANSWER, the script aborts and returns the termination code 6. The codes are "position dependent." If another user rewrote this script and placed the ABORT RING – NO ANSWER command before the other ABORT commands, aborting on the RING – NO ANSWER condition would return a termination code of 4 instead of the 6 it returns in our script.

A gated Reference

This appendix covers the syntax of the gated command and the gated configuration language for Gated 3.6—the publicly available version of gated. As a reference to the gated configuration language, this appendix stands on its own. But to fully understand how to configure gated, use this reference in conjunction with the sample configuration files in Chapter 7.

gated is constantly being improved. As it is upgraded, the command language changes. Refer to the latest manpages for the most recent information about gated.

The gated Command

The syntax of the gated command is:

```
gated [-v] [-c] [-C] [-n] [-N] [-t trace_options] [-f config_file] [trace_file]
```

The -c and -n command-line options debug the routing configuration file without impacting the network or the kernel routing table. Frequently, these debugging options are used with a test configuration identified by the -f config_file option:

-c

Tells gated to read the configuration file and check for syntax errors. When gated finishes reading the configuration file, it produces a snapshot of its status and then terminates. It writes the snapshot to */usr/tmp/gated_dump*. Running gated with the -c option does not require superuser privileges, and it is not necessary to terminate the active gated process.

-C

Checks the configuration file for syntax errors. gated exits with a status 1 if there are errors and 0 if there are none. Because this provides exit status, it is useful for script files.

-n

Tells gated not to update the kernel routing table. This is used to test the routing configuration with real routing data without interfering with system operation.

-f *config_file*

Tells gated to read the configuration from *config_file* instead of from the default configuration file, */etc/gated.conf*. Used in conjunction with the -c option, -f checks a new configuration without interfering with the currently running gated configuration.

The -v option causes gated to display its version number. When this is used, no other options are used because gated terminates immediately after displaying the version information.

The -N command-line option prevents gated from running in background mode as a daemon. This option is used when gated is started from *inittab*. By default, gated runs as a daemon.

The command-line arguments *trace_options* and *trace_file* are used for protocol tracing. The *trace_file* argument names the file to which the trace output is written. If a file is not specified, the trace is written to the standard output. Tracing usually produces a large amount of output.

The command-line options used for tracing are:

-t

This option turns on tracing. If -t is specified with no *trace_options*, gated defaults to general tracing, which traces normal protocol interactions and routing table changes. gated always logs protocol errors even if no tracing is specified. You can define several different *trace_options*, all of which are described later in this appendix. A few *trace_options* (detail, send, recv) cannot be specified on the gated command line. Two others are most useful when they are defined on the command line:

symbols

Traces the symbols read from the kernel, which is primarily of interest to developers debugging the interaction of gated and the kernel.

iflist

Traces the list of interfaces read from the kernel. Use this to determine what interfaces are detected by the kernel interface scan.

The advantage of placing a trace option on the command line is that it can trace activities that happen before the configuration file is processed. For the two options listed above, this is an essential advantage. For other options, it is not very important. Most trace options are specified in the configuration file. See the traceoptions command later in this appendix for more details.

Signal Processing

gated processes the following signals:

SIGHUP
> Tells gated to reread the configuration file. The new configuration replaces the one that gated is currently running. SIGHUP loads the new configuration file without interrupting gated service. SIGHUP is available for quick configuration changes. At most sites, the routing configuration changes infrequently. The few times you need to change to a new configuration, terminate gated and rerun it with the new configuration. This is a more accurate test of how things will run at the next boot.

SIGINT
> Tells gated to snapshot its current state to the file */usr/tmp/gated_dump*.

SIGTERM
> Tells gated to shut down gracefully. All protocols are shut down following the rules of that protocol. For example, EGP sends a CEASE message and waits for it to be confirmed. SIGTERM removes from the kernel routing table all routes learned via the exterior routing protocols. If you need to preserve those routes while gated is out of operation, use SIGKILL.

SIGKILL
> Tells gated to terminate immediately and dump core. Routes are not removed from the routing table, and no graceful shutdown is attempted.

SIGUSR1
> Tells gated to toggle tracing. If no trace flags are set, SIGUSR1 has no effect. But if tracing is enabled, the first SIGUSR1 causes gated to toggle off tracing and to close the trace file. The next SIGUSR1 turns tracing back on and opens the trace file. When the trace file is closed, it can be moved or removed without interfering with the operation of gated. Use this to periodically empty out the trace file to prevent it from becoming too large.

SIGUSR2
> Tells gated to check for changes in the status of the network interfaces.

The following is an example of gated signal handling. First, the SIGUSR1 signal is passed to the gated process using the process ID obtained from the *gated.pid* file (*/var/run/gated.pid* in this case).

```
# kill -USR1 'cat /var/run/gated.pid'
```

Next, the old trace file (*/usr/tmp/gated.log* in this case) is removed, and gated is passed another SIGUSR1 signal.

```
# rm /usr/tmp/gated.log
# kill -USR1 'cat /etc/gated.pid'
```

After receiving the second signal, gated opens a fresh trace file (still named */usr/tmp/gated.log*). An ls shows that the new file has been created.

```
# ls -l /usr/tmp/gated.log
-rw-rw-r--  1 root          105 Jul  6 16:41 /usr/tmp/gated.log
```

The gated Configuration Language

The gated configuration language is a highly structured language similar to C in appearance. Comments either begin with a #, or they begin with /* and end with */. gated configuration statements end with a semicolon, and groups of associated statements are enclosed in curly braces. The language structure is familiar to most Unix system administrators, and the structure makes it easy to see what parts of the configuration are associated with each other. This is important when multiple protocols are configured in the same file.

The configuration language is composed of nine types of statements. Two statement types, *directive statements* and *trace statements*, can occur anywhere in the *gated.conf* file and do not directly relate to the configuration of any protocol. These statements provide instructions to the parser and control tracing from within the configuration file. The other seven statement types are *options statements*, *interface statements*, *definition statements*, *protocol statements*, *static statements*, *control statements*, and *aggregate statements*. These statements must appear in the configuration file in the correct order, starting with options statements and ending with aggregate statements. Entering a statement out of order causes an error when parsing the file.

The remainder of this appendix provides a description of all commands in the gated configuration language, organized by statement type.

Directive Statements

Directive statements provide direction to the gated command language parser about "include" files. An include file is an external file whose contents are parsed into the configuration as if it were part of the original *gated.conf* file. Include files can contain references to other include files, and these references can be nested up to 10 levels deep.

The two directive statements are:

%include *filename*
> Identifies an include file. The contents of the file are "included" in the *gated.conf* file at the point in the *gated.conf* file where the %include directive is encountered. *filename* is any valid Unix filename. If *filename* is not fully qualified, i.e., does not begin with a /, it is considered to be relative to the directory defined in the %directory directive.

%directory *pathname*
> Defines the directory where the include files are stored. When it is used, gated looks in the directory identified by *pathname* for any include file that does not have a fully qualified filename.

Unless you have a very complex routing configuration, avoid using include files. In a complex environment, segmenting a large configuration into smaller, more easily understood segments can be helpful, but most gated configurations are very small. One of the great advantages of gated is that it combines the configuration of several different routing protocols into a single file. If that file is small and easy to read, segmenting the file unnecessarily complicates things.

Trace Statements

Trace statements allow you to control the trace file and its contents from within the *gated.conf* file. The trace statement is:

```
traceoptions
["trace_file" [replace] [size bytes[k|m] files n]]
[nostamp]
trace_options [except trace_options]
;
```

Its components are as follows:

trace_file
> Identifies the file that receives the trace output. It has exactly the same function as the *trace_file* argument on the gated command line.

replace
> Replaces the existing trace file. If you do not use this keyword, the trace output is appended to the current contents of the file.

size *bytes*[k|m] [files *n*]
> Limits the trace file to a maximum size of *bytes*. The optional k or m indicates thousands (k) or millions (m) of bytes. Thus 1000000 and 10m are equivalent entries. The size of the trace file cannot be less than 10k bytes. *n* defines the maximum number of trace files that should be saved. When the trace file reaches the maximum size, it is saved as *trace_file*.0, *trace_file*.1, *trace_file*.2 up to *trace_file*.*n*. The next save then overwrites *trace_file*.0. The value for *n* must be at least 2.

nostamp
> Specifies that trace lines should not begin with a timestamp. Timestamping each line of trace data is the default.

trace_options
> Defines the events to be traced by gated. Each trace option is specified by a keyword name. The available trace options are:

> Turns off all tracing.

all
> Turns on all types of global tracing.

general
> Turns on both normal and route tracing.

state
> Traces state machine transitions for protocols such as OSPF and BGP. The RFCs describe these protocols using *finite state machine* (FSM) diagrams or tables. The protocols transition from one state to another based on the occurrence of certain events. For example, the state might change from *idle* to *connect* when a *connection open* event occurs. This is a highly specialized trace flag, useful only to those who have a thorough understanding of the protocols involved. Use this option within the protocol statement to trace a specific protocol's transitions.

normal
> Traces normal protocol interactions. Errors are always traced.

policy
> Traces the application of routing policies. Use this to check that you have properly configured your routing policy.

task
> Traces system-level processing.

timer
> Traces the various timers used by a protocol or peer.

route
> Traces routing table changes. Use this to check that routes are properly installed by the protocol.

detail
> Traces the contents of the packets exchanged by the router. Must be specified before send or recv.

send
> Limits the detail trace to packets sent by this router.

recv
> Limits the detail trace to packets received by this router. Without these two options, all packets are traced when detail is specified.

symbols
> Traces the symbols read from the kernel at startup. See the -t command-line argument.

iflist
> Traces the kernel interface list. See the -t command-line argument.

parse
> Traces the lexical analyzer and parser.

adv
> Traces the allocation and release of blocks.

except *trace_options*
> Disables specific trace options. Must be used in conjunction with *trace_options* that enable a wide variety of tracing. For example, traceoptions all except state turns on all traces except for finite state machine tracing.

gated provides the flexibility for you to choose where you want to control tracing—on the command line or in the configuration file. By and large, the same trace options can be set on the gated command line or in the configuration file. detail, send, and recv can be set only in the configuration file.

Two others, symbols and iflist, are primarily used on the command line. Refer to the section on the gated command for a description of setting trace options with -t.

Some trace options are useful only for protocol developers and other experts. For most of us, general, which enables normal and route tracing, is an appropriate level of information for debugging routing problems. Occasionally, policy is useful for testing a routing policy. Most of the time, however, no tracing is needed.

Options Statements

Options statements define parameters that direct gated to do special internal processing. Options statements appear before any other configuration statements in the *gated.conf* file.

The options statement syntax is:

```
options
[nosend]
[noresolv]
[gendefault [preference preference] [gateway gateway]]
[syslog [upto] log_level]
[mark time]
;
```

An options statement can contain:

nosend
> Instructs the system not to send any packets. This option tests gated without actually sending out routing information. Use for RIP and HELLO. It is not yet implemented for BGP and is not useful for OSPF.

noresolv
> Instructs the system not to use the Domain Name System (DNS) to resolve hostnames and addresses. DNS failures can cause gated to deadlock during startup. Use this to prevent deadlock.

gendefault [preference *preference*] [gateway *gateway*]

    Generates a default route, with a preference of 20, when gated peers with an EGP or BGP neighbor. If gateway is not defined, the gateway in the generated route is the system itself, the default route is not installed in the kernel table, and this option is used only to advertise this system as a default gateway. If gateway is specified, the default route is installed in the kernel table with the specified router as the next hop. This option can be overridden with the nogendefault option.

syslog [upto] *log_level*

    Tells the system to use the setlogmask facility to control gated logging. See the setlogmask(3) manpage if this facility is available on your system.

mark *time*

    Sends a periodic timestamp message to the trace file. *time* defines how frequently the timestamp should be issued. Use this to determine if gated is running.

Interface Statements

An interface statement defines configuration options for the network interfaces. The *interface_list* identifies the interfaces affected by the configuration options. The interfaces in the list are identified by interface name (e.g., le0), by hostname, by IP address, or by the keyword all. The keyword all refers to every interface on the system. The interface name can refer to a single interface or a group of interfaces. For example, an interface name of eth0 refers to the interface eth0, whereas the name le refers to all installed interfaces that start with the letters le (which might include le0, le1, and le2). A hostname can be used if it resolves to only one address.

Most system administrators prefer to use the IP address to identify an interface. After all, IP addresses are inherently a part of TCP/IP, and it's TCP/IP routing that this file configures.

Additionally, remote systems know this interface by its IP address, not its interface name. Finally, DNS may provide more than one address for a hostname, and future Unix operating systems may allow more than one address per interface. IP addresses are safest.

gated supports four types of interfaces: loopback, broadcast, point-to-point, and nonbroadcast multiple access (NBMA). All of these are discussed in the text of this book except for NBMA. It is a multiple access interface, but the underlying network is not capable of broadcast. Examples are Frame Relay and X.25.

gated ignores any interface in the list that has an invalid local, remote, or broadcast address, or an invalid subnet mask. gated also ignores a point-to-point interface that has the same local and remote addresses. gated assumes that interfaces that are not marked UP by the kernel do not exist.

The syntax of the interfaces statement is:

```
interfaces {
    options
       [strictinterfaces]
       [scaninterval time]
       [ aliases-nexthop ( primary | lowestip | keepall ) ];
    interface interface_list
       [preference preference]
       [down preference preference]
       [passive]
       [simplex]
       [reject]
       [blackhole]
       [ AS autonomoussystem ];
    define address
       [broadcast address] | [pointopoint address]
       [netmask mask]
       [multicast] ;
} ;
```

The configuration options defined before the interface list are global options. The global options are:

strictinterfaces
> Generates a fatal error if an interface referenced in the configuration file is not found when gated scans the kernel at startup and is not listed in a define statement. (See the define option later in this section.) Normally a warning message is issued and gated continues running.

scaninterval time
> Specifies how often gated scans the kernel interface list for changes. The default is every 15 seconds on most systems, and 60 seconds on systems that pass interface status changes through the routing socket, such as BSD 4.4. Note that gated also scans the interface list on receipt of a SIGUSR2.

aliases-nexthop (primary | lowestip | keepall)
> Defines the next-hop address that gated installs for interface routes. primary, which is the default, uses the primary interface address as the gateway for an interface route. lowestip uses the lowest IP address as the next-hop address. keepall retains all interface routes in the kernel.

The interface command defines the interface_list and all of the options that affect the specified interfaces. Options available on this statement are:

preference preference
> Sets the preference for this interface. The value preference is a number between 0 and 255. gated prefers routes through interfaces with low preference numbers. The default preference for all directly attached network interfaces is 0.

down preference *preference*

Sets the preference used when gated believes an interface is not functioning properly. The default is 120.

passive

Prevents gated from downgrading the preference of the interface when it is not functioning properly. gated assumes that an interface is down when it stops receiving routing information through that interface. gated performs this check only if the interface is actively participating in a routing protocol.

simplex

Specifies that gated should not use packets generated by this system as an indication that the interface is functioning properly. Only packets from remote systems are used to indicate that the interface is operating.

reject | blackhole

Either of these keywords identifies the interface as the "blackhole interface" used to install rejected routes in the kernel. (See the control statements for more about rejected routes.) This is available only on BSD systems that have installed a reject/blackhole pseudo-interface.

AS *autonomoussystem*

Identifies the autonomous system number that gated should use when creating an AS path vector for this route. You should recall that some routing protocols, such as BGP, associate an AS path with a route.

The define *address* command lists interfaces that might not be present when gated scans the kernel interface list at startup. It overrides the strictinterfaces option for the interface defined by *address*. Possible options for the define command are:

broadcast *address*

Defines the broadcast address.

pointopoint *address*

Defines the local address for a point-to-point interface. (See Chapter 6 for a discussion of point-to-point interfaces.) When this option is used, the address on the define statement specifies the address of the remote host, and the address specified after the pointopoint keyword defines the local address. Don't use both broadcast and pointopoint in the same define.

netmask *mask*

Defines the subnet mask.

multicast

Specifies that the interface supports multicasting.

Definition Statements

Definition statements are general configuration statements that relate to more than one protocol. Definition statements must appear before any protocol statements in *gated.conf*. The three definition statements are:

autonomoussystem *asn* [loops *n*] ;
> Defines the autonomous system number (*asn*) used by BGP or EGP. The loops number defines the number of times this autonomous system may appear in an AS path for path vector protocols, such as BGP. The default value for *n* is 1.

routerid *address* ;
> Defines the router identifier used by BGP and OSPF. Use the address of your primary OSPF or BGP interface. By default, gated uses the address of the first interface it encounters.

martians {host *address* [allow]; *address* [mask *mask* | masklen *number*] [allow] ; default [allow] ; } ;
> Changes the list of addresses about which all routing information is ignored. Sometimes a misconfigured system sends out obviously invalid destination addresses. These invalid addresses, called *martians*, are rejected by the routing software. This command allows changes to the list of martian addresses. A martian address can be specified as a host address by using the host keyword before the address, or as a network address by simply specifying the address.

An address mask can be defined for a network address. The mask can be defined in dotted decimal notation using the mask keyword or as a numeric prefix length using the masklen keyword. The address masks mask 255.255.0.0 and masklen 16 are equivalent. If no address mask is specified, the natural mask is used. Specifying an address in the martians statement adds the address to the martians list. The allow keyword is used to remove an address from the martians list. When an address is removed from the martians list, it then becomes a valid address for routing.

gated contains a standard martian list of addresses that are known to be invalid. This is the default martian list. The option default allow removes all of the standard entries from the martians list and permits unrestricted routing. Don't do this if you're on a connected network.

Here is a sample of each definition statement:

```
autonomoussystem 249 ;
routerid 172.16.12.2 ;
martians {
        host 0.0.0.26 ;
        192.168.0.0 masklen 16 allow ; } ;
```

The statements in the sample perform the following functions:

- The autonomoussystem statement tells gated to use AS number 249 for its BGP or EGP packets.
- The routerid statement tells gated to use 172.16.12.2 as the router identifier for OSPF and BGP.
- The martians statement prevents routes to 0.0.0.26 from being included in the table, but it allows routes to the private IP addresses in the range 192.168.0.0 to 192.168.255.255.

Protocol Statements

Protocol statements enable or disable protocols and set protocol options. The protocol statements occur after the definition statements and before the static statements. There are many protocol statements, and more may be added at any time. There are statements for the various interior and exterior routing protocols and for other things that are not really routing protocols.

In this section we begin with the interior protocols, move on to the exterior protocols, and finish with the special "protocols."

The ospf Statement

```
ospf yes | no | on | off  [{
   defaults {
     preference preference ;
     cost cost ;
     tag [as] tag ;
     type 1 | 2 ;
     inherit-metric; } ;
   exportlimit routes ;
   exportinterval time ;
   traceoptions trace_options ;
   syslog [first count] [every count];
   monitorauthkey key ;
   backbone | area number {
     authtype 0 | 1 | none | simple ;
     stub [cost cost]  ;
     networks {
       address [mask mask | masklen number] [restrict]  ;
       host address [restrict]  ; } ;
     stubhosts {
       address cost cost ; } ;
     interface interface_list [nonbroadcast] [cost cost]  {
       pollinterval time ;
       routers {
       address [eligible]  ; } ;
       interface_parameters } ;
```

```
     virtuallink neighborid router_id transitarea area {
     interface_parameters } ;
} ; } ] ;
```

The ospf statement enables or disables the Open Shortest Path First (OSPF) routing protocol. By default, OSPF is disabled. It is enabled by specifying yes or on (it doesn't matter which you use) and it is disabled with no or off.

 For the sake of brevity, this text explains only the first occurrence of any *gated.conf* parameter if it is used the same way in subsequent commands. Only differences between commands are explained. For example, yes | no | on | off is not explained again because it is always used in the same way to enable or disable a protocol.

The ospf statement has many configuration parameters:

defaults
> Defines the defaults used when importing OSPF routes from an external autonomous system and announcing those routes to other OSPF routers. The link-state advertisement (LSA) used to announce these routes is called an ASE (autonomous system external) because it contains routes from external autonomous systems. See the description of OSPF in Chapter 7.

preference *preference*
> Defines the preference of OSPF ASE routes. The default is 150.

cost *cost*
> Defines the cost used when advertising a non-OSPF route in an ASE. The default is 1.

tag [as] *tag*
> Defines the OSPF ASE tag value. The tag is not used by the OSPF protocol but may be used by an export policy to filter routes. (See the export statement later in this appendix.) When the as keyword is specified, the tag field may contain AS path information.

type 1 | 2
> Defines the type of ASE used. The default is type 1. Type 1 contains routes learned from an external protocol that provides a metric directly comparable to the OSPF metric. The metric is added to the cost of reaching the border router when routes are advertised. A type 2 ASE contains routes learned from an exterior gateway protocol that does not provide a routing metric comparable to the OSPF metric. These routes are advertised with the cost of reaching the border router. See Chapter 7.

inherit-metric
> Directs gated to use the external metric for ASE routes if no metric is defined in the export statement.

exportlimit *routes*

> Defines the maximum number of ASE LSAs that will be flooded at one time. The default is 100.

exportinterval *time*

> Defines how frequently ASE link-state advertisements are flooded to the network. The default is once per second.

traceoptions *trace_options*

> Defines the tracing used to debug OSPF. In addition to the standard trace flags, OSPF supports:
>
> lsabuild
>
> > Traces construction of link-state advertisements (LSAs).
>
> spf
>
> > Traces the Shortest Path First (SPF) calculations.
>
> hello
>
> > Traces the OSPF HELLO packets.
>
> dd
>
> > Traces the OSPF Database Description packets.
>
> request
>
> > Traces the OSPF Link-State Request packets.
>
> lsu
>
> > Traces the OSPF Link-State Update packets.
>
> ack
>
> > Traces the OSPF Link-State Ack packets.

syslog [first *number*] [every *count*]

> Defines packet capture parameters. first specifies the number of packets captured for each type of OSPF packet. every specifies how often packets are captured after the initial group is captured. For example, if *count* is set to 50, every fiftieth packet of each type is captured.

monitorauthkey *password*

> Defines the password used for ospf_monitor queries. By default these queries are not authenticated. If monitorauthkey is specified, incoming queries must contain the specified password.

backbone | area *number*

> Defines the OSPF area of which this router is a member. Every router must belong to an area. If more than one area is configured, at least one must be the backbone. The backbone is defined using the backbone keyword. All other areas are defined by the area keyword and the number of the area, e.g., area 1. See Chapter 7 for a discussion of OSPF areas. Several configuration parameters are associated with each area:

stub [cost *cost*]

> Specifies that this is a stub area. A stub area is one in which there are no ASE routes. If a cost is specified, it is used to advertise a default route into the stub area.

networks

> Defines the range of networks contained within this area. The specified ranges are advertised into other areas as summary network LSAs and not as inter-area routes. If restrict is specified, the summary network LSAs are not advertised. The entries in the networks list are either specified as a host address by using the host keyword before the address, or as a network address by simply specifying the address. An address mask can be defined for a network address. The mask can be defined in dotted decimal notation using the mask keyword or as a numeric prefix length using the masklen keyword. The address masks mask 255.255.0.0 and masklen 16 are equivalent. If no address mask is specified, the natural mask is used. This option can reduce the amount of routing information propagated between areas.

stubhosts

> Lists the directly attached hosts, and their costs, that should be advertised as reachable from this router. List point-to-point interfaces here.

interface *interface_list* [nobroadcast] [cost *cost*]

> Defines the interfaces used by OSPF. If the keyword nobroadcast is specified, the interface connects to a nonbroadcast multiple access (NBMA) network. If nobroadcast is not used, the interface connects to a broadcast or a point-to-point network. Specify the cost of the interface with the cost keyword, e.g., cost 5. The default cost is 1. Two options are specific to NBMA interfaces:

pollinterval *time*

> Defines the time interval at which OSPF HELLO packets are sent to neighbors.

routers

> Lists all neighbors by address. The eligible keyword indicates if the neighbor can become a designated router.

All interfaces—NBMA and broadcast—can use these parameters:

enable | disable ;

> Enables or disables the interface.

retransmitinterval *time* ;

> Defines the number of seconds between link-state advertisement retransmissions.

transitdelay *time* ;

> Defines the estimated number of seconds required to transmit a link-state update over this interface. It must be greater than 0.

priority *priority* ;
> Defines this system's priority for the designated router election. *priority* is a number from 0 to 255. The router with the highest priority becomes the designated router. A router whose priority is 0 is ineligible to become the designated router. See Chapter 7 for a discussion of designated routers.

hellointerval *time* ;
> Defines the number of seconds between transmissions of HELLO packets.

routerdeadinterval *time* ;
> Defines the timeout before a neighbor is declared down. *time* is the maximum number of seconds this router will wait for a neighbor's HELLO packet.

auth [none | simple *password* | md5 *key*] ;
> Defines the type of authentication used to authenticate OSPF packets. none selects no authentication. simple selects password authentication. The *password* is specified as one to eight decimal digits separated by periods, a one- to eight-byte hexadecimal string preceded by 0x, or a one- to eight-character string in double quotes. md5 selects MD5 authentication. *key* is a valid MD5 cryptographic key.

virtuallink neighborid *router_id* transitarea *area*
> Defines a virtual link for the backbone area. The *router_id* is the router identifier of the remote router at the other end of the virtual link. The transit area must be one of the other areas configured on this system. All standard interface parameters defined above may be specified on a virtual link.

The rip Statement

```
rip yes | no | on | off [ {
    broadcast ;
    nobroadcast ;
    nocheckzero ;
    preference preference ;
    defaultmetric metric ;
    query authentication [none | [simple | md5 password]]  ;
    interface interface_list
       [noripin] | [ripin]
       [noripout] | [ripout]
       [metricin metric]
       [metricout metric]
       [version 1 | 2 [multicast | broadcast]]
       [[secondary] authentication [none | [simple | md5 password]] ;
    trustedgateways gateway_list ;
    sourcegateways gateway_list ;
    traceoptions trace_options ; } ] ;
```

The rip statement enables or disables RIP. By default RIP is enabled. The rip statement options are:

broadcast
> Forces gated to broadcast RIP update packets even if the system has only one network interface. By default, RIP updates are not broadcast if the system has only one network interface and are broadcast if it has more than one network interface; i.e., hosts do not broadcast updates and routers do.

nobroadcast
> Forces gated to *not* broadcast RIP update packets even if the system has more than one network interface. If a sourcegateways clause is present, routes are still unicast directly to that gateway. See sourcegateways later in this section.

notcheckzero
> Specifies that gated should not reject incoming version 1 RIP packets where the reserved fields are 0. Rejecting those packets is standard practice.

preference *preference* ;
> Sets the gated preference for routes learned from RIP. The default preference for these routes is 100.

defaultmetric *metric* ;
> Defines the metric used when advertising routes via RIP that were learned from other protocols. The default *metric* is 16, which to RIP indicates an unusable route. This means that by default, routes learned from other protocols are not advertised as valid routes by RIP. Set a lower value only if you want all routes learned from other protocols advertised at that metric.

query authentication [none | [simple | md5 *key*]] ;
> Specifies the authentication used for nonrouter query packets. The default is none. If simple is specified, the *key* is a 16-byte password. If md5 is specified, the *key* is a 16-byte value used with the packet contents to generate a Message Digest 5 cryptographic checksum.

interface *interface_list*
> Identifies the interfaces over which RIP runs and defines the configuration parameters of those interfaces. The *interface_list* can contain interface names, hostnames, IP addresses, or the keyword all. Possible parameters are:

> noripin
>> Tells system to ignore RIP packets received on this interface. The default is to listen to RIP packets on all nonloopback interfaces.

> ripin
>> Tells system to listen to RIP packets received on this interface. This is the default.

> noripout
>> Tells system not to send RIP packets out this interface. The default is to send RIP on all broadcast and nonbroadcast interfaces when in broadcast mode. See the nobroadcast option defined earlier in this list.

ripout

> Tells system to send RIP packets out this interface. This is the default.

metricin *metric*

> Specifies the RIP metric used for routes received on this interface. The default is the kernel interface metric plus 1, which is the default RIP hop count. If this metric is specified, it is used as the absolute value and is not added to the kernel metric.

metricout

> Specifies the RIP metric added to routes sent out this interface. The default is 0. This option can only increase the metric.

version 1 | 2 [multicast | broadcast]

> Identifies the version of RIP used for updates sent out this interface. Available versions are RIP 1 and RIP 2. RIP 1 is the default. If RIP 2 is specified and IP multicast is supported, full version 2 packets are sent via multicast. If multicast is not available, version 1–compatible version 2 packets are sent via broadcast. The keyword multicast, the default, specifies this behavior. The keyword broadcast specifies that RIP version 1–compatible version 2 packets should be broadcast on this interface, even if IP multicast is available. Neither keyword is used with version 1.

[secondary] authentication [none | simple | md5 *key*]

> Defines the RIP version 2 authentication used on this interface. The default authentication type is none. If simple is specified, the *key* is a 16-byte password. If md5 is specified, the *key* is a 16-byte value used with the packet contents to generate a Message Digest 5 cryptographic checksum. If secondary is specified, this defines the secondary authentication type. Packets are always sent using the primary authentication technique. The secondary authentication type is defined only for incoming packets. Inbound packets are checked against both the primary and secondary authentication methods before being discarded as invalid.

trustedgateways *gateway_list* ;

> Defines the list of gateways from which RIP accepts updates. The *gateway_list* is simply a list of hostnames or IP addresses. By default, all gateways on the shared network are trusted to supply routing information. But if the trustedgateways statement is used, only updates from the gateways in the list are accepted.

sourcegateways *gateway_list* ;

> Defines a list of gateways to which RIP sends packets directly. By default, RIP packets are broadcast or multicast to several systems on the shared network, but if this statement is used, RIP unicasts packets directly to the listed gateways.

traceoptions *trace_options*

> Defines tracing for RIP. RIP supports most of the standard tracing options as well as these packet-tracing options:

packets

> Traces all RIP packets.

request

> Traces the RIP information request packets, such as REQUEST, POLL, and POLLENTRY.

response

> Traces all RIP RESPONSE packets.

other

> Traces any other type of RIP packet.

The isis Statement

```
isis on | off {
    [ area areaid ; ]
    [ area auth simple key ; ]
    [ domain auth simple key ; ]
    [ domain-wide on | off ; ]
    [ export-defaults ; ]
    [ export-defaults level 1 | 2 ; ]
    [ export-defaults metric metric | inherit ; ]
    [ export-defaults metric-type internal | external ; ]
    [ external preference preference ; ]
    [ level 1 | 2 | 1 and 2 ; ]
    [ interface name | address [ {
        [ enable | disable ; ]
        [ auth simple key ; ]
        [ csn-interval interval [ level 1 | 2 | 1 and 2 ] ; ]
        [ dis-hello-interval interval [ level 1 | 2 | 1 and 2 ] ; ]
        [ encap [ iso | ip ] ; ]
        [ hello-interval interval [ level 1 | 2 | 1 and 2 ] ; ]
        [ hello-multiplier number [ level 1 | 2 | 1 and 2 ] ; ]
        [ lsp-interval interval ; ]
        [ level 1 | 2 | 1 and 2 ; ]
        [ max-burst number ; ]
        [ metric metric [ level 1 | 2 | 1 and 2 ] ; ]
        [ passive on | off ; ]
        [ priority priority [ level 1 | 2 | 1 and 2 ] ; ]
        [ retransmit-interval interval ; ]
    } ] ; ]
    [ overload-bit on | off ; ]
    [ preference preference ; ]
    [ psn-interval intervalt ; ]
    [ require-snp-auth on | off ; ]
    [ ribs unicast | unicast multicast ; ]
    [ spf-interval interval ; ]
    [ inet6 on | off ; ]
    [ summary-originate [ inet | inet6 ] {
        [network (mask mask | masklen n ) metric cost-value ; ]
    } ; ]
```

```
[ summary-filter [ inet | inet6 ] {
    [network mask mask | masklen number ; ]
} ; ]
[ systemid systemid ; ]
[ traceoptions traceoptions ; ]
[ config-time seconds ; ]
[ es-config-time seconds ; ]
[ hold-time seconds ; ]
};
```

The isis statement enables the IS-IS protocol. By default, it is disabled. The options that may appear in the isis statement are:

area *areaid*

> Adds area addresses to those configured automatically from the circuits. IS-IS area addresses are automatically configured based on the real circuits over which IS-IS runs. Up to three areas can be added using area statements.

area auth simple *key*

> Enables authentication for level 1 routing and selects the key. The format for *key* is one to eight decimal digits separated by periods, a one- to eight-byte hexadecimal string preceded by 0x, or a one- to eight-character string in double quotes. The same *key* format is used throughout the isis statement.

domain auth simple *key*

> Enables authentication and selects the key for level 2 routing.

export-defaults level 1 | 2

> Sets the protocol level used for exported routes. By default, a level 1 router exports at level 1, and a level 2 router supports both level 1 and 2.

export-defaults metric *metric* | inherit

> Defines the default metric used on routes exported as IS-IS from another protocol. The default is to use the metric already contained in the route, which is indicated by the inherit keyword.

export-defaults metric-type internal | external

> Defines the type of the metric used on routes exported as IS-IS from another protocol. The default is internal.

external preference *preference*

> Defines the preference of external routes learned from IS-IS. The default preference is 151.

level 1 | 2 | 1 and 2

> Sets the protocol level for this intermediate system. A level 1 system is an intra-area router. A level 1 system cannot have any level 2 interfaces. A level 2 system is an inter-area router, and it cannot have any level 1 interfaces. A level 1 and 2 system may have level 1, level 2, and level 1 and 2 interfaces. Additionally, individual options relating to protocol settings can be specified as level 1, level 2

or level 1 and 2 depending on the specific level for which the option is being set when the system supports level 1 and 2. The default is level 1 and 2.

interface *name* | *address*

Identifies the interfaces on which to run IS-IS. The default is all. The following options can be set for each interface:

enable | disable

enable or disable the interface. The default is enable.

auth simple *key*

Enables authentication and selects the authentication key for this interface.

csn-interval *interval* [level 1 | 2 | 1 and 2]

Sets the interval at which this system will multicast CSN packets if it is elected the Designated Intermediate System (DIS). The *interval* can be from 1 to 100 seconds.

dis-hello-interval *interval* [level 1 | 2 | 1 and 2]

Sets the interval at which this system will send hello messages if it is elected the DIS. The *interval* can be from 1 to 100 seconds.

encap [ip | iso]

Selects the type of encapsulation used. The default is ip.

hello-interval *interval* [level 1 | 2 | 1 and 2]

Defines the interval at which hello packets are sent on the interface. *interval* can be from 1 to 300 seconds.

hello-multiplier *number* [level 1 | 2 | 1 and 2]

Defines the number of hello packets that must be missed before a neighbor is considered "down." Thus if *number* is set to 3 and no hello packets are received from a neighbor in the amount of time in which three hello packets are normally received, the neighbor is considered down. *number* can be from 1 to 100.

lsp-interval *interval*

Defines the interval at which LSP packets are sent on the interface.

level 1 | 2 | 1 and 2 ;

Defines the protocol level used on this interface.

max-burst *number*

Defines the maximum number of packets that can be sent in a burst.

metric *metric* [level 1 | 2 | 1 and 2]

Defines the cost associated with this interface.

passive on | off

Indicates whether this interface should be treated as an active or passive interface.

priority *priority* [level 1 | 2 | 1 and 2]

> Sets the priority number used for the DIS election. *priority* is a value from 1 to 127.

retransmit-interval *interval*

> Defines the interval at which packets are retransmitted on the interface.

overload-bit on | off

Enables or disables use of the overload bit.

preference *preference*

Sets the gated preference for IS-IS routes. The default is 11.

psn-interval *interval*

Defines how often PSN packets are sent by this system. *interval* can be 1 to 20 seconds.

ribs unicast | unicast multicast

Defines the routing information base format used for IS-IS routes. The default is unicast.

spf-interval *interval*

Defines the amount of time to wait for more changes to occur before recalculating the routing table. *interval* can be from 1 to 60 seconds.

inet6 on | off

Enables support for IPv6 routing.

summary-originate

Defines how level 1 routes are summarized in this system's routing information base for level 2 routing. summary-originate is used only if this system is a level 2 router. *network* identifies the level 1 address received, and the network mask, defined as either a mask or a numeric mask length, aggregates the routes.

summary-filter

Defines how level 1 routes are summarized when this system advertises them through level 2 routing. summary-filter is used only if this system is a level 2 router.

systemid *systemid*

Defines the IS-IS system ID. If no system identifier is specified, the system ID portion of the first circuit's NSAP address is used.

traceoptions *traceoptions*

Defines the trace options used for IS-IS. The default is none.

The bgp Statement

```
bgp yes | no | on | off [{
    preference preference ;
    defaultmetric metric ;
    traceoptions trace_options ;
```

```
group type external peeras as_number
      | internal peeras as_number
      | igp peeras as_number proto proto
      | routing peeras as_number proto proto interface interface_list
      | test peeras as_number {
      allow {
          address mask mask | masklen number
          all
          host address } ;
      peer address
        [metricout metric]
        [localas as_number]
        [nogendefault]
        [gateway address]
        [preference preference]
        [preference2 preference]
        [lcladdr address]
        [holdtime time]
        [version number]
        [passive]
        [sendbuffer number]
        [recvbuffer number]
        [indelay time]
        [outdelay time]
        [keep all | none]
        [showwarnings]
        [noaggregatorid]
        [keepalivesalways]
        [v3asloopokay]
        [nov4asloop]
        [logupdown]
        [ttl ttl]
        [traceoptions trace_options]  ; }
  ; }] ;
```

This statement enables or disables BGP. By default, BGP is disabled. The default preference is 170. By default, BGP does not advertise a metric. Unlike the RIP metric, the BGP metric does not play a primary role in determining the best route. The BGP metric is simply an arbitrary 16-bit value that can be used as one criterion for choosing a route. The defaultmetric statement can be used to define a metric that BGP will use when advertising routes.

Trace options can be specified for all of BGP or for individual BGP peers. BGP supports most of the standard trace options as well as the following:

packets

    Traces all BGP packets. Traces BGP OPEN packets. Traces BGP UPDATE packets. Traces BGP KEEPALIVE packets.

BGP peers must be members of a group. The group statement declares the group, defines which peers are members of the group, and defines the group "type." Multiple group statements may be specified, but each must have a unique combination of type and autonomous system number. There are five possible group types:

group type external peeras *as_number*
> Specifies that BGP will run as a classic exterior gateway protocol. The peers listed in this group are members of an external autonomous system. Full policy checking is applied to all incoming and outgoing routes.

group type internal peeras *as_number*
> Specifies that BGP will be used to distribute routes to an internal group that has no traditional interior gateway protocol. Routes received from external BGP peers are re-advertised to this group with the received metric.

group type igp peeras *as_number* proto *proto*
> Specifies that BGP will be used to distribute path attributes to an internal group that runs an interior gateway protocol. BGP advertises the AS path, path origin, and transitive optional attributes if the path attributes are provided by the IGP's tag mechanism. *proto* is the name of the interior gateway protocol, e.g., proto ospf.

group type routing peeras *as_number* proto *proto* interface *interface_list*
> Specifies that BGP will be used internally to carry external routes, while an interior gateway protocol is used to carry only internal routes. Normally the routes learned by BGP from external autonomous systems are written in the routing table where they are picked up and distributed by an interior protocol to the local autonomous system. For this type of group, BGP distributes the external routes itself, and the interior protocol is limited to distributing only those routes that are interior to the local autonomous system. *proto* is the name of the interior protocol.

group type test peeras *as_number*
> Specifies that the members of this group are test peers. All routing information exchanged by test peers is discarded.

A group clause contains peer subclauses. Any number of peer subclauses may belong to a group. Peers are specified explicitly with a peer statement, or implicitly with the allow statement.

allow
> Any peer whose address is contained in the specified address range is a member of the group. The keyword all matches all possible addresses. The keyword host precedes an individual host address. The address and mask pairs define a range of addresses. Network masks can be defined with the keyword mask and an address mask written in dotted decimal notation, or with the keyword masklen and the prefix length written as a decimal number. All parameters for these peers must be defined in the group clause.

peer *address*
> The peer identified by *address* is a member of the group.

The BGP peer subclause allows the following parameters, which can also be specified on the group clause. If placed on the group clause, the parameters affect all peers in the group. The available options are:

metricout *metric*
> Defines the primary metric for routes sent to the peer. This overrides the default metric, a metric specified on the group, and any metric specified by export policy.

localas *as_number*
> Defines the local system's autonomous system number (asn). The default is to use the asn defined in the autonomoussystem statement.

nogendefault
> Prevents gated from generating a default route when BGP peers with this neighbor, even if gendefault is set in the options directive statement.

gateway *address*
> Identifies the next-hop gateway through which packets for this peer are routed. Use this only if the neighbor does not share a network with the local system. This option is rarely needed.

preference *preference*
> Defines the preference used for routes learned from this peer, which permits gated to prefer routes from one peer, or group of peers, over another.

preference2 *preference*
> Defines the "second" preference. In the case of a preference tie, the second preference is used to break the tie. The default value is 0.

lcladdr *address*
> Defines the address of the local interface used to communicate with this neighbor.

holdtime *time*
> Defines the number of seconds the peer should wait for a keepalive, update, or notification message before closing the connection. The value is sent to the peer in the Hold Time field of the BGP Open message. The value must be either 0 (no keepalives will be sent) or at least 3.

version *version*
> Identifies the version of the BGP protocol to use with this peer. By default, the version is negotiated when the connection is opened. Currently supported versions are 2, 3, and 4.

passive
> Specifies that gated should wait for the peer to issue an OPEN. By default, gated periodically sends OPEN messages until the peer responds.

`sendbuffer` *buffer_size*
`recvbuffer` *buffer_size*

Defines the size of the send and receive buffers. The default is 65535 bytes, which is the maximum. These parameters are not used on normally functioning systems.

`indelay` *time*
`outdelay` *time*

Implements "route dampening." `indelay` defines the number of seconds a route must be stable before it is accepted. `outdelay` is the number of seconds a route must be present in the gated routing database before it is exported to this peer. The default value for each is 0, meaning that these features are disabled. Use this only if the routing table is fluctuating so rapidly it is unstable.

`keep all`

Tells the system to retain routes learned from this peer even if the routes' AS paths contain our local AS number. Normally, routes that contain the local AS number are discarded as potential routing loops.

`showwarnings`

Tells the system to issue warning messages for events, such as duplicate routes, that are normally "silently ignored."

`noaggregatorid`

Sets the routerid in the aggregator attribute to 0. By default, it is set to the router identifier. Use this to prevent this router from creating aggregate routes with AS paths that differ from other routers in the AS.

`keepalivesalways`

Instructs the system to send a keepalive even when an update could have correctly substituted for one. Used for interoperability with some routers.

`v3asloopokay`

Allows advertisement of a route with a loop in the AS path (i.e., with an AS appearing more than once in the path) to version 3 external peers.

`nov4asloop`

Prevents a route with a loop in the AS path from being advertised to version 4 external peers. Used to avoid passing such routes to a peer that incorrectly forwards them to version 3 neighbors.

`logupdown`

Logs every time a BGP peer enters or leaves the ESTABLISHED state.

`ttl` *ttl*

Defines the IP ttl for local neighbors. By default it is set to 1. Use this option if the local neighbor discards packets sent with a ttl of 1. Not all Unix kernels allow the ttl to be specified for TCP connections.

The BGP trace options were covered previously.

The egp Statement

```
egp yes | no | on | off [{
    preference preference ;
    defaultmetric metric ;
    packetsize maxpacketsize ;
    traceoptions trace_options ;
    group [peeras as_number] [localas as_number] [maxup number] {
    neighbor address
    [metricout metric]
    [preference preference]
    [preference2 preference]
    [ttl ttl]
    [nogendefault]
    [importdefault]
    [exportdefault]
    [gateway address]
    [lcladdr address]
    [sourcenet network]
    [minhello | p1 interval]
    [minpoll | p2 interval]
    [traceoptions trace_options] ; }
  ; }] ;
```

This statement enables or disables EGP. By default, EGP is disabled. The default metric for announcing routes via EGP is 255, and the default preference for routes learned from EGP is 200.

The packetsize argument defines the size of the largest EGP packet that will be sent or accepted. maxpacketsize is the size in bytes. The default is 8192 bytes. If gated receives a packet larger than maxpacketsize, the packet is discarded, but maxpacketsize is increased to the size of the larger packet so that future packets won't have to be discarded.

The traceoptions statement defines the tracing for EGP. Tracing can be specified for the EGP protocol or for an individual EGP neighbor. The EGP trace options are:

packets
>   Traces all EGP packets.

hello
>   Traces EGP HELLO/I-HEARD-U packets.

acquire
>   Traces EGP ACQUIRE/CEASE packets.

update
>   Traces EGP POLL/UPDATE packets.

The egp statement has two clauses: the group clause and the neighbor clause. EGP neighbors must be part of a group, and all of the neighbors in a group must be members of the same autonomous system. Use the group clause to define parameters for a group of EGP neighbors. Values set in a group clause apply to all neighbor clauses in

the group. There can be multiple group clauses. The following parameters are set by
the group clause:

peeras

> Identifies the autonomous system number of the autonomous system to which
> the members of the group belong. If not specified, this number is learned from
> the neighbors.

localas

> Defines the local system's autonomous system number. The default is to use the
> asn defined in the autonomoussystem statement.

maxup

> Defines the number of EGP neighbors that gated is to acquire. The default is to
> acquire all listed neighbors.

The neighbor clause defines one EGP neighbor. The only part of the clause that is
required is the address argument, which is the hostname or IP address of the neighbor. All other parameters are optional. All of these optional parameters can also be
specified in the group clause if you want to apply the parameter to all neighbors. The
neighbor clause parameters are:

metricout *metric*

> Used for all routes sent to this neighbor. This value overrides the defaultmetric
> value set in the egp statement, but only for this specific neighbor.

preference *preference*

> Defines the preference used for routes learned from this neighbor, which per-
> mits gated to prefer routes from one neighbor, or group of neighbors, over
> another.

preference2 *preference*

> Defines the "second" preference. In the case of a preference tie, the second pref-
> erence is used to break the tie. The default value is 0.

ttl *ttl*

> Defines the IP ttl for local neighbors. By default, it is set to 1. Use this option if
> the local neighbor discards packets sent with a ttl of 1.

nogendefault

> Prevents gated from generating a default route when EGP peers with this neigh-
> bor, even if gendefault is set in the options directive statement.

importdefault

> Tells the system to accept the default route if it is included in this neighbor's
> EGP update. By default, it is ignored.

exportdefault

> Tells the system to send the default route in EGP updates to this EGP neighbor.
> Normally a default route is not included in an EGP update.

gateway *address*

Identifies the next-hop gateway through which packets for this neighbor are routed. Use this only if the neighbor does not share a network with the local system. This option is rarely needed.

lcladdr *address*

Defines the address of the local interface used to communicate with the neighbor.

sourcenet *network*

Changes the network queried in EGP POLL packets. By default, this is the shared network. However, if the neighbor does not share a network with your system, the neighbor's network address should be specified here. This parameter is normally not needed. Do not use it if you share a network with the EGP neighbor.

minhello | p1 *time*

Sets the interval between the transmission of EGP HELLO packets. The default HELLO interval is 30 seconds. If the neighbor fails to respond to three HELLO packets, the system stops trying to acquire the neighbor. Setting a larger interval gives the neighbor a better chance to respond. The interval can be defined as seconds, minutes:seconds, or hours:minutes:seconds. For example, a 3-minute interval could be specified as 180 (seconds), 3:00 (minutes), or 0:3:00 (no hours and 3 minutes). The keyword p1 can be used instead of the keyword minhello.

minpoll | p2 *time*

Sets the time interval between sending polls to the neighbor. The default is 120 seconds. If three polls are sent without a response, the neighbor is declared "down" and all routes learned from that neighbor are removed from the routing table. If a neighbor becomes congested and can't respond to rapid polls, this can cause the routing table to become very unstable. A longer polling interval provides a more stable, but less responsive, routing table. This interval is also defined as seconds, minutes:seconds, or hours:minutes:seconds.

The smux Statement

```
smux yes | no | on | off [ {
    port port ;
    password string ;
    traceoptions trace_options ; } ] ;
```

This command replaces the snmp statement used in previous versions of gated. The smux command controls whether gated informs the SNMP management software of its status. SNMP is not a routing protocol and is not started by this command. You must run SNMP software independently. This statement only controls whether gated keeps the management software apprised of its status. The default is on, so gated does inform SNMP of its status.

The smux statement supports three options:

port *port*
> Changes the SNMP port used by gated. By default, the SNMP daemon listens to port 199.

password *string*
> Enables password authentication and defines the password used.

traceoptions *trace_options*
> Traces the interactions between gated and the SNMP daemon. Three options are supported: packets, send, and receive.

The redirect Statement

```
redirect yes | no | on | off [{
    preference preference ;
    interface interface_list [noredirects | redirects]  ;
    trustedgateways gateway_list ;
    traceoptions trace_options ; } ] ;
```

This statement controls whether ICMP redirects are allowed to modify the kernel routing table. It does not prevent a system from sending redirects, only from listening to them. If no or off is specified, gated attempts to remove the effects of ICMP redirects from the kernel routing table whenever the redirects are detected. Remember that ICMP is part of IP, and the redirects may be installed in the kernel table before they are seen by gated. If you disable redirects, gated actively removes the redirected routes from the routing table. By default, ICMP redirects are enabled on hosts that quietly listen to interior routing protocols, and disabled on gateways that actively participate in interior routing protocols.

The default preference of a route learned from a redirect is 30, which can be changed with the preference option. The interface statement controls how redirects are handled on an interface-by-interface basis. Redirects are ignored if noredirects is specified, and are permitted if redirects, which is the default, is specified. The trustedgateways statement enables redirects on a gateway-by-gateway basis. By default, redirects are accepted from all routers on the local network. If the trustedgateways statement is used, only redirects received from a gateway listed in the *gateway_list* are accepted. The *gateway_list* is simply a list of hostnames or addresses. The *trace_options* defined on the traceoptions statement are the standard gated trace options.

The icmp Statement

```
icmp {
    traceoptions trace_options ; }
```

On some systems, gated listens to all ICMP messages but only processes the ICMP redirect packets. That processing is controlled by the redirect statement. In the future, more functionality may be added. At present the icmp statement is used only to enable tracing of ICMP messages. The tracing options supported by the icmp statement are:

packets
> Traces all ICMP packets.

redirect
> Traces ICMP REDIRECT packets.

routerdiscovery
> Traces ICMP ROUTER DISCOVERY packets.

info
> Traces ICMP informational packets.

error
> Traces ICMP error packets.

The routerdiscovery Statement

The Router Discovery Protocol informs hosts of the routers that are available on the network. It provides an alternative to static routes, routing protocols, and ICMP redirects for hosts that simply need to know the address of their default router. The Router Discovery Protocol is implemented as a server running on the router and a client running on the host. Both the server (router) software and the client (host) software are provided by gated.

First let's look at the server configuration statement:

```
routerdiscovery server yes | no | on | off [{
    traceoptions trace_options ;
    interface interface_list
      [minadvinterval time]
      [maxadvinterval time]
      [lifetime time] ;
    address interface_list
      [advertise | ignore]
      [broadcast | multicast]
      [ineligible | preference preference]  ;
} ] ;
```

The routerdiscovery statement for both the client and server supports tracing. The state trace flag can be used to trace finite state machine transitions. Router discovery packet tracing, however, is not done here. It is enabled via the ICMP statement.

The interface clause defines the physical interfaces and the parameters that apply to them. Only physical interfaces can be defined in the interface clause. Addresses are specified in the address clauses shown below. The interface parameters are:

maxadvinterval *time*

> Defines the maximum time interval between sending router advertisements. It must be more than 4 seconds and less than 30:00 minutes. The default is 10:00 minutes (600 seconds).

minadvinterval *time*

> Defines the minimum time interval between sending router advertisements. It must be no less than 3 seconds and no greater than maxadvinterval. The default is 0.75 times the maxadvinterval.

lifetime *time*

> Defines how long clients should consider the addresses in a router advertisement valid. It must be greater than maxadvinterval and no more than 2:30:00 (two hours, thirty minutes). The default is 3 times the maxadvinterval.

The address clause defines the IP addresses used and the parameters that apply to them. The address clause parameters are:

advertise | ignore

> advertise specifies that the address should be included in router advertisements, which is the default. ignore specifies that the address should not be included in router advertisements.

broadcast | multicast

> broadcast specifies that the address should be included in a broadcast router advertisement because some systems on the network do not support multicasting. This is the default if the router does not support multicasting.

> multicast specifies that the address should only be included in a multicast router advertisement. If the system does not support multicasting, the address is not advertised.

ineligible | preference *preference*

> Defines the preference of the address as a default router. *preference* is a 32-bit signed integer. Higher values mean the address is more preferable. Note that this is not gated preference. This is a value transmitted as part of the Router Discovery Protocol.

> The keyword ineligible assigns a preference of hex 80000000, which means the address is not eligible to be the default router. Hosts use ineligible addresses to verify ICMP redirects.

For routerdiscovery to work, the hosts must have the routerdiscovery client software. It is part of gated and is configured by the routerdiscovery client statement.

The routerdiscovery client statement

```
routerdiscovery client yes | no | on | off [{
    traceoptions trace_options ;
    preference preference ;
    interface interface_list
```

```
        [enable | disable | multicast]
        [quiet | solicit]  ;
  } ] ;
```

The client uses the same trace options as the server. Other options are different, however. The full list of client options is:

preference *preference* ;
> Defines the preference of default routes learned from routerdiscovery. The default is 55. Unlike the server statement, this is gated preference.

interface *interface_list*
> Defines the interfaces used by routerdiscovery.

enable | disable | multicast
> Enables or disables routerdiscovery on the interface. enable is the default. multicast forces gated to use multicasting for router discovery. If multicasting is unavailable, router discovery is not attempted. Normally, gated uses multicasting or broadcasting depending on what is available for the interface.

broadcast | multicast
> Specifies whether router solicitations should be broadcast or multicast on the interface. By default, router solicitations are multicast if that is supported; otherwise, router solicitations are broadcast. If the multicast keyword is specified and multicast is not available, the router solicitations are not sent. Generally, if these options are not specified, gated will do the right thing.

quiet | solicit
> Specifies whether router solicitations are sent on this interface. solicit, which is the default, sends router solicitations. quiet listens to Router Advertisements but does not send router solicitations.

The kernel Statement

```
kernel {
   options
     [nochange]
     [noflushatexit]
     [protosync];
   remnantholdtime  ;
   routes number ;
   flash
     [limit number]
     [type interface | interior | all]  ;
   background
     [limit number]
     [priority flash | higher | lower]  ;
   traceoptions trace_options ; } ;
```

The kernel statement defines the interactions between gated and the kernel.

options
> Defines three possible configuration options. These are:
>
> nochange
>> Limits gated to deletes and adds. Use on early versions of the routing socket code that have a malfunctioning change operation.
>
> noflushatexit
>> Prevents route deletions at shutdown. Normally, shutdown processing deletes routes that do not have a "retain" indication. Use to speed startup on systems with thousands of routes.
>
> protosync
>> Updates the kernel protocol field with the current gated protocol value.

remnantholdtime
> Holds routes read from the kernel forwarding table at startup for up to 3 minutes unless they are overridden.

routes *number*
> Defines the maximum number of routes gated will install in the kernel. By default, there is no limit to the number of routes in the kernel forwarding table.

flash
> Tunes the parameters used for flash updates. When routes change, the process of notifying the kernel is called a "flash update."
>
> limit *number*
>> Sets the maximum number of routes processed during one flash update. The default is 20. A value of −1 causes all route changes to be processed. Large updates can slow the processing of "time-critical" protocols. 20 is a good default.
>
> type interface | interior | all
>> Specifies the type of routes processed during a flash update. By default, only interface routes are installed during a flash update. interior specifies that interior routes are also installed, and all specifies that interior and exterior routes should be processed. Specifying flash limit -1 all causes all routes to be installed during the flash update, which mimics the behavior of previous versions of gated.

background
> Tunes the parameters used for background processing. Since only interface routes are normally installed during a flash update, most routes are processed in batches in the background.
>
> limit *number*
>> Sets the number of routes processed in one batch. The default is 120.

```
priority flash | higher | lower
```
> Sets the priority for processing batch updates. The default is lower, which means that batch updates are processed at a lower priority than flash updates. To process kernel updates at the same priority as flash updates, specify flash.

Many tracing options work for the kernel interface because, in many cases, the interface is handled as a routing protocol. The command-line trace options, symbols and iflist, provide information about the kernel. The kernel statement trace options are:

remnants
> Traces routes read from the kernel when gated starts.

request
> Traces gated kernel Add/Delete/Change operations.

The remaining trace options apply only to systems that use the routing socket to exchange routing information with the kernel.

info
> Traces informational messages received from the routing socket.

routes
> Traces routes exchanged with the kernel.

redirect
> Traces redirect messages received from the kernel.

interface
> Traces interface status messages received from the kernel.

other
> Traces any other messages received from the kernel.

static Statements

static statements define the static routes used by gated. A single static statement can specify several routes. The static statements occur after protocol statements and before control statements in the *gated.conf* file. To gated, static routes are any routes defined with static statements. However, unlike the routes in a static routing table, these routes can be overridden by routes with better preference values.

The structure of a static statement is:

```
static {
    [default] | [[host] address [mask mask | masklen n]] gateway gateways
      [interface interface_list]
      [preference preference]
      [retain]
      [reject]
```

```
        [blackhole]
        [noinstall] ;
    address [mask mask | masklen n] interface interface
        [preference preference]
        [retain]
        [reject]
        [blackhole]
        [noinstall] ;
} ;
```

The static statement has two different clauses. The one with the keyword gateway is
the one you'll use. This clause contains information similar to that provided by the
route command. A static route is defined as a destination address reached though a
gateway. The format of this clause is:

[default] | [[host] address [mask mask | masklen number]] gateway gateways
> Defines a static route through one or more gateways. The destination is defined
> by the keyword default (for the default route) or by a destination address. The
> destination address can be preceded by the keyword host, if it is a host address,
> or followed by an address mask. The address mask can be defined with the key-
> word mask and a dotted decimal address mask, or by the keyword masklen and a
> numeric prefix length. The listed gateways must be on a directly attached net-
> work. Possible configuration parameters are:

interface interface_list
> When specified, gateways in the gateway_list must be directly reachable
> through one of these interfaces.

preference preference
> Sets the gated preference for this static route. The default is 60.

retain
> Prevents this static route from being removed during a graceful shutdown.
> Normally, only interface routes are retained in the kernel forwarding table.
> Use this to provide some routing when gated is not running.

reject
> Installs this route as a "reject route." Packets sent to a reject route are
> dropped and an "unreachable" message is sent back to the source. Not all
> kernels support reject routes.

blackhole
> Installs this route as a "blackhole route." A blackhole route is the same as a
> reject route except the "unreachable" message is not sent.

noinstall
> Instructs the system to advertise this route via routing protocols but not to
> install it in the kernel forwarding table.

The other static statement clause uses the keyword interface instead of the keyword gateway. Use this clause only if you have a single physical network with more

than one network address—a rare occurrence. ifconfig normally creates only one destination for each interface. This special form of the static statement adds additional destinations to the interface.

    address [mask mask | masklen number] interface interface

The preference, retain, reject, blackhole, and noinstall options are the same as described above.

The default preference of a static route is 60, which prefers static routes over several other routing sources. If you want other types of routes to override static routes, use the preference argument on the static statement to increase the preference number. (Remember that high preference values mean less-preferred routes.)

The following example defines a static default route through gateway 172.16.12.1. The preference is set to 125 so that routes learned from RIP are preferred over this static route:

```
static {
    default gateway 128.66.12.1 preference 125 ;  } ;
```

Control Statements

The control statements define your routing policy. Often when administrators hear the terms "routing policy" or "policy-based routing," they assume that this is something done inside the routing protocol.

In reality, a routing policy is defined outside of the routing protocol in the configuration file. The policy defines what routes are accepted and what routes are advertised. gated does this with two control statements: import and export. The import statement defines which routes are accepted and from what sources those routes are accepted. The export statement defines which routes are advertised based on the source of the routes and the protocol used to advertise them.

The import and export statements use gated preference, routing metrics, routing filters, and AS paths to define routing policy. Preference and metrics are controlled by these keywords:

restrict
    Specifies that the routes are not to be imported, in the case of the import command, or exported in the case of the export command. This keyword blocks the use of a specific route.

preference preference
    Defines the preference value used when comparing this route to other routes. Preference is used when installing routes, not when advertising them.

metric metric
    Specifies the metric used when advertising a route.

Route filters match routes by destination address. Among other places, route filters are used on martians and import and export statements. A route matches the most specific filter that applies. Specifying more than one filter with the same destination, mask, and modifiers generates an error. Import and export route filters can be specified in the following ways:[*]

address [mask *mask* | masklen *number*] [exact | refines | between *n1* and *n2*]
> Defines a range of addresses using an address and an address mask. The address mask can be defined with the keyword mask and a mask written in dotted decimal notation, or with the keyword masklen and a numeric prefix length. If no mask is defined, the natural mask of the network is used. Three options can be used:

> exact
>> Matches a network, but no subnets or hosts of that network.

> refines
>> Matches subnets and/or hosts of a network, but not the network itself.

> between *n1* and *n2*
>> Matches an address where at least *n1* bits match and no more than *n2* bits match.

all
> Matches every possible address.

default
> Matches only the default route.

host *address*
> Matches an individual host address.

A routing filter that matches everything on network number 192.168.12.0 and the individual host 10.104.19.12 contains:

```
192.168.12.0 masklen 24 ; host 10.104.19.12 ;
```

When no route filtering is specified in an import or export statement, all routes from the specified source will match that statement. If any filters are specified, only routes that match the specified filters are imported or exported.

Border Gateway Protocol (BGP) is designed to support policy-based routing. A key feature of BGP is that it is a path-vector protocol. import and export statements allow you to use the AS path vector to enforce your routing policy.

---

[*] Route filters may include additional parameters. On import statements, they include a preference, and on export statements, a metric. *Preference* and *metric* were described previously.

An AS path lists the autonomous systems end-to-end for a route and provides an indication of the completeness of the path. Each autonomous system that a route passes through prepends its AS number to the beginning of the AS path.

The "origin" of the path indicates its completeness. An origin of igp indicates the route was learned from an interior routing protocol and is most likely complete. An origin of egp indicates the route was learned from an exterior routing protocol that does not support AS paths (EGP for example) and the path is most likely not complete.

When the path information is definitely not complete, an origin of incomplete is used. All of these origins can be specified in the import and export statements and therefore used in your routing policy. The keyword any is used when the policy applies to all origins.

The AS path can also be used in the control statements by defining an AS path regular expression.* The AS path regular expression provides a pattern-matching syntax used to filter routes based on the autonomous system numbers in the AS paths associated with those routes.

An AS path regular expression is a regular expression composed of autonomous system numbers and special operators. Table B-1 lists the AS path operators. The AS path operator operates on an AS path term, which is an autonomous system number; a dot (.), which matches any autonomous system number; or a parentheses-enclosed subexpression.

Table B-1. AS path operators

Symbol	Meaning
{m,n}	At least m and at most n repetitions
{m}	Exactly m repetitions
{m,}	m or more repetitions
*	0 or more repetitions
+	1 or more repetitions
?	0 or 1 repetition
aspath_term	aspath_term	Matches either the AS term on the left or the AS term on the right

A simple AS path regular expression might be:

```
import proto bgp aspath 164+ origin any restrict ;
```

This restricts all routes that have one or more occurrences of autonomous system number 164 in their path vector.

* AS path regular expressions are defined in RFC 1164.

The import Statement

The format of an import statement varies depending on the source protocol. The format of the import statements for the exterior gateway protocols is:

```
import proto bgp | egp autonomoussystem as_number
    [restrict] |
    [[preference preference] {
    route_filter [restrict | (preference preference)]] ; } ;
import proto bgp aspath aspath_regexp
    origin any | igp | egp | incomplete
    [restrict] |
    [[preference preference] {
    route_filter [restrict | (preference preference)]] ; } ;
```

BGP and EGP importation may be controlled by autonomous system number. BGP also can control importation using AS path regular expressions. Routes that are rejected by the routing policy are stored in the routing table with a negative preference. A negative preference prevents a route from being installed in the forwarding table or exported to other protocols. Handling rejected routes in this manner alleviates the need to break and reestablish a session if routing policy changes during a reconfiguration.

The format of the import statements for the RIP and redirect protocols is:

```
import proto rip | redirect
    [interface interface_list | gateway gateway_list]
    [restrict] |
    [[preference preference] {
    route_filter [restrict | (preference preference)]] ; } ;
```

This statement controls what routes are imported based on the source protocol, interface, and gateway. The order of precedence is from the most general (protocol) to the most specific (gateway). Unlike BGP and EGP, these protocols do not save routes that were rejected because these protocols have short update intervals.

The preference option is not used with RIP. RIP doesn't use preference to choose between routes of the same protocol. It uses the protocol metrics.

The format of the import statement for the OSPF protocol is:

```
import proto ospfase [tag ospf_tag] [restrict] |
    [[preference preference] {
    route_filter [restrict | (preference preference)]] ; } ;
```

Due to the nature of OSPF, only the importation of ASE routes can be controlled. Furthermore, it is only possible to restrict the importation of OSPF ASE routes when functioning as an AS border router. This requires you to specify an export ospfase statement in addition to the import ospfase statement. Specify an empty export statement to control importation of ASEs when no ASEs are being exported. (See the following section, "The export Statement.") If a tag is specified, the import statement applies only to routes with the tag. OSPF ASE routes that are rejected by policy are stored in the table with a negative preference.

OSPF routes are imported into the gated routing table with a preference of 10. Preference is not used to choose between OSPF ASE routes. OSPF costs are used for that purpose.

The export Statement

The syntax of the export statement is similar to the syntax of the import statement, and the meanings of many of the parameters are identical. An important difference between the two statements is that while route importation is controlled by source information, route exportation is controlled by both source and destination. Thus, export statements define where the routes will be sent and where they originated. The destination of the route advertisement is defined by the proto clause at the beginning of the export statement. The source of the routes is defined in the export list.

The export statement varies slightly for each protocol. To advertise routes via EGP and BGP, use this syntax:

```
export proto bgp | egp as as_number
  [restrict] |
  [[metric metric] {
   export_list ; }] ;
```

Routes are exported via EGP and BGP to the specified autonomous system. restrict blocks exports to the AS. Valid BGP or EGP metrics can be specified. If no export list is defined, only the direct routes of the attached interfaces are exported. If an export list is used, it must explicitly specify everything that should be exported.

To advertise routes via RIP, use this syntax:

```
export proto rip
  [interface interface_list | gateway gateway_list]
  [restrict] |
  [[metric metric] {
   export_list ; }] ;
```

Routes exported by RIP can be sent through a specific interface or to a specific gateway. Set metric if you plan to export static or internally generated default routes. The metric option is used only when exporting non-RIP routes via RIP.

If no export list is specified, RIP exports direct routes and RIP routes. If an export list is used, it must explicitly specify everything that should be exported.

To advertise routes via OSPF, use this syntax:

```
export proto osfpase [type 1 | 2] [tag ospf_tag]
  [restrict] |
  [[metric metric] {
   export_list ; }] ;
```

Only OSPF ASE routes can be exported by gated. There are two types of OSPF ASE routes, type 1 and type 2. They are described in Chapter 7 and earlier in this appendix. The default type is specified in the ospf protocol statement, but it can be overridden here. The *ospf_tag* is an arbitrary 32-bit number used to filter routing information. The default tag value is specified in the ospf protocol statement, but it can be overridden here.

The source of the routes advertised by a protocol is defined by the export list. Each of the commands listed above contains an export list option. Just like those commands, the export list syntax varies depending on the source protocol of the routes. The commands described above define the protocols that are used to advertise the routes. The export lists shown below describe the protocols from which the routes are obtained. The biggest confusion caused by the export list syntax is that it is almost identical to the syntax shown above. In both cases we define protocols, autonomous systems, interfaces, gateways, and so on. In the first case we are defining the protocols, interfaces, etc., to which routes are sent, and in this case we are defining the protocols, interfaces, etc., from which routes are received.

To export routes learned from BGP and EGP, use this export list syntax:

```
export proto bgp | egp autonomoussystem as_number
[restrict [noagg]] |
[[metric metric] {
  route_filter [restrict | metric metric] ; }] ;
```

This defines routes learned via BGP or EGP from a specific autonomous system. Routes can be restricted, or have a metric applied, based on matching the source AS number or the route filter. noagg can be used with restrict to prevent any aggregate routes from matching the filter.

When BGP is configured, gated assigns all routes an AS path. For interior routes, the AS path specifies igp as the origin and no autonomous systems in the AS path (the current AS is added when the route is exported). For EGP routes, the AS path specifies egp as the origin and the source AS as the AS path. For BGP routes, the AS path learned from BGP is used. If you run BGP, the export of all routes may be controlled by the AS path using this syntax:

```
proto proto | all
  aspath aspath_regexp origin any | igp | egp | incomplete
[restrict] |
[[metric metric] {
  route_filter [restrict | metric metric] ; }] ;
```

The source of the routes can be any one protocol (*proto*) or all protocols (all). The importation of routes can be controlled by matching their AS paths against the AS path regular expression (*aspath_regexp*) or by matching their addresses against the *route_filter*. Route filters and AS path regular expressions were explained previously.

To export routes learned from RIP, use this export list syntax:

```
proto rip
[interface interface_list | gateway gateway_list]
[restrict] |
[[metric metric] {
 route_filter [restrict | metric metric] ; }] ;
```

The export of RIP routes may be controlled by source interface, source gateway, or route filter.

To export routes learned from OSPF, use this export list syntax:

```
proto ospf | ospfase
[restrict] |
[[metric metric] {
 route_filter [restrict | metric metric] ; }] ;
```

The export of OSPF and OSPF ASE routes may be controlled by protocol and route filter. Exporting OSPF routes can also be controlled by *tag* using the following syntax:

```
proto proto | all tag tag
  [restrict] |
  [[metric metric] {
  route_filter [restrict | metric metric] ; }] ;
```

OSPF and RIP version 2 provide a tag field. For all other protocols, the tag is always 0. Routes may be selected based on the contents of the tag field.

There are other sources of routes that are not true routing protocols, and export lists can be defined for these sources. The two export lists for these sources are:

```
proto direct | static | kernel
[interface interface_list]
[restrict] |
[[metric metric] {
 route_filter [restrict | metric metric] ; }] ;
```

The export of these routes can be controlled based on the source "protocol" and the source interface. The "protocols" in this case are routes to direct interfaces, static routes, or routes learned from the kernel.

```
proto default | aggregate
[restrict] |
[[metric metric] {
 route_filter [restrict | metric metric] ; }] ;
```

The export of these routes may only be controlled based on source "protocol." default refers to routes created by the gendefault option. aggregate refers to routes created by the aggregate statements, the topic of the next section.

Aggregate Statements

Route aggregation is used by regional and national networks to reduce the number of routes advertised. With careful planning, large network providers can announce a few aggregate routes instead of hundreds of client network routes. Enabling aggregation is the main reason that CIDR blocks are allocated as contiguous address blocks.

Most of us don't have hundreds of routes to advertise. But we may have a classless address composed of a few class C addresses, and we may need to tell gated how to handle it. Older versions of gated automatically generated an aggregate route to a natural network using the old class A, B, and C concept; i.e., interface address 192. 168.16.1 created a route to 192.168.16.0. With the advent of classless interdomain routing, this can be the wrong thing to do. gated does not aggregate routes unless it is explicitly configured with the aggregate statement:

```
aggregate default | address [[mask mask | masklen number] [bgp]]
   [preference preference] [brief] {
   proto proto
     [as as_number | tag tag | aspath aspath_regexp]
     [restrict] |
     [[preference preference] {
       route_filter [restrict | (preference preference)]] ; } ;
```

Several options are available for the aggregate statement:

bgp
   Aggregations are to be formed using BGP protocol rules.

preference *preference;*
   Defines the preference of the resulting aggregate route. The default is 130.

brief
   Specifies that the AS path of the aggregate route should be the longest common AS path. The default is to build an AS path consisting of all contributing AS paths.

proto *proto*
   Only aggregate routes learned from the specified protocol. The value of *proto* may be any currently configured protocol. This includes the "protocols" direct, static, and kernel, discussed in the previous section; all for all possible protocols; and aggregate for other route aggregations.

as *as_number*
   Only aggregate routes learned from the specified autonomous system.

tag *tag*
   Only aggregate routes with the specified tag.

aspath *aspath_regexp*
   Only aggregate routes that match the specified AS path.

restrict
   Indicates routes that are not to be aggregated.

Routes that match the route filters may contribute to the aggregate route. A route may contribute only to an aggregate route that is more general than itself. Any given route may contribute to only one aggregate route, but an aggregate route may contribute to a more general aggregate.

A slight variation of aggregation is the generation of a route based on the existence of certain conditions. The most common usage for this is to create a default based on the presence of a route from a peer on a neighboring backbone. This is done with the generate statement:

```
generate default | address [mask mask | masklen number]
   [preference preference]
   [brief] {
   proto proto
     [as as_number | tag tag | aspath aspath_regexp]
     [restrict] |
     [[preference preference] {
     route_filter [restrict | preference preference]] ; } ;
} ;
```

The generate statement uses many of the same options as the aggregate statement. These options were described earlier in this appendix.

A named Reference

This appendix provides detailed information about named syntax and the commands and files used to configure it. This is primarily a reference to use in conjunction with the tutorial information in Chapter 8. This information is useful to any domain administrator.

The named Command

The server side of DNS is run by the name server daemon, named. The syntax of the named command is:[*]

```
named [-d level] [-p port] [[-b|c] configfile] [-q -r -f -v] [-u username]
[-g groupname] [-t path] [-w path] [configfile]
```

The options used on the named command line are:

-d level

Logs debugging information in the file *named.run*. The argument *level* is a number from 1 to 11. A higher *level* number increases the detail of the information logged, but even when *level* is set to 1, the *named.run* file grows very rapidly. Whenever you use debugging, keep an eye on the size of the *named.run* file and use ndc notrace or SIGUSR2 to close the file if it gets too large. Signal handling is covered in the next section.

It is not necessary to turn on debugging with the -d option to receive error messages from named. named displays error messages on the console and stores them in the *messages*, even if debugging is not specified. The -d option provides additional debugging information.

-p port

Defines the UDP/TCP port used by named. *port* is the port number used to connect to the remote name server. If the -p option is not specified, the standard

---

[*] Sun systems use in.named instead of named.

port (53) is used. Since port 53 is a well-known port, changing the port number makes the name server inaccessible to standard software packages. Therefore, -p is used only for testing.

-b *configfile* or -c *configfile*
Specifies the file named uses as its configuration file. By default the configuration file is */etc/named.conf*, but the -b or -c option allows the administrator to choose another configuration file. Note that using -b or -c is optional. As long as the filename used for *configfile* doesn't start with a dash, the -b or -c flag is not required. Any filename written on the named command line is assumed to be the configuration file, as the last item on the command line shows.

-q
Logs all incoming queries. named must be compiled with the QRYLOG option set to enable this type of logging.

-r
Turns off recursion. With this option set, the server will provide answers only for zones for which it is an authoritative server. It will not pursue the query through other servers or zones.

-f
Runs named in the foreground. Normally named is run as a background daemon.

-v
Displays the version number. The -v switch does not run named.

-u *username*
Sets the user ID under which the server runs after initializing. By default, named runs as root.

-g *groupname*
Set the group ID under which named runs after initializing. The group ID defaults to the master group of the user ID under which named is run.

-t *path*
Defines the path to the directory named uses when running chroot.

-w *path*
Defines the path of named's working directory. The default is the current directory. The directory option in the configuration file overrides this setting.

Signal Processing

named handles the following signals:

SIGHUP
Causes named to reread the *named.conf* file and reload the name server database. named then continues to run with the new configuration. If named is compiled with the FORCED_RELOAD option, this signal forces a slave server to transfer the zone from its master server. This signal has the same effect as ndc reload.

SIGINT

Causes named to dump its cache to *named_dump.db*. The dump file contains all of the domain information that the local name server knows. The file begins with the root servers and marks off every domain under the root that the local server knows anything about. If you examine this file, you'll see that it shows a complete picture of the information the server has learned. This signal has the same effect as ndc dumpdb.

SIGUSR1

Turns on debugging; each subsequent SIGUSR1 signal increases the level of debugging. Debugging information is written to *named.run* just as it is when the -d option is used on the named command line. Debugging does not have to be enabled with the -d option for the SIGUSR1 signal to work. SIGUSR1 allows debugging to be turned on when a problem is suspected, without stopping named and restarting it with the -d option. This signal has the same effect as ndc trace.

SIGUSR2

Turns off debugging and closes *named.run*. After issuing SIGUSR2, you can examine *named.run* or remove it if it is getting too large. This signal has the same effect as ndc notrace.

Optionally, some other signals can be handled by named. These additional signals require named to be compiled with the appropriate options to support the signals:

SIGILL

Writes statistics data to *named.stats*. named must be compiled with -DSTATS for this signal to work.

SIGSYS

Writes profiling data into the directory defined by the directory option in the *named.conf* file. named must be compiled with profiling to support this signal.

SIGTERM

Writes back the master and slave database files. This is used to save data modified by dynamic updates before the system is shut down. named must be compiled with dynamic updating enabled.

SIGWINCH

Toggles logging of all incoming queries via syslogd. named must be compiled with the QRYLOG option to support this. This signal has the same effect as ndc querylog.

named.conf Configuration Commands

The *named.conf* file defines the name server configuration and tells named where to obtain the name server database information. BIND 8 uses the following configuration commands: key, acl, options, logging, zone, server, controls, and trusted-keys. BIND 9 uses the same eight commands and adds the view command.

In addition to these configuration commands, both BIND 8 and BIND 9 provide an include statement used to load an external file that contains any of the configuration commands. For example:

```
include /var/named/keys
```

copies the file */var/named/keys*, which might be a file containing key and trusted-key commands into the *named.conf* file.

The key Statement

The key statement assigns an internal name used to reference an authentication method. key statements usually occur near the start of the configuration because forward references are not allowed. The syntax of the key statement for both BIND 8 and BIND 9 is:

```
key key_id {
    algorithm algorithm_id;
    secret secret_string;
};
```

key_id
> The name assigned to the authentication method.

algorithm_id
> The authentication algorithm used.

secret_string
> A base64-encoded key used by the algorithm.

The acl Statement

The acl command assigns a name to an address match list so that it can be referenced later in the configuration. Forward references are not allowed. The syntax of the acl command for both BIND 8 and BIND 9 is:

```
acl name {
    address_match_list
};
```

name
> An internal name for the list. There are four predefined names:

> any
>> Match every possible address.

> none
>> Match no address.

> localhost
>> Match every address assigned to the local host.

> localnet
>> Match every address where the network portion is the same as the network portion of any address assigned to the local hosts.

address_match_list

    A list of IP addresses written in dotted decimal notation with an optional address mask prefix. An exclamation point (!) before an address means "don't match" the value. An *address_match_list* can also contain the name of a previously defined access control list, including the four predefined names.

The trusted-keys Statement

The trusted-keys statement manually defines the public key for a remote domain when that key cannot be securely obtained from the network. The BIND 8 and BIND 9 syntax for the trusted-keys statement is:

```
trusted-keys {
    domain_name flags protocol algorithm key; [...]
};
```

domain_name

    The name of the remote domain.

flags, protocol, algorithm

    Attributes of the authentication method used by the remote domain.

key

    A base64-encoded string representing the remote domain's public key.

The server Statement

The server statement defines the characteristics of a remote server. The BIND 8 syntax is:

```
server address {
    [ bogus yes|no; ]
    [ support-ixfr yes|no; ]
    [ transfers number; ]
    [ transfer-format one-answer/many-answers; ]
    [ keys { key_id [key_id ... ] }; ]
};
```

The server statement applies to the remote server identified by *address*.

transfer-format

    Sets the format used for zone transfers with this server to either the more efficient many-answers format or the backward-compatible one-answer format.

bogus yes

    Prevents the local server from sending queries to this server. The default is no, which permits queries to the remote server.

support-ixfr yes

    Indicates that the remote server can support incremental transfers. no, which is the default, says that the remote server cannot perform incremental transfers.

transfers
: Defines the maximum number of concurrent inbound transfers permitted from this server.

keys
: Identifies the key required by the remote host for transaction security.

The BIND 9 server statement

The BIND 9 server statement syntax varies slightly. It is:

```
server address {
    [ bogus yes|no; ]
    [ provide-ixfr yes|no; ]
    [ request-ixfr yes|no; ]
    [ transfers number; ]
    [ transfer-format one-answer/many-answers; ]
    [ keys { key_id [key_id ... ] }; ]
};
```

All of the fields are the same as BIND 8, with the exception that support-ixfr has been replaced by two options:

provide-ixfr
: Indicates that the local server will provide incremental zone transfers to the remote server.

request-ixfr
: Indicates that the local server will request incremental zone transfers from the remote server.

The options Statement

The options statement defines global options for BIND and the DNS protocol. The BIND 8 syntax of the options command is:

```
options {
    [ version string; ]
    [ directory pathname; ]
    [ named-xfer pathname; ]
    [ dump-file pathname; ]
    [ memstatistics-file pathname; ]
    [ pid-file pathname; ]
    [ statistics-file pathname; ]
    [ auth-nxdomain yes|no; ]
    [ deallocate-on-exit yes|no; ]
    [ dialup yes|no; ]
    [ fake-iquery yes|no; ]
    [ fetch-glue yes|no; ]
    [ has-old-clients yes|no; ]
    [ host-statistics yes|no; ]
    [ multiple-cnames yes|no; ]
    [ notify yes|no; ]
```

```
    [ recursion yes|no; ]
    [ rfc2308-type1 yes|no; ]
    [ use-id-pool yes|no; ]
    [ treat-cr-as-space yes|no; ]
    [ also-notify { address-list; };
    [ forward only|first; ]
    [ forwarders { address-list; }; ]
    [ check-names master|slave|response  warn|fail|ignore; ]
    [ allow-query { address_match_list }; ]
    [ allow-transfer { address_match_list }; ]
    [ allow-recursion { address_match_list }; ]
    [ blackhole { address_match_list }; ]
    [ listen-on [ port ip_port ] { address_match_list }; ]
    [ query-source [address ip_addr|*] [port ip_port|*] ; ]
    [ lame-ttl number; ]
    [ max-transfer-time-in number; ]
    [ max-ncache-ttl number; ]
    [ min-roots number; ]
    [ serial-queries number; ]
    [ transfer-format one-answer|many-answers; ]
    [ transfers-in  number; ]
    [ transfers-out number; ]
    [ transfers-per-ns number; ]
    [ transfer-source ip_addr; ]
    [ maintain-ixfr-base yes|no; ]
    [ max-ixfr-log-size number; ]
    [ coresize size; ]
    [ datasize size; ]
    [ files size; ]
    [ stacksize size; ]
    [ cleaning-interval number; ]
    [ heartbeat-interval number; ]
    [ interface-interval number; ]
    [ statistics-interval number; ]
    [ topology { address_match_list }; ]
    [ sortlist { address_match_list }; ]
    [ rrset-order { order_spec ; [ order_spec ; ... ] ] };
};
```

There are almost a dozen different types of values for these options. Two options, check-names and transfer-format, accept keyword values. Boolean options accept either yes or no. All other options expect an appropriate value in a specific format. Some formats (*string*, *number*, *pathname*, *domain*, *type*, *class*, *ip_port*, and *ip_addr*) are self-explanatory. Some formats require a little explanation:.

address-list

A list of IP addresses separated by semicolons. This is more limited than an *address_match_list*.

address_match_list

A list of addresses, acl names, and key_ids.

order_spec

A multi-part rule that defines how resource records are ordered when multiple records are sent in response to a single query. The structure of an *order_spec* is:

[class *class*][type *type*][name "*domain*"] order *order*

class, *type* and *domain* are self-explanatory. *order* is one of three possible values:

fixed

The order in which records are defined in the zone file is maintained.

random

Resource records are shuffled into a random order.

cyclic

The resource records are rotated in a round-robin manner, which is the default order.

The BIND 8 options are:

version

The string returned when the server is queried for its version.

directory

The path of the working directory from which the server reads and writes files.

named-xfer

The path to the named-xfer program.

dump-file

The file where the database is dumped if named receives a SIGINT signal. The default filename is *named_dump.db*.

memstatistics-file

The file where memory usage statistics are written. The default filename is *named.memstats*.

pid-file

The file where the process ID is stored.

statistics-file

The file where statistics are written when named receives a SIGILL signal. The default filename is *named.stats*.

auth-nxdomain

yes, which is the default, causes the server to respond as an authoritative server.

deallocate-on-exit

yes writes memory usage to the *named.memstats* file. The default is no.

dialup

yes optimizes the server for a dial-up network operation. The default is no.

fake-iquery
> yes makes the server issue a fake reply instead of an error in response to inverse queries. The default is no.

fetch-glue
> yes, which is the default, retrieves all of the glue records for a response.

has-old-clients
> yes sets auth-nxdomain and maintain-ixfr-base to yes and rfc2308-type1 to no.

host-statistics
> yes keeps statistics on every host. The default is no.

multiple-cnames
> yes permits multiple CNAME records for a domain name. The default is no.

notify
> yes, which is the default, sends DNS NOTIFY messages when a zone is updated.

recursion
> yes, the default, recursively seeks answers to queries.

rfc2308-type1
> yes returns NS records with the SOA record for negative caching. no, the default, returns only the SOA record for compatibility with old servers.

use-id-pool
> yes tracks outstanding query IDs to increase randomness. no is the default.

treat-cr-as-space
> yes treats carriage returns as spaces when loading a zone file. no is the default.

also-notify
> Identifies unofficial name servers to which the server should send DNS NOTIFY messages.

forward
> first causes the server to first query the forwarders and then look for the answer itself. only causes the server to query only the forwarders.

forwarders
> Lists the IP addresses of the servers to which queries are forwarded. The default is not to use forwarding.

check-names
> Checks hostnames for compliance with the RFC specifications. Names can be checked when the master server loads the zone (master), when the slave transfers the zone (slave), or when a response is processed (response). If an error is detected, it can be ignored (ignore), a warning can be sent (warn), or the bad name can be rejected (fail).

allow-query
> Only queries from hosts in the address list will be accepted. The default is to accept queries from all hosts.

allow-transfer

> Only hosts in the address list are allowed to receive zone transfers. The default is to allow transfers to all hosts.

allow-recursion

> Only listed hosts are allowed to make recursive queries through this server. The default is to do recursive queries for all hosts.

blackhole

> Lists hosts from which this server will not accept queries.

listen-on

> Defines the interfaces and ports on which the server provides name service. By default, the server listens to the standard port (53) on all installed interfaces.

query-source

> Defines the address and port used to query other servers.

lame-ttl

> The amount of time a lame server indication will be cached. The default is 10 minutes.

max-transfer-time-in

> The maximum amount of time the server waits for an inbound transfer to complete. The default is 120 minutes (2 hours).

max-ncache-ttl

> The amount of time this server will cache negative answers. The default is 3 hours and the maximum acceptable value is 7 days.

min-roots

> The minimum number of root servers that must be reachable for queries involving the root servers to be accepted. The default is 2.

serial-queries

> The number of outstanding SOA queries a slave server can have at one time. The default is 4.

transfer-format

> one-answer transfers one resource record per message. many-answers transfers as many resource records as possible in each message.

transfers-in

> Sets the maximum number of concurrent inbound zone transfers. The default value is 10.

transfers-out

> Lists the number of concurrent outbound zone transfers.

transfers-per-ns

> Limits the number of concurrent inbound zone transfers from any one name server. The default value is 2.

transfer-source

> The IP address of the network interface this server uses to transfer zones from remote masters.

maintain-ixfr-base

> yes keeps a log of incremental zone transfers. no is the default.

max-ixfr-log-size

> Sets the maximum size of the incremental zone transfer log file.

coresize

> Sets the maximum size of a core dump file.

datasize

> Limits the amount of data memory the server may use.

files

> Limits the number of files the server may have open concurrently. The default is unlimited.

stacksize

> Limits amount of stack memory the server may use.

cleaning-interval

> Sets the time interval for the server to remove expired resource records from the cache. The default is 60 minutes.

heartbeat-interval

> Sets the time interval used for zone maintenance when the dialup option is set to yes. 60 minutes is the default.

interface-interval

> Sets the time interval for the server to scan the network interface list looking for new interfaces or interfaces that have been removed. The default is every 60 minutes.

statistics-interval

> Sets the time interval for the server to log statistics. The default is every 60 minutes.

topology

> Forces the server to prefer certain remote name servers over others. Normally, the server prefers the remote name server that is topologically closest to itself.

sortlist

> Defines a sort algorithm applied to resource records before sending them to the client.

rrset-order

> Specifies the ordering used when multiple records are returned for a single query.

The BIND 9 options statement

The BIND 9 syntax of the options command is:

```
options {
    [ version string; ]
    [ directory pathname; ]
    [ additional-from-auth yes|no; ]
    [ additional-from-cache yes|no; ]
    [ dump-file pathname; ]
    [ pid-file pathname; ]
    [ statistics-file pathname; ]
    [ auth-nxdomain yes|no; ]
    [ dialup yes|no; ]
    [ notify yes|no|explicit; ]
    [ notify-source [ip_addr|*] [port ip_port] ; ]
    [ notify-source-v6 [ip_addr|*] [port ip_port] ; ]
    [ recursion yes|no; ]
    [ recursive-clients number; ]
    [ tcp-clients number; ]
    [ also-notify { address-list; }; ]
    [ forward only|first; ]
    [ forwarders { address-list; }; ]
    [ allow-notify { address_match_list }; ]
    [ allow-query { address_match_list }; ]
    [ allow-transfer { address_match_list }; ]
    [ allow-recursion { address_match_list }; ]
    [ blackhole { address_match_list }; ]
    [ listen-on [ port ip_port ] { address_match_list }; ]
    [ listen-on-v6 [ port ip_port ] { address_match_list }; ]
    [ port ip_port; ]
    [ query-source [address ip_addr|*] [port ip_port|*] ; ]
    [ query-source-v6 [address ip6_addr|*] [port ip_port|*] ; ]
    [ lame-ttl number; ]
    [ max-transfer-time-in number; ]
    [ max-transfer-time-out number; ]
    [ max-transfer-idle-in number; ]
    [ max-transfer-idle-out number; ]
    [ max-refresh-time number; ]
    [ max-retry-time number; ]
    [ max-cache-ttl number; ]
    [ max-ncache-ttl number; ]
    [ min-refresh-time number; ]
    [ min-retry-time number; ]
    [ transfer-format one-answer|many-answers; ]
    [ transfers-in  number; ]
    [ transfers-out number; ]
    [ transfers-per-ns number; ]
    [ transfer-source ip_addr|*] [port ip_port|*]; ]
    [ transfer-source-v6 ip6_addr|*] [port ip_port|*]; ]
    [ coresize size; ]
    [ datasize size; ]
    [ files size; ]
    [ stacksize size; ]
```

```
[ cleaning-interval number; ]
[ heartbeat-interval number; ]
[ interface-interval number; ]
[ sortlist { address_match_list }; ]
[ sig-validity-interval number; ]
[ tkey-dhkey key_name key_tag; ]
[ tkey-domain domain; ]
[ zone-statistics yes|no; ]
};
```

Many BIND 9 options are the same as those used for BIND 8 and perform exactly the same functions. A few options have been added to BIND 9 to handle IPv6, which is an integral part of BIND 9. These options, `listen-on-v6`, `notify-source-v6`, `query-source-v6`, and `transfer-source-v6`, perform exactly the same functions as the like-named options do for IPv4. Many BIND 8 options are no longer needed because important functions have been incorporated into the new BIND 9 code. However, the list of options is no shorter because many new options have been added:

`additional-from-auth`
> yes, the default, causes the server to use information from any zone for which it is authoritative when completing the additional data section of a response.

`additional-from-cache`
> yes, the default, causes the server to use information from its cache when completing the additional data section of a response.

`notify-source`
> Defines the address and port used to send NOTIFY messages.

`recursive-clients`
> Defines the maximum number of outstanding recursive lookups the server will perform for its clients. The default is 1000.

`tcp-clients`
> Defines the maximum number of concurrent client connections. The default is 1000.

`allow-notify`
> Identifies the servers that are permitted to send NOTIFY messages to the slave servers.

`port`
> Defines the port number used by the server. The default is standard port 53.

`max-transfer-time-out`
> Defines the maximum time allowed for outbound zone transfers. The default is 2 hours.

`max-transfer-idle-in`
> Defines the maximum time that an inbound zone transfer will be allowed to sit idle. The default is 1 hour.

`max-transfer-idle-out`

> Defines the maximum time that an outbound zone transfer will be allowed to sit idle. The default is 1 hour.

`max-refresh-time`

> Sets the maximum refresh time this server will use when acting as a slave. This value overrides the refresh time set in the SOA record of the zone for which this server acts as a slave.

`max-retry-time`

> Sets the maximum retry time this server will use when acting as a slave. This value overrides the retry time set in the SOA record of the zone for which this server acts as a slave.

`max-cache-ttl`

> Sets the maximum amount of time this server will cache data. This value overrides the TTL values defined in the zone from which the data was retrieved.

`min-refresh-time`

> Sets the minimum refresh time this server will use when acting as a slave. This value overrides the refresh time set in the SOA record of the zone for which this server acts as a slave.

`min-retry-time`

> Sets the minimum retry time this server will use when acting as a slave. This value overrides the retry time set in the SOA record of the zone for which this server acts as a slave.

`sig-validity-interval`

> Defines the amount of time that digital signatures generated for automatic updates will be considered valid. The default is 30 days.

`tkey-dhkey`

> Identifies the Diffie-Hellman key used by the server to generate shared keys.

`tkey-domain`

> Defines the domain name appended to shared keys. Normally this is the server's domain name.

`zone-statistics`

> yes causes the server to collect statistics on all zones. The default is no.

Options change over time. Check the documentation that comes with the BIND 9 distribution for the latest list of options.

The logging Statement

The `logging` statement defines the logging options for the server. The `logging` statement can include two different types of subordinate clauses: the `channel` clause and the `category` clause. The BIND 8 syntax of the command is:

```
logging {
  [ channel channel_name {
      file pathname
        [ versions number|unlimited ]
        [ size size ]
    |syslog kern|user|mail|daemon|auth|syslog|lpr
                |news|uucp|cron|authpriv|ftp
                |local0|local1|local2|local3
                |local4|local5|local6|local7
    |null;

      [ severity critical|error|warning|notice
                  |info|debug [level]|dynamic; ]
      [ print-category yes|no; ]
      [ print-severity yes|no; ]
      [ print-time yes|no; ]
  }; ]

  [ category category_name {
    channel_name; [ channel_name; ... ]
  }; ]
  ...
};
```

The channel clause defines how logging messages are handled. Messages are written to a file (file), sent to syslog (syslog), or discarded (null). If a file is used, you can specify how many old versions are retained (version), how large the log file is allowed to grow (size), and the severity of the messages written to the log file (severity). You can specify that the time (print-time), category (print-category), and severity (print-severity) of the message be included in the log.

The category clause defines the types of messages sent to the channel. Thus the category clause defines what is logged, and the channel clause defines where it is logged. The categories are listed in Table C-1.

Table C-1. BIND 8 logging categories

Category	Type of messages logged
cname	Messages recording CNAME references.
config	Messages about configuration file processing.
db	Messages that log database operations.
default	Various types of messages. This is the default if nothing is specified.
eventlib	Messages containing debugging data from the event system.
insist	Messages that report internal consistency check failures.
lame-servers	Messages about lame server delegations.
load	Messages about loading the zone.
maintenance	Messages reporting maintenance events.
ncache	Messages about negative caching.

Table C-1. BIND 8 logging categories (continued)

Category	Type of messages logged
notify	Messages tracing the NOTIFY protocol.
os	Messages reporting operating system problems.
packet	Messages containing dumps of all of the packets sent and received.
panic	Messages generated by a fault that causes the server to shut down.
parser	Messages about configuration command processing.
queries	Messages about every DNS query received.
response-checks	Messages reporting the results of response checking.
security	Messages concerning the application of security criteria. These are most meaningful if allow-update, allow-query, and allow-transfer options are in use.
statistics	Messages containing server statistics.
update	Messages concerning dynamic updates.
xfer-in	Messages recording inbound zone transfers.
xfer-out	Messages recording outbound zone transfers.

The BIND 9 logging statement

The BIND 9 syntax of the logging command is:

```
logging {
   [ channel channel_name {
      file pathname
         [ versions number|unlimited ]
         [ size size ]
      |syslog kern|user|mail|daemon|auth|syslog|lpr
                   |news|uucp|cron|authpriv|ftp
                   |local0|local1|local2|local3
                   |local4|local5|local6|local7
      |stderr
      |null;

      [ severity critical|error|warning|notice
                   |info|debug [level]|dynamic; ]
      [ print-category yes|no; ]
      [ print-severity yes|no; ]
      [ print-time yes|no; ]
   }; ]

   [ category category_name {
      channel_name; [ channel_name; ... ]
   }; ]
   ...
};
```

The channel clause is essentially the same as it was in BIND 8 with the addition of stderr as a possible destination for messages. The category clause looks the same, but there has been a major change in the categories supported. One category has been renamed from db to database. A dozen categories are no longer supported: cname, eventlib, insist, load, maintenance, ncache, os, packet, panic, parser, response-check, and statistics. Six new categories have been added:

general
> A wide variety of messages.

resolver
> Messages relating to DNS resolution.

client
> Messages concerning processing of client requests.

network
> Messages relating to network operations.

dispatch
> Messages that trace packets sent to various server modules.

dnssec
> Messages that track the processing of the DNSSEC and TSIG protocols.

The zone Statement

The zone statement identifies the zone being served and defines the source of DNS database information. There are four variants of the zone statement: one for the master server, one for the slave servers, one for the root cache zone, and a special one for forwarding. The BIND 8 syntax of each variant is:

```
zone domain_name [ in|hs|hesiod|chaos ] {
    type master;
    file pathname;
    [ forward only|first; ]
    [ forwarders { address-list; }; ]
    [ check-names warn|fail|ignore; ]
    [ allow-update { address_match_list }; ]
    [ allow-query { address_match_list }; ]
    [ allow-transfer { address_match_list }; ]
    [ dialup yes|no; ]
    [ notify yes|no; ]
    [ also-notify { address-list };
    [ ixfr-base pathname; ]
    [ pubkey flags protocol algorithm key; ]
};

zone domain_name [ in|hs|hesiod|chaos ] {
    type slave|stub;
    [ file pathname; ]
    [ ixfr-base pathname; ]
    masters [port ip_port] { address-list };
    [ forward only|first; ]
    [ forwarders { address-list; }; ]
    [ check-names warn|fail|ignore; ]
```

```
[ allow-update { address_match_list }; ]
[ allow-query { address_match_list }; ]
[ allow-transfer { address_match_list }; ]
[ transfer-source ip_addr; ]
[ dialup yes|no; ]
[ max-transfer-time-in number; ]
[ notify yes|no; ]
[ also-notify { address-list };
[ pubkey flags protocol algorithm key; ]
};

zone "." [ in|hs|hesiod|chaos ] {
  type hint;
  file pathname;
  [ check-names warn|fail|ignore; ]
};

zone domain_name [in|hs|hesiod|chaos] {
  type forward;
  [ forward only|first; ]
  [ forwarders { address-list; }; ]
  [ check-names warn|fail|ignore; ]
};
```

The zone keyword is followed by the name of the domain. For the root cache, the domain name is always ".". The domain name is followed by the data class. This is always IN for Internet DNS service, which is the default if no value is supplied.

The type clause defines whether this is a master server, a slave server, a forwarded zone, or the hints file for the root cache. A stub server is a slave server that loads only the NS records instead of the entire domain.

The file clause for a master server points to the source file from which the zone is loaded. For the slave server, it points to the file to which the zone is written, and the master clause points to the source of the data written to the file. For the root cache, the file clause points to the hints file used to initialize the cache. A forwarded domain does not have a file clause because no data for the forwarded domain is stored on the local server.

With the exception of the pubkey option, all of the options available for the BIND 8 zone statement are covered earlier in this appendix. When defined in a zone statement, an option applies only to the specific zone. When specified in the options statement, an option applies to all zones. The specific settings for a zone override the global settings of the options statement.

The pubkey option defines the DNSSEC public encryption key for the zone when there is no trusted mechanism for distributing public keys over the network. pubkey defines the DNSSEC flags, protocol, and algorithm as well as a base64-encoded version of the key. The remote server that will be accessing this domain through DNSSEC defines the same settings using the trusted-key command described earlier in this appendix.

The BIND 9 zone statement

The BIND 9 syntax of the four zone statement variants is:

```
zone domain_name [ in|hs|hesiod|chaos ] {
  type master;
  file pathname;
  [ forward only|first; ]
  [ forwarders { address-list; }; ]
  [ allow-update { address_match_list }; ]
  [ allow-update-forwarding { address_match_list }; ]
  [ allow-query { address_match_list }; ]
  [ allow-transfer { address_match_list }; ]
  [ allow-notify { address_match_list }; ]
  [ dialup yes|no; ]
  [ notify yes|no|notify|notify-passive|refresh|passive; ]
  [ also-notify { address-list };
  [ database string; [...] ]
  [ update-policy { policy }; ]
  [ sig-validity-interval number; ]
  [ max-refresh-time number; ]
  [ max-retry-time number; ]
  [ max-transfer-idle-out number; ]
  [ max-transfer-time-out number; ]
  [ min-refresh-time number; ]
  [ min-retry-time number; ]
};

zone domain_name [ in|hs|hesiod|chaos ] {
  type slave|stub;
  [ file pathname; ]
  [ ixfr-base pathname; ]
  masters [port ip_port] { address-list };
  [ forward only|first; ]
  [ forwarders { address-list; }; ]
  [ check-names warn|fail|ignore; ]
  [ allow-update { address_match_list }; ]
  [ allow-update-forwarding { address_match_list }; ]
  [ allow-query { address_match_list }; ]
  [ allow-transfer { address_match_list }; ]
  [ transfer-source ip_addr; ]
  [ dialup yes|no|notify|notify-passive|refresh|passive; ]
  [ max-transfer-time-in number; ]
  [ notify yes|no; ]
  [ also-notify { address-list };
  [ max-refresh-time number; ]
  [ max-retry-time number; ]
  [ max-transfer-idle-in number; ]
  [ max-transfer-idle-out number; ]
  [ max-transfer-time-in number; ]
  [ max-transfer-time-out number; ]
  [ min-refresh-time number; ]
  [ min-retry-time number; ]
  [ transfer-source ip_addr|*] [port ip_port|*]; ]
  [ transfer-source-v6 ip6_addr|*] [port ip_port|*]; ]
```

```
};

zone "." [ in|hs|hesiod|chaos ] {
  type hint;
  file pathname;
};

zone domain_name [in|hs|hesiod|chaos] {
  type forward;
  [ forward only|first; ]
  [ forwarders { address-list; }; ]
};
```

BIND 9 uses the same four zone command variations as does BIND 8. The difference between the two versions of BIND is that they use different options. Most of the options shown in the BIND 9 syntax were explained in the discussion of the BIND 9 options statement. The two options that are unique to the BIND 9 zone statement are:

allow-update-forwarding
> Identifies the systems that are allowed to submit dynamic zone updates to a slave that will then be forwarded to the master.

database
> Specifies the type of database used for storing zone data. The default is rbt, which is the only database type supported by the standard BIND 9 executable.

The controls Statement

The BIND 8 controls statement defines the control channels used by ndc. ndc can use a Unix socket or a network socket as a control channel. The controls statement defines those sockets. The syntax is:

```
controls {
  [ inet ip_addr
    port ip_port
    allow { address_match_list; }; ]
  [ unix pathname
    perm file_permissions
    owner uid
    group gid; ]
};
```

The first three options, inet, port, and allow, define the IP address and the port number of a network socket and the access control list of those systems allowed to control named through that channel. Because BIND 8 has weak authentication, creating a control channel that is accessible from the network is a risky thing to do. Whoever gains access to that channel has control over the name server process.

The last four options, unix, perm, owner, and group, define the Unix control socket. The Unix socket appears as a file in the filesystem. It is identified by a normal file pathname, for example, /var/run/ndc. Like any file, the Unix socket is assigned the user ID (*uid*) of its owner and a valid group ID (*gid*). It is protected by standard file permissions. Only numeric *uid*, *gid*, and *file_permissions* values are acceptable. The *file_permissions* value must start with a 0. For example, to set owner read and write, group read, and world no permissions, the numeric value would be 0640.

The BIND 9 controls statement

The BIND 9 controls statement defines the control channels used by rndc. rndc performs the same functions as the older ndc program, but it can reliably be used over a network. The BIND 9 controls statement is:

```
controls {
  [ inet ip_addr|*
    port ip_port
    allow address_match_list;
    keys key_list; ]
};
```

In BIND 9, the controls statement always defines a network socket. However, strong authentication is used that requires cryptographic keys.

BIND 9 view Statement

The view statement allows the same zone to be viewed differently by different clients. This makes it possible to provide an internal view to clients within an organization, and a more limited, external view to clients in the outside world. The syntax of the view command is:

```
view view-name {
  match-clients { address_match_list };
  [ view-option; ... ]
  [ zone-statement; ... ]
};
```

view-name
> An arbitrary name used inside the configuration to identify this view. To prevent conflicts with keywords, *view-name* should be enclosed in quotes, e.g., "internal".

match-clients
> Defines the list of clients that will access the zone through this view.

view-option
> A standard BIND 9 option. Any option defined inside the view statement applies only to this view. This allows different options to be applied to the same zone depending on which view of the zone is being used.

zone-statement
> A standard BIND 9 zone statement. A complete zone statement is embedded inside the view statement to define the zone accessed through this view.

The view statement is available only in BIND 9. BIND 8 does not support views.

Zone File Records

Two types of entries are used to construct a zone file: *directives* that simplify constructing the file, and *standard resource records* that define the domain data contained in the zone file. While there are many types of standard resource records, there are only four directives. These are:

$INCLUDE *filename*

> Identifies a file that contains data to be included in the zone file. The data in the included file must be valid directives or standard resource records. $INCLUDE allows a large zone file to be divided into smaller, more manageable units.
>
> The *filename* specified on the command line is relative to the directory named on the directory option in the *named.conf* file. For example, if the *named.conf* file for *crab* points to /etc with the directory option, and a zone file on *crab* contains an $INCLUDE events.hosts statement, then the file */etc/events.hosts* would be included in that zone file. If you don't want the filename to be relative to that directory, specify a fully qualified name, such as */usr/dns/events.hosts*.

$ORIGIN *domainname*

> Changes the default domain name used by subsequent records in the zone file. Use this command to put more than one domain in a zone file. For example, an $ORIGIN events statement in the *wrotethebook.com* zone file sets the domain name to *events.wrotethebook.com*. All subsequent resource records would be relative to this new domain.
>
> The named software uses $ORIGIN statements to organize its own information. Dumping the named database, with ndc dumpdb, produces a single file containing all the information that the server knows. This file, *named_dump.db*, contains many $ORIGIN entries to place all of the domains that named knows about into a single file.

$TTL *time-to-live*

> Defines the default TTL value used on resource records that do not include a specific TTL. Each zone file should start with a $TTL directive to ensure that all resource records have a valid TTL. A purely numeric *time-to-live* field defines the TTL in seconds. An alphanumeric *time-to-live* format can also be used. For example, 1w sets the TTL to one week. The possible values for the alphanumeric format are:
>
> - w for week
> - d for day
> - h for hour
> - m for minute
> - s for second

$GENERATE *range template*

> Generates resource records for a range of values using a specific resource record template. *range* is a numeric range of values written in the form `low_value-high_value`. $GENERATE creates a resource record for each value in *range*. Thus a range of 1-9 would create nine distinct records. The type of records created is determined by the *template*. The *template* is composed of literal values that are written to the resource record exactly as shown in the *template*, and the symbol $ that is replaced by the current range value before the resource record is written. Therefore, if the current range value is 7 and the template is `$ CNAME $.first64`, the resource record generated is `7 CNAME 7.first64`.

These directives are helpful for organizing and controlling the data in a zone file, but all of the actual database information comes from standard resource records. All of the files pointed to by *named.conf* contribute to the DNS database, so all of these files are constructed from standard resource records.

Standard Resource Records

The format of standard resource records, sometimes called RRs, is defined in RFC 1033, the *Domain Administrators Operations Guide*. The format is:

```
[name] [ttl] class type data
```

The individual fields in the standard resource record are:

name

> This is the name of the object affected by this resource record. The named object can be as specific as an individual host, or as general as an entire domain. The string entered for *name* is relative to the current domain unless a fully qualified domain name is used.* Certain *name* values have special meaning. These are:

>> A blank name field denotes the current named object. The current name stays in force until a new name value is encountered in the name field. This permits multiple RRs to be applied to a single object without having to repeat the object's name for each record.

> ..

>> Two dots in the name field refer to the root domain. However, a single dot (the actual name of the root) also refers to the root domain, and is more commonly used.

---

* The FQDN must be specified all the way to the root; i.e., it must end with a dot.

@

A single at-sign (@) in the name field refers to the current origin. The origin is a domain name derived by the system from the current domain name, or explicitly set by the system administrator using the $ORIGIN command.

*

An asterisk in the name field is a wildcard character. It stands for a name composed of any string. It can be combined with a domain name or used alone. Used alone, an asterisk in the named field means that the resource record applies to objects with names composed of any string of characters plus the name of the current domain. Used with a domain name, the asterisk is relative to that domain. For example, *.uucp. in the name field means any string plus the string .uucp.

ttl

Time-to-live defines the length of time that the information in this resource record should be kept in the cache. When *ttl* is specified as a purely numeric value, it defines the length of time in seconds. *ttl* can also use the alphanumeric format described for the $TTL directive. If no value is set for *ttl*, it defaults to the value defined for the entire zone file by the $TTL directive.

class

This field defines the address class of the resource record. The Internet address class is IN. All resource records used by Internet DNS have IN in this field, but it is possible for a zone file to hold non-Internet information. For example, information used by the Hesiod server, a name server developed at MIT, is identified by HS in the class field, and chaosnet information is identified by a CH in the class field. All resource records used in this book have an address class of IN.

type

This field indicates the type of data this record provides. For example, the A type RR provides the address of the host identified in the name field. The most common standard resource record types are discussed in the following sections.

data

This field contains the information specific to the resource record. The format and content of the data field vary according to the resource record type. The data field is the meat of the RR. For example, in an A record, the data field contains the IP address.

In addition to the special characters that have meaning in the name field, zone file records use these other special characters:

;

The semicolon is the comment character. Use the semicolon to indicate that the remaining data on the line is a comment.

( )

Parentheses are the continuation characters. Use parentheses to continue data beyond a single line. After an opening parenthesis, all data on subsequent lines is considered part of the current line until a closing parenthesis.

\x

The backslash is an escape character. A non-numeric character following a back-slash (\) is taken literally, and any special meaning that the character may ordinarily have is ignored. For example, \; means a semicolon—not a comment.

\ddd

The backslash can also be followed by three decimal numbers. When the escape character is used in this manner, the decimal numbers are interpreted as an absolute byte value. For example, \255 means the byte value 11111111.

The same general resource record format is used for each of the resource records in a zone file. The most commonly used resource records are described below.*

Start of Authority record

The Start of Authority (SOA) record marks the beginning of a zone, and is usually the first record in a zone file. All of the records that follow are part of the zone declared by the SOA. Each zone has only one SOA record; the next SOA record encountered marks the beginning of another zone. Because a zone file is normally associated with a single zone, it normally contains only one SOA record.

The format of the SOA record is:

```
[zone] [ttl] IN SOA origin contact  (
                     serial
                     refresh
                     retry
                     expire
                     negative_cache_ttl  )
```

The components of the SOA record are:

zone

This is the name of the zone. Usually the SOA name field contains an at-sign (@). When used in an SOA record, the at-sign refers back to the domain name declared in the *named.conf* zone statement that points to this zone file.

ttl

Time-to-live is left blank on the SOA record.

IN

The address class is IN for all Internet RRs.

---

* There are more than 40 RRs, most of which are not used. For a description of all of them, see *Linux DNS Administration* by Craig Hunt (Sybex).

SOA

SOA is the resource record type. All the information that follows this is part of the data field and is specific to the SOA record.

origin

This is the hostname of the master server for this domain. It is normally written as a fully qualified domain name. For example, *crab* is the master server for *wrotethebook.com*, so this field contains *crab.wrotethebook.com.* in the SOA record for *wrotethebook.com*.

contact

The email address of the person responsible for this domain is entered in this field. The address is modified slightly. The at-sign (@) that usually appears in an Internet email address is replaced by a dot. Therefore, if *david@crab.wrotethe-book.com* is the mailing address of the administrator of the *wrotethebook.com* domain, the *wrotethebook.com* SOA record contains *david.crab.wrotethebook.com.* in the contact field.

serial

This is the version number of the zone file. It is a ten-digit numeric field usually entered as a simple number, e.g., 117. However, the composition of the number is up to the administrator. Some choose a format that shows the date the zone was updated, e.g., 2001061800. Regardless of the format, the important thing is that the serial number must increase every time the data in the zone file is modified.

The serial field is extremely important. It is used by the slave servers to determine if the zone file has been updated. To make this determination, a slave server requests the SOA record from the master server and compares the serial number of the data it has stored to the serial number received from the master server. If the serial number has increased, the slave server requests a full zone transfer. Otherwise it assumes that it has the most current zone data. You must increment the serial number each time you update the zone data. If you don't, the new data may not be disseminated to the slave servers.

refresh

This specifies the length of time that the slave server should wait before checking with the master server to see if the zone has been updated. Every *refresh* seconds, the slave server checks the SOA serial number to see if the zone file needs to be reloaded. Slave servers check the serial numbers of their zones whenever they restart. But it is important to keep the slave server's database current with the master server, so named does not rely on these unpredictable events. The *refresh* interval provides a predictable cycle for reloading the zone that is controlled by the domain administrator.

The value used in *refresh* is a number, up to eight digits long, that is the maximum number of seconds that the master and slave servers' databases can be out of sync. A low *refresh* value keeps the data on the servers closely synchronized, but a very low *refresh* value is not usually required. A value set lower than needed places an unnecessary burden on the network and the slave servers. The value used in *refresh* should reflect the reality of how often your DNS database is updated.

Most sites' DNS databases are very stable. Systems are added periodically, but not generally on an hourly basis. When you are adding a new system, you can assign the hostname and address of that system before the system is operational. You can then install this information in the name server database before it is actually needed, ensuring that it is disseminated to the slave servers long before it has to be used.

If extensive changes are planned, the *refresh* time can be temporarily reduced while the changes are underway. Therefore, you can normally set *refresh* time high, reducing load on the network and servers. Two (43200 seconds) to four (21600 seconds) times a day for *refresh* is adequate for many sites.

The process of retrieving the SOA record, evaluating the serial number, and, if necessary, downloading the zone file is called a *zone refresh*. Thus the name *refresh* is used for this value.

retry

This defines how long slave servers should wait before trying again if the master server fails to respond to a request for a zone refresh. *retry* is specified in seconds and can be up to eight digits long.

You should not set the *retry* value too low. If a master server fails to respond, the server or the network could be down. Quickly retrying a down system gains nothing and costs network resources. A slave server that backs up a large number of zones can have problems when *retry* values are short. If the slave server cannot reach the master servers for several of its zones, it can become stuck in a retry loop.* Avoid problems; use an hour (3600) or a half hour (1800) for the *retry* value.

expire

This defines how long the zone's data should be retained by the slave servers without receiving a zone refresh. The value is specified in seconds and is up to eight digits long. If after *expire* seconds the slave server has been unable to refresh this zone, it should discard all of the data.

expire is normally a very large value. 604800 seconds (about one week) is commonly used. This says that if there has been no answer from the master server to refresh requests repeated every *retry* seconds for the last 7 days, discard the data. Seven days is a good value, but much longer values are not unusual.

---

* The server may alternate between periods when it fails to respond and when it resolves queries, or it may display the error "too many open files."

negative_cache_ttl

The *negative_cache_ttl* field of the SOA record is the default time-to-live for negative information about this domain that is cached by remote servers. All servers cache answers and use those answers to respond to subsequent queries. Most of the answers cached by a server are standard resource records. Yet a name server can learn from an authoritative server that a specific resource record does not exist. This is also valuable information that should be cached.

The server keeps cached records as long as they are valid, and the TTL defines how long that is. Each resource record has a TTL, either a TTL defined specifically for that record or the default TTL defined by the $TTL directive. However, there is no resource record for negative information and thus no explicit TTL. It is the *negative_cache_ttl* that tells remote servers how long to cache negative information.

The *negative_cache_ttl* value is usually set to between 5 and 15 minutes. This is long enough to prevent repeated queries for nonexistent information from causing your server any trouble, but short enough for repeated queries caused by a remote user who knows that a system with a certain name will soon come online.

Most of the fields in the SOA record provide values used to keep the slave servers synchronized with the master server. These values are used to guarantee that the slave will periodically pull a copy of the zone from the master server. In addition to this, and completely independent of the settings on the SOA record, the master notifies the slaves when the zone is updated in order to push a copy of the zone down to the slave. Combining the master-initiated zone push and the slave-initiated zone pull ensures that the zone files on the master and its slaves stay tightly synchronized.

A sample SOA record for the *wrotethebook.com* domain is:

```
@    IN  SOA  crab.wrotethebook.com. david.crab.wrotethebook.com. (
              2001061801           ; serial
              21600                ; refresh four times a day
              1800                 ; retry every half hour
              604800               ; expire after 1 week
              900                  ; negative cache ttl is 15 minutes
     )
```

Notice the serial number in this SOA. The serial number is in the format *yyyymm-ddvv*, where *yyyy* is the year, *mm* is the month, *dd* is the day, and *vv* is the version written that day. This type of serial number allows the administrator to track what day the zone was updated. Adding the version number allows for multiple updates in a single day. This zone file was created June 18, 2001, and it is the first update that day.

This SOA record also says that *crab* is the master server for this zone and that the person responsible for this zone can be reached at the email address *david@crab.wrotethebook.com*. The SOA tells the slave servers to check the zone for changes four times a day and to retry every half hour if they don't get an answer. If they retry for an entire week and never get an answer, they should discard the data for this zone. Finally, if an RR does not exist in this zone and the remote server decides to cache that information, it should cache that information for 15 minutes.

Name Server record

Name Server (NS) resource records identify the authoritative servers for a zone. These records are the pointers that link the domain hierarchy together. NS records in the top-level domains point to the servers for the second-level domains, which in turn contain NS records that point to the servers for their subdomains. Name server records pointing to the servers for subordinate domains are required for these domains to be accessible. Without NS records, the servers for a domain would be unknown.

The format of the NS RR is:

> [*domain*] [*ttl*] IN NS *server*

domain
> The name of the domain for which the host specified in the server field is an authoritative name server.

ttl
> Time-to-live is usually blank.

IN
> The address class is IN.

NS
> The name server resource record type is NS.

server
> The hostname of a computer that provides authoritative name service for this domain.

> Usually domains have at least one server that is located outside the local domain. The server name cannot be specified relative to the local domain; it must be specified as a fully qualified domain name. To be consistent, many administrators use fully qualified names for all servers, even though it is not necessary for servers within the local domain.

Address record

The majority of the resource records in a forward-mapping zone file* are address records. Address records are used to convert hostnames to IP addresses, which is the most common use of the DNS database.

---

* Chapter 8 describes the various named configuration files.

The address RR contains the following:

> [*host*] [*ttl*] IN A *address*

host
> The name of the host whose address is provided in the data field of this record. Most often the hostname is written relative to the current domain.

ttl
> Time-to-live is usually blank.

IN
> The address class is IN.

A
> The address resource record type is A.

address
> The IP address of the host is written here in dotted decimal form, e.g., 172.16. 12.2.

A *glue record* is a special type of address record. Most address records refer to hosts within the zone, but sometimes an address record needs to refer to a host in another zone. This is done to provide the address of a name server for a subordinate domain. Recall that the NS record for a subdomain server identifies the server by name. An address is needed to communicate with that server, so an A record must also be provided. The address record, combined with the name server record, links the domains together—thus the term "glue record."

Mail Exchanger record

The Mail Exchanger (MX) record redirects mail to a mail server. It can redirect mail for an individual computer or an entire domain. MX records are extremely useful for domains that contain some systems that don't run SMTP server software. Mail addressed to those systems can be redirected to computers that do run server software. MX records are also used to simplify mail addressing by redirecting mail to servers that understand the simplified addresses.

The format of the MX RR is:

> [*name*] [*ttl*] IN MX *preference host*

name
> The name of a host or domain to which the mail is addressed. Think of this as the value that occurs after the @ in a mailing address. Mail addressed to this name is sent to the mail server specified by the MX record's host field.

ttl
> Time-to-live is usually blank.

IN
> The address class is IN.

MX

The mail exchanger resource record type is MX.

preference

A host or domain may have more than one MX record associated with it. The preference field specifies the order in which the mail servers are tried. Servers with low preference numbers are tried first, so the most preferred server has a preference of 0. Preference values are usually assigned in increments of 5 or 10, so that new servers can be inserted between existing servers without editing the old MX records.

host

The name of the mail server to which mail is delivered when it is addressed to the host or domain identified in the name field.

Here is how MX records work. If a remote system has mail to send to a host, it requests the host's MX records. DNS returns all of the MX records for the specified host. The remote server chooses the MX with the lowest preference value and attempts to deliver the mail to that server. If it cannot connect to that server, it will try each of the remaining servers in preference order until it can deliver the mail. If no MX records are returned by DNS, the remote server delivers the mail directly to the host to which the mail is addressed. MX records only define how to redirect mail. The remote system and the mail server perform all of the processing that actually delivers the mail.

Because the remote system will first try to use an MX record, many domain administrators include MX records for every host in the zone. Many of these MX records point right back to the host to which the mail is addressed, e.g., an MX for *crab* with a host field of *crab.wrotethebook.com*. These records are used to ensure that the remote computer first attempts delivery to the host, and uses the MX server only if the host cannot accept the mail.

An important use for MX records is to allow mail to non-Internet sites to be delivered using Internet-style addressing. MX records do this by redirecting the mail to computers that know how to deliver the mail to non-Internet networks. For example, sites using uucp can register an Internet domain name with UUNET. UUNET uses MX records to redirect Internet mail addressed to these non-connected sites to *uunet.uu.net*, which delivers the mail to its final destination via uucp.

Here are some MX examples. All of these examples are for the imaginary domain *wrotethebook.com*. In the first example, mail addressed to *clock.wrotethebook.com* is redirected to *crab.wrotethebook.com* with this MX record:

```
clock IN MX 10 crab
```

The second example is an MX record used to simplify mail addressing. People can send mail to any user in this domain without knowing the specific computer that the user reads his mail on. Mail addressed to *user@wrotethebook.com* is redirected by this MX record to *crab*, which is a mail server that knows how to deliver mail to every individual user in the domain.

```
wrotethebook.com. IN MX 10 crab.wrotethebook.com.
```

The last example is an MX record that redirects mail addressed to any *host* within the domain to a central mail server. Mail addressed to any host, *horseshoe.wrotethe-book.com*, *24seven.wrotethebook.com*, or *anything.wrotethebook.com*, is redirected to *crab*. This is the most common use of the wildcard character (*).

```
*.wrotethebook.com. IN MX 10 crab.wrotethebook.com.
```

In these examples, the *preference* is 10 so that a mail server with a lower preference number can be added to the zone without changing the existing MX record. Also notice that the hostnames in the first example are specified relative to the *wrotethe-book.com* domain, but the other names are not relative because they end in a dot. All of these names *could* have been entered as relative names because they all are hosts in the *wrotethebook.com* domain; fully qualified names were used only to vary the examples. Finally, the wildcard MX record applies only to hosts that do not have specific MX records. If the specific record for *clock* is in the same configuration as the wildcard record, the wildcard MX does not apply to *clock*.

Canonical Name record

The Canonical Name (CNAME) resource record defines an alias for the official name of a host. The CNAME record provides a facility similar to nicknames in the host table. The facility provides alternate hostnames for the convenience of users, and generic hostnames used by applications (such as *loghost* used by syslogd).

The CNAME record is frequently used to ease the transition from an old hostname to a new hostname. While it is best to avoid hostname changes by carefully choosing hostnames in the first place, not all changes can be avoided. When you do make a name change, it can take a long time before it becomes completely effective, particularly if the hostname is embedded in a mailing list run at a remote site. To reduce problems for the remote site, use a CNAME record until they can make the change.

The format of the CNAME record is:

```
nickname [ttl] IN CNAME host
```

nickname
> This hostname is an alias for the official hostname defined in the *host* field. The *nickname* can be any valid hostname.

ttl
> Time-to-live is usually blank.

IN
> The address class is IN.

CNAME

The canonical name resource record type is CNAME.

host

The canonical name of the host is provided here. This hostname must be the official hostname; it cannot be an alias.

One important thing to remember about the CNAME record is that all other resource records must be associated with the official hostname and not with the nickname. This means that the CNAME record should not be placed between a host and the list of RRs associated with that host. The example below shows a correctly placed CNAME record:

```
rodent      IN    A       172.16.12.2
            IN    MX      5 rodent.wrotethebook.com.
            IN    RP      alana.wrotethebook.com. alana
            IN    TXT     "Linux workstation in room A15"
mouse       IN    CNAME   rodent.wrotethebook.com.
```

In this example, the hostname *rodent* stays in force for the MX, RP, and TXT records because they all have blank name fields. The CNAME record changes the name field value to *mouse*, which is a nickname for *rodent*. Any RRs with blank name fields following this CNAME record would associate themselves with the nickname *mouse*, which is illegal. An improper CNAME placement is:

```
rodent      IN    A       172.16.12.2
mouse       IN    CNAME   rodent.wrotethebook.com.
            IN    MX      5 rodent.wrotethebook.com.
            IN    RP      alana.wrotethebook.com. alana
            IN    TXT     "Linux workstation in room A15"
```

This improperly placed CNAME record causes named to display the error message "mouse.wrotethebook.com has CNAME and other data (illegal)." Check */var/adm/ messages* for named error messages to ensure that you have not misplaced any CNAME records.

Domain Name Pointer record

The Domain Name Pointer (PTR) resource records are used to convert numeric IP addresses to hostnames. This is the opposite of what is done by the address record that converts hostnames to addresses. PTR records are used to construct the *in-addr. arpa* reverse domain files.

Many administrators ignore the reverse domains because things appear to run fine without them. Don't ignore them. Keep these zones up to date. Several programs use the reverse domains to map IP addresses to hostnames when preparing status displays. A good example is the netstat command. Some service providers use the reverse domains to track who is using their services. If they cannot map your IP address back to a hostname, they reject your connection.

The format of the PTR record is:

    name [ttl] IN PTR host

name

> The *name* specified here is actually a number. The number is defined relative to the current *in-addr.arpa* domain. Names in an *in-addr.arpa* domain are IP addresses specified in reverse order. If the current domain is *16.172.in-addr.arpa*, then the name field for *rodent* (172.16.12.2) is 2.12. These digits (2.12) are added to the current domain (*16.172.in-addr.arpa*) to make the name *2.12.16.172.in-addr.arpa*. Chapter 4 discusses the unique structure of *in-addr.arpa* domain names.

ttl

> Time-to-live is usually blank.

IN

> The address class is IN.

PTR

> The Domain Name Pointer resource record type is PTR.

host

> This is the fully qualified domain name of the computer whose address is specified in the name field. The host must be specified as a fully qualified name because the name cannot be relative to the current *in-addr.arpa* domain.

There are many examples of PTR records in the sample reverse-mapping zone file (*172.16.rev*) shown in Chapter 8.

Responsible Person record

The Responsible Person (RP) record identifies the point of contact for a host or domain. The format of the RP record is:

    [name] [ttl] IN RP mail_address text_pointer

name

> The name of the domain object for which the responsible person is defined.

ttl

> Time-to-live is usually blank.

IN

> The address class is IN.

RP

> The resource record type is RP.

mail_address

> The email address of the responsible person. The @ usually included in an email address is replaced with a dot. Thus, *craig@wrotethebook.com* becomes *craig.wrotethebook.com*.

text_pointer
> The domain name of a TXT record that contains additional information about the responsible person.

Here's an example of how an RP record is used with a TXT record:

```
crab.wrotethebook.com.    IN RP  craig.wrotethebook.com. crabRP
crabRP.wrotethebook.com. IN TXT "Craig Hunt (301)555-1234 X237"
```

The RP record states that the person responsible for *crab.wrotethebook.com* can be reached via email at *craig@wrotethebook.com* and that additional information about the person can be obtained in the TXT records for *crabRP.wrotethebook.com*. The TXT record provides the contact person's name and phone number.

Text record

The Text (TXT) resource record holds string data. The text data can be in any format. Some sites define a local format for the information. For example, a TXT record could hold the Ethernet address of a host at one site and a room number at another site.

The format of the TXT record is:

> [*name*] [*ttl*] IN TXT *string*

name
> The name of the domain object with which the string data is associated.

ttl
> Time-to-live is usually blank.

IN
> The address class is IN.

TXT
> The resource record type is TXT.

string
> The *string* field contains text data enclosed in quotation marks.

Host Information record

The Host Information (HINFO) resource record provides a short description of the hardware and operating system used by a specific host. The hardware and software are described using standard terminology defined in the *Assigned Numbers* RFC in the sections on *Machine Names* (hardware) and *System Names* (software). There are a large number of hardware and software designators listed in the RFC. Most names use the same general format. Names with embedded blanks must be enclosed in quotes, so some names have a dash (-) where you might expect a blank. A machine name is usually the manufacturer's name in uppercase letters separated from the model number by a dash. The system name is usually the manufacturer's operating system name written in uppercase letters. Naturally the rapid changes in the computer market constantly make the data in the *Assigned Numbers* RFC out of date. Because of this, many administrators make up their own values for machine names and system names.

The format of the HINFO record is:

```
[host] [ttl] IN HINFO hardware software
```

host
> The hostname of the computer whose hardware and software are described in the data section of this resource record.

ttl
> Time-to-live is usually blank.

IN
> The address class is IN.

HINFO
> HINFO is the resource record type. All of the information that follows is part of the HINFO data field.

hardware
> This field identifies the hardware used by this host. It contains the machine name defined in the *Assigned Numbers* RFC. This field must be enclosed in quotes if it contains any blanks. A single blank space separates the hardware field from the software field that follows it.

software
> This field identifies the operating system software this host runs. It contains the system name defined for this operating system in the *Assigned Numbers* RFC. Use quotes if the system name contains any blanks.

No widely used application makes use of the HINFO record; the record just provides information. Some security-conscious sites discourage its use. They fear that this additional information helps intruders narrow their attacks to the specific hardware and operating system that they wish to crack. The general-purpose TXT record is more often used to provide information about systems than is the HINFO record.

Well-Known Services record

The Well-Known Services (WKS) resource record names the network services supported by the specified host. The official protocol names and services names used on the WKS record are defined in the *Assigned Numbers* RFC. The simplest way to list the names of the well-known services is to cat the */etc/services* file on your system. Each host can have no more than two WKS records; one record for TCP and one for UDP. Because several services are usually listed on the WKS record, each record may extend through multiple lines.

The format of the WKS record is:

> [*host*] [*ttl*] IN WKS *address protocol services*

host
> The hostname of the computer that provides the advertised services.

ttl
> Time-to-live is usually blank.

IN
> The address class is IN.

WKS
> The resource record type is WKS. All of the information that follows is variable information for the WKS record.

address
> The IP address of the host written in dotted decimal format, e.g., 172.16.12.2.

protocol
> The transport-level protocol through which the service communicates—either TCP or UDP.

services
> The list of services provided by this host. As few or as many services as you choose may be advertised, but the names used to advertise the services must be the names found in the */etc/services* file. Items in the list of services are separated by spaces. Parentheses are used to continue the list beyond a single line.

There are no widely used applications that make use of this record. It is used only to provide general information about the system. Again, security-conscious sites may not wish to advertise their services. Some protocols, such as tftp and finger, are prime targets for intruders. The SRV record is more useful for providing information about the services offered by a specific server.

Server Selection record

The Server Selection (SRV) record provides a standardized way to locate network servers. The SRV record provides a standard convention for creating generic server names, and it adds features for server selection and load-balancing. The format of the SRV record is:

> *name* [*ttl*] IN SRV *preference weight port server*

name
> The SRV record has a unique *_service._protocol.name* format. Dots are used to separate the components in the name field just as in any domain name. The underscore characters (_) are used to prevent the service name and the protocol name from colliding with real domain names. *service* is the name of the offered service as listed in the */etc/services* file. *protocol* is the protocol name associated with that service in the */etc/services* file. *name* is a standard host or domain name

that would be found in any name field. Using these criteria, the name that could be used to find the FTP servers for the *wrotethebook.com* domain would be *_ftp. _tcp.wrotethebook.com.*

ttl

> Time-to-live is usually blank.

IN

> The address class is IN.

SRV

> The resource record type is SRV.

preference

> A number used to select the most preferred server when multiple SRV records exist for the same service. The server with the lowest number is the most preferred. All traffic is sent to the most preferred servers; servers with a higher preference number are used only if the preferred servers are not available.

weight

> A number that defines the share of traffic sent to a server, with 1 being the base. If server A has a weight of 1 and server B has a weight of 2, B gets twice as much traffic as A. *weight* is used only to balance the load among servers with the same preference number.

port

> The port number used for the specified service. Normally, this is the port number defined in the */etc/services* file for the specified service. But it is possible to specify a nonstandard port number for services equipped to use nonstandard numbers.

server

> The canonical hostname of the computer running the requested service.

A dhcpd Reference

This appendix covers the syntax of the dhcpd command and the *dhcpd.conf* configuration file. It is a reference to the Internet Software Consortium (ISC) Dynamic Host Configuration Protocol (DHCP) server, dhcpd. To fully understand how to configure and use dhcpd in realistic network environments, see the tutorial and sample configuration files in Chapter 9.

The information in this appendix is based on the version of dhcpd available at this writing. As a beta release, this software is bound to be upgraded and changed. Refer to the web page *http://www.isc.org/dhcp.html* for the most recent information about dhcpd. And remember, a DHCP implementation from another vendor will probably be configured in a completely different manner.

Compiling dhcpd

The source code for dhcpd can be obtained through the ISC web site at *http://www. isc.org* or via anonymous FTP at *ftp://ftp.isc.org/isc/dhcp*. The name of the compressed tar file will change as new versions are released. However, the latest release should be stored as *dhcp-latest.tar.gz*. Download, gunzip, and untar the file:

```
> ftp ftp.isc.org
Connected to pub1.bryant.vix.com.
220 pub1.bryant.vix.com FTP server ready.
Name (ftp.isc.org:craig): anonymous
331 Guest login ok, send your complete email address as password.
Password:
230 Guest login ok, access restrictions apply.
ftp> cd isc/dhcp
250 CWD command successful.
ftp> binary
200 Type set to I.
ftp> get dhcp-latest.tar.gz
200 PORT command successful.
150 Opening BINARY mode data connection for dhcp-latest.tar.gz
226 Transfer complete.
```

```
181892 bytes received in 17 secs (10 Kbytes/sec)
ftp> quit
221 Goodbye.
> gunzip dhcp-latest.tar.gz
> tar -xvf dhcp-latest.tar
drwxrwxr-x mellon/engsrc       0 2001-10-05 00:22:41 dhcp-3.0/
drwxrwxr-x mellon/engsrc       0 2001-10-05 00:22:32 dhcp-3.0/doc/
...
-rw-rw-r-- mellon/engsrc 150274 2001-08-23 12:25:51 dhcp-3.0/server/failover.c
-rw-rw-r-- mellon/engsrc  67711 2001-08-23 12:30:58 dhcp-3.0/server/mdb.c
-rw-rw-r-- mellon/engsrc  62087 2001-06-21 22:28:51 dhcp-3.0/server/omapi.c
-rw-rw-r-- mellon/engsrc   7612 2001-06-21 22:31:39 dhcp-3.0/server/salloc.c
-rw-rw-r-- mellon/engsrc  34248 2001-06-21 22:35:08 dhcp-3.0/server/stables.c
drwxrwxr-x mellon/engsrc       0 2001-10-05 00:22:42 dhcp-3.0/tests/
drwxrwxr-x mellon/engsrc       0 2001-10-05 00:22:42 dhcp-3.0/tests/failover/
-rw-rw-r-- mellon/engsrc   3585 2001-05-31 16:16:05 dhcp-3.0/tests/failover/dhcp-1.cf
-rw-rw-r-- mellon/engsrc   3463 2001-05-31 16:16:06 dhcp-3.0/tests/failover/dhcp-2.cf
-rwxrwxr-x mellon/engsrc    537 2001-05-31 16:16:07 dhcp-3.0/tests/failover/new-
failover
```

Change to the newly created directory and run configure. configure determines the type of Unix system you're running and creates the correct Makefile for that system. If configure cannot determine what version of Unix you're running, you must build your own Makefile by hand. Next, type make to compile the daemon. Finally, copy the daemon and the manpages to the correct directories:

```
# cd dhcp-3.0
# ./configure
System Type: linux
# make
cc -g      -c dhcpd.c -o dhcpd.o
cc -g      -c dhcp.c -o dhcp.o
cc -g      -c bootp.c -o bootp.o
...
nroff -man dhcpd.conf.5 >dhcpd.conf.cat5
# make install
```

The DHCP daemon should compile without errors. If you get compile errors or if configure cannot determine your system configuration, you should consider abandoning the compile and notifying the support group. Join the support group mailing list by going to *http://www.fugue.com/dhcp*. Once you join, send mail to the *dhcp-server@fugue.com* mailing list describing your configuration and the exact problem you have. The list is read by most of the people using dhcpd. Someone may have already solved your problem.

Simply installing dhcpd may not be all that is required. Read the *README* file very carefully. dhcpd runs on a wide variety of systems, including OSF/1, most recent BSD derivatives, Solaris, and Linux. It runs best on OSF/1 and BSD; on other systems it may have some limitations. For example, on both Solaris and Linux, it can support only one network interface. dhcpd also may require some system-specific configuration. Old systems with the Linux 2.0.0 kernel are an excellent example of this. To successfully run dhcpd on one of these old systems, add the following entry to the */etc/hosts* table:

```
255.255.255.255 all-ones
```

Next, add a specific route for the limited broadcast address, 255.255.255.255:

```
# route add -host all-ones dev eth0
```

To reinstall the limited broadcast address in the kernel routing table after each boot, add the following code to a startup script:

```
# Install the limited broadcast route and start DHCP
  if [ -f /etc/dhcpd.conf ]; then
    echo -n " dhcpd"
    route add -host all-ones dev eth0
    /usr/sbin/dhcpd    fi
```

The information needed to complete these extra configuration steps is clearly defined in the *README* file. Read it before you try to run dhcpd. Of course, this is not required for current versions of Linux, but it provides a good example of the type of special configuration that is sometimes required.

The dhcpd Command

The syntax of the dhcpd command is:

```
dhcpd [-p port] [-f] [-d] [-cf config-file] [-lf lease-file] [if0 [ifn]]
```

dhcpd usually is run without any command-line arguments. Most of the arguments are used only when testing and debugging. Two of the command-line arguments handle special configuration requirements:

-f

Runs dhcpd in foreground mode. By default, dhcpd runs as a background daemon process. Use -f when dhcpd is started from *inittab* on a System V Unix system.

if0 [...*ifn*]

Lists the interfaces on which dhcpd should listen for BOOTREQUEST packets. This is a whitespace-separated list of interface names. For example, dhcpd ec0 ec1 wd0 tells dhcpd to listen to interfaces ec0, ec1, and wd0. Normally this argument is not required. In most cases dhcpd locates all installed interfaces and eliminates the no-broadcast interfaces automatically. Use this argument only if it appears that dhcpd is failing to locate the correct interfaces.

All of the remaining command-line arguments are used for debugging or testing:

-p *port*

Causes dhcpd to listen to a nonstandard port. The well-known port for DHCP is 67. Changing it means that clients cannot talk to the server. On rare occasions this is done during testing.

`-d`

Routes error messages to stderr. Normally error messages are written via syslog with facility set to DAEMON.

`-cf` *config-file*

Causes dhcpd to read the configuration from the file identified by *config-file* instead of from *dhcpd.conf*. Use this only to test a new configuration before it is installed in *dhcpd.conf*. Use the standard file for production.

`-lf` *lease-file*

Causes dhcpd to write the address lease information to the file identified by *lease-file* instead of to *dhcpd.leases*. Use this only for testing. Changing the name of the lease file could cause dynamic addresses to be misallocated. Use this argument with caution.

Kill the dhcpd daemon with the SIGTERM signal. The process ID (PID) of the dhcpd daemon is found in the */var/run/dhcpd.pid* file. For example:

```
# kill -TERM 'cat /var/run/dhcpd.pid'
```

dhcpd uses three files. It writes its PID to */var/run/dhcpd.pid*, maintains a record of dynamic address leases in */var/db/dhcpd.leases*, and reads its configuration from */etc/dhcpd.conf*. These last two files are created by you. Create an empty lease file before you run dhcpd the first time, e.g., *touch /var/db/dhcpd.leases*. Create a configuration and store it in *dhcpd.conf*.

The dhcpd.conf Configuration File

When it starts, dhcpd reads its configuration from the */etc/dhcpd.conf* file. *dhcpd.conf* defines the network being served by the DHCP server and the configuration information the server provides to its clients.

dhcpd.conf is an ASCII text file. Comments in the file begin with a sharp sign (#). Keywords are case-insensitive. Whitespace can be used to format the file. Related statements are enclosed in curly braces. IP addresses can be entered as numeric addresses or as hostnames that resolve to addresses.

Statements in the configuration file define the topology of the network being served. In the documentation these statements are called "declarations" because they declare something about the network topology. The statements that define the topology are `shared-network`, `subnet`, `group`, and `host`. All of these can appear multiple times in the configuration file. The statements define a hierarchical structure. The `shared-network` contains subnets, and subnets can contain hosts.

Parameters and options can be associated with each of these statements. Parameters define things about the server and the protocol, such as the length of time for an address lease or where the boot file is located. The options provide the clients with values for the standard DHCP configuration options defined by the RFCs, for example, whether the client should enable IP forwarding. Parameters and options specified outside of a specific topology statement apply to all networks served by this server. Those specified in the group statement apply to all of the shared networks, subnets, or hosts grouped together by the statement. The shared-network statement options and parameters apply to all subnets on the shared network. Subnet options and parameters apply to everything on the subnet. Host options and parameters apply only to the individual host. Options applied at a general level can be overridden by the same option applied at a more specific level. Subnet options override global options and host options override subnet options. This structure allows the network administrator to define configuration information for the entire network and all of its parts.

In the following sections, we examine the syntax of all of the topology statements and all the parameters and options that can be associated with them. We include many more parameters and options than you will ever use, and there is no need to study them all. Use this reference to look up the details of individual parameters and options when you need them. See Chapter 9 for examples of how these statements, parameters, and options are actually used in a real-world configuration.

Topology Statements

group {[*parameters*] [*options*]}

> The group statement groups together shared-network, subnet, host, or other group statements to apply a set of parameters or options to all members of the group.

shared-network *name* {[*parameters*] [*options*] }

> The shared-network statement is used only if more than one IP subnet shares the same physical network. In most cases, different subnets are on different physical networks. The *name*, which must be provided, can be any descriptive name. It is used only in debugging messages. Parameters and options associated with the shared network are declared within the curly braces and apply to all subnets in the shared network. The subnets in a shared network must be defined within the curly braces of the shared-network statement. It is assumed that each shared-network statement contains at least two subnet statements; otherwise there is no need to use the shared-subnet statement. dhcpd cannot tell on which subnet of a shared network a client should boot. Therefore, dynamically allocated addresses are taken from the available range of all subnets on the shared network and assigned as needed.

subnet *address* mask *netmask* { [*parameters*] [*options*] }

> The subnet statement defines the IP address and address mask of every subnet the daemon will serve. The address and mask are used to identify the clients that belong to the subnet. The parameters and options defined within the curly braces apply to every client on the subnet. Every subnet physically connected to the server must have a subnet statement even if the subnet does not have any clients.

host *hostname* {[*parameters*] [*options*] }

> The host statement defines parameters and options for individual clients. Every BOOTP client must have a host statement in the *dhcpd.conf* file. For DHCP

clients, the host statement is optional. It is matched to an actual DHCP or BOOTP client by matching the dhcp-client-identifier provided by the client or by matching the hardware parameter to the hardware address of the client. BOOTP clients do not provide a dhcp-client-identifier, so use the hardware address for BOOTP clients. DHCP clients can be identified by either the dhcp-client-identifier or the hardware address.

Configuration Parameters

The parameter statements defined in this section control the operation of the DHCP server and the DHCP protocol. The standard DHCP configuration values that are passed to clients are defined in option statements, which are covered in the next section. Some parameter statements can be associated with any of the topology statements discussed above. Others can be used only with specific statements. These are noted in the description of the parameter.

range [dynamic-bootp] *low-address* [*high-address*] ;
> The range parameter defines the scope of addresses that are available for dynamic assignment by defining the lowest and highest IP addresses available for assignment. The range parameter must be associated with a subnet statement. All addresses in the scope of the range parameter must be in the subnet in which the range parameter is declared. The dynamic-bootp flag is specified if addresses may be automatically assigned to BOOTP clients as well as DHCP clients. The range parameter must be defined if you intend to use dynamic address assignment. If the subnet statement does not include a range parameter, dynamic address assignments are not made to clients on the subnet.

default-lease-time *seconds*;
> The life of an address lease in seconds that is used if the client does not request a specific lease length.

max-lease-time *seconds*;
> The maximum life of an address lease in seconds regardless of the lease length the client requests.

hardware *type address*;
> Defines a client's hardware address. At present, *type* must be either ethernet or token-ring. *address* must be an appropriate physical address for the type of hardware. The hardware parameter must be associated with a host statement. It is required for a BOOTP client to be recognized. It is optional for DHCP clients, for which it is an alternative to the dhcp-client-identifier option.

filename *file*;
> Identifies the boot file for diskless clients. *file* is an ASCII string enclosed in quotation marks.

server-name *name*;
> The hostname of the DHCP server that is provided to the client. *name* is an ASCII string enclosed in quotation marks.

next-server *name*;
>   The hostname or address of the server from which the boot file is to be loaded.

fixed-address *address*[, *address*...] ;
>   Assigns one or more fixed IP addresses to a host. The fixed-address parameter is valid only when associated with a host statement. If more than one address is supplied, the client is assigned the address that is valid for the subnet on which it is booting. If none of the addresses is valid for the subnet, no configuration data is sent to the client.

dynamic-bootp-lease-cutoff *date*;
>   Sets a termination date for addresses assigned to BOOTP clients. BOOTP clients don't have a way of renewing leases and don't know that address leases expire. By default, dhcpd assigns permanent addresses to BOOTP clients. This parameter changes that behavior. It is used only in special circumstances where the life of all systems is known in advance—for example, on a college campus where it is known that all student systems will be removed by June.

dynamic-bootp-lease-length *seconds*;
>   Defines the life of an address lease in seconds for an address automatically assigned to a BOOTP client. As noted above, BOOTP clients do not understand address leases. This parameter is used only in special circumstances where clients use a BOOTP boot PROM and run an operating system that supports DHCP. During the boot the client acts as a BOOTP client, but once it boots the client runs DHCP and knows how to renew a lease. Use this parameter, and the previous one, with caution.

get-lease-hostnames *flag*;
>   Tells dhcpd if it should send a DNS hostname to the client when it dynamically assigns it an IP address. If *flag* is true, dhcpd uses DNS to look up the hostnames for all dynamically assigned addresses, which dramatically slows DHCP performance. By default the *flag* is false, and no lookups are done.

use-host-decl-names *flag*;
>   Causes the name provided on the host statement to be supplied to the client as its hostname.

server-identifier *hostname*;
>   Defines the value sent in the server identifier option. The default is to send the first IP address of the network interface.

authoritative;
not authoritative;
>   Specifies whether or not the DHCP server is authoritative. The default is authoritative. not authoritative can be used if a DHCP server does not have the authority to set client addresses. It is possible to have a DHCP server that supports multiple networks and has address authority for some networks and no address authority for other networks.

`use-lease-addr-for-default-route` *flag;*

> Causes the leased IP address to be sent to the client as the default route in order to force Windows 95 clients to ARP for all IP addresses. This parameter is used only when the local router is the proxy ARP server. The `option routers` statement overrides this parameter.

`always-reply-rfc1048` *flag;*

> Sends responses that comply with RFC 1048 to a BOOTP client, even if that client does not send requests that comply with RFC 1048. This parameter is used when the server logs the message "(non-rfc1048)" for a BOOTP client's BOOTREQUEST. This parameter is generally used on a client-by-client basis. Upgrading the clients to DHCP is preferred.

`allow` *keyword;*
`deny` *keyword;*

> Determines whether or not the server responds to certain types of requests. *keyword* defines the type of request that is allowed or denied. There are three possible keyword values:
>
> `unknown-clients`
> > Determines whether the server dynamically assigns addresses to unknown clients. By default, dynamic addresses are assigned to unknown clients.
>
> `bootp`
> > Determines whether the server responds to BOOTP requests. By default, BOOTP requests are allowed.
>
> `booting`
> > Used inside a `host` declaration to specify whether the server responds to a particular client. By default, the DHCP server responds to all clients.

DHCP Options

The option statements available with dhcpd cover all of the standard DHCP configuration options currently defined in the RFCs. Furthermore, the syntax of the *dhcpd.conf* option statement is extensible. A new option can be identified by its decimal option code. All options are assigned a decimal option code, either in the RFC that describes the option, or in the vendor documentation if it is vendor-specific. The value assigned to the new option can be expressed as a string enclosed in quotes or as a colon-separated list of hexadecimal numbers. Imagine that a new DHCP option is created and assigned an option code of 133. Further, imagine that the value carried by this option is a 16-bit binary mask and that you want your clients to "turn on" the high-order 4-bits and "turn off" all other bits in the mask. You could add the following option to your configuration:

```
option option-133 F0:00
```

All option statements begin with the keyword `option`. The keyword is then followed by the name of the option and the value assigned to the option, in that order. In the example above, the option name is in the form `option-nnn`, where *nnn* is the decimal option code assigned to the option. In this manner, any new option that appears can be added to *dhcpd.conf* file. The value assigned to this imaginary option is F000.

Looking at the huge list of standard options, you may well wonder if they will ever need to be extended. The standard options are listed in the following section. The types of values that are assigned to options are:

Address
> An IP address written in dotted decimal notation, or a hostname that resolves to an address.

String
> A series of characters enclosed in quotation marks.

Number
> A numeric value.

Flag
> A switch containing either `true` or `false`, which can also be set as `1` or `0`, or `yes` or `no`.

In this book, the list of options is divided into "Commonly used options" and "Other options."

Commonly used options

`option subnet-mask` *mask*`;`
> Specifies the subnet mask in dotted decimal notation. If the subnet mask option is not provided, dhcpd uses the network mask from the `subnet` statement.

`option time-offset` *seconds*`;`
> Specifies the number of seconds this time zone is offset from Coordinated Universal Time (UTC).

`option routers` *address*`[,` *address*`...] ;`
> Lists the routers the client should use, in order of preference.

`option domain-name-servers` *address*`[,` *address*`...] ;`
> Lists the Domain Name System (DNS) name servers the client should use, in order of preference.

`option lpr-servers` *address* `[,` *address*`...] ;`
> Lists line printer (LPR) servers the client should use, in order of preference.

`option host-name` *host*`;`
> Defines the hostname the client should use.

`option domain-name` *domain*`;`
> Defines the domain name.

```
option interface-mtu bytes;
```
Defines the MTU the client should use. The minimum legal value for the MTU is 68.

```
option broadcast-address address;
```
Defines the broadcast address for the client's subnet.

```
option static-routes destination gateway[, destination gateway... ] ;
```
Lists the static routes the client should use. The default route cannot be specified in this manner. Use the routers option for the default route.

```
option trailer-encapsulation 0 | 1;
```
Specifies if the client should use trailer encapsulation. 0 means that the client shouldn't use trailer encapsulation, and 1 means that the client should use trailer encapsulation.

```
option nis-domain string;
```
A character string that defines the name of the Network Information Services (NIS) domain.

```
option nis-servers address[, address...] ;
```
Lists IP addresses of the NIS servers the client should use, in order of preference.

```
option dhcp-client-identifier string;
```
Used in the host statement to define the DHCP client identifier. dhcpd can use the client identifier to identify DHCP clients in lieu of the hardware address.

Other options

```
option time-servers address[, address...] ;
```
Lists the time servers the client should use, in order of preference.

```
option ien116-name-servers address[, address...];
```
Lists the IEN 116 name servers the client should use, in order of preference. IEN 116 is an obsolete name service. Avoid this and use DNS.

```
option log-servers address[, address...] ;
```
Lists the MIT-LCS UDP log servers the client should use, in order of preference.

```
option cookie-servers address[, address...] ;
```
Lists the cookie servers available to the client, in order of preference.

```
option impress-servers address[, address...] ;
```
Lists the Image Impress servers available to the client, in order of preference.

```
option resource-location-servers address[, address...] ;
```
Lists the Resource Location servers the client should use, in order of preference.

```
option boot-size blocks;
```
Specifies the number of 512-octet blocks in the boot file.

```
option merit-dump path;
```
path is a character string that identifies the location of the file the client should dump core to in the event of a crash.

option swap-server *address*;
 Specifies the IP address of the client's swap server.

option root-path *path*;
 path is a character string that identifies the location of the client's root disk.

option ip-forwarding 0 | 1;
 Specifies if the client should do IP forwarding. 0 disables IP forwarding, and 1 enables it.

option non-local-source-routing 0 | 1;
 Specifies if the client should allow non-local source routes. Source routes are a potential security problem, as they can be used by intruders to route data off the local network in ways not intended by the local network administrator. 0 disables forwarding of non-local source-routed datagrams, and 1 enables forwarding. 0 is the more secure setting.

option policy-filter *address mask*[, *address mask*...] ;
 Lists the IP addresses and masks that specify the only valid destination/mask pairs for incoming source routes. Any source-routed datagram whose next-hop address does not match one of the filters is discarded by the client.

option max-dgram-reassembly *bytes*;
 Defines, in bytes, the largest datagram the client should be prepared to reassemble. The value of *bytes* cannot be less than 576.

option default-ip-ttl *ttl* ;
 Defines the default time-to-live (TTL) for outgoing datagrams.

option path-mtu-aging-timeout *seconds*;
 Sets the number of seconds for timing out Path MTU values discovered by the mechanism defined in RFC 1191.

option path-mtu-plateau-table *bytes*[, *bytes*...] ;
 Defines a table of MTU sizes to use when performing Path MTU Discovery as defined in RFC 1191. The minimum MTU value cannot be smaller than 68.

option all-subnets-local 0 | 1;
 Tells the client if all subnets of the local network use the same MTU. 1 means that all subnets share the same MTU. 0 means that some subnets have smaller MTUs.

option perform-mask-discovery 0 | 1;
 Specifies if the client should use ICMP to discover the subnet mask. 0 enables ICMP mask discovery, and 1 disables it. Because the DHCP server can provide the correct subnet mask, ICMP mask discovery is rarely used on networks that have a DHCP server.

option mask-supplier 0 | 1;
 Specifies if the client should respond to ICMP subnet mask requests. 0 means that the client shouldn't respond, and 1 means that it should.

`option router-discovery 0 | 1;`
> Specifies if the client should use the Router Discovery mechanism defined in RFC 1256 to locate routers. 0 means it shouldn't, and 1 means it should perform router discovery. Because the DHCP server provides the correct list of routers, router discovery is rarely used on networks that have a DHCP server.

`option router-solicitation-address address;`
> Defines the address to which the client should transmit a router solicitation request if router discovery is enabled.

`option arp-cache-timeout seconds;`
> Defines the number of seconds entries are maintained in the ARP cache.

`option ieee802-3-encapsulation 0 | 1;`
> Specifies if the client should use Ethernet II (DIX) or IEEE 802.3 Ethernet encapsulation on the network. 0 tells the client to use Ethernet II and 1 tells the client to use IEEE 802.3 encapsulation.

`option default-tcp-ttl ttl;`
> Defines the default TTL for TCP segments. Possible values are 1 to 255.

`option tcp-keepalive-interval seconds;`
> The number of seconds TCP should wait before sending a keepalive message. 0 means that TCP should not generate keepalive messages. Keepalive messages are generally discouraged.

`option tcp-keepalive-garbage 0 | 1;`
> Specifies if the client should send TCP keepalive messages with an octet of garbage for compatibility with older implementations. 0 means don't send a garbage octet and 1 means send it. Keepalives are generally discouraged.

`option ntp-servers address[, address...] ;`
> Lists the IP addresses of the Network Time Protocol (NTP) servers the client should use, in order of preference.

`option netbios-name-servers address[, address...] ;`
> Lists the NetBIOS name servers (NBNS) the client should use, in order of preference.

`option netbios-dd-server address[, address...] ;`
> Lists the NetBIOS datagram distribution servers (NBDD) the client should use, in order of preference.

`option netbios-node-type type;`
> Defines the NetBIOS node type of the client. A type of 1 is a NetBIOS B-node; 2 is a P-node; 4 is an M-node; 8 is an H-node.

`option netbios-scope string;`
> A character string that defines the NetBIOS over TCP/IP scope parameter as specified in RFC 1001/1002.

option font-servers *address*[, *address*...] ;
> Lists the X Window System Font servers the client should use, in order of preference.

option x-display-manager *address*[, *address*...] ;
> Lists the systems running the X Window System Display Manager that the client should use, in order of preference.

option nisplus-domain *string*;
> Defines the NIS+ domain name.

option nisplus-servers *ip-address* [, *ip-address*...];
> Lists the NIS+ servers' IP addresses. Servers are listed in order of preference.

option tftp-server-name *string*;
> Identifies a TFTP boot server.

option bootfile-name *string*;
> Provides the name of the boot file found on the TFTP boot server.

option mobile-ip-home-agent *ip-address* [, *ip-address*...];
> Lists the IP addresses of Mobile IP home agents available to the client.

option smtp-server *ip-address* [, *ip-address*...];
> Lists the IP addresses of the SMTP servers in order of preference.

option pop-server *ip-address* [, *ip-address*...];
> Lists the IP addresses of POP3 servers in order of preference.

option nntp-server *ip-address* [, *ip-address*...];
> Lists the IP addresses of Network News Transport Protocol (NNTP) servers in order of preference.

option www-server *ip-address* [, *ip-address*...];
> Lists the IP addresses of web servers in order of preference.

option finger-server *ip-address* [, *ip-address*...];
> Lists the IP addresses of finger servers in order of preference.

option irc-server *ip-address* [, *ip-address*...];
> Lists the IP addresses of IRC servers in order of preference.

option streettalk-server *ip-address* [, *ip-address*...];
> Lists the IP addresses of StreetTalk servers in order of preference.

option streettalk-directory-assistance-server *ip-address* [, *ip-address*...];
> Lists the IP addresses of StreetTalk Directory Assistance (STDA) servers in order of preference.

A sendmail Reference

This appendix provides details of the syntax of the sendmail command, of the *sendmail.cf* file, and of the m4 macros that can be used to build that file. It describes where to obtain the latest source code for sendmail and how to compile it. This appendix is a reference, not a tutorial. Refer to Chapter 10 for a tutorial on sendmail configuration.

We start the appendix with information on locating, downloading, and compiling the latest version of sendmail.

Compiling sendmail

The source code for sendmail is available via anonymous FTP from *ftp.sendmail.org*, where it is stored in the *pub/sendmail* directory. sendmail is updated constantly. The following examples are based on sendmail 8.11.3. Remember that things will change for future releases. Always read the *README* files and installation documents that come with new software before beginning an installation.

To compile the sendmail program, download the compressed tar file as a binary file, and then uncompress and extract it with the tar command, shown below:

```
$ ftp ftp.sendmail.org
Connected to ftp.sendmail.org.
220 pub2.pa.vix.com FTP server ready.
Name (ftp.sendmail.org:craig): anonymous
331 Guest login ok, send your e-mail address as password.
Password:
230 Guest login ok, access restrictions apply.
Remote system type is UNIX.
Using binary mode to transfer files.
ftp> cd pub/sendmail
ftp> get sendmail.8.11.3.tar.gz
local: sendmail.8.11.3.tar.gz remote: sendmail.8.11.3.tar.gz
200 PORT command successful.
150 Opening BINARY mode data connection for sendmail.8.11.3.tar.gz
    (1347756 bytes).
226 Transfer complete.
```

```
1347756 bytes received in 18.68 Seconds (72.42 Kbytes/sec)
ftp> quit
221-You have transferred 1347756 bytes in 1 files.
221-Thank you for using the FTP service on pub2.pa.vix.com.
221 Goodbye.
$ cd /usr/local/src
$ tar -zxvf /home/craig/sendmail.8.11.3.tar.gz
```

Next, change to the *sendmail-8.11.3* directory created by the tar file, and use the Build script to compile the new sendmail program, as shown below:

```
$ cd sendmail-8.11.3
$ ./Build
Making all in:
/usr/local/src/sendmail-8.11.3/libsmutil
Configuration: pfx=, os=Linux, rel=2.2.10, rbase=2, rroot=2.2, arch=i586, sfx=,
variant=optimized
Using M4=/usr/bin/m4
Creating ../obj.Linux.2.2.10.i586/libsmutil using ../devtools/OS/Linux
Making dependencies in ../obj.Linux.2.2.10.i586/libsmutil
make[1]: Entering directory
      `/usr/local/src/sendmail-8.11.3/obj.Linux.2.2.10.i586/libsmutil'
cc -M -I. -I../../sendmail -I../../include -DNEWDB
      -DNOT_SENDMAIL debug.c
errstring.c lockfile.c safefile.c snprintf.c strl.c    >> Makefile
make[1]: Leaving directory
      `/usr/local/src/sendmail-8.11.3/obj.Linux.2.2.10.i586/libsmutil'
Making in ../obj.Linux.2.2.10.i586/libsmutil
make[1]: Entering directory
      `/usr/local/src/sendmail-8.11.3/obj.Linux.2.2.10.i586/libsmutil'
cc -O -I. -I../../sendmail -I../../include -DNEWDB
      -DNOT_SENDMAIL -c debug.c -o debug.o
cc -O -I. -I../../sendmail -I../../include -DNEWDB
      -DNOT_SENDMAIL -c errstring.c -o errstring.o

... Many, many, many lines deleted...

cc -O -I. -I../../sendmail -I../../include -DNEWDB
      -DNOT_SENDMAIL -c vacation.c -o vacation.o
cc -o vacation    vacation.o ../libsmdb/libsmdb.a
      ../libsmutil/libsmutil.a -ldb -lresolv -lcrypt -lnsl -ldl
groff -Tascii -man vacation.1 > vacation.0 ||
      cp vacation.0.dist vacation.0
make[1]: Leaving directory
      `/usr/local/src/sendmail-8.11.3/obj.Linux.2.2.10.i586/vacation'
```

Build detects the architecture of the system and builds the correct Makefile for your system. It then compiles sendmail using the newly created Makefile.

According to the documentation, running Build is all you need to do on most systems to compile sendmail. It works on Red Hat Linux and Solaris 8 systems. However, there are no guarantees. Your system may use nonstandard directories or lack certain libraries. You may need to provide compiler flags that are customized for your system.

If you have experience with compiling sendmail, you may be tempted to look for the compiler options in the Makefile in the sendmail distribution's source code directory. You may even remember setting compiler options in the Makefile at some time in the past, but that has changed. Now, compiler options are set in the files located in the *devtools* directory of the sendmail source code distribution.

The default compiler options are normally set in an operating system–specific file in the *devtools/OS* directory and changed in files you create specially for your server in the *devtools/Site* directory. The files in the *devtools/OS* directory are identified by operating system name; for example, the configuration file for Solaris 8 is named *SunOS5.8*. If your Solaris 8 system varies from the norm, create your own file in *devtools/Site* named *site.SunOS5.8.m4* that contains the corrected setting. Additionally, you can create a file named *site.config.m4* in the *devtools/Site* directory if the compiler options you wish to set relate more to the peculiarities of your site than they do to corrections of operating system settings. Build looks for and uses files with either of these names.

As the *.m4* file extension in these filenames implies, the commands that are used to define compiler options are m4 macros, not simple compiler options. Table E-1 lists the m4 commands that are used with sendmail 8.11.3 to control the compile process.

Table E-1. m4 compiler options

Command	Purpose
confBEFORE	Identifies files that must be created before the compile.
confBLDVARIANT	Requests OPTIMIZED, DEBUG, or PURIFY build variants.
confBUILDBIN	The path of the build support binaries.
confCC	The name of the C compiler.
confCCOPTS	Options to pass to the compiler.
confCOPY	The name of a program that copies files.
confDEPEND_TYPE	Name of a file in *devtools/M4/depend* that defines how to build dependencies.
confDEPLIBS	Dependent libraries for shared objects.
confEBINDIR	The path of the program executed by other programs.
confENVDEF	The -D flags passed to the compiler.
confFORCE_RMAIL	Forces installation of rmail.
confHFDIR	Path of the sendmail helpfile.
confHFFILE	Name of the helpfile.
confINCDIRS	The -I flags passed to the compiler.
confINCGRP	The group ID used for include files.
confINCMODE	The file permissions used for include files.
confINCOWN	The user ID used for include files.
confINCLUDEDIR	The path where include files are installed.
confINSTALL	The install program.

Table E-1. m4 compiler options (continued)

Command	Purpose
confINSTALL_RAWMAN	Install the unformatted manual pages.
confLDOPTS	Options for the linker.
confLIBDIR	Path to the install library files.
confLIBDIRS	The -L flags for the linker.
confLIBGRP	The group ID used for libraries.
confLIBMODE	The file permissions used for libraries.
confLIBOWN	The user ID used for libraries.
confLIBS	The -l flags passed to linker.
confLIBSEARCH	Names of the libraries searched during linking.
confLIBSEARCHPATH	Path of the libraries searched during linking.
confLINKS	Names of logical links to sendmail, e.g., newaliases.
confLN	The command used to create logical links.
confMAN1	The path of man1 files.
confMAN1EXT	The filename extension used for man1 files.
confMAN1SRC	The source for man1 pages.
confMAN3	The path of man3 files.
confMAN3EXT	The filename extension used for man3 files.
confMAN3SRC	The source for man3 pages.
confMAN4	The path of man4 files.
confMAN4EXT	The filename extension for man4 files.
confMAN4SRC	The source for man4 pages.
confMAN5	The path of man5 files.
confMAN5EXT	The filename extension used for man5 files.
confMAN5SRC	The source for man5 pages.
confMAN8	The path of man8 files.
confMAN8EXT	The filename extension used for man8 files.
confMAN8SRC	The source for man8 pages.
confMANDOC	The macros used to format manpages.
confMANGRP	The group ID used for manpage files.
confMANMODE	The file permission for manpages.
confMANOWN	The user ID used for manpage files.
confMANROOT	The root path of the various directories that contain formatted manpages.
confMANROOTMAN	The root path of the various directories that contain unformatted manpages.
confMAPDEF	Identifies the types of database support that should be compiled into sendmail.
confMBINDIR	The path in which the sendmail program is installed.
confNO_HELPFILE_INSTALL	If defined, no helpfile is installed.

Table E-1. m4 compiler options (continued)

Command	Purpose
confNO_MAN_BUILD	If defined, manpages are not created.
confNO_MAN_INSTALL	If defined, manpages are not installed.
confNO_STATISTICS_INSTALL	If defined, no statistics file is installed.
confNROFF	Identifies the command used to format manpages.
confOBJADD	Identifies objects that should be linked in to sendmail.
confOPTIMIZE	Flags passed to the compiler as ${O}.
confRANLIB	The path to the ranlib program.
confRANLIBOPTS	Options passed to ranlib.
confSBINDIR	The path of the directory in which commands such as makemap are stored.
confSBINGRP	The group ID used for setuid binaries.
confSBINMODE	The file permissions for setuid binaries.
confSBINOWN	The user ID used for setuid binaries.
confSHAREDLIB_EXT	The filename extension for shared libraries.
confSHAREDLIB_SUFFIX	The suffix used for shared objects.
confSHAREDLIBDIR	The path of the directory in which shared libraries are installed.
confSHELL	The pathname of the shell used inside make.
confSMOBJADD	Objects that should be linked in to sendmail.
confSMSRCADD	The C source files for the objects identified by confSMOBJADD.
confSMSRCDIR	The directory that contains the sendmail source code.
confSRCADD	The C source files for the objects identified by confOBJADD.
confSRCDIR	The root path of the source directories.
confSONAME	Linker flag for recording the shared object name.
confSTDIO_TYPE	Identifies the buffered file implementation used, i.e., portable or torek.
confSTDIR	The path where the statistics file is stored.
confSTFILE	The name of the statistics file.
confSTRIP	Identifies the program used to strip executables.
confSTRIPOPTS	Options passed to the strip program.
confUBINDIR	The path for user-executable programs.
confUBINGRP	The group ID used for user-executable binaries.
confUBINMODE	The file permissions used for user-executable binaries.
confUBINOWN	The user ID used for user-executable binaries.

Once sendmail compiles, it is installed by using the Build command with the install option, as shown here:

```
# ./Build install
Making all in:
/usr/local/src/sendmail-8.11.3/libsmutil
```

```
Configuration: pfx=, os=Linux, rel=2.2.10, rbase=2, rroot=2.2,
    arch=i586, sfx=, variant=optimized
Making in ../obj.Linux.2.2.10.i586/libsmutil
make[1]: Entering directory
    `/usr/local/src/sendmail-8.11.3/obj.Linux.2.2.10.i586/libsmutil'

... Many, many, many lines deleted...

Making in ../obj.Linux.2.2.10.i586/vacation
make[1]: Entering directory
    `/usr/local/src/sendmail-8.11.3/obj.Linux.2.2.10.i586/vacation'
install -c -o bin -g bin -m 555 vacation /usr/bin
install -c -o bin -g bin -m 444 vacation.0 /usr/man/man1/vacation.1
make[1]: Leaving directory
    `/usr/local/src/sendmail-8.11.3/obj.Linux.2.2.10.i586/vacation'
```

The Build command installs the manpages, the executables, the help file, and the status file in the correct directories for your system.

sendmail is now ready to run. The next section describes the syntax of the sendmail command.

The sendmail Command

The syntax of the sendmail command is deceptively simple:

```
sendmail [arguments] [address ...]
```

The syntax is deceptive because it hides the fact that there are a very large number of command-line arguments. Table E-2 lists all of them.

Table E-2. sendmail command-line arguments

Argument	Function
-U	Indicate initial user submission.
-V*envid*	Set the envelope ID to *envid*.
-N*dsn*	Set delivery status notification to *dsn*.
-M*xvalue*	Set macro *x* to *value*.
-R*return*	Set the part of the message returned with an error.
-B*type*	Set the MIME body type.
-p*protocol*	Set the receiving protocol and hostname.
-X*logfile*	Log all traffic in the indicated log file.
-f*addr*	Sender's machine address is *addr*.
-r *addr*	Obsolete form of -f.
-h *cnt*	Drop mail if forwarded *cnt* times.
-F*name*	Set the full name of this user to *name*.
-n	Don't do aliasing or forwarding.
-T*value*	Set the QueueTimeout option to *value*.

Table E-2. sendmail command-line arguments (continued)

Argument	Function
-t	Send to everyone listed in To:, Cc:, and Bcc:.
-bm	Deliver mail (default).
-bD	Run as a daemon in the foreground.
-ba	Run in arpanet mode.
-bs	Speak SMTP on input side.
-bd	Run as a daemon.
-bH	Clear the host status directory; equivalent to purgestat.
-bh	Display the host status report; equivalent to hoststat.
-bt	Run in test mode.
-bv	Verify addresses; don't collect or deliver mail.
-bi	Initialize the alias database.
-bp	Print the mail queue.
-bz	Create a parsed copy of the *sendmail.cf* file.
-q[*time*]	Process queued mail. Repeat at interval *time*.
-C*file*	Use *file* as the configuration file.
-c	Set the HoldExpensive option to true.
-d*level*	Set debugging level.
-e	Set the ErrorMode option.
-O*option*=*value*	Set option *option* to *value*.
-o*xvalue*	Set an option using its old single-character name.
-I	Alternate way to specify -bi.
-i	Ignore dots in incoming messages.
-m	Send to me, too.
-v	Run in verbose mode.
-s*addr*	Alternate form of -f.

Table E-2 lists over 30 command-line arguments. The table is a quick reference to all possible arguments, some of which are outdated in the latest version of sendmail. Perhaps the best-known argument that is now outdated is -bz. At one time it was used to preprocess the *sendmail.cf* file. The idea was that storing the processed configuration would enhance speed. This outdated switch does not work in the newest versions of sendmail. If you used this argument with an older version of sendmail you might mistakenly believe it is still needed. Attempting to run it with the current sendmail release will just return an error.

Several arguments are redundant forms of other switches. For example, -c, -e, -I, -m, -r, -T, and -s are all deprecated switches that have been replaced by newer arguments. All of the arguments that set *sendmail.cf* options, even those that are not deprecated, such as -i and -o, can be replaced with the -O switch. For example, the command line:

```
sendmail -m -s < mail.file
```

could be replaced by:

```
sendmail -OMeToo=true -OSaveFromLine=true < mail.file
```

The -O argument provides the distinct advantage of being able to set any *sendmail.cf* option. Arguments such as -m and -s set only one option each. The -O format is also easier to read and comprehend, particularly when the sendmail command is included inside a script.

Several of the command-line arguments from Table E-2 are covered in Chapter 10. These are:

-f

Allows trusted users to override the sender address on outgoing messages. For security reasons, it is disabled on some systems. Obsolete alternative forms of this argument are -r and -s.

-t

Reads the To:, Cc:, and Bcc: headers from standard input. Used to send a file that contains these headers or when typing in a test message, as in Chapter 10.

-bd

Runs sendmail in background mode, causing it to collect incoming mail. Use this argument on the sendmail command in the boot script.

-bt

Used to test sendmail address rewrite rules.

-bi

Initializes the aliases database. This is the same as the newaliases command covered in Chapter 10.

-q

Sets the time interval at which the mail queue is processed. Use on the sendmail command in the boot script.

-C

Loads an alternative sendmail configuration file. Use this to test the configuration before moving the new file to *sendmail.cf*.

-v

Permits you to view the exchange of SMTP commands in real time.

-bv

Verifies address processing without actually sending mail.

Other than the two arguments (-bd and -q) used on the sendmail command line in the boot script to process incoming mail, the most common use for sendmail arguments is debugging. From the list above, -bt, -C, -bv, -v, and -t are all used in Chapter 10 in debugging examples. Other debugging arguments are:

-bp

    Prints a list of mail that is queued for delivery. It is the same as the mailq command. Mail is queued when it cannot be delivered immediately because the remote host is temporarily unable to accept the mail. sendmail periodically processes the queue, based on the time interval you set with the -q argument, and attempts to deliver the mail in the queue. The queue can grow large enough to impede sendmail's performance if an important remote host is down. mailq shows how many items are queued as well as the source and destination of each piece of mail.

    When the queue requires immediate processing, invoke sendmail using -q with no time interval. This processes the entire queue. Some variations of the -q argument allow you to selectively process the queue. Use -qI*queue-id* to process only those queue entries with the specified queue identifier; -qR*recipient* to process only items being sent to the specified recipient; or -qS*sender* to process only mail sent from the specified sender. The mailq command displays the queue identifier, sender address, and recipient address for every item in the queue.

-o

    Sets a sendmail option for this one instantiation of sendmail, e.g., -oA/tmp/test-aliases. Use this argument to test alternative option settings without editing the *sendmail.cf* file. -o uses the old sendmail option syntax. An alternate form of the argument is -O, which uses the new option syntax, e.g., -OAliasFile=/tmp/test-aliases. See "sendmail Options" later in this appendix.

-d

    Sets the level of detail displayed when debugging sendmail code. Can be used to debug rewrite rules or to check configuration settings, e.g., sendmail -bt -d0.4. Most debug settings are useful only for sendmail source code debugging.

-h

    Sets the counter used to determine if mail is looping. By default, it is set to 30, which is a good operational value. When you are debugging a mail loop problem, set the hop count lower, e.g., -h10, to reduce the number of times a piece of mail is handled by the system. Otherwise, leave this value alone.

-bh

    Displays the persistent host status, if sendmail is configured to maintain this status. The host status displays the name of each remote host that mail was sent to, the time the status of that host was last updated, and the result of the last attempt to deliver mail to that host. The directory of host status files can grow very large. Use -bH to clean out the host status directory.

The remaining arguments are rarely used on the command line:

-B

> Indicates the MIME message body type. Acceptable values are either 7BIT or 8BITMIME.

-N

> Requests that the sender be notified of the delivery status of the mail. The default value is FAILURE, DELAY, which notifies the sender when mail delivery fails or is delayed in the queue. Other acceptable values are NEVER, to request that no status notifications be returned to the sender, and SUCCESS, to request notification of successful mail delivery.

-M

> Sets a macro value for this instantiation of sendmail. For example, entering the command -MMwrotethebook.com sets macro M to *wrotethebook.com*.

-p

> Sets the sending protocol and the sending host. This is equivalent to setting the internal s and r macros. If a system has more than one external mail protocol, for example, UUCP and SMTP, this forces the system to use a specific protocol for this piece of mail.

-R

> Sets the amount of information returned to the sender when a message cannot be delivered. This can be either HDRS for headers-only, or FULL for the headers and the full message body.

-U

> Indicates that this mail comes directly from a user interface and was not forwarded from a remote mail handler.

-V

> Inserts an "envelope ID" into the outbound message that is returned if message delivery fails.

-X

> Logs all mail messages to the specified log file. This rapidly produces an enormous log file.

-n

> Disables the processing of aliases and mail forwarding.

-bm

> Tells sendmail to deliver mail, which it will do anyway.

-ba

> Reads the header From: line to find the sender. It uses three-digit reply codes, and ends error lines with <CRLF>. This is an obsolete argument.

-bs

> Tells sendmail to use SMTP for incoming mail. When appropriate, sendmail will do this even without the -bs argument.

-i

Normally, an SMTP message terminates when a line containing only a dot is encountered. This argument tells sendmail to ignore the dots in incoming messages.

-m

Sends a copy of the mail to the person sending the mail. Normally this is done with a CC: or BCC: header in the message, not with the -m argument.

-bD

Runs sendmail as a foreground daemon so that it remains attached to the controlling terminal.

-F

Sets the sender's full name.

This is a complete list of sendmail command-line arguments at this writing. Some of these arguments were recently introduced. Others are obsolete in the latest version of sendmail. Check the manpage for your system to find out exactly what arguments are available on your system.

When the sendmail command is executed, it reads its configuration from the *sendmail.cf* file. A basic *sendmail.cf* file can be built from m4 macros that come with the sendmail source code. Chapter 10 provides examples of how this is done. The next section provides a complete list of the m4 macros that come with the sendmail distribution.

m4 sendmail Macros

The sendmail distribution comes with several sample configuration files. Chapter 10 provides an example of how the *tcpproto.mc* file is modified to produce a configuration file suitable for a Linux system. The prototype files are m4 macro configuration files that produce usable *sendmail.cf* files as output. The prototype files are located in the *sendmail/cf/cf* directory of the sendmail distribution. Use those prototypes as examples of reasonable sendmail configurations.

All of the sendmail configuration files are composed of the following m4 macros: [*]

divert

Directs the output of the m4 process.

dnl

Deletes all characters up to the next newline.

VERSIONID

Defines the version number of the *.mc* source file. RCS or SCCS version numbers are commonly used. This command is optional.

---

[*] By convention, m4 macros are shown in uppercase, and built-in m4 commands are shown in lowercase.

OSTYPE

Points to the m4 source file that contains the operating system–specific information for this configuration. This is required.

DOMAIN

Points to the m4 source file that contains configuration information specific to this domain. This is optional.

LOCAL_DOMAIN

Defines the hostname aliases for the server.

CANONIFY_DOMAIN

Defines domains that should be converted to canonical format even if the nocanonify feature is set.

CANONIFY_DOMAIN_FILE

Identifies a file that contains the list of domains that should be converted to canonical format even if the nocanonify feature is set.

GENERICS_DOMAIN

Defines domain names that should be processed through the genericstable database.

GENERICS_DOMAIN_FILE

Identifies a file that contains the list of domains that should be processed through the genericstable database.

LDAPROUTE_DOMAIN

Defines domains that should be routed according to directions found in the LDAP directory.

LDAPROUTE_DOMAIN_FILE

Identifies a file that lists the domains that should be routed according to directions found in the LDAP directory.

RELAY_DOMAIN

Defines the domains for which this server should relay mail.

RELAY_DOMAIN_FILE

Identifies a file that lists the domains for which this server should relay mail.

VIRTUSER_DOMAIN

Defines the virtual domains that should be processed through the virtusertable.

VIRTUSER_DOMAIN_FILE

Identifies a file that lists the virtual domains that should be processed through the virtusertable.

FEATURE

Points to an m4 source file that defines an optional sendmail feature. This is not required for m4 to process the *.mc* source file, but many configurations have multiple FEATURE entries.

MASQUERADE_AS

Defines the domain name used to masquerade outgoing mail.

MASQUERADE_DOMAIN

Defines domains that should be masqueraded.

MASQUERADE_DOMAIN_FILE

Identifies a file that lists the domains that should be masqueraded.

MASQUERADE_EXCEPTION

Defines a host that should not be masqueraded even if the domain is being masqueraded.

EXPOSED_USER

Defines usernames that prevent masquerading. If the user portion of the address contains one of these names, the host portion of the address is not masqueraded.

HACK

Points to an m4 source file that contains site-specific configuration information. This is a temporary configuration used to fix a temporary problem. The use of HACK is discouraged.

SITE

Identifies a locally connected UUCP host.

SITECONFIG

Points to a source file that contains m4 SITE commands that define the UUCP sites connected to this host. The format of the command is: SITECONFIG(*file, local-hostname, class*), which reads the UUCP hostnames from *file* into *class*.

UUCPSMTP

Maps a UUCP hostname to an Internet hostname.

define

Defines a local value. Most "defines" are done in the m4 source files that are called by the *.mc* file, not in the *.mc* file itself. It can define a value for a *sendmail. cf* macro, option, or other command.

undefine

Clears the value set for a configuration parameter.

MAILER

Points to an m4 source file that contains the configuration commands that define a sendmail mailer. At least one MAILER command must appear in the configuration file. Generally more than one MAILER command is used.

MAILER_DEFINITIONS

Heads a section of *sendmail.cf* commands that define a custom mailer.

MODIFY_MAILER_FLAGS

Overrides the flags defined for a mailer.

MAIL_FILTER

Defines a mail filter.

INPUT_MAIL_FILTER

> Defines a mail filter and the variables necessary to call the filter.

DAEMON_OPTIONS

> Defines runtime options for the sendmail daemon.

TRUST_AUTH_MECH

> Defines a list of trusted authorization mechanisms.

LOCAL_RULE_*n*

> Heads a section of code to be added to ruleset *n*, where *n* is 0, 1, 2, or 3. The code that follows the LOCAL_RULE_*n* command is composed of standard *sendmail.cf* rewrite rules.* The LOCAL_RULE_*n* command is rarely used.

LOCAL_RULESETS

> Heads a section of code that defines a custom ruleset.

LOCAL_USER

> Defines usernames that should be exempted from relaying even when local mail is being relayed.

LOCAL_NET_CONFIG

> Heads a section of *sendmail.cf* code that defines how mail destined for the local host is processed.

LOCAL_CONFIG

> Heads a section of code to be added to the *sendmail.cf* file after the local information section and before the rewrite rules. The section of code contains standard *sendmail.cf* configuration commands. This macro is rarely used.

The built-in m4 commands shown above—those listed in lowercase characters—are divided between those that control the flow of output and those that set macro values. The two commands that control the flow of output are dnl and divert. Text following the dnl command is not sent to the output file. Thus it is used at the beginning of a line on a comment. The divert(-1) command sends output to the "bit-bucket" and marks the start of a block of comments. The divert(0) command directs output to standard m4 processing. In addition to -1 and 0, the divert command accepts nine other numeric arguments: the values 1 to 9. These other values are used in the m4 macro source code to direct data to various parts of the *sendmail.cf* file. You will not use these values in your own configuration. Instead you will use other commands to direct data to specific parts of the *sendmail.cf* file.

The commands LOCAL_CONFIG, LOCAL_USER, LOCAL_RULESETS, MAILER_DEFINITION, LOCAL_NET_CONFIG, and LOCAL_RULE allow you to send data to various parts of the *sendmail.cf* file without using the various divert values directly. Commands such as LOCAL_CONFIG and MAILER_DEFINITION mark the start of raw *sendmail.cf* code that should be included in some part of the output

---

* The one exception to this is the UUCPSMTP macro that can be used in the local rule.

file. These commands make it possible for you to customize the *sendmail.cf* file in any possible way.

The built-in m4 commands define and undefine set macro values. define sets a variable to a value and undefine resets it to its default value. More configuration parameters can be controlled through the define command than through any other, and, correspondingly, more of this appendix is dedicated to define parameters than to anything else.

Almost half of the m4 macros act like the define command and simply set a parameter to a value. MASQUERADE_AS, MASQUERADE_DOMAIN, RELAY_DOMAIN, and VIRTUSER_DOMAIN_FILE are all examples of commands used to set variables.

The TRUST_AUTH_MECH macro is a good example of a macro that complements a define. As you'll see in the "define" section of this appendix, the parameter confAUTH_MECHANISMS can be used to define the trusted authentication mechanisms your server advertises to other servers. The TRUST_AUTH_MECH macro is the inverse of this. It identifies the mechanism that your server accepts from other servers. The same list of keywords used to configure the confAUTH_MECHA-NISMS parameter in the "define" section can be used to configure TRUST_AUTH_MECHANISMS.

The macro names OSTYPE, DOMAIN, FEATURE, MAILER, HACK, and SITE-CONFIG are all names of subdirectories within the *cf* directory. The value passed to each of these macros is the name of a file within the specified directory. For example, the command FEATURE(nouucp) tells m4 to load the file *nouucp.m4* from the *ostype* directory and process the m4 source code found there. The *.m4* source files pointed to by the OSTYPE, DOMAIN, FEATURE, and MAILER commands are built primarily from define and FEATURE commands.

Two of the macros that are also directory names, SITECONFIG and HACK, are rarely used. SITECONFIG points to a source file that contains SITE macros that define the UUCP sites connected to the local host. You create the file containing the SITE macros yourself and then invoke it with the SITECONFIG command. These commands, along with UUCPSMTP, are obsolete and maintained only for backward compatibility.

The HACK macro points to an m4 source file that contains a temporary site-specific fix to a sendmail problem. You create the file in the *hack* directory and then use the HACK command to add that file to the configuration. The use of hacks is discouraged and is generally unnecessary.

The following section provides additional information about the OSTYPE, DOMAIN, FEATURE, and MAILER macros and details of the various commands used to build the m4 source files they call. Chapter 10 provides an example of building a custom DOMAIN macro source file. The source files can contain any of the macros we have already mentioned as well as the additional ones documented below. The macro configuration (*.mc*) file also can contain any of the commands documented below. In fact, pretty much any macro can appear in any file.

To bring some order out of this chaos, the commands are organized according to the files they are most likely to appear in, which is similar to the organization found in the documentation that comes with the sendmail distribution. Just remember, actual implementation files may have a different organization. We start by examining the define macros and the FEATURE macros that are the primary building blocks of all the other files.

define

The syntax of the define macro is:

    define(`parameter', `value')

where *parameter* is the keyword name of a sendmail configuration parameter and *value* is the value assigned to that configuration parameter. The *parameter* and the *value* are normally enclosed in single quotes to prevent inappropriate macro expansion. These are not balanced quotes. The opening quote is a grave sign (`), and the closing quote is an apostrophe (').

Many of the configuration parameters that can be set using the define command are shown below. Most of the parameters correspond to sendmail options, macros, or classes. The name of the option, macro, or class set by the parameter is listed in the parameter description enclosed in square brackets ([]). Macro names begin with a dollar sign ($j), class names begin with a dollar sign and an equals sign ($=w), and options are shown with long option names (SingleThreadDelivery). To find out more about these parameters, see the descriptions of the macros, options, and classes they represent that are provided later in this appendix.

Because many define parameters are equivalent to options, macros, and classes, the command:

    define(`confDOMAIN_NAME', `rodent.wrotethebook.com')

placed in an m4 source file has the same effect as:

    Djrodent.wrotethebook.com

placed directly in the *sendmail.cf* file. If you compile and install a new version of sendmail, build your configuration with m4 and set values for macros, classes, and options with the m4 define macro.

The list of define parameters is quite long. However, because most of the parameters default to a reasonable value, they do not have to be explicitly set in the m4 source file. The default value of each parameter is shown in the listing—unless there is no default.

confMAILER_NAME

Default is MAILER-DAEMON. The sender name used on error messages. [$n]

confDOMAIN_NAME

The full hostname. [$j]

confCF_VERSION

The configuration file's version number. [$Z]

confFROM_HEADER

Default is $?x$x <$g>$|g. . The From: header format.

confRECEIVED_HEADER

Default is $?sfrom $s $.$?_($?s$|from $.$_) $.by $j ($v/$Z)$?r with r. id i?u for u.; $b . The Received: header format.

confCW_FILE

Default is */etc/sendmail.cw*. The file of local host aliases. [$=w]

confCT_FILE

Default is */etc/sendmail.ct*. The file of trusted usernames. [$=t]

confTRUSTED_USERS

Trusted usernames to add to *root*, *uucp*, and *daemon*.

confSMTP_MAILER

Default is esmtp. The mailer used for SMTP connections; must be smtp, smtp8, or esmtp.

confUUCP_MAILER

Default is uucp-old. The default UUCP mailer.

confLOCAL_MAILER

Default is local. The mailer used for local connections.

confRELAY_MAILER

Default is relay. The default mailer name for relaying.

confSEVEN_BIT_INPUT

Default is False. Forces input to seven bits. [SevenBitInput]

confEIGHT_BIT_HANDLING

Default is pass8. Defines how 8-bit data is handled. [EightBitMode]

confALIAS_WAIT

Default is 10m. The amount of time to wait for alias file rebuild. [AliasWait]

confMIN_FREE_BLOCKS

Default is 100. The minimum number of free blocks on the queue filesystem that must be available to accept SMTP mail. [MinFreeBlocks]

confMAX_MESSAGE_SIZE

Default is infinite. The maximum message size. [MaxMessageSize] confBLANK_SUB

> The character used to replace unquoted blank characters in email addresses. [BlankSub]

confCON_EXPENSIVE

> Default is False. Tells system to hold mail bound for mailers that have the e flag set until the next queue run. [HoldExpensive]

confCHECKPOINT_INTERVAL

> Default is 10. Tells system to checkpoint the queue files after this number of queued items are processed. [CheckpointInterval]

confDELIVERY_MODE

> Default is background. Sets the default delivery mode. [DeliveryMode]

confAUTO_REBUILD

> Default is False. Automatically rebuilds alias file. [AutoRebuildAliases]

confERROR_MODE

> Default is print. Defines how errors are handled. [ErrorMode]

confERROR_MESSAGE

> Points to a file containing a message that is prepended to error messages. [ErrorHeader]

confSAVE_FROM_LINES

> Tells system not to discard Unix From: lines. They are discarded if this is not set. [SaveFromLine]

confTEMP_FILE_MODE

> Default is 0600. File mode for temporary files. [TempFileMode]

confMATCH_GECOS

> Tells system to match the email username to the GECOS field. This match is not done if this is not set. [MatchGECOS]

confMAX_HOP

> Default is 25. The counter used to determine mail loops. [MaxHopCount]

confIGNORE_DOTS

> Default is False. Tells system to ignore dots in incoming messages. [IgnoreDots]

confBIND_OPTS

> Default is undefined. Sets options for DNS resolver. [ResolverOptions]

confMIME_FORMAT_ERRORS

> Default is True. Tells system to send MIME-encapsulated error messages. [SendMimeErrors]

confFORWARD_PATH

> Default is *$z/.forward.$w:$z/.forward*. Places to search for *.forward* files. [ForwardPath]

confMCI_CACHE_SIZE
> Default is 2. The number of open connections that can be cached. [Connection-CacheSize]

confMCI_CACHE_TIMEOUT
> Default is 5m. The amount of time inactive open connections are held in the cache. [ConnectionCacheTimeout]

confHOST_STATUS_DIRECTORY
> Directory in which host status is saved. [HostStatusDirectory]

confUSE_ERRORS_TO
> Default is False. Delivers errors using the Errors-To: header. [UseErrorsTo]

confLOG_LEVEL
> Default is 9. Level of detail for the log file. [LogLevel]

confME_TOO
> Default is False. Sends a copy to the sender. [MeToo]

confCHECK_ALIASES
> Default is False. Looks up every alias during alias file build. [CheckAliases]

confOLD_STYLE_HEADERS
> Default is True. Treats headers without special characters as old style. [OldStyle-Headers]

confDAEMON_OPTIONS
> SMTP daemon options. [DaemonPortOptions]

confPRIVACY_FLAGS
> Default is authwarnings. These flags restrict the use of some mail commands. [PrivacyOptions]

confCOPY_ERRORS_TO
> Address to receive copies of error messages. [PostmasterCopy]

confQUEUE_FACTOR
> Default is 600000. Used to calculate when a loaded system should queue mail instead of attempting delivery. [QueueFactor]

confDONT_PRUNE_ROUTES
> Default is False. Don't prune route-addresses to the minimum possible. [Dont-PruneRoutes]

confSAFE_QUEUE
> Create a queue file, then attempt delivery. This is not done unless this parameter is specified. [SuperSafe]

confTO_INITIAL
> Default is 5m. Maximum time to wait for the initial connect response. [Timeout.initial]

confTO_CONNECT

Default is 0. Maximum time to wait for a connect to complete. [Timeout.connect]

confTO_ICONNECT

Maximum time to wait for the very first connect attempt to a host. [Timeout.iconnect]

confTO_HELO

Default is 5m. Maximum time to wait for a HELO or EHLO response. [Timeout.helo]

confTO_MAIL

Default is 10m. Maximum time to wait for a MAIL command response. [Timeout.mail]

confTO_RCPT

Default is 1h. Maximum time to wait for a RCPT command response. [Timeout.rcpt]

confTO_DATAINIT

Default is 5m. Maximum time to wait for a DATA command response. [Timeout.datainit]

confTO_DATABLOCK

Default is 1h. Maximum time to wait for a block during DATA phase. [Timeout.datablock]

confTO_DATAFINAL

Default is 1h. Maximum time to wait for a response to the terminating ".". [Timeout.datafinal]

confTO_RSET

Default is 5m. Maximum time to wait for a RSET command response. [Timeout.rset]

confTO_QUIT

Default is 2m. Maximum time to wait for a QUIT command response. [Timeout.quit]

confTO_MISC

Default is 2m. Maximum time to wait for other SMTP command responses. [Timeout.misc]

confTO_COMMAND

Default is 1h. Maximum time to wait for a command to be issued. [Timeout.command]

confTO_IDENT

Default is 30s. Maximum time to wait for an IDENT query response. [Timeout.ident] `confTO_FILEOPEN`

Default is 60s. Maximum time to wait for a file open. [Timeout.fileopen]

`confTO_QUEUERETURN`

Default is 5d. Time until a message is returned from the queue as undeliverable. [Timeout.queuereturn]

`confTO_QUEUERETURN_NORMAL`

"Undeliverable" timeout for normal priority messages. [Timeout.queuereturn. normal]

`confTO_QUEUERETURN_URGENT`

"Undeliverable" timeout for urgent priority messages. [Timeout.queuereturn. urgent]

`confTO_QUEUERETURN_NONURGENT`

"Undeliverable" timeout for low priority messages. [Timeout.queuereturn.non-urgent]

`confTO_QUEUEWARN`

Default is 4h. Time until a "still queued" warning is sent about a message. [Timeout.queuewarn]

`confTO_QUEUEWARN_NORMAL`

Time until a "still queued" warning is sent for normal priority messages. [Timeout.queuewarn.normal]

`confTO_QUEUEWARN_URGENT`

Time until a "still queued" warning is sent for urgent priority messages. [Timeout.queuewarn.urgent]

`confTO_QUEUEWARN_NONURGENT`

Time until a "still queued" warning is sent for low priority messages. [Timeout. queuewarn.non-urgent]

`confTO_HOSTSTATUS`

Default is 30m. Time for stale host status information. [Timeout.hoststatus]

`confTIME_ZONE`

Default is USE_SYSTEM. Sets time zone from the system (USE_SYSTEM) or the TZ variable (USE_TZ). [TimeZoneSpec]

`confDEF_USER_ID`

Default is 1:1. Default user ID and group ID. [DefaultUser]

`confUSERDB_SPEC`

Path of the user database file. [UserDatabaseSpec]

`confFALLBACK_MX`

Backup MX host. [FallbackMXhost]

`confTRY_NULL_MX_LIST`

Default is False. Instructs system to connect to the remote host directly if the MX points to the local host. [TryNullMXList]

confQUEUE_LA

Default is 8. Sends mail directly to the queue when this load average is reached. [QueueLA]

confREFUSE_LA

Default is 12. Refuses incoming SMTP connections at this load average. [RefuseLA]

confMAX_DAEMON_CHILDREN

If set, refuses connection when this number of children is reached. [MaxDaemonChildren]

confCONNECTION_RATE_THROTTLE

Maximum number of connections permitted per second, if set. [ConnectionRateThrottle]

confWORK_RECIPIENT_FACTOR

Default is 30000. Factor used to lower the priority of a job for each additional recipient. [RecipientFactor]

confSEPARATE_PROC

Default is False. Delivers messages with separate processes. [ForkEachJob]

confWORK_CLASS_FACTOR

Default is 1800. The factor used to favor a high-priority job. [ClassFactor]

confWORK_TIME_FACTOR

Default is 90000. Factor used to lower the priority of a job for each delivery attempt. [RetryFactor]

confQUEUE_SORT_ORDER

Default is Priority. Sorts queue by Priority or Host order. [QueueSortOrder]

confMIN_QUEUE_AGE

Default is 0. Minimum time a job must be queued. [MinQueueAge]

confDEF_CHAR_SET

Default is unknown-8bit. Default character set for unlabeled 8-bit MIME data. [DefaultCharSet]

confSERVICE_SWITCH_FILE

Default is */etc/service.switch*. The path to the service switch file. [ServiceSwitchFile]

confHOSTS_FILE

Default is */etc/hosts*. The path to the hostnames file. [HostsFile]

confDIAL_DELAY

Default is 0s. Amount of time to delay before retrying a "dial on demand" connection. 0s means "don't retry." [DialDelay]

confNO_RCPT_ACTION

Default is none. Handling for mail with no recipient headers: do nothing (none); add To: header (add-to); add Apparently-To: header (add-apparently-to); add a

Bcc: header (add-bcc); add "To: undisclosed-recipients" header (add-to-undisclosed). [NoRecipientAction]

confSAFE_FILE_ENV

Default is undefined. chroot( ) to this directory before writing files. [SafeFileEnvironment]

confCOLON_OK_IN_ADDR

Default is True. Treats colons as regular characters in addresses. [ColonOkInAddr]

confMAX_QUEUE_RUN_SIZE

Default is 0. Limits the number of entries processed in a queue run. 0 means no limit. [MaxQueueRunSize]

confDONT_EXPAND_CNAMES

Default is False. If true, don't convert nicknames to canonical names. False means to convert. [DontExpandCnames]

confFROM_LINE

Default is From $g $d. The format of the Unix From: line. [UnixFromLine]

confOPERATORS

Default is .:%@!^/[ ]+. Address operator characters. [OperatorChars]

confSMTP_LOGIN_MSG

Default is $j sendmail $v/$Z; $b. The SMTP greeting message. [SmtpGreetingMessage]

confDONT_INIT_GROUPS

Default is False. If true, disable the initgroups(3) routine. False means to use the initgroups(3) routine. [DontInitGroups]

confUNSAFE_GROUP_WRITES

Default is False. If true, don't reference programs or files from group-writable *:include:* and *.forward* files. [UnsafeGroupWrites]

confDOUBLE_BOUNCE_ADDRESS

Default is postmaster. When errors occur sending an error message, send the second error message to this address. [DoubleBounceAddress]

confRUN_AS_USER

Default is undefined. Run as this user to read and deliver mail. [RunAsUser]

confSINGLE_THREAD_DELIVERY

Default is False. Force single-threaded mail delivery when set with HostStatusDirectory. [SingleThreadDelivery]

confALLOW_BOGUS_HELO

Defines normally illegal special characters that will be allowed in the DNS hostname on a HELO or EHLO command line. [AllowBogusHELO]

confAUTH_MECHANISMS

Defines a space-separated list of authentication mechanisms that will be advertised by this server. Possible values are GSSAPI, KERBEROS_V4, DIGEST-MD5, and CRAM-MD5. [AuthMechanisms]

confAUTH_OPTIONS

The AUTH= argument is added to the MAIL FROM header only when authentication succeeds if this is set to A. [AuthOptions]

confCACERT

Identifies a file containing a cryptographic certificate from a certificate authority. [CACERTFile]

confCACERT_PATH

Defines the path to the directory that contains the cryptographic certificates. [CACERTPath]

confCLIENT_CERT

Identifies the file containing the cryptographic certificate sendmail uses when it acts as client. [ClientCertFile]

confCLIENT_KEY

Identifies the file containing the private key associated with the certificate used when sendmail acts as a client. [ClientKeyFile]

confCLIENT_OPTIONS

Defines the port options used for outbound SMTP client connections. [Client-PortOptions]

confCONNECT_ONLY_TO

Limits connectivity. Used for testing by the sendmail developers. This is not used in production environments. [ConnectOnlyTo]

confCONTROL_SOCKET_NAME

Defines a socket used for managing the sendmail daemon. [ControlSocketName]

confCR_FILE

Points to the file that lists the hosts for which this server will relay mail. Defaults to */etc/mail/relay-domains*. [$=R]

confDEAD_LETTER_DROP

Defines the file where failed messages that could not be returned to the sender or sent to the postmaster are saved. [DeadLetterDrop]

confDEF_AUTH_INFO

Identifies the file that contains the authentication information used for outbound connections. [DefaultAuthInfo]

confDF_BUFFER_SIZE

Defines the maximum amount of buffer memory that will be used before a disk file is used. [DataFileBufferSize]

confDH_PARAMETERS

    Identifies the file that contains the DH parameters for the DSA/DH digital signature algorithm. [DHParameters]

confDONT_BLAME_SENDMAIL

    Tells sendmail to perform certain file security checks. By default, all checks are performed. This option weakens the security of your server. See the DontBlameSendmail option later in this appendix for a full list of the values that can be used with this parameter. [DontBlameSendmail]

confDONT_PROBE_INTERFACES

    Tells sendmail not to automatically accept the addresses of the server's network interfaces as valid addresses if set to true. Defaults to false. [DontProbeInterface]

confEBINDIR

    Defines the directory where executables for FEATURE(`local_lmtp') and FEATURE(`smrsh') are stored. The default directory is */usr/libexec*.

confLDAP_DEFAULT_SPEC

    Defines the defaults used for LDAP databases unless specifically overridden by a K command for an individual map. [LDAPDefaultSpec]

confMAX_ALIAS_RECURSION

    Aliases can refer to other aliases. This sets the maximum depth that alias references can be nested. The default is 10. [MaxAliasRecursion]

confMAX_HEADERS_LENGTH

    Defines the maximum length of the sum of all headers in bytes. [MaxHeadersLength]

confMAX_MIME_HEADER_LENGTH

    Defines the maximum length of MIME headers. [MaxMimeHeaderLength]

confMAX_RCPTS_PER_MESSAGE

    Defines the maximum number of recipients allowed for a piece of mail. [MaxRecipientsPerMessage]

confMUST_QUOTE_CHARS

    Adds characters to the list of characters that must be quoted when they are included in the user's full name ($x). The characters @,;:\()[] are always quoted. By default . and ' are added to the list. [MustQuoteChars]

confPID_FILE

    Specifies the path of the PID file. [PidFile]

confPROCESS_TITLE_PREFIX

    Identifies the string used on this system as the prefix for the process title in ps listings. [ProcessTitlePrefix]

confRAND_FILE

    Identifies the file that contains random data needed by STARTTLS if sendmail was not compiled with the HASURANDOM flag. [RandFile]

confREJECT_MSG

> Defines the message displayed when mail is rejected because of the access control database. Defaults to "550 Access denied".

confRRT_IMPLIES_DSN

> True tells sendmail to interpret a Return-Receipt-To: header as a request for delivery status notification (DSN). The default is false. [RrtImpliesDsn]

confSERVER_CERT

> Identifies the file that contains the cryptographic certificate used when this system acts as server. [ServerCertFile]

confSERVER_KEY

> Identifies the file that contains the private key associated with the cryptographic certificate used when this system acts as server. [ServerKeyFile]

confSINGLE_LINE_FROM_HEADER

> True forces a multiline From: line to a single line. The default is false. [SingleLineFromHeader]

confTO_RESOLVER_RETRANS

> Defines, in seconds, the retransmission timer for all resolver lookups. [Timeout.resolver.retrans]

confTO_RESOLVER_RETRANS_FIRST

> Defines, in seconds, the retransmission timer for the resolver lookup for the first attempt to deliver a message. [Timeout.resolver.retrans.first]

confTO_RESOLVER_RETRANS_NORMAL

> Defines, in seconds, the retransmission timer for all resolver lookups after the first attempt to deliver a message. [Timeout.resolver.retrans.normal]

confTO_RESOLVER_RETRY

> Defines the total number of times to retry a resolver query. [Timeout.resolver.retry]

confTO_RESOLVER_RETRY_FIRST

> Defines the number of times the resolver query for the first delivery attempt is retried. [Timeout.resolver.retry.first]

confTO_RESOLVER_RETRY_NORMAL

> Defines the number of times to retry resolver queries after the first delivery attempt. [Timeout.resolver.retry.normal]

confTRUSTED_USER

> Defines the user who controls the sendmail daemon and owns the files created by sendmail. Do not confuse this option with confTRUSTED_USERS. [TrustedUser]

confXF_BUFFER_SIZE

> Defines the maximum amount of buffer memory that can be used for a transcript file before the file must be written to disk. The default is 4096 bytes. [XScriptFileBufferSize]

define macros are the most common macros in the m4 source files. The next most commonly used macro is the FEATURE macro.

FEATURE

The FEATURE macro processes m4 source code from the *cf/feature* directory. Source files in that directory define optional sendmail features that you may wish to include in your configuration. The syntax of the FEATURE macro is:

```
FEATURE(name, [argument])
```

The FEATURE source file can be called with or without an optional argument. If an argument is passed to the source file, the argument is used by the source file to generate code for the *sendmail.cf* file. For example:

```
FEATURE(`mailertable', `hash /etc/mail/mailertable')
```

generates the code for accessing the mailertable and defines that table as being a hash database located in the file */etc/mail/mailertable*.

There are several features available in sendmail V8. They are all listed in Table E-3. The table provides the name of each feature and its purpose.

Table E-3. sendmail features

Name	Purpose
use_cw_file	Load $=w from */etc/mail/local-host-names*.
use_ct_file	Load $=t from */etc/mail/trusted-users*.
relay_based_on_MX	Relay mail for any site whose MX points to this server.
relay_entire_domain	Relay mail for any host in your domain.
relay_hosts_only	Only relay mail for hosts listed in the access database.
relay_local_from	Relay mail if the source is a local host.
relay_mail_from	Relay mail if the sender is listed as RELAY in the access database.
promiscuous_relay	Relay mail from any site to any site.
rbl	The obsolete Realtime Blackhole List feature has been replaced by dnsbl.
dnsbl	Reject mail from hosts listed in a DNS-based rejection list. Replaces rbl.
blacklist_recipients	Filter incoming mail based on values set in the access database.
delay_checks	Delay the check_mail and check_relay rulesets until check_rcpt is called.
loose_relay_check	Disable validity checks for addresses that use the % hack.
redirect	Support the .REDIRECT pseudo-domain.
no_default_msa	Allow the default configuration of the Message Submission Agent to be overridden by the DAEMON_OPTIONS macro.
nouucp	Don't include UUCP address processing.
nocanonify	Don't convert names with $[name$] syntax.
stickyhost	Treat "user" differently than "user@local.host".[a]

Table E-3. sendmail features (continued)

Name	Purpose
mailertable	Mail routing using a mailer table.
domaintable	Domain name mapping using a domain table.
access_db	Relay control using the access database.
bitdomain	Use a table to map bitnet hosts to Internet addresses.
uucpdomain	Use a table to map UUCP hosts to Internet addresses.
accept_unqualified_senders	Allow network mail from addresses that do not include a valid hostname.
accept_unresolvable_domains	Accept mail from hosts that are unknown to DNS.
always_add_domain	Add the local hostname to all locally delivered mail.
allmasquerade	Also masquerade recipient addresses.
limited_masquerade	Only masquerade hosts listed in $=M.
masquerade_entire_domain	Masquerade all hosts within the masquerading domains.
masquerade_envelope	Also masquerade envelope addresses. The default is to masquerade only header addresses.
genericstable	Use a table to rewrite local addresses.
generics_entire_domain	Map domain names identified in class G through the genericstable.
virtusertable	Map virtual domain names to real mail addresses.
virtuser_entire_domain	Map domain names through the virtusertable.
ldap_routing	Enable LDAP-based email routing.
nodns	Don't include DNS support.
nullclient	Forward all mail to a central server.
local_lmtp	Use mail.local with LMTP support.
local_procmail	Use procmail as the local mailer.
bestmx_is_local	Accept mail as local when it is addressed to a host that lists us as its MX server.
smrsh	Use smrsh as the prog mailer.

a See the discussion of "stickyhost" in the "DOMAIN" section later in this appendix.

The use_cw_file and the use_ct_file features are equivalent to Fw/etc/sendmail.cw and Fw/etc/sendmail.ct commands in the *sendmail.cf* file. See Chapter 10 for descriptions of host aliases ($=w) and trusted users ($=t).

The .REDIRECT pseudo-domain code returns an error message to the sender telling the sender to try a new address for the recipient. This is used to handle mail for people who no longer read mail at your site but who are still getting mail sent to a very old address. Enable this feature with the FEATURE(redirect) command and then add aliases for each obsolete mailing address in the form:

```
old-address new-address.REDIRECT
```

For example, assume that Edward Winslow is no longer a valid user of *crab.wrote-thebook.com*. Therefore, his old username, *ed*, should no longer accept mail. His new mailing address is *WinslowE@industry.com*. We enter the following alias in the */etc/aliases* file:

```
ed      WinslowE@industry.com.REDIRECT
```

Now when mail is sent to the *ed* account on *crab*, the following error is returned to the sender:

```
551 User not local; please try <WinslowE@industry.com>
```

Several of the FEATURE macros actually remove features from the *sendmail.cf* file instead of adding them. nouucp removes the code to handle UUCP addresses for systems that do not have access to UUCP networks, and nodns removes the code for DNS lookups for systems that do not have access to DNS. nocanonify disables the $[*name*]$ syntax that converts nicknames and IP addresses to canonical names. Finally, the nullclient feature strips everything out of the configuration except for the ability to forward mail to a single mail server via a local SMTP link. The name of the mail server is provided as the argument on the nullclient command line. For example, FEATURE(nullclient, ms.big.com) forwards all mail to *ms.big.com* without any local mail processing.

Several features relate to mail relaying and masquerading. Examples include sticky-host, relay_based_on_MX, allmasquerade, limited_masquerade, and masquerade_entire_domain. All of these features are covered in the "DOMAIN" section later in this appendix.

Several of the features define databases that are used to perform special address processing. All of these features accept an optional argument that defines the database. (See the sample mailertable command at the beginning of this section for an example of defining the database with the optional argument.) If the optional argument is not provided, the database description always defaults to hash -o /etc/mail/*filename*, where *filename* matches the name of the feature. For example, mailertable defaults to the definition hash -o /etc/mail/mailertable. The database features are:

mailertable

> Maps host and domain names to specific mailer:host pairs. If the host or domain name in the recipient addresses matches a key field in the mailertable database, it returns the mailer and host for that address. The format of mailertable entries is:
>
> > *domain-name mailer:host*
>
> where *domain-name* is either a full hostname (host plus domain) or a domain name. If a domain name is used it must start with a dot (.), and it will match every host in the specified domain.

domaintable

> Converts an old domain name to a new domain name. The old name is the key and the new name is the value returned for the key.

`bitdomain`

> Converts a Bitnet hostname to an Internet hostname. The Bitnet name is the key and the Internet hostname is the value returned. The `bitdomain` program that comes with sendmail can be used to build this database.

`uucpdomain`

> Converts a UUCP name to an Internet hostname. The key is the UUCP hostname and the value returned is the Internet hostname.

`genericstable`

> Converts a sender email address. The key to the database is either a username or a full email address (username and hostname). The value returned by the database is the new email address. `genericstable` is often used to convert the same address as those processed for masquerading and thus the features that affect masquerading and those that affect the `genericstable` conversion are set to exactly the same values. If you use the `genericstable` and you use masquerading, set GENERICS_DOMAIN and GENERICS_DOMAIN_FILE to the same values as MASQUERADE_DOMAIN and MASQUERADE_DOMAIN_FILE.

`virtusertable`

> Aliases incoming email addresses. Essentially, this is an extended alias database for aliasing addresses that are not local to this host. The key to the database is a full email address or a domain name. The value returned by the database is the recipient address to which the mail is delivered. If a domain name is used as a key, it must begin with an at-sign (@). Mail addressed to any user in the specified domain is sent to the recipient defined by the virtusertable database. Any hostname used as a key in the virtusertable database must also be defined in class w or class {VirtHost}. A hostname can be added to class w with the LOCAL_DOMAIN macro. Hostnames can be added to the {VirtHost} class using the VIRTUSER_DOMAIN macro. The {VirtHost} class can be loaded from a file using the VIRTUSER_DOMAIN_FILE macro.

Some features are important in the fight against spam because they help you control what mail your server will deliver or forward on for delivery. These are accept_unqualified_senders, accept_unresolvable_domains, access_db, blacklist_recipients, and dnsbl. The access database lists email sources and how mail from these sources should be treated. The dnsbl uses a special DNS database to reject mail from specific sources. The blacklist_recipients feature extends the access_db and dnsbl controls to email destinations as well as email sources. Two of the features, accept_unqualified_senders and accept_unresolvable_domains, weaken relay controls by allowing relaying for hosts or domains that cannot be found via DNS. Use care when adjusting these controls.

Two of the remaining FEATURE commands relate to domains. The always_add_domain macro makes sendmail add the local hostname to all locally delivered mail, even to those pieces of mail that would normally have just a username as an address.

The bestmx_is_local feature accepts mail addressed to a host that lists the local host as its preferred MX server as if the mail was local mail. If this feature is not used, mail bound for a remote host is sent directly to the remote host even if its MX record lists the local host as its preferred MX server. The bestmx_is_local feature should not be used if you use a wildcard MX record for your domain.

The last two features are used to select optional programs for the local and the prog mailers. local_procmail selects procmail as the local mailer. Provide the path to procmail as the argument in the FEATURE command. The smrsh feature selects the sendmail Restricted SHell (smrsh) as the prog mailer. smrsh provides improved security over */bin/sh*, which is normally used as the prog mailer. Provide the path to smrsh as the argument in the FEATURE command.

The FEATURE commands discussed in this section and the define macros discussed previously are used to build the m4 source files. The following sections describe the purpose and structure of the OSTYPE, DOMAIN, and MAILER source files.

OSTYPE

The source file for the OSTYPE macro defines operating system–specific parameters. Many operating systems are predefined. Look in the *sendmail/cf/ostype* directory for a full listing of the systems that are already defined.

OSTYPE source files are mostly composed of define macros. Table E-4 lists the define parameters most frequently associated with the OSTYPE source file and the function of each parameter. If a default value is assigned to a parameter, it is shown enclosed in square brackets after the functional description.

Table E-4. OSTYPE defines

Parameter	Function
ALIAS_FILE	Name of the alias file. [*/etc/mail/aliases*]
HELP_FILE	Name of the help file. [*/etc/mail/helpfile*]
QUEUE_DIR	Directory containing queue files. [*/var/spool/mqueue*]
STATUS_FILE	Name of the status file. [*/etc/mail/statistics*]
LOCAL_MAILER_PATH	The local mail delivery program. [*/bin/mail*]
LOCAL_MAILER_FLAGS	Local mailer flags added to "lsDFMAW5:/|@q". [Prmn9]
LOCAL_MAILER_ARGS	Arguments for local mail delivery. [mail -d $u]
LOCAL_MAILER_MAX	Maximum size of local mail.
LOCAL_MAILER_CHARSET	Character set for local 8-bit MIME mail.
LOCAL_MAILER_DSN_DIAGNOSTIC_ CODE	The delivery status notification code used for local mail. [X-Unix]
LOCAL_MAILER_EOL	The end-of-line character for local mail.
LOCAL_MAILER_MAXMSG	The maximum number of messages delivered with a single connection.

Table E-4. OSTYPE defines (continued)

Parameter	Function
LOCAL_SHELL_PATH	Shell used to deliver piped email. [*/bin/sh*]
LOCAL_SHELL_FLAGS	Flags added to lsDFM for the shell mailer. [eu9]
LOCAL_SHELL_ARGS	Arguments for the "prog" mail. [sh -c $u]
LOCAL_SHELL_DIR	Directory in which the shell should run. [*$z:/*]
USENET_MAILER_PATH	Program used for news. [*/usr/lib/news/inews*]
USENET_MAILER_FLAGS	Usenet mailer flags. [rDFMmn]
USENET_MAILER_ARGS	Arguments for the usenet mailer. [-m -h -n]
USENET_MAILER_MAX	Maximum size of usenet mail messages. [100000]
SMTP_MAILER_FLAGS	Flags added to "mDFMuX" for all SMTP mailers.
SMTP_MAILER_MAX	Maximum size of messages for all SMTP mailers.
SMTP_MAILER_ARGS	smtp mailer arguments. [IPC $h]
ESMTP_MAILER_ARGS	esmtp mailer arguments. [IPC $h]
DSMTP_MAILER_ARGS	dsmtp mailer arguments. [IPC $h]
SMTP8_MAILER_ARGS	smtp8 mailer arguments. [IPC $h]
RELAY_MAILER_ARGS	relay mailer arguments. [IPC $h]
RELAY_MAILER_FLAGS	Flags added to "mDFMuX" for the relay mailer.
RELAY_MAIL_MAXMSG	The maximum number of messages for the relay mailer delivered by a single connection.
SMTP_MAILER_CHARSET	Character set for SMTP 8-bit MIME mail.
SMTP_MAIL_MAXMSG	The maximum number of SMTP messages delivered by a single connection.
UUCP_MAILER_PATH	Path to the UUCP mail program. [*/usr/bin/uux*]
UUCP_MAILER_FLAGS	Flags added to "DFMhuU" for the UUCP mailer.
UUCP_MAILER_ARGS	UUCP mailer arguments. [uux - -r -z -a$g -gC $h!rmail ($u)]
UUCP_MAILER_MAX	Maximum size for UUCP messages. [100000]
UUCP_MAILER_CHARSET	Character set for UUCP 8-bit MIME mail.
FAX_MAILER_PATH	Path to the FAX program. [*/usr/local/lib/fax/mailfax*]
FAX_MAILER_ARGS	FAX mailer arguments. [mailfax $u $h $f]
FAX_MAILER_MAX	Maximum size of a FAX. [100000]
POP_MAILER_PATH	Path of the POP mailer. [*/usr/lib/mh/spop*]
POP_MAILER_FLAGS	Flags added to "lsDFMq" for the POP mailer. [Penu]
POP_MAILER_ARGS	POP mailer arguments. [pop $u]
PROCMAIL_MAILER_PATH	Path to the procmail program. [*/usr/local/bin/procmail*]
PROCMAIL_MAILER_FLAGS	Flags added to "DFM" for the Procmail mailer. [SPhnu9]
PROCMAIL_MAILER_ARGS	Procmail mailer arguments. [procmail -Y -m $h $f $u]
PROCMAIL_MAILER_MAX	Maximum size message for the Procmail mailer.
MAIL11_MAILER_PATH	Path to the mail11 mailer. [*/usr/etc/mail11*]

Parameter	Function
MAIL11_MAILER_FLAGS	Flags for the mail11 mailer. [nsFx]
MAIL11_MAILER_ARGS	mail11 mailer arguments. [mail11 $g $x $h $u]
PH_MAILER_PATH	Path to the phquery program. [/usr/local/etc/phquery]
PH_MAILER_FLAGS	Flags for the phquery mailer. [ehmu]
PH_MAILER_ARGS	phquery mailer arguments. [phquery -- $u]
QPAGE_MAILER_ARGS	qpage mailer arguments. [qpage -10 -m -P$u]
QPAGE_MAILER_FLAGS	Flags for the qpage mailer. [mDFMs]
QPAGE_MAILER_MAX	Maximum qpage mailer message size. [4096]
QPAGE_MAILER_PATH	Path to the qpage mailer. [/usr/local/bin/qpage]
CYRUS_MAILER_FLAGS	Flags added to "lsDFMnPq" for the cyrus mailer. [A5@/:|]
CYRUS_MAILER_PATH	Path to the cyrus mailer. [/usr/cyrus/bin/deliver]
CYRUS_MAILER_ARGS	cyrus mailer arguments. [deliver -e -m $h -- $u]
CYRUS_MAILER_MAX	Maximum size message for the cyrus mailer.
CYRUS_MAILER_USER	User and group used for the cyrus mailer. [*cyrus:mail*]
CYRUS_BB_MAILER_FLAGS	Flags added to "lsDFMnP" for the cyrusbb mailer.
CYRUS_BB_MAILER_ARGS	cyrusbb mailer arguments. [deliver -e -m $u]

Despite the long list of parameters in Table E-4, most OSTYPE macros are very short. There are a few reasons for this. First, many of the parameters in the table are redundant. They define the same things for different mailers, and no operating system uses all of the mailers. Second, the default values are often correct. A define only needs to be made if the operating system requires a value different from the default.

DOMAIN

The DOMAIN source file defines configuration parameters that are related to the local domain. Chapter 10 provides an example of a DOMAIN file built for the imaginary *wrotethebook.com* domain.

Table E-5 shows some define macros that commonly appear in DOMAIN files. (See the syntax of the define macro earlier.) This table lists the parameters and the function of each parameter. All of these parameters are used to define mail relay hosts. The value provided for each parameter is either a hostname, i.e., the name of a mail relay server, or a mailer:hostname pair where the mailer is the internal name of a local sendmail mailer and the hostname is the name of the remote mail relay server. If only a hostname is used, the mailer defaults to *relay*, which is the name of the SMTP relay mailer. If no values are provided for these parameters, the BITNET, DECNET, and FAX pseudo-domains are not used, and the local host must be able to handle its own UUCP and "local" mail.

Table E-5. Mail relay define macros

Parameter	Function
UUCP_RELAY	Server for UUCP-addressed email
BITNET_RELAY	Server for BITNET-addressed email
DECNET_RELAY	Server for DECNET-addressed email
FAX_RELAY	Server for mail to the .FAX pseudo-domain[a]
LOCAL_RELAY	Server for unqualified names
LUSER_RELAY	Server for apparently local names that really aren't local
MAIL_HUB	Server for all incoming mail
SMART_HOST	Server for all outgoing mail

[a] The "fax" mailer overrides this value.

The precedence of the relays defined by these parameters is from the most specific to the least specific. If both the UUCP_RELAY and the SMART_HOST relay are defined, the UUCP_RELAY is used for outgoing UUCP mail even though the SMART_HOST relay is defined as handling "all" outgoing mail. If you define both LOCAL_RELAY and MAIL_HUB, you must also use the FEATURE(stickyhost) command to get the expected behavior.

When the stickyhost feature is specified, LOCAL_RELAY handles all local addresses that do not have a host part, and MAIL_HUB handles all local addresses that do have a host part. If stickyhost is not specified and both relays are defined, the LOCAL_RELAY is ignored and MAIL_HUB handles all local addresses.

In addition to the defines shown in Table E-5, there is a group of macros that relate to masquerading and relaying that also appear in the DOMAIN source file. Some of these are used in the examples in Chapter 10. The macros are:

LOCAL_USER(*usernames*)

> Defines local usernames that should not be relayed even if LOCAL_RELAY or MAIL_HUB is defined. This command is the same as adding usernames to class L in the *sendmail.cf* file.

MASQUERADE_AS(*host.domain*)

> Converts the host portion of the sender address on outgoing mail to the domain name defined by *host.domain*. Sender addresses that have no hostname or that have a hostname found in the w class are converted. This has the same effect as defining *host.domain* for the M macro in the *sendmail.cf* file. See examples of MASQUERADE_AS and macro M in Chapter 10.

MASQUERADE_DOMAIN(*otherhost.domain*)

> Converts the host portion of the sender address on outgoing mail to the domain name defined by the MASQUERADE_AS command, if the host portion of the sender address matches *otherhost.domain*. This command must be used in

conjunction with MASQUERADE_AS. Its effect is the same as adding hostnames to class M in the *sendmail.cf* file. See Chapter 10.

MASQUERADE_DOMAIN_FILE(*filename*)

Loads *otherhost.domain* hostnames from the file identified by *filename*. This can be used in place of multiple MASQUERADE_DOMAIN commands. Its effect is the same as loading class M from a file by using the FM*filename* command in the *sendmail.cf* file.

MASQUERADE_EXCEPTION(*host.domain*)

This macro defines a host that is not masqueraded, even if it belongs to a domain that is being masqueraded. This allows you to masquerade an entire domain with the MASQUERADE_DOMAIN macro and then exempt a few hosts that should be exposed to the outside world.

EXPOSED_USER(*username*)

Disables masquerading when the user portion of the sender address matches *username*. Some usernames, such as root, occur on many systems and are therefore not unique across a domain. For those usernames, converting the host portion of the address makes it impossible to sort out where the message really came from and makes replies impossible. This command prevents the MASQUERADE_AS command from having an effect on the sender addresses for specific users. This is the same as setting the values in class E in the *sendmail.cf* file.

RELAY_DOMAIN(*otherhost.domain*)

This macro identifies a host for which mail should be relayed. The host identified in this manner is added to class R.

RELAY_DOMAIN_FILE(*filename*)

This macro identifies a file that contains a list of hosts for which mail should be relayed. This macro loads class R from the specified file.

There are several features that affect relaying and masquerading. We have already discussed FEATURE(stickyhost). Others are:

FEATURE(masquerade_envelope)

Causes envelope addresses to be masqueraded in the same way that sender addresses are masqueraded. See Chapter 10 for an example of this command.

FEATURE(allmasquerade)

Causes recipient addresses to be masqueraded in the same way that sender addresses are masqueraded. Thus, if the host portion of the recipient address matches the requirements of the MASQUERADE_AS command, it is converted. Don't use this feature unless you are positive that every alias known to the local system is also known to the mail server that handles mail for the masquerade domain.

FEATURE(limited_masquerade)

Limits masquerading to those hosts defined in class M. The hosts defined in class w are not masqueraded.

FEATURE(masquerade_entire_domain)

Causes MASQUERADE_DOMAIN to be interpreted as referring to all hosts within an entire domain. If this feature is not used, only an address that exactly matches the value defined by MASQUERADE_DOMAIN is converted. If this feature is used, all addresses that end with the value defined by MASQUERADE_DOMAIN are converted. For example, assume that the options MASQUERADE_AS(wrotethebook.com) and MASQUERADE_DOMAIN(sales.wrotethebook.com) are defined. If FEATURE(masquerade_entire_domain) is set, every hostname in the *sales.wrotethebook.com* domain is converted to *wrotethebook.com* on outgoing email. Otherwise, only the hostname *sales.wrotethebook.com* is converted.

Some features define how the server handles mail if it is the mail relay server. These features, which are mentioned in the "FEATURE" section earlier in this appendix, are:

FEATURE(access_db)

Adds the code necessary to use the access database. The access database maps a user, a domain name, or an IP address to a keyword that tells sendmail how to handle relaying for the host, domain, or network.

FEATURE(blacklist_recipient)

Uses the access database to control delivery of mail based on the recipient address. The basic access_db feature controls relaying and delivery based on the source of the message. This feature adds to that the ability to control mail relaying and delivery based on the destination.

FEATURE(dnsbl)

Controls mail delivery based on a DNS blacklist. Source addresses and destination addresses listed in the DNS blacklist database may be denied mail delivery or relay services.

FEATURE(promiscuous_relay)

Relays mail from any site to any site. Normally, sendmail does not relay mail. Mail relays can be abused by spammers and spoofers. Enable them with caution.

FEATURE(relay_entire_domain)

Relays mail from any domain defined in class M to any site.

FEATURE(relay_hosts_only)

Relays mail from any host defined in the access database or in class R.

FEATURE(relay_based_on_MX)

Relays mail from any site for which your system is the MX server.

FEATURE(relay_local_from)

Relays mail with a sender address that contains your local domain name.

Inbound mail can also be filtered to reduce the impact of spammers. Two macros are available for this purpose:

MAIL_FILTER(`name', `equates')
> This macro defines a mail filter using the Sendmail Mail Filter API syntax.

INPUT_MAIL_FILTER(`name', `equates')
> This macro defines a mail filter and sets up the call for that mail filter.

The DOMAIN source file is also used for features and macros that directly relate to DNS. These features are:

FEATURE(accept_unqualified_senders)
> This feature accepts mail even if the sender address does not include a hostname. Normally, only mail from a user directly logged on to the system is accepted without a hostname. This is a dangerous feature that should be used only on an isolated network.

FEATURE(accept_unresolvable_domains)
> This feature accepts mail from hostnames that cannot be resolved by DNS. This is a dangerous feature that is used only on systems that lack full-time DNS service.

FEATURE(always_add_domain)
> This feature adds the hostname of the system to all local mail. With this feature enabled on a server named *crab@wrotethebook.com*, mail from the local user *craig* to the local user *kathy* would be delivered as mail from *craig@crab@wrotethebook.com* to *kathy@crab@wrotethebook.com*.

FEATURE(bestmx_is_local)
> With this feature, mail addressed to any host that lists the local server as its MX server is accepted by the server as local mail.

The DNS macros are:

CANONIFY_DOMAIN(*domain*)
> This macro defines a domain name that will be passed to DNS for conversion to its canonical form even if the nocanonify feature is in use. Computers can be known by aliases. The official domain name of a host stored in DNS is called its canonical name. This macro is generally used to enable canonification of the local domain when nocanonify is in use.

CANONIFY_DOMAIN_FILE(*filename*)
> This macro identifies a file containing a list of domain names that should be converted to canonical form even if nocanonify has been selected.

LOCAL_DOMAIN(*alias-hostname*)
> This macro defines an alias for the local host. Mail addressed to the alias will be accepted as if it were addressed directly to the local host.

The macros and features described in this section are not limited to the DOMAIN source file. They can appear in any m4 source file, and, in fact, are often found in the macro control file. However, they are most naturally associated with the DOMAIN file as indicated by the documentation in the *cf/cf/README* file.

MAILER

It is possible that you will need to customize a file location in an OSTYPE file or that define domain-specific information in a DOMAIN file, but unless you develop your own mail delivery program you will not need to create a MAILER source file. Instead, you will need to invoke one or more existing files in your macro configuration file.

The available MAILER files are listed in Table E-6. This table lists each MAILER value and its function. These are invoked using the MAILER(*value*) command in the macro configuration (*.mc*) file, where *value* is one of the mailer names from the table.

Table E-6. MAILER values

Name	Function
local	The local and prog mailers
smtp	All SMTP mailers: smtp, esmtp, smtp8, and relay
uucp	All UUCP mailers: uucp-old (uucp) and uucp-new (suucp)
usenet	Usenet news support
fax	Fax support using FlexFAX software
pop	Post Office Protocol (POP) support
procmail	An interface for procmail
mail11	The DECnet mail11 mailer
phquery	The phquery program for CSO phone book
qpage	The QuickPage mailer used to send email to a pager
cyrus	The cyrus and cyrusbb mailers

Your macro configuration file should have a MAILER(local) and a MAILER(smtp) entry. This gives you the local and prog mailers required by sendmail, the smtp mailer for standard SMTP mail, the esmtp mailer for Extended SMTP, the smtp8 mailer for 8-bit MIME mail, and the relay mailer for the various mail relay servers mentioned in the "DOMAIN" section of this appendix. Selecting local and smtp provides everything you need for a standard TCP/IP installation.

Of all the remaining mailers, only uucp is widely used. uucp provides UUCP mail support for systems directly connected to UUCP networks. The uucp-old mailer supports standard UUCP mail, and the uucp-new mailer is used for remote sites that can handle multiple recipients in one transfer. The system needs the mailer that is correct for the capabilities of the remote site. Use class U to define the hostnames of systems that need the old mailer, and class Y for the names of remote systems that can work with the new mailer. Specify MAILER(uucp) after the MAILER(smtp) entry if your system has both TCP/IP and UUCP connections. Ordering the MAILER statements in this way adds two more mailers to the two standard UUCP mailers: the uucp-dom mailer to support standard domain names, and the uucp-uudom mailer to support standard domain names with a standard UUCP envelope.

The other mailers are rarely used:

usenet

> Modifies the sendmail rewrite rules to send local mail that contains ".usenet" in the username to the program inews. Instead of this mailer, choose a user mail agent that supports Usenet news. Don't hack sendmail to handle it.

fax

> This is an experimental mailer that supports HylaFax software.

pop

> On most systems, POP support is provided separately by the popd daemon, and the MAILER(pop) command is not used.

procmail

> Only provides an interface to procmail for use in the mailertable. The sendmail V8 distribution does not provide procmail. Even when procmail is used as the local mailer, as it is in Slackware Linux, the MAILER(procmail) command is not required.

mail11

> Only used on DECNET mail networks that use the mail11 mailer.

phquery

> Provides a name lookup program for the CSO phone book (ph) directory service. User directory services are usually configured in the user mail agent, not in sendmail.

qpage

> Provides an interface from email to pagers using the QuickPage program.

cyrus

> This is a local mail delivery program with a mailbox architecture. cyrus and cyrusbb mailers are not widely used.

This concludes our discussion of m4 macros. The output of all of the files and commands that go into the m4 processor is a *sendmail.cf* file. The remainder of this appendix provides additional details about the *sendmail.cf* configuration. The bulk of information about *sendmail.cf* is found in Chapter 10.

More sendmail.cf

Many options and flags can be used in configuring the *sendmail.cf* file. All of the important configuration parameters are covered in Chapter 10. But if you are unlucky enough to have a configuration that requires you to tweak one of the more obscure parameters, you will find all of them in the following tables.

sendmail Macros

The *sendmail.cf* file contains a large number of macro variables. Macros are useful because they can store values specific to your configuration and yet be referenced by a macro name that is independent of your configuration. This makes it possible to use a configuration file that is essentially the same on many different systems simply by varying the value stored in the macro. This appendix lists all of the internal sendmail macros in two tables. Table E-7 lists all of the macros that use single-character names.

Table E-7. Macros with single-character names

Macro	Contents
a	The date and time the mail was sent.
b	The current date in RFC 822 format.
B	The name of the Bitnet relay.
c	The number of times the mail has been forwarded.
C	The name of the DECnet relay.
d	The current date and time in ctime format.
E	Reserved for an X.400 relay.
f	The sender address.
F	The name of the FAX relay.
g	The sender address written as a full return address.
h	The recipient host.
H	The name of the mail hub.
i	The queue identifier.
j	The fully qualified domain name of the local computer.
k	The local system's UUCP node name.
L	The name of the LUSER_RELAY.
m	The name of the local domain.
M	The name used to masquerade outbound mail.
n	The sender name used for error messages.
p	The PID of the sendmail process running as a mail delivery agent.
r	The protocol used when the message was first received.
R	The name of the LOCAL_RELAY.
s	The hostname of the sender's machine.
S	The name of the SMART_HOST relay.

Table E-7. Macros with single-character names (continued)

Macro	Contents
t	A numeric representation of the current date and time.
u	The username of the recipient.
U	A local UUCP name that overrides the value of $k.
v	The version number of sendmail that is running.
V	The name of the UUCP relay for class V hosts.
w	The hostname of the local system.
W	The name of the UUCP relay for class W hosts.
x	The full name of the sender.
X	The name of the UUCP relay for class X hosts.
Y	The name of the UUCP relay for all other hosts.
z	The home directory of the recipient.
Z	The version number.
_	Sender address validated by identd.

The current version of sendmail allows macros to have multi-character names. Table E-8 lists the macros that use long names.

Table E-8. Reserved macros with long names

Macro	Contents
{auth_authen}	Identity of the authenticated user.
{auth_author}	Source of the authentication.
{auth_ssf}	The number of bits in the encryption key used by AUTH.
{auth_type}	The type of authentication mechanism used.
{bodytype}	The values from the ESMTP BODY parameter.
{cert_issuer}	The distinguished name of the certificate authority.
{cert_subject}	The distinguished name of the subject of the certificate.
{cipher_bits}	The length of the encryption key used for the connection.
{cipher}	The encryption technique used for the connection.
{client_addr}	The IP address of the remote client connected to TCP port 25.
{client_name}	The canonical name of the client connected to TCP port 25.
{client_port}	The source port number used by the remote client.
{client_resolve}	The keyword OK, FAIL, Forged or TEMP that indicates the result of a reverse DNS lookup using the client's IP address.
{currHeader}	The contents of the current header during header processing.
{daemon_addr}	The IP address of the network interface from which the daemon accepts mail. Normally 0.0.0.0 to indicate all interfaces.

Macro	Contents
{daemon_family}	The protocol family being used. Normally inet to indicate TCP/IP. Other values are inet6, iso, and ns.
{daemon_flags}	The flags set by the DaemonPortOption command, if any.
{daemon_info}	General information about the daemon.
{daemon_name}	The daemon name, which is usually Daemon1 unless a daemon name is defined by the Daemon-PortOptions command.
{daemon_port}	The port that the daemon is listening on, usually 25.
{deliveryMode}	The current delivery mode.
{envid}	The DSN ENVID value from the Mail From: header.
{hdrlen}	The length of the string stored in {currHeader}.
{hdr_name}	The name of the current header during header processing.
{if_addr}	The IP address of the network interface used by the current incoming connection.
{if_name}	The hostname assigned to the network interface used by the current incoming connection.
{mail_addr}	The user's mail address from the mail delivery triple created from the MAIL From: envelope header.
{mail_host}	The hostname from the mail delivery triple created from the MAIL From: envelope header.
{mail_mailer}	The mailer name from the mail delivery triple created from the MAIL From: envelope header.
{MessageIdCheck}	The value from the incoming Message-Id: header.
{ntries}	The number of delivery attempts.
{opMode}	The operating mode from the sendmail command line.
{queue_interval}	The length of time between queue runs defined by the -q command-line option.
{rcpt_addr}	The user's mail address from the mail delivery triple created from the RCPT To: envelope header.
{rcpt_host}	The hostname from the mail delivery triple created from the RCPT To: envelope header.
{rcpt_mailer}	The mailer name from the mail delivery triple created from the RCPT To: envelope header.
{server_addr}	The IP address of the remote server for the outgoing connection.
{server_name}	The name of the remote server for the outgoing connection.
{tls_version}	The TLS/SSL version used for the connection.
{verify}	The result of the verification process.

sendmail Classes

As the previous tables show, sendmail has many internal macros. It also has several internal classes. Most of these classes still use single-character names. A few use the newer long names. The full list of internal classes is shown in Table E-9.

Table E-9. Internal sendmail classes

Name	Contents
B	Domain names included in the bestmx-is-local process.
E	Usernames that should not be masqueraded.
G	Domains that should be looked up in the genericstable.
L	Local users that are not forwarded to MAIL_HUB or LOCAL_RELAY.
e	Supported MIME Content-Transfer-Encodings. Initialized to *7bit*, *8bit*, and *binary*.
k	The system's UUCP node names.
M	Domains that should be masqueraded.
m	All local domains for this host.
n	MIME body types that should never be 8- to 7-bit encoded. Initialized to *multipart/signed*.
q	MIME Content-Types that should not be Base64-encoded. Initialized to *text/plain*.
N	Hosts and domains that should not be masqueraded.
O	Characters that cannot be used in local usernames.
P	Pseudo-domain names, such as REDIRECT.
R	Domains for which this system will relay mail.
s	MIME message subtypes that can be processed recursively. Initialized to *rfc822*.
t	The list of trusted users.
U	The UUCP hosts that are locally connected.
V	The UUCP hosts reached via the relay defined by $V.
W	The UUCP hosts reached via the relay defined by $W.
X	The UUCP hosts reached via the relay defined by $X.
Y	Directly connected "smart" UUCP hosts.
Z	Directly connected UUCP hosts that use domain names.
.	A literal dot (.).
[	A literal left bracket ([).
{LDAPRoute}	A list of domains that can be rerouted based on LDAP lookups.
{VirtHost}	A list of hosts and domains that are valid virtual hostnames.
w	All hostnames this system will accept as its own.

sendmail Options

A large number of sendmail options can be set inside the sendmail configuration file. Chapter 10 provides the syntax of the option command in Table 10-1 and several examples of options. The complete list of options is:

`AliasFile=[class:]file, [class:]file...`

> Identifies the alias file(s). *class* is optional and defaults to `implicit`. Valid classes are `implicit`, `hash`, `dbm`, `stab` (internal symbol table) or `nis`. The selected database

class must be a database type that was compiled into `sendmail` on your system. *file* is the pathname of the alias file.

AliasWait=*timeout*

Wait *timeout* minutes for an "@:@" entry to appear in the alias database before starting up. When *timeout* expires, automatically rebuild the database if AutoRebuildAliases is set; otherwise, issue a warning.

AuthMechanisms=*list*

Advertise the listed authentication mechanisms.

AuthOptions=*list*

Lists the options supported with the SMTP AUTH argument.

AllowBogusHELO

Accept illegal HELO SMTP commands that don't contain a hostname.

AutoRebuildAliases

Automatically rebuild the alias database when necessary. The preferred method is to rebuild the alias database with an explicit newaliases command.

BlankSub=*c*

Use *c* as the blank substitution character to replace unquoted spaces in addresses. The default is to leave the spaces unchanged.

CACERTFile=*filename*

Identifies the file that contains the certificate of a certificate authority.

CACERTPath=*path*

Defines the path to the directory that contains the certificates of various certificate authorities.

CheckAliases

Check that the delivery address in each alias is valid when rebuilding the alias database. Normally this check is not done. Adding this check slows the database build substantially. This is a Boolean.

CheckpointInterval=*n*

Checkpoint the queue after every *n* items are processed to simplify recovery if your system crashes during queue processing. The default is 10.

ClassFactor=*fact*

The multiplier used to favor messages with a higher value in the Priority: header. Defaults to 1800.

ClientCertFile=*file*

Identifies the file that contains the certificate used when this system acts as a client.

ClientKeyFile=*file*

Identifies the file that contains the private key used when this system acts as a client.

ClientPortOptions=*options*

> Defines nonstandard settings used when this system acts as an SMTP client. *options* is a comma-separated list of *keyword=value* pairs. Valid *keyword=value* pairs are:

> Port=*port*
>
> > Defines the source port number the client uses for outbound connections. *port* can be specified by number or name. If a name is used, the name must be defined in */etc/services*. By default, the source port for an outbound connection is generated by the system for the connection.

> Addr=*address*
>
> > Defines the address of the network interface the client uses for outbound connections. The value for *address* can be written in dotted decimal notation or as a name. By default, any available interface is used.

> Family=*protocol*
>
> > Defines the protocol family used for the connection. inet, which is the default, is the protocol family for TCP/IP.

> SndBufSize=*bytes*
>
> > Defines the size of the send buffer.

> RcvBufSize=*bytes*
>
> > Defines the size of the receive buffer.

> Modifier=*flags*
>
> > Defines the daemon flags for the client. Only one flag, h, is available. The h flag tells the client to use the name assigned to the interface on the SMTP HELO or EHLO command.

ColonOkInAddr

> Accept colons in email addresses (e.g., *host:user*). Colons are always accepted in pairs in mail routing (*nodename::user*) or in RFC 822 group constructs (groupname: member1, member2, ...;). By default, this option is "on" if the configuration version level is less than 6.

ConnectionCacheSize=*n*

> The number of connections that can be held open (cached) by this instantiation of sendmail. The default is 1. The maximum is 4. 0 causes connections to be closed immediately after the data is sent, which is the traditional way sendmail operated.

ConnectionCacheTimeout=*timeout*

> The amount of time an inactive cached connection is held open. After *timeout* minutes of inactivity, it is closed. The default is 5 minutes.

ConnectionRateThrottle=*n*

> Limits the number of incoming connections accepted in any 1-second period to *n*. The default is 0, which means no limit.

ConnectOnlyTo=*address*
> Limits all SMTP connections to a single destination address. Used only for testing.

ControlSocketName=*path*
> Defines the path of the Unix control socket used to manage daemon connections. By default, this is not defined.

DaemonPortOptions=*options*
> Sets SMTP server options. The *options* are key=value pairs. The options are:

> Port=*portnumber*
>> where *portnumber* is any valid port number. It can be specified with the number or the name found in */etc/services*. The default is port 25, SMTP.

> Addr=*mask*
>> where *mask* is an IP address mask specified either in dotted decimal notation or as a network name. The default is INADDR-ANY, which accepts all addresses.

> Family=*addressfamily*
>> where *addressfamily* is a valid address family (see the ifconfig command). The default is INET, which allows IP addresses to be used.

> Listen=*n*
>> where *n* is the number of queued connections allowed. The default is 10.

> SndBufSize=*n*
>> where *n* is the send buffer size.

> RcvBufSize=*n*
>> where *n* is the receive buffer size.

DataFileBufferSize=*bytes*
> Defines the maximum amount of memory that can be used to buffer a data file.

DeadLetterDrop=*file*
> Defines the file where messages that cannot be returned to the sender or sent to the postmaster account are stored.

DefaultAuthInfo=*file*
> Defines the file that contains the authentication information needed for outbound connections.

DefaultCharSet=*charset*
> The character set placed in the Content-Type: header when 8-bit data is converted to MIME format. The default is unknown-8bit. This option is overridden by the Charset= field of the mailer descriptor.

DefaultUser=*user*[:*group*]
> The default user ID and group ID for mailers without the S flag in their definitions. If *group* is omitted, the group associated with *user* in the */etc/passwd* file is used. The default is 1:1.

DeliveryMode=*x*
>   Deliver in mode *x*, where *x* is i (interactive delivery), b (background delivery), q (queue the message), or d (defer until the queue run). The default is b.

DHParameters=*parameters*
>   Defines the DH parameters used for DSA/DH encryption.

DialDelay=*delaytime*
>   Delay *delaytime* seconds before redialing a failed connection on dial-on-demand networks. The default is 0 (no redial).

DontBlameSendmail=*options*
>   Disables sendmail's file security checks. *options* is a comma-separated list of keywords that disable specific security checks. The values for this option are set by the confDONT_BLAME_SENDMAIL define command in the m4 source file. The valid keywords for the *options* list are:

>   AssumeSafeChown
>>   Allow the chown command because it is only available to the root user.

>   ClassFileInUnsafeDirPath
>>   Accept any directory path in an F command.

>   DontWarnForwardFileInUnsafeDirPath
>>   Don't issue a warning about an unsafe path for the *.forward* file.

>   ErrorHeaderInUnsafeDirPath
>>   Accept the error header file regardless of its directory path.

>   FileDeliveryToHardLink
>>   Permit delivery to a file that is really a hard link.

>   FileDeliveryToSymLink
>>   Permit delivery to a file that is really a symbolic link.

>   ForwardFileInUnsafeDirPath
>>   Accept a *.forward* file even if it is in an unsafe directory.

>   ForwardFileInUnsafeDirPathSafe
>>   Accept program and file references from a *.forward* file even if it is in an unsafe directory.

>   ForwardFileIngroupWritableDirPath
>>   Accept a *.forward* file even if it is in a group-writable directory.

>   GroupWritableAliasFile
>>   Accept the *aliases* file even if it is group-writable.

>   GroupWritableDirPathSafe
>>   Accept all group-writable directories as "safe."

>   GroupWritableForwardFileSafe
>>   Accept a *.forward* file even if it is group-writable.

GroupWritableIncludeFileSafe
> Accept *:include:* files even if they are group-writable.

HelpFileinUnsafeDirPath
> Accept the help file even if it is in an unsafe directory.

IncludeFileInUnsafeDirPath
> Accept *:include:* files even if they are from unsafe directories.

IncludeFileInUnsafeDirPathSafe
> Accept program and file references from *:include:* files even if they are in an unsafe directory.

IncludeFileIngroupWritableDirPath
> Accept *:include:* files even if they are in a group-writable directory.

InsufficientEntropy
> Use STARTTLS even if the random seed generator for SSL is inadequate.

LinkedAliasFileInWritableDir
> Accept an *aliases* file that is a link in a writable directory.

LinkedClassFileInWritableDir
> Load class values from files that are links in writable directories.

LinkedForwardFileInWritableDir
> Accept *.forward* files that are links in writable directories.

LinkedIncludeFileInWritableDir
> Accept *:include:* files that are links in writable directories.

LinkedMapInWritableDir
> Accept database files that are links in writable directories.

LinkedServiceSwitchFileInWritableDir
> Accept a service switch file that is a link in a writable directory.

MapInUnsafeDirPath
> Accept database files that are in unsafe directories.

NonRootSafeAddr
> Don't flag file and program deliveries as unsafe when sendmail is not running as root.

RunProgramInUnsafeDirPath
> Run programs that are in writable directories.

RunWritableProgram
> Run programs that are group- or world-writable.

Safe
> Leave all of the safety checks on. This is the default.

TrustStickyBit
> Trust group- and world-writable directories if the sticky bit is set.

WorldWritableAliasFile

> Accept the *aliases* file even if it is world-writable.

WriteMapToHardLink

> Write to database files even if they are really hard links.

WriteMapToSymLink

> Write to database files even if they are really symbolic links.

WriteStatsToHardLink

> Write to the status file even if it is really a hard link.

WriteStatsToSymLink

> Write to the status file even if it is really a symbolic link.

DontExpandCnames

> Disable the $[*name*$] syntax used to convert nicknames to canonical names.

DontInitGroups

> Don't use the initgroups(3) call. This setting reduces NIS server load, but limits a user to the group associated with that user in */etc/passwd*.

DontProbeInterfaces

> If set to true, this stops sendmail from adding the names and addresses of the network interfaces to class w. The default is false, so interface names and addresses are stored in class w.

DontPruneRoutes

> Don't optimize explicit mail routes. Normally, sendmail makes a route as direct as possible. However, optimizing the route may not be appropriate for systems located behind a firewall.

DoubleBounceAddress=*error-address*

> Send the report of an error that occurs when sending an error message to *error-address*. The default is postmaster.

EightBitMode=*action*

> Handle undeclared 8-bit data by following the specified *action*. The possible actions are: s (strict), reject undeclared 8-bit data; m (mime), convert it to MIME; and p (pass), pass it through unaltered.

ErrorHeader=*file-or-message*

> Prepend *file-or-message* to outgoing error messages. If *file-or-message* is the path to a text file that is to be prepended, it must begin with a slash. If this option is not defined, nothing is prepended to error messages.

ErrorMode=*x*

> Handle errors messages according to *x*, where *x* is: p (print messages); q (give exit status but no messages); m (mail back messages); w (write messages to the user's terminal); or e (mail back messages and always give zero exit status). If this option is not defined, error messages are printed.

FallbackMXhost=*fallbackhost*
> Use *fallbackhost* as a backup MX server for every host.

ForkEachJob
> Run a separate process for every item delivered from the queue. This option reduces the amount of memory needed to process the queue.

ForwardPath=*path*
> The *path* to search for *.forward* files. Multiple paths can be defined by separating them with colons. The default is *$z/.forward*.

HelpFile=*file*
> The path to the help file.

HoldExpensive
> Queue mail for outgoing mailers that have the e (expensive) mailer flag. Normally mail is delivered immediately.

HostsFile=*path*
> The path to the hosts file. The default is */etc/hosts*.

HostStatusDirectory=*path*
> Directory in which host status information is stored so that it can be shared between sendmail processes. Normally, the status of a host or connection is only known by the process that discovers that status. To function, this option requires that ConnectionCacheSize be set to at least 1.

IgnoreDots
> Ignore dots in incoming messages. Dots cannot be ignored by SMTP mail because they are used to mark the end of a mail message.

LDAPDefaultSpec=*specification*
> The default specification used for LDAP databases.

LogLevel=*n*
> *n* indicates the level of detail stored in the log file. *n* defaults to 9, which is normally plenty of detail.

MatchGECOS
> Check the username from the email address against the GECOS field of the *passwd* file if it was not found in the alias database or in the username field of the *passwd* file. This option is not recommended.

MaxAliasRecursion=*n*
> Aliases can point to other aliases before finally resolving to the actual mail address. This option defines how deep aliases can be nested before resolving to a mail address. The default for *n* is 10.

MaxDaemonChildren=*n*
> Refuse connections when *n* children are processing incoming mail. Normally sendmail sets no arbitrary limit on child processes.

MaxHeadersLength=*bytes*
>   The maximum length allowed for all of the headers taken together.

MaxHopCount=*n*
>   Assume a message is looping when it has been processed more than *n* times. The default is 25.

MaxHostStatAge=*n*
>   Retain host status information for *n* minutes.

MaxMessageSize=*n*
>   The maximum message size advertised in response to the ESMTP EHLO. Messages larger than this are rejected.

MaxMimeHeaderLength=*size*
>   The maximum length of MIME header fields.

MaxQueueRunSize=*n*
>   The maximum number of items that can be processed in a single queue run. The default is no limit.

MaxRecipientsPerMessage=*n*
>   *n* limits the maximum number of recipients for a single message. If it is not specified, there is no limit.

MeToo
>   Send a copy to the sender.

MinFreeBlocks=*n*
>   Don't accept incoming mail unless *n* blocks are free in the queue filesystem.

MinQueueAge=*n*
>   Don't process any jobs that have been in the queue less than *n* minutes.

MustQuoteChars=*s*
>   The list of characters added to the set "@,;:\()[]" that must be quoted when used in the username part of an address. If MustQuoteChars is specified without an *s* value, it adds "." to the standard set of quoted characters.

NoRecipientAction=*action*
>   The *action* taken when a message has no valid recipient headers. *action* can be none to pass the message on unmodified, add-to to add a To: header using the recipient addresses from the envelope, add-apparently-to to add an Apparently-To: header, add-to-undisclosed to add a "To: undisclosed-recipients:;" header, or add-bcc to add an empty Bcc: header.

OldStyleHeaders
>   Allow spaces to delimit names. Normally, commas delimit names.

OperatorChars=*charlist*
>   The list of operator characters that are normally defined in macro o. The default is the standard set of operators. See the discussion of rewrite tokens and the use of operators in determining tokens in Chapter 10.

`ProcessTitlePrefix=`*`prefix`*
> A string used on the heading of process status reports.

`PostmasterCopy=`*`username`*
> Copy error messages to *username*. The default is not to send copies of error messages to the postmaster.

`PrivacyOptions=`*`options`*
> Set SMTP protocol *options*, where *options* is a comma-separated list containing one or more of these keywords:

> `public`
>> allow all commands

> `needmailhelo`
>> require HELO or EHLO before MAIL

> `needexpnhelo`
>> require HELO or EHLO before EXPN

> `noexpn`
>> disable EXPN

> `needvrfyhelo`
>> require HELO or EHLO before VRFY

> `novrfy`
>> disable VRFY

> `restrictmailq`
>> restrict `mailq` to users with group access to the queue directory

> `restrictqrun`
>> only *root* and the owner of the queue directory are allowed to run the queue

> `noreceipts`
>> don't return successful delivery messages

> `goaway`
>> disable all SMTP status queries

> `authwarnings`
>> put X-Authentication-Warning: headers in messages

`QueueDirectory=`*`directory`*
> The pathname of the queue directory.

`QueueFactor=`*`factor`*
> The factor used with the difference between the current load and the load average limit and with the message priority to determine if a message should be queued or sent immediately. The idea is to queue low-priority messages if the system is currently heavily loaded. It defaults to 600000.

`QueueLA=`*`n`*
> Queue messages when the system load average exceeds *n*. The default is 8.

QueueSortOrder=*sequence*

Sort the queue in the *sequence* specified, where *sequence* is: h (hostname sequence); t (submission time sequence); or p (message priority order). Priority ordering is the default.

RandFile=*file*

Points to a file that provides pseudo-random data for certain encryption techniques. This is used only if the compile option HASURANDOM is not available.

ResolverOptions=*options*

Set resolver options. Available option values are: debug, aaonly, usevc, primary, igntc, recurse, defnames, stayopen, and dnsrch. The option can be preceded by a plus (+) to turn it on or a minus (-) to turn it off. One other option, HasWildcardMX, is specified without a + or -. Simply adding HasWildcardMX turns the option on.

RrtImpliesDsn

If set to true, treat a Return-Receipt-To: header as a request for delivery service notification (DSN). The default is false.

RunAsUser=*userid*[:groupid]

Run sendmail under this user ID and group ID instead of under *root*. This may enhance security when sendmail is running on a well-maintained firewall. On general-purpose systems, this may decrease security because it requires that many files be readable or writable by this user ID.

RecipientFactor=*factor*

The priority of a job is lowered by this factor for each recipient so that jobs with large numbers of recipients have lower priority. Defaults to 30000.

RefuseLA=*n*

Refuse incoming SMTP connections when the system load average exceeds *n*. The default is 12.

RetryFactor=*factor*

The factor used to decrease the priority of a job every time it is processed, so that mail that cannot be delivered does not keep popping to the top of the queue. The default is 90000.

SafeFileEnvironment=*directory*

chroot(2) to *directory* before writing a file and refuse to deliver to symbolic links.

SaveFromLine

Save Unix-style From: lines at the front of headers. Normally they are discarded.

SendMIMEErrors

Send error messages in MIME format.

ServerCertFile=*file*

> Identifies the file that contains the certificate used when this system acts as a mail server.

ServerKeyFile=*file*

> Identifies the file that contains the private key used when this system acts as a mail server.

ServiceSwitchFile=*path*

> Identifies the *path* to a file that lists the methods used for various services. The ServiceSwitchFile contains entries that begin with the service name followed by the service method. sendmail checks for services named "aliases" and "hosts" and supports "dns", "nis", "nisplus", or "files" as possible service methods, assuming that support for all of these methods is compiled into this copy of sendmail. ServiceSwitchFile defaults to */etc/service.switch*. If that file does not exist, sendmail uses the following service methods: aliases are looked up in the aliases files, and hosts are looked up first using dns, then nis, and finally the hosts file. If the operating system has a built-in service switch feature, it is used and this option is ignored. See the description of the *nsswitch.conf* file in Chapter 9. It is a service switch file.

SevenBitInput

> Strip input to 7 bits for compatibility with old systems. This shouldn't be necessary.

SingleLineFromHeader

> For compatibility with some versions of Lotus Notes, unwrap From: lines that have embedded newlines into one long line.

SingleThreadDelivery

> Don't open more than one SMTP connection to a remote host at the same time. This option requires the HostStatusDirectory option.

SmtpGreetingMessage=*message*

> The greeting sent to the remote host when it connects to the SMTP server port. This is the value defined in macro e.

StatusFile=*file*

> Log summary statistics in *file*. By default, summary statistics are not logged.

SuperSafe

> Create a queue file, even when attempting immediate delivery.

TempFileMode=*mode*

> Use *mode* to set the access permissions for queue files. *mode* is an octal value. It defaults to 0600.

Timeout.*type*=*timeout*

> Set timeout values, where *type* is the thing being timed and *timeout* is the time interval before the timer expires. Table E-10 lists the valid *type* values, the event being timed, and the default *timeout* value for each type.

Table E-10. Timeout types

Type	Waiting for	Default
connect	A connection to complete	1m
control	A control socket transmission to complete	2m
iconnect	The connection to the first host in a message	5m
initial	Initial greeting message	5m
helo	Reply to HELO or EHLO command	5m
mail	Reply to MAIL command	10m
rcpt	Reply to RCPT command	1h
datainit	Reply to DATA command	5m
datablock	Data block read	1h
datafinal	Reply to terminating "."	1h
rset	Reply to RSET command	5m
quit	Reply to QUIT command	2m
misc	Reply to NOOP and VERB commands	2m
ident	IDENT protocol response	30s
fileopen	Open on a *.forward* or *:include:* file	60s
command	Command read	1h
queuereturn	Returning a queued message as undeliverable	5d
queuereturn.normal	Returning a normal message from the queue as undeliverable	5d
queuereturn.non-urgent	Returning a non-urgent message from the queue as undeliverable	7d
queuereturn.urgent	Returning an urgent message from the queue as undeliverable	2d
queuewarn	Warning that a message is still queued	4h
queuewarn.normal	Warning that a normal message is still queued	4h
queuewarn.non-urgent	Warning that a non-urgent message is still queued	12h
queuewarn.urgent	Warning that an urgent message is still queued	1h
resolver.retrans	A response to a resolver query	5s
resolver.retrans.first	A response to the first resolver query	5s
resolver.retrans.normal	A response to a normal resolver query	5s
resolver.retry	Sets the number of times to retry a resolver query	4
resolver.retry.first	Sets the number of times to retry the first resolver query	4
resolver.retry.normal	Sets the number of times to retry a normal resolver query	4
hoststatus	Removing stale host status	30m

TimeZoneSpec=*tzinfo*

Set the local time zone information to *tzinfo*. If TimeZoneSpec is not set, the system default is used; if set to null, the user's TZ variable is used.

TrustedUser=*users*

The list of users trusted to send mail using another user's name.

TryNullMXList

> Connect directly to any remote host that lists the local system as its most pre-ferred MX server, as if the remote host had no MX records. You are discouraged from using this option.

UnixFromLine=*fromline*

> Defines the format for Unix-style From: lines. This is the same as the value stored in macro l.

UnsafeGroupWrites

> Group-writable *:include:* and *.forward* files cannot reference programs or write directly to files. World-writable files always have these restrictions.

UseErrorsTo

> Send error messages to the addresses listed in the Errors-To: header. Normally, errors are sent to the sender address from the envelope.

UserDatabaseSpec=*udbspec*

> The user database specification.

UserSubmission

> Indicates that this is not relayed mail, but an initial submission directly from a Mail User Agent.

Verbose

> Run in verbose mode.

See Chapter 10 for examples of setting options.

sendmail Mailer Flags

Mailer flags are declared in the F field of the mailer definition. Each mailer flag is set by a single character that represents that flag. For example, F=lsDFMe sets six differ-ent flags. Table E-11 lists the single-character name and function of each flag.

Table E-11. sendmail mailer flags

Name	Function
C	Add *@domain* to addresses that do not have an @.
D	The mailer wants a Date: header line.
E	Add > to message lines that begin with From:.
e	This is an expensive mailer. See sendmail option c.
F	The mailer wants a From: header line.
f	The mailer accepts an -f flag from trusted users.
h	Preserve uppercase in hostnames.
I	The mailer will be speaking SMTP to another sendmail.
L	Limit the line lengths as specified in RFC 821.

Table E-11. sendmail mailer flags (continued)

Name	Function
l	This is a local mailer.
M	The mailer wants a Message-Id: header line.
m	The mailer can send to multiple users in one transaction.
n	Don't insert a Unix-style From: line in the message.
P	The mailer wants a Return-Path: line.
R	Use the MAIL FROM: return path rather than the return address.
r	The mailer accepts an -r flag from trusted users.
S	Don't reset the userid before calling the mailer.
s	Strip quotes off of the address before calling the mailer.
U	The mailer wants Unix-style From: lines.
u	Preserve uppercase in usernames.
X	Prepend a dot to lines beginning with a dot.
x	The mailer wants a Full-Name: header line.

See Chapter 10 for examples of mailer flag declaration within mailer definitions.

The sendmail K Command

The sendmail K command is used to define a database within the *sendmail.cf* file. The K command syntax is:

> K*name type* [*arguments*]

Chapter 10 provides examples of defining and using a sendmail database, and it describes the K command syntax. This appendix lists the valid *type* values and *arguments* that can be used with a K command.

The type field of the K command identifies what kind of database is being defined. There are several internal database types that are specific to sendmail, and several external types that rely on external database libraries. Support for the external database types must be compiled into sendmail by explicitly specifying the supported database types using the confMAPDEF command in a *devtools/OS* or *devtools/Site* file used by Build to compile sendmail. See the example of compiling sendmail earlier in this appendix.

The possible values for *type* are:

dbm

> The "new dbm" database format. It is accessed using the ndbm(3) library. Only supported if sendmail is compiled with NDBM defined.

btree

> The btree database format. It is accessed using the Berkeley db(3) library. Only supported if sendmail is compiled with NEWDB defined.

hash

> The hash database format. It is accessed using the Berkeley db(3) library. Only supported if sendmail is compiled with NEWDB defined.

nis

> NIS server lookups. sendmail must be compiled with NIS defined to support this.

nisplus

> NIS+ server lookups. sendmail must be compiled with NISPLUS defined to support this.

hesiod

> MIT hesiod server lookups. Support requires that sendmail is compiled with HESIOD defined.

ldap

> Searches using LDAP. sendmail must be compiled with LDAPMAP defined to support this. sendmail supports most of the standard command-line arguments of the ldapsearch program.

netinfo

> NeXT NetInfo lookups. Only supported if sendmail is compiled with NETINFO defined.

text

> Text file lookups. Requires no external database libraries or compile options. The format of the text database is defined with the key field, value field, and field delimiter flags. See the next section for a description of the K command flags.

ph

> CCSO Nameserver lookups.

program

> Queries are passed to an external program for resolution.

stab

> An internal symbols table database.

implicit

> The default internal sendmail format used for an alias file, if no type is defined for the file.

user

> A special sendmail type used to verify the existence of a user by using getpwnam(3).

host
> A special sendmail type used to convert nicknames and IP addresses to canonical names via the domain name server. This is an alternative form of the $[name]$ syntax.

sequence
> A special sendmail type used to define the order in which previously defined databases are searched. For example, assume that three databases (file1, file2, and file3) are defined by K commands. It is possible to add a fourth K command, Kallfiles sequence file3 file1 file2, that "combines" them together as *allfiles* and specifies that file3 is searched first, file1 second, and file2 third.

switch
> A special sendmail type that uses the service switch file to set the order in which database files are searched. The *argument* on a K command with a *type* of "switch" must be the name of a service in the service switch file. The values associated with the service name in the service switch file are used to create the names of databases that are searched in the order in which they are defined. For example, the command Kali switch aliases looks up the service switch entry for aliases. If it contains the value nis files, sendmail searches databases named *ali.nis* and *ali.files* in that order.

dequote
> A special sendmail type used to strip unwanted double quotes (") from email addresses.

arith
> An internal routine used for doing specific arithmetic functions.

bestmx
> An internal routine that retrieves the MX record for a host.

dns
> An internal routine that retrieves the address for a hostname.

null
> An internal routine that returns "Not found" for all lookups.

regex
> An internal routine that handles regular expressions.

Many of the possible type values do not refer to real databases. Several types are special values used only inside sendmail. Some refer to internal sendmail routines that are accessed from rewrite rules using the same syntax that would be used to access a database.

The argument that follows most of the real database types is a filename. The filename identifies the external file that contains the database. Only the basic filename is provided. sendmail adds an extension appropriate for the database type. For example, `Krealname dbm /usr/etc/names` becomes *lusr/etc/names.db* because *.db* is the correct extension for dbm databases.

In addition to a filename, the arguments field can contain optional flags:

-o

> This is an optional database. sendmail proceeds without error if the file is not found.

-N

> Valid database keys are terminated with a NULL character.

-O

> Valid database keys are never terminated with a NULL character. Never specify both -N and -O, which indicates that no keys are valid! It is safest to avoid both -N and -O and let sendmail determine the correct key structure unless you are positive about the correct flag.

-a*x*

> Append the string *x* to the value returned by a successful match.

-f

> Do not convert uppercase to lowercase before attempting to match the key.

-m

> Check that the key exists in the database, but do not replace the key with the value returned by the database.

-k*keycol*

> The location of the key within a database entry. For most databases, the key is the first field and this flag is not needed. For text file lookups, this flag is required and *keycol* is the column number in which the key begins.

-v*valcol*

> The location of the value within a database entry. For most databases, the value follows the key and the -v flag is not used. For text file lookups, this flag is required and specifies the column in which the value field begins.

-z*delim*

> The character that delimits fields within the database. By default, it is whitespace.

-t

> Allow database lookups that depend on remote servers to fail instead of queuing the mail for later processing. This is primarily used when you have DNS server problems. Normally, when a remote server fails to respond, the mail is put in the queue for later delivery. Setting this flag causes the mail to be immediately returned to the sender as undeliverable.

-s*spacesub*

> Use *spacesub* to replace space characters after processing an address against the dequote database.

-A

Accept values from duplicate keys. Most databases do not allow duplicate keys.

-q

Preserve any quotes contained in the key. Normally quotes are removed.

The full lists of database types and flags provided in this appendix will help you understand the K commands inserted into the *sendmail.cf* file by the m4 processor. Your own K commands will be much simpler. You will stick with a database type that is supported by your sendmail and makemap commands, and you will build simple databases designed to fulfill specific purposes. Chapter 10 provides examples of such databases, and the next section contains some simple scripts used to build those example databases.

Sample script

In Chapter 10, the *realnames* database is used to rewrite login usernames to the "firstname dot lastname" format for outbound email. The script shown below builds the *realnames* database from the */etc/passwd* file.

```
#! /bin/sh
#
# Eliminate "non-login" accounts
grep -v ':*:' /etc/passwd | \
# Eliminate "exposed" usernames, i.e. usernames defined
#  in class E as names that should not be re-written
grep -v ' root:' | \
# Replace delimiting colons with whitespace
sed 's/:/ /g' | \
# Output the username followed by firstname.lastname
awk '{ print $1, $5"."$6 }' > realnames
# Build the realnames database
makemap dbm realnames < realnames
```

Building *realnames* from the *passwd* file is completely dependent on the format of that file. The *passwd* file *must* have a consistent format for the GECOS field and a consistent way to identify a "non-user" account. A "non-user" account is not accessed by a user to log in or to collect email. It is normally a system account used by system or application software. A classic example is the *uucp* account. Every system has some way to mark that these accounts are not used for user logins. Some systems use an asterisk in the password field, while others use an exclamation mark, the letters NP, an x, or something else. The sample script assumes that an asterisk is used, which is the case on my Linux system. (My Solaris system uses an x.) Print out your *passwd* file to find out what it uses and modify the script accordingly.

The sample script also assumes that the first two values in the GECOS field are the user's first and last names separated by a blank. If the beginning of the GECOS field is in any other format, the script produces garbage. The procedure you use to add new users to your system should produce a consistent GECOS field. Inconsistency is the enemy of automation. The sample below shows a file that has inconsistencies, and the bad data it produces:

```
% cat /etc/passwd
root:oRd1L/vMzzxno:0:1:System Administrator:/:/bin/csh
nobody:*:65534:65534::/:
daemon:*:1:1::/:
sys:*:2:2::/:/bin/csh
bin:*:3:3::/bin:
uucp:*:4:8::/var/spool/uucppublic:
news:*:6:6::/var/spool/news:/bin/csh
ingres:*:7:7::/usr/ingres:/bin/csh
audit:*:9:9::/etc/security/audit:/bin/csh
craig:1LrpKlz8sYjw:198:102:Craig Hunt:/home/craig:/bin/csh
dan:RSU.NYlKuFqzh2:214:885:Dan Scribner:/home/dan:/bin/csh
becca:monfTHdnjj:101:102:"Becky_Hunt":/home/becca:/bin/csh
dave:lniuhugfds:121:885:David H. Craig:/home/dave:/bin/csh
kathy:TUVigddehh:101:802:Kathleen S McCafferty:/home/kathy:/bin/csh
% build.realnames
% cat realnames
craig Craig.Hunt
dan Dan.Scribner
becca "Becky_Hunt"./home/becca
dave David.H.   kathy Kathleen.S
```

Your *passwd* file may have grown over time under the control of several different system administrators. It may be full of inconsistencies. If it is, clean it up before you run the script to build email aliases, and then maintain it consistently.

Solaris httpd.conf File

The web server configuration described in Chapter 11 is based on the default *httpd. conf* file delivered with Solaris 8. That file is listed in its entirety in this appendix for those readers who want to see the complete configuration and examples of the individual directives described in Chapter 11.

Lines that begin with # are comments. Many of the comments describe the function and syntax of individual configuration directives. Use the comments as an additional source of information about the directives covered in Chapter 11.

The complete contents of the Solaris 8 *httpd.conf* file are listed here.

```
#
# Based upon the NCSA server configuration files originally by Rob McCool.
#
# This is the main Apache server configuration file.  It contains the
# configuration directives that give the server its instructions.
# See <URL:http://www.apache.org/docs/> for detailed information about
# the directives.
#
# Do NOT simply read the instructions in here without understanding
# what they do.  They're here only as hints.  If you are unsure
# consult the online docs. You have been warned.
#
# After this file is processed, the server will look for and process
# /etc/apache/srm.conf and then /etc/apache/access.conf
# unless you have overridden these with ResourceConfig and/or
# AccessConfig directives here.
#
# The configuration directives are grouped into three basic sections:
#  1. Directives that control the operation of the Apache server process
#     as a whole (the 'global environment').
#  2. Directives that define the parameters of the 'main' or 'default'
#     server, which responds to requests that aren't handled by a virtual
#     host. These directives also provide default values for the settings
#     of all virtual hosts.
#  3. Settings for virtual hosts, which allow Web requests to be sent to
#     different IP addresses or hostnames and have them handled by the
#     same Apache server process.
```

```
#
# Configuration and logfile names: If the filenames you specify for many
# of the server's control files begin with "/" (or "drive:/" for Win32),
# the server will use that explicit path.  If the filenames do *not* begin
# with "/", the value of ServerRoot is prepended -- so "logs/foo.log"
# with ServerRoot set to "/usr/local/apache" will be interpreted by the
# server as "/usr/local/apache/logs/foo.log".
#

### Section 1: Global Environment
#
# The directives in this section affect the overall operation of Apache,
# such as the number of concurrent requests it can handle or where it
# can find its configuration files.
#

#
# ServerType is either inetd, or standalone.  Inetd mode is only supported
# on Unix platforms.
#
ServerType standalone

#
# ServerRoot: The top of the directory tree under which the server's
# configuration, error, and log files are kept.
#
# NOTE!  If you intend to place this on an NFS (or otherwise network)
# mounted filesystem then please read the LockFile documentation
# (available at <URL:http://www.apache.org/docs/mod/core.html#lockfile>);
# you will save yourself a lot of trouble.
#
# Do NOT add a slash at the end of the directory path.
#
ServerRoot "/var/apache"

#
# The LockFile directive sets the path to the lockfile used when Apache
# is compiled with either USE_FCNTL_SERIALIZED_ACCEPT or
# USE_FLOCK_SERIALIZED_ACCEPT. This directive should normally be left at
# its default value. The main reason for changing it is if the logs
# directory is NFS mounted, since the lockfile MUST BE STORED ON A LOCAL
# DISK. The PID of the main server process is automatically appended to
# the filename.
#
#LockFile /var/apache/logs/accept.lock

#
# PidFile: The file in which the server should record its process
# identification number when it starts.
#
PidFile /var/run/httpd.pid

#
# ScoreBoardFile: File used to store internal server process information.
```

```
# Not all architectures require this.  But if yours does (you'll know
# because this file will be  created when you run Apache) then you *must*
# ensure that no two invocations of Apache share the same scoreboard file.
#
ScoreBoardFile /var/run/httpd.scoreboard


#
# In the standard configuration, the server will process this file,
# srm.conf, and access.conf in that order.  The latter two files are
# now distributed empty, as it is recommended that all directives
# be kept in a single file for simplicity.  The commented-out values
# below are the built-in defaults.  You can have the server ignore
# these files altogether by using "/dev/null" (for Unix) or
# "nul" (for Win32) for the arguments to the directives.
#
#ResourceConfig /etc/apache/srm.conf
#AccessConfig /etc/apache/access.conf


#
# Timeout: The number of seconds before receives and sends time out.
#
Timeout 300


#
# KeepAlive: Whether or not to allow persistent connections (more than
# one request per connection). Set to "Off" to deactivate.
#
KeepAlive On


#
# MaxKeepAliveRequests: The maximum number of requests to allow
# during a persistent connection. Set to 0 to allow an unlimited amount.
# We recommend you leave this number high, for maximum performance.
#
MaxKeepAliveRequests 100


#
# KeepAliveTimeout: Number of seconds to wait for the next request from
# the same client on the same connection.
#
KeepAliveTimeout 15


#
# Server-pool size regulation.  Rather than making you guess how many
# server processes you need, Apache dynamically adapts to the load it
# sees --- that is, it tries to maintain enough server processes to
# handle the current load, plus a few spare servers to handle transient
# load spikes (e.g., multiple simultaneous requests from a single
# Netscape browser).
#
# It does this by periodically checking how many servers are waiting
# for a request.  If there are fewer than MinSpareServers, it creates
# a new spare.  If there are more than MaxSpareServers, some of the
# spares die off.  The default values are probably OK for most sites.
```

```
#
MinSpareServers 5
MaxSpareServers 10

#
# Number of servers to start initially --- should be a reasonable ballpark
# figure.
#
StartServers 5

#
# Limit on total number of servers running, i.e., limit on the number
# of clients who can simultaneously connect --- if this limit is ever
# reached, clients will be LOCKED OUT, so it should NOT BE SET TOO LOW.
# It is intended mainly as a brake to keep a runaway server from taking
# the system with it as it spirals down...
#
MaxClients 150

#
# MaxRequestsPerChild: the number of requests each child process is
# allowed to process before the child dies.  The child will exit so
# as to avoid problems after prolonged use when Apache (and maybe the
# libraries it uses) leak memory or other resources.  On most systems,
# this isn't really needed, but a few do have notable leaks
# in the libraries. For these platforms, set to something like 10000
# or so; a setting of 0 means unlimited.
#
# NOTE: This value does not include keepalive requests after the initial
#       request per connection. For example, if a child process handles
#       an initial request and 10 subsequent "keptalive" requests, it
#       would only count as 1 request towards this limit.
#
MaxRequestsPerChild 0

#
# Listen: Allows you to bind Apache to specific IP addresses and/or
# ports, in addition to the default. See also the <VirtualHost>
# directive.
#
#Listen 3000
#Listen 12.34.56.78:80

#
# BindAddress: You can support virtual hosts with this option. This
# directive is used to tell the server which IP address to listen to. It
# can either contain "*", an IP address, or a fully qualified Internet
# domain name. See also the <VirtualHost> and Listen directives.
#
#BindAddress *

#
# Dynamic Shared Object (DSO) Support
#
```

```
# To be able to use the functionality of a module which was built as a DSO
# you have to place corresponding `LoadModule' lines at this location so
# the directives contained in it are actually available _before_ they are
# used. Please read the file README.DSO in the Apache 1.3 distribution for
# more details about the DSO mechanism and run `httpd -l' for the list of
# already built-in (statically linked and thus always available) modules
# in your httpd binary.
#
# Note: The order is which modules are loaded is important.  Don't change
# the order below without expert advice.
#
# Example:
# LoadModule foo_module libexec/mod_foo.so
LoadModule vhost_alias_module /usr/apache/libexec/mod_vhost_alias.so
LoadModule env_module         /usr/apache/libexec/mod_env.so
LoadModule config_log_module  /usr/apache/libexec/mod_log_config.so
LoadModule mime_magic_module  /usr/apache/libexec/mod_mime_magic.so
LoadModule mime_module        /usr/apache/libexec/mod_mime.so
LoadModule negotiation_module /usr/apache/libexec/mod_negotiation.so
LoadModule status_module      /usr/apache/libexec/mod_status.so
LoadModule info_module        /usr/apache/libexec/mod_info.so
LoadModule includes_module    /usr/apache/libexec/mod_include.so
LoadModule autoindex_module   /usr/apache/libexec/mod_autoindex.so
LoadModule dir_module         /usr/apache/libexec/mod_dir.so
LoadModule cgi_module         /usr/apache/libexec/mod_cgi.so
LoadModule asis_module        /usr/apache/libexec/mod_asis.so
LoadModule imap_module        /usr/apache/libexec/mod_imap.so
LoadModule action_module      /usr/apache/libexec/mod_actions.so
LoadModule speling_module     /usr/apache/libexec/mod_speling.so
LoadModule userdir_module     /usr/apache/libexec/mod_userdir.so
LoadModule alias_module       /usr/apache/libexec/mod_alias.so
LoadModule rewrite_module     /usr/apache/libexec/mod_rewrite.so
LoadModule access_module      /usr/apache/libexec/mod_access.so
LoadModule auth_module        /usr/apache/libexec/mod_auth.so
LoadModule anon_auth_module   /usr/apache/libexec/mod_auth_anon.so
LoadModule dbm_auth_module    /usr/apache/libexec/mod_auth_dbm.so
LoadModule digest_module      /usr/apache/libexec/mod_digest.so
LoadModule proxy_module       /usr/apache/libexec/libproxy.so
LoadModule cern_meta_module   /usr/apache/libexec/mod_cern_meta.so
LoadModule expires_module     /usr/apache/libexec/mod_expires.so
LoadModule headers_module     /usr/apache/libexec/mod_headers.so
LoadModule usertrack_module   /usr/apache/libexec/mod_usertrack.so
LoadModule unique_id_module   /usr/apache/libexec/mod_unique_id.so
LoadModule setenvif_module    /usr/apache/libexec/mod_setenvif.so
LoadModule perl_module        /usr/apache/libexec/libperl.so

#  Reconstruction of the complete module list from all available modules
#  (static and shared ones) to achieve correct module execution order.
#  [WHENEVER YOU CHANGE THE LOADMODULE SECTION ABOVE UPDATE THIS, TOO]
ClearModuleList
AddModule mod_vhost_alias.c
AddModule mod_env.c
AddModule mod_log_config.c
AddModule mod_mime_magic.c
```

```
AddModule mod_mime.c
AddModule mod_negotiation.c
AddModule mod_status.c
AddModule mod_info.c
AddModule mod_include.c
AddModule mod_autoindex.c
AddModule mod_dir.c
AddModule mod_cgi.c
AddModule mod_asis.c
AddModule mod_imap.c
AddModule mod_actions.c
AddModule mod_speling.c
AddModule mod_userdir.c
AddModule mod_alias.c
AddModule mod_rewrite.c
AddModule mod_access.c
AddModule mod_auth.c
AddModule mod_auth_anon.c
AddModule mod_auth_dbm.c
AddModule mod_digest.c
AddModule mod_proxy.c
AddModule mod_cern_meta.c
AddModule mod_expires.c
AddModule mod_headers.c
AddModule mod_usertrack.c
AddModule mod_unique_id.c
AddModule mod_so.c
AddModule mod_setenvif.c
AddModule mod_perl.c


#
# ExtendedStatus controls whether Apache will generate "full" status
# information (ExtendedStatus On) or just basic information
# (ExtendedStatus Off) when the "server-status" handler is called. The
# default is Off.
#
#ExtendedStatus On

### Section 2: 'Main' server configuration
#
# The directives in this section set up the values used by the 'main'
# server, which responds to any requests that aren't handled by a
# <VirtualHost> definition.  These values also provide defaults for
# any <VirtualHost> containers you may define later in the file.
#
# All of these directives may appear inside <VirtualHost> containers,
# in which case these default settings will be overridden for the
# virtual host being defined.
#


#
# If your ServerType directive (set earlier in the 'Global Environment'
# section) is set to "inetd", the next few directives don't have any
# effect since their settings are defined by the inetd configuration.
```

```
# Skip ahead to the ServerAdmin directive.
#

#
# Port: The port to which the standalone server listens. For
# ports < 1023, you will need httpd to be run as root initially.
#
Port 80

#
# If you wish httpd to run as a different user or group, you must run
# httpd as root initially and it will switch.
#
# User/Group: The name (or #number) of the user/group to run httpd as.
#  . On SCO (ODT 3) use "User nouser" and "Group nogroup".
#  . On HPUX you may not be able to use shared memory as nobody, and the
#    suggested workaround is to create a user www and use that user.
#  NOTE that some kernels refuse to setgid(Group) or semctl(IPC_SET)
#  when the value of (unsigned)Group is above 60000;
#  don't use Group #-1 on these systems!
#
User nobody
Group nobody

#
# ServerAdmin: Your address, where problems with the server should be
# e-mailed.  This address appears on some server-generated pages, such
# as error documents.
#
ServerAdmin you@your.address

#
# ServerName allows you to set a host name which is sent back to clients
# for your server if it's different than the one the program would get
# (i.e., use "www" instead of the host's real name).
#
# Note: You cannot just invent host names and hope they work. The name you
# define here must be a valid DNS name for your host. If you don't
# understand this, ask your network administrator. If your host
# doesn't have a registered DNS name, enter its IP address here.
# You will have to access it by its address (e.g., http://123.45.67.89/)
# anyway, and this will make redirections work in a sensible way.
#
#ServerName new.host.name

#
# DocumentRoot: The directory out of which you will serve your
# documents. By default, all requests are taken from this directory, but
# symbolic links and aliases may be used to point to other locations.
#
DocumentRoot "/var/apache/htdocs"

#
# Each directory to which Apache has access, can be configured with
```

```
# respect to which services and features are allowed and/or disabled in
# that directory (and its subdirectories).
#
# First, we configure the "default" to be a very restrictive set of
# permissions.
#
<Directory />
    Options FollowSymLinks
    AllowOverride None
</Directory>

#
# Note that from this point forward you must specifically allow
# particular features to be enabled - so if something's not working as
# you might expect, make sure that you have specifically enabled it
# below.
#

#
# This should be changed to whatever you set DocumentRoot to.
#
<Directory "/var/apache/htdocs">

#
# This may also be "None", "All", or any combination of "Indexes",
# "Includes", "FollowSymLinks", "ExecCGI", or "MultiViews".
#
# Note that "MultiViews" must be named *explicitly* --- "Options All"
# doesn't give it to you.
#
    Options Indexes FollowSymLinks

#
# This controls which options the .htaccess files in directories can
# override. Can also be "All", or any combination of "Options",
# "FileInfo", "AuthConfig", and "Limit"
#
    AllowOverride None

#
# Controls who can get stuff from this server.
#
    Order allow,deny
    Allow from all
</Directory>

#
# UserDir: The name of the directory which is appended onto a user's home
# directory if a ~user request is received.
#
UserDir public_html

#
# Control access to UserDir directories.  The following is an example
# for a site where these directories are restricted to read-only.
```

```
#
#<Directory /home/*/public_html>
#    AllowOverride FileInfo AuthConfig Limit
#    Options MultiViews Indexes SymLinksIfOwnerMatch IncludesNoExec
#    <Limit GET POST OPTIONS PROPFIND>
#        Order allow,deny
#        Allow from all
#    </Limit>
#    <Limit PUT DELETE PATCH PROPPATCH MKCOL COPY MOVE LOCK UNLOCK>
#        Order deny,allow
#        Deny from all
#    </Limit>
#</Directory>

#
# DirectoryIndex: Name of the file or files to use as a pre-written HTML
# directory index.  Separate multiple entries with spaces.
#
DirectoryIndex index.html

#
# AccessFileName: The name of the file to look for in each directory
# for access control information.
#
AccessFileName .htaccess

#
# The following lines prevent .htaccess files from being viewed by
# Web clients.  Since .htaccess files often contain authorization
# information, access is disallowed for security reasons.  Comment
# these lines out if you want Web visitors to see the contents of
# .htaccess files.  If you change the AccessFileName directive above,
# be sure to make the corresponding changes here.
#
# Also, folks tend to use names such as .htpasswd for password
# files, so this will protect those as well.
#
<Files ~ "^\.ht">
    Order allow,deny
    Deny from all
</Files>

#
# CacheNegotiatedDocs: By default, Apache sends "Pragma: no-cache" with
# each document that was negotiated on the basis of content. This asks
# proxy servers not to cache the document. Uncommenting the following line
# disables this behavior, and proxies will be allowed to cache the
# documents.
#
#CacheNegotiatedDocs

#
# UseCanonicalName:  (new for 1.3)  With this setting turned on, whenever
# Apache needs to construct a self-referencing URL (a URL that refers back
```

```
# to the server the response is coming from) it will use ServerName and
# Port to form a "canonical" name.  With this setting off, Apache will
# use the hostname:port that the client supplied, when possible.  This
# also affects SERVER_NAME and SERVER_PORT in CGI scripts.
#
UseCanonicalName On


#
# TypesConfig describes where the mime.types file (or equivalent) is
# to be found.
#
TypesConfig /etc/apache/mime.types


#
# DefaultType is the default MIME type the server will use for a document
# if it cannot otherwise determine one, such as from filename extensions.
# If your server contains mostly text or HTML documents, "text/plain" is
# a good value.  If most of your content is binary, such as applications
# or images, you may want to use "application/octet-stream" instead to
# keep browsers from trying to display binary files as though they are
# text.
#
DefaultType text/plain


#
# The mod_mime_magic module allows the server to use hints from the
# contents of the file itself to determine its type.  The MIMEMagicFile
# directive tells the module where the hint definitions are located.
# mod_mime_magic is not part of the default server (you have to add
# it yourself with a LoadModule [see the DSO paragraph in the 'Global
# Environment' section], or recompile the server and include
# mod_mime_magic as part of the configuration), so it's enclosed in an
# <IfModule> container. This means that the MIMEMagicFile directive will
# only be processed if the module is part of the server.
#
<IfModule mod_mime_magic.c>
    MIMEMagicFile /etc/apache/magic
</IfModule>


#
# HostnameLookups: Log the names of clients or just their IP addresses
# e.g., www.apache.org (on) or 204.62.129.132 (off).
# The default is off because it'd be overall better for the net if people
# had to knowingly turn this feature on, since enabling it means that
# each client request will result in AT LEAST one lookup request to the
# nameserver.
#
HostnameLookups Off


#
# ErrorLog: The location of the error log file.
# If you do not specify an ErrorLog directive within a <VirtualHost>
# container, error messages relating to that virtual host will be
# logged here.  If you *do* define an error logfile for a <VirtualHost>
```

```
# container, that host's errors will be logged there and not here.
#
ErrorLog /var/apache/logs/error_log


#
# LogLevel: Control the number of messages logged to the error_log.
# Possible values include: debug, info, notice, warn, error, crit,
# alert, emerg.
#
LogLevel warn


#
# The following directives define some format nicknames for use with
# a CustomLog directive (see below).
#
LogFormat "%h %l %u %t \"%r\" %>s %b \"%{Referer}i\" \"%{User-Agent}i\"" combined
LogFormat "%h %l %u %t \"%r\" %>s %b" common
LogFormat "%{Referer}i -> %U" referer
LogFormat "%{User-agent}i" agent


#
# The location and format of the access logfile (Common Logfile Format).
# If you do not define any access logfiles within a <VirtualHost>
# container, they will be logged here.  Contrariwise, if you *do*
# define per-<VirtualHost> access logfiles, transactions will be
# logged therein and *not* in this file.
#
CustomLog /var/apache/logs/access_log common


#
# If you would like to have agent and referer logfiles, uncomment the
# following directives.
#
#CustomLog /var/apache/logs/referer_log referer
#CustomLog /var/apache/logs/agent_log agent


#
# If you prefer a single logfile with access, agent, and referer
# information (Combined Logfile Format) you can use the following
# directive.
#
#CustomLog /var/apache/logs/access_log combined


#
# Optionally add a line containing the server version and virtual host
# name to server-generated pages (error documents, FTP directory listings,
# mod_status and mod_info output etc., but not CGI generated documents).
# Set to "EMail" to also include a mailto: link to the ServerAdmin.
# Set to one of:  On | Off | EMail
#
ServerSignature On


#
# Aliases: Add here as many aliases as you need (with no limit). The
```

```
# format is    Alias fakename realname
#
# Note that if you include a trailing / on fakename then the server will
# require it to be present in the URL.  So "/icons" isn't aliased in this
# example, only "/icons/"..
#
Alias /icons/ "/var/apache/icons/"

<Directory "/var/apache/icons">
    Options Indexes MultiViews
    AllowOverride None
    Order allow,deny
    Allow from all
</Directory>

Alias /manual/ "/usr/apache/htdocs/manual/"

#
# ScriptAlias: This controls which directories contain server scripts.
# ScriptAliases are essentially the same as Aliases, except that
# documents in the realname directory are treated as applications and
# run by the server when requested rather than as documents sent to the
# client. The same rules about trailing "/" apply to ScriptAlias
# directives as to Alias.
#
ScriptAlias /cgi-bin/ "/var/apache/cgi-bin/"

#
# "/var/apache/cgi-bin" should be changed to whatever your ScriptAliased
# CGI directory exists, if you have that configured.
#
<Directory "/var/apache/cgi-bin">
    AllowOverride None
    Options None
    Order allow,deny
    Allow from all
</Directory>

#
# Redirect allows you to tell clients about documents which used to exist
# in your server's namespace, but do not anymore. This allows you to tell
# the clients where to look for the relocated document.
# Format: Redirect old-URI new-URL
#

#
# Directives controlling the display of server-generated directory
# listings.
#

#
# FancyIndexing is whether you want fancy directory indexing or standard
#
```

```
IndexOptions FancyIndexing

#
# AddIcon* directives tell the server which icon to show for different
# files or filename extensions.  These are only displayed for
# FancyIndexed directories.
#
AddIconByEncoding (CMP,/icons/compressed.gif) x-compress x-gzip

AddIconByType (TXT,/icons/text.gif) text/*
AddIconByType (IMG,/icons/image2.gif) image/*
AddIconByType (SND,/icons/sound2.gif) audio/*
AddIconByType (VID,/icons/movie.gif) video/*

AddIcon /icons/binary.gif .bin .exe
AddIcon /icons/binhex.gif .hqx
AddIcon /icons/tar.gif .tar
AddIcon /icons/world2.gif .wrl .wrl.gz .vrml .vrm .iv
AddIcon /icons/compressed.gif .Z .z .tgz .gz .zip
AddIcon /icons/a.gif .ps .ai .eps
AddIcon /icons/layout.gif .html .shtml .htm .pdf
AddIcon /icons/text.gif .txt
AddIcon /icons/c.gif .c
AddIcon /icons/p.gif .pl .py
AddIcon /icons/f.gif .for
AddIcon /icons/dvi.gif .dvi
AddIcon /icons/uuencoded.gif .uu
AddIcon /icons/script.gif .conf .sh .shar .csh .ksh .tcl
AddIcon /icons/tex.gif .tex
AddIcon /icons/bomb.gif core

AddIcon /icons/back.gif ..
AddIcon /icons/hand.right.gif README
AddIcon /icons/folder.gif ^^DIRECTORY^^
AddIcon /icons/blank.gif ^^BLANKICON^^

#
# DefaultIcon is which icon to show for files which do not have an icon
# explicitly set.
#
DefaultIcon /icons/unknown.gif

#
# AddDescription allows you to place a short description after a file in
# server-generated indexes.  These are only displayed for FancyIndexed
# directories.
# Format: AddDescription "description" filename
#
#AddDescription "GZIP compressed document" .gz
#AddDescription "tar archive" .tar
#AddDescription "GZIP compressed tar archive" .tgz

#
```

```
# ReadmeName is the name of the README file the server will look for by
# default, and append to directory listings.
#
# HeaderName is the name of a file which should be prepended to
# directory indexes.
#
# The server will first look for name.html and include it if found.
# If name.html doesn't exist, the server will then look for name.txt
# and include it as plaintext if found.
#
ReadmeName README
HeaderName HEADER


#
# IndexIgnore is a set of filenames which directory indexing should ignore
# and not include in the listing.  Shell-style wildcarding is permitted.
#
IndexIgnore .??* *~ *# HEADER* README* RCS CVS *,v *,t


#
# AddEncoding allows you to have certain browsers (Mosaic/X 2.1+)
# uncompress information on the fly. Note: Not all browsers support this.
# Despite the name similarity, the following Add* directives have nothing
# to do with the FancyIndexing customization directives above.
#
AddEncoding x-compress Z
AddEncoding x-gzip gz tgz


#
# AddLanguage allows you to specify the language of a document. You can
# then use content negotiation to give a browser a file in a language
# it can understand.  Note that the suffix does not have to be the same
# as the language keyword --- those with documents in Polish (whose
# net-standard language code is pl) may wish to use "AddLanguage pl .po"
# to avoid the ambiguity with the common suffix for perl scripts.
#
AddLanguage en .en
AddLanguage fr .fr
AddLanguage de .de
AddLanguage da .da
AddLanguage el .el
AddLanguage it .it


#
# LanguagePriority allows you to give precedence to some languages
# in case of a tie during content negotiation.
# Just list the languages in decreasing order of preference.
#
LanguagePriority en fr de


#
# AddType allows you to tweak mime.types without actually editing it, or
# to make certain files to be certain types.
#
```

```
# For example, the PHP3 module (not part of the Apache distribution - see
# http://www.php.net) will typically use:
#
#AddType application/x-httpd-php3 .php3
#AddType application/x-httpd-php3-source .phps

AddType application/x-tar .tgz

#
# AddHandler allows you to map certain file extensions to "handlers",
# actions unrelated to filetype. These can be either built into the server
# or added with the Action command (see below)
#
# If you want to use server side includes, or CGI outside
# ScriptAliased directories, uncomment the following lines.
#
# To use CGI scripts:
#
#AddHandler cgi-script .cgi

#
# To use server-parsed HTML files
#
#AddType text/html .shtml
#AddHandler server-parsed .shtml

#
# Uncomment the following line to enable Apache's send-asis HTTP file
# feature
#
#AddHandler send-as-is asis

#
# If you wish to use server-parsed imagemap files, use
#
#AddHandler imap-file map

#
# To enable type maps, you might want to use
#
#AddHandler type-map var

#
# Action lets you define media types that will execute a script whenever
# a matching file is called. This eliminates the need for repeated URL
# pathnames for oft-used CGI file processors.
# Format: Action media/type /cgi-script/location
# Format: Action handler-name /cgi-script/location
#

#
# MetaDir: specifies the name of the directory in which Apache can find
# meta information files. These files contain additional HTTP headers
# to include when sending the document
```

```
#
#MetaDir .web

#
# MetaSuffix: specifies the file name suffix for the file containing the
# meta information.
#
#MetaSuffix .meta

#
# Customizable error response (Apache style)
#   these come in three flavors
#
#     1) plain text
#ErrorDocument 500 "The server made a boo boo.
#  n.b.  the (") marks it as text, it does not get output
#
#     2) local redirects
#ErrorDocument 404 /missing.html
#  to redirect to local URL /missing.html
#ErrorDocument 404 /cgi-bin/missing_handler.pl
#  N.B.: You can redirect to a script or a document using
#  server-side-includes.
#
#     3) external redirects
#ErrorDocument 402 http://some.other_server.com/subscription_info.html
#  N.B.: Many of the environment variables associated with the original
#  request will *not* be available to such a script.

#
# The following directives modify normal HTTP response behavior.
# The first directive disables keepalive for Netscape 2.x and browsers
# that spoof it. There are known problems with these browsers.
# The second directive is for Microsoft Internet Explorer 4.0b2
# which has a broken HTTP/1.1 implementation and does not properly
# support keepalive when it is used on 301 or 302 (redirect) responses.
#
BrowserMatch "Mozilla/2" nokeepalive
BrowserMatch "MSIE 4\.0b2;" nokeepalive downgrade-1.0 force-response-1.0

#
# The following directive disables HTTP/1.1 responses to browsers which
# are in violation of the HTTP/1.0 spec by not being able to grok a
# basic 1.1 response.
#
BrowserMatch "RealPlayer 4\.0" force-response-1.0
BrowserMatch "Java/1\.0" force-response-1.0
BrowserMatch "JDK/1\.0" force-response-1.0

#
# Allow status reports with the URL of http://servername/server-status
# Change the ".your_domain.com" to match your domain to enable.
#
#<Location /server-status>
```

```
#     SetHandler server-status
#     Order deny,allow
#     Deny from all
#     Allow from .your_domain.com
#</Location>


#
# Allow remote server configuration reports, with the URL of
#  http://servername/server-info (requires that mod_info.c be loaded).
# Change the ".your_domain.com" to match your domain to enable.
#
#<Location /server-info>
#     SetHandler server-info
#     Order deny,allow
#     Deny from all
#     Allow from .your_domain.com
#</Location>


#
# There are reports of people trying to abuse an old bug from pre-1.1
# days.  This bug involved a CGI script distributed as a part of Apache.
# By uncommenting these lines you can redirect these attacks to a logging
# script on phf.apache.org.  Or, you can record them yourself, using the
# script support/phf_abuse_log.cgi.
#
#<Location /cgi-bin/phf*>
#     Deny from all
#     ErrorDocument 403 http://phf.apache.org/phf_abuse_log.cgi
#</Location>


#
# Proxy Server directives. Uncomment the following lines to
# enable the proxy server:
#
#<IfModule mod_proxy.c>
#ProxyRequests On
#
#<Directory proxy:*>
#     Order deny,allow
#     Deny from all
#     Allow from .your_domain.com
#</Directory>


#
# Enable/disable the handling of HTTP/1.1 "Via:" headers.
# "Full" adds the server version; "Block" removes outgoing Via: headers
# Set to one of: Off | On | Full | Block
#
#ProxyVia On


#
# To enable the cache as well, edit and uncomment the following lines:
# (no cacheing without CacheRoot)
#
```

```
#CacheRoot "/var/apache/proxy"
#CacheSize 5
#CacheGcInterval 4
#CacheMaxExpire 24
#CacheLastModifiedFactor 0.1
#CacheDefaultExpire 1
#NoCache a_domain.com another_domain.edu joes.garage_sale.com

#</IfModule>
# End of proxy directives.

### Section 3: Virtual Hosts
#
# VirtualHost: If you want to maintain multiple domains/hostnames on your
# machine you can setup VirtualHost containers for them.
# Please see the documentation at <URL:http://www.apache.org/docs/vhosts/>
# for further details before you try to setup virtual hosts.
# You may use the command line option '-S' to verify your virtual host
# configuration.

#
# If you want to use name-based virtual hosts you need to define at
# least one IP address (and port number) for them.
#
#NameVirtualHost 12.34.56.78:80
#NameVirtualHost 12.34.56.78

#
# VirtualHost example:
# Almost any Apache directive may go into a VirtualHost container.
#
#<VirtualHost ip.address.of.host.some_domain.com>
#     ServerAdmin webmaster@host.some_domain.com
#     DocumentRoot /www/docs/host.some_domain.com
#     ServerName host.some_domain.com
#     ErrorLog logs/host.some_domain.com-error_log
#     CustomLog logs/host.some_domain.com-access_log common
#</VirtualHost>

#<VirtualHost _default_:*>
#</VirtualHost>

#<IfModule mod_perl.c>
#
#<Location /perl-status>
#     SetHandler perl-script
#     PerlHandler Apache::Status
#     order deny,allow
#     deny from all
#     allow from yourhost
#</Location>
#
#</IfModule>
```

RFC Excerpts

Chapter 13 refers to specific TCP/IP headers that are documented here. This is not an exhaustive list of headers; only the headers used in the troubleshooting examples in Chapter 13 are covered:

- IP Datagram Header, as defined in RFC 791, *Internet Protocol*
- TCP Segment Header, as defined in RFC 793, *Transmission Control Protocol*
- ICMP Parameter Problem Message Header, as defined in RFC 792, *Internet Control Message Protocol*

Each header is presented using an excerpt from the RFC that defines the header. These are not exact quotes; the excerpts have been slightly edited to better fit this text. However, the importance of using primary sources for troubleshooting protocol problems is still emphasized. These headers are provided here to help you follow the examples in Chapter 13. For real troubleshooting, use the real RFCs. You can obtain your own copies of the RFCs by following the instructions at the end of this appendix.

IP Datagram Header

This description is taken from pages 11 to 15 of RFC 791, *Internet Protocol*.

```
Internet Header Format

 0                   1                   2                   3
 0 1 2 3 4 5 6 7 8 9 0 1 2 3 4 5 6 7 8 9 0 1 2 3 4 5 6 7 8 9 0 1
+-+-+-+-+-+-+-+-+-+-+-+-+-+-+-+-+-+-+-+-+-+-+-+-+-+-+-+-+-+-+-+-+
|Version|  IHL  |Type of Service|          Total Length         |
+-+-+-+-+-+-+-+-+-+-+-+-+-+-+-+-+-+-+-+-+-+-+-+-+-+-+-+-+-+-+-+-+
|         Identification        |Flags|      Fragment Offset    |
+-+-+-+-+-+-+-+-+-+-+-+-+-+-+-+-+-+-+-+-+-+-+-+-+-+-+-+-+-+-+-+-+
|  Time to Live |    Protocol   |        Header Checksum         |
+-+-+-+-+-+-+-+-+-+-+-+-+-+-+-+-+-+-+-+-+-+-+-+-+-+-+-+-+-+-+-+-+
|                        Source Address                         |
+-+-+-+-+-+-+-+-+-+-+-+-+-+-+-+-+-+-+-+-+-+-+-+-+-+-+-+-+-+-+-+-+
```

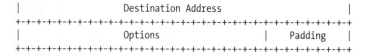

```
|                     Destination Address                     |
+-+-+-+-+-+-+-+-+-+-+-+-+-+-+-+-+-+-+-+-+-+-+-+-+-+-+-+-+-+-+-+-+
|                    Options                    |    Padding   |
+-+-+-+-+-+-+-+-+-+-+-+-+-+-+-+-+-+-+-+-+-+-+-+-+-+-+-+-+-+-+-+-+
```

Version: 4 bits

   The Version field indicates the format of the internet header.
   This document describes version 4.

IHL: 4 bits

   Internet Header Length is the length of the internet header in 32
   bit words. The minimum value for a correct header is 5.

Type of Service: 8 bits

   The Type of Service indication the quality of service desired.
   The meaning of the bits is explained below.

      Bits 0-2: Precedence.
      Bit   3: 0 = Normal Delay,   1 = Low Delay.
      Bits   4: 0 = Normal Throughput, 1 = High Throughput.
      Bits   5: 0 = Normal Reliability 1 = High Reliability.
      Bit 6-7: Reserved for Future Use.

         0   1   2   3   4   5   6   7
      +-----+-----+-----+-----+-----+-----+-----+-----+
      | | | | | | |
      | PRECEDENCE | D | T | R | 0 | 0 |
      | | | | | | |
      +-----+-----+-----+-----+-----+-----+-----+-----+

         Precedence

            111 - Network Control
            110 - Internetwork Control
            101 - CRITIC/ECP
            100 - Flash Override
            011 - Flash
            010 - Immediate
            001 - Priority
            000 - Routine

Total Length: 16 bits

   Total Length is the length of the datagram, measured in octets
   (bytes), including internet header and data.

Identification: 16 bits

   An identifying value assigned by the sender to aid in assembling
   the fragments of a datagram.
```
```

Flags: 3 bits

   Various Control Flags. The Flag bits are explained below:

      Bit 0: reserved, must be zero
      Bit 1: (DF) 0 = May Fragment, 1 = Don't Fragment.
      Bit 2: (MF) 0 = Last Fragment, 1 = More Fragments.

        0   1   2
      +---+---+---+
      | | D | M |
      | 0 | F | F |
      +---+---+---+

Fragment Offset: 13 bits

   This field indicates where in the datagram this fragment belongs.
   The fragment offset is measured in units of 8 octets (64 bits).
   The first fragment has offset zero.

Time to Live: 8 bits

   This field indicates the maximum time the datagram is allowed to
   remain in the internet system.

Protocol: 8 bits

   This field indicates the Transport Layer protocol that the data
   portion of this datagram is passed to. The values for various
   protocols are specified in the "Assigned Numbers" RFC.

Header Checksum: 16 bits

   A checksum on the header only. Since some header fields change
   (e.g., time to live), this is recomputed and verified at each
   point that the internet header is processed. The checksum
   algorithm is:

      The checksum field is the 16 bit one's complement of the one's
      complement sum of all 16 bit words in the header. For purposes
      of computing the checksum, the value of the checksum field is
      zero.

Source Address: 32 bits

   The source IP address. See Chapter 2 for a
   description of IP addresses.

Destination Address: 32 bits

   The destination IP address. See Chapter 2 for a description of IP
   addresses.

Options: variable

The options may or may not appear in datagrams, but they must be implemented by all IP modules (host and gateways). No options were used in any of the datagrams examined in Chapter 13.

TCP Segment Header

This description is taken from pages 15 to 17 of RFC 793, *Transmission Control Protocol*.

TCP Header Format

```
    0                   1                   2                   3
    0 1 2 3 4 5 6 7 8 9 0 1 2 3 4 5 6 7 8 9 0 1 2 3 4 5 6 7 8 9 0 1
   +-+-+-+-+-+-+-+-+-+-+-+-+-+-+-+-+-+-+-+-+-+-+-+-+-+-+-+-+-+-+-+-+
   |          Source Port          |       Destination Port        |
   +-+-+-+-+-+-+-+-+-+-+-+-+-+-+-+-+-+-+-+-+-+-+-+-+-+-+-+-+-+-+-+-+
   |                        Sequence Number                        |
   +-+-+-+-+-+-+-+-+-+-+-+-+-+-+-+-+-+-+-+-+-+-+-+-+-+-+-+-+-+-+-+-+
   |                    Acknowledgment Number                      |
   +-+-+-+-+-+-+-+-+-+-+-+-+-+-+-+-+-+-+-+-+-+-+-+-+-+-+-+-+-+-+-+-+
   | Data |           |U|A|P|R|S|F|                                |
   | Offset| Reserved |R|C|S|S|Y|I|            Window              |
   |       |           |G|K|H|T|N|N|                                |
   +-+-+-+-+-+-+-+-+-+-+-+-+-+-+-+-+-+-+-+-+-+-+-+-+-+-+-+-+-+-+-+-+
   |           Checksum            |         Urgent Pointer        |
   +-+-+-+-+-+-+-+-+-+-+-+-+-+-+-+-+-+-+-+-+-+-+-+-+-+-+-+-+-+-+-+-+
   |                    Options                    |    Padding    |
   +-+-+-+-+-+-+-+-+-+-+-+-+-+-+-+-+-+-+-+-+-+-+-+-+-+-+-+-+-+-+-+-+
   |                             data                              |
   +-+-+-+-+-+-+-+-+-+-+-+-+-+-+-+-+-+-+-+-+-+-+-+-+-+-+-+-+-+-+-+-+
```

Source Port: 16 bits

  The source port number.

Destination Port: 16 bits

  The destination port number.

Sequence Number: 32 bits

  The sequence number of the first data octet (byte) in this segment (except when SYN is present). If SYN is present the sequence number is the initial sequence number (ISN) and the first data octet is ISN+1.

Acknowledgment Number: 32 bits

  If the ACK control bit is set, this field contains the value of the next sequence number the sender of the segment is expecting to receive. Once a connection is established this is always sent.

Data Offset: 4 bits

The number of 32 bit words in the TCP Header. This indicates
where the data begins. The TCP header (even one including options)
is an integral number of 32 bits long.

Reserved: 6 bits

Reserved for future use. Must be zero.

Control Bits: 6 single-bit values (from left to right):

  URG: Urgent Pointer field significant
  ACK: Acknowledgment field significant
  PSH: Push Function
  RST: Reset the connection
  SYN: Synchronize sequence numbers
  FIN: No more data from sender

Window: 16 bits

The number of data octets (bytes) the sender of this segment is
willing to accept.

Checksum: 16 bits

The checksum field is the 16 bit one's complement of the one's
complement sum of all 16 bit words in the header and text.

Urgent Pointer: 16 bits

This field contains the current value of the urgent pointer as a
positive offset from the sequence number in this segment. The
urgent pointer points to the sequence number of the octet
following the urgent data. This field is only be interpreted
in segments with the URG control bit set.

Options: variable

Options may occupy space at the end of the TCP header and are a   multiple of 8
bits in length.

ICMP Parameter Problem Message Header

This description is taken from pages 8 and 9 of RFC 792, *Internet Control Message
Protocol*.

Parameter Problem Message

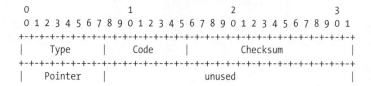

```
+-+-+-+-+-+-+-+-+-+-+-+-+-+-+-+-+-+-+-+-+-+-+-+-+-+-+-+-+-+-+-+-+
|       Internet Header + 64 bits of Original Data Datagram      |
+-+-+-+-+-+-+-+-+-+-+-+-+-+-+-+-+-+-+-+-+-+-+-+-+-+-+-+-+-+-+-+-+
```

Type

   12

Code

   0 = pointer indicates the error.

Checksum

   The checksum is the 16-bit ones's complement of the one's
   complement sum of the ICMP message starting with the ICMP Type.
   For computing the checksum , the checksum field should be zero.

Pointer

   If code = 0, identifies the octet where an error was detected.

Internet Header + 64 bits of Data Datagram

   The internet header plus the first 64 bits of the datagram that   elicited
this error response.

Retrieving RFCs

Throughout this book, we have referred to many RFCs. These are the Internet documents used for everything from general information to the definitions of the TCP/IP protocol standards. As a network administrator, there are several important RFCs that you'll want to read. This section describes how you can obtain them.

RFCs are available at *http://www.ietf.org*. Follow the RFC Pages link from that home page. The page that appears allows you to retrieve an RFC by specifying its number. The page also has links to the RFC Index and the RFC Editor Web Pages. The index is useful for general browsing. It helps you map RFC names to numbers, and it tells you when an RFC has been updated or replaced. Figure G-1 shows a network administrator scrolling through the index looking for RFC 1122.

Of even more interest are the RFC Editor Web Pages. Selecting this link takes you to *http://www.rfc-editor.org*, where you can select RFC Search and Retrieval. The page that is displayed provides access to a hyperlinked RFC index and to a search tool that allows you to look for RFC titles, numbers, authors, or keywords.

Assume you want to find out more about the SMTP service extensions that have been proposed for Extended SMTP. Figure G-2 shows the first page displayed as a result of this query.

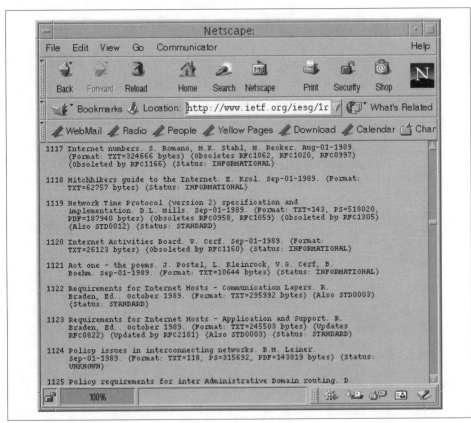

Figure G-1. The RFC index

The Web provides the most popular and best method for browsing through RFCs. However, if you know what you want, anonymous FTP can be a faster way to retrieve a specific document. RFCs are stored at *ftp.ietf.org* in the *rfc* directory. This stores the RFCs with filenames in the form *rfcnnnn.txt* or *rfcnnnn.ps*, where *nnnn* is the RFC number and *txt* or *ps* indicates whether the RFC is ASCII text or PostScript. To retrieve RFC 1122, FTP to *ftp.ietf.org* and enter get rfc/rfc1122.txt at the ftp> prompt. This is generally a very quick way to get an RFC if you know what you want.

Retrieving RFCs by Mail

While anonymous FTP is the fastest way and the Web is the best way to get an RFC, they are not the only ways. You can also obtain RFCs through electronic mail. Electronic mail is available to many users who are denied direct access to Internet services because they are on a nonconnected network or are sitting behind a restrictive firewall. Also, there are times when email provides sufficient service because you don't need the document quickly.

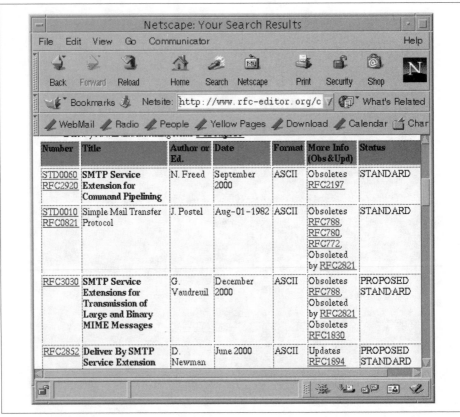

Figure G-2. An RFC web search

Retrieve RFCs through email by sending mail to *mailserv@ietf.org*. Leave the Subject: line blank. Request the RFC in the body of the email text, preceding the pathname of the RFC with the keyword FILE. In this example, we request RFC 1258.

```
% mail mailserv@ietf.org
Subject:
FILE /rfc/rfc1258.txt
^D
```

The technique works very well. In the time it took to type these paragraphs, the requested RFC was already in my mailbox.

Index

Symbols

! flag (Linux routing table), 39
? option (arp module), 110
(sharp sign)
    automounter comments, 251
    host table comments, 52
    inittab file comments, 126
$- symbol (sendmail pattern matching), 310
$@ symbol (sendmail pattern
          matching), 311
$ symbol (sendmail transformation), 313
$> symbol (sendmail transformation), 313

Numbers

7bit (MIME encoding type), 71
8bit (MIME encoding type), 71

A

A flag (Linux routing table), 39
-a option (exportfs command), 242
A records
    named.ca file, 220
    nslookup command, 229
ABORT keyword (chat), 499
ACCEPT keyword (iptables command), 431
access control
    Apache
        document level, 369
        file level, 369
        overview, 365
        user authentication, 366–369
    language extensions, 414

packet filtering, 427
security
    overview, 409
    shell command, 413
    tcpd, 410–413
    wrapper package, 409
    wrapper package, 409
    xinetd, 416–418
access.conf (Apache configuration file), 338
AccessFileName directive (Apache), 364
access_times parameter (xinetd), 417
acdirmax= option (vfstab file), 246
acdirmin= option (vfstab file), 246
Acknowledgment Number field (TCP
          headers), 20
Acknowledgment Segment (TCP
          headers), 21
acl statement (named.conf file), 551
aclok option (share command), 236
acquire (EGP trace option), 529
acquiring a neighbor (EGP), 189
acregmax= option (vfstab file), 246
acregmin= option (vfstab file), 246
actimeo= option (vfstab file), 246
action field (inittab file), 126
active keyword (routed command), 181
active-filter option (pppd), 487
add keyword (dbmmanage command), 368
add keyword (route command), 173
AddEncoding directive (httpd.conf file), 352
AddIcon directive (Apache), 351
AddIconByEncoding directive (Apache), 351
AddIconByType directive (Apache), 351
Additional (DNS response packets), 469

We'd like to hear your suggestions for improving our indexes. Send email to *index@oreilly.com*.

additional-from-auth parameter (named BIND 9 options statement), 560
additional-from-cache (named BIND 9 options statement), 560
AddLanguage directive (httpd.conf file), 352
AddModule directive (httpd.conf file), 343
  Solaris modules, 343
address argument (ifconfig command), 135
address blocks, 27
address conversion database (sendmail), 294
address field (chap-secrets file), 161
Address field (netstat command), 137
address option (share command), 238
address records, 576
address resolution, 43
Address Resolution Protocol (see ARP)
Address value (dhcpd option statement), 594
addresses, 4, 24
  assigning
    contiguous blocks, 33
    ifconfig command, 135
  bit masks, 27, 32
  broadcast, 26
  cache initialization file, 219–221
  CIDR, 33
  classes of, 30
  conversion database (sendmail), 294
  datagrams, 27
  default gateway, need for, 84
  default masks, identifying, 30
  DHCP, assigning, 79
  dynamic allocation, dhcpd.conf file, 275
  expected utilization rate, 90
  host, 30
    assigning, 93
  interpreting, 30
  IPv6, 34
  limited broadcast, 80
  loopback
    converting to localhost, 222
    localhost, 53
  martians (gated), 513
  multicast, 26
  natural mask, 30–32
  Network Access Layer, 12
  network growth, effect on addressing schemes, 32
  obtaining, 86–88
  official, assessing need for, 88–91
  overriding (sendmail), 606
  registries, obtaining from, 90
  reserved, 26
  resolution of, 43
  reverse domains, 92
  rewrite rules, testing (sendmail), 606
  routing tables, reducing size of, 33
  sendmail
    transformation databases, 329–332
    transforming, 311–316
  share command and, 238
  shortage of, 34
  spoofing, 87
  subnet mask, defining, 94, 97
  subnet masks
    creating, 28
    RFCs, 29
  subnets, 28–30
  timing out, 80
  translating
    forward-mapping zone files, 225–227
    reverse zone files, 223–225
    troubleshooting, 444–447
  translation, overview, 87
  unicast, 26
  uniqueness of, 86
  verifying (sendmail), 606
  (see also IP addresses)
address-list option (named), 554
address_match_list option (named), 554
AddType directive (httpd.conf file), 352
adduser keyword (dbmmanage command), 368
admin-c field (RIPE database), 93
adopts, 384
adv (gated), 509
Advanced Research Projects Agency (ARPA), 2
advanced router option (Linux kernel configuration), 118
advertise parameter (gated), 534
aero domain, 56
aggregate statement (gated), 545
Alias directive (httpd.conf file), 349
aliases
  hostnames, 53
  network services, 47
  sendmail, overview, 288
aliases database (sendmail), 606
aliases file, 64
  email addresses, 64
  NIS map, 268
  sendmail, location of, 288

aliases-nexthop (gated), 511
AliasFile option (sendmail), 302
ALL keyword (security), 411
All (Options directive setting), 363
Allow from directive (Directory
       containers), 366
allow keyword parameter (dhcpd), 593
allow-ip option (pppd), 487
allow-notify (named), 560
AllowOverride directive (Apache), 365
AllowOverride directives (Directory
       containers), 364
allow-query option (named), 556
allow-recursion option (named), 557
allow-transfer option (named), 557
also-notify option (named), 556
alternative (MIME data subtype), 71
always-reply-rfc1048 flag parameter
       (dhcpd), 593
amd command, 250
American Registry for Internet Numbers
       (ARIN), 91
anon=uid option (share command), 236
Answer (DNS response packets), 469
Apache
   access controls
      document level, 369
      file level, 369
      overview, 365
      user authentication, 366–369
   AllowOverride directive, 365
   conditional logging, 357
   configuring
      overview, 338
      Solaris, 339–341
   directives
      AccessFileName, 364
      AuthName, 366
      AuthType, 366
      BrowserMatch, 353
      configuration, 344
      directory indexing, 351
      DocumentRoot, 348
      Group, 347
      HostnameLookups, 353
      httpd process control, 346
      KeepAlive, 352
      KeepAliveTimeout, 352
      LogFileFormat, 354–357
      MaxKeepAliveRequests, 352
      MaxRequestsPerChild, 347
      MaxSpareServer, 347
      MinSpareServer, 346
      performance tuning, 352–353
      Require, 367
      StartServer, 347
      Timeout, 353
      User, 347
   directory indexes, 351
   directory-level configuration control, 364
   DocumentRoot directive, 340
   DSO modules, 342
   encryption, 370–378
   httpd processes, managing, 346
   httpd.conf file
      configuration directives, 344
      dynamically loadable
         modules, 342–344
      overview, 341
   installing, overview, 334–336
   launching
      daemons at bootup, 336
      without rebooting, 336
   MIME file types, defining, 351
   monitoring, 378
   multi-homed servers, options, 360
   obtaining, 337
   OpenSSL, 370
   packages, locating names of, 335
   proxy servers, caching options, 359
   security
      CGI scripts, 361
      overview, 361
      SSI, 362
   server options, controlling, 363–364
   virtual hosts, defining, 360
Applicability Statements (AS), 5
Application Layer, 22
   OSI Model, 8
application (MIME data content type), 70
applications
   port numbers, 22
   protocols for, 46
   security
      removing unnecessary, 402
      updating, 402
architecture
   Internet routing, 35–37
   TCP/IP models, 9–11
area auth simple parameter (gated), 522
area parameter
   gated isis statement, 522
   gated ospf statement, 516
areas (OSPF hierarchy), 185

arguments
    gated command, 504
    ifconfig command, 135
    sendmail command, 287, 604–609
    sendmail K command, 658
arguments field (inet.conf file), 131
Argv field (sendmail), 306
arith (sendmail K command value), 657
ARP (Address Resolution Protocol), 43
    enabling and disabling, 146
arp command, 43
    troubleshooting with, 444–447
arp, diagnostic troubleshooting, 439
arp module, options, 110
ARPA (Advanced Research Projects
        Agency), 2
ARPAnet, 2
AS (Applicability Statements), 5
AS (autonomous system), 36
AS (gated), 512
as parameter (gated), 546
AS path (routing policies), 541
ASCII, MIME encoding, 71
Asian Pacific Network Information Center
        (APNIC), 91
ASNs (autonomous system numbers)
    obtaining, 99
    routing databases, registering, 100
aspath parameter (gated), 546
aspppd command (Solaris), 164
asymmetric encryption, 419
Asynchronous PPP Daemon (aspppd), 164
asyncmap option (pppd), 487
at command, security considerations, 405
ATTEMPT option (xinetd), 417
attempts option (resolv.conf file), 210
audio (MIME data content type), 71
auth option (pppd), 160, 487
    configuring PPP servers, 163
authentication, 387
    Apache, 366–369
        document-level access controls, 369
        file-level access controls, 369
    dedicated connections and, 153
    OSPF, 188
    protocols, pppd command, 160
    shadow password files, 388–391
    share command, 237
    ssh, 400
AuthName directive (Apache), 366
auth-nxdomain option (named), 555
authoritative parameter (dhcpd), 592

authoritative servers, 60
    DNS, 54
Authority (DNS response packets), 469
AuthType directive (Apache), 366
autofs script, 250
auto_home map, 251
auto_master file, configuration, 250
automatically allocating addresses
        (DHCP), 79
automounter (NFS), 249
    configuration files, 250
    daemon, 250
autonomous system external (ASE)
        routes, 201
autonomous system numbers (see ASNs)
autonomous systems (AS), 36
autonomoussystem (gated), 513

B

B flag (Linux routing table), 39
backbone parameter (gated), 516
backbones (OSPF hierarchy), 185
background mode (sendmail), 606
background parameter (gated), 536
base64 (MIME encoding type), 72
basic (MIME data subtype), 71
bastion host (firewalls), 427
beep command (dip), 481
Berkeley Internet Name Domain (see BIND)
Best Current Practices (BCP) RFCs, 6
bestmx (sendmail K command value), 657
bg option (vfstab file), 246
BGP (Border Gateway Protocol), 36, 190
    autonomous system numbers, 99
    group types, 526
    peers, 525
bgp parameter (gated), 546
bgp statement (gated), 524
bilateral agreements (routing), 37
binary data, 70
binary files, security considerations, 405
binary (MIME encoding type), 72
BIND (Berkeley Internet Name
        Domain), 207, 210
    BIND 9
        controls statement, 568
        logging statement, 563
        options statement, 559
        server statement, 553
        view statement, 568
        zone statement, 566

caching-only servers, configuring, 212
configurations, 206
directives, 218
master name, configuring, 214
named command, configuring, 211
named.conf file, 212
overview, 205
slave, configuring, 215
Unix DNS, 60
BindAddress option (multi-homed
        servers), 360
bit mask, 32
    addresses, 27
    routing tables, 40
bitdomain (sendmail database feature), 628
biz domain, 56
blackhole (gated), 512
blackhole option (named), 557
blackhole parameter (gated), 538
Boolean values (printcap file), 253
BOOTP (Bootstrap Protocol), 78
    clients, automatic address
            assignment, 276
    DHCP, 78
bootp command (dip), 481
BOOTPROTO (Linux configuration
        value), 142
Bootstrap Protocol (see BOOTP)
bootup
    Apache daemons, launching, 336
    ifconfig command-line, persistence
        of, 149
    mounted directories and, 245
    share command persistence, 238
    Solaris, 108
    (see also startup files)
Border Gateway Protocol (see BGP)
break command (dip), 481
brief parameter (gated), 546
broadcast address argument (ifconfig
        command), 135
broadcast addresses, 26
    assigning, ifconfig command, 144
BROADCAST flag (ifconfig command), 140
broadcast (gated), 512
broadcast GRE over IP option (Linux kernel
        configuration), 119
BROADCAST (Linux configuration
        value), 142
broadcast parameter (gated)
    rip statement, 519
    routerdiscovery statement, 534
browseable parameter (smb.config file), 263

BrowserMatch directive (Apache), 353
BSD Unix
    configuration file, 120
        devices statement, 122
        options statement, 121
        pseudo-device statement, 121
    default configuration, overriding, 149
    fstab files, 245
    startup files, 124
    static routing, adding to startup
            scripts, 177
bsdcomp option (pppd), 487
btree (sendmail K command value), 656
buffer overruns, avoiding, 148
Bugtraq web site, 385
Build script, sendmail, compiling, 600
byte numbering, synchronizing, 20

C

C command (sendmail), 300
C flag (Linux routing table), 39
cable testers, 438
cables (Ethernet), length restrictions, 95
cache initialization file, 219–221
CacheDefaultExpire option (proxy server
        caching), 360
CacheGcInterval option (proxy server
        caching), 359
CacheLastModifiedFactor option (proxy
        server caching), 359
CacheMaxExpire option (proxy server
        caching), 359
CacheNegotiatedDocs option (proxy server
        caching), 359
CacheRoot option (proxy server
        caching), 359
caches
    DNS, 55
    dump files
        cache & data section, 462–465
        hints section, 465–467
        zone tables, 461
    name servers, troubleshooting, 460
    proxy servers, options, 359
    routing tables, 40
CacheSize option (proxy server caching), 359
caching-only servers, 60, 207
    configuration, 212
    configuration files, 222
Caldera Linux httpd.conf file, location, 338
call option (pppd), 487
cannot connect error (SMTP), 64

canonical names, 227
CANONIFY_DOMAIN macro
        (sendmail), 610
CANONIFY_DOMAIN_FILE macro
        (sendmail), 610
CAs (Certificate Authorities), 377
cat command (gpg), 423
category clause (named logging
        statement), 562
cdtrcts option (pppd), 487
CERT (Computer Emergency Response
        Team) web site, 385
certificates, 372
    CAs, 377
    validity of, 375
cf/cf directory (sendmail sample
        configuration files), 291
CGI (Common Gateway Interface), security
        considerations, 361
changed field (RIPE database), 93
CHAP (Challenge Handshake Authentication
        Protocol), 160
chap-interval option (pppd), 487
chap-max-challenge option (pppd), 487
chap-restart option (pppd), 487
chap-secrets file, 160
Charset field (sendmail), 307
chat, 501
    escape sequences, 500
    keywords, 499
    options, 498
    overview, 497
    syntax, 498
    termination code, 502
chat command, 159
chat scripts, PPP, 158
chatkey command (dip), 482
check keyword (dbmmanage
        command), 368
check-names option (named), 556
checksums, TCP, 19
chkconfig command (Apache), 336
CIDR (Classless Inter-Domain Routing), 33
class (DSN error code), 315
class field (resource records), 571
classes
    IP addresses, 30
    sendmail, 300, 640
        E, 322
        M, 322
        P, 320
        w, 319

classful routing, 182
Classless Inter-Domain Routing (CIDR), 33
cleaning-interval option (named), 558
ClearModuleList directive (httpd.conf
        file), 342
client field (chap-secrets file), 161
clients, NFS, 234
CLOSE command (IMAP), 69
CNAME (Canonical Name) records, 579
    forward-mapping zone files, 227
Collis field (netstat command), 137
com domain, 56
commands
    IMAP, 67
    POP, 66
    SMTP, 62
        source code, 63
comment parameter (smb.config file), 263
comments
    automounter configuration file, 251
    host table, 52
    inittab file, 126
Common Gateway Interface (see CGI)
communications, OSI Model, 6–9
compiler options, sendmail, 601
compiling
    dhcpd, 586
    sendmail, 599–604
conditionals, sendmail macros, 300
config command (dip), 482
configuration
    Apache
        overview, 338
        Solaris, 339–341
    auto_master file, 250
    automounter, 250
    BIND, 206
    caching-only servers, 212
    DHCP
        dhcpd file, 273–277
        overview, 272
    dip (dial-up IP), 154
    DNS, resource records, 216
    email networks, 106
    files, Unix startup, 124
    gated, 193–195
        exterior gateways, 199–202
        host, 196
        interior gateways, 197–199
        samples, 195
        testing, 202–203

httpd.conf file
  directives, 344
  dynamically loadable
    modules, 342–344
  overview, 341
ifconfig startup files, 149
IMAP servers, 282
information, distributing, 106
interfaces, Linux file locations, 141
kernel
  dynamically loadable
    modules, 109–114
  overview, 108
Line Printer, 256
Linux kernel, 115
  Ethernet, 117
  help, 117
  options, 117
loopback interface, Solaris, 138
macro configuration file, 636
master name servers, 214
named command, 211
NFS, exports file, 239–242
options, 117
POP servers, 281
PPP
  chat scripts, 158
  dial-up connections, 154–158
  servers, 162–163
  Solaris, 163
pppd command, dedicated
    connections, 153
printcap file, 252–255
resolvers, 207
  sample, 210
routing, 171
Samba name server, 266
Samba servers, 259–263
sendmail
  define class command, 300
  define macro command, 299
  headers command, 304
  m4 macros, 609–614
  mailers command, 305
  overview, 297
  precedence command, 303
  set option command, 302
  set ruleset command, 317
  testing, 606
  trusted users command, 303
  version level command, 298

sendmail.cf file, 637
  creating with m4 macros, 291–295
  local information, 319–322
  modifying, 319
  Options section, 322
  overview, 290
  samples, 290
  structure, 295
  testing, 323–326
  testing rewrite rules, 326–329
slave servers, 215
startup files, static routing and, 177
system, planning, 84
configuration commands (named.conf
    file), 212
configuration files
  BSD Unix, 120
    devices statement, 122
    options statement, 121
    pseudo-device statement, 121
  Solaris, 109
    syslog.conf, 53
configuration servers
  DHCP, 78
  overview, 76
  RARP, 77
connect option (pppd), 488
connect option (pppd command), 159
connect-delay option (pppd), 488
connected networks, 85
connection-orientation, TCP, 19
connections
  point-to-point, defining with ifconfig
    command, 148
  troubleshooting with ping
    command, 440, 441
Content-Transfer-Encoding header
    (MIME), 71
Content-Type header (MIME), 70
control script (system initialization), 128
control statements (gated), 539
controls statement (named command), 567
coop domain, 56
core gateways, 35
coresize option (named), 558
cost
  address translation, 87
  Internet connection considerations, 85
  routing, 179
  routing metric, 147
counting to infinity problem (routing), 181
  avoiding, 183

cron command, security considerations, 405
crtscts option (pppd), 488
crtscts option (pppd command), 153
   configuring PPP servers, 163
Cybercop (automated system
        monitoring), 408
cyrus mailer, 637

D

D command (sendmail), 299
D flag (Linux routing table), 38
DAEMON_OPTIONS macro
        (sendmail), 612
DARPA (Defense Advanced Research
        Projects Agency), 2
DATA command (SMTP), 63
data delivery, 24
data field (resource records), 571
Data Link Layer (OSI Model), 9
Data Link Layer Protocol, 152
data value (DNS resource records), 217
databases
   address conversion (sendmail), 294
   Apache, user authentication, 367
   gpg, 422
   sendmail
      address transformation, 316, 329–332
      local information section
         (configuration file), 321
   Unix r commands, 396
databits command (dip), 482
datagrams, 10, 27
   forwarding, 16
   fragmenting, 15
   headers, 47, 679–682
      protocol numbers, 45
   martians, 87
   Network Access Layer
      IP addresses, 12
   overview, 13
   routing, 14
   (see also packets)
datasize option (named), 558
dbm (sendmail K command value), 655
dbmmanage command, 368
DCA (Defense Communications Agency), 2
DDN (Defense Data Network), 2
DDNS (Dynamic DNS), 80
deallocate-on-exit option (named), 555
debug option (pppd), 488
debug option (resolv.conf file), 209

debugging
   nslookup tool, 228–232
   sendmail arguments, 607
   (see also testing)
dec command (dip), 482
decentralized network administration, 28
--decrypt option (gpg), 423
dedicated connections, pppd command,
        configuring, 153
default command (dip), 482
default domain names, 59
default gateway, 41
   address, 84
   addresses, need for, 84
default keyword (route command), 173
default masks, indentifying, 30
default route (network addresses), 26
default-asyncmap option (pppd), 488
defaultdomain file, 269
DefaultIcon directive (Apache), 351
default-lease-time parameter (dhcp.conf
        file), 274
default-lease-time parameter (dhcpd), 591
defaultmetric parameter (gated), 519
default-mru option (pppd), 488
defaultroute option (pppd), 153, 488
defaults parameter (gated), 515
DefaultType directive (httpd.conf file), 351
Defense Advanced Research Projects Agency
        (DARPA), 2
Defense Communications Agency (DCA), 2
Defense Data Network (DDN), 2
define class command (sendmail), 300
define macro command (sendmail), 299
define macro (sendmail), 611, 614–625
definition fields (sendmail mailers), 305
deflate option (pppd), 488
DEL command (POP), 66
DELETE command (IMAP), 69
delete keyword
   dbmmanage command, 368
   route command, 173
deleting email, POP servers, 66
Delivery Status Notification (see DSN)
demand option (pppd), 488
denial of service (DoS), 383
Deny from directive (Directory
        containers), 365
deny keyword parameter (dhcpd), 593
depmod command (Linux), 113
dequote (sendmail K command value), 657
descr field (RIPE database), 93

designated routers (OSPF), 187
Destination Address
  datagram headers, 14
  TCP headers, 27
Destination field
  Linux routing table, 38, 40
  routing tables, 172
Destination Port, 22
Destination Port numbers (UDP), 18
Destination Unreachable Message
    (ICMP), 17
destination values (routing tables), 40
detail
  DSN error code, 315
  gated trace statements, 508
dev/cua3 argument (pppd command), 153
device drivers
  Ethernet, loading, 113
  installing, pkgadd command, 109
DEVICE (Linux configuration value), 142
devices statement (BSD Unix kernel
    configuration), 122
dgram field (inet.conf file), 130
dh value (share command), 237
DHCP (Dynamic Host Configuration
    Protocol), 78
  dhcpd file, 273–277
  operational principles, 80
  overview, 272
  system configuration information,
    distributing to end-users, 106
dhcpd
  command-line options, 588
  common options, 594
  compiling, 586
  mailing list, 587
  option statement, 593
  other options, 595–598
  parameter statements, 591
  syntax, 588
dhcpd.conf file, 273, 589
  parameters, 274
  range parameter, 275
  topology statements, 590
DHCPDISCOVER packet, 80
DHCPOFFER packet, 81
dial command (dip), 156, 482
dial-up connections, 153
  dip
    sample script file, 484
    script file, 480–484
    syntax, 479

PPP, configuring, 154–158
  pppd, syntax, 486
  scripts, troubleshooting, 168
dial-up IP (see dip)
dialup option (named), 555
dig (debugging tool), 467–471
digest (MIME data subtype), 71
Dijkstra Shortest Path First (SPF)
    algorithm, 185
dip command, 158
dip (dial-up IP)
  configuring, 154
  options, 479
  sample script file, 484
  script file, 480–484
  syntax, 479
direct delivery (SMTP), 64
direct map configuration file
    (automounter), 250
directed graphs (OSPF), 185
directives
  Apache
    configuration, 344
    directory-level configuration
      control, 365
    httpd process control, 346
    log files, 354–357
    MIME file types, 351
    performance tuning, 352–353
    user authentication, 366
    web server document locations, 348
  BIND, 218
  httpd.conf file, configuration, 344
  zone files, creating, 569
directories
  Apache, configuration control, 364
  indexing, Apache, 351
Directory containers (Apache), 348–351
  server options, controlling, 363–364
Directory directive (httpd.conf file), 348
Directory field (sendmail), 307
directory option (named), 555
directory sharing
  mounting remote directories, 243
  NFS
    daemons, 234
    overview, 233
  Samba, 263
  Unix, 235
DirectoryIndex option (Apache), 350
disconnect option (pppd), 488
distance-vector algorithms, routing, 178

Distfiles, 279
distributed servers, managing, 277
divert macro (sendmail), 609
dmesg command, network interfaces,
      determining avaliable, 136
dnl command, 291
dnl macro (sendmail), 609
DNS (Domain Name System), 22
   authoritative servers, 54
   BIND
      configurations, 206
      configuring resolvers, 207, 210
      directives, 218
      overview, 205
   caching-only servers, configuring, 212
   compared to NIS, 61
   domain hierarchy, 55
   domains, creating, 57
   host tables and, 53
   master name servers, configuring, 214
   name server record pointers, 58
   named command, configuring, 211
   named.conf file, 212
   overview, 54
   resource records, 216
   slave servers, configuring, 215
   system configuration, 84
   top-level domains, 55
   Unix, BIND, 60
dns proxy option (nmbd command), 266
dns proxy parameter (smb.config file), 262
dns (sendmail K command value), 657
documentation, Internet address
      requests, 90
DocumentRoot directive (Apache), 340
   web server document locations, 348
domain administration, 61
domain auth simple parameter (gated), 522
domain entry (resolv.conf file), 208
domain field (RIPE database), 93
DOMAIN macro (sendmail), 610
Domain Name Pointer (PTR) records, 580
domain name registrars, 57
domain name servers, system
      configuration, 84
Domain Name System (see DNS)
domain names, 59
   obtaining, 101
   registering, 102
domain names (Linux), 239
domain option (pppd), 488

domain option (share command), 238
domain setting (smb.config file), 261
DOMAIN source file
   DNS features, 635
   DNS macros, 635
DOMAIN source file (sendmail), 631
domainname command, 269
domains
   cache initialization file, 219–221
   caching-only server, 207
   DNS
     creating, 57
     hierarchy, 55
     top-level, 55
   downloading for inspection, nslookup
      command, 231
   in-addr.arpa, 92
   master name server, 206
   NIS, 269
   slave server, 207
   zones, 206
domaintable (sendmail database
      feature), 627
DoS (denial of service), 383
dotted decimal notation (IP addresses), 25
down preference (gated), 512
draft standards (RFCs), 5
Driver Options field (printconf-gui), 254
DROP keyword (iptables command), 431
dsmtp mailer, 292
DSN (Delivery Status Notification), error
      codes, 315
DSO (Dynamic Shared Object), 342
dump files
   cache & data section, 462–465
   hints section, 465–467
   zone tables, 461
dumpdb command, 461
dump-file option (named), 555
DURATION option (xinetd), 416
dynamic address allocation, dhcpd.conf
      file, 275
dynamic assignment, 94
Dynamic DNS (DDNS), 80
Dynamic Host Configuration Protocol (see
      DHCP)
dynamic routing, 171
dynamic routing tables, 97
Dynamic Shared Object (DSO), 342
dynamically allocated ports, 49
dynamically assigning addresses, 79

dynamically loadable modules, 109–114
    httpd.conf file, 342–344
dynamic-bootp argument (dhcpd range
        parameter), 276
dynamic-bootp-lease-cutoff parameter, 276
    dhcpd, 592
dynamic-bootp-lease-length parameter, 276
    dhcpd, 592

E

echo command (dip), 482
Echo Message (ICMP), 17
edu domain, 56
EGP (Exterior Gateway Protocol), 36, 189
    trace options, 529
egp statement (gated), 529
EHLO command (ESMTP), 72
elective protocols, 5
email
    copies, sending (sendmail), 609
    deleting, POP servers, 66
    delivery status notification
            (sendmail), 608
    encapsulated messages, 71
    IMAP, 67–69
    logging (sendmail), 608
    MIME, 69–74
    POP, 65–67
    queue processing time, 287
        sendmail, 606
    services, planning, 105
    SMTP, 62–65
    (see also sendmail)
encapsulation
    email messages, 71
    Network Access Layer, 12
    OSI layers, 10
encoding
    binary data (MIME), 72
    text data (MIME), 72
encrypt passwords option (smb.config
        file), 262
encryption, 418
    Apache, 370–378
    public key, 419
        stunnel, 423–425
        tools, 421–423
    symmetric, 420
end users, system configuration information,
        distributing to, 106
End-of line field (sendmail), 307

endpoint option (pppd), 489
end-to-end routes, 43
enterprise networks, 85
environment variables,
        LOCALDOMAIN, 208
equal-cost multi-path routing (OSPF), 188
equivalent hosts, 396
error codes (DSN), 315
error detection, 13
error messages
    named command, 228
    Unreachable Port, 452
error parameter (gated), 533
error recovery, 13
errors
    dhcpd, when compiling, 587
    SMTP, cannot connect, 64
escape option (pppd), 488
escape sequences, chat, 500
ESMTP (Extended SMTP), 72
    private extensions, 74
esmtp mailer, 292
Ethernet
    addresses, 12
        translation, 43
        translation, troubleshooting, 444–447
    BSD Unix, support, 122
    device drivers
        loading, 113
        Red Hat 7.1, 113
    length restrictions, 95
    Linux kernel configuration, 117
    MTU, 148
    networks, 12
    packet fragmentation, 16
    promiscuous mode, enabling and
            disabling, 146
    Solaris, ifconfig command, 135
    subdividing segments, 448
ethers file, 77
    NIS map, 268
except (gated), 509
EXCEPT keyword (security), 412
ExecCGI (Options directive setting), 363
executable files, security considerations, 405
exit command (dip), 157, 482
EXIT option (xinetd), 417
expected utilization rate (IP addresses), 90
experimental protocols, 6
EXPN command
    ESMTP, 74
    SMTP, 64

export statement (gated), 539, 543–545
exportdefault parameter (gated), 530
export-defaults level parameter (gated), 522
export-defaults metric parameter
        (gated), 522
export-defaults metric-type parameter
        (gated), 522
exportfs command, 242
exporting directories (see directory sharing)
exportinterval parameter (gated), 516
exportlimit parameter (gated), 516
exports file
    exportfs command, 242
    NFS, 239–242
EXPOSED_USER macro (sendmail), 611,
        633
EXPUNGE command (IMAP), 69
Extended Internet Daemon (xinetd), 132
Extended SMTP (ESMTP), 72
    private extensions to, 74
ExtendedStatus option (httpd.conf file), 378
Exterior Gateway Protocol (see EGP)
exterior routing protocols
    BGP, 190
    EGP, 189
    gated sample configuration, 199–202
    overview, 188
external preference parameter (gated), 522
External-body (MIME data subtype), 71

F

F command (sendmail), 300
fake-iquery option (named), 556
FancyIndexing keyword, 351
fax mailer, 637
FEATURE macro (sendmail), 292, 610,
        625–629
features
    DOMAIN source file, 633
    sendmail, 625
FETCH command (IMAP), 69
fetch-glue option (named), 556
fg option (vfstab file), 246
file option (pppd), 489
file servers, 104
file sharing, 75
    mounting remote directories, 243
    NFS
        daemons, 234
        overview, 233
    Unix, 235
File Transfer Protocol (see FTP)

filename parameter (dhcpd), 591
FILES = (Distfiles), 280
Files directive (httpd.conf file), 348
files option (named), 558
filtering routers, 430
    iptables command, 430
FIN bit (TCP), 20
find command, locating httpd.conf file, 338
firewalls
    filtering routers, 430
    functions of, 428
    iptables command, 430
    overview, 425–428
FIRST (Forum of Incident Response and
        Security Teams), 385
fixed-address parameter (dhcpd), 592
Flag value (dhcpd option statement), 594
Flags field, 16
    Linux routing table, 38, 40
    routing tables, 172
    sendmail, 306
flash parameter (gated), 536
Flg field (netstat command), 138
flow control
    Acknowledgment Segment, 21
    ICMP, 17
flush command (dip), 156
FollowSymLinks (Options directive
        setting), 363
Format of Headers (generic-linux.cf
        section), 296
Forum of Incident Response and Security
        Teams (FIRST), 385
forward only option (named.conf file), 214
forward option (named), 556
forwarders option
    named options statement, 556
    named.conf file, 213
forwarding datagrams, 16
forwarding, sendmail, 289
forward-mapping zone file, 211, 225–227
FQDN (fully qualified domain name), 59
Fragmentation Offset field, 16
fragmenting datagrams, 15
frames, 10
    Network Access Layer, 12
FreeBSD, network interface support, 123
fstab files, 245
FTP (File Transfer Protocol), 22
    distributed servers, managing, 278
fully qualified domain name (FQDN), 59
FYI (For Your Information) RFCs, 6

G

G flag (Linux routing table), 38
gated
  aggregate statement, 545
  bgp statement, 524
  command-line arguments, 504
  command-line options, 503
  configuration language
    definition statements, 513
    directive statements, 506
    interface statements, 510–512
    options statements, 509
    overview, 506
    protocol statements, 514
    trace statements, 507
  configuration statements, 194
  configuring, 193–195
  control statements, 539
  egp statement, 529
  export statement, 539, 543–545
  generate statement, 547
  icmp statement, 532
  import statement, 539, 542
  isis statement, 521
  kernel statement, 535
  ospf statement, 514
  overview, 191
  preference values, 192
  redirect statement, 532
  rip statement, 518
  routerdiscovery client statement, 534
  routerdiscovery statement, 533
  routing filters, 540
  sample configurations
    exterior gateways, 199–202
    host, 196
    interior gateways, 197–199
    overview, 195
    testing, 202–203
  signal processing, 505
  smux statement, 531
  startup files, 203
  static statements, 537
  syntax, 503
gated.conf file, 193
gateway addresses, need for, 84
gateway argument (route command), 174
Gateway field (Linux routing table), 38, 40
gateway parameter (gated), 527, 531
Gateway to Gateway Protocol (GGP), 35

gateways, 14
  autonomous system numbers,
    obtaining, 99
  core, 35
  data delivery, 24
  default, 41
  exterior, gated sample
    configuration, 199–202
  interior, gated sample
    configuration, 197–199
  mail, 105
  routing, planning, 97–99
  routing tables, 37
    adding to, 173
  subnetting, advantages, 95
gateways file (Solaris), routed command, 180
gdc command, testing gated
    configurations, 203
gendefault (gated), 510
general (gated), 508
$GENERATE directive (zone files), 219, 570
  reverse domain delegations, 224
generate statement (gated), 547
GENERIC kernel file (BSD Unix), 120
Generic Routing Encapsulation (GRE), 119
generic-linux.cf, modifying
  local information, 319–322
  Options section, 322
  overview, 319
GENERICS_DOMAIN macro
    (sendmail), 610
GENERICS_DOMAIN_FILE macro
    (sendmail), 610
genericstable (sendmail), 294, 628
--gen-key option (gpg), 422
Genmask field (Linux routing table), 38, 40
geographic domains (DNS), 55
get command (dip), 156, 482
get-lease-hostnames (dhcpd), 275, 592
GGP (Gateway to Gateway Protocol), 35
GID (group ID)
  exports file, 240
  mapping users to, 241
Gigabit Ethernet switches, 448
global section (smb.conf file), 260
GNU Privacy Guard (gpg), 421
goto command (dip), 483
gov domain, 56
gpg (GNU Privacy Guard), 421
graphic images, still, 70
GRE (Generic Routing Encapsulation), 119

GRE tunnels over IP option (Linux kernel configuration), 119
grep command, troubleshooting routing, 450
group clause
  gated bgp statement, 526
  gated egp statement, 530
Group directive (Apache), 347
group statement (dhcpd), 590
group statements (dhcpd.config file), 277
group types (BGP), 526
grpid option (vfstab file), 246

H

H command (sendmail), 304
H flag (Linux routing table), 38
HACK macro (sendmail), 611
hand tools, hardware maintenance, 438
handshaking, 13, 19
  port numbers and, 49
HANGUP command (chat), 502
hard option (vfstab file), 246
hardware
  detecting, Solaris reconfigure file and, 109
  distance limitations, subnetting and, 95
  Linux, device driver installation, 113
  maintenance tools, 438
  network interfaces, identifying installed, 124
  OSI Physical Layer, 9
  subnetting and, 28
hardware parameter (dhcpd), 591
hash mark (#) for comments, 52
hash (sendmail K command value), 656
has-old-clients option (named), 556
HDLC (High-level Data Link Control), 152
Header (DNS response packets), 469
HeaderName directive (Apache), 351
headers
  datagrams, 13
    port numbers, 47
    protocol numbers, 45
  ICMP parameter problem, 683
  IP datagrams, 679–682
  MIME, 70
    Content-Transfer-Encoding, 71
  protocol stack, 10
  sendmail, 606
    H command, 304
    precedence, 304
  TCP segment, 19, 682

heartbeat-interval option (named), 558
hello command, 72
hello (EGP trace option), 529
Hello packets (OSPF), 187
Hello protocol, overview, 179
help
  dip, 155, 483
  Linux kernel configuration, 117
HELP command
  ESMTP, 74
  SMTP, 64
hesiod (sendmail K command value), 656
heterogeneous networks, 4
hide-password option (pppd), 489
High-level Data Link Control (HDLC), 152
high-volume end-user (organizational type), 89
HINFO (Host Information) records, 582
hints (cache initialization file), 219–221
historic protocols, 6
holdoff option (pppd), 489
holdtime parameter (gated), 527
home section (smb.conf file), 263
hop count, routing, 179
host addresses, assigning, 93
  (see also IP addresses)
Host Information (HINFO) records, 582
HOST option (xinetd), 416
host (sendmail K command value), 657
host statement (dhcpd), 590
host statements (dhcpd.config file), 276
host tables, 52–54
  limitations of, 54
hostname file (Solaris), 141
hostname option (share command), 237
HostnameLookups directive (Apache), 353
hostnames, 52
  aliases, 53
  canonical names, 227
  locating host tables, 52–54
  selecting, 103
  sendmail, class w, 319
  share command and, 237
hosts
  bastion, 427
  gated configuration, 196
  grouping, dhcpd.conf file, 277
  multi-homed, 14
  peers, 51
  routing tables, 37
  trusted, 396

values, exports file, 239
virtual (Apache), 360
HOSTS = (Distfiles), 280
hosts file, 52
    ifconfig command and, 135
    mask values, storing, 143
    NIS maps, 61, 268
hosts.allow file (security), 410–413
hosts.deny (security), 410–413
hosts.equiv file, security considerations, 396, 405
hosts.lpd file, security considerations, 405
host-statistics option (named), 556
htdocs directory (Solaris), 340
HTTP (Hypertext Transfer Protocol), 22
http (MIME data subtype), 71
http_core.c (DSO module), 342
httpd processes, managing, 346
httpd.conf (Apache configuration file), 338
    access controls
        document level controls, 369
        file level controls, 369
        overview, 365
        user authentication, 366–369
    configuration directives, 344
    directives
        configuration, 344
        MIME file types, 351
    dynamically loadable modules, 342–344
    location of, 338
    overview, 341
    server options, controlling, 363–364
    Solaris configuration, 339–341
    web server document locations, 348
httpd.conf file, 661–678
Hypertext Transfer Protocol (HTTP), 22

I flag (Linux routing table), 39
IANA (Internet Assigned Numbers
        Authority)
    address requests, 91
    protocol and port numbers, 45
ICANN (Internet Corporation for Assigned
        Names and Numbers)
    domain name registrars, 57
    domain names, registering, 101
ICMP (Internet Control Message
        Protocol), 17
    Echo Message, 17
    Redirect Message, 17
    Source Quench Message, 17

ICMP parameter problem header, 683
ICMP Redirect, 176
icmp statement (gated), 532
ICMP Unreachable Port message, 452
Identification field, 16
idle option (pppd), 489
IDRP (InterDomain Routing Protocol), 190
Ierrs field (netstat command), 137
IETF (Internet Engineering Task Force)
    IPv6, 33
    protocol development, 4
if command (dip), 483
Iface field (Linux routing table), 39
ifcfg file (Linux), 141
ifcfg-eth0 file (Linux), 144
ifconfig command, 77, 110
    arguments, 135
    ARP, enabling and disabling, 146
    broadcast addresses, assigning, 144
    diagnostic troubleshooting, 439
    Ethernet promiscuous mode, enabling and
        disabling, 146
    IP addresses, assigning, 141–142
    MTU, changing, 148
    network interfaces
        checking, 139
        determining available, 139
        enabling and disabling, 145
    overview, 134
    routing metric, changing, 146
    Solaris
        configuring PPP, 164
        Ethernet, 135
    startup files, 149
    subnet masks, assigning, 143–144
    troubleshooting with, 443
iflist (gated), 508
ignore parameter (gated), 534
IHL (Internet Header Length) field, 14
image (MIME data content type), 70
IMAP (Internet Message Access
        Protocol), 67–69
    commands, 67
    servers, configuring, 282
implicit (sendmail K command value), 656
import keyword (dbmmanage
        command), 368
import statement (gated), 539, 542
importdefault parameter (gated), 530
IN value (DNS resource records), 217
inactivity_timeout statement (Solaris
        PPP), 164

in-addr.arpa domains, 92
inc command (dip), 483
$INCLUDE directive (zone files), 218, 569
include files, gated, 506
Includes (Options directive setting), 364
IncludesNOEXEC (Options directive
        setting), 364
indefinite tokens (sendmail pattern
        matching), 310
indelay parameter (gated), 528
indexes, directory (Apache), 351
Indexes (Options directive setting), 364
index=file option (share command), 236
index.html file (Apache), 340
IndexIgnore directive (Apache), 351
IndexOptions directive (httpd.conf file), 351
indirect map configuration file
        (automounter), 250
ineligible parameter (gated), 534
inet6 option (resolv.conf file), 210
inet6 parameter (gated), 524
inetd, 129–132
inetd.conf file
    fields, 130
    NFS daemons, starting, 235
info domain, 56
info parameter (gated)
    icmp statement, 533
    kernel statement, 537
information disclosure (security risk), 382
informational RFCs, 6
init command (dip), 483
init script option (pppd), 489
init.d/httpd script (Apache), 336
Initial Sequence Number (ISN), 20
inittab file, runlevels and, 126
INPUT_MAIL_FILTER macro
        (sendmail), 612
insmod command (Linux), 112
--install option (rpm), 335
installation
    Apache, overview, 334–336
    PPP, 153
    sendmail, 603
int domain, 56
InterDomain Routing Protocol (IDRP), 190
interface argument (ifconfig command), 135
interface parameter
    gated isis statement, 523
    gated kernel statement, 537
    gated ospf statement, 517
    gated rip statement, 519
    gated static statements, 538

interface-interval option (named), 558
interfaces
    configuring
        checking, 139
        ifconfig command, 134
        troubleshooting, 443
    connectors (OSI Physical Layer), 9
    determining avaiable, 136–139
    enabling and disabling, ifconfig
        command, 145
    gated support, 510
    hardware, identifying installed, 124
    serial lines, overview, 150
interior routing protocols
    gated sample configuration, 197–199
    OSPF, 184
    overview, 178
    RIP, 179
    routed command, 180–184
Intermediate System to Intermediate System
        (see IS-IS)
internal classes, sendmail, 640
Internet, 36
    architecture, routing, 35–37
    growth of, 3
        effect on addressing schemes, 32
    history of, 2
    tier-one providers, 3
Internet Assigned Numbers Authority (see
        IANA)
Internet Control Message Protocol (see
        ICMP)
Internet Control Protocol (IPCP), 152
Internet Corporation for Assigned Names
        and Numbers (see ICANN)
Internet end user (organizational type), 88
Internet Engineering Task Force (see IETF)
Internet Header Length (IHL) field, 14
Internet Layer, 12
    ICMP, 17
    IP datagrams, 13
        forwarding, 16
        fragmenting, 15
        routing, 14
Internet Protocol (see IP)
Internet Routing Registry (see IRR)
Internet Service Providers (see ISPs)
Internet standards (RFCs), 5
intr option (vfstab file), 246
intranets, 85
    defined, 3
intruder detection, 404

IP addresses
  assigning
    contiguous blocks of, 33
    ifconfig command, 135, 141–142
  bit masks, 32
  broadcast, 26
    assigning, 144
  CIDR, 33
  classes, 30
  data delivery, 24
  datagrams, 27
  default masks, identifying, 30
  dotted decimal notation, 25
  expected utilization rate, 90
  hostnames, 52
    locating with dig, 468
  interpreting, 30
  IPv6, 34
  loopback, localhost, 53
  multicast, 26
  natural mask, 30–32
  network growth, effect on addressing
    schemes, 32
  nslookup and, 229
  obtaining, 27, 86–88
  official, assessing need for, 88–91
  pppd command and, 153
  registries, obtaining addresses from, 90
  resolution, 43
  reverse domains, 92
  routing tables, reducing size of, 33
  share command and, 238
  shortage of, 34
  structure, 27
  subnet masks
    assigning, 143–144
    creating, 28
    RFCs, 29
  subnets, 28–30
  translation
    forward-mapping zone files, 225–227
    overview, 87
    reverse zone files, 223–225
    troubleshooting, 444–447
  unicast, 26
  uniqueness of, 86
IP datagram header, 679–682
IP (Internet Protocol)
  datagrams, 13
  forwarding datagrams, 16
  fragmenting datagrams, 15
  overview, 13

  RFC 791, 51
  routing datagrams, 14
  versions, 12
ip module, ip_forwarding variable, 111
IPADDR (Linux configuration value), 142
IPCP (Internet Control Protocol), 152
ipcp-accept-local option (pppd), 489
ipcp-accept-remote option (pppd), 489
ipcp-max-configure option (pppd), 489
ipcp-max-failure option (pppd), 489
ipcp-max-terminate option (pppd), 489
ipcp-restart option (pppd), 489
ip_forwarding variable (ip module),
    configuring, 111
Ipkts field (netstat command), 137
ipparam option (pppd), 490
iptables command
    filtering routers, 430
    samples, 432
IPv4 flag (ifconfig command), 140
IPv6, 33, 34
    demand for, 35
    efficiency of, 34
ipv6 option (pppd), 490
ipv6cp-max-configure option (pppd), 490
ipv6cp-max-failure option (pppd), 490
ipv6cp-max-terminate option (pppd), 490
ipv6cp-restart option (pppd), 490
ipv6cp-use-ipaddr option (pppd), 490
ipv6cp-use-persistent option (pppd), 490
IRR (Internet Routing Registry), 36, 100
IRs (Internet Registries), address requests, 91
IS-IS (Intermediate System to Intermediate
    System), overview, 179
isis statement (gated), 521
ISN (Initial Sequence Number), 20
ISPs (Internet Service Providers), 3
    addresses, assigning, 27
    as organizational type, 89
ISS (automated system monitoring), 408

J

j macro (sendmail), inspecting, 320

K

K command (sendmail), 655–659
    address transformation, 317
kdebug option (pppd), 490
keep all parameter (gated), 528
KeepAlive directive (Apache), 352
KEEPALIVE messages (BGP), 190

keepalivesalways parameter (gated), 528
KeepAliveTimeout directive (Apache), 352
kernel
    configuration
        dynamically loadable
            modules, 109–114
        overview, 108
    configuring, Linux, 115, 117
    recompiling, 114
kernel level autoconfiguration (Linux kernel
        configuration), 118
kernel statement (gated), 535
kernel/drv directory, 110
Kernel/User netlink socket option (Linux
        kernel configuration), 117
key statement (named.conf file), 551
keywords
    chat, 499
    dbmmanage command, 368
    FancyIndexing, 351
    netmask, 143
    route command, 173
    (see also directives)
keyword/value pairs, ifconfig syntax, 135
KNOWN keyword (tcpd access
        control), 412
krb4 value (share command), 237
ktune option (pppd), 490

L

L flag (Linux routing table), 39
label field (inittab file), 126
lame-ttl option (named), 557
LanguagePriority directive (httpd.conf
        file), 352
laptop computers, as troubleshooting
        tool, 438
last command, security and, 406
layers
    OSI Model, 7
    TCP/IP models, 9–11
lcladdr parameter
    gated bgp statement, 527
    gated egp statement, 531
LCP (Link Control Protocol), 152
lcp-echo-failure option (pppd), 490
lcp-echo-interval option (pppd), 490
lcp-max-configure option (pppd), 490
lcp-max-failure option (pppd), 491
lcp-max-terminate option (pppd), 491
lcp-restart option (pppd), 491
ldap (sendmail K command value), 656

LDAPROUTE_DOMAIN macro
        (sendmail), 610
LDAPROUTE_DOMAIN_FILEmacro
        (sendmail), 610
leases, DHCP, 79
level parameter (gated), 522
lib/modules directory, 113
lifetime parameter (gated), 534
limited broadcast addresses, 80
limited use protocols, 5
Line Printer (LP), configuring, 256
Linelimit field (sendmail), 307
Link Control Protocol (LCP), 152
linkname option (pppd), 491
Link-State Advertisement (LSA), 187
link-state database (OSPF), 186
link-state protocols, 184
Linux
    broadcast addresses, setting, 145
    commands
        depmod, 113
        dmesg, 136
        insmod, 112
        lsmod, 112
        modprob, 112
        rmmod, 113
    domain names, 239
    Ethernet promiscuous mode, enabling and
            disabling, 146
    filesystem type, specifying, 244
    fstab files, 245
    ifcfg-eth0 file, 144
    interface configuration files, 141
    kernel configuration, 108, 115
        Ethernet, 117
        help, 117
        options, 117
    loadable modules, 111
    minicom, 166
    mount options, 248
    named.conf file, caching-only
            servers, 212
    netstat -in command output, 138
    network interfaces, checking status, 140
    NFS, exports file, 239–242
    NIS domains, 269
    NIS server, initializing, 269
    point-to-point connections, defining, 149
    printcap configuration tool, 254
    rc.local script, 129
    rc.sysinit script, 127
    routing cache, examining, 40

routing metric, changing, 147
routing tables, 38
    adding routes, 174
runlevels, 125
sendmail startup script, 287
serial ports, troubleshooting, 165
smb.config file, location, 259
static routing, adding to startup
        scripts, 177
Listen option (multi-homed servers), 360
listen-on option (named), 557
load printers parameter (smb.config
        file), 260
LoadModule directive (httpd.conf file), 342
Local Information (generic-linux.cf
        section), 296
Local Internet Registry (organizational
        type), 89
LOCAL keyword (security), 411
local mailer, 305
local option (pppd), 491
localas parameter
    gated bgp statement, 527
    gated egp statement, 530
LOCAL_CONFIG macro (sendmail), 612
LOCALDOMAIN environment variable, 208
LOCAL_DOMAIN macro (sendmail), 610
localhost, converting from loopback
        address, 222
localhost file, 211
local_IP_address:remote_IP_address option
        (pppd), 486
LOCAL_NET_CONFIG macro
        (sendmail), 612
LOCAL_RULE_n macro (sendmail), 612
LOCAL_RULESETS macro (sendmail), 612
LOCAL_USER
    m4 sendmail macro, 612
    sendmail macro, 632
Location directive (httpd.conf file), 348
lock option (pppd command), 160, 491
lockd command (NFS), 235
log file parameter (smb.config file), 261
log files
    Apache, conditional logging, 357
    Apache directives, 354
    monitoring, 404
    sendmail, 608
    share command, 236
    xinetd, 416
log option (share command), 236
logfd option (pppd), 491

logfile option (pppd), 491
LogFormat directive (Apache), 354–357
logging statement (named command), 561
loghost (Solaris hostname), 53
login activity, security considerations, 406
login option (pppd), 491
login scripts, PPP servers, configuring, 162
LOGOUT command (IMAP), 69
logupdown parameter (gated), 528
loopback addresses, 26
    converting to localhost, 222
    localhost, 53
    named.conf file, 213
    routing tables, 172
loopback interface (Solaris), configuring, 138
loopback route, 41
lp files, 256
lpadmin command, 256
lpd, 252
    printcap file, 252–255
lpq command, 256
lpr command, 76, 255
lprm command, 256
lpsystem command, 257
lp/Systems file, 257
LSA (Link-State Advertisement), 187
lsmod command (Linux), 112

M

M command (sendmail), 305
m configuration option (Linux kernel), 117
M flag (Linux routing table), 39
m4 macros
    sendmail compiler options, 601–603
    sendmail configuration files, 609–614
        creating, 291–295
macros
    configuration file, 636
    define, 614
    DNS, 635
    DOMAIN source file, 632
    FEATURE, 625
    m4, 609
    OSTYPE, 629
    sendmail, conditionals, 300
    sendmail.cf file, 638
mail gateways, 105
mail relay servers, sendmail features, 634
mail relays, 105
mail servers, 105
    IMAP servers, configuring, 282
    POP servers, configuring, 281

mail services, 62
  IMAP, 67–69
  MIME, 69–74
  POP, 65–67
  SMTP, 62–65
mail11 mailer, 637
Mailer Definitions (generic-linux.cf
      section), 296
mailer flags, sendmail, 654
MAILER macro (sendmail), 292, 611
MAILER source file, 636
MAILER_DEFINITIONS macro
      (sendmail), 611
mailers (sendmail), 292
  definition fields, 305
  definitions, 307
  M command, 305
mailertable (sendmail database feature), 627
MAIL_FILTER macro (sendmail), 611
mailing lists, dhcpd, 587
maintain-ixfr-base option (named), 558
maintenance hand tools, 438
make command, variations of, 115
make config command, 115
make menu config command, 115
make xconfig command, 115
makemap command (sendmail), 294
manual routing, 171
manually allocating addresses (DHCP), 79
mapping users to UIDs/GIDs (Linux exports
      file), 241
maps
  auto_home, 251
  automounter configuration, 250
  NIS, 61
mark (gated), 510
martians, 87
  gated, 513
MASQUERADE_AS (sendmail macro), 611,
      632
MASQUERADE_DOMAIN (sendmail
      macro), 611, 632
MASQUERADE_DOMAIN_FILE (sendmail
      macro), 611, 633
MASQUERADE_EXCEPTION (sendmail
      macro), 611, 633
masquerading
  sendmail features, 633
  sendmail macros, 632
master map configuration file
      (automounter), 250
master name server, 206
  configuration, 214

master server, 60
max log size parameter (smb.config file), 261
maxadvinterval parameter (gated), 534
max-cache-ttl (named), 561
MaxClients directive (Apache), 347
maxconnect option (pppd), 491
maxfail option (pppd), 491
maximum transmission unit (see MTU)
max-ixfr-log-size option (named), 558
MaxKeepAliveRequests directive
      (Apache), 352
max-lease-time parameter (dhcpd), 274, 591
max-ncache-ttl option (named), 557
max-refresh-time (named), 561
MaxRequestsPerChild directive
      (Apache), 347
max-retry-time (named), 561
Maxsize field (sendmail), 307
MaxSpareServers directive (Apache), 347
max-transfer-idle-in (named), 560
max-transfer-idle-out (named), 561
max-transfer-time-in option (named), 557
max-transfer-time-out (named), 560
maxup parameter (gated), 530
MAXWEEKS (passwd file value), 389
memstatistics-file option (named), 555
message (MIME data), 71
Message Precedence (generic-linux.cf
      section), 296
messages
  ICMP, 17
  UDP, 10
metric argument (route command), 174
Metric field (Linux routing table), 39, 40
metric keyword (routed command), 181
metric (routing)
  changing, ifconfig command, 146
  gated preference values, 192
metricout parameter
  gated bgp statement, 527
  gated egp statement, 530
mil domain, 56
MILNET, 2
MIME (Multipurpose Internet Mail
      Extensions), 69–74
  defining, Apache, 351
  message body type (sendmail), 608
MIME protocol, Presentation Layer, 8
minadvinterval parameter (gated), 534
minhello parameter (gated), 531
minicom, troubleshooting modems, 166
minpoll parameter (gated), 531
min-refresh-time (named), 561

min-retry-time (named), 561
min-roots option (named), 557
MinSpareServers directive (Apache), 346
MINWEEKS (passwd file value), 390
mixed (MIME data subtype), 71
mobile systems, dynamic address
        allocation, 79
mod_auth (Apache module), 367
mode command (dip), 157, 483
MODE variable (sendmail), 287
modem command (dip), 483
modem option (pppd), 159, 491
    configuring PPP servers, 163
modems, troubleshooting, 166
MODIFY_MAILER_FLAGS macro
        (sendmail), 611
modlist option (ifconfig command), kernel
        modules listing, 110
modprobe command (Linux), 112
mod_so.c (DSO module), 342
mod_ssl module (Apache), 370
module dependencies, 112
modules
    Apache, user authentication, 367
    arp, options, 110
    httpd.conf file, dynamically
        loadable, 342–344
    Linux
        listing, 112
        removing, 112, 113
monitorauthkey parameter (gated), 516
monitoring
    security considerations, 404
        find command, 405
        intruder detection, 404
        login activity, 406
mount command, 244
mount options, Linux, 248
mountall command, 247
mountd command, 234
mounthost= option (fstab file), 248
mounting directories, 234
    mount command, 244
    remote, 243
mountport= option (fstab file), 248
mountprog= option (fstab file), 248
mountvers= option (fstab file), 248
mp option (pppd), 491
mpeg (MIME data subtype), 71
mpshortseq option (pppd), 492
mrru option (pppd), 492
mru option (pppd), 492

ms-dns option (pppd), 492
ms-wins option (pppd), 492
Mtu field (netstat command), 137
MTU (maximum transmission unit), 16
    changing, ifconfig command, 148
    DHCP and, 275
mtu option (pppd), 492
multicast addresses, 26, 30
MULTICAST flag (ifconfig command), 140
multicast (gated), 512
multicast parameter (gated), 534
multicast routing option (Linux kernel
        configuration), 119
multicasting option (Linux kernel
        configuration), 118
multi-homed
    hosts, 14
    servers, options, 360
    sites, ASNs, 100
multi-homed host firewall architecture, 427
multilink option (pppd), 492
multipart (MIME data content type), 71
multiple-cnames option (named), 556
multiplexing, 45
    data delivery, 24
MultiViews (Options directive setting), 364
museum domain, 56
MX (mail exchange) records, 577
MX records
    forward-mapping zone files, 226
    nslookup command and, 229

N

n configuration option (Linux kernel), 117
$n symbol (sendmail transformation), 311
name domain, 56
name field (inet.conf file), 130
Name field (netstat command), 137
name field (resource records), 570
name option (pppd), 492
name servers, 456, 457, 459, 460
    classifications, 60
    dig debugging tool, 467–471
    Samba, 266
    software, 60
    system configuration, 84
Name Service Switch file, 271
name services, 22
    BIND, overview, 205
    domain names, obtaining, 101
name value (DNS resource records), 217

named command, 205
  BIND 9 statements
    controls, 568
    logging, 563
    options, 559
    server, 553
    view, 568
    zone, 566
  command-line options, 548
  configuring, 211
  controls statement, 567
  error messages, 228
  logging statement, 561
  running, 227
  signal processing, 549
  syntax, 548
  zone statement, 564
named server daemon, 60
named.ca file, 219–221
named.conf file, 211
  caching-only servers, 212
  configuration commands, 550
  overview, 212
named.local file, 222
named-xfer option (named), 555
nameserver entry (resolv.conf file), 208
namlen= option (fstab file), 248
NAPs (Network Access Points), 36
NAT (network address translation)
  compared to proxy servers, 88
  non-connected networks, 85
  overview, 87
  scalability, 88
National Institute of Standards and
      Technology (see NIST)
National Science Foundation (NSF),
      NSFNet, 2
natural mask, 30–32
NBT (NetBIOS over TCP/IP), 259
NCC (Network Control Center), 36
ndc command, 227
ndd command, configuration options, 110
ndots option (resolv.conf file), 209
neighbor clause (gated), 530
Nessus (automated system monitoring), 407
net domain, 56
net keyword (routed command), 180
NetBIOS
  file sharing and, 75
  Samba and, 259
NetBIOS over TCP/IP (NBT), 259
Net/Dest field (netstat command), 137

Netfilter Configuration option (Linux kernel
      configuration), 119
netgroup option (share command), 238
netinfo (sendmail K command value), 656
netmask command (dip), 483
netmask (gated), 512
netmask keyword, 143
NETMASK (Linux configuration value), 142
netmask mask argument (ifconfig
      command), 135
netmask option (pppd), 492
netmasks file (Solaris), 144
netstat
  diagnostic troubleshooting, 439
  -nr command, 41
netstat command
  network interfaces, determining
      available, 136
  routing, troubleshooting, 450
  troubleshooting with, 447
netstat -in command
  fields, 137
  Linux output, 138
Network Access Layer, 11, 12
Network Access Points (see NAPs)
network adapters, Linux kernel
      configuration, 117
network address translation (see NAT)
network administration
  decentralized, 28
  defined, 1
  hostnames, 52
  remote administrators, contacting, 454
  routing and, 97
  security information resources, 385
Network Control Center (NCC), 36
Network Control protocols, 152
network file, NIS domains, 269
Network File System (see NFS)
Network Information Center (see NIC)
Network Information Service (see NIS)
Network Layer (OSI Model), 9
NETWORK (Linux configuration
      value), 142
network numbers, 30
@network option (share command), 238
Network packet filtering option (Linux
      kernel configuration), 118
network services
  configuration servers, 76
    DHCP, 78, 272
    RARP, 77

defined, 51
DNS, 54, 205–232
email, planning, 105
file servers, 104
file sharing, 75
inetd, 129–132
Linux kernel configuration, 117
mail, 62
    IMAP, 67–69
    MIME, 69–74
    POP, 65–67
    SMTP, 62–65
name servers, running, 227
name servers, Samba, 266
NFS
    configuring, 235
    daemons, 234
    mounting remote directories, 243
    overview, 233
NIS, 61
port numbers and, 46
print servers, 76
    Line Printer, 256
    lpd, 252
    lpr command, 255
    overview, 252
    printcap file, 252–255
restoring, 131
Samba, overview, 259
sendmail, 285–332, 599–660
Network Terminal Protocol (see telnet)
Network unreachable error (ping
        command), 440
networks
    access troubleshooting
        arp command, 444–447
        ifconfig file, 443
        netstat command, 447
    autonomous systems, 36
    configuring, startup files, 149
    connected vs. non-connected, 85
    enterprise, 85
    heterogeneous, 4
    interconnecting dissimilar physical
        networks, 95
    interface configuration
        checking, 139
        ifconfig command, 134
    interface support (BSD Unix), 123
    interfaces
        determining available, 136–139
        enabling and disabling, 145

intranets, 85
    MTU (maximum transmission unit), 16
    packet fragmentation, 16
    packet switching, 13
    private, 85
    routing, planning, 97–99
    services
        aliases, 47
        port numbers, 46
        sockets, 48
    subnet masks, distributing, 96
    support, FreeBSD, 123
    topology, 25
    traffic, reducing, 448
networks file, NIS map, 268
newaliases command (sendmail), 289
news (MIME data subtype), 71
newsgroups, security information, 385
next-server parameter (dhcpd), 592
nfs directory, 235
NFS (Network File System), 22, 75
    automounter, 249
        configuration files, 250
    daemons, 234
    distributed servers, managing, 278
    exports file, 239–242
    mount command, 244
    overview, 233
    Unix
        configuring, 235
        mounting remote directories, 243
    vfstab files, options, 245
nfs.client file, 235
nfsd command, 234
nfslogd command, 234
nfsprog= option (fstab file), 248
nfs.server file, 235
nfsvers= option (fstab file), 248
NIC (Network Information Center), host
        tables, 54
NIS (Network Information Service)
    domains, 269
    host tables and, 54
    maps, 61, 268
        initializing, 269
    Name Service Switch file, 271
    NIS+, 271
    overview, 61
nis (sendmail K command value), 656
nisplus (sendmail K command value), 656

NIST (National Institute of Standards and Technology), Computer Security Division web site, 385
nmbd command (Samba), 266
No answer error (ping command), 441
noac option (vfstab file), 246
no_access parameter (xinetd), 417
noaccomp option (pppd), 492
noaggregatorid parameter (gated), 528
noauth option (pppd), 492
nobsdcomp option (pppd), 492
NoCache option (proxy server caching), 360
noccp option (pppd), 492
no-check-names option (resolv.conf file), 210
nocrtscts option (pppd), 493
nocto option (fstab file), 248
nodefaultroute option (pppd), 493
nodeflate option (pppd), 493
nodetach option (pppd), 159, 493
nodtrcts option (pppd), 493
noendpoint option (pppd), 493
nogendefault parameter
    gated bgp statement, 527
    gated egp statement, 530
noinstall parameter (gated), 538
nointr option (vfstab file), 246
noip option (pppd), 493
noipdefault option (pppd), 493
noipv6 option (pppd), 493
noktune option (pppd), 493
nolock option (fstab file), 248
nolog option (pppd), 493
nomagic option (pppd), 493
nomp option (pppd), 493
nompshortseq option (pppd), 493
nomultilink option (pppd), 493
non-authoritative servers, 60
non-connected networks, 85
None (Options directive setting), 364
none value (share command), 237
non-encoded binary data, 72
non-standards track protocols, types of, 6
nopcomp option (pppd), 493
nopersist option (pppd), 493
nopredictor1 option (pppd), 494
noproxyarp option (pppd), 494
noquota option (vfstab file), 247
noresolv (gated), 509
normal (gated), 508
nosend (gated), 509
nostamp (gated), 507

nosub option (share command), 236
nosuid option
    share command, 237
    vfstab file, 246
not authoritative parameter (dhcpd), 592
not recommended protocols, 6
notify option (named), 556
notify-source (named), 560
NOTRAILERS flag (ifconfig command), 140
notty option (pppd), 494
nov4asloop parameter (gated), 528
novj option (pppd), 494
novjccomp option (pppd), 494
-nr command, 41
NS (name server) records, 576
    forward-mapping zone files, 226
    named.ca file, 220
    named.local file, 222
    pointers, 58
    reverse zone files, 223
nserver field (RIPE database), 93
NSFNet, 2
    routing policy database, 36
nslookup (debugging tool), 228–232
    diagnostic troubleshooting, 439
    name service, checking with, 456–460
nsswitch.conf file, 271
null (sendmail K command value), 657
Number value (dhcpd option statement), 594
numeric values (printcap file), 253

0

O command (sendmail), 302
-o option (exportfs command), 242
octet data, MIME encoding, 71
octet-stream (MIME data subtype), 70
Oerrs field (netstat command), 137
official Internet addresses, assessing need for, 88–91
ONBOOT (Linux configuration value), 142
one-time passwords, 392
    OPIE, 393–395
ONEX command (ESMTP), 74
only_from parameter (xinetd), 417
OPEN messages (BGP), 190
Open Shortest Path First (see OSPF)
open standards protocol development, 4
Open Systems Interconnect Reference Model (see OSI)
OpenSSL (Apache), 370

OPIE (One-time Passwords in
    Everything), 393–395
Opkts field (netstat command), 137
option statement (dhcpd), 593
Options directive (Apache), 363–364
options entry (resolv.conf file), 209
Options field (DHCP), 78
options parameter (gated), 536
options statement
    BSD Unix kernel configuration, 121
    named.conf file, 553–558
OPTIONS variable (sendmail), 287
Order directive (Directory containers), 365
order_spec option (named), 555
org domain, 56
organizational domains (DNS), 55
organizational types, 88
$ORIGIN directive (zone files), 218, 569
OSI (Open Systems Interconnect Reference
    Model), 7
    Application Layer, 8
    Data Link Layer, 9
    layers, 7
    Network Layer, 9
    Physical Layer, 9
    Presentation Layer, 8
    Session Layer, 8
    Transport Layer, 9
OSPF (Open Shortest Path First), 22
    designated routers, 187
    directional graphs, 185
    equal-cost multi-path routing, 188
    Hello packets, 187
    hierarchy of routing areas, 184
    link-state database, 186
    LSA (Link-State Advertisement), 187
    overview, 179
    security, 188
ospf statement (gated), 514
OSTYPE macro (sendmail), 291, 610, 629
other parameter (gated), 537
outdelay parameter (gated), 528
overload-bit parameter (gated), 524
overriding sender addresses (sendmail), 606

P

P command (sendmail), 303
packages
    Apache, locating names of, 335
    wrapper, security, 409, 410–413
packet filtering, 427
    snoop and, 471–472
Packet socket option (Linux kernel
    configuration), 117
packet switching networks, 13
packets, 10
    capturing, BSD Unix support, 122
    DHCPDISCOVER, 80
    DHCPOFFER, 81
    filtering, 427
    fragmentation, avoiding, 148
    gateways, 14
    Hello (OSPF), 187
    MTU (maximum transmission unit), 16
    routing, 14
    routing tables, 37
    (see also datagrams)
packets option
    BGP, 525
    EGP tracing, 529
packets parameter (gated), 533
PAP (Password Authentication
    Protocol), 160
papcrypt option (pppd), 494
pap-max-authreq option (pppd), 494
pap-restart option (pppd), 494
pap-secrets file, 160
pap-timeout option (pppd), 494
PAR (Positive Acknowledgment with
    Re-transmission), 19
parallel (MIME data subtype), 71
parameter statements (dhcpd), 591
parameters
    define m4 macro, 614–625
    dhcpd.conf file, 274
    gated
        aggregate statement, 546
        bgp statement, 527
        egp statement, 530
        icmp statement, 533
        isis statement, 522
        kernel statement, 535
        ospf statement, 515
        rip statement, 518
        routerdiscovery statement, 533
        smux statement, 532
        static statements, 538
    iptables command, 431
    printcap file, 253
parity command (dip), 483
parse (gated), 509
partial (MIME data subtype), 71
PASS command (POP), 66
pass-filter option (pppd), 494

passive (gated), 512
passive keyword (routed command), 181
passive option (pppd command), 494
    configuring PPP servers, 163
passive parameter (gated), 527
PASSLENGTH (passwd file value), 390
passwd command (Solaris), 389
passwd file, 262
    default values, 389
    PPP servers, configuring, 162
    sample script, 659
    security considerations, 405
Password Authentication Protocol
        (PAP), 160
password command (dip), 157, 483
password parameter (gated), 532
passwords
    aging, 388
    authentication, OSPF, 188
    databases, user authentication
        (Apache), 367
    one-time, 392
        OPIE, 393–395
    Samba, 262
    selecting, 391
    user authentication, 387
        shadow password files, 388–391
Path fields (sendmail), 306
path section (Solaris PPP configuration), 164
pattern matching, sendmail rewrite
        rules, 309
PCM (pulse code modulation), 71
peer subclause (gated), 527
peeras parameter (gated), 530
peers, 8
    BGP, 190, 525
    network servers, 51
performance
    address translation, 87
    Apache, directives, 352–353
    packet fragmentation, avoiding, 148
perimeter networks (firewalls), 427
permanent addresses
    assigning (dhcpd.conf file), 276
    fixed (DHCP), 79
persist option (pppd), 494
ph (sendmail K command value), 656
phquery mailer, 637
PID option (xinetd), 416
PidFile directive (httpd.conf file), 350
pid-file option (named), 555

ping command, 17
    diagnostic troubleshooting, 439
    implementing, 441
    routing tables and, 172
    troubleshooting with, 440
pkgadd command, Solaris device
        drivers, 109
plain text (MIME data subtype), 70
plugin option (pppd), 495
plumb option (loopback interface
        configuration), 138
pointers, 58
    name server record, 58
pointopoint (gated), 512
point-to-point connections, defining (ifconfig
        command), 148
Point-to-Point Protocol (see PPP)
poison reverse (routing), 183
policies
    routing, BGP and, 190
    security, creating, 386
policy (gated), 508
policy routing database (NFSnet), 36
polls (EGP), 189
POP (Post Office Protocol), 65–67
    commands, 66
    MAILER command, 637
    servers, configuring, 281
port command (dip), 156, 483
Port directive (httpd.conf file), 346
port (named), 560
port numbers, 22, 45, 46, 47
    data delivery, 24
    Unix, 47
port= option (vfstab file), 246
port parameter (gated), 532
portmapper, 48
ports, 9
    DHCP, 81
    DNS, 55
    IMAP, 67
    POP, 65
    sendmail, 286
    SMTP, 62
PortSentry (automated system
        monitoring), 408
Positive Acknowledgment with
        Re-transmission (PAR), 19
posix option (vfstab file), 247
PostScript (MIME data subtype), 70

PPP (Point-to-Point Protocol)
   BSD Unix support, 122
   chat scripts, 158
   configuring Solaris, 163
   dialup connections, configuring, 154–158
   installing, 153
   overview, 152
   pppd command, 153
   security, 160–162
   servers, configuring, 162–163
pppd command, 153
   authentication protocols, 160
   dedicated connection configuration, 153
   invoking dial-up scripts, 159
   options, 154, 486
   PPP servers, configuring, 162
   security, 160–162
   signal processing, 497
   syntax, 486
ppp/options file, 154
ppp/options.device file, 154
ppprc file (ppd), 154
PRDB (policy routing database), 36
precedence command (sendmail), 303
predictor1 option (pppd), 495
preference (gated), 511
preference parameter
   gated aggregate statement, 546
   gated bgp statement, 527
   gated egp statement, 530
   gated isis statement, 524
   gated rip statement, 519
   gated routerdiscovery statement, 534
   gated static statements, 538
prefix-length (IP addresses), 27
Presentation Layer (OSI Model), 8
primary servers, 60
print command (dip), 483
print jobs, commands, 256
print servers, 76
   network services, print servers, 104
printcap file, 252–255
printcap name parameter (smb.config
    file), 260
printconf-gui, 254
Printer Driver field (printconf-gui), 254
printer services
   Line Printer, configuring, 256
   lpd, 252
     printcap file, 252–255
   lpr command, 255
   overview, 252

printers, sharing, Samba, 265–266
printing parameter (smb.config file), 260
private key, 419
private networks, 85
privgroup option (pppd), 495
pro domain, 56
process field (inittab file), 127
process status command, httpd,
     locating, 334
processes, httpd, managing, 346
procmail mailer, 637
prog mailer, 305
program (sendmail K command value), 656
promiscuous mode (Ethernet), enabling and
     disabling, 146
proposed standards (RFCs), 5
proto= option (vfstab file), 247
proto parameter (gated), 546
protocol field (inet.conf file), 130
protocol numbers, 45
   datagram headers, 17
protocols
   Application Layer, 22
   Internet Layer, 12
    ICMP, 17
    IP, 13, 14, 15, 16
   Network Access Layer, 11
   non-standards track, 6
   open standards development, 4
   peers, 8
   routing
    BGP, 190
    EGP, 189
    exterior, 188
    gated, 191
    interior, 178
    OSPF, 184
    RIP, 179
    RIP-2, 184
    routed command, 180–184
    selecting, 191
   stack, 7
    headers, 10
   standards, 4, 4–6
   tracing, gated, 504
   Transport Layer, 18
    TCP, 19
    UDP, 18
   troubleshooting
    ftp failure, 474–478
    overview, 471
    snoop, 471–472

protocols file (/etc/protocols), 45, 268
proxy servers
    caching options, 359
    compared to NAT boxes, 88
    non-connected networks, 85
    scalability, 88
    security, 88
proxyarp command (dip), 483
proxyarp option (pppd), 495
ProxyRequests option (proxy server
        caching), 359
ProxyVia option (proxy server caching), 359
ps command, Apache software, locating, 334
psend command (dip), 483
pseudo-device statement, BSD Unix kernel
        configuration, 121
psn-interval parameter (gated), 524
PTR (Domain Name Pointer) records, 580
    named.local file, 222
    reverse zone records, 224
pty option (pppd), 495
public key encryption, 370, 419
    ssh, 400
    stunnel, 423–425
    tools, 421–423
public option
    share command, 237
    vfstab file, 247
pubring.gpg file, 422
pulse code modulation (PCM), 71

Q

-q option (routed command), 180
QoS and/or fair queue option (Linux kernel
        configuration), 119
qpage mailer, 637
query authentication parameter (gated), 519
--query option (rpm), 335
query types (dig), 467
query-response applications, UDP and, 18
query-source option (named), 557
Question (DNS response packets), 469
Queue field (netstat command), 138
QUEUE keyword (iptables command), 431
QUEUEINTERVAL variable (sendmail), 287
quicktime (MIME data subtype), 71
QUIT command
    POP, 66
    SMTP, 63
quit command (dip), 483
quota option (vfstab file), 247
quoted-printable (MIME encoding type), 72

R

R command (sendmail), 309
r commands (Unix)
    disabling, 401
    security considerations, 395–399
R flag (Linux routing table), 38
-r option (exportfs command), 242
RADB (Routing Arbiter Database), 36
    registering in, 100
range parameter (dhcpd), 275, 591
RARP (Reverse Address Resolution
        Protocol), 77
RAs (Routing Arbiters), 36
raw field (inet.conf file), 130
rc.local script
    BSD Unix, 149
    Linux, 129
    routing startup scripts, 177
rc.sysinit script, Linux, 127
rdist command, 279
reachability information
    autonomous systems, 36
    EGP, 189
    exterior routing protocols, 188
read access (filesystems), 236
ReadmeName directive (Apache), 351
receive option (pppd), 495
Recipient field (sendmail), 306
recommended protocols, 5
reconfigure file (Solaris), 109
record option (pppd), 495
RECORD option (xinetd), 417
recursion option (named), 556
recursive searches (DNS), 58
recursive servers (DNS), 58
recursive-clients (named), 560
recv (gated), 508
recvbuffer parameter (gated), 528
Red Hat Linux
    caching-only servers, configuring, 212
    DSO modules, 342
    Ethernet device drivers, 113
    httpd.conf file, location, 338
    named command, running, 227
    NIS domains, 269
    printcap configuration tool, 254
    sendmail, startup script, 287
    updating, 403
Redirect Message (ICMP), 17, 38
redirect parameter (gated), 533, 537
redirect statement (gated), 532
redirection, routing, 176

Ref field (Linux routing table), 39, 40
refuse-chap option (pppd), 495
refuse-pap option (pppd), 495
regex (sendmail K command value), 657
Regional Internet Registries (IRs), address
  requests, 91
registered hosts, 54
registries, addresses, obtaining from, 90
reject (gated), 512
reject parameter (gated), 538
relay mailer, 292
RELAY_DOMAIN (sendmail macro), 610,
  633
RELAY_DOMAIN_FILE (sendmail
  macro), 610, 633
reliability
  address translation, 87
  interface configuration methods, 142
  TCP, 19
remnantholdtime parameter (gated), 536
remnants parameter (gated), 537
Remote File Distribution Program, 279
Remote Procedure Calls (see RPCs)
remotename option (pppd), 495
replace (gated), 507
REPORT keyword (chat), 499
request parameter (gated), 537
Requests for Comments (see RFCs)
Require directive (Apache), 367
require-chap option (pppd), 495
required protocols, 5
require-pap option (pppd), 495
Reseaux IP Europeens (see RIPE)
reserved addresses, 26
reset command (dip), 156, 483
resolv.conf file, 206, 207
  entries, 208
  sample configuration, 210
resolver code, 60
resolver software (name service), 60
resolver-only configurations, 60
resolvers, 206
  configuring, 207, 210
  sample configuration, 210
resource records, 570
  DNS, 216
resources, security, 433
Responsible Person (RP) records, 581
restrict parameter (gated), 546
retain parameter (gated), 538
RETR command (POP), 66
retrans= option (vfstab file), 247

re-transmission, 19
retry= option (vfstab file), 247
RETURN keyword (iptables command), 431
Reverse Address Resolution Protocol
  (RARP), 77
reverse domains, 92
reverse zone file, 223–225
reverse-mapping zone file, 211
rewrite rules (sendmail), 309
  pattern matching, 309
  transformation field, 311–316
  transformation with database, 316
Rewriting Rules (generic-linux.cf
  section), 296
RFC 791, 51, 679
RFC 792, 683
RFC 793, 682
RFC 821, 62
RFC 822, 70
RFC 826, 12
RFC 894, 12
RFC 919, 144
RFC 1033, 206, 216, 570
RFC 1035, 469
RFC 1055, 151
RFC 1172, 152
RFC 1281, 387, 434
RFC 1470, 438
RFC 1521, 70
RFC 1661, 152
RFC 1812, 29
RFC 1869, 72
RFC 1878, 29
RFC 1918, 86
RFC 2050, 90
RFC 2060, 67
RFC 2196, 382, 434
RFC 2901, 88
rfc2308-type1 option (named), 556
rfc822 (MIME data subtype), 71
RFCs (Requests for Comments)
  Network Access Layer, 12
  obtaining on Web, 684
  obtaining through email, 685
  protocol development, 5
  subnet masks, 29
rhosts file, security considerations, 398, 405
ribs unicast parameter (gated), 524
richtext text (MIME data subtype), 70
RIP (Routing Information Protocol), 40, 179
  ifconfig command and, 147
  limitations, 181

RIP *(continued)*
  overview, 178
  routed command, 180–184
rip statement (gated), 518
RIP-2, 184
RIPE Network Control Center, 36
RIPE (Reseaux IP Europeens), 36
  database fields, 92
RIPE-181 standard, 36
rmmod command (Linux), 113
ro option
  exports file, 240
  share command, 236
root access
  preventing, exports file, 240
  share command and, 237
root domain (DNS), 55
root hints file, 211
root servers
  cache initialization files, 219
  DNS, 55
root_squash setting (exports file), 240
rotate option (resolv.conf file), 210
route command, 173
route filters, 201
route (gated), 508
routed command, 179
  gateways file, 180
  implementing, 180
routerdiscovery parameter (gated), 533, 534
routerid (gated), 513
routers
  filtering, 430
    iptables command, 430
  interconnecting dissimilar physical
    networks, 95
  multicast addresses, 26
routes parameter (gated), 536, 537
routing, 170, 192
  bilateral agreements, 37
  classful, 182
  common configurations, 171
  consolidated, 33
  data delivery, 24
  databases, registering, 100
  datagrams, 14
  distance-vector algorithms, 178
  domains, 36
  filters, gated and, 540
  gated, 191
  Internet architecture, 35–37
  planning, 97–99

poison reverse, 183
policies, AS path, 541
protocols, 170
  BGP, 190
  EGP, 189
  exterior, 188
  interior, 178
  OSPF, 184
  RIP, 179
  RIP-2, 184
  routed command, 180–184
  selecting, 191
  system configuration and, 84
  redirection, 176
  slow convergence problem, 181
  split horizon, 183
  triggered updates, 183
  troubleshooting, 450
    traceroute command, 451
Routing Arbiter Database (see RADB)
Routing Arbiters (RAs), 36
Routing Information Protocol (see RIP)
routing tables, 37
  bit mask, 40
  cache, 40
  contents of, 171–173
  default gateways, 41
  deleting routes, RIP, 179
  destination values, 40
  dynamic, 97
  end-to-end routes, 43
  informational fields, 40
  Linux, 38
  loopback route, 41
  metric, changing with ifconfig
    command, 146
  ping command, 172
  reducing size of, 33
  routd command, 179
  Solaris, 41
  static, 97
    adding routes, 174–177
    creating, 173
routing updates (RIP), 180
RP (Responsible Person) records, 581
RPCs (Remote Procedure Calls), port
  numbers, 48
rquotad command, 235
rrset-order option (named), 558
RS232C connectors, 9
rsize= option (vfstab file), 247
rulesets (sendmail), 317

runlevel field (inittab file), 126
runlevels
    inittab file, 126
    System V startup, 125
RUNNING flag (ifconfig command), 140
rw option
    exports file, 240
    share command, 236

S

S command (sendmail), 317
SAINT (automated system monitoring), 408
Samba
    daemon, 259
    directory sharing, 263
    name servers, 266
    overview, 259
    passwords, 262
    printer sharing, 76, 265–266
    server, configuring, 259–263
SANS (System Administration, Networking
        and Security) Institute web
        site, 386
SARA (automated system monitoring), 408
SAY command (chat), 500
scalability
    address translation compared to proxy
        servers, 88
    DNS, 54
    gateway hierarchy, 36
    host tables, 54
scaninterval (gated), 511
ScoreBoardFile directives (httpd.conf
        file), 350
scp (secure copy), 400
screened subnet firewall architecture, 426
ScriptAlias directive (httpd.conf file), 349
scripts, system initialization, 127
search entry (resolv.conf file), 208
sec= option (vfstab file), 247
secondary servers, 60
secret field (chap-secrets file), 161
secring.gpg file, 422
sec=type option (share command), 237
secure servers, bastion hosts, 427
security, 501
    access control
        language extensions, 414
        overview, 409
        shell command, 413
        tcpd, 410–413
    aclok option (share command), 236

address spoofing, 87
address translation, 88
applications
    removing unnecessary, 402
    updating, 402
authentication
    shadow password files, 388–391
    ssh, 400
chat, 501
dedicated connections and, 153
distributing responsibility, 384
    subnets, 384
encryption, 418
    public key, 419
    public key tools, 421–423
    stunnel, 423–425
    symmetric, 420
firewalls
    filtering routers, 430
    functions of, 428
    iptables command, 430
    overview, 425–428
information resources, 385
Internet connection considerations, 85
passwords
    one-time, 392
    OPIE, 393–395
    selecting, 391
planning, overview, 382
policies, creating, 386
PPP, 160–162
proxy servers, 88
r commands (Unix), 395–399
    disabling, 401
resources, 433
risks, 85
    types of, 382
Samba, encrypted passwords, 262
ssh, 399–402
system monitoring, 404
    find command, 405
    intruder detection, 404
    login activity, 406
trusted hosts, 396
user authentication, 387
vendors, information mailing lists, 385
web servers
    CGI scripts, 361
    overview, 361
    SSI, 362
security parameter (smb.config file), 261
segment header, 682

segments, 10
  format, 19
  TCP headers, 19
SELECT command (IMAP), 69
send command (dip), 157, 484
send (gated), 508
sendbuffer parameter (gated), 528
Sender fields (sendmail), 306
sendmail, 285–332, 599–660
  aliases, overview, 288
  classes
    E, 322
    M, 322
    P, 320
    w, 319
  command-line arguments, 604–609
  compiling, 599–604
  configuration commands, 298
  configuration file
    creating with m4 macros, 291–295
    local information, 319–322
    modifying, 319
    Options section, 322
    overview, 290
    samples, 290
    structure, 295
    testing, 323–326
    testing rewrite rules, 326–329
  configuration options, 293
  configuring
    define class command, 300
    define macro command, 299
    headers command, 304
    mailers command, 305
    overview, 297
    precedence command, 303
    set option command, 302
    set ruleset command, 317
    trusted users command, 303
    version level command, 298
  as daemon, 286
  databases, address
    transformation, 329–332
  define m4 macro, 614–625
  DOMAIN source file
    DNS features, 635
    DNS macros, 635
  Domain source file, 631
  FEATURE macro, 625–629
  forwarding, 289
  installing, 603
  internal classes, 640

  K command, 655–659
  m4 macros, 609–614
  macros, conditionals, 300
  mailer definitions, 307
  mailer flags, 654
  MAILER source file, 636
  masquerading features, 633
  masquerading macros, 632
  options, 641–654
  OSTYPE macro, 629
  overview, 285
  queue processing time, 287
  relay features, 634
  rewrite rules, 309
    pattern matching, 309
    transformation fields, 311–316
    transformation with database, 316
  SMTP, receiving, 286
  source code distribution web site, 291
  spam macros, 635
  test commands, 326
  (see also email)
sendmail.cf file
  configuring, 637
  creating with m4 macros, 291–295
  modifying
    local information, 319–322
    Options section, 322
    overview, 319
  overview, 290
  samples, 290
  structure, 295
  testing, 323–326
  testing rewrite rules, 326–329
Sequence Number field, TCP headers, 20
sequence (sendmail K command value), 657
Serial Line IP protocol, BSD Unix
    support, 122
serial lines
  connections, troubleshooting, 165–169
  overview, 150
  protocols, SLIP, 151
serial ports, troubleshooting, 165
serial-queries option (named), 557
server field
  chap-secrets file, 161
  inet.conf file, 130
Server Message Block (SMB), 75
Server Selection (SRV) records, 584
server setting (smb.config file), 261
Server Side Includes (see SSI)
server statement (named.conf file), 552

server string parameter (smb.config file), 260
ServerAdmin defines (httpd.conf file), 345
ServerAdmin values (Apache), changing
    (Solaris), 339
server-identifier parameter (dhcpd), 592
ServerName (httpd.conf file), 345
server-name parameter (dhcpd), 591
ServerRoot directive (httpd.conf file), 345
servers
    caching-only, 207
        configuration, 212
    configuration, 76
        DHCP, 78
        RARP, 77
    distributed, management, 277
    DNS, authoritative, 54
    IMAP
        configuring, 282
        testing, 68
    mail, 105
    master name, 206
        configuration, 214
    name, classifications, 60
    NFS, 234
    POP, configuring, 281
    PPP, configuring, 162–163
    root, 55
        cache initialization files, 219
    Samba, configuring, 259–263
    slave, 207
        configuration, 215
    TCP/IP networks compared to PC LAN
        servers, 51
    (see also Apache; web servers)
ServerType directive (httpd.conf file), 346
service extensions, SMTP, 73
services file, NIS map, 268
Session Layer (OSI Model), 8, 9
set option command (sendmail), 302
SetEnvIf directive (Apache), 372
setgid files, share command and, 237
setuid files, share command and, 237
sftp (secure shell), 400
shadow password files, 388–391
share command
    options, 236
    persistence, 238
share setting (smb.config file), 261
shared media networks, 449
shared-network statement (dhcpd), 590
sharp sign (#)
    automounter comments, 251
    comments, 52

comments in host table, 52
    inittab file, 126
shell command
    dip, 484
    security, 413
shell files, security considerations, 405
showmount command, 243
show-password option (pppd), 495
showwarnings parameter (gated), 528
SIGHUP
    gated signal processing, 505
    named signal processing, 549
    pppd signal processing, 497
SIGILL (named signal processing), 550
SIGINT
    gated signal processing, 505
    named signal processing, 550
    pppd signal processing, 497
SIGKILL (gated signal processing), 505
signal processing
    gated, 505
    named command, 549
    pppd, 497
SIGSYS (named signal processing), 550
SIGTERM
    gated signal processing, 505
    named signal processing, 550
SIGUSR1
    gated signal processing, 505
    named signal processing, 550
    pppd signal processing, 497
SIGUSR2
    named signal processing, 550
    pppd signal processing, 497
SIGUSR2 (gated signal processing), 505
sig-validity-interval (named), 561
SIGWINCH (named signal processing), 550
silent option (pppd), 495
Simple Mail Transfer Protocol (see SMTP)
simplex (gated), 512
SITE macro (sendmail), 611
SITECONFIG macro (sendmail), 611
size bytes (gated), 507
size field (lsmod command), 112
skey command (dip), 484
slave servers, 60, 207
    configuring, 215, 222
sleep 2 command (dip), 157
sleep command (dip), 484
SLIP END character, 151
SLIP ESC character, 151
SLIP (Serial Line IP), 151
    limitations, 151

SMB (Server Message Block), 75
smb.conf file, 259
  directory sharing, 263
  global section, 260
  home section, 263
  name server configuration, 266
  printer sharing, 265
smbd command, 259
smbpasswd file, 262
smtp mailer, 292
SMTP (Simple Mail Transfer Protocol), 22,
    62–65
  commands, 62
    source code, 63
    viewing, 606
  ESMTP (Extended SMTP), 72
    private extensions to, 74
  sendmail, 286
    required macros, 293
  service extensions, 72, 73
smtp8 mailer, 292
smux statement (gated), 531
snoop
  diagnostic troubleshooting, 439
  troubleshooting protocols, 471–472
    ftp failure, 474–478
Snort (automated system monitoring), 408
SOA (Start of Authority) records, 572–576
  forward-mapping zone files, 226
  named.local file, 222
  reverse zone files, 223
socket options parameter (smb.config
    file), 262
sockets, 9, 48–50
soft option (vfstab file), 245
Solaris
  AddModule directive, modules
    referenced, 343
  Apache
    configuring, 339–341
    Directory containers, 348
  bootup, 108
  broadcast addresses, setting, 145
  configuration files
    command-line option to override
      location, 345
    syslog.conf, 53
  device drivers, installing, 109
  dmesg command, 136
  DSO modules, 342
  dynamically loadable modules, 109
  Ethernet, ifconfig command, 135

filesystem type, specifying, 244
hostname file, 141
httpd.conf file, 661–678
  configuration directives, 344
  location, 338
ifconfig command, syntax, 135
IndexOptions directive (Apache), 351
kernel configuration, 108
loghost alias, 53
mountall command, 247
named command, running, 227
netmasks file, 144
network interfaces, checking status, 139
NFS, daemon locations, 235
physical network address, 77
ping command option, 442
point-to-point connections, defining, 149
PPP, configuring, 163
printers, configuring, 258
rc.script files, 149
routed command, running, 180
routing metric, changing, 147
routing tables, 41
runlevels, 129
sendmail, 287
serial ports, troubleshooting, 165
shadow password files, 388
share command, 236–239
SMTP extensions, 74
static routing, adding to startup
    scripts, 177
System V startup, 129
vfstab files, options, 245
sortlist command, 209
sortlist entry (resolv.conf file), 208
sortlist option (named), 558
source field (RIPE database), 93
Source Port, 22
Source Port numbers (UDP), 18
Source Quench Message (ICMP), 17
sourcegateways parameter (gated), 520
sourcenet parameter (gated), 531
spam
  preventing (sendmail features), 628
  sendmail macros, 635
speed command (dip), 156, 484
SPF (Dijkstra Shortest Path First)
    algorithm, 185
spf-interval parameter (gated), 524
spoofing IP addresses, 87
squash entries (exports file), 240
srm.conf (Apache configuration file), 338

SRV (Server Selection) records, 584
ssh (secure shell), 399–402
sshd (secure shell daemon), 399
ssh-keygen (secure shell), 400
SSI (Server Side Includes), security
    considerations, 362
ssl CA certFile parameter (smb.config
    file), 262
SSL (Secure Sockets Layer)
    Apache, 370–378
    certificates, creating, 373
SSLCertificateFile directive (Apache), 372
SSLCertificateKeyFile directive
    (Apache), 372
SSLEngine directive (Apache), 372
SSLOptions directive (Apache), 372
stab (sendmail K command value), 656
stack (protocol), 7
    headers, 10
stacksize option (named), 558
standard resource records, 570
standards
    categories of, 5
    protocols, 4, 4–6
standards track RFCs, maturity levels, 5
start argument (sendmail), 287
Start of Authority (see SOA records)
StartServers directive (Apache), 347
startup files
    gated, 203
    ifconfig command, 149
    inetd, 129
    mountall command, 247
    sendmail, 286
    static routing, 177
    Unix configuration, 124
    xinetd, 132
    (see also bootup)
STAT command (POP), 66
statd command, 235
state (gated), 508
static address assignment, 94
static routing, 171
    startup files, 177
    tables, 97
        adding routes, 174–177
        creating, 173
static statements (gated), 537
statistics-file option (named), 555
statistics-interval option (named), 558
STDs (standards RFCs), 5
stopbits command (dip), 484
store and forward protocols, 64

STORE command (IMAP), 69
stream field (inet.conf file), 130
streams, 10
strictinterfaces (gated), 511
String value (dhcpd option statement), 594
string values (printcap file), 253
stub areas (OSPF hierarchy), 185
stubhosts parameter (gated), 517
stunnel (public key encryption), 423–425
subdirectories, share command and, 236
subdividing Ethernet segments, 448
subdomains, 57
subject (DSN error code), 315
subnet addresses, 28–30
subnet masks
    assigning, ifconfig command, 143–144
    creating, 28
    defining, 94, 97
    distributing, 96
    RFCs, 29
    system configuration, 84
subnet security, distributing
        responsibility, 384
subnet statement (dhcpd), 275, 590
subnetting
    need for, 94
    organization purposes for, 95
    plans, RFCs, 90
    topological reasons for, 95
summary-filter parameter (gated), 524
summary-originate parameter (gated), 524
switch (sendmail K command value), 657
symbols
    gated trace statements, 508
    sendmail pattern matching, 309
SymLinksIfOwnerMatch (Options directive
        setting), 364
symmetric encryption, 419, 420
SYN bit, TCP headers, 19
sync option (pppd), 495
synchronization, TCP byte numbering, 20
sys value (share command), 237
syslog (gated), 510
syslog parameter (gated), 516
syslog.conf configuration file, 53
system administration
    defined, 1
    distributed servers, managing, 277
system configuration
    end users, distributing to, 106
    initialization scripts, 127
    planning, 84
system file, Solaris configuration, 109

System V
  Line Printer configuration, 257
  vfstab files, options, 245
System V startup model, 125
  inittab file, 126
  runlevels, 125
systemid systemid parameter (gated), 524

T

T command (sendmail), 303
tag parameter (gated), 546
task (gated), 508
TCP (Transmission Control Protocol), 19
TCP Explicit Congestion Notification
      support option (Linux kernel
      configuration), 119
tcp option (fstab file), 248
TCP segment header, 682
TCP syncookie support option (Linux kernel
      configuration), 119
tcp-clients (named), 560
tcpd (security), 410–413
TCP/IP
  architecture, 9–11
  defined, 1
  hardware independence, 4
  history, 2
  need for, 4
  serial lines, overview, 150
TCP/IP networking option (Linux kernel
      configuration), 118
tcpproto.mc file, 291
tech-c field (RIPE database), 93
Technical Specification (TS) standards, 5
telnet, 22, 48
TempFileMode option (sendmail), 302
termination code (chat), 502
terminfo file, 257
terminology, OSI model, 6–9
test commands (sendmail), 326
test mode (dip), 155
testing
  chat scripts, 159
  IMAP servers, 68
  NIS servers, 270
  routing tables, 175
  sendmail address rewrite rules, 606
  sendmail configuration, 606
  sendmail.cf file, 323–326
    rewrite rules, 326–329
  (see also debugging)

text
  MIME data content type, 70
  sendmail K command value, 656
threat assessment (security), types of
      threat, 382
three-way handshake, 19
tier-one providers, 3
timeo= option (vfstab file), 245
timeout command (dip), 484
Timeout directive (Apache), 353
TIMEOUT keyword (chat), 499
timeout option (resolv.conf file), 209
timeout, Solaris PPP, 164
timeout values, sendmail, 652
Timeout.queuereturn option (sendmail), 302
timer (gated), 508
tkey-dhkey (named), 561
tkey-domain (named), 561
top-level domains (DNS), 55
topology, 25
topology option (named), 558
topology statements (dhcpd), 590
trace_file (gated), 507
trace_options (gated), 507
traceoptions parameter
  gated isis statement, 524
  gated ospf statement, 516
  gated rip statement, 520
  gated smux statement, 532
traceroute command, 451
  diagnostic troubleshooting, 439
tracing protocols, gated, 504
transfer-format option (named), 557
transfers-in option (named), 557
transfer-source option (named), 558
transfers-out option (named), 557
transfers-per-ns option (named), 557
transformation field (sendmail rewrite
      rules), 311–316
transformation metasymbols (sendmail), 311
transforming addresses, sendmail, 311–316
  creating databases, 329–332
  databases, 316
translation, IP addresses, 43
Transmission Control Protocol (TCP), 19
Transport Layer, 9, 18
  TCP, 19
  UDP, 18
Transport Layer (OSI Model), 9
treat-cr-as-space option (named), 556
triggered updates (routing), 183

Tripwire (automated system monitoring), 407
troubleshooting, 456
  basic ideas, 436
  cache corruption, 460
  dig debugging tool, 467–471
  effect on by setting ifconfig values, 142
  name servers, 456
    cache corruption, 460
    slave servers, 459
    spotty service, 457
  network access
    arp command, 444–447
    ifconfig command, 443
    netstat command, 447
  nslookup tool, 228–232
  overview, 435
  ping command and, 440
    implementing, 441
  protocols
    ftp failure, 474–478
    overview, 471
    snoop, 471–472
  remote administrators, contacting, 454
  routing, 450
    traceroute command, 451
  serial connections, 165–169
  slave servers, 459
  spotty service, 457
  tools, 438
TRUST_AUTH_MECH macro (sendmail), 612
trusted hosts, 396
trusted users command (sendmail), 303
Trusted Users (generic-linux.cf section), 296
trustedgateways parameter (gated), 520
trusted-keys statement (named.conf file), 552
/tryflags command (sendmail), 328
TS (Technical Specification) standards, 5
$TTL directive (zone files), 218, 569
ttl field (resource records), 571
ttl parameter
  gated bgp statement, 528
  gated egp statement, 530
ttl value (DNS resource records), 217
tunneling option (Linux kernel configuration), 119
TXT records, 582
type field
  inet.conf file, 130
  resource records, 571

Type field (sendmail), 307
type value (DNS resource records), 217

U

U flag (Linux routing table), 38
-u option (exportfs command), 242
udp option (fstab file), 248
UDP (User Datagram Protocol), 9
  Transport Layer, 18
uid field (inet.conf file), 130
UID (user ID)
  exports file, 240
  mapping users to, 241
  share command, 236
undefine macro (sendmail), 611
unicast addresses, 26
unicast multicast parameter (gated), 524
--uninstall option (rpm), 335
Unix
  BSD
    configuration file, 120
    devices statement, 122
    options statement, 121
    pseudo-device statement, 121
  configuration files, startup, 124
  dynamically loadable modules, 109–114
  ifconfig command, overview, 134
  lpr command, 76
  Network Access Layer, 12
  NIS maps, 268
  port numbers, 47
  protocol numbers, 45
  r commands
    disabling, 401
    security considerations, 395–399
  routing tables, 41
  serial ports, troubleshooting, 165
  services, 46
  TCP/IP and, 2
Unknown host error (ping command), 440
UNKNOWN keyword (security), 412
Unreachable Port message, 452
UP flag (ifconfig command), 140
update (EGP trace option), 529
update keyword (dbmmanage command), 368
UPDATE messages (BGP), 190
updates (EGP), 189
updetach option (pppd), 496
Use field (Linux routing table), 39, 40
Use Nice field (sendmail), 307

UseCanonicalName directive (httpd.conf file), 345
use_ct_file (sendmail), 626
use_cw_file (sendmail), 626
use-host-decl-names parameter (dhcpd), 592
usehostname option (pppd command), 160, 496
use-id-pool option (named), 556
use-lease-addr-for-default-route parameter (dhcpd), 593
usenet mailer, 637
usepeerdns option (pppd), 496
user authentication (see authentication)
USER command (POP), 66
User Datagram Protocol (see UDP)
User directive (Apache), 347
user option (pppd), 496
user (sendmail K command value), 656
user setting (smb.config file), 261
USERCTL (Linux configuration value), 142
UserDir directive (httpd.conf file), 350
Userid field (sendmail), 307
USERID option (xinetd), 416
UUCP protocol, 64
uucpdomain (sendmail database feature), 628
UUCPSMTP macro (sendmail), 611

V

V command (sendmail), 298
V.35 connectors, 9
v3asloopokay parameter (gated), 528
variables
    environment, LOCALDOMAIN, 208
    LogFormat directive (Apache), 355
vendors, security information mailing lists, 385
VERB command (ESMTP), 74
vers= option (vfstab file), 247
version level command (sendmail), 298
version numbers, sendmail configuration file modifications, 321
version option (named), 555
version parameter (gated), 527
VERSIONID macro (sendmail), 291, 609
vfstab files, options, 245
video (MIME data content type), 71
view keyword (dbmmanage command), 368
virtual hosts (Apache), 360
virtuallink neighborid parameter (gated), 518
VIRTUSER_DOMAIN macro (sendmail), 610

VIRTUSER_DOMAIN_FILE macro (sendmail), 610
virtusertable (sendmail database feature), 628
VLSM (variable-length subnet masks), 97
VRFY command (SMTP), 64

W

wait command (dip), 157, 484
wait ogin> command (dip), 157
wait-status field (inet.conf file), 130
WANs (wide area networks), serial lines and, 150
WARNWEEKS (passwd file value), 390
web pages, passwords, selecting, 392
web servers
    benefits, 333
    monitoring, 378
    multi-homed, options, 360
    proxies, caching options, 359
    security
        CGI scripts, 361
        overview, 361
        SSI, 362
    SSL, 370–378
web sites
    Apache, 337
    automated system monitoring tools, 407
    autonomous system numbers (ASNs), applications for, 99
    Bugtraq, 385
    CERT, 385
    dhcpd, 586, 587
    domain names, registering, 101
    Ethernet device driver source code, 114
    exploits (security), 386
    FIRST (Forum of Incident Response and Security Teams), 385
    gated, 193
    IANA, 45
    Internet Registries membership applications, 91
    Linux kernel source code, 115
    NIST Computer Security Division, 385
    OpenSSL, 370
    OPIE, 393
    RADB, registering in, 100
    reverse domains, 92
    RFCs, 684
    Samba, 259

SANS (System Administration,
Networking and Security)
Institute, 386
sendmail, 291, 599
welcome option (pppd), 496
well-known ports, 48
well-known services, 45
Well-Known Services (WKS) records, 583
Whisker (automated system
monitoring), 408
who command, security and, 404
whois database, 91
contacting remote administrators, 454
wide area networks (see WANs)
Window field, TCP headers, 21
Windows, Samba overview, 259
window=seconds option (share
command), 237
wins proxy option (nmbd command), 267
wins server option (nmbd command), 267
wins support option (nmbd command), 266
WKS (Well-Known Services) record, 583
workgroup parameter (smb.config file), 260
wrapper package, security, 409
tcpd, 410–413
writable parameter (smb.config file), 263
write access (filesystems), 236
wsize= option (vfstab file), 247

X

X.25 networks, packet fragmentation, 16
X.400 protocol, 64
XDR protocol, Presentation Layer, 8
xinetd (Extended Internet Daemon), 132
access control, 416–418
xinetd.conf file, 132
security considerations, 405
xonxoff option (pppd), 496
x-token (MIME encoding type), 72

Y

y configuration option (Linux kernel), 117
ypbind command, 270
ypcat command, testing NIS servers, 270
ypcat -x command, NIS maps, 268

Z

zone files, 60
address records, 576
CNAME records, 579
creating, 569
displaying, 459
$GENERATE directive, 219
HINFO records, 582
$INCLUDE directive, 218
MX records, 577
NS records, 576
$ORIGIN directive, 218
PTR, 580
RP records, 581
SOA records, 572–576
SRV records, 584
$TTL directive, 218
TXT records, 582
WKS records, 583
zone statement
named command, 564
named.conf file, 213, 215
zone tables (cache dump files), 461
zone transfers, 207
zone-c field (RIPE database), 93
zones, 206
caching-only server, 207
master name server, 206
slave server, 207
zone-statistics (named), 561

About the Author

Craig Hunt has worked with computer systems for the last 25 years. His first computer job was as a programmer and systems programmer for the federal government. He left the government to work for Honeywell on the WWMCCS network in the days before TCP/IP, back when the global network used NCP. After Honeywell, Craig went to work for the National Institute of Standards and Technology (NIST) where he built their first enterprise TCP/IP network, administered the central servers on that network, and eventually moved into network research. Craig left NIST to work full time writing and teaching about Linux, Unix, and networking. In addition to *TCP/IP Network Administration*, Craig has written four other books, co-authored two, and edited five. He teaches Linux, Unix, and networking tutorials at major conferences such as USENIX and LinuxWorld. To find out more about what he is doing, visit his web site at *http://www.wrotethebook.com*.

Craig lives with his wife and youngest daughter in Gaithersburg, Maryland. He loves the outdoors, and has a newly discovered passion for exploring it on his mountain bike.

Colophon

Our look is the result of reader comments, our own experimentation, and feedback from distribution channels. Distinctive covers complement our distinctive approach to technical topics, breathing personality and life into potentially dry subjects.

The animal on the cover of *TCP/IP Network Administration* is a land crab. Land crabs are found in tropical America, West Africa, and the Indo-Pacific region where they can be found living in burrows in fields, swamps, and mangrove thickets. They occasionally are found as far as five miles inland, returning to the sea to spawn. Land crabs are a subgroup of over 4,500 species of crabs. Classified with shrimp, lobster, and crayfish, crabs differ from these in their tail structure. Unlike the rest of their order, crabs' tails are curled under their thorax. In addition, their carapaces tend to be unusually broad. Though land crabs in the United States commonly grow to weigh no more than 18 ounces and measure 4 or 5 inches across, crabs in general range in size from less than a centimeter across to the largest, the Japanese spider crab, whose claws can span 12 feet.

Emily Quill was the production editor and copyeditor for *TCP/IP Network Administration*, Third Edition. Jeffrey Holcomb and Jane Ellin provided quality control. Derek Di Matteo and Sue Willing provided production assistance. Tom Dinse wrote the index.

Edie Freedman designed the cover of this book, using a 19th-century engraving from the Dover Pictorial Archive. Emma Colby produced the cover layout with Quark-XPress 4.1 using Adobe's ITC Garamond font.

Melanie Wang designed the interior layout, based on a series design by David Futato. Neil Walls converted the files from Microsoft Word to FrameMaker 5.5.6 using tools created by Mike Sierra. The text font is Linotype Birka; the heading font is Adobe Myriad Condensed; and the code font is LucasFont's TheSans Mono Condensed. The illustrations that appear in the book were produced by Robert Romano and Jessamyn Read using Macromedia FreeHand 9 and Adobe Photoshop 6. The tip and warning icons were drawn by Christopher Bing.

Other Titles Available from O'Reilly

Network Administration

DNS and BIND, 4th Edition

By Paul Albitz & Cricket Liu
4th Edition April 2001
622 pages, ISBN 0-596-00158-4

DNS and BIND, 4th Edition, covers
the new 9.1.0 and 8.2.3 versions of
BIND as well as the older 4.9 version.
There's also more extensive coverage
of NOTIFY, IPv6 forward and reverse mapping, transaction signatures and the new DNS Security Extensions;
and a section on accommodating Windows 2000 clients,
servers, and Domain Controllers.

Internet Core Protocols: The Definitive Guide

By Eric Hall
1st Edition February 2000
472 pages, Includes CD-ROM
ISBN 1-56592-572-6

*Internet Core Protocols: The Definitive
Guide* provides the nitty-gritty details
of TCP, IP, and UDP. Many network problems can only
be debugged by working at the lowest levels—looking
at all the bits traveling back and forth on the wire. This
guide explains what those bits are and how to interpret
them. It's the only book on Internet protocols written
with system and network administrators in mind.

Network Troubleshooting Tools

By Joseph D. Sloan
1st Edition August 2001
364 pages, ISBN 0-596-00186-X

Network Troubleshooting Tools helps
you sort through the thousands of
tools that have been developed for
debugging TCP/IP networks and
choose the ones that are best for your needs. It also
shows you how to approach network troubleshooting
using these tools, how to document your network so
you know how it behaves under normal conditions, and
how to think about problems when they arise so you
can solve them more effectively.

Managing NFS and NIS, 2nd Edition

*By Hal Stern, Mike Eisler &
Ricardo Labiaga*
2nd Edition July 2001
510 pages, ISBN 1-56592-510-6

This long-awaited new edition of a
classic, now updated for NFS Version
3 and based on Solaris 8, shows how
to set up and manage a network filesystem installation.
Managing NFS and NIS is the only practical book devoted
entirely to NFS and the distributed database NIS; it's a
"must-have" for anyone interested in Unix networking.

sendmail, 3rd Edition

By Bryan Costales with Eric Allman
2rd Edition December 2002 (est.)
1000 pages (est.), ISBN 1-56592-839-3

Versions 8.10 through 8.12 of the sendmail program differ so significantly
from earlier versions that a massive
rewrite of our best-selling reference
was called for. With so many web sites now seeking to
make mail delivery efficient, there's a new chapter on
performance tuning, and because sendmail 8.10 and
above are now rich in anti-spam features, a chapter on
handling spam has been added. Also new to this edition
is coverage of other programs supplied with sendmail,
such as vacation and makemap. These additional programs are pivotal to sendmail's daily operation. Altogether, versions 8.10 through 8.12 include dozens of new
features, options, and macros, and this greatly expanded
edition thoroughly addresses each.

Hardening Cisco Routers

By Thomas Akin
1st Edition February 2002
192 pages, ISBN 0-596-00166-5

This small, handy reference helps system and network administrators make
sure their Cisco routers are secure.
Because it's about securing the routers
themselves, and not the entire network, it's highly practical. The book includes Cisco Router Security Checklists
for quick reference, not to mention value-added topics
that incorporate the most current thinking about security: DoS attack mitigation, router auditing, and FBI rec-
ommendations on incident response.

Network Administration

Essential SNMP

By Douglas Mauro & Kevin Schmidt
1st Edition July 2001
326 pages, ISBN 0-596-00020-0

This practical guide for network and
system administrators introduces
SNMP along with the technical background to use it effectively. But the
main focus is on practical network administration: how
to configure SNMP agents and network management
stations, how to use SNMP to retrieve and modify variables on network devices, how to configure management software to react to traps sent by managed devices.
Covers all SNMP versions through SNMPv3.

Unix Backup & Recovery

By W. Curtis Preston
1st Edition November 1999
734 pages, Includes CD-ROM
ISBN 1-56592-642-0

This guide provides a complete
overview of all facets of Unix backup
and recovery and offers practical,
affordable backup and recovery solutions for environments of all sizes and budgets. It explains everything
from freely available backup systems to large-scale commercial utilities.

T1: A Survival Guide

By Matthew Gast
1st Edition August 2001
304 pages, ISBN 0-596-00127-4

This practical, applied reference to T1
for system and network administrators brings together in one place the
information you need to set up, test,
and troubleshoot T1. You'll learn what components you
need to build a T1 line; how the components interact to
transmit data; how to adapt the T1 to work with data
networks using standardized link layer protocols; troubleshooting strategies; and working with vendors.

Cisco IOS in a Nutshell

By James Boney
1st Edition December 2001
608 pages, ISBN 1-56592-942-X

This two-part reference covers IOS
configuration for the TCP/IP protocol
family. The first part includes chapters
on the user interface, configuring lines
and interfaces, access lists, routing protocols, and dial-on-demand routing and security. The
second part is a classic O'Reilly-style quick reference to
all the commands you need to work with TCP/IP and
the lower-level protocols on which it relies, with lots of
examples of the most common configuration steps for
the routers themselves.

Cisco IOS Access Lists

By Jeff Sedayao
1st Edition June 2001
272 pages, ISBN 1-56592-385-5

This book focuses on a critical aspect
of the Cisco IOS—access lists, which
are central to securing routers and
networks. Administrators cannot
implement access control or traffic routing policies
without them. The book covers intranets, firewalls, and
the Internet. Unlike other Cisco router titles, it focuses
on practical instructions for setting router access policies rather than the details of interfaces and routing protocol settings.

O'REILLY®

To order: *800-998-9938* • *order@oreilly.com* • *www.oreilly.com*
Online editions of most O'Reilly titles are available by subscription at *safari.oreilly.com*
Also available at most retail and online bookstores.

Security

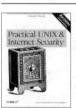

Practical UNIX & Internet Security, 2nd Edition

By Simson Garfinkel & Gene Spafford
2nd Edition April 1996
1004 pages, ISBN 1-56592-148-8

This second edition of the classic *Practical UNIX Security* is a complete rewrite of the original book. It's packed with twice the pages and offers even more practical information for Unix users and administrators. It covers features of many types of Unix systems, including SunOS, Solaris, BSDI, AIX, HP-UX, Digital Unix, Linux, and others. Contents include Unix and security basics, system administrator tasks, network security, and appendices containing checklists and helpful summaries.

Building Internet Firewalls, 2nd Edition

By Elizabeth D. Zwicky, Simon Cooper & D. Brent Chapman
2nd Edition June 2000
894 pages, ISBN 1-56592-871-7

Completely revised and much expanded, this second edition of the highly respected and bestselling *Building Internet Firewalls* now covers Unix, Linux, and Windows NT. It's a practical and detailed guide that provides step-by-step explanations of how to design and install firewalls, and how to configure Internet services to work with a firewall. It covers a wide range of services and protocols. It also contains a complete list of resources, including the location of many publicly available firewalls construction tools.

Incident Response: Planning & Management

By Kenneth R. van Wyk & Richard Forno
1st Edition August 2001
234 pages, ISBN 0-596-00130-4

Incident Response has the technical and administrative information organizations need for planning how to handle computer-related incidents. The book describes and compares a variety of problem-solving approaches, and outlines techniques and procedures for an incident response team to use. In addition, *Incident Response* describes several types of tools for investigating incidents and lists extensive online resources.

Network Security with OpenSSL

By John Viega, Matt Messier & Pravir Chandra
1st Edition June 2002
384 pages, ISBN 0-596-00270-X

OpenSSL is a popular and effective open source version of SSL/TLS, the most widely used protocol for secure network communications. The only guide available on the subject, Network Security with OpenSSLdetails the challenges in securing network communications, and shows you how to use OpenSSL tools to best meet those challenges. Focused on the practical, this book provides only the information that is necessary to use OpenSSL safely and effectively.

Web Security, Privacy & Commerce, 2nd Edition

By Simson Garfinkel with Gene Spafford
2nd Edition November 2001
786 pages, ISBN 0-596-00045-6

Web Security, Privacy & Commerce cuts through the front-page sensationalism and examines the major issues facing e-commerce. It reveals what the real risks are and how to minimize them. Dramatically expanded from the first edition, it includes new information about PKI, privacy, and e-commerce and examines what works or doesn't work on today's Web. Destined to be the classic reference on web security risks and the techniques and technologies that protect users, organizations, systems, and networks.

SSH, The Secure Shell: The Definitive Guide

By Daniel J. Barrett & Richard Silverman
1st Edition January 2001
558 pages, ISBN 0-596-00011-1

SSH (Secure Shell) is a popular, robust, TCP/IP-based product for network security and privacy, supporting strong encryption and authentication. *SSH, The Secure Shell: The Definitive Guide* covers SSH in detail for both system administrators and end users, from the basics up to advanced case studies. You'll learn how to install and maintain SSH, configure servers and clients in simple and complex ways, apply SSH to practical problems, protect other TCP applications through forwarding (tunneling), and troubleshoot a wide variety of difficulties. Coverage includes SSH1, SSH2, OpenSSH, and F-Secure SSH for Unix, plus Windows and Macintosh implementations.

O'REILLY®

To order: *800-998-9938* • *order@oreilly.com* • *www.oreilly.com*
Online editions of most O'Reilly titles are available by subscription at *safari.oreilly.com*
Also available at most retail and online bookstores.

Security

802.11 Security

By Bruce Potter & Bob Fleck
1st Edition November 2002 (est.)
350 pages (est.), ISBN 0-596-00290-4

This book shows how to secure 802.11-based wireless networks focusing particularly on the 802.11b specification. Includes detailed coverage of security issues unique to wireless networking, such as Wireless Access Points (WAP), bandwidth stealing, and the problematic Wired Equivalent Privacy component of 802.11. You will learn how to configure a wireless client and set up a WAP using either Linux or FreeBSD. Controlling network access and encrypting client traffic are also covered thoroughly.

Securing Windows NT/2000 Servers for the Internet

By Stefan Norberg
1st Edition November 2000
200 pages, 1-56592-768-0

In recent years, Windows NT and 2000 systems have emerged as viable platforms for Internet servers, but securing Windows for Internet use is a complex task. This concise guide simplifies the task by paring down installation and configuration instructions into a series of security checklists for security administration, including hardening servers for use as "bastion hosts," performing secure remote administration with OpenSSH, TCP Wrappers, VNC, and the new Windows 2000 Terminal Services.

RADIUS

By Jonathan Hassell
1st Edition September 2002 (est.)
304 pages (est.), ISBN 0-596-00322-6

This new book provides a complete, detailed guide into the underpinnings of the RADIUS protocol, with particular emphasis on the utility of user accounting. Author Jonathan Hassell also provides practical suggestions for using an open-source variation called FreeRADIUS, giving the reader background in both RADIUS theory and practice.

Database Nation: The Death of Privacy in the 21st Century

By Simson Garfinkel
Softcover Edition January 2001
336 pages, 0-596-00105-3

As the 21st century begins, advances in technology endanger our privacy in ways never before imagined. This newly revised update of the popular hardcover edition, *Database Nation: The Death of Privacy in the 21st Century*, is the compelling account of how invasive technologies will affect our lives in the coming years. It's a timely, far-reaching, entertaining, and thought-provoking look at the serious threats to privacy facing us today.

O'REILLY®

To order: *800-998-9938* • *order@oreilly.com* • *www.oreilly.com*
Online editions of most O'Reilly titles are available by subscription at *safari.oreilly.com*
Also available at most retail and online bookstores.

How to stay in touch with O'Reilly

1. Visit our award-winning web site

http://www.oreilly.com/

★ "Top 100 Sites on the Web"—PC Magazine
★ CIO Magazine's Web Business 50 Awards

Our web site contains a library of comprehensive product information (including book excerpts and tables of contents), downloadable software, background articles, interviews with technology leaders, links to relevant sites, book cover art, and more. File us in your bookmarks or favorites!

2. Join our email mailing lists

Sign up to get email announcements of new books and conferences, special offers, and O'Reilly Network technology newsletters at:

http://www.elists.oreilly.com

It's easy to customize your free elists subscription so you'll get exactly the O'Reilly news you want.

3. Get examples from our books

To find example files for a book, go to:

http://www.oreilly.com/catalog

select the book, and follow the "Examples" link.

4. Work with us

Check out our web site for current employment opportunities:

http://jobs.oreilly.com/

5. Register your book

Register your book at:

http://register.oreilly.com

6. Contact us

O'Reilly & Associates, Inc.
1005 Gravenstein Hwy North
Sebastopol, CA 95472 USA
TEL: 707-827-7000 or 800-998-9938
         (6am to 5pm PST)
FAX: 707-829-0104

order@oreilly.com
For answers to problems regarding your order or our products. To place a book order online visit:

http://www.oreilly.com/order_new/

catalog@oreilly.com
To request a copy of our latest catalog.

booktech@oreilly.com
For book content technical questions or corrections.

corporate@oreilly.com
For educational, library, and corporate sales.

proposals@oreilly.com
To submit new book proposals to our editors and product managers.

international@oreilly.com
For information about our international distributors or translation queries. For a list of our distributors outside of North America check out:

http://international.oreilly.com/distributors.html

O'REILLY®

To order: *800-998-9938* • *order@oreilly.com* • *www.oreilly.com*
Online editions of most O'Reilly titles are available by subscription at *safari.oreilly.com*
Also available at most retail and online bookstores.